COLLEGE ACCOUNTING
Twelfth Edition

PARTS 1–2

Arthur E. Carlson, PhD
Professor of Accounting
School of Business Administration
Washington University, St. Louis

James A. Heintz, DBA, CPA
Professor of Accounting
Indiana University
Bloomington, Indiana

Published by
SOUTH-WESTERN PUBLISHING CO.

A84

CINCINNATI   WEST CHICAGO, IL   DALLAS   PELHAM MANOR, NY   LIVERMORE, CA

PREFACE

College Accounting is designed for students of accounting, business administration, computer science, and secretarial science. An understanding of the principles of business accounting is essential for anyone who desires a successful career in business, in many of the professions, and in many branches of government. Those who manage or operate a business, its owners, its prospective owners, its present and prospective creditors, governmental taxing authorities, and other government agencies have need for various types of information. Accounting systems are designed to fill such needs. The particular practices followed are tailored to meet the requirements and the circumstances in each case. However, the same accounting principles underlie all of the practices—just as the same principles of structural engineering apply to the construction of a single-car garage and of a fifty-floor steel and concrete office building.

This twelfth edition of College Accounting continues the pattern of earlier editions—explanations of principles with examples of practices. Numerous forms and documents are illustrated. Because the terminology of accounting is undergoing gradual change, the currently preferred terms are used throughout the textbook. Diagrams, flow charts, and color are used both to facilitate understanding and, in the case of many of the color illustrations, to conform to practice. This twelfth edition continues to include "Chapter Objectives" at the beginning of each chapter, "Building Your Accounting Knowledge" review questions at the end of each chapter section (there are one or more sections per chapter), and "Expanding Your Business Vocabulary" terms at the end of each chapter. In addition, a feature entitled "Applying Accounting Concepts" has been added at the end of each chapter section to provide immediate learning reinforcement.

Chapter 6 has been expanded and retitled Accounting for Purchases and Payments, and Chapter 7 has been expanded and retitled Accounting for Sales and Collections. Chapter 6 presents both the gross-price and net-price bases of accounting for cash discounts and provides exercise material using both bases. However, the primary emphasis is on the net-price basis, because of its growing use in current practice. Chapters 8, 9, and 10 use the net-price basis exclusively for the same reason.

Chapter 13 introduces ACRS (Accelerated Cost Recovery System) depreciation and expands the discussion of like-kind and unlike-kind exchanges of assets. In addition, the corporation section of Chapter 16 has been streamlined to deal primarily with transaction analysis.

The textbook is organized to facilitate the use of various supplementary learning aids. Workbooks containing study assignments correlated with the chapter sections are available. Each workbook study assignment (called a report) includes an exercise on principles and one or more problems bearing on the material discussed in the related section of the textbook. A compilation of check figures for selected workbook problems is available for distribution to students. Additional accounting problems to be used for either supplementary or remedial work are included following Chapters 5, 10, 15, and 20. Three practice sets (the first two of which are entirely new) are available: the first involves the accounting records of a professional person (Vance J. Zarmer, a computer consultant), the second involves the accounting records of a retail computer store (MicroWorld), and the third involves the accounting records of a wholesale and retail bakery business (the partnership of Spinner & Thomas). These sets provide realistic work designed to test the student's ability to apply the knowledge of accounting principles which has been gained from studying the textbook and completing the workbook assignments. Upon completion of each practice set, a test is provided to determine the student's ability to interpret intelligently the records and financial statements of the enterprise. A comprehensive periodic testing program is provided. Tests are available for use following completion of Chapters 2, 5, 7, 10, 12, 15, 17, and 20. In addition, a test bank is available for instructors who wish to construct their own tests.

The authors acknowledge their indebtedness and express their appreciation to the considerable number of accounting instructors, business executives, accountants, and other professional people whose suggestions contributed to the preparation of this textbook.

A. E. Carlson
J. A. Heintz

CONTENTS

PARTS 1 & 2 — CHAPTERS 1-20

1	**The Nature of Business Accounting**	**1**
	The Accounting Process	3
	The Double-Entry Framework	13
2	**Accounting Procedure**	**26**
	Journalizing Transactions	27
	Posting to the Ledger: The Trial Balance	39
	The Financial Statements	48
3	**Accounting for Cash**	**55**
	Cash Receipts and Cash Payments	56
	Banking Procedures	65
4	**Payroll Accounting**	**85**
	Employee Earnings and Deductions	86
	Payroll Taxes Imposed on the Employer	105
5	**Accounting for a Personal Service Enterprise**	**117**
	The Cash Basis of Accounting for a Personal Service Enterprise	118
	Work at Close of the Fiscal Period	137
1-5	**Supplementary Practical Accounting Problems**	**154**
6	**Accounting for Purchases and Payments**	**167**
	Source Documents and Associated Records for Purchases and Payments	168
	Accounting Procedures for Purchases and Payments	183

7 **Accounting for Sales and Collections** 199
Source Documents and Associated Records For Sales and
  Collections 200
Accounting Procedures for Sales and Collections 214

8 **Accrual Accounting Applied to a Small Retail Business** 227
Principles and Procedures 228
Illustration of Accounting Procedure 244

9 **The Periodic Summary** 279
End-of-Period Work Sheet 280
The Financial Statements 290

10 **Adjusting and Closing Accounts at End of Accounting
Period** 307
Adjusting Entries 308
Closing Procedure 314

6-10 **Supplementary Practical Accounting Problems** 329

11 **Accounting for Notes and Interest** 341

12 **Accounting for Inventory and Prepaid Expenses** 362
Merchandise Inventory 363
Prepaid Expenses 377

13 **Accounting for Property, Plant, and Equipment** 387
Land, Buildings, and Equipment 389
Accounting Procedure 403

14 **Internal Accounting Control** 418
Internal Accounting Control Concepts 419
Application in the Expenditure Cycle 423
Application in the Revenue Cycle 440

15 **Accounting Concepts and Accepted Practices** 456
Basic Concepts in Financial Accounting 457
Accepted Accounting Practices 464

11-15 **Supplementary Practical Accounting Problems** 471

16 **Accounting For Owner's Equity** 481
The Single Proprietorship 482
The Partnership 490
The Corporation 506

17   **Accrual Accounting Applied to a Medium-Scale Wholesale-Retail Business**   **522**

18   **Accounting Procedure at Year End**   **551**
Summary and Supplementary Year End Work Sheets   552
Adjusting, Closing, and Reversing Entries   566

19   **The Annual Report**   **577**
The Income Statement   578
The Balance Sheet   585
The Statement of Changes in Financial Position   590

20   **Interim Financial Statements**   **604**

16-20   **Supplementary Practical Accounting Problems**   **625**

INDEX

CHAPTER 1

The Nature of
Business Accounting

CHAPTER OBJECTIVES

Careful study of this chapter should enable you to:

- Describe business accounting as it applies to profit-seeking enterprises.

- Define certain business accounting terms.

- Explain how selected business transactions affect the business entity, using the accounting equation.

- Explain the nature of the income statement and the balance sheet, and how they relate to one another.

- Explain the double-entry framework.

- Explain the function of the trial balance.

The purpose of business accounting is to provide information about the current operating results and financial condition of an enterprise to individuals, agencies, and organizations who have the need and the right to be so informed. These user groups normally include:

1. The **owners** of the business—both present and prospective.
2. The **managers** of the business—managers may or may not own the business. Often the owners and the managers are the same persons.
3. The **creditors**, or **suppliers**, of the business—both present and prospective. Creditors or suppliers are those who supply goods and services on credit— meaning that payment need not be made on the date of purchase. The creditor category also includes banks and individuals who lend money to the business.

4. **Government agencies**—local, state, and national. For purposes of regulation and taxation, various governmental agencies must be given certain financial information.

In connection with many businesses, some or all of the following also make use of accounting information: customers or clients, labor unions, competitors, trade associations, stock exchanges, commodity exchanges, financial analysts, and financial writers.

Although the information needed by all types of users is not identical, most want data regarding (1) the results of operations—net income or loss—for the most recent period and (2) the financial status of the business as of the most current date available. The demand for the greatest quantity and variety of information usually comes from the managers of the business. They constantly need up-to-the-minute information about the financial activities of every department in their organization. Because accounting relates to so many phases of business, it is not surprising that there are several fields of accounting specialization such as tax work, cost accounting, computer-based accounting systems design and installation, management consulting, and budget preparation.

Many accountants have but one employer whereas others become qualified as public accountants and offer their services as independent contractors or advisors. Public accountants perform various functions. One of their major activities is auditing. This involves the application of standard review and testing procedures to the records of an enterprise to be certain that acceptable accounting policies and practices have been consistently followed. The purpose of the audit is to provide an independent opinion that the financial information about a business is fairly presented. Public accountants frequently extend their activities into the area of "management consulting"—a term that covers a variety of specialized management service assignments. Some states license individuals as **Public Accountants** or **Registered Accountants**, although this practice is disappearing. All states grant the designation of **Certified Public Accountant** (CPA) to those who meet various prescribed requirements, including the passing of a uniform examination prepared by the American Institute of Certified Public Accountants.

A uniform examination is also offered in numerous cities throughout the country by the Institute of Management Accounting of the National Association of Accountants, leading to the designation of **Certified Management Accountant** (CMA). This certificate is designed to give professional status to managerial accountants. Still another uniform examination is offered under similar conditions by the Institute of Internal Auditors, leading to the designation of **Certified Internal Auditor** (CIA). This certificate affords professional status to accountants who review the operating and accounting control procedures adopted by their employers.

All of the foregoing comments have related to accounting and accountants in connection with profit-seeking organizations. There are thousands of not-for-profit organizations such as governments, educational institutions, churches, and hospitals that also need to accumulate and dispense information. These organizations also engage a large number of accountants. While the "rules of the game" are somewhat different in not-for-profit organizations, much of the record keeping is identical with that found in profit-seeking organizations.

The accountant is responsible for accumulating and dispensing the financial information needed by users. Since such activities touch upon nearly every aspect of business operation and since financial information is communicated in accounting terms, accounting is said to be the "language of business." Anyone intending to engage in any type of business activity should learn this language.

THE ACCOUNTING PROCESS

Business accounting may be defined as the art of analyzing and recording financial transactions and certain business-related economic events in a manner that classifies and summarizes the information and reports and interprets the results. The accounting process itself provides the basis for this definition.

Analyzing is the first step in the accounting process. The accountant must look at a transaction or event that has occurred and determine its fundamental significance to the business so that the relevant information may be properly processed.

Recording traditionally meant writing something by hand. Much of the record keeping in accounting still is done manually, however, technological advances have introduced a variety of bookkeeping machines which typically combine the major attributes of typewriters, calculators, cathode ray tubes, and electro-mechanical printing. The initial processing can take the form of (1) terminal keyboard input directly into a computer, (2) diskettes prepared by keyboard input not directly connected to a computer, or (3) special characters that can be magnetically or electronically "read" from source documents and thus used to feed information directly into a computer. Because of the multiple ways information may be processed, the term "data entry" may be substituted for the term "recording" in the accounting process.

Classifying relates to the process of sorting or grouping like things together rather than merely keeping a simple, diary-like narrative record of numerous and varied transactions and events.

Summarizing is the process of bringing together various items of information to determine or explain a result.

Final processing , or **reporting**, refers to the process of communicating the results. In accounting, it is common to use tabular arrangements rather than narrative-type reports. Sometimes, a combination of the two is used.

Interpreting refers to the steps taken to direct attention to the significance of various matters and relationships. Percentage analyses and ratios often are used to help explain the meaning of certain related bits of information. Footnotes to financial reports and special captions may also be valuable in the interpreting phase of accounting.

Accounting and Bookkeeping

A person involved with or responsible for such functions as accounting information systems design, accounting policy making, data analysis, report preparation, and report interpretation may be referred to as an accountant. A person who records or enters information in accounting records may be referred to as a bookkeeper. Bookkeeping is the processing phase of the accounting information processing system. That term goes back to the time when formal accounting records were in the form of books—pages bound together. While this still is sometimes the case, modern practice favors the use of loose-leaf or computer-generated records and cards. When the language catches up with practice, the designation information processor or "record keeper" may replace "bookkeeper."

Accounting Elements

A business entity is a particular individual, association, or other organization for which formal records are kept and periodic reports are made. Properties of value that are owned by a business entity are called assets.

Assets. Properties such as money, accounts receivable, merchandise, furniture, fixtures, machinery, buildings, and land are common examples of business assets. An account receivable is an unwritten promise by a customer to pay at a later date for goods sold or for services rendered.

It is possible to conduct a business or a professional practice with very few assets. A medical doctor, for example, may have relatively few assets, such as money, accounts receivable, instruments, laboratory equipment, and office equipment. In many cases, however, numerous assets are necessary. A merchant must have a large selection of merchandise to sell and store equipment with which to display the merchandise. A manufacturer must have an inventory of parts and materials, tools and various sorts of machinery with which to make or assemble the product.

Liabilities. A legal obligation of a business to pay a debt is a business liability. Debts can be paid with money, goods, or services, but usually are paid in cash. Liabilities represent one type of ownership interest in a business—an outside interest.

The most common liabilities are accounts payable and notes payable. An account payable is an unwritten promise to pay a supplier for property purchased on credit or for a service rendered. Formal written promises to pay suppliers or lenders specified sums of money at definite future times are known as notes payable. A business also may have one or more types of taxes payable classified as a liability.

Owner's Equity. The amount by which the business assets exceed the business liabilities is termed the owner's equity in the business. The word "equity" used in this sense represents a second type of ownership interest in a business—an inside interest. The terms proprietorship, net worth, or capital are sometimes used as synonyms for owner's equity. If there are no business liabilities, the owner's equity in the business is equal to the total amount of the assets of the business.

A business that is owned by one person traditionally is called a proprietorship. The person owning the interest in a business is known as the proprietor. A distinction must be made between the business assets and liabilities and nonbusiness assets and liabilities that a proprietor may have. For example, the proprietor probably owns a home, clothing, and a car, and perhaps owes the dentist for dental service. These are personal, nonbusiness assets and liabilities. The formal accounting records for the enterprise will relate to the business entity only; any nonbusiness assets and liabilities of the proprietor should be excluded. While the term "owner's equity" can be used in a very broad sense, its use in accounting is nearly always limited to the meaning: business assets minus business liabilities.

Frequent reference will be made to the owner's acts of investing money or other property in the business and to the withdrawal of money or other property from the business. In either case, property is changed from the category of a nonbusiness asset to a business asset or vice versa. These distinctions are important if the owner is going to make decisions based on the financial condition and results of the business apart from nonbusiness affairs.

The Accounting Equation

The relationship between the three basic accounting elements can be expressed in the form of a simple equation known as the accounting equation.

ASSETS = LIABILITIES + OWNER'S EQUITY

This equation reflects the fact that outsiders and insiders have an interest in all of the assets of a business. When the amounts of any two of these elements are known, the third can always be calculated.

LIABILITIES = ASSETS − OWNER'S EQUITY

OWNER'S EQUITY = ASSETS − LIABILITIES

For example, Jane Buelt has business assets on December 31 in the sum of $60,400. The business liabilities on that date consist of $2,400 owed for supplies purchased on account and $3,000 owed to a bank on a note. The owner's equity element of the business may be calculated by subtracting the total liabilities from the total assets, $60,400 − $5,400 = $55,000. These facts about the business can also be expressed in equation form as follows:

ASSETS	**= LIABILITIES**	**+ OWNER'S EQUITY**
$60,400	$5,400	$55,000

A closer examination of the owner's equity will show how the equation maintains equality. One way to increase the owner's equity in the business is to increase the assets. To increase the assets and owner's equity, Buelt may (1) invest more money or other property in the business or (2) operate the business profitably.

For example, if one year later the assets are $91,400 and the liabilities are $5,200, the status of the business would be as follows:

ASSETS	**= LIABILITIES**	**+ OWNER'S EQUITY**
$91,400	$5,200	$86,200

The fact that Buelt's equity in the business had increased by $31,200 (from $55,000 to $86,200) does not prove that she had made a profit (often called net income) equal to the increase. Increases and decreases in owner's equity must be analyzed. If the records indicated that she invested additional money during the year in the amount of $14,000 and did not withdraw any funds for personal use, the remainder of the increase in her equity ($17,200) would have been due to profit (net income).

If the records indicated she invested no additional funds, withdrew assets in an amount of $18,800 cash for personal use, and increased her equity by $50,000 as a result of a profitable operation, the net effect would also account for the $31,200 ($50,000 − $18,800) increase. It is essential that the business records show the changes in owner's equity due to events that are part of regular business operations and the changes in owner's equity due to investments and withdrawals of assets by the owner.

Transactions

Any activity of an enterprise which involves the exchange of values is referred to as a transaction. These values typically are expressed in terms of money, but may also be expressed as the market values of goods and services. Buying and selling property and performing services are common transactions. The following typical transactions are analyzed to show that each represents an exchange of values.

Typical Transactions	Analysis of Transactions
1. Purchased equipment for cash, $1,500.	Money was exchanged for equipment.
2. Received cash in payment of professional fees, $400.	Professional service was rendered in exchange for money.
3. Paid office rent, $300.	Money was exchanged for the right to use property.
4. Paid an amount owed to a supplier, $825.	Money was given in settlement of a debt that may have resulted from the purchase of property on account or from services rendered by a supplier.
5. Paid wages in cash, $175.	Money was exchanged for services rendered.
6. Borrowed $3,500 at a bank giving a 10 percent interest-bearing note due in 30 days.	A liability known as a note payable was incurred in exchange for money.
7. Purchased office equipment on account, $600.	A liability known as an account payable was incurred in exchange for office equipment.

Effect of Transactions on the Accounting Equation

Each transaction affects one or more of the three basic accounting elements. For example, in transaction (1) the purchase of equipment for cash represents both an increase and a decrease in assets. The assets increased because equipment was acquired; the assets decreased because cash was disbursed. The office equipment in transaction (7) was purchased on account, thereby creating a liability. The transaction results in an increase in assets (equipment) with a corresponding increase in liabilities (accounts payable). Neither of these transactions has any effect upon the owner's equity element of the equation.

The effect of any transaction on the basic elements of the accounting equation may be indicated by increasing or decreasing a specific asset, liability or owner's equity account. To illustrate: assume that Gray Dorsey, an attorney, decided to go into practice for himself. During the first month of this venture (June, 1986), the following transactions relating to the practice took place:

Transaction (a)

An Increase in an Asset Offset by an Increase in Owner's Equity

Dorsey opened a bank account with a deposit of $10,000. This transaction caused the new business to receive the asset cash; and since Dorsey contributed the assets, the owner's equity element was increased by the same amount. As a result of this transaction, the equation for the business would appear as follows:

ASSETS	=	LIABILITIES + OWNER'S EQUITY
Cash		Gray Dorsey, Capital
(a) $10,000		$10,000

Transaction (b)

An Increase in an Asset Offset by an Increase in a Liability

Dorsey purchased office equipment (desk, chairs, file cabinet, etc.) for $4,900 on 30 days credit. This transaction caused the asset office equipment to increase by $4,900 and resulted in an equal increase in the liability accounts payable. Updating the foregoing equation by this transaction gives the following result:

	ASSETS		=	LIABILITIES	+ OWNER'S EQUITY
	Cash	+ Office Equipment		Accounts Payable	Gray Dorsey, Capital
Bal.	$10,000				$10,000
(b)		$4,900		$4,900	
Bal.	$10,000	$4,900		$4,900	$10,000

Transaction (c)

An Increase in One Asset Offset by a Decrease in Another Asset

Dorsey purchased office supplies (stationery, legal pads, pencils, etc.) for cash, $760. This transaction caused a $760 increase in the asset office supplies that exactly offset the $760 decrease in the asset cash. The effect on the equation is as follows:

	ASSETS				LIABILITIES	+	OWNER'S EQUITY
	Cash	Office + Equipment	Office + Supplies	=	Accounts Payable		Gray Dorsey, Capital
Bal.	$10,000	$4,900			$4,900		$10,000
(c)	− $760		$760				
Bal.	$9,240	$4,900	$760		$4,900		$10,000

Transaction (d)

A Decrease in an Asset Offset by a Decrease in a Liability

Dorsey paid $2,800 on account to the company from which the office equipment was purchased. (See Transaction (b).) This payment caused the asset cash and the liability accounts payable both to decrease $2,800. The effect on the equation is as follows:

	ASSETS				LIABILITIES	+	OWNER'S EQUITY
	Cash	Office + Equipment	Office + Supplies	=	Accounts Payable		Gray Dorsey, Capital
Bal.	$9,240	$4,900	$760		$4,900		$10,000
(d)	− 2,800				− 2,800		
Bal.	$6,440	$4,900	$760		$2,100		$10,000

Transaction (e)

An Increase in an Asset Offset by an Increase in Owner's Equity Resulting from Revenue

Dorsey received $2,000 cash from a client for professional services. This transaction caused the asset cash to increase $2,000, and since the cash was received for services performed by the business, the owner's equity increased by the same amount. The effect on the equation is as follows:

	ASSETS				LIABILITIES	+	OWNER'S EQUITY
	Cash	Office + Equipment	Office + Supplies	=	Accounts Payable		Gray Dorsey, Capital
Bal.	$6,440	$4,900	$760		$2,100		$10,000
(e)	2,000						2,000
Bal.	$8,440	$4,900	$760		$2,100		$12,000

Transaction (f)

A Decrease in an Asset Offset by a Decrease in Owner's Equity Resulting from Expense

(1) Dorsey paid $400 for office rent for June. This transaction caused the asset cash to be reduced by $400 with an equal reduction in owner's equity. The effect on the equation is as follows:

	ASSETS				LIABILITIES	+ OWNER'S EQUITY
	Cash	+ Office Equipment	+ Office Supplies	=	Accounts Payable	Gray Dorsey, Capital
Bal.	$8,440	$4,900	$760		$2,100	$12,000
(f1) −	400					− 400
Bal.	$8,040	$4,900	$760		$2,100	$11,600

(2) Dorsey paid a bill for telephone service, $49. This transaction, like the previous one, caused a decrease in the asset cash with an equal decrease in the owner's equity. The effect on the equation is as follows:

	ASSETS				LIABILITIES	+ OWNER'S EQUITY
	Cash	+ Office Equipment	+ Office Supplies	=	Accounts Payable	Gray Dorsey, Capital
Bal.	$8,040	$4,900	$760		$2,100	$11,600
(f2) −	49					− 49
Bal.	$7,991	$4,900	$760		$2,100	$11,551

The Financial Statements

A set of records that make up an accounting data base is maintained to fill a variety of needs. Foremost is to provide source data for use in preparing various reports, including those referred to as financial statements. The two most important of these are the income statement and the balance sheet.

The Income Statement. The income statement, sometimes called the profit and loss statement or operating statement, shows the net income (net profit) or net loss for a specified period of time and how it was calculated. A very simple income statement has been prepared relating to the business of Gray Dorsey for the first month's operation, June, 1986. This statement contains information that was obtained by analysis of the changes in the owner's equity element of the business for the month. This element went from zero to $11,551. Part of this increase, $10,000, was due to the initial investment made by Dorsey. Since an owner's investment is not classified as income or expense of the business, it is not considered in the income statement. The remainder of the increase, $1,551, was due to Dorsey's earning income and incurring expense. Transaction (e) involved revenue of $2,000; transactions (f1) and (f2) involved expenses of $400 and $49, respectively. Taken together, these transactions explain the net income of $1,551, as it appears in the following statement:

Gray Dorsey, Attorney
Income Statement
For the Month of June, 1986

Professional fees		$2,000
Expenses:		
Rent expense...	$400	
Telephone expense	49	449
Net income for month.....................................		$1,551

The Balance Sheet. The balance sheet, sometimes called a statement of financial position or statement of financial condition, shows the assets, liabilities, and owner's equity of a business at a specified date. The following is a balance sheet for Dorsey's business as of June 30, 1986.

Gray Dorsey, Attorney
Balance Sheet
June 30, 1986

Assets		Liabilities	
Cash	$ 7,991	Accounts payable	$ 2,100
Office supplies	760		
Office equipment	4,900	**Owner's Equity**	
		Gray Dorsey, capital	11,551
		Total liabilities and	
Total assets	$13,651	owner's equity	$13,651

The foregoing accounting process can be illustrated with the following diagram:

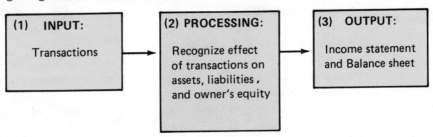

1. Transactions in which property or services are bought or sold by an enterprise provide the necessary input for the accounting information system.
2. Recognizing the effect of these transactions on the assets, liabilities, and owner's equity of an enterprise is the processing function of the accounting information system.
3. The accounting data base that is updated in the processing function provides the source data for the output of the accounting information system—the income statement and the balance sheet.

BUILDING YOUR ACCOUNTING KNOWLEDGE

1. Identify four user groups normally interested in financial information about a business enterprise.
2. Which group of information users usually demands the greatest quantity and variety of information? Why?
3. Why is accounting called the "language of business?"
4. What is the major difference between a public accountant and a management accountant? An internal auditor?
5. Identify the six major phases of the accounting process, and indicate what is done in each phase.
6. Why is it necessary to distinguish between the business assets and liabilities and the nonbusiness assets and liabilities of the single proprietor?
7. In what other way than by making a profit can the owner's equity in a proprietorship be increased?
8. In what other way than by suffering a loss can the owner's equity in a proprietorship be decreased?

APPLYING ACCOUNTING CONCEPTS

Exercise 1-1. Fred Hand has started his own business. During the first month (March 19--), the following transactions occurred. Show the effect of each transaction on the basic elements of the accounting equation: Assets = Liabilities + Owner's Equity.

1. Invested $12,000 cash in the business.
2. Purchased office supplies for cash, $800.
3. Purchased office equipment for $3,100 on account.
4. Received $2,200 cash from a client for services rendered.
5. Paid $3,100 on account to the company from which office equipment was purchased.
6. Paid $500 for office rent for the month.

Exercise 1-2. Refer to Exercise 1-1 and answer the following questions:

1. Fred   Hand's   net   income   for   the   first   month   of   operations   was $_____.

2. Fred Hand's initial cash investment in the business was $_____.

3. Fred Hand's total owner's equity at the end of the first month of operations was
   $_____.

**Report
No. 1-1**

> *A workbook of study assignments is provided for use with this textbook.
> Each study assignment is referred to as a report. The work involved in com-
> pleting Report No. 1-1 requires a knowledge of the principles developed in
> the preceding textbook discussion. Before proceeding with the following dis-
> cussion, complete Report No. 1-1 in accordance with the instructions given
> in the study assignments.*

THE DOUBLE-ENTRY FRAMEWORK

The meanings of the terms asset, liability, and owner's equity were
explained in the preceding pages. Examples were given to show how
each business transaction causes a change in one or more of the three
basic accounting elements. Transaction (a) shown on page 8 involved
an increase in an asset with a corresponding increase in owner's equity.
Transaction (b) involved an increase in an asset which caused an equal
increase in a liability. Transaction (c) involved an increase in one asset
which was offset by a decrease in another. Each of the transactions
illustrated a dual effect. This is always true. A change, increase or
decrease, in any asset, any liability, or in owner's equity is always
accompanied by an offsetting change within the basic accounting
elements.

The fact that each transaction has two aspects—a dual effect upon
the accounting elements—provides the basis for what is called double-
entry bookkeeping. This term describes a processing system that
involves entering the two aspects that are involved in every transaction. Double entry does not mean that a transaction is entered twice;
instead, it means that both of the two aspects of each transaction are
entered.

Double entry is known to have been practiced for at least 500 years.
The method has endured largely because it has several virtues; it is
orderly, fairly simple, and very flexible. There is no transaction that
cannot be entered in a double-entry manner. Double entry promotes
accuracy. Its use makes it impossible for certain types of error to
remain undetected for very long. For example, if one aspect of a transaction is properly entered but the other aspect is overlooked, it will
soon be found that the records as a whole are "out of balance." The
accountant then knows that something is wrong, reviews the transaction to discover the trouble and then makes the needed correction.

The Account

It has been explained previously that the assets of a business may consist of a number of items, such as cash, accounts receivable, merchandise, equipment, buildings, and land. The liabilities may consist of one or more items, such as accounts payable and notes payable. A separate record should be kept of each asset and of each liability. Later it will be shown that a separate record should also be kept of the increases and decreases in owner's equity.

A form or record used to keep track of the increases and decreases in each item that result from business transactions is known as an account. There are many types of account forms in general use. They may be ruled on sheets of paper and bound in a book form or kept in a loose-leaf binder; they may be ruled on cards and kept in a file of some sort; or they may be developed as computer print-outs. The following is an illustration of a standard account form.

Standard Form of Account

The three major parts of the standard account form are (1) the title and the account number, (2) the debit or left side, and (3) the credit or right side. This account form is designed to facilitate the entering of the essential information regarding each transaction that affects the account. Each account should be given an appropriate title that will indicate whether it is an asset, a liability, or an owner's equity account.

Before any entries are made in an account, the title and number of the account should be entered on the horizontal line at the top of the form. The standard account form is divided into two equal parts or sections which are ruled identically to facilitate entering increases and decreases. The left side is called the debit side, while the right side is called the credit side. The Date columns are used for entering the dates of transactions. The Item columns may be used for entering a brief description of a transaction when deemed necessary. The Posting Reference columns will be discussed later. The amount column on the left is headed "Debit" while that on the right is headed "Credit." The Debit and Credit columns are used for entering the amounts of `transactions.

To determine the balance of an account at any time, it is necessary only to total the amounts in the Debit and Credit columns, and calculate the difference between the two totals. To save time, a T account is commonly used for instructional purposes. It consists of a two-line drawing resembling the capital letter T and is sometimes referred to as a skeleton form of account.

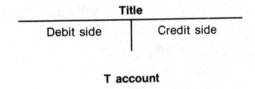

Title

Debit side | Credit side

T account

Debits and Credits

To debit an account means to enter an amount on the left or debit side of the account. To credit an account means to enter an amount on the right or credit side of the account. The abbreviation for debit is Dr. and for credit Cr. (based on the Latin terms "debere" and "credere"). Sometimes the word charge is used as a substitute for debit. Increases in assets are entered on the left side of the accounts; increases in liabilities and in owner's equity are entered on the right side of the accounts. Decreases in assets are entered on the right side of the accounts; decreases in liabilities and in owner's equity are entered on the left side of the accounts. Entering increases and decreases in the accounts in this manner will reflect the basic equality of assets to liabilities plus owner's equity (Assets = Liabilities + Owner's Equity); at the same time it will maintain equality between the total amounts debited to all accounts and the total amounts credited to all accounts (Debits = Credits). These basic relationships may be illustrated in the following manner:

ASSETS	=	LIABILITIES + OWNER'S EQUITY

All Asset Accounts	
Debit to enter increases (+)	Credit to enter decreases (−)

All Liability Accounts	
Debit to enter decreases (−)	Credit to enter increases (+)

All Owner's Equity Accounts	
Debit to enter decreases (−)	Credit to enter increases (+)

TOTAL DEBITS	=	TOTAL CREDITS

Use of Asset, Liability, and Owner's Equity Accounts

To illustrate the application of the double-entry process in handling transactions that affect asset, liability, and owner's equity accounts, the transactions discussed on pages 8-10 will be analyzed and their effect on the accounting elements will be indicated by showing the proper entries in T accounts. As before, the transactions are identified by letters; dates are omitted intentionally.

Transaction (a)

An Increase in an Asset Offset by an Increase in Owner's Equity

Gray Dorsey, an attorney, started a business by investing $10,000 in cash.

Cash		Gray Dorsey, Capital	
(a) 10,000			(a) 10,000

Analysis: As a result of this transaction the business acquired an asset, cash. The amount of money invested represents Dorsey's equity in the business; thus the amount of the asset cash is equal to the owner's equity in the business. Separate accounts are kept for the asset cash and for the owner's equity. To enter the transaction as an increase in an asset and an increase in owner's equity, the cash account was debited and Dorsey's capital account was credited for $10,000.

Transaction (b)

An Increase in an Asset Offset by an Increase in a Liability

Purchased office equipment (desk, chairs, file cabinet, etc.) for $4,900 on 30 days' credit.

Office Equipment		Accounts Payable	
(b) 4,900			(b) 4,900

Analysis: As a result of this transaction the business acquired a new asset, office equipment. The debt incurred as a result of purchasing the equipment on 30 days' credit is a liability, accounts payable. Thus, the outside interest in the business has increased by $4,900. Separate accounts are kept for office equipment and for accounts payable. The purchase of office equipment caused an increase in the assets of the business. Therefore, the asset account, Office Equipment, was debited for $4,900. The purchase also caused an increase in a liability. There-fore the liability account, Accounts Payable was credited for $4,900.

Transaction (c)

An Increase in One Asset Offset by a Decrease in Another Asset

Purchased office supplies (stationery, legal pads, pencils, etc.) for cash, $760.

Cash			Office Supplies	
(a) 10,000	(c) 760		(c) 760	

Analysis: As a result of this transaction the business acquired a new asset, office supplies. The addition of this asset was offset by a decrease in the asset cash. Notice there is no change in total assets. To enter the transaction properly, Office Supplies was debited and Cash was credited for $760. This is the second entry in the cash account; the account was previously debited for $10,000 when Transaction (a) was entered.

It is proper to enter office supplies as an asset at the time of purchase even though they will become an expense when used. The procedure in accounting for supplies used will be discussed later.

Transaction (d)

A Decrease in an Asset Offset by a Decrease in a Liability

Paid $2,800 on account to the company from which the office equipment was purchased. (See Transaction (b).)

Cash				Accounts Payable			
(a)	10,000	(c)	760	(d)	2,800	(b)	4,900
		(d)	2,800				

Analysis: This transaction resulted in a decrease in the liability accounts payable with a corresponding decrease in the asset cash; hence, it was entered by debiting Accounts Payable and by crediting Cash for $2,800. Note that this is the second entry in the accounts payable account and the third entry in the cash account. At this point in time, the outside interest in the business has decreased by $2,800.

Revenue and Expense

The owner's equity element of a business entity or professional enterprise may be increased in two ways as follows:

1. The owner may invest additional money or other property in the enterprise. Such investments result in an increase both in the assets of the enterprise and in the owner's equity, but they do not further enrich the owner. More property merely is invested in the enterprise and less property outside of the enterprise.
2. Revenue may be derived from sales of goods or services, or from other sources.

As used in accounting, the term revenue in nearly all cases refers to an increase in the owner's equity in a business resulting from transactions involving asset inflows other than the investment of assets in the business by its owner. In most cases, an increase in owner's equity due to revenue results from an addition to the assets without any change in the liabilities. Often it is cash that is increased. However, an increase in cash and other assets can occur in connection with several types of transactions that do not involve revenue. For this reason, revenue is often defined in terms of a change in owner's equity rather than a change in assets. Any transaction that causes owner's equity to increase, except for investments in the business by its owner, involves revenue.

The owner's equity element of a business entity or professional enterprise may be decreased in two ways as follows:

1. The owner may withdraw assets (cash or other property) from the business enterprise.
2. Expenses may be incurred in operating the enterprise.

As used in accounting, the term expense in nearly all cases means a decrease in the owner's equity in a business caused by transactions involving asset outflows other than a withdrawal by the owner. When an expense is incurred, either the assets are reduced or the liabilities are increased. In either event, owner's equity is reduced. If a transaction causing a reduction is not a withdrawal of assets by the owner, an expense is incurred. Common examples of expense are rent of office or store, salaries of employees, telephone service, supplies consumed, and many types of taxes.

If during a specified period of time, the total increases in owner's equity resulting from revenue exceed the total decreases resulting from expenses, it may be said that the excess represents the net income or net profit for the period.

> **Revenue > Expenses = Net Profit**

On the other hand, if the expenses of the period exceed the revenue, such excess represents a **net loss** for the period.

> **Expenses > Revenue = Net Loss**

The time interval used in the measurement of net income or net loss can be determined by the owner. It may be a month, a quarter (three months), a year, or some other period of time. Any accounting period of twelve months' duration is usually referred to as a fiscal year. The fiscal year frequently coincides with the calendar year.

Transactions involving revenue and expense always cause a change in the owner's equity element of an enterprise. Such changes could be entered by debiting an account called Owner's Equity for expense and crediting it for revenue. If this practice were followed, however, the credit side of the owner's equity account would contain a mixture of increases due to revenue and to the investment of assets in the business by the owner, while the debit side would contain a mixture of decreases due to expenses and to the withdrawal of assets from the business by the owner. In order to determine the net income or the net loss for each accounting period, a careful analysis of the owner's equity account would be required. It is, therefore, better practice to enter revenue and expenses in separate accounts.

When a transaction produces revenue, the amount of the revenue should be credited to an appropriate revenue account. When a transaction involves expense, the amount of the expense should be debited to an appropriate expense account. The relationship of these accounts to the owner's equity account and the application of the debit and credit theory to the accounts are indicated in the following diagram:

All Owner's Equity Accounts

Debit	Credit
to enter	to enter
decreases	increases
(−)	(+)

All Expense Accounts

Debit	Credit
to enter	to enter
increases	decreases
(+)	(−)

All Revenue Accounts

Debit	Credit
to enter	to enter
decreases	increases
(−)	(+)

The revenue and expense accounts are called temporary owner's equity accounts because it is customary to close them into the owner's equity account (which sets their balances back to zero) at the end of each accounting period. It is important to recognize that the credit side of each revenue account is serving temporarily as a part of the credit side of the owner's equity account. Increases in owner's equity are entered as credits. Thus increases in owner's equity resulting from revenue should be credited to revenue accounts. The debit side of each expense account is serving temporarily as a part of the debit side of the owner's equity account. Decreases in owner's equity are entered as debits. Thus decreases in owner's equity resulting from expense should be debited to expense accounts.

Use of Revenue and Expense Accounts

To illustrate the application of the double-entry process in handling transactions that affect revenue and expense accounts, the transactions discussed on pages 9-10 will be analyzed and their effect on the accounting elements will be indicated by showing the proper entries in T accounts. These transactions represent a continuation of the transactions completed by Gray Dorsey, an attorney, in the conduct of his practice. (See pages 16-18 for Transactions (a) to (d)).

Transaction (e)

An Increase in an Asset Offset by an Increase
in Owner's Equity Resulting from Revenue

Received $2,000 in cash from a client for professional services rendered.

Cash				Professional Fees	
(a)	10,000	(c)	760	(e)	2,000
(e)	2,000	(d)	2,800		

Analysis: This transaction results in an increase in the asset cash with a corresponding increase in owner's equity because of revenue from professional fees. To enter the transaction properly, Cash was debited and an appropriate account for the revenue was credited for $2,000. Accounts should always be given a descriptive title that will aid in classifying them in relation to the accounting elements. In this case the revenue account was given the title, Professional Fees. Note that this is the fourth entry in the cash account and the first entry in the account, Professional Fees.

Transaction (f)

A Decrease in an Asset Offset by a Decrease
in Owner's Equity Resulting from Expense

1. Paid $400 for office rent for one month.

Cash				Rent Expense	
(a)	10,000	(c)	760	(f1)	400
(e)	2,000	(d)	2,800		
		(f1)	400		

Analysis: This transaction resulted in a decrease in the asset cash with a corresponding decrease in owner's equity because of expense. To enter the transaction properly, Rent Expense was debited and Cash was credited for $400. This is the first entry in the rent expense account and the fifth entry in the cash account.

2. Paid bill for telephone service, $49.

Cash				Telephone Expense	
(a)	10,000	(c)	760	(f2)	49
(e)	2,000	(d)	2,800		
		(f1)	400		
		(f2)	49		

Analysis: This transaction is identical with the previous one except that telephone expense rather than rent expense was the reason for the decrease in owner's equity. To enter the transaction properly, Telephone Expense was debited and Cash was credited for $49. This is the first entry in the telephone expense account and the sixth entry in the cash account.

The Trial Balance

It is a fundamental principle of the double-entry framework that the sum of the assets is always equal to the sum of the liabilities and owner's equity. In order to maintain this equality in entering transactions, the sum of the debit entries must always be equal to the sum of the credit entries. To determine whether this equality has been maintained, it is customary to take a trial balance periodically. A trial balance is a list of all of the accounts showing the title and balance of each account. The balance of any account is the amount of difference between the total debits and the total credits to that account. To determine the balance of each account, first the debit and credit amount columns should be totaled. This procedure is called footing the amount columns as shown in the following illustration:

Cash			
(a)	10,000	(c)	760
(e)	2,000	(d)	2,800
7,991	*12,000*	(f1)	400
		(f2)	49
			4,009

If there is only one item entered in a column, no footing is necessary. To find the balance of an account, it is necessary only to determine the difference between the footings by subtraction.

Since asset and expense accounts are debited for increases, these accounts normally have debit balances. Since liability, owner's equity, and revenue accounts are credited to enter increases, these accounts normally have credit balances. The balance of an account should be entered on the side of the account that has the larger total. The footings and balances of accounts should be entered in small figures just below the last entry, preferably in pencil. If the two footings of an account are equal in amount, the account is said to be in balance.

The accounts of Gray Dorsey are reproduced below. To show their relationship to the fundamental accounting equation, the accounts are arranged in three columns under the headings of Assets, Liabilities, and Owner's Equity. The footings and the balance are printed in italics. Note the position of the footings directly under the debit and credit amount columns of the cash account, and the position of the balance on the left side of the cash account. (The balance of the accounts payable account is shown on the right side in italics.) It is not necessary to enter the balances of the other accounts because there are entries on only one side of those accounts.

ASSETS	=	LIABILITIES	+	OWNER'S EQUITY

Cash		Accounts Payable		Gray Dorsey, Capital	
(a) 10,000	(c) 760	(d) 2,800	(b) 4,900		(a) 10,000
(e) 2,000	(d) 2,800		*2,100*		
7,991 12,000	(f1) 400				
	(f2) 49				
	4,009				

Office Supplies		Professional Fees	
(c) 760			(e) 2,000

Office Equipment		Rent Expense	
(b) 4,900		(f1) 400	

		Telephone Expense	
		(f2) 49	

The following is a trial balance of Gray Dorsey's accounts. The trial balance was taken on June 30, 1986; therefore, this date is shown on the third line of the heading. The trial balance shows that the debit and credit totals are equal in amount. This is proof that in entering Transactions (a) to (f) inclusive the total of the debits was equal to the total of the credits.

Gray Dorsey, Attorney Trial Balance June 30, 1986		
Account	Dr. Balance	Cr. Balance
Cash	7991 00	
Office Supplies	760 00	
Office Equipment	4900 00	
Accounts Payable		2100 00
Gray Dorsey, Capital		10000 00
Professional Fees		2000 00
Rent Expense	400 00	
Telephone Expense	49 00	
	14100 00	14100 00

Gray Dorsey's Trial Balance

A trial balance is not a formal statement or report. Normally, it is never seen by anyone except the accountant or bookkeeper. It is used as an aid in preparing the income statement and the balance sheet. If the trial balance is studied in conjunction with the income statement and the balance sheet shown on page 11, it will be seen that those statements could have been prepared quite easily from the information that this trial balance provides.

BUILDING YOUR ACCOUNTING KNOWLEDGE

1. Identify at least three ways in which account forms may be developed and kept.
2. What are the three major parts of the standard account form?
3. What is the standard form of account designed to facilitate?
4. Explain the basis of the abbreviations "Dr." for debit and "Cr." for credit.
5. What word is sometimes used as a substitute for debit?
6. In most cases an increase in owner's equity due to revenue results from what event?
7. When an expense is incurred, what may be the effect on the assets? What may be the effect on the liabilities?
8. What is the purpose of the trial balance?

APPLYING ACCOUNTING CONCEPTS

Exercise 1-3. For each of the transactions in Exercise 1-1, show the effect on the accounting elements by preparing proper entries in appropriate asset, liability, owner's equity, revenue, and expense T accounts.

Exercise 1-4. Refer to Exercise 1-3. Prepare a trial balance for Fred Hand's business at the end of the first month of operations.

Report No. 1-2

Refer to the study assignments and complete Report No. 1-2 in accordance with the instructions given therein. The work involved in completing the assignment requires a knowledge of the principles developed in the preceding discussion. Any difficulty experienced in completing the report will indicate a lack of understanding of these principles. In such event further study, using the vocabulary words below, should be helpful. After completing the report, you may continue with the textbook discussion in Chapter 2 until the next report is required.

EXPANDING YOUR BUSINESS VOCABULARY

What is the meaning of each of the following terms?

account **(p. 14)**

accountant **(p. 4)**

accounting equation **(p. 6)**

account payable **(p. 5)**

account receivable **(p. 4)**

assets **(p. 4)**

auditing **(p. 2)**

balance **(p. 22)**

balance sheet **(p. 11)**

bookkeeper **(p. 4)**

business accounting **(p. 3)**

business entity **(p. 4)**

capital **(p. 5)**

charge **(p. 15)**

credit **(p. 15)**

credit balances **(p. 22)**

debit **(p. 15)**

debit balances **(p. 22)**

double-entry bookkeeping **(p. 13)**

expense **(p. 19)**

fiscal year **(p. 19)**

footing **(p. 22)**

in balance **(p. 23)**

income statement **(p. 10)**

information processor **(p. 4)**

input **(p. 12)**

liability **(p. 5)**

net income **(p. 19)**

net loss **(p. 19)**

net worth **(p. 5)**

notes payable **(p. 5)**

operating statement **(p. 10)**

output **(p. 12)**

owner's equity **(p. 5)**

processing **(p. 12)**

profit and loss statement **(p. 10)**

proprietorship **(p. 5)**

revenue **(p. 18)**

statement of financial condition
   (p. 11)

statement of financial position **(p. 11)**

temporary owner's equity
   accounts **(p. 20)**

transaction **(p. 7)**

trial balance **(p. 22)**

T account **(p. 15)**

CHAPTER 2

Accounting Procedure

CHAPTER OBJECTIVES

Careful study of this chapter should enable you to:

- Recognize the flow of the financial data in an accounting information system—the basic accounting cycle.

- Explain the purpose of a book of original entry.

- Describe the chart of accounts as a means of classifying financial information, using an account numbering system.

- Perform the journalizing and posting process.

- Prepare the income statement and the balance sheet.

The double-entry framework of accounting was explained and illustrated in the preceding chapter. To avoid complicating these principles, the mechanics of collecting and classifying information about business transactions were ignored. In actual practice, the first record of a transaction, sometimes called the source document, is in the form of a business paper, such as a check stub, receipt, cash register tape, sales ticket, or purchase invoice. The information supplied by source documents is an aid in analyzing transactions to determine their effect upon the accounts.

This chapter traces the flow of relevant financial data through the accounting information system. The functions of a book of original entry and a set of accounts are described, and their uses in the journalizing and posting process are explained and illustrated. The role of the chart of accounts in classifying financial information also is described and illustrated. Finally, the procedures for preparing the trial balance,

26

and the income statement and balance sheet from trial balance information, are explained and illustrated.

JOURNALIZING TRANSACTIONS

A collection of the double-entry records of the transactions of a business is called a journal. The act of entering transactions in a journal is called journalizing. It is necessary to analyze each transaction before it can be journalized properly. The purpose of a series of journal entries is to provide a chronological record of all transactions completed by the business showing the date of each transaction, titles of the accounts to be debited and credited, and the amounts of the debits and credits. The journal then provides all the information needed to transfer the debits and credits to the proper accounts. When the accounts are grouped together, they collectively comprise a ledger. The flow of data concerning transactions can be illustrated in the following manner:

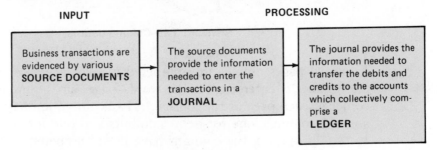

INPUT   PROCESSING

| Business transactions are evidenced by various **SOURCE DOCUMENTS** | The source documents provide the information needed to enter the transactions in a **JOURNAL** | The journal provides the information needed to transfer the debits and credits to the accounts which collectively comprise a **LEDGER** |

Source Documents

The term source document covers a wide variety of forms and papers. Almost any document that provides information about a business transaction can be called a source document.

<u>SOURCE DOCUMENTS</u>

Examples:
1. Check stubs or carbon copies of checks
2. Receipt stubs, carbon copies of receipts, cash register tapes, or memos of cash register totals.
3. Copies of sales tickets or sales invoices issued to customers or clients
4. Purchase invoices received from suppliers

Provide information about:
Cash payments

Cash receipts

Sales of goods or services

Purchases of goods or services

The Journal

A journal is commonly referred to as a book of original entry because the first formal accounting record of a transaction is made in a journal from source document information. The format of the pages of a journal varies with the type and size of an enterprise and the nature of its operations. Although a wide variety of journals are used in business, the simplest form of journal is a two-column journal. The following is a standard form of such a journal.

| | JOURNAL | | | PAGE |
DATE	DESCRIPTION	POST. REF.	DEBIT	CREDIT
①	②	③	④	⑤

Standard Two-Column Journal

Journal pages usually are numbered in sequence, and the appropriate number is entered after the word "page" in the upper right-hand corner of each page of the journal. A two-column journal has only two amount columns, one for debit amounts and one for credit amounts. In the illustration, the columns have been numbered to facilitate the following discussion.

Column 1 is the Date column. The year is entered in small figures at the top of the column immediately below the column heading and need only be repeated at the top of each new page unless an entry for a new year is made farther down on the page. The Date column is a double column, the perpendicular single rule being used to separate the month from the day. Thus in entering the date, the name of the month should be entered in full or abbreviated to the left of the single line. The number designating the day of the month should be entered to the right of this line. The name of the month need only be shown for the first entry on a page unless an entry for a new month is made farther down on the page.

Column 2 is generally referred to as the Description or explanation column. The Description column is used to enter the titles of the accounts affected by each transaction, together with a description of the transaction. Two or more accounts are affected by each transaction, and the titles of all accounts must be entered. The titles of the accounts debited are entered first, followed by the titles of the accounts credited. A separate line should be used for each account title. The titles of the accounts to be debited are entered at the extreme left of the column, while the titles of the accounts to be credited are usually indented one-half inch (about 1.3 centimeters). The description should be entered immediately following the credit entry and indented an additional one-half inch.

Column 3 is the Posting Reference column sometimes referred to as a folio column. No entries are made in this column at the time of journalizing the transactions; such entries are made only at the time of posting which is the process of entering the debit and credit elements in the proper accounts in the ledger. This procedure will be explained in detail later in this chapter.

Column 4, the Debit amount column, is a column in which the amount that is to be debited to an account should be entered on the same line on which the title of that account appears in the description column.

Column 5, the Credit amount column, is a column in which the amount that is to be credited to an account should be entered on the same line on which the title of that account appears in the description column.

Journalizing

Journalizing involves entering the significant information concerning each transaction either (1) at the time the transaction occurs or (2) subsequently, but in the chronological order in which it and the other transactions occurred. For every transaction, the entry should include the date, the title of each account affected, the amounts, and a brief description. Before a transaction can be entered properly, it must be analyzed in order to determine:

1. Which accounts are affected by the transaction.
2. What effect the transaction has upon each of the accounts involved, that is, whether the balance of each affected account is increased or decreased.

To illustrate the journalizing process, assume that a business purchased an electronic calculator on June 25 for $125 in cash. The asset accounts affected are Office Equipment and Cash. Office Equipment was increased and Cash was decreased upon purchase of the calculator. The following information would be entered in a two-column journal.

JOURNAL					PAGE	
	DATE	DESCRIPTION	POST. REF.	DEBIT	CREDIT	
1	*1986 June 25*	*Office Equipment*		*12500*		1
2		*Cash*			*12500*	2
3		*Purchased an electronic calculator.*				3
4						4

The Chart of Accounts

In analyzing a transaction prior to journalizing it, the accountant or bookkeeper must know which accounts are being kept. When an accounting information system is established for a new business, the first step is to decide which accounts are required. The accounts used will depend upon the information needed or desired. Ordinarily, it is desirable to keep a separate account for each type of asset and each type of liability, since it is certain that information will be desired in regard to what is owned and what is owed. A permanent owner's equity or capital account should be kept in order that information may be available as to the owner's interest in the business. Furthermore, it is advisable to keep separate accounts for each type of revenue and each kind of expense. The revenue and expense accounts are temporary accounts that are used in entering increases and decreases in owner's equity from day-to-day business transactions apart from changes caused by the owner's investments and withdrawals. The specific accounts to be kept for entering increases and decreases in owner's equity depend upon the nature and sources of the revenue and the nature of the expenses incurred in earning the revenue.

A professional person or an individual engaged in operating a small enterprise may need to keep relatively few accounts. On the other hand, a large business may need to keep a great many accounts because of the complexity of the operation. Regardless of the number, accounts can be segregated into the three major classes, assets, liabilities, and owner's equity, and should be grouped according to these classes in the ledger. Asset accounts are placed first, liability accounts second, and owner's equity accounts, including revenue and expense accounts, last. A list of all the accounts used by a business is called a chart of accounts. It has become a general practice to give each account a number and to keep the accounts in numerical order. The numbering usually follows a consistent pattern and becomes a code. For example, asset accounts may be assigned numbers that always start with "1," liability accounts with "2," owner's equity accounts with "3," revenue accounts with "4," and expense accounts with "5."

To illustrate, assume that on December 1, 1986, Victor Pearce enters the employment agency business under the name of The Victor Pearce Placement Service. Since the accounts are to be kept on the calendar-year basis, the first accounting period will be for one month only, that is, for the month of December. A two-column journal and a ledger will be used. There will not be a need for many accounts at present because the business is new but additional accounts may be added as the need arises. The following is a chart of the accounts for The Victor Pearce Placement Service:

THE VICTOR PEARCE PLACEMENT SERVICE

CHART OF ACCOUNTS

Assets*
- 111 Cash
- 151 Office Supplies
- 191 Office Equipment

Liabilities
- 218 Accounts Payable

Owner's Equity
- 311 Victor Pearce, Capital
- 311.1 Victor Pearce, Drawing**

Revenue
- 411 Placement Fees

Expenses
- 541 Rent Expense
- 542 Salary Expense
- 543 Travel and Entertainment Expense
- 544 Telephone Expense
- 545 Office Supplies Expense
- 562 Miscellaneous Expense

*Words in heavy type represent headings and not account titles.
**The number of this account will have four digits with a decimal point separating the third and fourth digit. The first three digits will be the same as the capital account to indicate that its balance is subtracted from the capital account balance on the balance sheet. A similar procedure will be followed for all accounts whose balances are subtracted from other related account balances on the financial statements.

Journalizing Procedure Illustrated

To illustrate journalizing procedures, the transactions completed by The Victor Pearce Placement Service through December 31, 1986, will be journalized. A narrative of the transactions follows which provides all of the information needed in journalizing the transactions. Some of the transactions are analyzed to explain their effect upon the accounts. The analysis will immediately follow the journal entry.

THE VICTOR PEARCE PLACEMENT SERVICE

NARRATIVE OF TRANSACTIONS

Monday, December 1, 1986

Pearce invested $4,000 cash in a business enterprise to be known as the Victor Pearce Placement Service.

JOURNAL					PAGE /
DATE	DESCRIPTION	POST. REF.	DEBIT	CREDIT	
1986 Dec. 1	Cash		400000		1
	Victor Pearce, Capital			400000	2
	Original investment in				3
	placement service.				4

Analysis: As a result of this transaction, the business acquired the asset cash in the amount of $4,000. Since Pearce contributed this asset, the transaction caused an increase of $4,000 in owner's equity. Accordingly, the entry for the transaction is a debit to Cash and a credit to Victor Pearce, Capital, for $4,000.

Note that the following steps are involved:

1. Since this was the first entry on the journal page, the year is entered at the top of the Date column.
2. The month (abbreviated) and day are entered on the first line in the Date column.
3. The title of the account to be debited, Cash, is entered on the first line at the extreme left of the Description column. The amount of the debit, $4,000, is entered on the same line in the Debit column.
4. The title of the account to be credited, Victor Pearce, Capital, is entered on the second line indented one-half inch from the left side of the Description column. The amount of the credit, $4,000, is entered on the same line in the Credit column.
5. The explanation of the entry is entered on the next line indented an additional one-half inch. The second line of the explanation is also indented the same distance as the first.

Wednesday, December 3

Paid office rent for December, $450.

	3	Rent Expense		45000		5
		Cash			45000	6
		Paid December rent.				7

Analysis: This transaction resulted in an increase in an expense, with a corresponding decrease in the asset cash. The increase in the expense represents a decrease in owner's equity. The transaction is entered by debiting Rent Expense and by crediting Cash for $450.

Pearce ordered several pieces of office equipment. Since the dealer did not have in stock what Pearce wanted, the articles were ordered from the factory. Delivery is not expected until the latter part of the month. Pending arrival of the equipment, the dealer loaned Pearce some used office equipment. No entry is required until the new equipment is received.

Friday, December 5

Purchased office supplies from the S. G. Adams Co. on account, $368.

8	5	Office Supplies		368 00		8
9		Accounts Payable			368 00	9
10		S. G. Adams Co.				10

Analysis: In this transaction, the business acquired a new asset which represented an increase in the total assets. A liability was also incurred because of the purchase on account. The transaction is entered by debiting Office Supplies and crediting Accounts Payable for $368. As these supplies are consumed, the amount will become an expense of the business.

Monday, December 8

Paid the General Telephone Co. $45 covering the cost of installing a telephone in the office, together with the first month's service charges payable in advance.

11	8	Telephone Expense		45 00		11
12		Cash			45 00	12
13		Paid telephone bill.				13

Analysis: This transaction caused an increase in an expense and a corresponding decrease in the asset cash. The transaction is entered by debiting Telephone Expense and by crediting Cash for $45.

Tuesday, December 9

Paid $11 for a subscription to a trade journal.

14	9	Miscellaneous Expense		11 00		14
15		Cash			11 00	15
16		Trade journal sub.				16

Analysis: This transaction resulted in an increase in an expense and a corresponding decrease in the asset cash. The transaction is entered by debiting Miscellaneous Expense and by crediting Cash for $11.

Wednesday, December 10

Received $300 from Dore Hainer's employer for placement services rendered.

17	10 Cash	300 00	
18	Placement Fees		300 00
19	Placed Dore Hainer.		

Analysis: This transaction resulted in an increase in the asset cash with a corresponding increase in revenue from placement fees. The transaction is entered by debiting Cash and by crediting Placement Fees for $300. In keeping the accounts, Pearce follows the practice of not entering revenue until it is received in cash. This practice is common to professional and personal service enterprises.

Friday, December 12

Paid the Apex Travel Service $195 for an airplane ticket to be used the next week for a placement officer's convention trip.

20	12 Travel & Entertainment Expense	195 00	
21	Cash		195 00
22	Airplane fare-convention.		

Analysis: This transaction resulted in an increase in an expense and a corresponding decrease in the asset cash. The transaction is entered by debiting Travel and Entertainment Expense and by crediting Cash for $195.

Monday, December 15

Paid Ida Early $300 covering her salary for the first half of the month. Early is employed by Pearce as a secretary and bookkeeper at a salary of $600 a month.

23	15 Salary Expense	300 00	
24	Cash		300 00
25	Paid secretary's salary.		

Analysis: This transaction resulted in an increase in salary expense with a corresponding decrease in the asset cash. The transaction is entered by debiting Salary Expense and by crediting Cash for $300. (The matter of payroll taxes is purposely ignored at this point. These taxes will be discussed in detail in Chapter 4.)

Note that the Posting Reference column has been left blank in the eight preceding journal entry illustrations. This is because the column is not used until the amounts are posted to the accounts in the ledger, a process to be described starting on page 40. Account numbers are shown in the Posting Reference column of the journal illustrated on pages 37 and 38, since the illustration shows how the journal appears after the posting has been completed.

The journal entries for the following transactions (as well as for those to this point) are illustrated on pages 37 and 38.

Wednesday, December 17

Received $750 from Michael Dorf's employer for placement services rendered.

Friday, December 19

Pearce withdrew $1,000 for personal use.

Analysis: Amounts of cash withdrawn for personal use by the owner of a business enterprise represent a decrease in owner's equity. Although the amounts withdrawn might be entered as debits to the owner's capital account, it is better practice to enter withdrawals in a separate account, Victor Pearce, Drawing, since this makes it easier to summarize the owner's withdrawals. This transaction is entered in the journal by debiting Victor Pearce, Drawing, and by crediting Cash for $1,000.

Monday, December 22

Received $800 from Julia Buser's employer for placement services rendered.

Wednesday, December 24

Paid $75 membership dues in the American Society for Personnel Administration.

Monday, December 29

Received the office equipment ordered December 3. These items were purchased on account from Interiors Unlimited for $3,500. The dealer removed the used equipment that had been loaned to Pearce.

Tuesday, December 30

Paid the S. G. Adams Co. $368 for the office supplies purchased on December 5.

Analysis: This transaction caused a decrease in the liability accounts payable with a corresponding decrease in the asset cash. The transaction is entered by debiting Accounts Payable and by crediting Cash for $368.

Received from Deanna Einspahr's employer $600 for placement services rendered.

Wednesday, December 31

Paid Early $300 covering her salary for the second half of the month.

Office supplies used during the month, $62.

Analysis: Refer to the transaction of December 5, and note that office supplies amounting to $368 were purchased and were recorded as an asset. By taking an inventory, counting the supplies in stock at the end of the month, Pearce was able to determine that $306 of supplies were on hand. This meant that the expense of supplies used during the month amounted to $62 ($368 − $306). The total expenses for the month of December would not be reflected properly if the supplies used during the month were not taken into consideration. Therefore, the expense of supplies used is entered by debiting the expense account, Office Supplies Expense, and by crediting the asset account, Office Supplies, for $62.

Note that in the journal illustrated on pages 37 and 38 there are no blank lines between the entries. Some bookkeepers leave a blank line after the explanation of each entry. This practice is acceptable, though not recommended, because it provides an opportunity for dishonest persons to alter one or more entries.

Proving The Journal

Because a double entry is made for each transaction, the equality of debit and credit entries on each page of the journal may be proved merely by totaling the amount columns. The total of each column is

	DATE	DESCRIPTION	POST. REF.	DEBIT	CREDIT	
1	1986 Dec. 1	Cash	111	400000		1
2		Victor Pearce, Capital	311		400000	2
3		Original investment in				3
4		placement service				4
5	3	Rent Expense	541	45000		5
6		Cash	111		45000	6
7		Paid December rent.				7
8	5	Office Supplies	151	36800		8
9		Accounts Payable	218		36800	9
10		S. G. Adams Co.				10
11	8	Telephone Expense	544	4500		11
12		Cash	111		4500	12
13		Paid telephone bill.				13
14	9	Miscellaneous Expense	562	1100		14
15		Cash	111		1100	15
16		Trade journal sub.				16
17	10	Cash	111	30000		17
18		Placement Fees	411		30000	18
19		Placed Dore Hainer.				19
20	12	Travel & Entertainment Expense	543	19500		20
21		Cash	111		19500	21
22		Airplane fare - convention.				22
23	15	Salary Expense	542	30000		23
24		Cash	111		30000	24
25		Paid secretary's salary.				25
26	17	Cash	111	75000		26
27		Placement Fees	411		75000	27
28		Placed Michael Dorf.				28
29	19	Victor Pearce, Drawing	311.1	100000		29
30		Cash	111		100000	30
31		Withdrawn for personal use.				31
32	22	Cash	111	80000		32
33		Placement Fees	411		80000	33
34		Placed Julia Buser.				34
35	24	Miscellaneous Expense	562	7500		35
36		Cash	111		7500	36
37		A. S. P. A. dues.				37
38	29	Office Equipment	191	350000		38
39		Accounts Payable	218		350000	39
40		Interiors Unlimited		1179400	1179400	40

VICTOR PEARCE PLACEMENT SERVICE

(continued on next page)

JOURNAL					PAGE 2	

	DATE		DESCRIPTION	POST. REF.	DEBIT	CREDIT	
1	*1986* Dec	30	Accounts Payable	218	36800		1
2			Cash	111		36800	2
3			S. G. Adams Co.				3
4		30	Cash	111	60000		4
5			Placement Fees	411		60000	5
6			Placed Deanna Einspahr				6
7		31	Salary Expense	542	30000		7
8			Cash	111		30000	8
9			Paid secretary's salary.				9
10		31	Office Supplies Expense	545	6200		10
11			Office Supplies	151		6200	11
12			Expense of supplies				12
13			used during December.				13
14					133000	133000	14

VICTOR PEARCE PLACEMENT SERVICE
(concluded)

entered as a footing immediately under the last entry. When a page of the journal is filled, the footings may be entered just under the last single horizontal ruled line at the bottom of the page as shown in the illustration on page 37. When it is desirable to prove the equality of debits and credits on a page that is not filled, the footings should be entered immediately under the last entry as shown in the foregoing illustration.

BUILDING YOUR ACCOUNTING KNOWLEDGE

1. Where are the first formal double-entry records of business transactions usually made?

2. Name a source document that provides information about each of the following types of business transactions:
(a) cash payment
(b) cash receipt
(c) sale of goods or services
(d) purchase of goods or services

3. What information usually is entered in each of the following columns of the journal?
(a) Date column
(b) Description column
(c) Debit amount column
(d) Credit amount column

4. What is the first step in establishing an accounting information system for a new business?

5. Name the five types of financial statement items for which it is ordinarily found desirable to keep separate accounts.
6. Which two types of accounts are temporarily used to enter increases and decreases in owner's equity from most day-to-day business transactions?
7. In what order are the accounts customarily placed in the ledger?

APPLYING ACCOUNTING CONCEPTS

Exercise 2-1. Rudy Hanes operates a personnel agency. Journalize the following transactions which occurred during the first month of operations (June, 19--). Use two-column journal paper. Identify the entries by inserting the transaction number in the Date column.

1. Hanes invested $15,000 cash in the business.
2. Paid office rent, $600.
3. Purchased office furniture from Indy Office Supply on account, $3,200.
4. Received $800 from Mary Wrona's employer for placement services rendered.
5. Paid Indy Office Supply $1,500 on account.

Exercise 2-2. Rose Thomas operates a consulting business. Journalize the following transactions which occurred during the first month of operations (January, 19--). Use two-column journal paper. Identify the entries by inserting the transaction number in the Date column.

1. Thomas invested $12,000 cash in the business.
2. Paid office rent, $700.
3. Paid Smithburn Telephone Company $52 for telephone installation and first month's service charges.
4. Paid $20 for a subscription to a trade journal.
5. Received $1,800 from Mary Alexer for consulting services rendered.
6. Purchased office supplies from HPR Co. on account, $650.
7. Paid office secretary $850 covering her salary for the first month.

**Report
No. 2-1**

Refer to the study assignments and complete Report No. 2-1. To complete this assignment correctly, the principles developed in the preceding discussion must be understood. Review the text assignment if necessary. After completing the report, continue with the following textbook discussion until the next report is required.

POSTING TO THE LEDGER; THE TRIAL BALANCE

The purpose of a journal is to provide a chronological record of financial transactions expressed as debits and credits to accounts. Accounts are kept to supply management with desired information in summary form. Collectively, the accounts are known as the general ledger, or often simply as "the ledger." The account forms may be on sheets of paper or on cards. When on sheets of paper, the sheets may be bound in book form or kept in a loose-leaf binder. Usually a separate page or card is used for each account. The accounts should be classified properly in the ledger; that is, the asset accounts should be grouped together, the liability accounts together, and the owner's equity accounts together. Proper grouping of the accounts in the ledger is an aid in preparing the various reports desired by the owner. Pearce decided to keep all of the accounts for the placement service in a loose-leaf ledger. The numbers shown in the service's chart of accounts on page 31 were used as a guide in arranging the accounts in the ledger. The ledger is reproduced on pages 42-44. Note that the accounts are in numerical order.

Since Pearce makes few purchases on account, a separate account is not kept for each supplier. When invoices are received for items purchased on account, the invoices are reviewed and entered in the journal by debiting the proper accounts and by crediting Accounts Payable. The credit balance of Accounts Payable indicates the total amount owed to suppliers. After each invoice is entered, it is filed in an unpaid invoice file, where it remains until it is paid in full. When an invoice in paid in full, it is removed from the unpaid invoice file and then filed under the name of the supplier for future reference. The balance of the accounts payable account may be proved at any time by determining the total of the unpaid amounts of the invoices.

Posting

The process of transferring information from the journal to the ledger is known as posting. All amounts entered in the journal should be posted to the accounts kept in the ledger in order to summarize the results. Such posting may be done daily or at frequent intervals. The ledger is not a reliable source of information until all of the transactions entered in the journal have been posted. Since the accounts provide the information needed in preparing financial statements, an accurate posting procedure must be maintained.

Posting from the journal to the ledger involves entering the following information in the accounts:

1. The date of each transaction.
2. The amount of each transaction.
3. The page of the journal from which each transaction is posted.

The posting procedure also requires that after the page of the journal has been posted to the ledger account, the number of that account should be entered in the Posting Reference column in the journal so as to provide a cross-reference between the journal and the ledger.

The first entry of the placement service to be posted from the journal occurred on December 1, 1986, and required a debit to cash of $4,000. The posting is, as shown in the following illustration, accomplished by (1) entering the year, "1986," the month, abbreviated "Dec.," and the day, "1," in the Date column of the cash account, (2) entering the amount, $4,000, in the Debit column, (3) entering the number "1" in the Posting Reference column since the posting came from Page 1 of the journal, and (4) entering the cash account number 111 in the Posting Reference column of the journal on the same line as the debit to Cash for $4,000. The same pattern is followed in posting the credit part of the entry, $4,000, to Victor Pearce, Capital, Account No. 311.

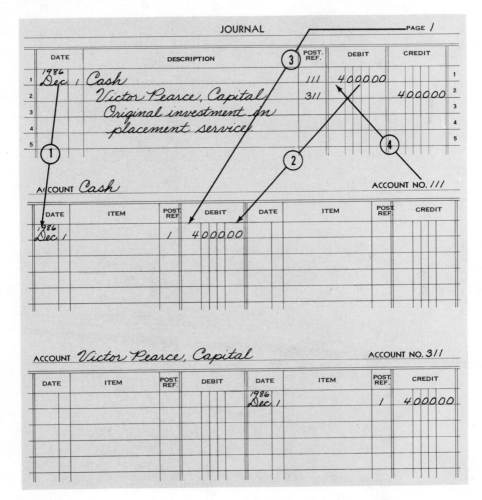

As shown in the journal of The Victor Pearce Placement Service (reproduced on pages 37 and 38) and its ledger (reproduced below and on pages 43-44), a similar procedure is followed in posting every amount from the journal. Note also that in the ledger, the year "1986" is entered only at the top of each Date column, and that the month "Dec." is entered only with the first posting to an account.

ACCOUNT Cash   ACCOUNT NO. 111

DATE	ITEM	POST. REF.	DEBIT	DATE	ITEM	POST. REF.	CREDIT
1986 Dec. 1		1	4000 00	1986 Dec. 3		1	450 00
10		1	300 00	8		1	45 00
17		1	750 00	9		1	11 00
22		1	800 00	12		1	195 00
30	3,706.00	2	600 00 / 6450 00	15		1	300 00
				19		1	1000 00
				24		1	75 00
				30		2	368 00
				31		2	300 00 / 2744 00

ACCOUNT Office Supplies   ACCOUNT NO. 151

DATE	ITEM	POST. REF.	DEBIT	DATE	ITEM	POST. REF.	CREDIT
1986 Dec. 5	306.00	1	368 00	1986 Dec. 31		2	62 00

ACCOUNT Office Equipment   ACCOUNT NO. 191

DATE	ITEM	POST. REF.	DEBIT	DATE	ITEM	POST. REF.	CREDIT
1986 Dec. 29		1	3500 00				

ACCOUNT Accounts Payable   ACCOUNT NO. 218

DATE	ITEM	POST. REF.	DEBIT	DATE	ITEM	POST. REF.	CREDIT
1986 Dec. 30		2	368 00	1986 Dec. 5		1	368 00
				29	3,500.00	1	3500 00 / 3868 00

The Victor Pearce Placement Service Ledger
(continued on next page)

ACCOUNT _Victor Pearce, Capital_   ACCOUNT NO. 311

DATE	ITEM	POST. REF.	DEBIT	DATE	ITEM	POST. REF.	CREDIT
				1986 Dec. 1		1	4000 00

ACCOUNT _Victor Pearce, Drawing_   ACCOUNT NO. 311.1

DATE	ITEM	POST. REF.	DEBIT	DATE	ITEM	POST. REF.	CREDIT
1986 Dec. 19		1	1000 00				

ACCOUNT _Placement Fees_   ACCOUNT NO. 411

DATE	ITEM	POST. REF.	DEBIT	DATE	ITEM	POST. REF.	CREDIT
				1986 Dec. 10		1	300 00
				17		1	750 00
				22		1	800 00
				30		2	600 00
							2450 00

ACCOUNT _Rent Expense_   ACCOUNT NO. 541

DATE	ITEM	POST. REF.	DEBIT	DATE	ITEM	POST. REF.	CREDIT
1986 Dec. 3		1	450 00				

ACCOUNT _Salary Expense_   ACCOUNT NO. 542

DATE	ITEM	POST. REF.	DEBIT	DATE	ITEM	POST. REF.	CREDIT
1986 Dec. 15		1	300 00				
31		2	300 00				
			600 00				

The Victor Pearce Placement Service Ledger
(continued)

ACCOUNT *Travel & Entertainment Expense*   **ACCOUNT NO.** *543*

DATE	ITEM	POST. REF.	DEBIT	DATE	ITEM	POST. REF.	CREDIT
1986 Dec. 12		1	19500				

ACCOUNT *Telephone Expense*   **ACCOUNT NO.** *544*

DATE	ITEM	POST. REF.	DEBIT	DATE	ITEM	POST. REF.	CREDIT
1986 Dec. 8		1	4500				

ACCOUNT *Office Supplies Expense*   **ACCOUNT NO.** *545*

DATE	ITEM	POST. REF.	DEBIT	DATE	ITEM	POST. REF.	CREDIT
1986 Dec. 31		2	6200				

ACCOUNT *Miscellaneous Expense*   **ACCOUNT NO.** *562*

DATE	ITEM	POST. REF.	DEBIT	DATE	ITEM	POST. REF.	CREDIT
1986 Dec. 9		1	1100				
24		1	7500				
			8600				

The Victor Pearce Placement Service Ledger
(concluded)

As shown in the preceding discussion, when the posting is completed, the same information is provided in both the journal and the ledger as to the date, the amount, and the effect of each transaction. A cross-reference from each book to the other book is provided by the Posting Reference column. Each entry in the journal may be traced to the ledger by referring to the account numbers indicated in the Posting Reference column of the journal. The cross reference also makes it possible to trace the entry in the ledger to the journal by referring to the page indicated in the Posting Reference column. Note that the account numbers were inserted in the Posting Reference column of the journal on pages 37 and 38. This was done as each part of the posting was completed.

The Trial Balance

As indicated in Chapter 1, the purpose of a trial balance is to prove that the totals of the debit and credit balances in the ledger accounts are equal. In a double-entry framework, equality of debit and credit balances in the ledger must be maintained. A trial balance may be taken daily, weekly, monthly, or whenever desired. Before taking a trial balance, all transactions should be journalized and the posting should be completed in order that the effect of all transactions to date will be reflected in the ledger accounts.

Footing Accounts. Prior to taking a trial balance it is necessary to (1) foot—add the amounts entered on the debit and credit side of each account and (2) determine the balance of each account. The footing process is illustrated in the following manner. The footings are entered immediately below the last item in both the debit and credit amount columns of the account. The footings should be entered in small figures close to the preceding line so that they will not interfere with the placing of an item on the next ruled line. At the same time, the balance (the difference between the footings) is computed and entered in small figures in the Item column of the account on the side with the larger footing. In other words, if an account has a debit balance, the balance should be entered in the Item column on the debit or left side of the account just below the line on which the last regular entry appears and in line with the footing. If the account has a credit balance. the balance should be entered in the Item column on the credit or right side of the account just below the line in which the last regular entry appears.

DATE	ITEM	POST. REF.	DEBIT	DATE	ITEM	POST. REF.	CREDIT
1986 Dec. 1		1	4 0 0 00	1986 Dec. 3		1	4 5 0 00
10		1	3 0 0 00	8		1	4 5 00
17		1	7 5 0 00	9		1	1 1 00
22		1	8 0 0 00	12		1	1 9 5 00
30	3,706.00	2	6 0 0 00 6 4 5 0 00	15		1	3 0 0 00
				19		1	1 0 0 0 00
				24		1	7 5 00
				30		2	3 6 8 00
				31		2	3 0 0 00 2 7 4 4 00

ACCOUNT Cash   ACCOUNT NO. 111

In the ledger shown on pages 42-44, the accounts have been footed and the footings and the balances are entered. When only one item has been posted to an account, regardless of whether it is a debit or a credit amount, no footing is necessary.

Care should be used in computing the balances of the accounts. If an error is made in adding the amount columns or in determining the difference between the footings, the error will be carried to the trial balance and considerable time may be required to locate the mistake. Most accounting errors result from carelessness. For example, a bookkeeper may enter an account balance on the wrong side of an account by mistake or may enter figures so carelessly that they may be misread later. Care in entering the amounts is just as important as accuracy in determining the footings and the balances.

Preparing the Trial Balance. It is important that the following procedure be followed in preparing a trial balance:

1. Head the trial balance showing (a) the name of the individual, firm, or organization, (b) the title of the report, "Trial Balance," and (c) the date. The date shown is the day of the last transaction that is included in the accounts, which is usually the last day of a month. A December 31 trial balance might be prepared by the bookkeeper on January 3, however, the accounts should reflect only transactions through December 31.
2. List the account titles in order, showing each account number.
3. Enter the account balances, placing debit balances in the left amount column and credit balances in the right amount column.
4. Add the columns and enter the totals, placing a single line across the amount columns above the totals and a double line below the totals in the manner shown in the illustration at the top of page 47.

A trial balance is usually prepared on ruled paper though it can be prepared on plain paper if desired. The illustration on page 47 shows the trial balance as of December 31, 1986, of the ledger of The Victor Pearce Placement Service.

Even though the trial balance indicates that the ledger is in balance, there still may be errors in the ledger. For example, if a journal entry has been made in which the wrong accounts were debited or credited, or if an item has been posted to the wrong account, the ledger will still be in balance. It is important, therefore, that extreme care be used in preparing the journal entries and in posting them to the ledger accounts.

BUILDING YOUR ACCOUNTING KNOWLEDGE.

1. What useful purpose is served by proper grouping of the accounts in the ledger?
2. When does the ledger become a reliable source of information?
3. Name the three elements of information normally entered in each ledger account involved in the posting process.

Victor Pearce Placement Service
Trial Balance
December 31, 1986

Account	Acct No.	Dr. Balance	Cr. Balance
Cash	111	370600	
Office Supplies	151	30600	
Office Equipment	191	350000	
Accounts Payable	218		350000
Victor Pearce, Capital	311		400000
Victor Pearce, Drawing	311.1	100000	
Placement Fees	411		245000
Rent Expense	541	45000	
Salary Expense	542	60000	
Travel & Entertainment Expense	543	19500	
Telephone Expense	544	4500	
Office Supplies Expense	545	6200	
Miscellaneous Expense	562	8600	
		995000	995000

Model Trial Balance

4. What information is entered in the Posting Reference column of the journal as each amount is posted to the proper account in the ledger?
5. Where should the footings of an account be entered?
6. Where should the balance of an account be entered?
7. Explain why there still may be errors in the ledger even though the trial balance indicates that the ledger is in balance. Give examples of two such types of errors.

APPLYING ACCOUNTING CONCEPTS

Exercise 2-3. **(a)** Using T accounts, post the journal entries from Exercise 2-1 to appropriate accounts **(b)** Foot the accounts, enter the balances, and prepare a trial balance.

Exercise 2-4. **(a)** Using T accounts, post the journal entries from Exercise 2-2 to appropriate accounts. **(b)** Foot the accounts, enter the balances, and prepare a trial balance.

**Report
No. 2-2**

Refer to the study assignments and complete Report No. 2-2. To complete this assignment correctly, the principles developed in the preceding discussion must be understood. Review the text assignment if necessary. After completing the report, continue with the following textbook discussion until the next report is required.

THE FINANCIAL STATEMENTS

The transactions completed by The Victor Pearce Placement Service during the month of December were entered in a two-column journal (see pages 37 and 38). The debits and credits were subsequently posted to the proper accounts in a ledger (see pages 42-44). At the end of the month, a trial balance was taken as a means of proving that the equality of debits and credits had been maintained throughout the journalizing and posting process (see page 47).

Although the trial balance of The Victor Pearce Placement Service taken as of December 31 lists all of the accounts, shows the amounts of their debit and credit balances, and proves the equality of these debit and credit balances, it does not clearly present all of the information that Pearce may need regarding the results of operations during the month or the status of the business at the end of the month. To meet these needs, it is the usual practice for a small personal service enterprise to prepare two financial statements—the income statement and the balance sheet. Preparation of the financial statements is the last step in the flow of the financial data through the accounting information system. This flow can be illustrated as follows:

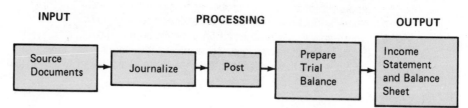

The Income Statement

An income statement is an itemized statement for the purpose of providing information regarding the results of operations during a specified period of time. It is a statement of the changes in owner's equity resulting from the revenue and expenses of a specific period (month, quarter, or year). Such changes are entered originally in temporary owner's equity accounts known as revenue and expense accounts. Changes in owner's equity resulting from investments or withdrawals of assets by the owner are not included in the income statement because they involve neither revenue nor expense.

The **heading** of an income statement consists of the following:

1. The name of the business.
2. The title of the statement.
3. The period of time covered by the statement.

The **body** of an income statement consists of (1) an itemized list of the sources and amounts of revenue received during the period, and (2) an itemized list of the various expenses incurred during the period. The income statement reflects the **matching** concept (matching the revenues and expenses of a business on a periodic basis). It is said that this matching process is the "heart" of income measurement.

The following income statement prepared from the Victor Pearce Placement Service trial balance shows the results of operations for the month ended December 31, 1986.

Victor Pearce Placement Service		
Income Statement		
For the Month Ended December 31, 1986		
Revenue:		
Placement fees		$ 245000
Expenses:		
Rent expense	$ 45000	
Salary expense	60000	
Travel & entertainment expense	19500	
Telephone expense	4500	
Office supplies expense	6200	
Miscellaneous expense	8600	
Total expenses		143800
Net income		$ 101200

Income Statement

The financial statements usually are prepared first on ruled paper. Such copies may then be typed or word processed on a microcomputer so that a number of copies will be available for those who are interested in examining the statements. Since the processed copies are not on lined paper, dollar signs are included in the preliminary draft so that the typist or word processor will understand just where they are to be inserted. Note that a dollar sign is placed beside the first amount in each column and the first amount below a ruling in each column. The income statement illustrated is shown on two-column paper; however, the columns do not have any debit-credit significance. The only source of revenue was placement fees that amounted to $2,450. The total expenses for the month amounted to $1,438. The revenue exceeded the expenses by $1,012. This represents the amount of the **net income** for the month. If the total expenses had exceeded the total revenue, the excess would have represented a **net loss** for the month. The information provided by the income statement of The Victor Pearce Placement Service may be summarized in equation form as follows:

REVENUE	−	EXPENSES	=	NET INCOME
$2,450	−	$1,438	=	$1,012

It is apparent that the income statement is more informative than the trial balance as to the results of operations for December. The trial balance contains the necessary data for preparing the income statement, but the income statement presents the data in a more meaningful way.

The Balance Sheet

The **balance sheet** is an itemized statement of the assets, liabilities, and owner's equity of a business enterprise as of a specified date. Its purpose is to provide information regarding the status of these basic accounting elements as of the close of business on the date indicated in the heading.

The **heading** of a balance sheet contains the following:

1. The name of the business.
2. The title of the statement.
3. The date of the statement as of the close of business on that day.

The **body** of a balance sheet consists of an itemized list of the assets, the liabilities, and the owner's equity, the latter being the difference between the total amount of the assets and the total amount of the liabilities. A balance sheet for The Victor Pearce Placement Service showing the status of the business when it closed on December 31, 1986, is reproduced on pages 52 and 53. The balance sheet illustrated is arranged like a standard account with the assets listed on the left side and the liabilities and owner's equity listed on the right side. The information provided by the balance sheet of The Victor Pearce Placement Service may be summarized in equation form as follows:

ASSETS	=	LIABILITIES	+	OWNER'S EQUITY
$7,512	=	$3,500	+	$4,012

The trial balance was the source of the information needed in listing the assets and liabilities in the balance sheet. The amount of the owner's equity may be determined by subtracting the total liabilities from the total assets. Thus, Pearce's equity as of December 31, 1986, is as follows:

Total assets	$7,512
Less total liabilities	3,500
Owner's equity	$4,012

The owner's equity may also be determined by taking into consideration the following factors:

1. The **amount invested** in the enterprise by Pearce on December 1, as shown by the capital account.
2. The amount of the **net income** of The Victor Pearce Placement Service for December, as shown by the income statement.
3. The total **amount withdrawn** for personal use during December, as shown by Pearce's drawing account.

The trial balance on page 47 shows that Pearce's equity in The Victor Pearce Placement Service on December 1 amounted to $4,000. This is supported by the credit balance of the capital account. The income statement on page 49 shows that the net income of the service for December amounted to $1,012. The trial balance also shows that the amount withdrawn by Pearce for personal use during the month amounted to $1,000. This is supported by the debit balance of the drawing account. On the basis of this information, Pearce's equity in the Victor Pearce Placement Service as of December 31, 1986, is as follows:

Amount of capital, December 1		$4,000
Net income for December	$1,012	
Less amount withdrawn for personal use during the month	1,000	12
Capital as of close of business, December 31		$4,012

BUILDING YOUR ACCOUNTING KNOWLEDGE

1. What is the purpose of an income statement?
2. Why are changes in owner's equity resulting from investments or withdrawals of assets by the owner not included in the income statement?

Victor Pearce
Balance
December

	Assets					
Cash		# 370600				
Office supplies		30600				
Office equipment		350000				
Total assets			# 751200			

Balance Sheet—Account Form
(Left Page)

3. What are the three parts of the heading of an income statement?
4. What is the purpose of a balance sheet?
5. What are the three parts of the heading of a balance sheet?
6. What is the source of information for preparing both the income statement and the balance sheet?
7. Owner's equity can be calculated by subtracting total liabilities shown by the balance sheet from total assets shown by the balance sheet. What three factors may be used to prove the amount of owner's equity calculated in this manner?

APPLYING ACCOUNTING CONCEPTS

Exercise 2-5. Dawn Glow operates a beauty salon. The following is the trial balance for Glow's business as of September 30, 19--, the first month of operations.

Glow Beauty Salon
Trial Balance
September 30, 19--

Cash	111	1,683	
Supplies	151	610	
Equipment	191	4,150	
Accounts Payable	218		319
Dawn Glow, Capital	311		6,000
Dawn Glow, Drawing	311.1	625	
Customer Fees	411		1,451
Rent Expense	541	400	
Telephone Expense	544	42	
Supplies Expense	545	260	
		7,770	7,770

Placement Service
Sheet
31, 1986

	Liabilities			
Accounts payable		$350000		
Total liabilities			$350000	
	Owner's Equity			
Victor Pearce, capital:				
Capital, Dec. 1, 1986		$400000		
Net income	$1,012.00			
Less withdrawals	1,000.00			
Net increase		1200		
Capital, Dec. 31, 1986			401200	
Total liabilities and owner's equity			$751200	

Balance Sheet—Account Form
(Right Page)

Prepare an income statement for the Glow Beauty Salon for the month of September.

Exercise 2-6. Refer to Exercise 2-5 and prepare a balance sheet in account form for the Glow Beauty Salon as of September 30.

Report No. 2-3

Refer to the study assignments and complete Report 2-3. This assignment provides a test of your ability to apply the principles developed in Chapters 1 and 2 of this textbook. The textbook and the study assignments go hand in hand, each serving a definite purpose in the learning process. Inability to solve correctly any problem included in the report indicates that you have failed to master the principles developed in the textbook. Further study, with the aid of the vocabulary list on page 54, should be helpful in this regard. After completing the report, you may proceed with Chapter 3 until the next report is required.

EXPANDING YOUR BUSINESS VOCABULARY

What is the meaning of each of the following terms:

balance (p. 45)

balance sheet (p. 50)

book of original entry (p. 28)

capital account (p. 30)

chart of accounts (p. 30)

Credit amount column (p. 29)

cross reference (p. 41)

Date column (p. 28)

Debit amount column (p. 29)

Description column (p. 28)

foot (p. 45)

general ledger (p. 40)

income statement (p. 48)

journal (p. 27)

journalizing (p. 27)

matching concept (p. 49)

net income (p. 50)

net loss (p. 50)

owner's equity (p. 30)

posting (p. 40)

Posting Reference column (p. 29)

source document (p. 27)

two-column journal (p. 28)

CHAPTER 3

Accounting for Cash

CHAPTER OBJECTIVES

Careful study of this chapter should enable you to:

- Explain the meanings of the term "cash" as it is used in accounting.

- Describe **internal control** as it relates to the handling of cash.

- Explain the operation of a petty cash fund and prepare a special multi-column record of cash payments.

- Describe banking procedures relating to the use of commercial bank checking accounts, and prepare a bank statement reconciliation.

In the preceding chapters, the purpose and nature of business accounting, transaction analysis, and the double entry framework were introduced. Explanations and illustrations were given of (1) **journalizing** (entering transactions in a journal — a book of original entry), (2) **posting** (transferring the entries to the accounts that, taken together, comprise the general ledger), (3) taking a trial balance, and (4) using the latter to prepare an income statement and a balance sheet (two basic and important financial statements).

This chapter is devoted to a discussion of the handling of and accounting for cash receipts and cash payments. Included in the discussion are the nature of the cash account, cash proof, and the operation of and accounting for a petty cash fund. Also included in the discussion are the operation of both bank checking and savings accounts, the functions performed by commonly used bank forms, and the process of reconciling the bank statement.

CASH RECEIPTS AND CASH PAYMENTS

The term "cash" has several different, though not completely distinctive, meanings. In a very narrow sense, cash means currency and coins. In a broader sense, cash includes checks, drafts, and money orders. All of these, including currency and coins, are sometimes called cash items. Usually, any reference to the cash receipts of a business relates to the receipt of checks, drafts, and money orders payable to the business, as well as to the receipt of currency and coins. The cash account balance, as well as the amount shown for cash in a balance sheet, normally includes cash and cash items on hand plus the amount on deposit in one or more bank checking accounts. On the balance sheet, it is rather rare to make a distinction between "cash on hand" and "cash in bank," but sometimes this is done.

A good policy for a business enterprise to adopt is a system of internal control which requires that all cash and cash items it receives be deposited daily in a bank. When this is done, its total cash receipts will equal its total deposits in the bank. It is also a good policy to make arrangements with the bank so that all checks and other cash items received by the business from customers or others in the usual course of business will be accepted by the bank for deposit only. This will cause the records of cash receipts and payments of the business to agree item by item with the bank's record of deposits and withdrawals.

The Cash Account

The cash account is debited when cash is increased and credited when cash is decreased. This account normally has a debit balance.

Cash Receipts. Cash and cash items received by a business are known as cash receipts. It is vital that an accurate and timely record be kept of cash receipts. When the volume of the receipts is large both in number and in amount, procedures designed to reduce the danger of mistake and embezzlement (the unauthorized taking of business cash by an employee) should be followed. When numerous receipts of currency and coins are accepted from customers who have purchased goods or services, it is customary to use a cash register. Such a machine classifies items sold and amounts. A cash register may also have the capability of accumulating subtotals by departments and calculating sales taxes.

When money comes in by mail (nearly always as checks), a presupplied form showing the remitter's name, address, and the amount on the enclosed check or money order is usually enclosed. A good example of this is the top part of a monthly statement that the customer has received as shown in the following illustration:

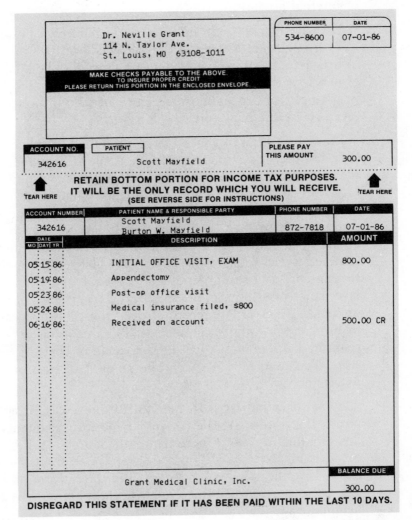

Sometimes a written receipt must be prepared by the business. A copy of the receipt or the returned portion of the monthly statement provides the source document for the cash received. In any case, the initial record of each amount received should be prepared by someone other than the accountant to provide good internal control. The money received, including checks and money orders, is placed in the custody of whoever is authorized to handle bank deposits and cash on hand. The accountant uses the initial records in preparing proper journal entries for cash receipts. Under such a plan, the accountant does not actually handle any cash; instead cash receipts are entered from documents prepared by other persons. The procedure of having transactions involving cash handled by two or more persons reduces the danger of embezzlement and is one of the important features of a system of internal accounting control.

Cash Payments. Cash and cash items paid by a business are known as cash payments. Payments may be made in cash or by bank check. When a payment is made in cash, a receipt should be obtained as evidence of the payment. When a payment is made by bank check, it is not necessary to obtain a receipt since the canceled check that is returned by the bank serves as a receipt.

Proving Cash. The process of determining whether the amount of cash, both on hand and in the bank, is the same amount that exists in the accounting records is called proving cash. Cash should be proved at least once a week and, more often if the volume of cash transactions is large. The first step is to determine from the ledger the amount of the cash account balance. The most recent cash account balance is determined by adding the total of the receipts to the opening balance and subtracting the total of the payments. The result should be equal to the amount of cash on deposit in the bank as reflected in the check-book stubs plus the total of currency, coins, checks, and money orders on hand. An up-to-date record of cash in bank is maintained — usually by using check stubs to show deposits as well as checks drawn, and the resulting balance after each deposit made or check drawn. (See check stubs illustrated on page 74.) The amount of cash on hand must be determined by actual count.

Cash Short and Over. If the effort to prove cash is not successful, it means that either (1) the records of receipts, payments, and cash on deposit contain one or more data entry errors, (2) the physical count of cash not deposited is incorrect, or (3) a shortage or an overage exists. If verifications of the records and the cash count do not uncover any error, it is evident that some mistake must have been made in handling cash.

Finding that cash is slightly short or over is not unusual. If there are numerous cash transactions, it is difficult to avoid occasional errors in making change. There is always the danger of shortages due to dishonesty, but most discrepancies are the result of mistakes. Many businesses have a special ledger account entitled Cash Short and Over which is used to keep track of day-to-day shortages and overages of cash. If, in the effort to prove cash, it is found that a shortage exists, the amount is treated as a cash payment transaction involving a debit to Cash Short and Over and a credit to Cash. Any overage discovered is regarded as a cash receipt transaction involving a credit to Cash Short and Over and a debit to Cash.

To illustrate, if cash was $2 short at the end of the day, the entry would be as follows:

Cash Short and Over 2.00
   Cash 2.00

Conversely, if cash was $3 over, the entry would be as follows:

Cash 3.00
   Cash Short and Over 3.00

By the end of the fiscal year, it is likely that the cash short and over account will have both debits and credits. If the total of the debits exceeds the total of the credits, the balance represents an expense or loss; if the reverse is the case, the balance represents revenue.

The Petty Cash Fund

When all cash receipts are deposited in a bank, an office fund known as a petty cash fund may be established for paying small items. ("Petty" means small or little.) Such a fund eliminates the necessity of writing checks for relatively small amounts.

Operating a Petty Cash Fund. To establish a petty cash fund, a check is written for the amount that is to be set aside in the fund. The amount may be $50, $100, $200, or any amount considered necessary. The check is made payable to the person who will have custody of the fund. That person's name, followed by a comma and the words, "Petty Cashier" appears on the check as the payee. When the check is cashed by the bank, the money is placed in a cash drawer, a cash register, or a safe at the depositor's place of business; and a designated individual in the office is authorized to make payments from the fund. The person responsible for the fund should be able to account for the full amount of the fund at any time.

Payments from the fund should not be made without obtaining some sort of receipt in return. A special form of receipt, showing the name of the payee, the purpose of the payment, and the account to be charged for each petty cash payment, is known as a petty cash voucher. A form of petty cash voucher is shown on page 60. Such a voucher should be used for each expenditure.

The check written to establish the petty cash fund may be entered in the journal by debiting Petty Cash Fund and by crediting Cash.

Petty Cash Voucher

No. ___4___   Date _December 11, 1986_

Paid to _Deborah Douglas_   Amount

For _American Cancer Society_   25 | 00

Charge to _Charitable Contributions Expense_

Remittance received:

Deborah Douglas   Approved by _John E. Berra_

Petty Cash Voucher

When it is necessary to replenish the fund, the petty cashier usually prepares a statement of the payments, properly classified. A check is then written for the exact amount of the total payments. This check is entered in the journal by debiting the proper accounts indicated in the statement and by crediting Cash.

To illustrate, assume that on June 1, Suzanne's Fashions established a petty cash fund for $100, and that on June 30 the fund was replenished for $85.25 after classifying and totaling the petty cash vouchers. The journal entries for these transactions are:

June 1 Petty Cash Fund	100.00	
Cash		100.00
To establish petty cash fund.		
30 Automobile Expense	22.00	
Supplies Expense	32.00	
Postage Expense	26.00	
Miscellaneous Expense	5.25	
Cash		85.25
Replenishment of petty cash fund.		

The petty cash fund is thus a revolving fund. The petty cash account balance does not change in amount unless the fund is increased or decreased. The actual amount of cash in the fund plus the total of the petty cash vouchers should be equal to the amount originally deposited in the petty cash fund. This commonly used method for handling petty cash is referred to as the imprest method.

Petty Cash Payments Record. When a petty cash fund is maintained, it is good practice to keep a formal record of all payments from the fund. The petty cash payments record is a special multi-column record that supplements the regular accounting records. No posting is done from this special record. Various types of records also called *auxiliary records* have been designed for this purpose. One of the standard forms is illustrated on pages 62 and 63. The headings of the Distribution columns may vary with each enterprise, depending upon the desired classification of the expenditures. The headings represent accounts that eventually are to be charged for the expenditures. The desired headings may either be printed on the form or they may be typed or written in. Often account numbers instead of account titles are used in the headings to indicate the accounts to be charged.

The petty cashier should have a document for each payment made from the petty cash fund. Whether or not a receipt or receipted invoice is obtained, the petty cashier should prepare a voucher. The vouchers should be numbered consecutively.

A typical petty cash payments record is reproduced on pages 62 and 63. It is a part of the records of John E. Berra, a business consultant. Since Berra is out of the office much of the time, a petty cash fund is provided from which his secretary is authorized to make petty cash payments not to exceed $35 each. A narrative of the petty cash transactions completed by Judy Singler, Berra's secretary, during the month of December follows:

JOHN E. BERRA

NARRATIVE OF PETTY CASH TRANSACTIONS

Dec. 1 Issued check for $200 payable to Judy Singler, Petty Cash Fund Cashier. The check is cashed and the proceeds placed in a petty cash fund.

This transaction is entered in the journal by debiting Petty Cash Fund and by crediting Cash. A memorandum entry is also made in the Description column of the petty cash payments record reproduced on pages 62 and 63.

	JOURNAL			PAGE
DATE	DESCRIPTION	POST. REF.	DEBIT	CREDIT
Dec. 1	Petty Cash Fund		200 00	
	Cash			200 00
	To establish petty cash			
	fund.			

PAGE 1		PETTY CASH PAYMENTS				
	DAY	DESCRIPTION	VOU. NO.	TOTAL AMOUNT	Tel. Exp.	Auto Exp.
1		AMOUNTS FORWARDED				
2	1	Received in fund		200.00		
3	5	Automobile repairs	1	22 80		22 80
4	8	Client luncheon	2	12 75		
5	9	John E. Berra, personal use	3	30 00		
6	11	American Cancer Society	4	25 00		
7	15	Typewriter repairs	5	13 25		
8	17	Traveling expense	6	14 50		
9	19	Washing automobile	7	6 00		6 00
10	22	Postage expense	8	9 50		
11	23	Care and Counseling, Inc.	9	15 00		
12	29	Postage stamps	10	40 00		
13	30	Long distance call	11	4 80	4 80	28 80
14				193 60	4 80	28 80
15	31	Balance		6.40		
16	31	Received in fund		193.60		
17		Total		200.00		

John E. Berra's Petty Cash Payments Record (Left Page)

During the month of December, the following payments were made from the petty cash fund:

5 Paid $22.80 to Bill Glasgow of Glasgow's Auto for having the company automobile serviced. Petty Cash Voucher No. 1.

8 Reimbursed Berra $12.75 for the amount spent in entertaining a client at lunch. Petty Cash Voucher No. 2.

9 Gave Berra $30 for personal use. Petty Cash Voucher No. 3.

This item is entered in the Amount column provided at the extreme right of the petty cash payments record since no special distribution column has been provided for entering amounts withdrawn by the owner for personal use.

11 Gave the American Cancer Society a $25 donation. Petty Cash Voucher No. 4.

15 Paid $13.25 for typewriter repairs. Petty Cash Voucher No. 5.

17 Reimbursed Berra $14.50 for traveling expenses. Petty Cash Voucher No. 6.

19 Paid $6.00 to Gary Bronson of Gary's Car Care for having the company automobile washed. Petty Cash Voucher No. 7.

22 Paid $9.50 for mailing a package. Petty Cash Voucher No. 8.

23 Donated $15 to Care and Counseling, Inc. Petty Cash Voucher No. 9.

FOR MONTH OF *December* 1986   PAGE *1*

Post. Exp.	*Char. Cont. Exp.*	*Travel + Ent. Exp.*	*Misc. Exp.*		ACCOUNT	AMOUNT	
							1
							2
							3
		12 75					4
					John E. Berra, Drawing	30 00	5
	25 00						6
			13 25				7
		14 50					8
							9
9 50							10
	15 00						11
40 00							12
							13
49 50	40 00	27 25	13 25			30 00	
49 50	40 00	27 25	13 25			30 00	14
							15
							16
							17

John E. Berra's Petty Cash Payments Record (Right Page)

29 Paid $40 for postage stamps. Petty Cash Voucher No. 10.

30 Reimbursed Berra $4.80 for a long distance telephone call made from a public telephone. Petty Cash Voucher No. 11.

Proving the Petty Cash Payments Record. To prove the petty cash payments record, it is first necessary to foot all of the amount columns. The sum of the footings of the Distribution columns should equal the footing of the Total Amount column. After proving the footings, the totals are entered and the record is ruled as shown in the illustration. The illustration shows that a total of $193.60 was paid out during December. Since this is an appropriate time to replenish the petty cash fund, the following statement of the payments for December is prepared:

Statement of Petty Cash Payments for December

Telephone Expense	$ 4.80
Automobile Expense	28.80
Postage Expense	49.50
Charitable Contributions Expense	40.00
Travel and Entertainment Expense	27.25
Miscellaneous Expense	13.25
John E. Berra, Drawing	30.00
Total payments	$193.60

The statement of petty cash payments provides the information for the issuance of a check for $193.60 to replenish the petty cash fund. On December 31, Berra issued a check for $193.60 payable to Judy Singler, Petty Cashier to replenish the petty cash fund. This transaction was treated as a compound entry in the journal by debiting the proper accounts and by crediting Cash for the total amount of the expenses. A compound entry is one that affects more than two accounts, with the sum of the debits equal to the sum of the credits. Such an entry is usually required for petty cash fund replenishment. The entry is posted from the journal to the affected ledger accounts.

	DATE	DESCRIPTION	POST. REF.	DEBIT	CREDIT	
	JOURNAL				PAGE 15	
1	Dec. 31	Telephone Expense		4 80		1
2		Automobile Expense		28 80		2
3		Postage Expense		49 50		3
4		Charitable Contributions Expense		40 00		4
5		Travel + Entertainment Expense		27 25		5
6		Miscellaneous Expense		13 25		6
7		John E Berra, Drawing		30 00		7
8		Cash			193 60	8
9		Replenishment of petty				9
10		cash fund.				10

After the petty cash payments record is footed and ruled, the balance in the fund and the amount received to replenish the fund may be entered in the Description column below the ruling as shown in the illustration. It is customary to carry the total forward to the top of a new page as a memorandum entry before entering any of the transactions for the following month.

BUILDING YOUR ACCOUNTING KNOWLEDGE

1. What is the usual source documentation of cash receipts when they are numerous and presented in person? What form of source documentation usually accompanies money that comes in by mail?
2. Why should transactions involving cash be handled by two or more persons?
3. Why is it not unusual to find that the cash balance at the time of proof is slightly short or over?
4. What does a debit balance in the cash short and over account represent? What does a credit balance in this account represent?
5. What is the purpose of a petty cash fund?
6. What should be obtained from the receiving party each time a petty cash payment is made?

7. From what source is the information obtained for issuing a check to replenish the petty cash fund?

APPLYING ACCOUNTING CONCEPTS

Exercise 3-1. **(a)** In attempting to prove cash, a shortage of $8.40 is found. Prepare the appropriate journal entry to recognize this shortage. **(b)** Assume that cash was found to be over by $2.25. Prepare the appropriate journal entry to recognize the overage.

Exercise 3-2. **(a)** On July 1, Mary Sue's Dance Studio established a petty cash fund for $150. Prepare the journal entry for this transaction. **(b)** The following payments were made from the fund in July:

Telephone Expense	$ 5.10
Automobile Expense........	33.40
Supplies Expense	27.25
Postage Expense...........	13.90
Miscellaneous Expense	15.00
Total payments.........	$ 94.65

Prepare the journal entry to replenish the fund on July 31.

Report No. 3-1

Refer to the study assignments and complete Report No. 3-1. After completing the report, proceed with the textbook discussion until the next report is required.

BANKING PROCEDURES

A bank is a financial institution that receives deposits, lends money, makes collections, and renders a variety of other services, such as providing vaults for the safekeeping of valuables, handling trust funds, and buying and selling securities and insurance for its customers. Most banks offer facilities for both checking accounts and savings accounts.

Checking Account

The majority of all money payments in the United States are made by checks. A piece of commercial paper drawn on funds in a bank account and payable on demand is called a check. Such a paper involves three original parties: (1) the depositor who orders the bank to pay a certain amount of money—known as the drawer; (2) the bank in which the drawer has money on deposit—known as the drawee; and (3) the person directed to receive the money—known as the payee. The drawer and payee may be the same person, though the payee named in such a case usually is "Cash."

A check is **negotiable** (meaning that the right to receive the money can be transferred to someone else) if it complies with the following requirements: (1) it is in writing; (2) it is signed by the drawer; (3) it contains an unconditional order to pay a specified amount of money; (4) it is payable on demand; and (5) it is payable to the order of another party or to the bearer. The payee transfers the right to receive the money by **indorsing** the check. This procedure requires stamping or writing his or her name and sometimes other pertinent information on the back of the check. If the payee simply signs on the back of the check, customarily near the left end, the signature is called a **blank indorsement**. This makes the check payable to any bearer. If there are added words such as "For deposit," "Pay to any bank or banker," or "Pay to Ed Eck only," it is called a **restrictive indorsement**. A widely used business practice when indorsing checks for deposit is to use a rubber stamp similar to that shown in the following illustration:

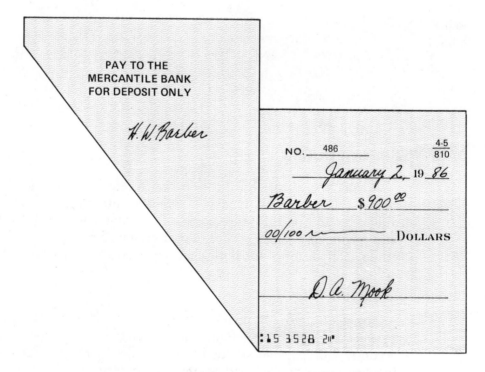

Restrictive Indorsement for Deposit (Rubber Stamp)

Important activities in connection with using a checking account are: (1) opening the account, (2) making deposits, (3) making withdrawals, (4) entering banking transactions, and (5) reconciling the bank statement.

Opening a Checking Account. To open a checking account with a bank, it is necessary to obtain the approval of an official of the bank and to make an initial deposit. Money, checks, bank drafts, money orders, and other cash items usually are accepted for deposit, subject to their verification as to amount and validity.

Banks usually require new depositors to sign their names on a card or form as an aid in verifying the depositor's signature on checks that may be issued, on cash items that may be indorsed for deposit, and on other business papers that may be presented to the bank. The form a depositor signs to give the bank a sample signature is called a signature card. If desired, depositors may authorize others to sign checks and other business forms on their behalf. A person who is so authorized is required to sign the depositor's name along with his or her own signature on a signature card and on all documents subsequently executed on behalf of the depositor. To aid in identification, the depositor's social security number is also shown. A signature card is one of the safeguards that a bank uses to protect its own interests as well as the interests of its depositors.

Making Deposits. To make a deposit with a bank, it is necessary to use certain forms prescribed by that bank and to observe the rules of the bank with regard to acceptable and unacceptable deposit items. In preparing the deposit, paper money should be arranged in the order of the denominations, the smaller denominations being placed on top. The bills should be all stacked face up and top up. Coins (pennies, nickels, dimes, quarters, half dollars and dollars) that are to be deposited in considerable quantities should be wrapped in coin wrappers, which the bank provides, unless the bank has a coin-sorting machine. The name and account number of the depositor should be written on the outside of each coin wrapper as a means of identification in the event that a mistake has been made in counting the coins. All checks being deposited must be indorsed. As mentioned earlier, the indorsement on the check illustrated on page 66 was made by means of a rubber stamp.

Deposit Ticket. A printed form with a detailed listing of items being deposited is called a deposit ticket. Banks provide these forms for depositors. A filled-in deposit ticket, typical of the type that most banks provide, is reproduced on page 68. Note that the number of the depositor's account is preprinted at the bottom in numbers that can

Checking Deposit	Mercantile Trust Company N.A. 8th and Locust St. Louis, MO 63166-5023	MERCANTILE BANK

Depositor agrees and Mercantile Trust Company N.A. accepts business on condition that items received for deposit or collection are accepted under the terms and conditions of the Bank's rules and regulations and the Bank Collection Code of the State of Missouri, now in effect or as may be amended from time to time.

Items deposited after 2:00 p.m. will be credited next business day.

Date ____October 13, 1986____   Number of checks listed   3

For credit of Account No. ____16 3247 5____

Name ____H. W. Barber____

____2815 Springridge Dr., St. Louis, MO 63129-9892____

	Dollars	Cents
Currency	934	00
Coin	42	63
Coupons	0	
Checks 4-21	320	80
80-459	680	00
4-5	590	00
Total Deposit	2,567	43

⑈081000210⑆ 16 3247 5⑈

Deposit Ticket

be "read" by electronic equipment used by banks. These numbers are called **MICR numbers**, which stands for magnetic ink character recognition. This series of digits, which is also preprinted at the bottom of all of the depositor's checks, is actually a code used in sorting and routing deposit slips and checks. In the first set of digits, 081000210, the first "8" indicates that the bank is in the Eighth Federal Reserve District. The third digit "1" is the reserve bank or branch serving the district. The fourth digit "0" indicates whether the item is for immediate credit or deferred credit. The number "21" is a number assigned to the Mercantile Bank. The last number position ("0" in this case) is a check digit position and may be used to verify the accuracy of the eight preceding digits in computer processing. This numbering method, known as **ABA numbers**, was established by the American Bankers Association, for use in sorting and routing deposit tickets. The second set of digits, 16-3247-5, is the number assigned by the Mercantile Bank to H. W. Barber's account.

It is not unusual for a depositor to receive a duplicate deposit ticket receipted by a bank teller. However, a more common practice today is to obtain a machine-printed receipt from the bank, which serves as a source document of the deposit. In preparing a deposit ticket, the date, number of checks, and account number should be written in the spaces provided. The amounts of cash represented by currency, coins, matured bond coupons and checks that are deposited should be entered in the amount column of the deposit ticket on the lines provided for these items.

Each check to be deposited should be listed on a separate line of the deposit ticket as shown in the illustration. In listing checks on the deposit ticket, the instructions of the bank should be observed in describing the checks for identification purposes. Banks usually prefer that depositors identify checks being deposited by showing the ABA number of the bank on which the check is drawn. This number is frequently located in the upper right hand corner of the check. The ABA number for the first check listed on the deposit ticket is $\frac{4\text{-}21}{810}$. The number "4" is the number assigned to the city in which the bank is located and the number "21" is assigned to the specific bank. The denominator "810" is the check routing number, but only the numerator is used in identifying the deposit.

The total of the cash and other items deposited should be entered on the deposit ticket. The deposit ticket, together with the cash and the other items deposited, should be delivered to the receiving teller of the bank. The teller processes the deposit ticket and gives the depositor a machine-printed receipt.

A depositor may personally obtain cash at the time of making a deposit by indicating on the deposit ticket what portion of the total of items listed is to be returned to him or her, with the remainder to constitute the deposit. Alternatively, a check may be drawn payable to the depositor, or usually, just to "Cash."

Most banks use teller-operated machines in preparing machine-printed receipts for deposits. The use of such machines saves the time required to make manual entries and eliminates the need for making duplicate copies of deposit tickets. Such machines are not only time-saving, but they also promote accuracy in the handling of deposits.

The deposits handled by each teller during the day may be accumulated in the teller-operated machine so that at the end of the day the total amount of the deposits received by the teller is automatically recorded by the machine. This amount may be proved by counting the cash and cash items accepted by a teller for deposit during the day.

Deposits by Mail. Bank deposits may be made by mail since it may not always be convenient to make deposits over the counter. Such deposits should consist exclusively of checks. When deposits are made by mail, the bank may provide the depositor with a supply of deposit tickets, and a self-addressed, prestamped envelope. A machine-printed receipt for the deposit is subsequently returned by the bank.

Night Deposits. Many banks provide night deposit service. A common practice is for the bank to have a night safe with an opening on the exterior of the bank building. Upon signing a night depository contract, the bank supplies the depositor with a key to the outside door of the safe, together with a bag that has an identifying number and in which valuables may be placed, and two keys to the bag itself. Once the depositor places the bag in the night deposit safe, it cannot be retrieved because it moves to a vault in the bank that is accessible to bank employees only. Since only the depositor is provided with keys to the bag, the depositor or an authorized representative must go to the bank to unlock the bag. The depositor may or may not deposit the funds that had been placed previously in the night deposit safe.

Night deposit banking service is especially valuable to those individuals and concerns that accumulate cash and other cash items which they cannot take to the bank during regular banking hours and that do not have safe facilities in their own places of business.

Dishonored Checks. A check that a bank refuses to pay is described as a dishonored check. A depositor guarantees all items deposited and is liable to the bank for the amount involved if any item is not honored when presented for payment. When a check or other cash item is deposited with a bank and is not honored upon presentation to the bank upon which it is drawn, the depositor's bank may charge the amount of the dishonored item to the depositor's account or may present it to the depositor for reimbursement. It is not uncommon for checks that have been deposited to be returned to the depositor for various reasons accompanied with a debit advice. As indicated on the following debit advice, the most common reason for checks being returned unpaid is that they are NSF checks ("not sufficient funds" remain in the drawer's account to cover them).

Debit	Mercantile Trust Company N.A. 8th and Locust St. Louis, MO 63166-5023	**MERCANTILE BANK**

Statement Copy   Date _June 16, 1986_

Dishonored check - not sufficient funds $84.75

Debit

    H. W. Barber   Account No.   Total $84.75

                     16 3247 5   Dept.__Checking

                                      By__K. a. W.

⑆081000210 16 3247 5⑈

Debit Advice

Issuance of a check on a bank without sufficient funds on deposit with that bank to cover the check when it is presented for payment is called an overdraft. Under the laws of most states, issuance of such a check is illegal. When a dishonored check is charged to the depositor's account, the amount should be deducted from the balance shown on the depositor's checkbook stub.

Most overdraft checks are not the result of any dishonest intent on the part of the drawer of such checks. The depositor either thought that there was money in the account when the check was written, due to an error in keeping the checkbook, or expected to get a deposit to the bank in time to "cover" the check before it reached the bank for payment. It is commonly considered to be something of a disgrace to the drawer of a check if the bank will not honor (pay) it. In recent years, many banks have made available plans that guarantee that all checks, within prescribed limits as to amount, will be honored even if the depositor's balance is too low. This amounts to a prearrangement with the bank to make a loan to the depositor, and in some cases, interest may be automatically computed and charged against the depositor's account. These plans have been given names such as "Ready Reserve Account," "Instant Cash," and others. Arrangements of this sort are parts of larger plans that involve such things as picture checks, no minimum balance requirement, bank statements that list checks paid in numerical order, check guarantee cards, travelers checks without fee, safe-deposit boxes, and even bank credit cards. The bank may charge a monthly fee for any or all of these services. Such comprehensive plans are not widely subscribed to by businesses (in contrast to individuals).

Postdated Check. A check dated after the date that the check was written and issued is known as a **postdated check**. For example, a check written and issued on March 1 is dated March 15. The recipient of the postdated check should not deposit it before the date specified on the check (March 15) because it is not legally acceptable as cash until that date. One reason for issuing a postdated check may be that the maker does not have sufficient funds in the bank at the time of issuance which in this case is March 1, but expects to have a sufficient amount on deposit by the time the check is presented for payment on or after the date of the check (March 15). When a postdated check is presented to the bank on which it is drawn and payment is not made, it is handled by the bank in the same manner as any other dishonored check and the payee should treat it as a dishonored check. Generally, it is not considered good practice for a business to issue postdated checks.

Making Withdrawals. The amount deposited in a bank checking account may be withdrawn either by the depositor or by any other person who is properly authorized to make withdrawals from the depositor's account. Such withdrawals are accomplished by the use of plastic cards inserted in automated teller machines or by the use of checks signed by the depositor or by others having the authority to sign checks drawn on the account.

Automated Teller Machines. Many banks now make automated teller machines available at all times to depositors. Although such machines may be used to make deposits, they are used far more frequently to make withdrawals.

Each depositor electing to use automated teller machines is provided with a plastic card and a secret code number. The depositor inserts the card into the machine, keys in the "password" code number, presses another key to indicate either (1) a withdrawal or (2) a deposit, and then keys in the amount. The machine next asks for a keyed-in verification ("yes" or "no") of the amount and—after a slight pause—instructs the depositor to open a drawer or door on the front of the machine.

If the transaction is a withdrawal, the cash requested can be found and removed. If a deposit, the deposit ticket and deposit items are placed in the drawer or compartment. The machine then asks the depositor whether another transaction will take place, and if the keyed-in answer is "no," the drawer or compartment locks automatically. The depositor then removes the plastic card from the machine, which deactivates it until the next depositor arrives.

Checkbook. Checks used by businesses are usually bound in the form of a book with two or three blank checks to a page and perforated so that they may be removed singly. Checks may be provided by the bank (often for a charge) or purchased directly from firms that specialize in the manufacture of check forms.

To the left of each check is a small form called a check stub that contains space to record all relevant information about the check. Sometimes the depositor is provided with a checkbook that, instead of containing stubs, is accompanied by a small register book in which the relevant information is noted. The information contained on the stub or on the register includes the check number, date, payee, amount, the purpose of the check and often the account to be charged, along with the bank balance before the check was issued, current deposits if any, and the resulting balance after issuing the check.

The depositor's name and address normally are printed on each check and the MICR numbers are shown along the bottom edge. Often the check number is preprinted in the upper right corner. Sometimes, checks come bound in the form of a pad. There may be a blank page after each check for use in making a carbon copy of the check. The copy is not a check; it is merely a copy of what was typed or written on the original check and provides the essential information for making an entry in the formal records.

Preparing a Check. The first step in preparing a check is to complete the check stub or check register. This plan insures that the drawer will retain a record of each check issued. Second, the name of the payee is entered on the check. Third, the amount of the check is entered on the check in both figures and words. If the amount shown on the check in figures does not agree with the amount shown in words, the bank usually contacts the drawer for the correct amount or returns the check unpaid.

Care must be used in entering the amount on the check in order to avoid any possibility that the payee or a subsequent holder may change the amount. If the instructions below are followed in the preparation of a check, it will be difficult to change the amount.

1. The amount shown in figures should be entered so that there is no space between the dollar sign and the first digit of the amount.
2. The amount stated in words should be entered beginning at the extreme left on the line provided for this information. The cents should be entered in the form of a common fraction; if the check is for an even number of dollars, use two ciphers or the word "no" as the numerator of the fraction. If a vacant space remains, a line should be drawn from the amount stated in words to the word "Dollars" on the same line with it, as shown on the illustration on page 74.

A machine frequently used to print the amount of a check in figures and in words is known as a checkwriter. The use of a checkwriter is desirable because it practically eliminates the possibility of changing the amount of a check.

As the fourth step in preparing a check, the purpose for which a check is drawn is often noted in the lower left-hand corner of the check itself. Indicating the purpose on the check provides information for the benefit of the payee and provides a specific receipt for the drawer. In the fifth step, the signature of the drawer is written on the lower right hand corner of the check in the same manner as on the signature card.

Each check issued by a depositor will be returned by the bank on which it is drawn after the check has been paid. Canceled checks are returned to the depositor with the bank statement, which is usually sent by mail each month. Canceled checks will have been indorsed by the payee and any subsequent holders. They constitute receipts that the depositor should retain for future reference. They may be attached to the stubs from which they were removed originally or they may be filed as received.

Electronic Processing of Checks. It is now nearly universal practice

Checks and Stubs

to use checks that, like deposit tickets, can be processed by MICR (magnetic ink character recognition) equipment. Imprinted in magnetic ink along the lower margin of the check is a series of magnetic numbers or digits in the form of a code that indicates (1) the identity of the Federal Reserve district in which the bank is located and a routing number, (2) the identity of the bank, and (3) the account number assigned to the depositor. Sometimes the check number is also imprinted. In processing checks with electronic equipment, the first bank that handles the check imprints the amount in magnetic ink characters to further aid in the processing of the check. The amount is printed directly below the signature line in the lower right-hand corner of the check.

Checks imprinted with the bank's number, the depositor's number, and the amount — all in MICR characters — can be posted electronically to the customer's account. The two checks reproduced above illustrate magnetic ink characters along the lower margins, as well as check stubs properly completed.

Entering Banking Transactions. A depositor should keep a record of the transactions completed with the bank. The checkbook stubs, as shown in the illustration on page 74, serve this purpose. The record consists of detailed information concerning each check written and an amount column in which are recorded (1) the balance brought forward, (2) the amount of deposits to be added, and (3) the amount of each check to be subtracted. The purpose is to keep a detailed record of deposits made and checks issued and to indicate the balance in the checking account after each check is drawn.

As the amount of each check is entered in the journal, a check mark is placed immediately after the account title written on the stub to indicate that the check has been entered. When the canceled check is subsequently received from the bank, the amount shown on the stub may be checkmarked to indicate that the canceled check has been received.

Records   Kept by a Bank. The usual transactions completed by a bank with a depositor are:

1. Accepting deposits made by the depositor.
2. Paying checks issued by the depositor.
3. Lending money to the depositor.
4. Collecting the amounts of various kinds of commercial paper, such as matured notes or bonds and bond interest coupons, for the account of the depositor.
5. Buying and selling securities and insurance for the depositor.

The bank keeps an account for each depositor. Each transaction affecting the depositor's account is entered by either debiting or crediting the depositor's account, depending upon the effect of the transaction.

When a bank accepts a deposit, the account of the depositor is credited (increased) for the amount of the deposit. The deposit increases the bank's liability to the depositor. When the bank pays a check that has been drawn on the bank, it debits (decreases) the account of the depositor for the amount of the check. If the bank makes a collection for the depositor, the net amount of the collection is credited to the account. At the same time, the bank notifies the depositor that the collection has been made using a form (credit advice) similar to the illustration shown on page 76.

Bank Statement. A statement of account issued to each depositor once a month by a bank is called a bank statement. An illustration of a widely used form of bank statement is shown on page 77. Some banks provide statements that also present information regarding savings accounts and loan accounts, for those depositors who have such accounts. Very commonly, however, a separate statement is furnished for each type of account.

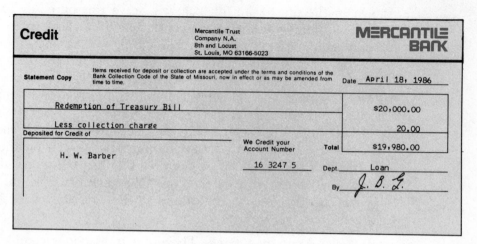

Credit Advice

The statement illustrated is for a checking account. It is a report showing (1) the balance on deposit at the beginning of the period, (2) the amounts of deposits and credits added during the period (credits), (3) the amounts of withdrawals by check and other charges subtracted during the period (debits), (4) the balance on deposit at the end of the period, (5) the average daily balance during the period, and (6) the minimum balance in the period. With the bank statement, the depositor also receives all checks paid by the bank during the period, together with any other forms representing items charged to the account.

Reconciling the Bank Statement. A depositor ordinarily keeps one or more records of bank-related transactions. A bank also keeps records of transactions with each depositor. The depositor's records of transactions with the bank should be brought into agreement with the bank's records of transactions with the depositor at periodic intervals — usually once a month.

As soon as possible after a bank statement is received, the depositor should try to make it agree with the bank balance record kept on the check stubs, a procedure known as reconciling the bank statement. The balance shown on the bank statement may not be the same as the amount shown on the check stubs for one or more of the following reasons:

1. Checks issued during the period may not have been presented to the bank for payment before the statement was prepared. These are known as **outstanding checks.** Some of the checks issued may fall into this category.

2. Deposits may not have been entered by the bank on the bank statement. These are known as **deposits in transit.** Such a deposit may have been mailed, or placed in the automated teller or night depository and not entered by the bank until the day following the date of the statement.

Statement

MERCANTILE BANK

	Reference Number	16 3247 5	Page Number

H. W. Barber
2815 Springridge Dr.
St. Louis, MO 63129-9892

	Statement Date	Nov. 21, 1986
	Statement Instructions	

Beginning Balance	No. of Deposits and Credits	We have added these deposits and credits totaling	No. of Withdrawals and Charges	We have subtracted these withdrawals and charges totaling	Resulting in a statement balance of
$2,721.51	2	$2,599.31	15	$3,572.73	

Document Count	Average daily balance this statement period		Minimum balance this statement period:		
17	$2,258.18			Date 11/18/86	Amount $1,748.09

If your account does not balance, please see reverse side and report any discrepancy to our Customer Service Department.

Date	Deposits and Credits	Withdrawals and Charges				Balance
		Previous Statement				2,721.51
10/27		242.00				2,479.51
10/28		68.93	58.00			2,352.58
10/29	867.00					3,219.58
11/3	1,732.31	19.88	228.11	452.13	94.60	4,157.17
11/10		2,000.00	32.42	64.08	210.87	1,849.80
11/18		18.00	23.31	58.60	1.80 SC	1,748.09

AD - Credit Advance	EC - Error Correction	LS - List of Checks	RT - Returned Check	TC - Transfer to Checking
CM - Credit Memo	FB - Fingertip Banking	M - Credit or Debit Memo	SC - Service Charge	TR - Wire Transfer
CR - Deposit	IC - Internal Credit (float)	OD - Overdrawn	SP - Sure Pay	
DM - Debit Memo	IE - Internal Entry	RC - Return Check Charge	ST - Savings Transfer	

Depositor agrees and Bank accepts business upon the terms and conditions of Bank's rules and regulations now in effect or as may be hereafter adopted.

Bank Statement

3. The bank may have credited the depositor's account for an amount collected, but the depositor may not as yet have noted it on the check stubs since the credit advice has not yet been received.

4. Service charges or other charges may appear on the bank statement that the depositor has not entered on the check stubs.

5. The depositor may have erred in keeping the bank account record.

6. The bank may have erred in keeping its account with the depositor.

Each bank usually provides a form for completing the bank reconciliation on the back of the bank statement. If a depositor is unable to reconcile the bank statement, a report on the matter should be made to the bank immediately.

The following is a suggested procedure in reconciling the bank statement:

1. The amount of each deposit entered on the bank statement is compared with the amount entered on the check stubs. Any deposit entered on the check stub but not entered on the bank statement should be added to the bank statement balance as a deposit in transit.

2. The amount of each canceled check is compared both with the amount entered on the bank statement and with the amount entered on the depositor's check stubs. When making this comparison, it is a good plan to place a check mark by the amount entered on each check stub to indicate that the canceled check has been returned by the bank and its amount verified.

3. The outstanding checks are listed, totaled, and deducted from the bank balance. The information needed for this list may be obtained by examining the check stubs and noting the amounts that have not been checkmarked.

4. The amounts of any items listed on the bank statement that represent credits or charges to a depositor's account which have not been entered on the check stubs are added to or deducted from the balance on the check stubs and are entered in the journal that is being used for cash receipts and payments.

5. Any error discovered on the check stubs or bank statement will require an adjustment to the check stub balance or bank balance depending on the nature of the error. A journal entry will also be necessary to correct for any check stub errors.

After completion of the foregoing procedure, the adjusted balance shown on the check stubs should equal the adjusted bank balance. A reconciliation of the bank balance shown in the statement reproduced on page 77 with the most recent check stub balance is as follows:

H. W. BARBER
Reconciliation of Bank Statement
November 21, 1986

1. Balance, November 21, per bank statement		$1,748.09
2. Add deposit, November 21		782.91
		$2,531.00
3. Less checks outstanding, November 21:		
No. 525	$163.00	
No. 530	28.47	
No. 532	247.20	438.67
4. Adjusted bank balance...........................		$2,092.33
5. Balance, November 21, per check stub		$2,095.03
6. Less: Bank service charge	$1.80	
7. Error on stub for Check No. 503.............	.90	2.70
8. Adjusted check stub balance.....................		$2,092.33

In making the reconciliation of the H. W. Barber bank statement as of November 21, 1986, the following steps, which correspond with the numbers in the reconciliation, were completed:

1. The November 21 bank balance, $1,748.09, was copied from the bank statement.

2. A deposit of $782.91, placed in the night depository on November 21 and therefore not shown on the bank statement, was added to the November 21 bank balance to agree with the check stub that reflected the deposit on that date.

3. The outstanding Checks Nos. 525, 530, and 532 were listed, totaled, and $438.67 was subtracted from the bank balance. These checks had not been presented to the bank for payment and thus were not returned with the bank statement.

4. The adjusted bank balance as of the close of business November 21 was calculated as $2,092.33.

5. The check stub balance as of November 21 was copied from the last check stub bearing that date, in the amount of $2,095.03.

6. A bank service charge of $1.80 shown at the bottom of the bank statement was subtracted from the check stub balance.

7. A checkbook error was discovered. Check No. 503 was written for $19.88 and entered in the check stub as $18.98. This error required the check stub balance to be decreased by $.90.

8. The adjusted check stub balance as of the close of business, November 21, was calculated as $2,092.33 and was equal to the adjusted November 21 bank balance.

In step number 6, a bank service charge was mentioned. A service charge may be made by a bank for the handling of checks and other items. The basis and the amount of such charges vary with different banks in different localities.

When a bank statement indicates that a service charge has been made, the depositor should enter the amount of the service charge by debiting an expense account, such as Miscellaneous Expense, and by crediting Cash.

Miscellaneous Expense	....	1.80
Cash	....	1.80
Bank service charge for November.		

The error noted in step number 7 was discovered when the canceled checks that were returned with the bank statement were matched against the check stubs. It was found that, although Check No. 503 had been written for $19.88, the amount was shown as $18.98 on its stub. This is called a transposition error, because the "9" and the "8" were transposed; i.e., their order was reversed. On Stub No. 503, and the others that followed, the bank balance shown was $.90 overstated. The correct amount, $19.88, should be shown on Stub No. 503, and the bank balance shown on the stub of the last check used should be corrected by reducing the amount by $.90. If Check No. 503 was in payment of a telephone bill, an entry should be made debiting Telephone Expense and crediting Cash. Alternatively, since such a small amount was involved, the debit might be made to Miscellaneous Expense.

Telephone Expense or Miscellaneous Expense	.90	
Cash..		.90
Correction of checkbook error.		

Keeping a Ledger Account for Each Bank

As explained previously, the depositor may keep a checkbook for each bank account. The depositor may also keep a ledger account for each bank. The title of such an account usually is the name of the bank. Sometimes, more than one account is kept with a bank, in which case each account should be correctly labeled. Such terms as "commercial," "executive," and "payroll" are used to identify the accounts.

The bank account is debited for the amount of each deposit and should be credited for the amount of each check written. The account should also be debited or credited for any other items that may have been handled directly by the bank, including collections and service charges.

When both a cash on hand account and a bank account are kept in the ledger, the following procedure should be observed in entering transactions affecting these accounts:

1. Cash receipts are entered as debits to the cash on hand account.
2. Cash payments and bank deposits are entered as credits to the cash on hand account.
3. Cash deposits and bank collections are entered as debits to the cash in bank account.
4. Checks written and bank charges are entered as credits to the cash in bank account.

Under this method of accounting for cash and banking transactions, the cash on hand account will be in balance when all cash on hand has been deposited in the bank. When this account is in balance, it means that the account has a zero balance since the total of the debits is equal to the total of the credits. To prove the balance of the cash on hand account at any time, it is necessary only to count the cash and cash items on hand and to compare the total with the cash on hand account balance. To prove the cash in bank account balance, it is necessary to reconcile the bank statement in the same manner in which it was reconciled when only a memorandum record of bank transactions was kept on the check stubs.

The cash on hand account can be dispensed with when a cash in bank account is kept in the ledger and all cash receipts are deposited daily in the bank. All payments except small amounts paid from a petty cash fund are made by check. If all cash received during the month has been deposited before the accounts are closed at the end of the month, the total amount of the bank deposits will equal the total cash receipts for the month. If all payments during the month are made by check, the total amount of checks issued will be the total cash payments for the month.

Cash—on Hand		Cash—Mercantile Bank	
Debit	Credit	Debit	Credit
(1) For all receipts of cash and cash items.	(2) For all payments in cash. For all bank deposits.	(3) For all deposits. For collection of amounts for the depositor, such as notes from customers and bond coupons.	(4) For all checks written. For all service charges. For all other charges, such as for dishonored checks.

Savings Account

When a savings account is opened in a bank, a signature card must be signed by the depositor. By signing the signature card, the depositor agrees to abide by the rules and regulations of the bank. These rules and regulations vary with different banks and may be altered and amended from time to time. At this time, a passbook may be given to the depositor. This is a small book in which the bank teller enters the date and amount of each deposit or withdrawal. The passbook is to be presented at the bank or mailed to the bank along with a deposit or withdrawal slip, each time money is deposited or withdrawn from the account. An alternative practice for depositing or withdrawing money from a savings account is to give the depositor a small register for recording deposits and withdrawals and a pad of deposit-withdrawal forms. This procedure eliminates the use of the passbook. Each time a deposit or withdrawal from savings is made, the appropriate part of one of the forms is filled in, signed, entered in the register and presented or mailed to the bank with deposit items or other documents. The bank gives a machine-printed receipt to the depositor or returns it by mail. There should be a separate savings account in the ledger to enter these activities. Sometimes, the name of the bank is in the title of the account, for example, "Cash—Mercantile Bank Savings Account."

At least once each quarter, the bank mails a credit advice to the depositor, indicating the amount of interest credited to the account. This should be entered in the depositor's register upon receipt. If a passbook is used, it should be presented or mailed to the bank, so that the credit advice can be entered by a teller. The depositor should also enter the amount in the business accounts by a debit to the cash account and by a credit to Interest Earned. The interest is revenue earned whether withdrawn or not and is taxable to the depositor.

```
Cash—Mercantile Bank Savings Account ....................... xxx
     Interest Earned .............................................. xxx
          Quarterly interest earned.
```

Traditionally, the principal differences between a savings account and a checking account are that interest is paid regularly by the bank on a savings account and withdrawals from a savings account may be made at the bank or by mail by the depositor or an authorized agent. Depositors use checking accounts primarily as a convenient means of making payments, while savings accounts are used primarily as a means of accumulating funds with interest.

An increasingly common practice is for the bank to combine savings and checking accounts and get depositor permission to make automatic transfers of funds from the savings portion to the checking portion whenever the latter falls below a specified minimum balance. This amounts to giving the depositor an interest-earning checking account.

Interest-Earning Checking Accounts

Many checking accounts now earn interest on their average daily balances. The amount of such interest usually is determined and reported monthly on the depositor's bank statement. Such accounts commonly specify that a minimum balance must be maintained, and higher rates of interest may be offered if depositors agree to maintain larger minimum balances.

Electronic Funds Transfer

Electronic funds transfer (EFT) uses a computer rather than money or checks to complete transactions with the bank. Increasingly, this approach is being used to meet payrolls, process social security payments, and pay for retail purchases.

If employees agree to sign authorization forms, each pay period their employers will send a magnetic tape containing payroll information directly to the bank. The bank's computer will then debit the employer's account for the total payroll and credit each employee's checking account. The U.S. government will, on authorization, process social security payments in a similar manner. Customers of retail stores can insert special pre-coded plastic cards in store terminals and automatically transfer cash from their checking accounts to the store's checking account at the bank in payment for their purchases.

BUILDING YOUR ACCOUNTING KNOWLEDGE

1. Name the five requirements with which a check must comply in order to be negotiable.
2. Why do banks usually require a new depositor to fill out a signature card? Why may more than one name appear on a signature card?
3. What is the reason for a depositor to obtain a printed receipt from the bank teller?
4. Describe the use of MICR numbers in the electronic processing of checks.
5. Briefly describe how a depositor uses an automated teller machine.
6. Name the six major dollar amounts summarized on a bank statement.
7. If a depositor is unable to reconcile a bank statement, what should be done?
8. What journal entry should a depositor make when a bank statement indicates that there has been a service charge?
9. What is the primary purpose of a checking account? What is the primary purpose of a savings account?
10. Name three applications of electronic funds transfer in current use.

APPLYING ACCOUNTING CONCEPTS

Exercise 3-3. The following information relates to the bank account of Kim's Bridal Shop on August 31:

Balance, August 31, per check stub		$2,241.06
Balance, August 31, per bank statement		1,955.54
August 31 deposit not shown on bank statement		695.00
Bank service charge shown on bank statement.......		2.25
Checks outstanding, August 31:		
No. 320	$147.50	
No. 323	38.14	
No. 331	226.09	411.73

Prepare a reconciliation of the bank statement with the check stub balance as of August 31.

Exercise 3-4. **(a)** A depositor's bank statement shows a service charge of $3.15. Prepare the journal entry for this service charge. **(b)** Comparison of the cancelled checks with the check stubs revealed that Check No. 211 which had been written for $17.47 was shown as $14.77 on the check stub. Check No. 211 was used to pay a telephone bill of $17.47. Prepare the journal entry to correct this error.

Report No. 3-2

Refer to the study assignments and complete Report No. 3-2. This assignment provides a test of your ability to apply the principles developed in the first three chapters of the textbook. Further study, with the aid of the vocabulary list below, may be helpful in this regard. After completing the report, you may proceed with the textbook discussion in Chapter 4 until the next report is required.

EXPANDING YOUR BUSINESS VOCABULARY

What is the meaning of each of the following terms?

ABA numbers **(p. 68)**
automated teller machines **(p. 72)**
bank **(p. 65)**
bank statement **(p. 75)**
blank indorsement **(p. 66)**
cash **(p. 56)**
cash payments **(p. 58)**
cash receipts **(p. 56)**
cash register **(p. 56)**
Cash Short and Over **(p. 58)**
check **(p. 65)**
check stub **(p. 72)**
checkwriter **(p. 73)**
compound entry **(p. 64)**
credit advice **(p. 75)**
debit advice **(p. 70)**
deposit ticket **(p. 67)**
deposits in transit **(p. 76)**
dishonored check **(p. 70)**
drawee **(p. 66)**
drawer **(p. 65)**
electronic funds transfer **(p. 82)**

embezzlement **(p. 56)**
imprest method **(p. 60)**
indorsing **(p. 66)**
internal control **(pp. 56, 57)**
MICR numbers **(p. 68)**
NSF checks **(p. 70)**
negotiable **(p. 66)**
outstanding checks **(p. 76)**
overdraft **(p. 70)**
passbook **(p. 81)**
payee **(p. 66)**
petty cash fund **(p. 59)**
petty cash payments record **(p. 61)**
petty cash voucher **(p. 59)**
postdated check **(p. 71)**
proving cash **(p. 58)**
reconciling the bank statement **(p. 76)**
restrictive indorsement **(p. 66)**
signature card **(p. 67)**
transposition error **(p. 79)**

CHAPTER 4

Payroll Accounting

CHAPTER OBJECTIVES

Careful study of this chapter should enable you to:

- Explain and perform the three major functions of payroll accounting: (1) determination of employee earnings and deductions, (2) determination of employer payroll taxes, and (3) proper data entry of the expenses, liabilities, and cash payments in connection with (1) and (2).

- Explain those government laws and regulations that primarily affect payroll accounting.

- Describe and prepare selected forms and records that are required or desirable in payroll accounting.

- Explain selected record-keeping methods and procedures used in the payroll area in connection with a computer-based accounting information system.

Employers need to maintain detailed and accurate payroll accounting records for both financial and legal reasons. The financial reason is simply that payroll expenditures represent a major part of the total expenditures of most companies. Payroll accounting records provide data useful in the analysis, classification, and control of these expenditures. In addition, payroll accounting information is invaluable in contract discussions with labor unions, in the settlement of company-union grievances, and in determining employee pension benefits.

The legal reason for maintaining payroll accounting records is that employers are required by federal, state, and local laws to do so. Companies must accumulate payroll data both for the business as a whole and for each employee. Clearly, accurate payroll accounting is essential to the survival of most businesses.

EMPLOYEE EARNINGS AND DEDUCTIONS

The first step in determining the amount to be paid to an employee is to calculate the employee's total or gross earnings for the pay period. The second step is to determine the amounts of deductions that are required either by law or by specific agreement between the employer and the employee. Depending upon a variety of circumstances, either or both of these steps may be relatively simple or quite complicated. An examination of the factors that must be considered in performing these two steps follows.

Employees and Independent Contractors

Not every individual who performs services for a business is considered to be an employee. A public accountant, lawyer, or management consultant who sells services to a business does not necessarily become its employee. Neither does a plumber nor an electrician who is hired to make specific repairs or installations on business property. These people are told what to do, but not how to do it, and the compensation that they receive for their services is called a fee. Any person who agrees to perform a service for a fee and is not subject to the control of those for whom the service is performed is called an independent contractor.

In contrast, an employee is one who is under the control and direction of an employer with regard to the performance of services. The difference between an independent contractor and an employee is an important legal distinction. The nature and extent of the responsibilities of the contractor and the client to each other and to third parties are quite different from the mutual obligations of the employer and the employee. Of particular importance for payroll accounting purposes is the fact that the various government laws and regulations regarding employee deductions, employer payroll taxes, records, and reports apply only to employees.

Types of Compensation

Compensation for managerial or administrative services usually is called salary. A salary normally is expressed in biweekly, monthly, or annual terms. Compensation either for skilled or for unskilled labor usually is referred to as wages. Wages ordinarily are expressed in terms of hours, weeks, or pieces of accomplishment. The terms salaries and wages often are used interchangeably in practice.

Supplements to basic salaries or wages of employees include bonuses, commissions, cost-of-living adjustments, pension and profit sharing plans, and vacation pay. Compensation also may take the form of goods, lodging, meals, or other property, and as such is measured by the fair market value of the property or service given in payment for the employee's efforts. This chapter demonstrates proper accounting for basic salaries and wages of employees paid in cash.

Determination of Total Earnings

An employee's earnings commonly are based on the time worked during the payroll period. Sometimes earnings are based on units of output or of sales during the period. Compensation based on time requires a record of the time worked by each employee. If there are only a few employees, a record of times worked may be kept in a memorandum book. Where there are many employees, time clocks commonly are used to record time spent on the job each day. With time clocks, a time card is provided for each employee and the clock is used to record arrival and departure times on the card. Alternatively, plastic cards or badges encoded with basic employee data are now being used in computer-based timekeeping systems. Whatever method is used, the total time worked during the payroll period must be computed.

Employees often are entitled to compensation at more than their regular rate of pay for work during certain hours or on certain days. If the employer is engaged in Interstate Commerce, the Federal Fair Labor Standards Act (commonly known as the Wages and Hours Law) provides that all employees covered by the Act must be paid one and one-half times the regular rate for all hours worked over 40 per week. Labor-management agreements often require extra pay for certain hours or days. In such cases, hours worked in excess of eight per day or work on Sundays and specified holidays may be paid for at higher rates.

To illustrate, assume that the company which employs Harry Falk pays time and a half for all hours worked in excess of 40 per week and double time for work on Sunday. Falk's regular rate is $10 per hour; and during the week ended April 11, Falk worked nine hours each day Monday through Friday, six hours on Saturday and four on Sunday. Falk's total earnings or gross pay for the week ended April 11, is computed as follows:

40 hours @ $10	$400
11 hours @ $15	165*
4 hours (on Sunday) @ $20	80
Total earnings for the week ...	$645

*Falk worked 9 hours each day Monday through Friday and 6 hours on Saturday—a total of 51 hours. Forty hours would be paid for at the regular rate and 11 hours at time and a half.

An employee who is paid a regular biweekly, monthly or annual salary may also be entitled to premium pay for any overtime. If this is the case, it is necessary to compute the regular hourly rate of pay before computing the overtime rate. To illustrate, assume that Gail Smith receives a regular salary of $1,800 a month and that Smith is entitled to overtime pay at the rate of one and one-half times the regular hourly rate for any time worked in excess of 40 hours per week. Smith's overtime pay is computed as follows:

```
$1,800 × 12 months ....... $21,600 annual pay
$21,600 ÷ 52 weeks ....... $415.38 pay per week
$415.38 ÷ 40 hours ....... $10.38 pay per regular hour
$10.38 × 1½ ............. $15.57 overtime pay per hour
```

Deductions from Total Earnings

An employee's take-home or net pay typically is significantly less than the total earnings or gross pay. The difference between an employee's gross and net pay generally can be explained by three factors: (1) employee FICA (Federal Insurance Contributions Act) tax withheld by the employer, (2) employee federal income taxes (and state and city income taxes where applicable) withheld by the employer, and (3) other deductions based on special agreements between the employer and the employee.

Employees' FICA Tax Withheld. The Federal Insurance Contributions Act (FICA) requires most employers to withhold certain amounts from employees' earnings for contributions to the old-age, survivors, and disability insurance (OASDI) and health insurance for the aged (HIP) programs. These withheld amounts are commonly referred to as FICA taxes.

Each employee is required to have a social security number for payroll accounting purposes. An illustration of a completed form SS-5, the official form used in applying for an account number is shown on page 89.

The earnings base against which the FICA tax is applied and the tax rate have been changed several times since the law was first enacted and are subject to change by Congress at any time in the future. These base and rate changes, however, do not affect the accounting principles and procedures for payroll. Therefore, for the sake of convenience in this chapter, the rate is assumed to be 6.0% of taxable wages paid during the calendar year for OASDI plus 1.5% for HIP for a total FICA rate of 7.5%. It is also assumed that the first $47,000 of earnings paid to each employee in any calendar year is taxable. Any amount of compensation paid in excess of $47,000 is assumed to be exempt from the tax.

FORM SS-5 — APPLICATION FOR A SOCIAL SECURITY NUMBER CARD
(Original, Replacement or Correction)

MICROFILM REF. NO. (SSA USE ONLY)

Unless the requested information is provided, we may not be able to issue a Social Security Number (20 CFR 422-103(b))

INSTRUCTIONS TO APPLICANT ▶	Before completing this form, please read the instructions on the opposite page. You can type or print, using pen with dark blue or black ink. Do not use pencil.		
NAA NAME TO BE SHOWN ON CARD	First MARK	Middle CARL	Last PENNO
NAB 1 FULL NAME AT BIRTH (IF OTHER THAN ABOVE)	First	Middle	Last
ONA OTHER NAME(S) USED			

STT 2 MAILING ADDRESS	1546 Swallow Dr.	(Street/Apt. No., P.O. Box, Rural Route No.)			
CTY CITY St. Louis	**STE** STATE Missouri	**ZIP** ZIP CODE 63144-4752

CSP 3 CITIZENSHIP (Check one only)	**SEX 4** SEX	**ETB 5** RACE/ETHNIC DESCRIPTION (Check one only) (Voluntary)
☒ a. U.S. citizen	☒ MALE	☐ a. Asian, Asian-American or Pacific Islander (Includes persons of Chinese, Filipino, Japanese, Korean, Samoan, etc., ancestry or descent)
☐ b. Legal alien allowed to work		☐ b. Hispanic (Includes persons of Chicano, Cuban, Mexican or Mexican-American, Puerto Rican, South or Central American, or other Spanish ancestry or descent)
☐ c. Legal alien not allowed to work	☐ FEMALE	☐ c. Negro or Black (not Hispanic) ☐ d. Northern American Indian or Alaskan Native
☐ d. Other (See instructions on Page 2)		☒ e. White (not Hispanic)

DOB 6 DATE OF BIRTH ▶	MONTH 10	DAY 17	YEAR 64	**AGE 7** PRESENT AGE 18	**PLB 8** PLACE OF BIRTH ▶	CITY Whitehall	STATE OR FOREIGN COUNTRY Wisconsin	**FCI** ☐

MNA 9 MOTHER'S NAME AT HER BIRTH	First Margaret	Middle F.	Last (Her maiden name) Mueller
FNA FATHER'S NAME	First Carl	Middle E.	Last Penno

PNO 10 a. Has a Social Security number card ever been requested for the person listed in item 1?	☐ YES(2) ☒ NO(1) ☐ Don't know(1)	If yes, when: ➡	MONTH	YEAR
b. Was a card received for the person listed in item 1?	☐ YES(3) ☒ NO(1) ☐ Don't know(1)	If you checked yes to a or b, complete items c through e; otherwise go to item 11.		
SSN c. Enter Social Security number assigned to the person listed in item 1	☐☐☐ — ☐☐ — ☐☐☐☐			
NLC d. Enter the name shown on the most recent Social Security card issued for the person listed in item 1		**PDB** e. Date of birth correction (See Instruction 10 on page 2) ▶	MONTH	DAY	YEAR

DON 11 TODAY'S DATE ▶	MONTH 5	DAY 23	YEAR 83	**12** Telephone number where we can reach you during the day. Please include the area code. ▶	HOME 961-3739	OTHER

ASD WARNING: Deliberately furnishing (or causing to be furnished) false information on this application is a crime punishable by fine or imprisonment, or both.

13 YOUR SIGNATURE *Mark Penno*	**14** YOUR RELATIONSHIP TO PERSON IN ITEM 1 ☒ Self ☐ Other (Specify)

Application for Social Security Number (Form SS-5)

State and Local Taxes. In addition to the foregoing federal requirements, a few states require employers to withhold a percentage of the employees' wages for unemployment compensation benefits or for disability benefits. In some states and cities, employers are also required to withhold a percentage of the employees' wages for other types of payroll taxes.

Employees' Income Tax Withheld. Under federal law, employers are required to withhold certain amounts from the total earnings of each employee to be applied toward the payment of the employee's federal income tax. The amount to be withheld each pay period is based on (1) the total earnings of the employee, (2) the marital status of the employee, (3) the number of withholding allowances claimed by the employee, and (4) the length of the employee's pay period.

Each employee is required to furnish the employer with an Employee's Withholding Allowance Certificate, Form W-4, showing marital status and the number of allowances claimed. The marital status of the taxpayer and the number of allowances claimed determine the dollar amount of earnings subject to withholding tax. According to 1984 federal income tax laws, $2,300 for single taxpayers and $3,400 for married taxpayers filing jointly is excluded from withholding tax. These amounts on which no withholding tax is levied are known as zero bracket amounts, that is, they represent income brackets or levels at which the withholding tax is zero. A withholding allowance is an allowance of $1,000 on which no federal income tax is withheld from the employee's pay. Each federal income taxpayer is permitted one personal withholding allowance, one for a spouse, and one for each dependent who qualifies. Thus, the taxpayer is entitled to one or more exemptions of $1,000 each from federal income tax based on family status and dependency relationships. The law specifies the relationship that must exist, the extent of support required, and the amount of support that must be provided in order for a person to qualify as a dependent.

In addition to these withholding allowances for personal, spouse, and dependent exemptions, a taxpayer can qualify for two other types of withholding allowances. First, one special withholding allowance can be claimed by each single taxpayer who has only one job, or each married taxpayer whose spouse is not employed. Second, additional withholding allowances are permitted to taxpayers who anticipate child-care tax credits or large itemized deductions. In order to claim one or more additional withholding allowances, an employee's expected total earnings, credits, and itemized deductions for the coming year have to be estimated. Based on these expected total earnings and itemized deductions, the schedule illustrated on page 91 is used to determine the number of additional withholding allowances to which the employee is entitled. An allowance certificate completed by Mark Carl Penno is shown on page 91.

To illustrate the use of the schedule, Mark Penno is married, has a spouse who is not employed, and has one dependent child. Penno expects earnings of $28,500 and itemized deductions of $5,500 in the coming year. As computed in the schedule, Penno is therefore entitled to 1 additional withholding allowance. On line 1 of the W-4 form, Penno claims 6 allowances, calculated as follows:

Form **W-4** (Rev. January 1984)	Department of the Treasury—Internal Revenue Service **Employee's Withholding Allowance Certificate**		OMB No. 1545-0010
1 Type or print your full name MARK CARL PENNO	**2** Your social security number 393 58 8194		

Home address (number and street or rural route) 1546 Swallow Dr.	**3** Marital Status	☐ Single ☒ Married ☐ Married, but withhold at higher Single rate **Note:** If married, but legally separated, or spouse is a nonresident alien, check the Single box.
City or town, State, and ZIP code St. Louis, MO 63144-4752		

4 Total number of allowances you are claiming (from line F of the worksheet on page 2) **6**

5 Additional amount, if any, you want deducted from each pay   . . . . $ -0-

6 I claim exemption from withholding because (see instructions and check boxes below that apply):

 a ☐ Last year I did not owe any Federal income tax and had a right to a full refund of **ALL** income tax withheld, **AND**

 b ☐ This year I do not expect to owe any Federal income tax and expect to have a right to a full refund of
  ALL income tax withheld. If both a and b apply, enter the year effective and "EXEMPT" here ▶ [Year]

 c If you entered "EXEMPT" on line 6b, are you a full-time student? . . . . ☐ Yes ☐ No

Under penalties of perjury, I certify that I am entitled to the number of withholding allowances claimed on this certificate, or if claiming exemption from withholding, that I am entitled to claim the exempt status.

Employee's signature ▶ *Mark Penno*   Date ▶ January 3 , 1986

7 Employer's name and address (**Employer: Complete 7, 8, and 9 only if sending to IRS**) | **8** Office code | **9** Employer identification number

Withholding Allowance Certificate (Form W-4)

Personal allowances:
 Self. 1
 Wife 1   2
Special withholding allowance. 1
Allowance for dependent 1
Additional withholding allowances 2
Total withholding allowances. 6

Penno's Withholding Allowance Schedule

Most employers use the wage-bracket method of determining the amount of tax to be withheld from an employee's pay by tracing the employee's gross pay for a specific time period into the appropriate wage-bracket table provided by the Internal Revenue Service. These tables cover monthly, semimonthly, biweekly, weekly, and daily or miscellaneous periods, and there are separate tables for single and married taxpayers. Copies may be obtained from any local Internal Revenue Service office. A portion of a weekly income tax wage-bracket withholding table for married persons is illustrated on page 92. To use this table, assume that Mark Penno (who claims 6 allowances) had gross earnings of $425 for the week ending December 19, 1986. On the line showing the tax on wages of "at least $420, but less than $430," in the column headed "6 withholding allowances," $37.90 is given as the amount to be withheld.

Whether the wage-bracket method or some other method is used in computing the amount of tax to be withheld, the sum of the taxes withheld from an employee's wages only approximates the tax on actual income derived solely from wages. An employee may be liable for a tax larger than the amount withheld. This additional tax will be remitted with the employee's federal income tax return. On the other hand, the amount of the taxes withheld by the employer may be greater than the employee's actual tax liability. In such an event, the employee will be entitled to a refund of the excess taxes withheld, or the excess can be applied to the employee's tax liability for the following year.

Several states and cities have adopted state and city income tax procedures. Some of these states and cities supply employers with withholding allowance certificate forms and income tax withholding tables that are similar in concept and appearance to those used by the federal Internal Revenue Service. Other states determine the amount to be withheld merely by applying a fixed percentage to the federal withholding amount.

WEEKLY Payroll Period — Employee MARRIED — Effective January 1, 1984*

And the number of withholding allowances claimed is—											
the wages are—		0	1	2	3	4	5	6	7	8	9	10
At least	But less than	The amount of income tax to be withheld shall be—										
310	320	38.80	35.50	32.20	29.00	25.70	22.40	19.20	16.10	13.80	11.50	9.20
320	330	40.50	37.20	33.90	30.70	27.40	24.10	20.90	17.60	15.00	12.70	10.40
330	340	42.20	38.90	35.60	32.40	29.10	25.80	22.60	19.30	16.20	13.90	11.60
340	350	43.90	40.60	37.30	34.10	30.80	27.50	24.30	21.00	17.70	15.10	12.80
350	360	45.60	42.30	39.00	35.80	32.50	29.20	26.00	22.70	19.40	16.30	14.00
360	370	47.30	44.00	40.70	37.50	34.20	30.90	27.70	24.40	21.10	17.90	15.20
370	380	49.30	45.70	42.40	39.20	35.90	32.60	29.40	26.10	22.80	19.60	16.40
380	390	51.50	47.40	44.10	40.90	37.60	34.30	31.10	27.80	24.50	21.30	18.00
390	400	53.70	49.50	45.80	42.60	39.30	36.00	32.80	29.50	26.20	23.00	19.70
400	410	55.90	51.70	47.50	44.30	41.00	37.70	34.50	31.20	27.90	24.70	21.40
410	420	58.10	53.90	49.60	46.00	42.70	39.40	36.20	32.90	29.60	26.40	23.10
420	430	60.30	56.10	51.80	47.70	44.40	41.10	37.90	34.60	31.30	28.10	24.80
430	440	62.50	58.30	54.00	49.80	46.10	42.80	39.60	36.30	33.00	29.80	26.50
440	450	64.70	60.50	56.20	52.00	47.80	44.50	41.30	38.00	34.70	31.50	28.20
450	460	66.90	62.70	58.40	54.20	50.00	46.20	43.00	39.70	36.40	33.20	29.90
460	470	69.40	64.90	60.60	56.40	52.20	47.90	44.70	41.40	38.10	34.90	31.60
470	480	71.90	67.10	62.80	58.60	54.40	50.10	46.40	43.10	39.80	36.60	33.30
480	490	74.40	69.60	65.00	60.80	56.60	52.30	48.10	44.80	41.50	38.30	35.00
490	500	76.90	72.10	67.30	63.00	58.80	54.50	50.30	46.50	43.20	40.00	36.70
500	510	79.40	74.60	69.80	65.20	61.00	56.70	52.50	48.30	44.90	41.70	38.40
510	520	81.90	77.10	72.30	67.50	63.20	58.90	54.70	50.50	46.60	43.40	40.10
520	530	84.40	79.60	74.80	70.00	65.40	61.10	56.90	52.70	48.40	45.10	41.80
530	540	86.90	82.10	77.30	72.50	67.70	63.30	59.10	54.90	50.60	46.80	43.50
540	550	89.40	84.60	79.80	75.00	70.20	65.50	61.30	57.10	52.80	48.60	45.20
550	560	91.90	87.10	82.30	77.50	72.70	67.90	63.50	59.30	55.00	50.80	46.90
560	570	94.70	89.60	84.80	80.00	75.20	70.40	65.70	61.50	57.20	53.00	48.80
570	580	97.50	92.10	87.30	82.50	77.70	72.90	68.10	63.70	59.40	55.20	51.00
580	590	100.30	94.90	89.80	85.00	80.20	75.40	70.60	65.90	61.60	57.40	53.20
590	600	103.10	97.70	92.30	87.50	82.70	77.90	73.10	68.30	63.80	59.60	55.40
600	610	105.90	100.50	95.10	90.00	85.20	80.40	75.60	70.80	66.00	61.80	57.60

*As of the date of printing, the above Weekly Federal Income Tax Withholding Table is the most current available.

Portion of Weekly Federal Income Tax Wage-Bracket Withholding Table for Married Persons

Other Deductions. In addition to the compulsory deductions from employee earnings for FICA and income taxes, there are many other possible deductions that generally are voluntary and depend on specific agreements between the employee and employer. Some examples of these deductions are for:

1. United States savings bond purchases.
2. Life, accident or health insurance premiums.
3. Credit union deposits.
4. Pension plan payments.
5. Charitable contributions.

Payroll Records

The needs of management and the requirements of various federal and state laws make it necessary for employers to keep records that will provide the following information for each employee:

1. Name, address, and social security number.
2. The gross amount of earnings, the date of payment, and the period of employment covered by each payroll.
3. The gross amount of earnings accumulated since the first of the year.
4. The amount of any taxes or other items withheld.

Regardless of the number of employees or type of business, three types of payroll records usually need to be prepared by the employer. They are: (1) the payroll register or payroll journal; (2) the payroll check with earnings statement attached; and (3) the earnings record of the individual employee (on a weekly, monthly, quarterly, or annual basis). While these records can be prepared either by manual or by automated methods, payroll is a major application of computer-based accounting systems.

Record-Keeping Methods. A purely manual system is one in which all records, journals and ledgers are prepared by hand. Such systems are rare today. Even very small businesses use cash registers, electronic calculators and other machines in performing accounting tasks. In this sense, virtually all accounting information systems today are at least partially automated, i.e., they use some kind of machines in the accounting process.

In a manual system, all employee data on the payroll records, such as name, address, social security number, pay rate, hours worked, current earnings, and taxes withheld, are determined, calculated, and entered by hand. In such a system, it often is necessary to enter the same data a number of times. For example, identical employee earnings amounts would be entered on the payroll register, paycheck, and earnings record.

Automated systems can be broken down into two types: mechanical and electronic. A mechanical system is one in which various types of accounting machines are used for posting accounts, billing customers, entering payroll, and printing paychecks. An electronic system is one in which data are processed using electronic computers. On the following pages, a payroll register, payroll check, and individual employee's earnings record that were prepared using a microcomputer are illustrated.

In a mechanical system, much of the payroll information is entered simultaneously on the payroll register, paycheck, and earnings record. This is an example of the write-it-once principle. It is often desirable to enter data on a number of documents and records at the same time, because each time the same information is recopied there is another chance for an error. Many accounting machines are available that perform these functions. Most of these machines also are capable of performing the arithmetic operations necessary in preparing the payroll. Each pay period, accounting personnel still need to provide input to the machines indicating information such as employee name, social security number, gross earnings, taxes withheld, and other deductions.

In a system using electronic computers, not only are the payroll register, paycheck, and earnings record generated simultaneously, but a number of inputs need not be repeated each pay period. Computers have the ability to store internally large amounts of information, such as employee names, social security numbers, withholding allowances, pay rates, FICA and income tax withholding rates, and earnings to date. They also can perform the arithmetic and logic functions required in payroll accounting. In a given pay period, based on inputs of employee social security numbers and hours worked, the computer can supply the related employee names and other data and calculate gross earnings, all appropriate deductions, and net pay. The computer can then print the paychecks and the payroll register, and update the employee's earnings records.

Both mechanical and electronic processing systems also are available through companies external to an employer's business. These companies, known as service bureaus (or automation companies), perform payroll accounting, among other accounting functions, for businesses on a contract basis. A common approach is for the employer to provide a service bureau with whatever inputs the employer would need if the payroll were being prepared on the employer's own mechanical or electronic payroll system. The service bureau then processes these inputs and provides the employer with the completed payroll register, paychecks, and updated employee earnings records. The use of service bureaus is diminishing as a result of rapid growth in the use of personal computer systems.

Computers are also used with payroll accounting systems on a time sharing basis. This refers to the use of a single computer by a number of small- to medium-sized businesses who share time on the computer. Thus it is possible for businesses that cannot afford their own computer to have the use of one by sharing it with other companies. Companies using time sharing have record keeping and processing situations similar to those for companies having their own computers. The main difference is that communication between time sharing users and the computer is normally by means of special telephone lines, remote computer terminals, and other electronic devices at each business location. Time sharing also is diminishing in use as personal computer systems increase in use, largely because the latter are believed to be less costly.

An important point to note in connection with this discussion of payroll record-keeping methods is that the same inputs and outputs are required in all of the different systems. Even given an electronic computer with substantial data stored in its memory, the inputs required for payroll processing have to be provided to the system at some point in time. The outputs in the form of a payroll register, paychecks, and employee earnings records are basically the same under all of the different systems. This means that the illustrations of payroll records under any of these systems are quite similar. For the sake of convenience and in order to avoid duplication, the illustrations in this chapter are based on a computer system only. The forms and procedures illustrated are equally applicable to a manual or a mechanical system.

Payroll Register. A payroll register is a multi-column form used to assemble, compute, and summarize the data required at the end of each payroll period. The payroll register used by Central States Diversified, Inc., for the payroll period ended December 19, 1986, is illustrated on pages 96 and 97. The columnar headings are basically self-explanatory. Detailed information on earnings, taxable earnings, deductions, and net pay is summarized for each employee.

Central States Diversified, Inc., has eight employees. James Gunther and Harry Wool each claim only one allowance because each has two jobs. Linda Swaney claims two allowances because she has only one job. Mary Roback claims only two withholding allowances because her spouse also works. Pamela Bloodgood, Russell Shaw, and Paulus

Tamin each get the special withholding allowance. In addition, Bloodgood and Tamin each get one additional withholding allowance, and Tamin has one child.

In this example, assume that the first $47,000 of earnings received in any calendar year is subject to FICA tax. None of the eight employees has exceeded this limit. In addition to their use in determining the employees' FICA tax, the columns for taxable earnings are needed for determining the employer's payroll taxes. These taxes are discussed on pages 105-107.

Regular deductions are made from the earnings of employees for FICA tax, federal income tax, and city earnings tax. In addition, voluntary deductions are made for the company pension plan (which is a voluntary plan), health insurance, the company credit union, and for the United Way contribution, according to agreement with individual employees. Gunther and Roback have each authorized Central States Diversified, Inc., to withhold $20 each week for their United Way contributions.

After the data for each employee have been entered, the amount columns in the payroll register should be footed and the footings verified as shown on page 97. In a computer-based accounting system, the software package for the payroll application will perform this proof without need for separate verification. An error in the payroll register could cause the payment of an incorrect amount to an employee or remittance of an incorrect amount to the companies or government agencies for whom funds are deducted from the employees' gross pay.

PAYROLL

NAME	EMPLOYEE NUMBER	NUMBER OF ALLOW.	MARITAL STATUS	EARNINGS				TAXABLE EARNINGS	
				REGULAR	OVERTIME	TOTAL	CUMULATIVE TOTAL	UNEMPLOY-MENT COMP.	FICA
BLOODGOOD, PAMELA D.	1	4	M	320.00		320.00	16,320.00		320.00
GUNTHER, JAMES B.	2	1	S	360.00	40.00	400.00	20,400.00		400.00
PENNO, MARK C.	3	6	M	425.00		425.00	22,025.00		425.00
ROBACK, MARY F.	4	2	M	650.00	75.00	725.00	35,850.00		725.00
SHAW, RUSSELL J.	5	3	M	340.00		340.00	17,340.00		340.00
SWANEY, LINDA L.	6	2	S	450.00	50.00	500.00	25,000.00		500.00
TAMIN, PAULUS	7	5	M	390.00		390.00	20,650.00		390.00
WOOL, HARRY	8	1	S	300.00		300.00	6,300.00	300.00	300.00
				3,235.00	165.00	3,400.00	163,885.00	300.00	3,400.00

Payroll Register—Computer Prepared (Left Page)

Regular earnings	$3,235.00	
Overtime earnings	165.00	
Gross earnings	$3,400.00	
Deductions:		
FICA tax	$255.01	
Federal income tax	463.70	
City earnings tax.................	102.00	
Pension plan	42.50	
Health insurance premiums........	46.00	
Credit union	37.50	
United Way	40.00	986.71
Net amount of payroll		$2,413.29

Payroll Check. Employees may be paid in cash or by check. In some cases today, the employee does not even handle the paycheck. Rather, salary is paid via a direct deposit of the check or electronic funds transfer by the employer to the employee's bank. The employee receives the deduction stub from the check and a printed deposit receipt. Payment by check or direct deposit is strongly preferred because it provides better internal accounting control. Many businesses prepare a single check for the net amount of the total payroll and deposit it in a special payroll bank account. Individual paychecks are then drawn on that account for the amount due to each employee. Data needed to prepare an individual paycheck for each employee are contained in the payroll register. (In a computer-based system, the paychecks normally are prepared at the same time as the payroll register.) The employer furnishes a statement of payroll deductions to each employee along with each wage payment. Paychecks with detachable stubs, like the

REGISTER

| | | | DEDUCTIONS | | | | | | | |
FICA TAX	FEDERAL INCOME TAX	CITY TAX	PENSION PLAN	HEALTH INS.	CREDIT UNION	UNITED WAY	TOTAL	DATE	NET PAY	CK. NO.
24.00	27.40	9.60	10.00		7.50		78.50	DEC. 19,'86	241.50	409
30.00	66.90	12.00			7.50	20.00	136.40	DEC. 19,'86	263.60	410
31.88	37.90	12.75		10.00			92.53	DEC. 19,'86	332.47	411
54.38	130.20	21.75	12.00	13.00	7.50	20.00	258.83	DEC. 19,'86	466.17	412
25.50	34.10	10.20	12.00	13.00	7.50		102.30	DEC. 19,'86	237.70	413
37.50	89.30	15.00	8.50				150.30	DEC. 19,'86	349.70	414
29.25	36.00	11.70		10.00	7.50		94.45	DEC. 19,'86	295.55	415
22.50	41.90	9.00					73.40	DEC. 19,'86	226.60	416
255.01	463.70	102.00	42.50	46.00	37.50	40.00	986.71		2,413.29	

Payroll Register—Computer Prepared (Right Page)

one for Mark Penno illustrated on page 100, are widely used for this purpose. Before such a check is deposited or cashed, the stub should be detached and retained by the employee as a permanent record of earnings and payroll deductions.

Employee's Earnings Record. A separate record of each employee's earnings, called an employee's earnings record, is kept in order to provide the information needed in preparing the various federal, state, and local reports required of employers. A computer-prepared employee's earnings record used by Central States Diversified, Inc., for Mark C. Penno during the last two quarters of the current calendar year is illustrated below and on page 99.

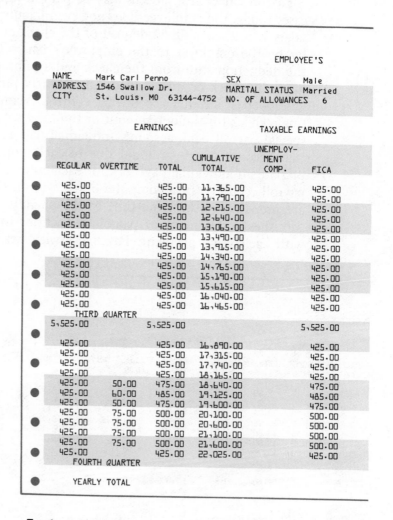

EMPLOYEE'S

NAME	Mark Carl Penno			SEX	Male
ADDRESS	1546 Swallow Dr.			MARITAL STATUS	Married
CITY	St. Louis, MO 63144-4752			NO. OF ALLOWANCES	6

	EARNINGS			TAXABLE EARNINGS	
				UNEMPLOY-	
			CUMULATIVE	MENT	
REGULAR	OVERTIME	TOTAL	TOTAL	COMP.	FICA
425.00		425.00	11,365.00		425.00
425.00		425.00	11,790.00		425.00
425.00		425.00	12,215.00		425.00
425.00		425.00	12,640.00		425.00
425.00		425.00	13,065.00		425.00
425.00		425.00	13,490.00		425.00
425.00		425.00	13,915.00		425.00
425.00		425.00	14,340.00		425.00
425.00		425.00	14,765.00		425.00
425.00		425.00	15,190.00		425.00
425.00		425.00	15,615.00		425.00
425.00		425.00	16,040.00		425.00
425.00		425.00	16,465.00		425.00
THIRD QUARTER					
5,525.00		5,525.00			5,525.00
425.00		425.00	16,890.00		425.00
425.00		425.00	17,315.00		425.00
425.00		425.00	17,740.00		425.00
425.00		425.00	18,165.00		425.00
425.00	50.00	475.00	18,640.00		475.00
425.00	60.00	485.00	19,125.00		485.00
425.00	50.00	475.00	19,600.00		475.00
425.00	75.00	500.00	20,100.00		500.00
425.00	75.00	500.00	20,600.00		500.00
425.00	75.00	500.00	21,100.00		500.00
425.00	75.00	500.00	21,600.00		500.00
425.00		425.00	22,025.00		425.00
FOURTH QUARTER					
YEARLY TOTAL					

Employee's Earnings Record—Computer Prepared (Left Page)

This record usually is kept on separate sheets or cards, which may be filed alphabetically or by employee number for ready reference. The information printed on this form is obtained from the payroll register in a computer-based system, in which the employee's earnings record can be updated simultaneously with the preparation of the payroll register. This is done with multiple-copy forms and special paper, which can be machine-separated after printing.

Penno's earnings for the last half of the year up to December 19 are shown on this form. The entry for the pay period ended December 19 is the same as that in the payroll register illustrated on pages 96 and 97.

EARNINGS RECORD

DEPARTMENT	Maintenance			SOCIAL SECURITY NUMBER	393 58 8194
OCCUPATION	Service			DATE OF BIRTH	October 17, 1964
PAY RATE	$425 weekly			DATE EMPLOYED	January 3, 1983
EMPLOYEE NO.	3			DATE EMPLOYMENT TERMINATED	

DEDUCTIONS

FICA TAX	FEDERAL INCOME TAX	CITY TAX	PENSION PLAN	HEALTH INS.	CREDIT UNION	UNITED WAY	TOTAL	DATE	NET PAY	CK. NO.
31.88	37.90	12.75		10.00			92.53	JULY 4, '86	332.47	219
31.88	37.90	12.75		10.00			92.53	JULY 11, '86	332.47	227
31.88	37.90	12.75		10.00			92.53	JULY 18, '86	332.47	235
31.88	37.90	12.75		10.00			92.53	JULY 25, '86	332.47	243
31.88	37.90	12.75		10.00			92.53	AUG. 1, '86	332.47	251
31.88	37.90	12.75		10.00			92.53	AUG. 8, '86	332.47	259
31.88	37.90	12.75		10.00			92.53	AUG. 15, '86	332.47	267
31.88	37.90	12.75		10.00			92.53	AUG. 22, '86	332.47	275
31.88	37.90	12.75		10.00			92.53	AUG. 29, '86	332.47	283
31.88	37.90	12.75		10.00			92.53	SEPT. 5, '86	332.47	291
31.88	37.90	12.75		10.00			92.53	SEPT. 12, '86	332.47	299
31.88	37.90	12.75		10.00			92.53	SEPT. 19, '86	332.47	307
31.88	37.90	12.75		10.00			92.53	SEPT. 26, '86	332.47	315
414.44	492.70	165.75		130.00			1,202.89		4,322.11	
31.88	37.90	12.75		10.00			92.53	OCT. 3, '86	332.47	323
31.88	37.90	12.75		10.00			92.53	OCT. 10, '86	332.47	331
31.88	37.90	12.75		10.00			92.53	OCT. 17, '86	332.47	339
31.88	37.90	12.75		10.00			92.53	OCT. 24, '86	332.47	347
35.63	46.40	14.25		10.00			106.28	OCT. 31, '86	368.72	355
36.38	48.10	14.55		10.00			109.03	NOV. 7, '86	375.97	363
35.63	46.40	14.25		10.00			106.28	NOV. 14, '86	368.72	371
37.50	52.50	15.00		10.00			115.00	NOV. 21, '86	385.00	379
37.50	52.50	15.00		10.00			115.00	NOV. 28, '86	385.00	387
37.50	52.50	15.00		10.00			115.00	DEC. 5, '86	385.00	395
37.50	52.50	15.00		10.00			115.00	DEC. 12, '86	385.00	403
31.88	37.90	12.75		10.00			92.53	DEC. 19, '86	332.47	411

Employee's Earnings Record—Computer Prepared (Right Page)

OFFICE PAYROLL

CSD **CENTRAL STATES DIVERSIFIED, INC.**
5221 NATURAL BRIDGE ST. LOUIS, MO. 63115-8230
PLANTS ST LOUIS - PALATKA, FLA

NUMBER 411

4-97/810

DATE	NAME	DOLLARS	CENTS
Dec. 19, '86	MARK C. PENNO	$ 332	47 A N D

PAY TO THE ORDER OF

BY _William C. Bonohou_

CENTRAL STATES DIVERSIFIED, INC.

MOUND CITY TRUST CO.
ST. LOUIS, MO.

⑆081000974⑆   49 053 2⑆

CSD **CENTRAL STATES DIVERSIFIED, INC.**
ST. LOUIS, MO.
STATEMENT OF EARNINGS

EARNINGS				TAXABLE EARNINGS		DEDUCTIONS										
REGULAR	OVERTIME	TOTAL	CUMULATIVE TOTAL	UNEMPLOYMENT COMP.	FICA	FICA TAX	FEDERAL INC. TAX	CITY TAX	PENSION PLAN	HEALTH INS.	CREDIT UNION	UNITED WAY	TOTAL	DATE	NET PAY	CK. NO.
425.00		425.00	22,025.00		425.00	31.88	37.90	12.75		10.00			92.53	Dec. 19, '86	332.47	411
20,375.00	1,650.00	22,025.00	22,025.00		22,025.00	1,651.88	1,895.90	676.25		484.00			4,708.03	Yr-to-Date	17,316.97	

NON-NEGOTIABLE

Paycheck and Deduction Stub—Computer Prepared

The payroll register is a summary of the earnings of all employees for each pay period, while the earnings record is a summary of the annual earnings of each employee. The earnings record illustrated on pages 98 and 99 is designed so that quarterly and yearly totals can be accumulated. Thus the form provides a complete record of the earnings of an employee for the year—information that is needed in preparing an annual report to the employee and the Internal Revenue Service on a form called a Wage and Tax Statement. This report is explained in the following section. The earnings record also provides information on an employee's quarterly earnings, which is needed for filing quarterly reports to government agencies on various forms. These reports will be discussed later in this chapter.

Wage and Tax Statement

Not later than January 31 of each year, the law requires employers to furnish each employee from whom income taxes have been withheld an annual report called a Wage and Tax Statement, Form W-2, showing the total amount of wages paid and the amount of such tax withheld during the preceding calendar year. A completed form W-2 is illustrated.

[Form W-2]

1 Control number 22222 For Paperwork Reduction Act Notice, see back of Copy D. OMB No. 1545-0008	For Official Use Only		
2 Employer's name, address, and ZIP code	**3** Employer's identification number 43 0211630	**4** Employer's State number 21 686001	
Central States Diversified, Inc. 5221 Natural Bridge St. Louis, MO 63115-8230	**5** Stat. employee ☐ Deceased ☐ Legal rep ☐ 942 emp. ☐ Subtotal ☐ Void ☐		
	6 Allocated tips	**7** Advance EIC payment	
8 Employee's social security number 393 58 8194	**9** Federal income tax withheld $1,933.80	**10** Wages, tips, other compensation $22,450.00	**11** Social security tax withheld $1,683.76
12 Employee's name (first, middle, last) Mark Carl Penno	**13** Social security wages $22,450.00	**14** Social security tips	
1540 Swallow Dr. St. Louis, MO 63144-4752	**16** *		
	17 State income tax	**18** State wages, tips, etc.	**19** Name of State
15 Employee's address and ZIP code	**20** Local income tax $689.00	**21** Local wages, tips, etc. $22,450.00	**22** Name of locality St.Louis,Co.

Wage and Tax Statement (Form W-2)

If the employee's wages are subject to FICA tax as well as federal, state, or local income tax, the employer must report total wages paid and the amounts deducted both for income tax and for FICA tax. Information for this purpose is contained in the employee's earnings record.

The employer's identification number appearing on the Wage and Tax Statement is an identification number assigned to the employer by the Internal Revenue Service. An employer who employs one or more persons must file for an identification number. This number must be shown on all reports required of Central States Diversified, Inc., under the Federal Insurance Contributions Act.

Wage and Tax Statements must be prepared in quadruplicate. Copy A goes to the Social Security Administration. Copies B and C are furnished to the employee; Copy B must be sent in with the employee's federal income tax return, and Copy C is for the employee's files. Copy D is kept by the employer as part of the accounting records. In states or cities which have state or city income tax withholding laws, two more copies are furnished. Copy 1 is sent by the employer to the appropriate state or city tax department, and Copy 2 is sent by the employee with the state or city income tax return.

Accounting for Employee Earnings and Earnings Deductions

In accounting for employee earnings and deductions from earnings, it is desirable to keep separate accounts for (1) earnings and (2) earnings deductions. Various account titles are used in entering wages, such as Payroll Expense, Salaries Expense, and Salaries and Commissions Expense. The accounts needed in entering earnings deductions depend upon what deductions are involved. It helps in understanding the accounting for these deductions if we recognize that in withholding amounts from employees' earnings, the employer basically is serving as an agent for various groups such as the federal government, insurance companies, and credit unions. Amounts that are withheld and deducted from an employee's gross earnings must be paid by the employer to these groups. Therefore, a separate account should be kept for the liability incurred under each type of deduction, such as employee income tax, FICA tax, and insurance premiums. Examples of several of the major accounts involved in payroll accounting and of a typical journal entry for payroll are presented in the following sections.

Payroll Expense. This is an expense account which is debited for the total amount of the gross earnings of all employees for each pay period. Sometimes separate payroll accounts are kept for the employees of different departments. Thus separate accounts may be kept for Office Salaries Expense, Sales Salaries Expense, and Factory Payroll Expense.

Payroll Expense

Debit	
to enter gross earnings of employees for each pay period.	

FICA Tax Payable. This is a liability account which is credited for (1) the FICA tax withheld from employees' earnings and (2) the FICA tax imposed on the employer. FICA taxes imposed on the employer are discussed later in the chapter. The account should be debited for amounts paid to the Internal Revenue Service. When all of the FICA taxes have been paid, the account should be in balance.

FICA Tax Payable

Debit	Credit
to enter payment of FICA tax previously withheld or imposed.	to enter FICA taxes (1) withheld from employees' earnings and (2) imposed on the employer.

Employees Income Tax Payable. This is a liability account which should be credited for the total income tax withheld from employees' earnings. The account is debited for amounts paid to a bank depository for the Internal Revenue Service. When all of the income taxes withheld have been paid, the account will be in balance. A city or state earnings tax payable account is used in a similar manner.

Employees Income Tax Payable

Debit	Credit
to enter payment of income tax previously withheld.	to enter income tax withheld from employees' earnings.

Other Deductions. Pension Plan Deductions Payable is a liability account which is credited with amounts withheld from employees' earnings for any pension plan contributions. The account should be debited for the subsequent payment of these amounts to the pension plan trustee. Accounts for health insurance premiums payable, credit union contributions payable, and United Way contributions payable are similarly used.

Journalizing Payroll Transactions. The information needed to properly enter the payment of employee wages and salaries is contained in the payroll register. The totals at the bottom of the columns of the payroll register on pages 96 and 97 provide the basis for the following two-column journal entry for wages paid on December 19, 1986:

Dec. 19 Payroll Expense	3,400.00	
FICA Tax Payable		255.01
Employees Income tax Payable		463.70
City Earnings Tax Payable		102.00
Pension Plan Deductions Payable		42.50
Health Insurance Premiums Payable		46.00
Credit Union Contributions Payable		37.50
United Way Contributions Payable		40.00
Cash		2,413.29
Payroll for week ended December 19.		

These amounts are posted to payroll expense and liability accounts such as those illustrated in the preceding paragraphs.

BUILDING YOUR ACCOUNTING KNOWLEDGE

1. Why is it important for payroll accounting purposes to distinguish between an employee and an independent contractor?
2. Name three factors that generally explain the difference between an employee's gross pay and net pay.
3. Identify the four factors that determine the amount of federal income tax that is withheld from an employee's pay each pay period.
4. What factors determine the number of withholding allowances to which a taxpayer is entitled?
5. Identify the three types of payroll records usually needed by an employer.
6. Describe the information contained in the payroll register.
7. Why is it important to foot and verify the footings of the payroll register after the data for each employee have been entered?
8. Distinguish between the payroll register and the employee earnings record.
9. Explain what an employer does with the amounts withheld from an employee's pay.

APPLYING ACCOUNTING CONCEPTS

Exercise 4-1. Linda Lion's regular hourly rate is $9. She receives time and a half for any time worked over 40 hours a week, and double time for work on Sunday. During the past week, Lion worked 8 hours each day Monday through Thursday, 10 hours on Friday, and 6 hours on Sunday.

Compute Lion's gross pay for the past week.

Exercise 4-2. The payroll register of DSC Company for the payroll period ended December 5 showed the following amount column totals:

Regular earnings	$3,980.00
Overtime earnings	206.00
Deductions:	
FICA tax	$ 314.04
Federal income tax	571.92
City earnings tax	125.09
Pension plan	53.45
Health insurance	57.50
Credit union............	47.00
United Way	50.00

Based on the foregoing payroll register amounts, prepare the two-column journal entry for the payment of wages on December 5.

Report No. 4-1

Complete Report No. 4-1 in the study assignments and submit your working papers to the instructor for approval. After completing the report, continue with the following textbook discussion until the next report is required.

PAYROLL TAXES IMPOSED ON THE EMPLOYER

The various taxes discussed thus far have had one thing in common—they all were levied on the employee. The employer withholds them from the employees' earnings only for the purpose of subsequently paying them to some agency or organization. They do not represent any additional expense of the employer.

In addition to these employee taxes, however, certain taxes are also imposed directly on the employer for various purposes, such as: old-age, survivors, and disability insurance benefits; hospital insurance benefits for the aged; and unemployment, relief, and welfare. Most employers are subject to payroll taxes imposed under the Federal Insurance Contributions Act (FICA) and the Federal Unemployment Tax Act (FUTA). An employer may also be subject to the payroll tax imposed under the unemployment compensation laws of one or more states. This tax is commonly called a **State Unemployment Tax**. All of these employer taxes do represent additional payroll expenses of the employer, as will be demonstrated in subsequent sections.

Employer's FICA Tax

The taxes imposed under the Federal Insurance Contributions Act are levied on employers for exactly the same amounts as employees. As explained on page 88, the rate and the taxable earnings base of the tax may be changed by Congress at any time. It was assumed in this chapter that the combined rate (OASDI and HIP) is 7.5% and the base is $47,000. Thus the employer would be required to pay the employer's share of the FICA tax at a rate of 7.5% on the first $47,000 of each employee's earnings. Any amount of earnings paid to an employee during a year in excess of $47,000 is exempt from FICA tax. (Note that a total of 15% of each employee's taxable earnings—the employer's share and the employee's share—must be paid periodically to an authorized bank or the Internal Revenue Service.)

Employer's FUTA Tax

Under the Federal Unemployment Tax Act, a payroll tax, called the FUTA tax, is levied on employers for the purpose of financing the cost of administering the federal-state unemployment compensation program. This tax is levied only on employers and is not deducted from employees' earnings. Employers who employ one or more persons for at least one day in each of 20 or more calendar weeks in a calendar year, or who pay wages of $1,500 or more in any calendar quarter are subject to this tax. The federal law imposes a specific rate of tax on a specific earnings base but allows a substantial credit against this levy for amounts paid into state unemployment compensation programs. Since all states have such programs, the amounts actually paid to the federal government by most employers are substantially less than the legal maximum. Most of the total amount of tax levied under the FUTA program typically is paid to the state governments.

As in the case of the FICA tax, Congress can and does change both the rate and the taxable base of the FUTA tax from time to time. At present a rate of 6.2% with a credit of 5.4% for payments to state unemployment programs is assumed. The difference, 0.8% (6.2% - 5.4%) is the effective federal rate. Further, the taxable base is the first $7,000 of compensation paid to each employee during the calendar year. Note that both the rate and base are substantially lower than the 7.5% and $47,000 for the FICA tax. It is also important to note that all of the payroll taxes relate to gross wages paid—not to wages earned. Sometimes wages are earned in one quarter or year, but not paid until the following period.

Employer's State Unemployment Tax

All of the states and the District of Columbia have enacted unemployment compensation laws providing for the payment of benefits to qualified unemployed workers. The cost of administering the state unemployment compensation laws is borne by the federal government. Under the federal law an appropriation is made for each year by the Congress from which grants are made to the states to meet the proper administrative costs of their unemployment compensation laws. As a result of this provision, the entire amount paid into the state funds may be used for the payment of benefits to qualified workers. While in general there is considerable uniformity in the provisions of the state laws, there are many variations in coverage, rates of tax imposed, and benefits payable to qualified workers. The date of payment of unemployment taxes also varies from state to state, and a penalty generally is imposed on the employer for late payment. Not all employers covered by the Federal Unemployment Tax Act are covered by the unemployment compensation laws of the states in which they have employees. But most employers of one or more individuals are covered by the federal law.

There are frequent changes in the state laws with respect to coverage, contribution rates required, eligibility to receive benefits, and amounts of benefits payable. Under the laws of most states there is a merit-rating system which provides a tax-saving incentive to employers to stabilize employment. Under this system, an employer's rate may be considerably less than the maximum rate if steady work is provided for the employees, i.e., if none or very few of the employer's workers have applied for unemployment compensation. If an employer is qualified for a lower state rate, the full credit of 5.4% would still be allowed in computing the federal unemployment tax due.

To illustrate the merit-rating system and the functioning of the federal-state unemployment tax program as a whole, assume that an employer has a favorable merit rating and is required to pay only 2.0% rather than 5.4% to the state government. If an employee earns $5,000, this employer would be required to pay a total of $140 in unemployment taxes; $100 to the state government and $40 to the federal government, calculated as follows:

Taxable earnings	$5,000
State unemployment tax rate	× 2.0%
State unemployment tax	$ 100
Taxable earnings	$5,000
Total FUTA rate	6.2%
Credit for state program	5.4%
	× 0.8%
Federal unemployment tax	$ 40

For purposes of the payroll discussions that follow in this textbook, assume that a favorable merit rating exists and employers are required to pay only 2.7% rather than 5.4% to the state unemployment programs.

Accounting for Employer Payroll Taxes

In accounting for employer payroll taxes, it is acceptable either to use separate accounts for FICA Tax Expense, FUTA Tax Expense, and State Unemployment Tax Expense, or to enter all of these taxes in a single account such as Payroll Taxes Expense. Liabilities for FICA, FUTA, and state unemployment taxes normally should be entered in separate accounts. Examples of the payroll taxes expense and liability accounts and a typical journal entry for payroll taxes are presented in the following sections.

Payroll Taxes Expense. All of the payroll taxes imposed on an employer under the federal and state social security laws are an expense of the employer. For the purpose of this discussion, it is assumed that a single account entitled Payroll Taxes Expense is used in summarizing such taxes. This is an expense account which is debited for all payroll taxes imposed on the employer.

Payroll Taxes Expense	
Debit	
to enter FICA, FUTA, and state unemployment taxes imposed on the employer.	

FICA Tax Payable. This is the same liability account that was illustrated on page 103 and was used to recognize the FICA tax withheld from employees' earnings. As used here, the account is credited to enter the FICA tax imposed on the employer. The account is debited when the tax is paid to the Internal Revenue Service. When all of the FICA taxes have been paid, the account should be in balance.

FICA Tax Payable	
Debit	Credit
to enter payment of FICA tax.	to enter FICA taxes (1) withheld from employees' earnings and (2) imposed on the employer.

FUTA Tax Payable. In entering the federal unemployment tax, it is customary to keep a separate liability account entitled FUTA Tax Payable. This is a liability account which is credited for the tax imposed on employers under the Federal Unemployment Tax Act. The account is debited for amounts paid to apply on such taxes. When all of the FUTA taxes have been paid, the account should be in balance.

FUTA Tax Payable

Debit	Credit
to enter payment of FUTA tax.	to enter FUTA tax imposed on the employer.

State Unemployment Tax Payable. In entering the tax imposed under state unemployment compensation laws, it is customary to keep a separate liability account entitled State Unemployment Tax Payable. This is a liability account which is credited for the tax imposed on employers under the state unemployment compensation laws. The account is debited for the amount paid to apply on such taxes. When all of the state taxes have been paid, the account should be in balance. Some employers who are subject to taxes imposed under the laws of several states keep a separate liability account for the tax imposed by each state.

State Unemployment Tax Payable

Debit	Credit
to enter state unemployment tax paid.	to enter state unemployment tax imposed on the employer.

Journalizing Employer's Payroll Taxes. The payroll taxes imposed on employers may be entered periodically, such as monthly or quarterly. It is more common to enter such taxes at the time that wages are paid so that the employer's liability for such taxes and related expenses may be entered in the same period as the wages on which the taxes are based.

The information needed to properly enter employer payroll taxes is contained in the payroll register such as the one illustrated on pages 96 and 97. The totals at the bottom of the two columns for "Taxable Earnings" headed "Unemployment Comp." and "FICA" indicate the total employee earnings on which employer taxes would be levied. The FICA taxable earnings for the pay period involved amounted to $3,400.00. Assuming that the combined rate of the tax imposed on the employer was 7.5%, which is the same as the rate of the tax imposed on each employee, the tax would amount to $255.01. The only earnings in the payroll register that were subject to unemployment compensation taxes were Wool's earnings for the year because they had not exceeded the $7,000 taxable base. Wool just started working for Central States Diversified, Inc., on July 28, 1986. Federal and State unemployment taxes in this situation can be computed as follows:

```
State unemployment tax, 2.7% of $300..... $ 8.10
FUTA tax, 0.8% of $300................... 2.40
Total unemployment taxes ............... $10.50
```

The following two-column journal entry would therefore be made for the employer payroll taxes expense on wages paid on December 19. These amounts would be posted to payroll taxes expense and liability accounts such as those illustrated in the preceding paragraphs.

```
Dec. 19 Payroll Taxes Expense ........................... 265.51
            FICA Tax Payable.............................         255.01
            FUTA Tax Payable ...........................           2.40
            State Unemployment Tax Payable..............           8.10
            Employer payroll taxes for the week ended
            December 19.
```

An alternative approach employed by some businesses is to enter employer payroll taxes only when they are paid. Under this approach, the above entry would not be made on December 19. Instead, if the employer taxes on Central States Diversified's November 1986 payroll totaled $1,065.73, and were due on December 15, 1986, the following journal entry would be made:

```
Dec. 15 Payroll Taxes Expense ...................... 1,065.73
            Cash .......................................       1,065.73
            Employer payroll taxes for November.
```

The business illustrated in the following chapter accounts for employer payroll taxes in this manner.

It is important to note in connection with these illustrations the total cost incurred by an employer in order to employ a person. The employer must of course pay the gross wages of an employee, either in whole or in part to the employee, or in part to various government agencies and other organizations. In addition to these gross wages, however, the employer must pay payroll taxes on wages paid to an employee up to certain dollar limits. To illustrate this point, assume that an employee earns $25,000 for a year. The total cost of this employee to the employer can be calculated as follows:

```
Gross wages ............................. $25,000
Employer FICA tax, 7.5% of $25,000 .......   1,875
State unemployment tax, 2.7% of $7,000 ...     189
FUTA tax, 0.8% of $7,000 .................      56
                                          $27,120
```

Thus, the total cost to an employer of employing a person whose stated compensation is $25,000 is not $25,000, but $27,120. Employer payroll taxes clearly are a significant cost of doing business.

Filing Returns and Making Payroll Tax Payments

Employer responsibilities for filing reports and making payroll tax payments can be broken down into two areas: (1) responsibility with respect to FICA and federal income taxes, and (2) responsibility with respect to state and federal unemployment taxes. These two areas are discussed in the following sections.

Responsibilities for FICA and Federal Income Taxes. Federal reporting and payment regulations deal jointly with requirements for employee FICA taxes withheld, federal income taxes withheld, and employer FICA taxes. When the cumulative amount withheld from employees for FICA and income tax purposes plus the cumulative amount of employer FICA tax exceeds certain specified dollar amounts as of particular dates, an employer is required to deposit the amount in a Federal Reserve bank or branch or in some other authorized commercial bank depository. The dollar amounts and dates have been changed several times in recent years and are subject to change at any time in the future. In general, large employers are required to make deposits about every four days. Medium-size employers generally are required to make deposits by the 15th of the following month. In contrast, very small employers need not make a deposit but pay the accumulated liability at the end of the following month. For the sake of convenience in this chapter, it is assumed that the cumulative amount of FICA and income taxes at the end of each month must be deposited by the 15th of the following month.

At the time any one of these tax deposits is made, the employer should submit to the depository bank a completed copy of the Federal Tax Deposit Form 8109. An example of this form is shown on page 112.

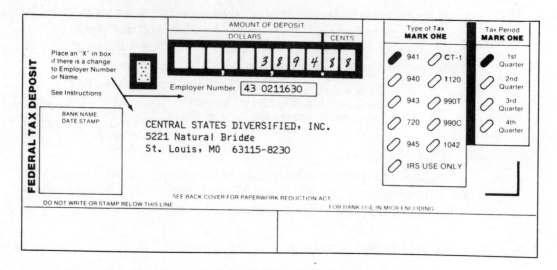

Federal Tax Deposit Form (Form 8109)

To illustrate the accounting procedure for entering the payment of employees' FICA and income taxes withheld and employer's FICA tax, assume that on January 26, Central States Diversified, Inc., issued a check in payment of the following taxes imposed with respect to wages paid during the first four payroll weeks of January:

Employees' income tax withheld from wages ...		$1,854.80
FICA tax:		
Withheld from employees' wages	$1,020.04	
Imposed on employer	1,020.04	2,040.08
Amount of check		$3,894.88

The journal entry for this transaction would be as follows:

Jan. 26 FICA Tax Payable.............................	2,040.08	
Employees Income Tax Payable	1,854.80	
Cash.......................................		3,894.88
Remitted $3,894.88 in payment of taxes.		

Another major form that the employer must file in connection with employee FICA and income taxes withheld and cumulative employer FICA taxes is Form 941. This is the Employer's Quarterly Federal Tax Return which must be filed with the Internal Revenue Service by the end of the month following the end of each quarter involved. A completed copy of Form 941 which would be used by Central States Diversified, Inc., on April 30, 1987, to file for the quarter ended March

27, 1987, is shown on page 114. This form summarizes employee FICA and federal income taxes withheld and employer FICA taxes due for the quarter. Portions of the information needed to complete Form 941 are obtained from the payroll register.

Responsibilities for State and Federal Unemployment Taxes. The amount of the tax imposed on employers under the state unemployment compensation laws must be remitted to the proper state office by the end of the month following the close of each calendar quarter involved. Each state provides an official form to be used in making a return of the taxes due. To illustrate the accounting procedure for entering the payment of state unemployment taxes, assume that a check for $842.40 was issued on April 30 in payment of state unemployment compensation taxes on wages paid during the preceding quarter ended March 27. This transaction would be entered in a two-column journal as follows:

Apr. 30 State Unemployment Tax Payable 842.40
          Cash 842.40
          Paid state unemployment tax.

Federal unemployment tax must be computed on a quarterly basis. If the amount of the employer's liability under the Federal Unemployment Tax Act during any quarter is more than $100, the total must be paid to a Federal Reserve Bank or some other authorized depository by the last day of the first month following the close of the quarter. If the amount is $100 or less, no deposit is necessary, but this amount must be added to the amount subject to deposit for the next quarter. When a federal unemployment tax deposit is made, the employer should submit to the bank a completed copy of the Federal Tax Deposit of Unemployment Taxes, Form 508. This form is similar to Form 8109, which was illustrated on page 112.

In addition to these quarterly reports and deposits, employers are required to submit an annual report of federal unemployment tax on Form 940 to the District IRS Center by the end of the month following the close of the calendar year. Form 940 is not illustrated here. Any federal unemployment tax due for the last quarter or for other periods during the year would be submitted with Form 940.

To illustrate the accounting procedure for payment of federal unemployment tax, assume that a check for $87.20 was issued on January 30 in payment of federal unemployment tax on wages paid during the preceding three quarters ended December 26. This transaction

Form **941** (Rev. January 1984) Department of the Treasury Internal Revenue Service	**Employer's Quarterly Federal Tax Return** ► For Paperwork Reduction Act Notice, see page 2.	OMB No. 1545-0029

		T
		FF

Your name, address, employer identification number, and calendar quarter of return. (If not correct, please change.)

►

Name (as distinguished from trade name)	Date quarter ended March 27, 1987
Trade name, if any **Central States Diversified, Inc.**	Employer identification number **43 0211630**
Address and ZIP code **5221 Natural Bridge, St. Louis, MO 63115-8230**	

FD	
FP	
I	
T	

If address is different from prior return, check here ► ☐

Record of Federal Tax Liability
(Complete if line 13 is $500 or more)

See the instructions under rule 4 on page 4 for details before checking these boxes.
Check only if you made eighth-monthly deposits using the 95% rule. . . . . ► ☐
Check only if you are a first-time 3-banking-day depositor. . . . . ► ☐

If you are not liable for returns in the future, write "FINAL" . . . . ►
Date final wages paid . . . . ►

Complete for First Quarter Only

	Date wages paid Day	Tax liability
First month of quarter	1st-3rd A	
	4th-7th B	974.20
	8th-11th C	
	12th-15th D	975.38
	16th-19th E	
	20th-22nd F	973.20
	23rd-25th G	
	26th-last H	972.10
I	Total . . ►	3,894.88
Second month of quarter	1st-3rd I	
	4th-7th J	
	8th-11th K	964.14
	12th-15th L	
	16th-19th M	962.66
	20th-22nd N	
	23rd-25th O	963.52
	26th-last P	960.30
II	Total . . ►	3,850.62
Third month of quarter	1st-3rd Q	
	4th-7th R	
	8th-11th S	1,006.54
	12th-15th T	
	16th-19th U	1,008.13
	20th-22nd V	
	23rd-25th W	1,007.28
	26th-last X	1,006.40
III	Total . . ►	4,028.35
IV	Total for quarter (add lines I, II, and III) . .	11,773.85

1 a Number of employees (except household) employed in the pay period that includes March 12th . . ►   **8**
b If you are a subsidiary corporation AND your parent corporation files a consolidated Form 1120, enter parent corporation's employer identification number (EIN) ►

2	Total wages and tips subject to withholding, plus other compensation . . . . ►	41,875	00
3	**a** Income tax withheld from wages, tips, pensions, annuities, sick pay, gambling, etc. . . . . . ►	5,492	60
	b Backup withholding . . . . ►	-0-	
	c Total income tax withheld (add lines 3a and 3b) . ►	5,492	60
4	Adjustment of withheld income tax for preceding quarters of calendar year:		
	a From wages, tips, pensions, annuities, sick pay, gambling, etc. . . . . ►	-0-	
	b From backup withholding . . . . ►	-0-	
	c Total adjustments (add lines 4a and 4b) . . . ►	-0-	
5	Adjusted total of income tax withheld (line 3c as adjusted by line 4c)	5,492	60
6	Taxable social security wages paid: $____41,875 00 X 15.0% . .	6,281	25
7	**a** Taxable tips reported: $_____ X 7.5%	-0-	
	b Tips deemed to be wages (see instructions): $_____ X 7.5%	-0-	
8	Total social security taxes (add lines 6, 7a, and 7b) . .	6,281	25
9	Adjustment of social security taxes (see instructions) ►	-0-	
10	Adjusted total of social security taxes	6,281	25
11	Total taxes (add lines 5 and 10) . . . . ►	11,773	85
12	Advance earned income credit (EIC) payments, if any ►	-0-	
13	Net taxes (subtract line 12 from line 11). This must equal line IV (plus line IV of Schedule A (Form 941) if you have treated backup withholding as a separate liability.) . . . . ►	11,773	85
14	Total deposits for quarter, including any overpayment applied from a prior quarter, from your records . . . . ►	11,773	85
15	Undeposited taxes due (subtract line 14 from line 13. Enter here and pay to Internal Revenue Service . . . . . ►	-0-	
16	If line 14 is more than line 13, enter overpayment here ► $_____ and check if to be: ☐ Applied to next return, or ☐ Refunded.		

Under penalties of perjury, I declare that I have examined this return, including accompanying schedules and statements, and to the best of my knowledge and belief it is true, correct, and complete.

Signature ► *William C. Bouchein*   Title ► Treasurer   Date ► Apr. 30. 1987

Please file this form with your Internal Revenue Service Center (see instructions on "Where to File").   Form **941** (Rev. 1-84)

Employer's Quarterly Federal Tax Return and Quarterly Report (Form 941)

would be entered in a two-column journal as follows:

```
Jan. 30 FUTA Tax Payable..................................  87.20
        Cash .............................................          87.20
        Paid federal unemployment tax.
```

BUILDING YOUR ACCOUNTING KNOWLEDGE

1. Why do employer payroll taxes represent an additional expense to the employer, whereas the various employee payroll taxes do not?
2. What is the purpose of the FUTA tax and who must pay it?
3. Why is most of the total amount of the tax levied under the FUTA program typically paid to the state governments?
4. Describe how a state merit-rating system works to reduce an employer's unemployment tax rate.
5. Identify all items that are debited or credited to the FICA Tax Payable account.
6. What accounts are affected when employer payroll tax expenses are properly recorded?
7. Explain why an employee whose gross salary is $20,000 costs an employer more than $20,000 to employ.
8. What is the purpose of the Employer's Quarterly Federal Tax Return Form 941?

APPLYING ACCOUNTING CONCEPTS

Exercise 4-3.   John Weimer operates a business in a state with a state unemployment tax rate of 2.7%, but he qualifies for a 1.2% rate because of his merit rating. The gross payroll for the period ending April 18 is $4,000, all of which is subject to state and federal unemployment taxes.

Compute **(a)** the state unemployment tax and **(b)** the federal unemployment tax for Weimer's payroll for the period ending April 18. (Assume a total FUTA tax rate of 3.5%.)

Exercise 4-4.   PR Company's gross payroll for the period ending May 9 is $4,500. All of the earnings are subject to FICA tax at a rate of 7.5%. Only $2,400 of the earnings are subject to state unemployment tax at a rate of 2.7%, and FUTA tax at a rate of 0.8%.

Prepare the two-column journal entry for PR Company's employer payroll taxes expense for wages paid on May 9.

Exercise 4-5.   George Ernest employs Paula Brown at a salary of $20,000 a year. Ernest is subject to employer FICA taxes at a rate of 7.5% on the salary. In addition, Ernest must pay state unemployment tax at a rate of 2.7% and federal unemployment tax at a rate of 0.8% on the first $7,000 of Brown's salary.

Compute the total cost to Ernest of employing Brown for the year.

Exercise 4-6. On June 15, Timly Company paid the following taxes imposed on the wages paid in the four preceding weekly payrolls:

Employees' income tax withheld from wages		$1,217.40
FICA tax:		
Withheld from employees' wages	$701.30	
Imposed on employer	701.30	1,402.60
Amount of check		$2,620.00

Prepare the two column journal entry for the payment of these taxes.

Report No. 4-2

Complete Report No. 4-2 in the study assignments and submit your working papers to the instructor for approval. After completing the report, you may continue with the textbook discussion in Chapter 5 until the next report is required.

EXPANDING YOUR BUSINESS VOCABULARY

What is the meaning of each of the following terms?

additional withholding allowances **(p. 90)**

automated systems **(p. 94)**

direct deposit **(p. 97)**

electronic system **(p. 94)**

employee **(p. 86)**

earnings record **(p. 93)**

employee's earnings record **(p. 98)**

employer's identification number **(p. 102)**

fee **(p. 86)**

FICA taxes **(p. 88)**

FUTA tax **(p. 106)**

gross pay **(p. 88)**

independent contractor **(p. 86)**

manual system **(p. 93)**

mechanical system **(p. 94)**

merit-rating system **(p. 107)**

net pay **(p. 88)**

payroll register **(pp. 93, 95)**

salary **(p. 86)**

service bureaus **(p. 94)**

special withholding allowance **(p. 90)**

State Unemployment Tax **(p. 105)**

time sharing **(p. 95)**

wage-bracket method **(p. 91)**

wages **(p. 86)**

withholding allowance **(p. 90)**

write-it-once principle **(p. 94)**

zero-bracket amounts **(p. 90)**

CHAPTER 5

Accounting for a Personal Service Enterprise

CHAPTER OBJECTIVES

Careful study of this chapter should enable you to:

- Combine the basic ideas, procedures, forms, and records that have been described and illustrated thus far into a real-world accounting system.

- Describe the cash basis of accounting and to recognize the limits of its application.

- Explain and prepare a multi-column book of original entry (the combination journal) and a four-column form of balance-column ledger.

- Explain and perform the following end-of-period steps in the accounting process:
  1. Determine needed adjustments to the accounts.
  2. Prepare an end-of-period work sheet.
  3. Prepare financial statements with the aid of the work sheet.
  4. Journalize and post adjusting entries.
  5. Journalize and post closing entries
  6. Prepare a post-closing trial balance.

A personal service enterprise is one in which the principal source of revenue is compensation for services rendered to a business firm or to a person. This is in contrast to a mercantile enterprise which buys merchandise for resale and a manufacturing enterprise which makes and sells one or more products. There are two major types of personal service enterprises:

1. Business enterprises
2. Professional enterprises

Personal service business enterprises include real estate, insurance, advertising, transportation, storage, entertainment, brokerage, and various other firms. Personal service professional enterprises include attorneys, physicians, dentists, public accountants, management consultants, engineers, architects, artists, and educators. The principal source of revenue for individuals engaged in these two types of enterprises is usually the compensation received for rendering personal services.

The purpose of this chapter is to illustrate accounting procedures for a personal service enterprise, Vance Zarmer, Computer Consultant. To this end, a multi-column combination journal and a four-column form of balance-column ledger are introduced. The use of an eight-column work sheet to facilitate preparing financial statements, adjusting the accounts, and closing the temporary owner's equity accounts is explained and demonstrated. Finally, a post-closing trial balance is presented.

THE CASH BASIS OF ACCOUNTING FOR A PERSONAL SERVICE ENTERPRISE

Accounting for revenue on a cash basis, cash basis revenue, means that no entry of revenue is made in the accounts until the cash is received for the services performed. Some services may be rendered in one period but the revenue from them will not be accounted for until received in the succeeding period. The business or professional person using the cash basis of accounting takes the view that there is no revenue until it is received in such a form that it can be spent. One cannot "spend" the promise of a customer or client to pay some money.

The cash basis is widely used in accounting for the revenue of a personal service enterprise. It is acceptable for federal and state income tax purposes. Under this basis, revenue is recognized not only when cash is received but also when certain other types of transactions or events occur. For example, any property or service that is accepted in lieu of cash for services rendered is treated as revenue to the extent of its fair market value at the time received. Revenue from interest on a savings account is said to be a constructive receipt if it is credited to the depositor's account or set apart so that it can be drawn upon. Such interest need not actually be received in cash or be withdrawn immediately.

Accounting for expenses on the cash basis, cash basis expense, generally means that expenses are not entered in the accounts until paid for in cash. Consequently, a certain expense may be incurred in one period and entered in the accounts in the succeeding period. In the case of many expenses of a recurring nature, however, this situation is not considered to be a significant problem. If, for example, twelve monthly telephone bills of about the same amount are paid during each year, little importance is attached to the fact that the bill that is paid and entered as an expense in January is really for service that was received in December.

An exception to the cash basis of accounting for expenses is made in connection with most plant and equipment. For example, it would be unreasonable to consider the entire cost of a building or piece of equipment to be an expense of the period in which these assets were purchased. It is expected that these assets will serve for a number of years. Their cost less any expected scrap or salvage value should be allocated over their estimated useful lives. The part of the original cost of the asset that is assigned to each period expected to benefit from its use is described as depreciation expense. Such expense cannot be calculated with precise accuracy. Still, this allocation results in a far more equitable periodic net income (profit) or loss measurement than one that simply considers the costs of such assets to be entirely expenses of the period in which they were purchased.

Another exception to the cash basis of accounting for expenses is sometimes made in connection with supplies purchased and later used. If the amount of money so invested is substantial and at the end of the accounting period a considerable quantity of expensive supplies is still on hand, an effort is made to determine the cost of those items which are on hand, so that only the cost of the supplies used will be treated as an expense of the period. If both the quantity and the cost of the items on hand at the end of an accounting period are small, the usual practice is to consider the total cost of all items purchased during that accounting period to be an expense of that period.

Illustration of Accounting Procedure

As an aid in applying the principles and procedures involved in keeping the accounts of a personal service enterprise on the cash basis, a system of accounts for Vance Zarmer, a computer consultant, will be described. While certain distinctive problems may arise in keeping the accounts of any specific enterprise, it will be found that the principles are generally the same; hence, the system of accounts used by Zarmer may readily be adapted to the needs of any personal service enterprise regardless of whether it is of a professional or a business nature.

Chart of Accounts

The following illustration is Zarmer's chart of accounts. Note that all account numbers beginning with 1 relate to assets; 2, liabilities; 3,

VANCE ZARMER, COMPUTER CONSULTANT

CHART OF ACCOUNTS

Assets*
    111 Cash
    112 Petty Cash
    191 Office Equipment
    191.1 Accumulated Depreciation—
           Office Equipment

Liabilities
    211 FICA Tax Payable
    214 Employees Income Tax
         Payable

Owner's Equity
    311 Vance Zarmer, Capital
    311.1 Vance Zarmer, Drawing
    331 Expense and Revenue
         Summary

Revenue
    411 Professional Fees

Expenses
    541 Rent Expense
    542 Salary Expense
    543 Travel and Entertainment
         Expense
    544 Telephone Expense
    545 Forms and Supplies Expense
    546 Automobile Expense
    547 Depreciation Expense
    548 Insurance Expense
    549 Charitable Contributions
         Expense
    551 Payroll Taxes Expense
    562 Miscellaneous Expense

*Words in bold type represent headings and not account titles.

owner's equity; 4, revenue; and 5, expenses. Account numbers that have four digits with a decimal point between the third and fourth digit represent contra accounts meaning "opposite" or "offsetting" accounts. A contra account is used with a related account to bring about a decrease in the net amount of the two account balances. This system of account numbering permits the addition of new accounts as they may be needed without disturbing the numerical order of the existing accounts.

Most of the accounts in the chart have been discussed and their use illustrated in the preceding chapters. Three notable exceptions are: Accumulated Depreciation — Office Equipment (No. 191.1), Depreciation Expense (No. 547), and Expense and Revenue Summary (No. 331). Each of these will be explained and its use illustrated as the need for the account arises in the narrative of transactions on pages 143–145. Except for Depreciation Expense, every debit to an expense account arises in connection with a cash payment. Note that there is no asset account for forms and supplies. In this illustration, the cost of all business forms and supplies purchased is debited (charged) to Forms and Supplies Expense, Account No. 545. The cost of any unused forms and supplies that may be on hand at the end of the year is ignored because such quantities normally are very small. The car that Zarmer uses for business purposes is leased. The monthly car rental and the cost of gasoline, oil, lubrication, washing, and automobile insurance are charged to Automobile Expense, Account No. 546. The cost of all other types of insurance that relate to the enterprise, such as workers' compensation, "errors and omissions" insurance (normally carried by computer consultants), and fire insurance on the office equipment and contents, is charged to Insurance Expense, Account No. 548, when the premiums on the policies are paid.

Accounting Records

Zarmer uses the following accounting records:

1. General records
   (a) Combination journal
   (b) General ledger
2. Auxiliary records
   (a) Petty cash payments record
   (b) Employees' earnings records
   (c) Copies of statements rendered to clients (billings for fees) with collections noted thereon

Combination Journal. The two-column journal can be used to enter every transaction of a business enterprise. However, in most businesses, there are many similar transactions that involve the same account or accounts. Outstanding examples are receipts and payments of cash. Suppose that in a typical month there are 30 transactions that result in an increase in cash and 40 transactions that cause a decrease in cash. In a two-column journal, this would require entering the word "Cash" 70 times, using a journal line each time. A considerable saving of time and space would result if two columns were added to the journal: one for debits to Cash and the other for credits to Cash. Other Debit and Credit columns in the journal can be used for amounts that belong in other accounts. At the end of the month, the special columns for cash debits and credits are totaled. The total of the Cash Debit column is posted as one amount to the debit side of the cash account and the total of the Cash Credit column is posted as one amount to the credit side of the cash account. Thus, instead of receiving 70 postings, Cash receives only two, one debit and one credit. Posting would require much less time and the danger of posting error would be reduced.

There is no reason to limit special journal columns to those for cash. If there are other accounts frequently used in the entering of transactions, special columns may be used to assemble all amounts that have the same effect on the account. More space and time may be saved. A journal with such special columns, and in addition a General Debit column and a General Credit column to take care of changes in accounts infrequently involved, is called a combination journal.

Zarmer uses a combination journal as the only record of original entry. The following is a reproduction of a portion of this journal. It

has eight amount columns, two at the left and six at the right of the Description column. The headings of the amount columns (as they read from left to right on the journal page) are as follows:

Cash
  Debit
  Credit
General
  Debit
  Credit
Professional Fees Credit
Salary Expense Debit
Wage Deductions
  FICA Tax Payable Credit
  Employees Income Tax Payable Credit

Each of the six special columns is justified because there are enough transactions requiring entries in the accounts indicated by each of the column headings to warrant this arrangement, which will help make the data entry process more efficient. A narrative of transactions completed by Zarmer during the month of December, 19--, is given on pages 124–132. These transactions are entered in the combination journal on pages 128–131. Note that before any transactions are entered in this journal, a memo notation of the bank balance at the start of the month, "Balance $6,993.65", is entered in the Description column just after the words "Amounts Forwarded."

General Ledger. Zarmer uses a balance-column account form, which has four amount columns: a debit column, a credit column, and two balance columns — one for debit balances and one for credit balances.

DATE	ITEM	POST. REF.	DEBIT	CREDIT	BALANCE DEBIT	BALANCE CREDIT

ACCOUNT   **ACCOUNT NO.**

Balance-Column Account Form

The standard two-column account form illustrated up to now is still used by some, but the four-column balance-column account form is used more frequently and has the advantage of providing a specific place for the account balance to be entered after each amount is posted. Posting to the ledger may be done after each transaction, at the end of the week, or at month end. Zarmer prefers to post the General column accounts of the combination journal at the end of the week and the column totals at the end of the month.

Zarmer's general ledger is reproduced on pages 133–136. In each instance, the balance of the account as of December 1 has been entered. This is done by (1) entering the date (Dec. 1, 19--) on the first line in the Date column of each account, (2) entering the word "Balance" in the Item column, (3) entering a check mark ($\sqrt{}$) in the Post. Ref. column (to show that each balance amount was not posted from the combination journal), and (4) entering the amount of the balance in the appropriate (Debit or Credit) Balance column of each account. The balance should **not** be entered in either the Debit or Credit amount column.

Two accounts are omitted: Expense and Revenue Summary (No. 331) and Depreciation Expense (No. 547). They are not included because neither had a balance on December 1, and neither received any debits or credits as a result of the cash receipt and payment transactions in December. These accounts are not used until the end-of-year process of adjusting and closing the accounts takes place. This procedure will be explained and illustrated on pages 143–147.

Auxiliary Records. The auxiliary records included in Zarmer's accounting information system are not reproduced in this chapter. The petty cash payments record that is used as a source document for the December 31 entry (see page 132) to replenish petty cash is almost identical in form to the one illustrated in Chapter 3 on pages 62–63. An employee's earnings record, similar to the one illustrated in Chapter 4 on pages 98 and 99, is maintained for each employee. Zarmer has two employees: Frank Cornich, a full-time systems analyst and programmer, and Donna Straits, a part-time secretary. Zarmer keeps a file for each client which includes, among other things, a copy of the contract or agreement with the client. This agreement stipulates the fee for the engagement and the time of payment (or payments, if the fee is to be paid in installments—which is the usual case). A copy machine copy of each statement or billing for fees earned is placed in each client's file. When money is received from a client, the date and amount are noted on the copy of the billing in addition to the formal entry made in the combination journal.

Transactions and Entries During the Fiscal Period

VANCE ZARMER, COMPUTER CONSULTANT

NARRATIVE OF TRANSACTIONS

Friday, December 5

Issued Check No. 431 for $560.05 to Frank Cornich, systems designer (full-time), in payment of his salary for the week: $750.00 less income tax withholding, $133.70, and FICA tax withholding, $56.25.[1]

Since the individual posting of Cornich's salary is not required, a check mark was placed in the Posting Reference column of the combination journal at the time the transaction was entered. The check mark notes that there is nothing entered in the General Debit and Credit columns on that line.

Issued Check No. 432 for $199.35 to Donna Straits, secretary (part-time), in payment of her salary for the week: $250.00 less income tax withholding, $31.90, and FICA tax withholding, $18.75.

Issued Check No. 433 for $850 to Bryan Reid for December office rent.

Note that the account title Rent Expense was recorded in the Description column and that $850 was debited in the General Column and credited in the Cash column.

---

[1]Because the cash basis method of accounting is used, Zarmer's share of FICA taxes and federal and state unemployment taxes is not entered until they are actually paid. FICA taxes for both Zarmer as an employer and the two employees normally are paid once each month. (See the second entry for December 15 on page 126.) Federal unemployment taxes normally are paid in January, and state unemployment taxes are paid in January, April, July, and October. In either of the latter two cases, the entry is a debit to Payroll Taxes Expense (No. 551) and a credit to Cash (No. 111).

Payroll Taxes Expense...   xxx
    Cash   xxx
        To pay federal and state unemployment taxes.

End-of-the-Week Work

(1) Proved the footings of the combination journal.

To be sure that the debits entered in the journal are equal to the credits, the journal must be **proved**. Each amount column is footed and the sum of the footings of the debit columns and the sum of the footings of the credit columns compared. This is known as a **proof of footings**. The footings are entered in small figures immediately below the last regular entry. If these sums are not the same, the journal entries must be examined to discover and correct the errors. The footings should be proved frequently. When the transactions are numerous, it is advisable to prove the footings daily. The footings must be proved when a page of the journal is filled to be sure that no error is carried forward to a new page. Proof of the footings is essential at the end of the month before the journal is ruled or any column totals are posted. The following is a proof of the footings of Zarmer's combination journal.

	CASH		Ck. No	DAY	DESCRIPTION	Post. Ref.	GENERAL		PROFESSIONAL FEES CR.	SALARY EXPENSE DR.	WAGE DEDUCTIONS	
DEBIT		CREDIT					DEBIT	CREDIT			FICA TAX PAY. CR.	EMP. INC. TAX PAY. CR.
					AMOUNTS FORWARDED *Balance* 6,993 65							
		560 05	431	5	*Frank Cornich*	✓				750 00	56 25	133 70
		199 35	432	5	*Donna Straits*	✓				250 00	18 75	31 90
		850 00	433	5	*Rent Expense* 5,384 25	541	850 00			1000 00	75 00	165 60
		1609 40										

(2) Proved the cash balance (Beginning balance, $6,993.65 — cash credits $1,609.40 = $5,384.25, end-of-week balance), and entered the new balance in the Description column following the third transaction of December 5.

(3) Posted the entry from the General Debit column of the combination journal to the rent expense account in the general ledger, Account No. 541. The date, "5," was entered in the Date column of this account; the code, "CJ 28," was entered in the "Post. Ref." column; the amount, $850.00, was entered in the Debit column, and the updated balance, $10,200.00, was entered in the Debit Balance column.

The code, "CJ 28," in the Post. Ref. column indicates that this entry was posted from page 28 of the Combination Journal. Finally, the number, "541," was entered in the Post. Ref. column of the combination journal on the line with Rent Expense, to show the "ledger address" to which this amount was posted.

Monday, December 8

Received a check for $1,400 from Phyllis Davis, a client, for services billed Nov. 24 and deposited it in the bank.

In the journal on page 126 note that the client's name is entered in the Description column and that a check mark is placed in the Posting Reference column.

Wednesday, December 10

Issued Check No. 434 for $58.40 to Elinor Spiller, an insurance agent, in payment of the one-year premium on a fire insurance policy covering Zarmer's office equipment and contents.

Friday, December 12

Issued Check No. 435 for $560.05 to Frank Cornich and Check No. 436 for $199.35 to Donna Straits in payment of salaries for the week.

End-of-the-Week Work

(1) Proved the footings of the combination journal. Total debits ($1,400.00 + $908.40 + $2,000.00 = $4,308.40) equal total credits ($2,427.20 + $1,400.00 + $150.00 + $331.20 = $4,308.40). (2) Proved the cash balance ($6,993.65 + $1,400.00 − $2,427.20 = $5,966.45), and entered the new balance in the Description column following the second transaction of December 12. (3) Posted the entry from the General Debit column of the combination journal to the proper general ledger account.

PAGE 28		COMBINATION JOURNAL			FOR MONTH OF December 19— — PAGE 28						
CASH		CK.	DAY	DESCRIPTION	POST.	GENERAL		PROFESSIONAL	SALARY EXPENSE	WAGE DEDUCTIONS	
DEBIT	CREDIT	NO.			REF.	DEBIT	CREDIT	FEES CR.	DR.	FICA TAX PAY. CR.	EMP. INC. TAX PAY. CR.
1400 00			8	Phyllis Davis	✓			1400 00			
	58 40	434	10	Insurance Expense	548	58 40					
	560 05	435	12	Frank Cornich	✓				750 00	56 25	133 70
1400 00	199 35	436	12	Donna Straits	✓						
	2427 20					908 40		1400 00	2358 88	158 88	331 20

Monday, December 15

Received a check for $2,000 from Goods Stores, Inc., a client, for services billed Dec. 1 and deposited it in the bank.

Issued Check No. 437 for $1,262.40 to the City Bank, a United States depository, in payment of the following taxes:

Employees' income tax withheld during November		$ 662.40
FICA tax imposed:		
On employees (withheld during November)	$300.00	
On the employer	300.00	600.00
Total		$1,262.40

This payment involved three factors in addition to the decrease in the cash balance: (1) payment of the recorded liability, Employees Income Tax Payable, Account No. 214, of $662.40; (2) payment of the recorded liability, FICA

Tax Payable, Account No. 211, of $300; and **(3)** payment of the unrecorded liability of $300, the employer's FICA tax relating to the taxable earnings paid in November. To enter the transaction correctly, the first two amounts ($662.40 and $300) are debited to the proper liability accounts, since the tax liability was being decreased, and the third amount is debited to Payroll Taxes Expense, Account No. 551, resulting in an increase in the employer's expenses. Note that three lines were needed in the combination journal. A Tax Deposit Form was presented at the bank in payment of the taxes. A photocopy of the form was made and retained as a record of the deposit.

Tuesday, December 16

Issued Check No. 438 for $139.21 to UARCO Business Forms Co. in payment for supplies.

Received a check for $3.60 from Elinor Spiller, the insurance agent, to whom Zarmer had sent a check (No. 434) on December 10 in the amount of $58.40 in payment of the premium on a fire insurance policy covering office equipment and contents. The check for $3.60 was accompanied by a letter from Spiller explaining that a clerical error was made in preparing the invoice for the policy. The correct amount was $54.80—not $58.40. Zarmer's check for $58.40 had been deposited before the mistake was discovered. Accordingly, Spiller sent the check for $3.60 as a refund of the excess premium and the check was deposited in the bank.

This insurance premium refund check was entered in the combination journal by a debit to Cash, Account No. 111, and a credit to Insurance Expense, Account No. 548, in the amount of $3.60. Since the entry for Check No. 434 has already been posted as a debit to Insurance Expense, this manner of handling is required. Note that the error resulted from the fact that the clerk in Spiller's office had made a **transposition error**—a mistake well known to accountants. The intention was to type $54.80 but $58.40 was typed instead. The "4" and the "8" were placed in the wrong order—they were transposed.

Wednesday, December 17

Issued Check No. 439 for $4,000 to Zarmer for personal use.

Thursday, December 18

Issued Check No. 440 for $170.80 to the O'Daniel Auto Leasing Co. in payment of one month's rent of the leased automobile used by Zarmer for business purposes.

This payment was recorded by a debit to Automobile Expense, Account No. 546.

Friday, December 19

Issued Check No. 441 for $560.05 to Frank Cornich and Check No. 442 for $199.35 to Donna Straits in payment of salaries for the week. Issued Check No. 443 for $100 to American Heart Association.

PAGE 28   COMBINATION JOURNAL

	CASH DEBIT	CASH CREDIT	CK. NO.	DAY	DESCRIPTION	POST. REF.
1					AMOUNTS FORWARDED *Balance 6,993.65*	
2		560 05	431	5	Frank Cornich	✓
3		199 35	432	5	Donna Straits	✓
4		850 00 / 1699 48	433	5	Rent Expense *5,384.25*	541
5	1400 00			8	Phyllis Davis	✓
6		58 40	434	10	Insurance Expense	548
7		560 05	435	12	Frank Cornich	✓
8		199 35 / 2427 20	436	12	Donna Straits	✓
9	1400 00 / 2000 00			15	Goods Stores, Inc. *5,966.45*	✓
10		1262 40	437	15	Employees Income Tax Payable	214
11					FICA Tax Payable	211
12					Payroll Taxes Expense	551
13		139 21	438	16	Forms and Supplies Expense	545
14	3 60			16	Insurance Expense	548
15		4000 00	439	17	Vance Farmer, Drawing	311.1
16		170 80	440	18	Automobile Expense	546
17		560 05	441	19	Frank Cornich	✓
18		199 35	442	19	Donna Straits	✓
19	3403 60	100 00 / 8859 01	443	19	Charitable Contribution Expense *1,538.24*	549
20		48 35	444	22	Automobile Expense	546
21		24 75	445	22	Miscellaneous Expense	562
22		39 60	446	23	Telephone Expense	544
23	1400 00			24	L. R. Frames	✓
24		118 22	447	24	Forms and Supplies Expense	545
25		560 05	448	26	Frank Cornich	✓
26	4803 60	199 35 / 9849 33	449	26	Donna Straits	✓
27	4803 60	9849 33		26	Carried Forward *1,947.92*	
28						

Combination Journal (Left Page)

End-of-the-Week Work

(1) Proved the footings of the combination journal. (2) Proved the cash balance ($1,538.24). (3) Posted each entry individually from the General Debit and General Credit columns of the combination jour-

FOR MONTH OF *December*   19--   PAGE 28

GENERAL DEBIT	GENERAL CREDIT	PROFESSIONAL FEES CR.	SALARY EXPENSE DR.	FICA TAX PAY. CR.	EMP. INC. TAX PAY. CR.	
						1
			750 00	56 25	133 70	2
			250 00	18 75	31 90	3
850 00						4
850 00		1400 00	1000 00	75 00	165 60	5
						6
58 40			750 00	56 25	133 70	7
			250 00	18 75	31 90	8
908 40		1400 00 / 2000 00	2000 00	150 00	331 20	9
662 40						10
300 00						11
300 00						12
139 21						13
	3 60					14
4000 00						15
170 80						16
			750 00	56 25	133 70	17
			250 00	18 75	31 90	18
1000 00						19
6580 81	3 60	3400 00	3000 00	225 00	496 80	20
48 35						21
	24 75					22
	39 60	1400 00				23
						24
118 22			750 00	56 25	133 70	25
			250 00	18 75	31 90	26
6811 73	3 60	4800 00	4000 00	300 00	662 40	27
6811 73	3 60	4800 00	4000 00	300 00	662 40	28

Combination Journal (Right Page)

nal to the proper general ledger accounts. When the entry of December 15 relating to Check No. 437 was posted, debits were made to Employees Income Tax Payable, Account No. 214, and FICA Tax Payable, Account No. 211, which caused those accounts to be in balance.

Monday, December 22

Issued Check No. 444 for $48.35 to Tom's Service Center in payment for gasoline, oil and lubrication purchased on credit during the past month. All of these purchases related to the expense of operating the leased automobile used for business purposes.

Issued Check No. 445 for $24.75 to Belcher Typewriter Service in payment of charges for cleaning and repairing office typewriter.

> The amount of this check was charged to Miscellaneous Expense, Account No. 562.

Tuesday, December 23

Issued Check No. 446 for $39.60 to The Tinker Bell Telephone Co. in payment of statement just received showing charges for local and long-distance business calls, during the past month.

PAGE 29   COMBINATION JOURNAL

| | CASH | | CK. | DAY | DESCRIPTION | POST. |
DEBIT		CREDIT	No.			REF.
1	4 8 0 3 60	9 8 4 9 33		26	AMOUNTS FORWARDED *Balance 1,947 92*	
2		1 4 8 75	450	29	*Travel + Entertainment Expense*	543
3	1 6 0 0 00			30	*F + M Seafood Markets*	✓
4		1 0 2 92	451	31	*Vance Farmer, Drawing*	311
5					*Travel + Entertainment Expense*	543
6					*Forms and Supplies Expense*	545
7					*Automobile Expense*	546
8					*Charitable Contribution Expense*	549
9					*Miscellaneous Expense*	562
10		5 6 0 05	452	31	*Frank Cornich*	✓
11		1 9 9 35	453	31	*Donna Straits*	✓
12	6 4 0 3 60	10 8 6 0 40				
	6 4 0 3 60	10 8 6 0 40			*2,536.85*	
13	(111)	(111)				

Combination Journal (Left Page) *(concluded)*

Wednesday, December 24

Received a check for $1,400 from L. R. Frames, a client, for services billed Dec. 10 and deposited it in the bank.

Issued Check No. 447 for $118.22 to Corporate Business Systems in payment for supplies purchased.

Friday, December 26

Issued Check No. 448 for $560.05 to Frank Cornich and Check No. 449 for $199.35 to Donna Straits in payment of salaries for the week.

End-of-the-Week Work

(1) Proved the footings of the combination journal. (2) Proved the cash balance ($1,947.92). (3) Posted each entry individually from the General Debit column of the combination journal.

> Because a page of the combination journal was filled after Check No. 449 was entered, the footings of the columns were proved and entered as totals on the last line of the page, and the words "Carried Forward" were placed in the Description column. The totals were entered in the appropriate columns on the top line of the next page. The cash balance was entered in the Description column of the new page just after the words "Amounts Forwarded."

FOR MONTH OF *December*   19--   PAGE 29

GENERAL DEBIT	GENERAL CREDIT	PROFESSIONAL FEES CR.	SALARY EXPENSE DR.	FICA TAX PAY. CR.	EMP. INC. TAX PAY. CR.	
6811 73	3 60	4800 00	4000 00	300 00	662 40	1
148 75						2
		1600 00				3
22 75						4
36 25						5
16 50						6
6 80						7
12 50						8
8 12						9
			750 00	56 25	133 70	10
			250 00	18 75	31 90	11
7063 40	3 60	6400 00	5000 00	375 00	828 00	12
7063 40	3 60	6400 00	5000 00	375 00	828 00	
(√)	(√)	(411)	(542)	(211)	(214)	13

Combination Journal (Right Page) *(concluded)*

Monday, December 29

Issued Check No. 450 for $148.75 to Memorial Country Club in payment of food and beverage charges for one month.

> The amount of this check was charged to Travel and Entertainment Expense, Account No. 543. Zarmer uses the facilities of the club to entertain prospective clients.

Tuesday, December 30

Received a check for $1,600 from F & M Seafood Markets, a client, for services billed Dec. 16 and deposited it in the bank.

Wednesday, December 31

Issued Check No. 451 for $102.92 to replenish the petty cash fund. Following is a summary of the petty cash payments for the month of December prepared from the Petty Cash Payments Record:

Vance Zarmer, Drawing	$ 22.75
Travel and Entertainment Expense	36.25
Forms and Supplies Expense	16.50
Automobile Expense	6.80
Charitable Contributions Expense	12.50
Miscellaneous Expense	8.12
Total payments	$102.92

Issued Check No. 452 for $560.05 to Frank Cornich and Check No. 453 for $199.35 to Donna Straits in payment of salaries for the partial week. Because of the holiday, Cornich and Straits were off for the rest of the week.

Routine-End-of-the-Month Work

(1) Proved the footings and entered the totals in the combination journal. (2) Proved the cash balance ($2,536.85). (3) Completed the individual posting from the General Debit column of the combination journal. (4) Completed the summary posting of the six special-column totals of the combination journal and ruled the journal as illustrated on pages 130–131. Note that the number of the account to which the total is posted was written in parentheses just below the total, and that check marks in parentheses were placed below the General Debit and General Credit column totals to indicate that these amounts were not posted. Also note that the ledger accounts were balanced at the time that they were posted. (5) Prepared a trial balance of the ledger accounts.

> Usually a trial balance at the end of a month is prepared using two-column paper. However, because Zarmer has chosen the calendar year for the fiscal

year (a common, but by no means universal practice), the trial balance at the end of December is placed in the first two amount columns of a form known as a work sheet. The need for and preparation of a work sheet are explained and illustrated on pages 137–141.

ACCOUNT *Cash*   ACCOUNT NO. *111*

DATE	ITEM	POST. REF.	DEBIT	CREDIT	BALANCE DEBIT	BALANCE CREDIT
19-- Dec. 1	Balance	✓			699365	
31		CG29	640360		1339725	
31		CG29		1086040	253685	

ACCOUNT *Petty Cash Fund*   ACCOUNT NO. *112*

DATE	ITEM	POST. REF.	DEBIT	CREDIT	BALANCE DEBIT	BALANCE CREDIT
19-- Dec. 1	Balance	✓			30000	

ACCOUNT *Office Equipment*   ACCOUNT NO. *191*

DATE	ITEM	POST. REF.	DEBIT	CREDIT	BALANCE DEBIT	BALANCE CREDIT
19-- Dec. 1	Balance	✓			4021080	

ACCOUNT *Accumulated Depreciation-Office Equipment*   ACCOUNT NO. *191.1*

DATE	ITEM	POST. REF.	DEBIT	CREDIT	BALANCE DEBIT	BALANCE CREDIT
19-- Dec. 1	Balance	✓				965470

ACCOUNT *FICA Tax Payable*   ACCOUNT NO. *211*

DATE	ITEM	POST. REF.	DEBIT	CREDIT	BALANCE DEBIT	BALANCE CREDIT
19-- Dec. 1	Balance	✓				30000
15		CG28	30000		-0-	-0-
31		CG29		37500		37500

Vance Zarmer, Computer Consultant—General Ledger

ACCOUNT *Employees Income Tax Payable*   ACCOUNT NO. 214

DATE	ITEM	POST. REF.	DEBIT	CREDIT	BALANCE DEBIT	BALANCE CREDIT
19-- Dec 1	Balance	✓				66240
15		CJ28	66240		-0-	-0-
31		CJ29		82800		82800

ACCOUNT *Vance Zarmer, Capital*   ACCOUNT NO. 311

DATE	ITEM	POST. REF.	DEBIT	CREDIT	BALANCE DEBIT	BALANCE CREDIT
19-- Dec 1	Balance	✓				3815200

ACCOUNT *Vance Zarmer, Drawing*   ACCOUNT NO. 311.1

DATE	ITEM	POST. REF.	DEBIT	CREDIT	BALANCE DEBIT	BALANCE CREDIT
19-- Dec 1	Balance	✓			4421075	
17		CJ28	400000		4821075	
31		CJ29	2275		4823350	

ACCOUNT *Professional Fees*   ACCOUNT NO. 411

DATE	ITEM	POST. REF.	DEBIT	CREDIT	BALANCE DEBIT	BALANCE CREDIT
19-- Dec 1	Balance	✓				11924000
31		CJ29		640000		12564000

ACCOUNT *Rent Expense*   ACCOUNT NO. 541

DATE	ITEM	POST. REF.	DEBIT	CREDIT	BALANCE DEBIT	BALANCE CREDIT
19-- Dec 1	Balance	✓			935000	
5		CJ28	85000		1020000	

Vance Zarmer, Computer Consultant—General Ledger (Continued)

ACCOUNT Salary Expense   **ACCOUNT NO.** 542

DATE		ITEM	POST. REF.	DEBIT	CREDIT	BALANCE	
						DEBIT	CREDIT
Dec. 19--	1	Balance	✓			4700000	
	31		CJ29	500000		5200000	

ACCOUNT Travel & Entertainment Expense   **ACCOUNT NO.** 543

DATE		ITEM	POST. REF.	DEBIT	CREDIT	BALANCE	
						DEBIT	CREDIT
Dec. 19--	1	Balance	✓			332595	
	29		CJ29	14875		347470	
	31		CJ29	3625		351095	

ACCOUNT Telephone Expense   **ACCOUNT NO.** 544

DATE		ITEM	POST. REF.	DEBIT	CREDIT	BALANCE	
						DEBIT	CREDIT
Dec. 19--	1	Balance	✓			141804	
	23		CJ28	3960		145764	

ACCOUNT Forms and Supplies Expense   **ACCOUNT NO.** 545

DATE		ITEM	POST. REF.	DEBIT	CREDIT	BALANCE	
						DEBIT	CREDIT
Dec. 19--	1	Balance	✓			603386	
	16		CJ28	13921		617307	
	24		CJ28	11822		629129	
	31		CJ29	1650		630779	

ACCOUNT Automobile Expense   **ACCOUNT NO.** 546

DATE		ITEM	POST. REF.	DEBIT	CREDIT	BALANCE	
						DEBIT	CREDIT
Dec. 19--	1		✓			292753	
	18		CJ28	17080		309833	
	22		CJ28	4835		314668	
	31		CJ29	680		315348	

Vance Zarmer, Computer Consultant—General Ledger (Continued)

ACCOUNT *Insurance Expense*   ACCOUNT NO. 548

DATE		ITEM	POST. REF.	DEBIT	CREDIT	BALANCE	
						DEBIT	CREDIT
19--Dec	1	Balance	✓			62840	
	10		CJ28	5840		68680	
	16		CJ28		360	68320	

ACCOUNT *Charitable Contributions Expense*   ACCOUNT NO. 549

DATE		ITEM	POST. REF.	DEBIT	CREDIT	BALANCE	
						DEBIT	CREDIT
19--Dec	1	Balance	✓			123500	
	19		CJ28	10000		133500	
	31		CJ29	1250		134750	

ACCOUNT *Payroll Taxes Expense*   ACCOUNT NO. 551

DATE		ITEM	POST. REF.	DEBIT	CREDIT	BALANCE	
						DEBIT	CREDIT
19--Dec	1	Balance	✓			401500	
	15		CJ28	30000		431500	

ACCOUNT *Miscellaneous Expense*   ACCOUNT NO. 562

DATE		ITEM	POST. REF.	DEBIT	CREDIT	BALANCE	
						DEBIT	CREDIT
19--Dec	1	Balance	✓			36012	
	22		CJ28	2475		38487	
	31		CJ29	812		39299	

Vance Zarmer, Computer Consultant—General Ledger *(Concluded)*

Study Assignment: Report No. 5-1, Part B, Problem 1, in the study assignments may be completed at this time at the option of your instructor.

WORK AT CLOSE OF THE FISCAL PERIOD

As soon as possible after the end of the fiscal period, the owner (or owners) of an enterprise wants to be provided with (1) an income statement covering the period just ended, and (2) a balance sheet as of the last day of the period. To provide these statements, the accountant must consider certain matters that have not been entered in the daily routine of events. For example, in the case of Zarmer's enterprise, depreciation of office equipment for the past year is one such matter. Furthermore, the revenue accounts, the expense accounts, and the account showing the owner's withdrawals have performed their function for the period just ended (in this case, the calendar year) and need to be made ready to receive the entries of the new period. In the language of accountants, "the books must be adjusted and closed." Actually, only the temporary owner's equity accounts—those for revenue, expense and the owner's drawings—are closed, but the remark quoted is widely used to describe what takes place at this time.

The End-Of-Period Work Sheet

To facilitate (1) the preparing of the financial statements, (2) the making of needed adjustments in the accounts, and (3) the closing of the temporary owner's equity accounts, it is common practice to prepare an end-of-period work sheet. Because of the nature of Zarmer's enterprise, an eight-column work sheet is adequate. Note that the heading states that it is for the year ended December 31, 19--. The income statement columns relate to the full year, and the balance sheet columns show the financial position as of the last day of the fiscal period.

Vance Zarmer, Computer Consultant
Work Sheet
For the Year Ended December 31, 19--

ACCOUNT TITLE	ACCT. NO.	TRIAL BALANCE		ADJUSTMENTS		INCOME STATEMENT		BALANCE SHEET	
		DEBIT	CREDIT	DEBIT	CREDIT	DEBIT	CREDIT	DEBIT	CREDIT
1									
2									
3									
4									
5									
6									

The first pair of columns of the work sheet illustrated on page 140 shows the trial balance taken after the routine posting for the month of December has been completed. Note that the account Depreciation Expense (No. 547) is included in the list of accounts and account numbers even though the account has no balance at this point. The second pair of columns, headed "Adjustments," shows the manner in which the expense of estimated depreciation of office equipment for the year affects the accounts. The trial balance shows that the account Office Equipment (No. 191) has a balance of $40,210.80, and that the balance of the account Accumulated Depreciation—Office Equipment (No. 191.1) is $9,654.70. No new equipment was purchased during the year and there were no sales or retirements of such property during the year. Accordingly, the balances of these two accounts have not changed during the year. The two accounts are closely related: the debit balance of the office equipment account indicates the cost of the assets, and the credit balance of the accumulated depreciation account indicates the amount of this cost that has been charged off as depreciation in past years—that is, up to January 1 of the current year. The difference between the cost of the asset and the accumulated depreciation, $30,556.10 ($40,210.80 − $9,654.70) is described as the undepreciated cost of the office equipment. This amount is also called the book value of the equipment. A better description of the difference is "cost yet to be charged to expense."

Since the year has just ended, it is necessary to enter as an expense the estimated depreciation for the year. Zarmer estimates that the various items of office equipment have average useful lives of ten years and that any scrap or salvage value at the end of that time is likely to be so small that it can be ignored. Accordingly, estimated depreciation expense for the year is calculated to be $4,021.08 ($40,210.80 ÷ 10 years). This expense needs to be entered on the work sheet so that it will be considered when the financial statements are prepared. Later it will be journalized and posted to the ledger accounts. As shown in the foregoing illustration, the entry is made on the work sheet as follows: $4,021.08 is placed in the Adjustments Debit column on the line for

Vance Zarmer, Computer Consultant
Work Sheet
For the Year Ended December 31, 19--

ACCOUNT TITLE	ACCT. NO.	TRIAL BALANCE DEBIT	TRIAL BALANCE CREDIT	ADJUSTMENTS DEBIT	ADJUSTMENTS CREDIT	INCOME STATEMENT DEBIT	INCOME STATEMENT CREDIT	BALANCE SHEET DEBIT	BALANCE SHEET CREDIT
Office Equipment	191	40210 80						40210 80	
Accum. Depr.-Office Equip.	191.1		9654 70		402108				13675 78
Depreciation Expense	547			402108		402108			

Depreciation Expense and the same amount is placed in the Adjustments Credit column on the line for Accumulated Depreciation. Since there are no more adjustments, the Debit and Credit columns are totaled.

The next step is to combine each amount in the Trial Balance columns with the amount, if any, in the Adjustments columns and to extend the total into the Income Statement or Balance Sheet columns. Revenue and expense account balances are extended to the Income Statement columns and balance sheet account balances to the Balance Sheet columns. Note that the new amount for Accumulated Depreciation—Office Equipment, $13,675.78 ($9,654.70 + $4,021.08) appears in the Balance Sheet Credit column, and that the depreciation expense of $4,021.08 appears, along with all other expenses, in the Income Statement Debit column.

Each of the last four columns is then totaled. The total of the Income Statement Credit column exceeds the total of the Income Statement Debit column by $38,250.37—the calculated net income for the year. That amount, so designated, is placed in the Income Statement Debit column to bring the pair of Income Statement columns into balance. When the same amount, $38,250.37, is placed in the Balance Sheet Credit column, the last pair of columns is brought into balance. The final totals of the last four columns are entered at the bottom of the work sheet.

Vance Zarmer, Computer Consultant
Work Sheet
For the Year Ended December 31, 19--

ACCOUNT TITLE	ACCT. NO.	TRIAL BALANCE		ADJUSTMENTS		INCOME STATEMENT		BALANCE SHEET	
		DEBIT	CREDIT	DEBIT	CREDIT	DEBIT	CREDIT	DEBIT	CREDIT
		17464970	17464970	402108	402108	8738963	12564000	9128115	5303078
Net Income						3825037			3825037
						12564000	12564000	9128115	9128115

The reason for adding the net income for the year, $38,250.37, to the Balance Sheet Credit column causing its total to equal the total of the Balance Sheet Debit column is explained as follows. The amounts for the assets and liabilities in the last pair of columns are up-to-date amounts. However, the Zarmer equity account is not up-to-date. In this example, the equity account of $38,152.00 reflects the balance of the account at the beginning of the year. It is affected during the year by withdrawals and net income. The contra owner's equity drawing

Vance Zarmer, Computer Consultant
Work Sheet
For the Year Ended December 31, 19--

#	ACCOUNT TITLE	ACCT. NO.	TRIAL BALANCE DEBIT	TRIAL BALANCE CREDIT	ADJUSTMENTS DEBIT	ADJUSTMENTS CREDIT	INCOME STATEMENT DEBIT	INCOME STATEMENT CREDIT	BALANCE SHEET DEBIT	BALANCE SHEET CREDIT
1	Cash	111	2536 85						2536 85	
2	Petty Cash Fund	112	3000 00						3000 00	
3	Office Equipment	191	40210 80						40210 80	
4	Accum. Depr.-Office Equip.	191.1		9654 70		4021 08				13675 78
5	FICA Tax Payable	211		375 00						375 00
6	Employee's Inc. Tax Payable	214		828 00						828 00
7	Vance Zarmer, Capital	311		38152 00						38152 00
8	Vance Zarmer, Drawing	311.1	48233 50						48233 50	
9	Professional Fees	411		125640 00				125640 00		
10	Rent Expense	541	10200 00				10200 00			
11	Salary Expense	542	52000 00				52000 00			
12	Travel & Entertainment Exp.	543	3510 95				3510 95			
13	Telephone Expense	544	1457 64				1457 64			
14	Forms & Supplies Expense	545	6307 79				6307 79			
15	Automobile Expense	546	3153 48				3153 48			
16	Depreciation Expense	547			4021 08		4021 08			
17	Insurance Expense	548	683 20				683 20			
18	Charitable Cont. Expense	549	1347 50				1347 50			
19	Payroll Taxes Expense	551	4315 00				4315 00			
20	Miscellaneous Expense	562	392 99				392 99			
21			174649 70	174649 70	4021 08	4021 08	87389 63	125640 00	91281 15	53030 78
22	Net Income						38250 37			38250 37
23							125640 00	125640 00	91281 15	91281 15
24										
25										

Vance Zarmer, Computer Consultant—End-of-Period Work Sheet

account balance of $48,233.50 has been extended to the debit column of the Balance Sheet to offset the equity account. It is also necessary to enter the net income of $38,250.37 in the credit column of the Balance Sheet to show the increase in the owner's equity due to the successful operation of the business during the year. The explanation is that there has been a profit from operations during the year (increasing owner's equity) as well as withdrawals for personal expenses (decreasing owner's equity) that have caused the owner's equity element to adjust to $28,168.87. This can be expressed in the form of the following equation:

Owner's Equity at Start of Period	+	Net Income for the Period	+ Investments	− Withdrawals	=	Owner's Equity at End of Period
$38,152.00	+	$38,250.37	+ 0	− $48,233.50	=	$28,168.87

The correct amounts for assets and liabilities and two of the three factors (owner's equity at start of period and withdrawals) needed to determine the correct amount of the owner's equity as of December 31, are already in the Balance Sheet columns. Therefore, the amount of the third factor—the net income for the year—has to be included so that those columns will reflect the basic equation: Assets = Liabilities + Owner's Equity. The implications of the net decrease in owner's equity will be discussed later in the chapter.

The Financial Statements. The work sheet supplies all of the information needed to prepare an income statement and a balance sheet. These statements for Zarmer's enterprise are shown on page 142.

Three features of the balance sheet should be noted:

1. Its format is the **report form of balance sheet**—the liabilities and the owner's equity sections are shown below the assets section. An alternative is the **account form of balance sheet**, in which the assets are at the left, and the liabilities and the owner's equity sections are at the right. (See the balance sheet of The Victor Pearce Placement Service on pages 52-53.)

2. The assets are classified on the basis of whether they are current or property, plant and equipment. **Current assets** include cash and any other assets that will be converted into cash within one year or the normal operating cycle of the business, whichever is longer. This cycle is the period of time required to purchase supplies and services and convert them back into cash. Zarmer's enterprise does not have any current assets other than cash. The amount shown includes both the cash in the bank account and petty cash. The **property, plant, and equipment** are assets which are expected to serve for many years.

3. All of the liabilities are classified as current, since they must be paid in the near future. Obligations which need not be paid until more than one year has passed are classified as **long-term liabilities**, but Zarmer has no debts of this type.

Vance Zarmer, Computer Consultant
Income Statement
For the Year Ended December 31, 19--

Professional fees		$125,640.00
Professional expenses:		
Rent expense	$10,200.00	
Salary expense	52,000.00	
Travel and entertainment expense	3,510.95	
Telephone expense	1,457.64	
Forms and supplies expense	6,307.79	
Automobile expense	3,153.48	
Depreciation expense	4,021.08	
Insurance expense	683.20	
Charitable contributions expense	1,347.50	
Payroll taxes expense	4,315.00	
Miscellaneous expense	392.99	
Total professional expenses		87,389.63
Net income		$ 38,250.37

Vance Zarmer, Computer Consultant—Income Statement

Vance Zarmer, Computer Consultant
Balance Sheet
December 31, 19--

Assets

Current assets:		
Cash		$ 2,836.85
Property, plant, and equipment:		
Office equipment	$40,210.80	
Less accumulated depreciation	13,675.78	26,535.02
Total assets		$29,371.87

Liabilities

Current liabilities:		
FICA tax payable	$ 375.00	
Employees income tax payable	828.00	
Total current liabilities		$ 1,203.00

Owner's Equity

Vance Zarmer, capital:			
Capital, January 1, 19--		$38,152.00	
Net income for year	$38,250.37		
Withdrawals for year	48,233.50	(9,983.13)	
Capital, December 31, 19--			28,168.87
Total liabilities and owner's equity			$29,371.87

Vance Zarmer, Computer Consultant—Balance Sheet

The $9,983.13 net decrease in owner's equity shown on Zarmer's year-end balance sheet was the amount by which his withdrawals during the year, $48,233.50, exceeded the firm's net income for the year of $38,250.37. The owner of a small personal service enterprise makes periodic withdrawals during the year in anticipation of a certain year-end net income. Zarmer has been overly optimistic in estimating the results of operations.

Zarmer can make a one-time additional cash investment of about $10,000 to restore his equity to its beginning-of-year level. However, a more permanent solution will require: (1) increasing the amounts of professional fees, (2) obtaining more engagements, (3) decreasing certain expenses, (4) decreasing the amounts of his periodic withdrawals, or (5) a combination of two or more of the above actions.

Rounded Amounts in Statements and Schedules. The foregoing income statement and balance sheet could be presented by rounding to the nearest dollar. The rule adopted for rounding is: If the cents in the amount are 50 or more, raise the first digit left of the decimal point by one; if 49 or less, drop the cents. Thus, $37.73 would become $38; $37.38 would become $37.

Adjusting Entries for a Personal Service Enterprise. The amounts in the financial statements must agree with the ledger account balances. To speed up the preparation of the statements, a work sheet was used to adjust accounts and accumulate income statement and balance sheet information. Subsequently, these adjustments will have to be formally entered in the journal and posted to the accounts. Such entries are called **adjusting entries**.

As shown below in the partial Combination Journal illustration, the heading "Adjusting Entry" is centered at the top of the Description column on a new page (Page 30) of this journal. The title of the account debited, "Depreciation Expense," is entered in the Descrip-

				GENERAL	
DAY	**DESCRIPTION**	**POST. REF.**	**DEBIT**	**CREDIT**
	GENERAL JOURNAL FOR MONTH OF *December* 19--			PAGE *30*	
1	AMOUNTS FORWARDED				
2	*31*	*Adjusting Entry*			
3		*Depreciation Expense*	547	402 08	
4		*Accumulated Depr.- Office Equipment*	191.1		402 08
5					
6					

tion column on the next available line, along with the debit amount, "$4,021.08," in the General Debit column. The title of the account credited, "Accumulated Depreciation—Office Equipment," is indented in the Description column on the following line, and the credit amount, "$4,021.08," is entered in the General Credit column. The two numbers in the Post. Ref. column, "547" and "191.1," are entered later when this entry is posted to the general ledger.

The following illustration shows how the two accounts affected by the entry, Depreciation Expense (No. 547) and Accumulated Depreciation—Office Equipment (No. 191.1), appear after the entry is posted. After this posting is completed, the balance of the depreciation expense account agrees with the amount shown in the income statement, and the balance of the accumulated depreciation account is the same as the amount shown in the balance sheet.

ACCOUNT Accumulated Depreciation—Office Equipment   ACCOUNT NO. 191.1

DATE		ITEM	POST. REF.	DEBIT	CREDIT	BALANCE	
						DEBIT	CREDIT
19-- Dec.	1	Balance	✓				9654 70
	31		CG30		4021 08		13675 78

ACCOUNT Depreciation Expense   ACCOUNT NO. 547

DATE		ITEM	POST. REF.	DEBIT	CREDIT	BALANCE	
						DEBIT	CREDIT
19-- Dec.	31		CG30	4021 08		4021 08	

Closing Entries for a Personal Service Enterprise. As in the case of the adjusting entry, the closing entries are made as of December 31. Note that the work sheet provides all of the data needed to prepare the adjusting and closing entries. The purpose and use of Expense and Revenue Summary, Account No. 331, as its name indicates, is to summarize the amounts of expense and revenue which are reasons for changes in owner's equity other than investments and withdrawals by the owner.

The revenue and expense accounts and the account for Vance Zarmer, Drawing (No. 311.1) have served their purpose for the year 19--, and the balance of each of these accounts needs to be reduced to zero, or closed, in order to make the accounts ready for entries in the following year. This is accomplished by closing entries that will have to be formally entered in the journal and posted to the accounts. The expense and revenue summary account will assist in closing the expense and revenue accounts.

The procedures for closing the temporary accounts under the double-entry system are:

1. For revenue accounts with credit balances: debit the account for its balance and credit Expense and Revenue Summary.
2. For expense accounts with debit balances: debit the expense and revenue summary account and credit the temporary account for its balance.
3. Close the expense and revenue summary account to the Vance Zarmer capital account.
4. Close the Vance Zarmer drawing account to the capital account.

These procedures can be illustrated with the following diagram:

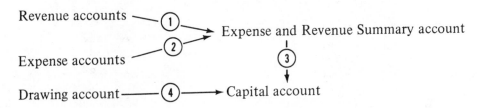

The journal entries reflecting the above procedures are as follows:

1. The $125,640 credit balance of Professional Fees, Account No. 411 is closed to (transferred to the credit side of) Expense and Revenue Summary, Account No. 331.
2. The debit balances of all eleven expense accounts (Nos. 541 through 549, 551, and 562) which, in total, amounted to $87,389.63, are closed to (transferred to the debit side of) Expense and Revenue Summary (No. 331).
3. The result of entries (1) and (2) is a credit balance of $38,250.37—the net income for the year—in Expense and Revenue Summary (No. 331). This was closed to Vance Zarmer, Capital (No. 311).
4. The $48,233.50 debit balance of Vance Zarmer, Drawing, Account No. 311.1, was closed to Vance Zarmer, Capital (No. 311).

These journal entries are shown in general journal form at the top of page 146. These are followed by an illustration of the effects of the closing procedures on Vance Zarmer's capital and drawing accounts, and expense and revenue summary account. Note that the net effect of the four closing entries is a decrease in the credit balance of the account for Vance Zarmer, Capital (No. 311) of $9,983.13—the excess of withdrawals for the year, $48,233.50, over net income for the year, $38,250.37.

GENERAL JOURNAL FOR MONTH OF *December* 19-- PAGE 30

	DAY	DESCRIPTION	POST. REF.	GENERAL DEBIT	GENERAL CREDIT	
1		AMOUNTS FORWARDED				1
2	31	*Closing Entries*				2
3		*Professional Fees*	411	12564000		3
4		*Expense and Revenue Summary*	331		12564000	4
5		*Expense and Revenue Summary*	331	8738963		5
6		*Rent Expense*	541		1020000	6
7		*Salary Expense*	542		5200000	7
8		*Travel + Entertainment Expense*	543		351095	8
9		*Telephone Expense*	544		145764	9
10		*Forms and Supplies Expense*	545		630779	10
11		*Automobile Expense*	546		315348	11
12		*Depreciation Expense*	547		402108	12
13		*Insurance Expense*	548		68320	13
14		*Charitable Contributions Expense*	549		134750	14
15		*Payroll Taxes Expense*	551		431500	15
16		*Miscellaneous Expense*	562		39299	16
17		*Expense and Revenue Summary*	331	3825037		17
18		*Vance Zarmer, Capital*	311		3825037	18
19		*Vance Zarmer, Capital*	311	4823350		19
20		*Vance Zarmer, Drawing*	311.1		4823350	20
21				29951350	29951350	21

ACCOUNT *Vance Zarmer, Capital* ACCOUNT NO. 311

DATE	ITEM	POST. REF.	DEBIT	CREDIT	BALANCE DEBIT	BALANCE CREDIT
19-- Dec. 1	Balance	✓				3815200
31		CJ30		3825037		7640237
31		CJ30	4823350			2816887

ACCOUNT *Vance Zarmer, Drawing* ACCOUNT NO. 311.1

DATE	ITEM	POST. REF.	DEBIT	CREDIT	BALANCE DEBIT	BALANCE CREDIT
19-- Dec. 1	Balance	✓			4421075	
17		CJ28	400000		4821075	
31		CJ29	2275		4823350	
31		CJ30		4823350	-0-	-0-

ACCOUNT	Expense and Revenue Summary				ACCOUNT NO. 331	
DATE	ITEM	POST. REF.	DEBIT	CREDIT	BALANCE DEBIT	BALANCE CREDIT
19-- Dec. 31		CJ30		12564000		12564000
31		CJ30	8738963			3825037
31		CJ30	3825037		-0-	-0-

Balancing the Closed Accounts. After posting the closing entries, all of the temporary owner's equity accounts are closed, and they are balanced in the manner shown in the following illustrations. (Note that zeros are entered in the Debit Balance and Credit Balance columns in each account on the line with the closing entry.)

ACCOUNT	Professional Fees				ACCOUNT NO. 411	
DATE	ITEM	POST. REF.	DEBIT	CREDIT	BALANCE DEBIT	BALANCE CREDIT
19-- Dec. 1	Balance	✓				11924000
31		CJ29		640000		12564000
31		CJ30	12564000		-0-	-0-

ACCOUNT	Rent Expense				ACCOUNT NO. 541	
DATE	ITEM	POST. REF.	DEBIT	CREDIT	BALANCE DEBIT	BALANCE CREDIT
19-- Dec. 1	Balance	✓			935000	
5		CJ28	85000		1020000	
31		CJ30		1020000	-0-	-0-

ACCOUNT	Salary Expense				ACCOUNT NO. 542	
DATE	ITEM	POST. REF.	DEBIT	CREDIT	BALANCE DEBIT	BALANCE CREDIT
19-- Dec. 1	Balance	✓			4700000	
31		CJ29	500000		5200000	
31		CJ30		5200000	-0-	-0-

Vance Zarmer, Computer Consultant—Closed General Ledger Accounts

ACCOUNT Travel & Entertainment Expense   **ACCOUNT NO.** 543

DATE	ITEM	POST. REF.	DEBIT	CREDIT	BALANCE DEBIT	BALANCE CREDIT
19-- Dec 1	Balance	✓			332595	
29		CJ29	14875		347470	
31		CJ29	3625		351095	
31		CJ30		351095	- 0 -	- 0 -

ACCOUNT Telephone Expense   **ACCOUNT NO.** 544

DATE	ITEM	POST. REF.	DEBIT	CREDIT	BALANCE DEBIT	BALANCE CREDIT
19-- Dec 1	Balance	✓			141804	
23		CJ28	3960		145764	
31		CJ30		145764	- 0 -	- 0 -

ACCOUNT Forms and Supplies Expense   **ACCOUNT NO.** 545

DATE	ITEM	POST. REF.	DEBIT	CREDIT	BALANCE DEBIT	BALANCE CREDIT
19-- Dec 1	Balance	✓			603386	
16		CJ28	13921		617307	
24		CJ28	11822		629129	
31		CJ29	1650		630779	
31		CJ30		630779	- 0 -	- 0 -

ACCOUNT Automobile Expense   **ACCOUNT NO.** 546

DATE	ITEM	POST. REF.	DEBIT	CREDIT	BALANCE DEBIT	BALANCE CREDIT
19-- Dec 1	Balance	✓			292753	
18		CJ28	17080		309833	
22		CJ28	4835		314668	
31		CJ29	680		315348	
31		CJ30		315348	- 0 -	- 0 -

Vance Zarmer, Computer Consultant—Closed General Ledger Accounts
(continued)

ACCOUNT *Depreciation Expense*   ACCOUNT NO. 547

DATE	ITEM	POST. REF.	DEBIT	CREDIT	BALANCE DEBIT	BALANCE CREDIT
19-- Dec 31		CG30	402108		402108	
31		CG30		402108	-0-	-0-

ACCOUNT *Insurance Expense*   ACCOUNT NO. 548

DATE	ITEM	POST. REF.	DEBIT	CREDIT	BALANCE DEBIT	BALANCE CREDIT
19-- Dec 1	Balance	✓			62840	
10		CG28	5840		68680	
16		CG28		360	68320	
31		CG30		68320	-0-	-0-

ACCOUNT *Charitable Contributions Expense*   ACCOUNT NO. 549

DATE	ITEM	POST. REF.	DEBIT	CREDIT	BALANCE DEBIT	BALANCE CREDIT
19-- Dec 1	Balance	✓			123500	
19		CG28	10000		133500	
31		CG29	1250		134750	
31		CG30		134750	-0-	-0-

ACCOUNT *Payroll Taxes Expense*   ACCOUNT NO. 551

DATE	ITEM	POST. REF.	DEBIT	CREDIT	BALANCE DEBIT	BALANCE CREDIT
19-- Dec 1	Balance	✓			401500	
15		CG28	30000		431500	
31		CG30		431500	-0-	-0-

ACCOUNT *Miscellaneous Expense*   ACCOUNT NO. 562

DATE	ITEM	POST. REF.	DEBIT	CREDIT	BALANCE DEBIT	BALANCE CREDIT
19-- Dec 1	Balance	✓			36012	
22		CG28	2475		38487	
31		CG29	812		39299	
31		CG30		39299	-0-	-0-

Vance Zarmer, Computer Consultant—Closed General Ledger Accounts
(concluded)

Updating Owner's Equity Accounts. After the temporary owner's equity accounts are closed, the permanent owner's equity accounts are updated to prepare them to receive entries in the next fiscal period. Only one of Zarmer's owner's equity accounts needs to be updated: Vance Zarmer, Capital, Account No. 311. This account was shown on page 145 and is reproduced below as it appears after the third and fourth closing entries illustrated on page 146 are posted.

DATE	ITEM	POST. REF.	DEBIT	CREDIT	BALANCE DEBIT	BALANCE CREDIT
Dec 1	Balance	✓				38 15 2 00
31		CJ30		38 250 37		76 402 37
31		CJ30	48 233 50			28 168 87

ACCOUNT Vance Zarmer, Capital   ACCOUNT NO. 311

Vance Zarmer, Computer Consultant—Updating Owner's Equity

Post-Closing Trial Balance. After posting the closing entries, it is advisable to take a post-closing trial balance to prove the equality of the debit and credit balances in the general ledger accounts. The following is the post-closing trial balance of Zarmer's ledger:

Vance Zarmer, Computer Consultant
Post-Closing Trial Balance
December 31, 19--

Account	Acct. No.	Dr. Balance	Cr. Balance
Cash	111	2 536 85	
Petty Cash Fund	112	300 00	
Office Equipment	191	40 210 80	
Accumulated Depreciation—Office Equipment	191.1		13 675 78
FICA Tax Payable	211		375 00
Employees Income Tax Payable	214		828 00
Vance Zarmer, Capital	311		28 168 87
		43 047 65	43 047 65

Vance Zarmer, Computer Consultant—Post-Closing Trial Balance

The Accounting Cycle

The steps involved in handling all of the transactions and events completed during an accounting period, beginning with placing data in a book of original entry and ending with a post-closing trial balance, are referred to collectively as the accounting cycle. This chapter has illustrated a complete accounting cycle. A brief summary of the various steps follows:

1. Journalize the transactions.
2. Post to the ledger accounts.
3. Take a trial balance.
4. Determine the needed adjustments.
5. Complete an end-of-period work sheet.
6. Prepare an income statement and a balance sheet.
7. Journalize and post the adjusting and closing entries.
8. Balance the closed accounts and update certain owner's equity accounts.
9. Take a post-closing trial balance.

In visualizing the accounting cycle, it is important to realize that steps (3) through (9) in the foregoing list are performed as of the last day of the accounting period. This does not mean that they are done on the last day. The accountant may not be able to do any of these things until the first few days (sometimes weeks) of the next period. Nevertheless, the work sheet, statements, and entries are prepared as of the closing date. While the journalizing of transactions in the new period proceeds in regular fashion, entries relating to the new period are normally not posted to the general ledger until the steps relating to the period just ended have been completed.

BUILDING YOUR ACCOUNTING KNOWLEDGE

1. How does a personal service enterprise differ from a mercantile enterprise? From a manufacturing enterprise?
2. Describe the process of accounting for revenue on a cash basis.
3. Describe the process of accounting for expenses on a cash basis.
4. What is the chief advantage of Vance Zarmer's system of account numbering?
5. How does the use of the combination journal save time and space in entering cash transactions?
6. What is the principal advantage of the four-column balance-column account form over the standard two-column account form?
7. Name two elements that are normally added to and one element that is normally deducted from owner's equity at the start of the fiscal period to produce owner's equity at the end of the fiscal period.
8. List the nine steps in Vance Zarmer's accounting cycle.

APPLYING ACCOUNTING CONCEPTS

Exercise 5-1. Rudy Gorch completed the following transactions during the first week of March, 19--.

1. Received a check for $900 from Paula Dern for services rendered.
2. Issued Check No. 210 for $362.75 to HB Supply Co. in payment for supplies.
3. Issued Check No. 211 for $96.40 to Protector Insurance Co. in payment of one-year premium on business liability insurance policy.
4. Issued Check No. 212 for $500 to Gorch for personal use.
5. Received a check for $850 from Mark Joseph for services rendered.
6. Issued Check No. 213 for $100 to United Way.
7. Issued Check No. 214 for $290.60 to Freida Vesvardez in payment of salary for the week: $400 less income tax withholding of $79.40, and FICA tax withholding, $30.

Prepare a combination journal using the same format and account titles as illustrated in the chapter. The balance in the cash account on March 1 is $3,210.66. Enter the foregoing transactions in the combination journal. (In the Day column, enter the transaction number.)

Exercise 5-2. Refer to Exercise 5-1. At the end of the current year, Rudy Gorch needs to make an adjusting entry for the estimated depreciation expense for the year on his office equipment. The equipment cost $7,450 two years ago and is being depreciated at a rate of 10% per year.

Make the adjusting entry to recognize the depreciation expense on the office equipment.

Exercise 5-3. The following is the trial balance for the current year ended December 31, 19-- for Jessica Roebuck's counseling service.

Jessica Roebuck's Counseling Service
Trial Balance
December 31, 19--

Cash	111	6,187.39	
Office Equipment	191	7,200.00	
Accum. Depr.—Office Equipment	191.1		720.00
Accounts Payable	218		500.00
Jessica Roebuck, Capital	311		10,000.00
Jessica Roebuck, Drawing	311.1	21,264.99	
Professional Fees	411		33,490.55
Rent Expense	541	8,400.00	
Telephone Expense	544	760.20	
Supplies Expense	545	394.51	
Depreciation Expense	547		
Insurance Expense	548	405.00	
Miscellaneous Expense	562	98.46	
		44,710.55	44,710.55

(a) Prepare an eight-column work sheet making the necessary entry in the Adjustments columns to record the depreciation of office equipment, $720. Extend the totals to the Income Statement or Balance Sheet columns. (b) Prepare an income statement for the year ended December 31. (c) Prepare a balance sheet in report form as of December 31.

Report No. 5-1

Complete Report No. 5-1 in the study assignments and submit your working papers to the instructor for approval. After completing the report you will then be given instructions as to the work to be done next.

EXPANDING YOUR BUSINESS VOCABULARY

What is the meaning of each of the following terms?

account form of balance sheet **(p. 141)**

accounting cycle **(p. 151)**

adjusting entries **(p. 143)**

balance-column account form **(p. 122)**

book value **(p. 138)**

business enterprises **(p. 118)**

cash basis expense **(p. 118)**

cash basis revenue **(p. 118)**

closing entries **(p. 144)**

combination journal **(p. 121)**

constructive receipt **(p. 118**

contra accounts **(p. 120)**

current assets **(p. 141)**

depreciation expense **(p. 119)**

end-of-period work sheet **(p. 137)**

long-term liabilities **(p. 141)**

manufacturing enterprise **(p. 117)**

mercantile enterprise **(p. 117)**

personal service enterprise **(p. 117)**

post-closing trial balance **(p. 150)**

professional enterprises **(p. 118)**

proof of footings **(p. 125)**

property, plant and equipment **(p. 141)**

proved **(p. 125)**

report form of balance sheet **(p. 141)**

transposition error **(p. 127)**

undepreciated cost **(p. 138)**

CHAPTERS 1–5

Supplementary Practical Accounting Problems

The following problems supplement those in Reports 1-1 through 5-1 of the Part 1 Study Assignments. These problems are numbered to indicate the chapter of the textbook with which they correlate. For example, Problem 1-A and Problem 1-B correlate with Chapter 1. Loose-leaf stationery should be used in solving these problems. The paper required includes plain ruled paper, two-column journal paper, two-column and three-column statement paper, ledger paper, and work sheet paper.

PROBLEM 1-A   Accounting Elements—Equation Form

B. Peterson owns a real estate agency. As of December 31, Peterson owned the following property that related to the business: cash, $2,648; office equipment, $3,612; and an automobile, $8,110. At the same time, Peterson owed business creditors, $2,966.

Required: (1) On the basis of the foregoing information, compute the amounts of the accounting elements and show them in equation form. (2) Assume that during the following year there is an increase in Peterson's business assets of $1,990 and a decrease in the business liabilities of $455. Indicate the changes in the accounting elements by showing them in equation form after the changes have occurred.

PROBLEM 1-B   T Account Format; Trial Balance

W. Barbier, an insurance agent who has been employed by a large local firm, decides to go into business. Barbier's business transactions for the first month of operations were as follows:

a. Barbier invested $20,000 cash in the business.
b. Paid office rent for one month, $370.
c. Purchased office equipment from the McLennon Office Equipment Co. (a supplier), $2,400 on account.
d. Paid telephone bill, $59.
e. Received $4,000 for services rendered to B. Fife.
f. Paid $1,500 to the McLennon Office Equipment Co., on account.
g. Received $2,250 for services rendered to O. Taylor.
h. Paid $800 salary to office secretary.

Required: (1) On a plain sheet of paper, rule eight T accounts and enter the following titles: Cash; Office Equipment; Accounts Payable; W. Barbier, Capital; Professional Fees; Rent Expense; Telephone Expense; and Salary Expense. (2) Enter the foregoing transactions directly in the accounts. (3) Foot the accounts and enter the balances where necessary. (4) Prepare a trial balance of the accounts, using a sheet of two-column journal paper.

PROBLEM 2-A Journal Entries

Following is a narrative of the transactions completed by Tom Dernier, an attorney, during the first month of Dernier's business operations:

Oct. 1 Dernier invested $10,000 cash in the business.
  1 Paid office rent, $700.
  3 Purchased office furniture for $2,300.
  3 Paid $152.75 for installation of telephone and for one month's service.
  4 Received $1,000 from Tasty Delights Co. for legal services rendered.
  5 Purchased stationery and supplies on account from F. Parker Stationery Co. for $367.20.
  6 Paid $38 for subscription to the Legal Eagle magazine. (Charge to Miscellaneous Expense.)
  8 Paid $60 to Dr. Pete Gruber, a dentist, for dental service performed for Dernier. (This is equivalent to a withdrawal of $60 by Dernier for personal use. Charge to drawing account.)
  10 Received $750 from R. Grant for legal services rendered.
  12 Paid $311 for an airplane ticket for a business trip.
  14 Paid other traveling expenses, $411.30.
  19 Received $900 from Starfinder, Inc. for legal services rendered.
  20 Paid account of F. Parker Stationery Co. in full, $367.20.
  31 Paid $700 monthly salary to secretary.
  31 Office supplies used during the month were $83.

Required: Journalize the foregoing transactions, using a sheet of two-column journal paper. Number the pages and use both sides of the sheet, if necessary. Select the account titles from the chart of accounts shown at the top of page 156.

After journalizing the transactions, prove the equality of the debits and credits by footing the amount columns. Enter the footings in pencil immediately under the line on which the last entry appears.

Chart of Accounts

Assets
111 Cash
151 Stationery and Supplies
191 Office Furniture

Liabilities
218 Accounts Payable

Owner's Equity
311 Tom Dernier, Capital
311.1 Tom Dernier, Drawing

Revenue
411 Professional Fees

Expenses
541 Rent Expense
542 Salary Expense
543 Traveling Expense
544 Telephone Expense
545 Stationery and Supplies
　　　Expense
562 Miscellaneous Expense

PROBLEM 2-B   Journal Entries; Posting; Trial Balance

Leo Toomey is an architect. Following is the trial balance of Toomey's business taken as of September 30, 19--.

Leo Toomey, Architect
Trial Balance
September 30, 19--

Account	Acct. No.	Dr. Balance	Cr. Balance
Cash	111	2,957.85	
Automobile	184	11,650.70	
Office Equipment	191	7,900.71	
Accounts Payable	218		3,107.36
Leo Toomey, Capital	311		4,987.45
Leo Toomey, Drawing	311.1	9,655.00	
Professional Fees	411		29,990.00
Rent Expense	541	3,825.00	
Automobile Expense	543	840.30	
Telephone Expense	544	604.11	
Electric Expense	545	186.55	
Charitable Contributions Expense	549	205.00	
Miscellaneous Expense	562	259.59	
		38,084.81	38,084.81

A narrative of transactions completed by Toomey during the month of October follows:

Oct.　1　(Saturday) Paid one month's rent, $425.
　　　3　Paid telephone bill, $81.77.
　　　3　Paid electric bill, $14.36.
　　　5　Received $1,050 from The Spa Restaurant for services rendered.
　　　7　Paid a garage bill, $101.75.

Oct. 10 Received $400 from R. Colavito for services rendered.
12 Paid Crestview Country Club, $207.50. (Charge to Toomey's drawing account.)
15 Toomey withdrew $400 for personal use.
17 Paid Kessinger's Office Supply, $250 on account.
19 Received $650 from Lansing Construction Co. for services rendered.
24 Gave the Heart Fund, $50.
26 Paid the American Institute of Architects $200 for annual membership dues and fees.
29 Received $2,100 from Sever and Sever, attorneys-at-law, for professional services.
31 Toomey withdrew $500 for personal use.

Required: (1) Journalize the October transactions, using a sheet of two-column journal paper. Number the pages and use both sides of the sheet, if necessary. Foot the amount columns. (2) Open the necessary accounts, using the standard account form of ledger paper. Allow one page for each account. Enter the October 1 balances as shown in the September 30 trial balance and post the journal entries for October. (3) Foot the ledger accounts and enter the balances. (4) Prove the balances by taking a trial balance as of October 31. Use a sheet of two-column journal paper for the trial balance.

PROBLEM 2-C Income Statement; Balance Sheet

The following is the trial balance of Lissy Company.

Lissy Company
Trial Balance
March 31, 19--

Account	Acct. No.	Dr. Balance	Cr. Balance
Cash	111	8,311.69	
Stationery and Supplies	151	2,408.67	
Office Furniture	191	5,170.77	
Notes Payable	216		1,610.00
Accounts Payable	218		2,088.18
M. D. Lissy, Capital	311		9,113.11
M. D. Lissy, Drawing	311.1	375.82	
Professional Fees	411		5,374.36
Rent Expense	541	410.00	
Salary Expense	542	791.67	
Traveling Expense	543	406.11	
Telephone Expense	544	39.77	
Stationery and Supplies Expense	545	66.76	
Miscellaneous Expense	562	204.39	
		18,185.65	18,185.65

Required: (1) Prepare an income statement for the Lissy Company showing the results of the first month of operations, March. Use a sheet of two-column statement paper for the income statement. (2) Prepare a balance sheet in account form showing the financial condition of the company as of March 31. Two sheets of two-column statement paper may be used for the balance sheet. List the assets on one sheet and the liabilities and owner's equity on the other sheet.

PROBLEM 3-A   Journalizing; Posting; Trial Balance

Jerry North operates a hypnosis clinic for people who want to quit smoking. The only book of original entry for the business is a two-column journal and the standard form of account in the general ledger is used. Following is the trial balance of the business taken as of November 30.

North's Hypnosis Clinic
Trial Balance
November 30, 19--

Account	Acct. No.	Dr. Balance	Cr. Balance
Cash	111	4,000.00	
Equipment	181	455.00	
Accounts Payable	218		207.15
Jerry North, Capital	311		1,755.30
Jerry North, Drawing	311.1	10,400.00	
Hypnosis Fees	411		18,200.00
Rent Expense	541	4,125.00	
Electric Expense	543	294.62	
Telephone Expense	544	302.14	
Supplies Expense	545	409.91	
Miscellaneous Expense	562	161.47	
Cash Short and Over	563	14.31	
		20,162.45	20,162.45

Narrative of Transactions for December

Dec.	1	(Thursday) Paid December rent in advance, $375.
	1	Paid electric bill, $33.88.
	2	Paid telephone bill, $41.20.
	2	Received cash and checks for hypnotic services, $555.
	6	Paid $23.60 for repair of broken window.
	9	Received cash and checks for hypnotic services, $835.
	13	Purchased new table and chairs from Bigotti's Furniture Co. on credit, $132.
	16	Received cash and checks for hypnotic services, $400.

Dec. 19 Paid $10 for having snow shoveled.
20 Paid $73.46 for supplies.
22 Paid Hensley's Furniture Co. $100 on account.
23 Received cash and checks for hypnotic services, $960.
27 North withdrew $400 for personal use.
30 Received cash and checks for hypnotic services, $350.
30 When cash was proved, a cash shortage of $6.50 was found.

Required: (1) Journalize the December transactions. For the journal use two sheets of two-column journal paper and number the pages, 11 and 12. (2) Open the necessary ledger accounts. Allow one page for each account and number the accounts. Enter the December 1 balances and post the journal entries. Foot the journal. (3) Take a trial balance.

PROBLEM 3-B Petty Cash Payments; Statement of Petty Cash Payments

Lauri Roth, a pet store owner, had a balance of $150 in the petty cash fund as of April 1. During April, the following petty cash transactions were completed for the Pet Palace.

April 2 Paid $17.37 for typewriter repairs. Petty Cash Voucher No. 41.
6 Paid for long-distance telephone call, $4.50. Petty Cash Voucher No. 42.
8 Gave $4 for Girl Scout cookies. Petty Cash Voucher No. 43.
9 Paid garage for washing car, $12. Petty Cash Voucher No. 44.
12 Gave Roth's son, $20. (Charge to Lauri Roth, Drawing.) Petty Cash Voucher No. 45.
14 Paid for postage stamps, $12. Petty Cash Voucher No. 46.
17 Paid for newspaper for month, $11.30. Petty Cash Voucher No. 47.
22 Paid for window washing, $15. Petty Cash Voucher No. 48.
27 Paid UPS $22.50 for package. (Charge to Lauri Roth, Drawing.) Petty Cash Voucher No. 49.
28 Paid for car oil and lubrication, $9.50. Petty Cash Voucher No. 50.
30 Rendered report of petty cash payments for month and received the amount needed to replenish the petty cash fund.

Required: **(1)** Enter the foregoing transactions in a petty cash payments record (a page of work sheet paper may be used), distributing the payments as follows:

Lauri Roth, Drawing	Postage Expense
Automobile Expense	Miscellaneous Expense
Telephone Expense	

(2) Prove the petty cash payments record by footing the amount columns and proving the totals. Enter the totals and rule the amount columns with single and double lines. **(3)** Prepare a statement of the petty cash payments for April. **(4)** Bring down the balance in the petty cash fund below the ruling in the Description column. Enter the amount received to replenish the fund and enter the total.

PROBLEM 3-C   Bank Reconciliation

Yuri Djokovich, who owns a bicycle shop, completed the following transactions with the Fidelity National Bank during the month of July:

July	3 (Monday) Balance in bank per record kept on check stubs	$5,988.62	July	11 Check No. 218	$ 90.00
	3 Deposit	3,000.00		11 Check No. 219	101.00
	3 Check No. 208	406.30		13 Check No. 220	900.00
	3 Check No. 209	75.00		14 Check No. 221	115.39
	4 Check No. 210	600.00		14 Check No. 222	500.00
	4 Check No. 211	291.14		14 Deposit	800.00
	5 Check No. 212	99.00		17 Check No. 223	265.00
	6 Check No. 213	171.15		18 Check No. 224	489.07
	7 Check No. 214	208.92		21 Check No. 225	140.07
	7 Check No. 215	125.00		21 Deposit	1,936.42
	7 Check No. 216	188.50		24 Check No. 226	8.36
	7 Deposit	436.12		25 Check No. 227	266.61
	10 Check No. 217	800.00		27 Check No. 228	804.39
				28 Check No. 229	425.00
				31 Check No. 230	1,010.00
				31 Deposit	2,054.71

Required: **(1)** Prepare a reconciliation of the bank statement for July which indicated a balance of $5,707.02 on July 31, with Checks Nos. 216, 226, 229, and 230 outstanding. The July 31 deposit is not shown on the bank statement, and a service charge of $6.10 has been deducted. **(2)** Prepare the journal entry for the bank service charge for July.

PROBLEM 4-A   Payroll Register

Following is a summary of the hours worked, rates of pay, and other relevant information concerning the employees of the Arfax Mining Co., Jack Cooben, owner, for the week ended Saturday, November 6. Employees are paid at the rate of time and one half for all hours worked in excess of 8 in any day or 40 in any week.

No.	Name	Allowances Claimed	M	T	W	T	F	S	Regular Hourly Rate	Cumulative Earnings Jan. 1 - Oct. 31
1	Allodi, Steve	1	8	8	8	8	8	6	$9.00	$16,720
2	Cash, Norm	5	8	9	8	8	8	4	9.25	16,435
3	Fine, Larry	3	8	8	8	8	8	0	8.00	14,180
4	Gorley, Linda	2	8	8	8	9	8	4	7.00	12,805
5	Portman, Joe	1	8	8	8	8	8	4	9.00	16,040
6	Theile, Terry	3	8	8	8	8	6	0	8.50	15,165

Allodi and Gorley each have $5 withheld this payday for group life insurance. Cash and Theile each have $12 withheld this payday for private hospital insurance. Portman has $3 withheld this payday as a contribution to the United Way.

Required: (1) Using plain ruled paper size 8 1/2″ × 11″, rule a payroll register form similar to that reproduced on pages 96 and 97, and insert the necessary columnar headings. Enter on this form the payroll for the week ended Saturday, November 6. Refer to the Weekly Income Tax Table on page 92 to determine the amounts to be withheld from the wages of each worker for income tax purposes. All of Cooben's employees are married. Seven and one-half percent of the taxable wages of each employee should be withheld for FICA tax. Checks Nos. 611 through 616 were issued to the employees. Complete the payroll record by footing the amount columns, proving the footings, entering the totals, and ruling. (2) Assuming that the wages were paid on November 10, enter the payment on a sheet of two-column journal paper.

PROBLEM 4-B   Journal Entries—Payroll and Payroll Taxes

The Overbrook Mall employs twelve people. They are paid by checks on the 15th and the last working day of each month. The entry to record each payroll includes the liabilities for the amounts withheld. The expense and liabilities arising from the employer's payroll taxes are recorded on each payday. Following is a narrative of the transactions completed during the month of January that relate to payrolls and payroll taxes:

Jan. 15 Payroll for first half of month:

Total salaries		$6,320.00
Less amounts withheld:		
FICA tax...................................	$474.00	
Employees' income tax	984.60	1,458.60
Net amount paid		$4,861.40

15 Payroll taxes imposed on employer:
FICA tax, 7.5%
State unemployment tax, 2%
FUTA tax, 0.8%

29 Paid $3,994.20 for December's payroll taxes:
FICA tax, $1,966.80
Employees' income tax withheld, $2,027.40

29 Paid state unemployment tax for quarter ended December 31, $766.90.

29 Paid balance due on FUTA tax for last half of year ended December 31, $318.65.

30 Payroll for last half of month:

Total salaries		$6,175.00
Less amounts withheld:		
FICA tax...................................	$463.13	
Employees' income tax	942.00	1,405.13
Net amount paid		$4,769.87

30 Payroll taxes imposed on employer:
All salaries taxable; rates same as on January 15.

Required: (1) Journalize the foregoing transactions, using two-column journal paper. (2) Foot the debit and credit amount columns as a means of proof.

PROBLEM 5-A Combination Journal

Gary Knowles operates a plumbing service. Knowles' revenue consists entirely of compensation for personal services rendered, and accounts are kept on the cash basis. The chart of accounts is shown at the top of page 163.

The following transactions were completed by Knowles during the month of June, 19--:

June   3 Issued Check No. 261 for $311 to the Crane Co. for plumbing supplies.

       4 Issued Check No. 262 for $62 to MCI Telephone Co. for telephone service.

       6 Received check for $1,200 from Bailly Middle School for services rendered.

Assets
111 Cash
181 Plumbing Equipment
181.1 Accumulated Depreciation—
Plumbing Equipment
185 Truck
185.1 Accumulated Depreciation—
Truck

Liabilities
211 FICA Tax Payable
214 Employees Income Tax
Payable

Owner's Equity
311 Gary Knowles, Capital
311.1 Gary Knowles, Drawing
331 Expense and Revenue
Summary

Revenue
411 Plumbing Fees

Expenses
542 Salary Expense
544 Telephone Expense
545 Supplies Expense
546 Truck Expense
547 Depreciation Expense
548 Repairs Expense
551 Payroll Taxes Expense
562 Miscellaneous Expense

June 10 Received a check for $800 from Burger Boy Restaurant for services rendered.

12 Issued Check No. 263 for $69 to Lefty's Service Station for servicing truck.

14 Issued Check No. 264 for $324 to part-time assistant, Roger Adank, in payment of salary for first half of month: $400 less income tax withholding, $46, and FICA tax withholding, $30.

14 Received check for $3,650 from Wacky Water Slide for services rendered.

18 Issued Check No. 265 for $440 for plumbing supplies.

20 Issued Check No. 266 for $146 to Al's Machine Shop for repairs to plumbing equipment.

21 Issued Check No. 267 for $1,400 to Gary Knowles for personal use.

25 Received check for $675 from University Apartments for services rendered.

27 Issued Check No. 268 for $84 to Lefty's Service Station for gasoline bill.

28 Issued Check No. 269 for $324 to part-time assistant, Roger Adank, in payment of salary for second half of the month. (See explanation of Check No. 264 issued on June 14.)

Required: (1) Prepare a combination journal with eight amount columns and enter Knowles' June transactions. The headings of the amount columns are as follows:

Cash
  Deposits 111 Dr.
  Checks 111 Cr.

Plumbing Fees 411 Cr.

Salary Expense 542 Dr.

General
  Debit
  Credit

Wage Deductions
  FICA Tax Payable 211 Cr.
  Employees Income Tax Payable 214 Cr.

The balance in the cash account on June 1 is $3,647. **(2)** Foot and prove the combination journal. **(3)** Enter all appropriate posting references in the combination journal, assuming all general ledger posting had been completed.

PROBLEM 5-B   Work Sheet; Adjusting Entries; Income Statement; Balance Sheet

Tawny Griffith is an engineer engaged in professional practice. Griffith's revenue consists entirely of compensation for personal services rendered, and accounts are kept on the cash basis. The following is the trial balance for the current year ending December 31:

Tawny Griffith, Engineer
Trial Balance
December 31, 19--

Account	Acct. No.	Dr. Balance	Cr. Balance
Cash	111	8,602.57	
Automobiles	185	19,640.00	
Accumulated Depreciation—Automobiles	185.1		3,928.00
Office Equipment	191	4,096.00	
Accumulated Depreciation—Office Equipment	191.1		327.68
FICA Tax Payable	211		403.60
Employees Income Tax Payable	214		594.90
Accounts Payable	218		3,488.86
Tawny Griffith, Capital	311		19,932.13
Tawny Griffith, Drawing	311.1	52,000.00	
Professional Fees	411		108,290.00
Rent Expense	541	11,040.00	
Salary Expense	542	34,000.00	
Automobile Expense	546	2,638.21	
Depreciation Expense	547		
Charitable Contributions Expense	549	755.00	
Payroll Taxes Expense	551	2,550.00	
Miscellaneous Expense	562	1,643.39	
		136,965.17	136,965.17

Required: (1) Prepare an eight-column work sheet making the necessary entries in the Adjustments columns for the depreciation of the following assets:

Office equipment, 8%, $327.68
Automobiles, 20%, $3,928.00

(2) Prepare the following financial statements (round all amounts to the nearest dollar): (a) an income statement for the year ended December 31, and (b) a balance sheet in report form as of December 31.

PROBLEM 5-C Work Sheet; Financial Statements; Adjusting and Closing Entries

Monty Cleese operates an automobile ferrying service between various islands and mainland ports located in the Puget Sound and downtown Seattle. The following is a trial balance of Cleese's general ledger accounts:

Cleese's Ferry Boat Service
Trial Balance
December 31, 19--

Account	Acct. No.	Dr. Balance	Cr. Balance
Cash	111	11,640.00	
Office Equipment	191	3,985.00	
Accumulated Depreciation—Office Equipment	191.1		1,434.60
Ferrying Equipment	192	184,225.00	
Accumulated Depreciation—Ferrying Equipment	192.1		99,481.60
FICA Tax Payable	211		765.00
Employees Income Tax Payable	214		920.00
Accounts Payable	218		14,370.00
Monty Cleese, Capital	311		64,746.00
Monty Cleese, Drawing	311.1	22,000.00	
Ferrying Revenue	411		166,955.40
Rent Expense	541	10,800.00	
Salary Expense	542	44,328.00	
Office Expense	545	2,696.00	
Maritime Expense	546	64,042.00	
Depreciation Expense	547		
Charitable Contributions Expense	549	200.00	
Payroll Taxes Expense	551	3,324.60	
Miscellaneous Expense	562	1,432.00	
		348,672.60	348.672.60

Required: **(1)** Prepare an eight-column work sheet making the necessary adjustments for the depreciation of long-term assets as shown:

Property	Rate of Depreciation	Amount of Depreciation
Office equipment	12%	$ 478.20
Ferrying equipment	18%	33,160.50

(2) Prepare an income statement for the year ended December 31. (Round all amounts to the nearest dollar.) (3) Prepare a balance sheet in report form as of December 31. (Round all amounts to the nearest dollar.) (4) Using two-column journal paper, prepare the entries required: (a) to adjust the general ledger accounts so that they will be in agreement with the financial statements; (b) to close the temporary owner's equity accounts on December 31. (Use Account No. 331 for Expense and Revenue Summary.) Foot the amount columns of the journal.

CHAPTER 6

Accounting for Purchases and Payments

CHAPTER OBJECTIVES

Careful study of this chapter should enable you to:

- Explain why the cash basis of periodic income determination usually is unsuited to a merchandise business, and why the accrual basis gives a more meaningful measure of periodic income.

- Describe and use the following source documents:

    1. Purchase requisition
    2. Purchase order
    3. Purchase invoice

    4. Freight bill
    5. Credit memorandum

- Define **trade discounts, cash discounts,** and the most common **terms of purchase**.

- Define the terms **purchases, purchases discounts, purchases returns and allowances, merchandise inventory,** and **cost of goods sold**.

- Explain and use the **gross price** and **net-price bases** of entering purchase invoices and processing such invoices for payment.

- Explain and use a special journal for purchases of merchandise.

- Describe subsidiary records that support amounts in general ledger accounts, specifically—

    1. A file of unpaid suppliers invoices—the ''invoice'' method, or
    2. A subsidiary accounts payable ledger—the ''ledger account'' method.

- Explain and use a special journal for all cash payments.

In the preceding chapter, accounting practices suitable for a personal service enterprise were discussed and illustrated. Except for depreciation, the net income for the year was calculated on the cash basis. Revenue was not recorded until money was received for the service performed. Similarly, most expenses were not recorded until paid in cash, even though many of the payments were for items of value received and consumed in a prior period or for things to be received and consumed in a later period. An exception to this practice was made for depreciation, since it is unrealistic to consider the entire cost of an asset such as office equipment (expected to be used for many years) to be an expense only of the month or year of purchase. The cost of plant and equipment assets is spread as expense over their expected useful lives.

The cash basis, even when slightly modified, is not technically perfect; but it has the virtues of simplicity and ease of understanding. This basis has proved to be quite satisfactory for most personal service enterprises. In the case of business enterprises whose major activity is the purchase of merchandise for resale, however, the cash basis of periodic income determination usually does not give a meaningful or useful measure of net income or net loss. There are two reasons why this is true: (1) Merchandising businesses commonly purchase and sell merchandise "on account" or "on credit"—meaning that payment is postponed a few days or weeks. The amount of cash paid or collected in any accounting period is almost never the same as the amount of purchases or sales of that period. (2) Merchandising businesses normally start and end each period with a stock of goods on hand for resale, and the dollar amount of this stock is not likely to be the same at both points of time.

The purpose of this chapter is to describe and explain the common accounting practices for handling purchases of merchandise and the subsequent payment of invoices for such purchases. The setting is that of a small retail enterprise using the accrual basis of periodic income determination. Commonly used source documents for purchases and payments will be discussed and illustrated, and special journals for purchases and cash payments will be introduced and explained.

SOURCE DOCUMENTS AND ASSOCIATED RECORDS FOR PURCHASES AND PAYMENTS

Merchandise for resale and other property for use in the operation of a business enterprise may be purchased either for cash or on account. In a small enterprise the buying may be done by the owner or by an employee, and may require only part-time attention. In a large enterprise a purchasing department may be maintained with a manager and staff who devote their entire time to buying activities. The successful operation of a purchasing department requires an efficient organization as well as the proper equipment.

A flowchart showing some of the major documents commonly used in the purchases function of a merchandise business is presented below. Each of these documents is explained in the following sections.

| Purchase Requisition | → | Purchase Order | → | Receiving Report | → | Purchase Invoice |

The Purchase Requisition

A form used to request the responsible person or department to purchase merchandise or other property is known as a purchase requisition. Such requests may come from any person or department of an enterprise. Purchase requisitions should be numbered consecutively to prevent the loss or misuse of the forms. Usually they are prepared in duplicate, with the original copy going to the person responsible for purchasing and the duplicate copy being retained by the person or department originating the requisition.

The following purchase requisition specifies merchandise wanted in

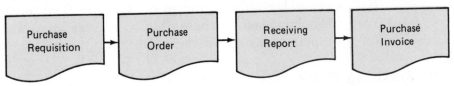

MicroWorld
1099 E. Louisiana, Indianapolis, IN 46202-3322

PURCHASE REQUISITION NO. A-106

DATE ISSUED	March 26, 19--
DATE REQUIRED	April 12, 19--
REQUIRED FOR DEPARTMENT	Computer Software
DELIVER TO	Faye J. Quinn

ORDER FROM
MLT Software
1439 E. Broad St.
Columbus, OH 43205-9892

QUANTITY	DESCRIPTION
5	Word Pro, No. F20386
4	Spellmaster, No. N10367

SALESCLERK'S MEMORANDUM

PLACED BY	Emily Green
APPROVED BY	Faye J. Quinn
PURCHASE ORDER NO.	312

DATE   March 26, 19--
ISSUED TO
MLT Software
1439 E. Broad St.
Columbus, OH 43205-9892

Purchase Requisition

computer software. The merchandising business known as MicroWorld is owned by Faye J. Quinn. It is organized into several store areas. Requisitions for merchandise originate with the salespersons responsible for the particular areas. After the purchase requisition shown in the illustration was approved by Quinn, an order was placed with MLT Software, a manufacturer of computer software, as indicated by the memorandum at the bottom of the form. The purchase requisition, when approved, is the authority to order the merchandise or other property described in the requisition.

The Purchase Order

A written order by the buyer for merchandise or other property specified in the buyer company's purchase requisition is known as a purchase order. A purchase order may be prepared on a printed stock form, on a specially designed form, or on an order blank furnished by a supplier of goods or services. Purchase orders should be numbered consecutively. Usually they are prepared with multiple copies. The original copy goes to the supplier or vendor—the person or firm from whom the merchandise or other property is ordered. Sometimes the duplicate copy also goes to the supplier. If this is the case, this copy—called the "acknowledgment copy"—will have a space for the supplier's signature to indicate the acceptance of the order. Such acceptance creates a formal contract. The signed acknowledgment copy is then returned to the ordering firm. Sometimes a copy of the purchase order is sent to the salesperson or department of the company that requisitioned the purchase. In many organizations a copy of the purchase order is sent to a receiving clerk. Some firms require that the accounting department receive a copy of the purchase order to provide a basis for verifying the charges made by the supplier. A variety of practices are followed with respect to requisitioning purchases, placing orders, verifying goods received and charges made, recording purchases, and paying suppliers. Each business adopts procedures best suited to its particular needs.

The purchase order at the top of page 171 shows the same quantity and description of the merchandise ordered as specified in the purchase requisition reproduced on page 169. The unit prices shown in the purchase order are those quoted by the supplier and it is expected that the merchandise will be billed at such prices.

The Purchase Invoice

A source document prepared by the seller that lists the items shipped, their cost, and the method of shipment is commonly referred

M MicroWorld

PURCHASE ORDER NO. ___312___

1099 E. Louisiana, Indianapolis, IN 46202-3322

DATE March 26, 19-- DELIVER BY April 12, 19--	
TERMS 2/10, n/30	MLT Software
SHIP BY AJax Transfer Co.	1439 E. Broad St.
FOB Columbus	Columbus, OH 43205-9892

QUANTITY	DESCRIPTION	UNIT PRICE
5	Word Pro, No. F20386	210.00
4	Spellmaster, No. N10367	71.50

Faye J. Quinn

Purchase Order

to as an invoice. From the viewpoint of the seller, it is considered a sales invoice; from the viewpoint of the buyer, it is considered a purchase invoice.

A purchase invoice may be received by the buyer before or after delivery of the merchandise or other property ordered. As invoices are received, it is customary for the buyer to number them consecutively. These numbers should not be confused with the suppliers' numbers, which represent their sale numbers. After being numbered, each purchase invoice is compared with a copy of the purchase order to determine that the quantity, description, prices, and the terms agree and that the method of shipment and the date of delivery conform to the instructions and specifications. A separate approval form may be used, or approval may be stamped on the invoice by means of a rubber stamp. If a separate approval form is used, it may be stapled to or pasted on the invoice form.

The following is an example of a purchase invoice. A rubber stamp was used to imprint the approval form on the face of the invoice. When the merchandise is received, the salesperson may compare the contents of the shipment with a copy of the purchase order, or may prepare a receiving report indicating the contents of the shipment. In the latter event, the receiving report and the purchase order must be compared by someone from either the purchasing or the accounting area. After the prices and extensions are verified, the invoice is held in an unpaid invoice file until it is paid.

Back Orders. If the supplier is unable to ship immediately a part or all of the merchandise ordered, the portions not shipped are known as back orders. Nevertheless, the supplier may send an invoice for the complete order, indicating on it what has been back ordered and when such items will be shipped. The purchase invoice reproduced below

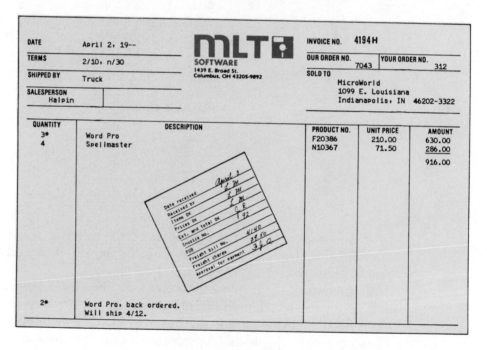

Purchase Invoice

indicates that while 5 copies of Word Pro were ordered, only 3 were shipped by MLT Software. Notice of this shortage was indicated on the invoice. In this instance, only the items shipped were billed.

Trade Discounts. Many manufacturers and wholesalers quote list prices (printed) which are subject to special discounts. Special discounts on list prices granted to customers to encourage their patronage are known as trade discounts. Such arrangements make possible the publication of catalogs with quotations of prices that will not be subject to frequent changes. Some firms, such as those dealing in hardware and jewelry, publish catalogs listing thousands of items. Such catalogs are costly, and considerable loss might be involved when price changes occur if it were not for the fact that discount rates may be changed without changing the list or catalog prices. This practice also has the advantage of permitting retail dealers to display catalogs to their customers without revealing what the items of merchandise cost the dealers.

When an invoice is subject to a trade discount, the discount is usually shown as a deduction from the total amount of the invoice. For example, if the invoice shown on page 172 had been subject to a trade discount of 10%, the discount would be stated in the body of the invoice in the following manner:

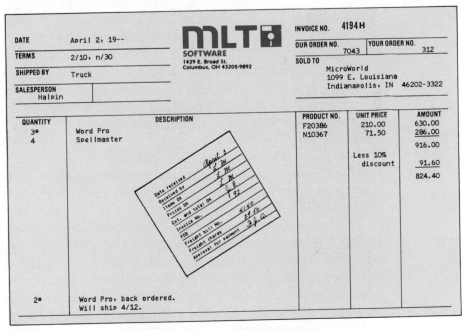

Purchase Invoice with Trade Discount

In entering such an invoice in the books, the amount to be used is the net amount, $824.40, after deducting the trade discount of $91.60. Trade discounts represent a reduction in the price of the merchandise and should not be entered in the accounts of either the seller or the buyer.

Sometimes a series or chain of trade discounts is allowed. For example, if the list prices are subject to discounts of 20%, 10%, and 5%, each discount is computed separately on the successive net amounts. Assume that the gross amount of an invoice is $100 and discounts of 20%, 10%, and 5% are allowed. The net amount is determined as follows:

Gross amount of invoice	$100.00
Less 20%	20.00
Balance	$ 80.00
Less 10%	8.00
Balance	$ 72.00
Less 5%	3.60
Net amount	$ 68.40

In entering this invoice only the net amount, $68.40, is used.

Cash Discounts. Many firms follow the practice of allowing cash discounts, which are discounts from quoted prices, as an inducement for prompt payment of invoices. The terms of payment should be clearly indicated on the invoice. The terms specified on the invoice reproduced on page 172 are "2/10, n/30." This means that a discount of 2% will be allowed if payment is made within 10 days from the date of the invoice (April 2), that is, if payment is made by April 12.

If the invoice is paid on or before April 12, 2% of $916 or $18.32, is deducted and a check for $897.68 may be issued in full settlement of the invoice. After April 12, no discount will be allowed and the total amount of $916 must be paid not later than 30 days after the date of invoice, that is, by May 2.

Cash discounts often are not entered at the time of entering purchase invoices, even though it may be the policy of a firm to pay all invoices in time to get the benefit of any cash discounts offered. For example, the invoice reproduced on page 172 shows that the amount of $916 was entered in the books. The cash discount taken at time of payment on or before April 12 would be accounted for by crediting a purchases discount account at the time of recording the check issued in settlement of the invoice. At the end of the period, the credit balance of the purchases discount account is shown in the income statement as a deduction from the cost of goods purchased.

This approach to accounting for purchases, which is known as the gross-price basis, would involve the following journal entries. If the purchases was entered on April 3, the following entry in two-column journal form would be made:

19--			
April 3	Purchases	916.00	
	Accounts Payable		916.00

If the invoice was paid on April 12, the following entry would be made:

```
19--
April 12 Accounts Payable.............................. 916.00
         Cash...........................................        897.68
         Purchases Discounts...........................         18.32
```

On the other hand, if the invoice was not paid until April 20, the following entry would be made:

```
19--
April 30 Accounts Payable.............................. 916.00
         Cash...........................................       916.00
```

An alternative approach to accounting for purchases that is being used by a growing number of businesses today is the net-price basis of entering purchase invoices. The net-price basis of entering purchase invoices assumes that nearly all discounts will be taken. The purchases are therefore entered at invoice price *less* all available discounts. If the purchase invoice is not paid within the discount period, the amount of the discount is debited to a special purchases discounts lost account at the time that the invoice is paid.

In the case of the invoice previously described, if the purchase was entered on April 3, the following entry in two-column journal form would be made:

```
19--
April 3  Purchases...................................... 897.68
         Accounts Payable..............................        897.68
```

If the invoice was paid on April 12, the following entry (also in two-column journal form) would be made:

```
19--
April 12 Accounts Payable.............................. 897.68
         Cash...........................................        897.68
```

However, if the invoice was not paid until April 20, the following two-column journal entry would be made:

19--		
April 20 Accounts Payable...............................	897.68	
Purchases Discounts Lost........................	18.32	
Cash...		916.00

The net-price basis of handling purchases discounts assumes that the discounts usually will be taken because of the lower costs of buying that result. The purchases discounts lost account is an expense account that reminds Quinn of occasional accounting employee carelessness.

When the net-price basis is used, care must be taken to see that the amount on the face of the invoice agrees with the amount entered in the accounts. Notice, for example, that the amount on the face of the invoice on page 172 is $916, whereas the amount entered on April 3 is $897.68. This potential problem is solved in either of two ways. First, at the time the invoice is received, the buyer can simply enter on the face of the invoice the discount in dollars and the net amount due. Alternatively, many vendors show on the face of the invoice both the gross and net amounts. An example of this is the following MLT Software invoice to MicroWorld.

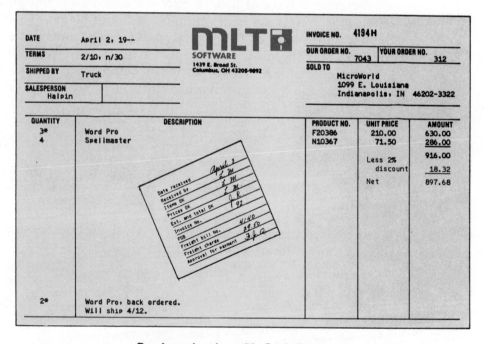

Purchase Invoice with Cash Discount

Sometimes an invoice is subject to both trade and cash discounts. In such cases the trade discount should be deducted from the gross amount of the invoice before the cash discount is computed and deducted. For example, if the invoice reproduced on page 173 were subjected to a trade discount of 10% and the terms were 2/10, n/30, the net amount payable within 10 days from the date of the invoice should be computed in the following manner:

Amount of invoice	$916.00
Less trade discount, 10%	91.60
Amount subject to cash discount	$824.40
Less cash discount, 2%	16.49
Net amount payable	$807.91

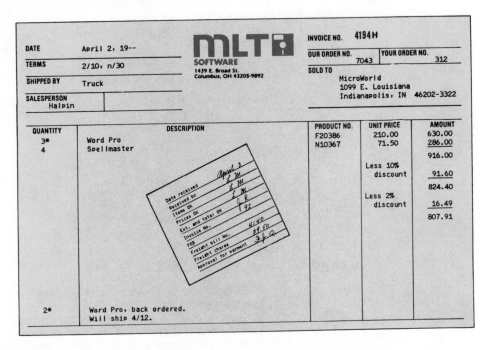

Purchase Invoice with Cash and Trade Discounts

Usually an entire invoice must be paid within the time specified to obtain the benefit of any cash discount offered. However, in some instances, the purchaser is allowed the usual cash discount for partial payment of an invoice within the time specified. Thus, if instead of paying the entire invoice of MLT Software, MicroWorld made a payment of $286 on the invoice by April 12, MLT Software might agree to allow MicroWorld the cash discount of 2%. In this case, the amount of the discount is computed in the following manner:

100% = Amount for which MicroWorld should receive credit
100% − 2% = 98%
$286 ÷ 98% = $291.84
$291.84 − $286.00 = $5.84 discount

This transaction would be entered by MicroWorld (shown in two-column journal form) as follows:

```
19--
April 12  Accounts Payable.................................. 286.00
              Cash...........................................        286.00
```

If the balance of the invoice is paid on April 20, the following computation will be made:

$824.40   Total subject to cash discount
 291.84   Amount for which MicroWorld received credit
$532.56   Amount still due

$532.56 × 2% = $10.65 amount of discount lost
$532.56 − $10.65 = $521.91 amount still owed to supplier

The entry shown in two-column journal form on April 20 would be as follows:

```
19--
April 20  Accounts Payable.................................. 521.91
              Purchases Discounts Lost........................ 10.65
              Cash...........................................        532.56
```

Purchase Invoice Terms. The terms commonly used in connection with purchase invoices are interpreted as follows:

30 days	The amount of the invoice must be paid within 30 days from its date.
2/10, n/30	A discount of 2% is allowed if payment is made within 10 days from the date of the invoice; otherwise, the total amount of the invoice must be paid within 30 days from its date.
2/EOM, n/60	A discount of 2% is allowed if payment is made before the end of the month; otherwise, the total amount of the invoice must be paid within 60 days from its date.
4/10 EOM	A discount of 4% is allowed if payment is made within 10 days after the end of the current month.
COD	Collect on delivery. The amount of the invoice must be paid at the time the merchandise is delivered.
FOB Shipping Point	Free on board at point of origin of the shipment. Under such terms the buyer must pay all transportation costs and assume all risks from the time the merchandise is accepted for shipment by the carrier.
FOB Destination	Free on board at destination of the shipment. The seller will pay the transportation costs and will assume all responsibility for the merchandise until it reaches the carrier's delivery point at destination.

Payment of Invoice. Assuming that MicroWorld pays the April 2 invoice of MLT Software on April 12, the purchase invoice is removed from the unpaid invoice file and another rubber stamp is used to imprint the notation "Paid" and the date of payment "4/12/--" on the face of the invoice. The check number and amount paid are then entered on the proper lines, and the check is issued to the supplier. The following illustration shows the "paid" invoice and related check. Note that the check is for $807.91 (the invoice amount of $824.40 less the 2% cash discount).

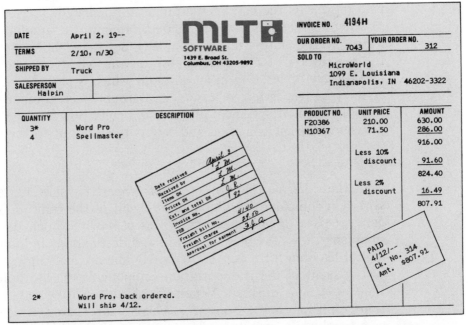

Paid Invoice with Related Check

After the check is mailed to the supplier, the purchase invoice is placed in a "paid invoice" file in alphabetic order by supplier's name.

COD Purchases. Merchandise or other property may be purchased on COD terms, that is, collect on delivery or cash on delivery. COD shipments may be received by parcel post, express, or freight. When shipments are received by parcel post or express, the recipient must pay for the property at the time of delivery. The bill may include transportation charges and COD fees. In any event, the total amount paid represents the cost of the property purchased.

When COD shipments are made by freight, the amount to be collected by the transportation company is entered immediately below the description of the merchandise on the bill. A copy of the sales invoice may be inserted in an envelope which is pasted to the outside of the package, carton, or case. The transportation company then collects the amount specified, plus a COD collection fee, at the time of delivering the merchandise, and remits the amount to the shipper.

The Freight Bill

At the time merchandise or other property is delivered to a transportation company for shipment, an agent of the transportation company prepares a document known as a waybill which describes the shipment, shows the point of origin and destination, and indicates any special handling that may be required. The original copy is forwarded to the agent of the transportation company at the location to which the shipment is directed. When the shipment arrives at the destination, a bill for the transportation charges is prepared, which is known as a freight bill. Sometimes the recipient of the shipment is required to pay the freight bill before the property can be obtained. The following is a reproduction of a freight bill.

TO		1530 E. Mason Columbus, OH 43205-8919				
MicroWorld 1099 E. Louisiana Indianapolis, IN 46202-3322		**AJAX TRANSFER CO.**				
		ORIGINAL FREIGHT BILL		NUMBER **4140**		
FROM		CODE 3	TERMINAL Columbus	SHIPPER NO. C 02473		
MLT Software 1439 E. Broad St. Columbus, OH 43205-9892		FOR OFFICE USE ONLY				
		NAME		PRO	DIV	
		DATE April 3, 19--				
PIECES	DESCRIPTION	WEIGHT	RATE	PREPAID	COLLECT	
2	Packages Software	2 lbs.	14.75		29.50	
		C. O. D. AMOUNT		FEE	DRIVER COLLECT	
ARTICLES LISTED HAVE BEEN RECEIVED IN GOOD CONDITION BY _L. M._ DATE Apr. 3						

Freight Bill

Trucking companies usually make what is known as a "store-to-door delivery." Freight shipments made by railroad or airline may also be delivered to the recipient's place of business at no extra charge. In case such service is not rendered by the transportation company, it may be necessary for the recipient to employ a local drayage company to transport the merchandise from the freight warehouse to the place of business. In such a case, the drayage company will submit a bill for its services, which is known as a **drayage bill.**

The Credit Memorandum

Ordinarily the buyer expects to receive the merchandise or other property ordered and pays for it at the agreed price in accordance with the terms specified in the purchase invoice. However, part or all of the merchandise or other property may be returned to the supplier for various reasons, such as the following:

1. It may not conform to the specifications in the purchase order.
2. A mistake may have been made in placing the order and the supplier may give permission for it to be returned.
3. It may have been delayed in shipment and thus, the buyer cannot dispose of it. This sometimes happens with seasonal goods, such as style merchandise handled by a clothing store.

If the merchandise received is damaged or unsatisfactory or the prices charged are not in accord with an existing agreement or with previous quotations, an adjustment may be made that is referred to as an allowance.

When merchandise is to be returned to the supplier for credit, a debit memorandum — essentially, a formal request for credit to be granted by the supplier — is usually issued by the buyer for the purchase price of the merchandise returned. Upon receipt of the merchandise, the supplier usually issues a document, known as a credit memorandum, confirming the amount of the credit allowed. A filled-in credit memorandum is reproduced on page 182. This form indicates that MLT Software has given MicroWorld credit for the return of one Spellmaster software package. Note that MLT Software has shown on the face of the credit memorandum both the gross and net amount of the credit. This information is needed by MicroWorld because they use the net-price basis for entering credit memorandums. This is consistent with MicroWorld's treatment of purchase invoices.

mLT SOFTWARE
1439 E. Broad St.
Columbus, OH 43205-9892

Credit Memorandum

Date

April 9, 19--

To

MicroWorld
1099 E. Louisiana
Indianapolis, IN 46202-3322

We Credit Your Account As Follows

Description	Quantity	Unit Price	Extension	Total
Spellmaster, No. N10367	1	71.50	71.50	71.50
Less 2% discount				1.43
Net credit				70.07

Credit Memorandum

BUILDING YOUR ACCOUNTING KNOWLEDGE

1. What are two major reasons why the cash basis of accounting does not result in meaningful income or loss determination for a merchandising business?
2. Why should purchase requisitions be numbered consecutively?
3. Why should a purchase invoice be compared with a copy of the related purchase order after having been numbered consecutively upon receipt?
4. How is a trade discount usually shown on an invoice?
5. How does accounting for cash discounts differ under the net-price and gross-price methods of accounting for purchases?
6. What does the net-price basis of entering purchase invoices assume with regard to the taking of all available discounts? Why is this assumption made?
7. If an invoice is subject to both trade and cash discounts, which type of discount should be deducted from the gross invoice amount first?
8. What is done with the purchase invoice at the time of its payment?
9. What is the purpose of a waybill?
10. When does a buyer usually issue a debit memorandum?
11. When does a supplier usually issue a credit memorandum?

APPLYING ACCOUNTING CONCEPTS

Exercise 6-1. McCaghren Office Equipment and Supply purchased the following merchandise:

15 Electronic printing calculators . . . . $ 59.95 each
10 Electric self-correcting typewriters . . . . .   850.00 each
5 Microcomputers . . . .   1,995.00 each

The amount of the purchase is subject to a trade discount of 10% and credit terms of 2/10, n/30.

The following transactions occurred during the month of November:

Nov. 5 Purchased merchandise on account.

Nov. 15 Issued a check for the amount due.

(a) Journalize the following transactions in two-column journal form using the gross-price basis of entering invoices. **(b)** Give the appropriate two-column journal entry if the payment is not made until December 5.

Exercise 6-2. Using the information from Exercise 6-1 **(a)** Journalize the transactions that occurred on November 5 and November 15 in two-column journal form using the net-price basis. **(b)** Give the appropriate journal entry if the payment is not made until December 5.

Exercise 6-3. Lorance Heating and Air Conditioning owes Sheldon-Air $2,024 (gross amount) for merchandise purchased on June 26. The credit terms of the purchase were 4/10, n/30. Sheldon-Air allows cash discounts on partial payments. Lorance Heating and Air Conditioning uses the net-price basis of entering purchase invoices.

The following transactions occurred in June and July:

June 26 Purchased merchandise on account.

July   5 Made a partial payment of $1,500.

July 26 Paid the balance due on the account. (Take into account the amount of credit received on July 5 and the amount of discount lost.)

Journalize the foregoing transactions in two-column journal form.

**Report
No. 6-1**

Complete Report No. 6-1 in the study assignments and submit your working papers to the instructor for approval. Then continue with the following textbook discussion until Report No. 6-2 is required.

ACCOUNTING PROCEDURES FOR PURCHASES AND PAYMENTS

The word purchase can refer to the act of buying almost anything or, if used as a noun, to the thing that is bought. In connection with the accounting for a merchandising business, however, the term usually refers to merchandise. A reference to "purchases for the year," unless qualified in some way, relates to the merchandise purchased for resale, stock in trade.

A stock of goods held for resale at any time in the normal course of business is known as merchandise inventory. Determining the value of this inventory at the beginning, during, and at the end of the accounting period is an important factor in the periodic determination of net income for a merchandising business. Net purchases is the cost of merchandise purchased during the period less (1) the amount of any discounts — purchases discounts — granted by suppliers to encourage prompt payment of their invoices, (2) the cost of goods returned — purchases returns — to suppliers because they have proved to be unsatisfactory or unwanted, and (3) the amount of any allowances— purchases allowances — (price reductions for damaged or defective goods received) made by suppliers.

In entering transactions concerned with purchases of merchandise, it is desirable to keep at least the following accounts:

1. Purchases
2. Purchases Discounts Lost (or Purchases Discounts)
3. Purchases Returns and Allowances

Under the accrual basis of accounting, which will be discussed in detail in Chapter 8, the cost of goods sold must be determined periodically in order that it can be matched against the net sales revenue of the related period. Cost of goods sold (really merchandise inventory expense) is simply defined by the following formula:

$$\begin{array}{ccc} & \text{Merchandise} & \text{Merchandise} \\ \text{Cost of} & \text{Inventory,} & \text{Inventory,} \\ \text{Goods Sold} = \text{Beginning of Period} & + \text{ Net Purchases } - & \text{End of Period} \end{array}$$

Purchases Account

The purchases account is a temporary owner's equity account in which the cost of all merchandise purchased during the accounting period is entered. The account is debited for the cost of the merchandise purchased. If the purchase is for cash, the cash account is credited; if purchased on account, Accounts Payable should be credited. For example, MicroWorld purchased from Compumate, Inc., merchandise on account for $920.

The purchases account may also be debited for any transportation charges, such as freight, express, and parcel post charges, that increase the cost of the merchandise purchased. The common practice, however, is to charge these items to a separate account.

Purchases

Debit	
to enter the cost of merchandise purchased.	

Purchases   920

    Accounts Payable   920

Purchases Discounts Lost (or Purchases Discounts) Account

The purchases discounts lost account is a temporary owner's equity account in which the expense of failing to take advantage of suppliers' discounts is entered. This account is needed when the net-price method of accounting for purchases is used. The account is debited for the amount of any discount lost as a result of paying a supplier's invoice after the discount period is past. Accounts Payable should be debited at the same time for the net amount of the invoice, and Cash should be credited for the sum of the two debits.

Purchases Discounts Lost

Debit	
to enter the expense of discounts lost because of late payment of invoices	

Although purchases discounts lost could be debited directly to Purchases, it is better to debit the account Purchases Discounts Lost. There will then be a separate record of the expense of careless invoice payment. If discounts lost are large in proportion to gross purchases, action may be necessary to improve the functioning of the supplier invoice payment system.

As an example, consider the journal entry previously illustrated on page 176:

Accounts Payable 897.68

Purchases Discounts Lost 18.32

    Cash 916.00

This entry would be made in the cash payments journal on a single line, using the General Debit and Accounts Payable Debit columns (see the cash payments journal illustration on page 192). "Purchases Discounts Lost" would be entered in the Account Debited column.

Under the gross-price basis of accounting for purchases, the purchases discounts account is used rather than the purchases discounts lost account. The use of the purchases discounts account was illustrated with the journal entries on page 175.

Purchases Returns and Allowances Account

The purchases returns and allowances account is a temporary owner's equity account in which purchases returns and allowances are entered. The account is credited for the cost of any merchandise returned to suppliers and for any allowances received from suppliers that decrease the cost of the merchandise purchased. The offsetting debit is to Accounts Payable if the goods were purchased on account, or to Cash if a refund is received because the purchase was originally for cash. Allowances may be received from suppliers for merchandise delivered in poor condition or for merchandise that does not meet specifications as to quality, weight, size, color, grade, or style.

Purchases Returns and Allowances
Credit
to enter the cost of merchandise returned and allowances received.

Although purchases returns and allowances may be credited directly to Purchases, it is better to credit the account Purchases Returns and Allowances. There will then be a record of the amount of gross purchases and the total amount of returns and allowances. If returns and allowances are large in proportion to gross purchases, a weakness in purchasing operations is indicated. It may be that better sources of supply should be sought or that purchase specifications should be stated more clearly.

As an example, consider the credit memorandum for $71.50 illustrated on page 182 that was received from MLT Software, for one Spellmaster software package that was returned by MicroWorld. As explained on page 181, this credit memorandum should be entered at the net price amount of $70.07 in a two-column journal as follows:

Accounts Payable	70.07	
Purchases Returns and Allowances		70.07

If a separate accounts payable ledger is kept, this amount should also be posted as a debit to the individual account of MLT Software, in that ledger. This procedure will be discussed further in the next section.

Accounts Payable

In order that the owner or manager may know both the amount owed to the individual suppliers (sometimes referred to as "creditors"), and the total amount owed to all suppliers, it is advisable to keep an individual record of each supplier and a summary or controlling ledger account. A summary account in the general ledger that represents the total liability to all the suppliers at any point in time is known as Accounts Payable. The credit balance of the account at the beginning of the period represents the total amount owed to suppliers from prior accounting periods. During the period, the account is credited for the amount of any transactions involving increases and is debited for the amount of any transactions involving decreases in the amounts owed to suppliers. At the end of the period, the credit balance of the liability account again represents the total amount owed to all the suppliers.

It is also necessary to keep a record of the transactions completed with each supplier in order that information may be readily available as to the amount owed to each supplier and as to when each invoice should be paid. Two widely used methods of accounting for purchases on account are described in the following paragraphs.

The Invoice Method. Under the invoice method, it is customary to keep a chronological record of the purchase invoices received and to file them systematically by due date in an "unpaid invoices" file. All other documents representing transactions completed with suppliers are filed with the purchase invoices. After an invoice is paid, it is filed alphabetically by the supplier name in a "paid invoices" file. In this way, the "unpaid invoices" file represents a detailed listing of the liabilities to individual suppliers for individual invoices. The total amount of unpaid invoices should equal the balance in the accounts payable account. Special filing equipment or computerized files facilitate the use of this method.

The Ledger Account Method. Under the ledger account method, a chronological record of the purchase invoices received from each supplier is kept in an individual ledger account. A separate ledger containing individual accounts with suppliers arranged in alphabetical order is called a subsidiary accounts payable ledger.

Purchases Journal

All of the transactions of a merchandising business can be entered in an ordinary two-column journal or in a combination journal. However, in many enterprises purchase transactions occur frequently. Since most purchases are made on account, such transactions may be entered advantageously in a special journal. A journal designed for entering only purchases of merchandise on account is called a purchases journal. The following is a sample purchases journal.

	DATE	INVOICE NO.	FROM WHOM PURCHASED	POST. REF.	AMOUNT	
	1986					
1	Apr. 4	631	Compumate, Inc.	✓	6825 00	1
2	8	632	Minisoft	✓	2009 70	2
3	9	633	E H M Corp.	✓	7944 15	3
4	17	634	Printmaster Co.	✓	10419 90	4
5	23	635	Telecomp, Inc.	✓	3214 50	5
6	30		Purchases Dr.–Accounts Payable Cr.	511/218	30413 25	6
7						7
8						8

PURCHASES JOURNAL   PAGE 8

Purchases Journal

Note that in entering each purchase invoice, the following information is placed in the purchases journal:

1. Date on which the invoice is received
2. Number of the invoice, i.e., the number assigned by the buyer
3. From whom purchased (the supplier)
4. Amount of the invoice

With this form of purchases journal, each transaction can be entered on one horizontal line. The numbers "511/218" in the Post. Ref. column on the last line of the Purchases Journal indicate that the total was posted twice—to Purchases, Account No. 511, as a debit, and to Accounts Payable, Account No. 218, as a credit.

If an individual ledger account is not kept with each supplier, the purchase invoices should be filed immediately after they have been entered in the purchases journal. It is preferable that they are filed according to due date in an unpaid invoice file. If an individual ledger account is kept with each supplier, the invoices normally are used to post to the supplier accounts, after which the invoices are properly filed.

The unpaid invoice file is usually arranged with a division for each month with folders numbered 1 to 31 in each division. This makes it possible to file each unpaid invoice according to its due date which facilitates payment of the invoices on or before their due dates. Since certain invoices may be subject to discounts if paid within a specified time, it is important that they are handled in such a manner that payment is made in sufficient time to get the benefit of the discounts.

If a partial payment is made on an invoice, a notation of the payment should be made on the invoice, and it should be retained in the unpaid invoice file until paid in full. If credit is received because of returns and allowances, a notation of the amount of the credit should be made on the invoice so that the adjusted balance due will be indicated. As mentioned earlier, when an invoice is paid in full, the payment should be noted on the invoice, and the invoice then transferred from the unpaid invoice file to the paid invoice file. It is considered a good policy to pay each invoice in full. Paying specific invoices in full simplifies the accounting process for both the buyer and the seller.

The paid invoice file is usually arranged in alphabetic order according to the names of suppliers. This facilitates updating the file for all paid invoices, and all other vouchers or documents representing transactions with suppliers, in such a manner that a complete history of the business done with each supplier is maintained.

Posting From the Purchases Journal

At the end of the month, the Amount column of the purchases journal is totaled and the ruling completed as illustrated. A process referred to as summary posting is then performed by posting the total of the purchases on account for the month to the ledger as a debit to Purchases and as a credit to Accounts Payable. The titles of both accounts and the posting reference may be entered on one horizontal line of the purchases journal as shown in the illustration. A proper cross-reference should be provided by entering the page of the purchases journal preceded by the initial "P" in the Posting Reference column of the ledger account and by entering the account number in the Posting Reference column of the purchases journal.

The summary posting from MicroWorld's purchases journal to the ledger accounts on April 30 is illustrated on page 193.

ACCOUNT *Accounts Payable*						ACCOUNT NO. 218	
DATE	ITEM	POST. REF.	DEBIT	CREDIT	BALANCE		
					DEBIT	CREDIT	
1986 Apr. 30		P8		3041325		3041325	

ACCOUNT *Purchases*						ACCOUNT NO. 511	
DATE	ITEM	POST. REF.	DEBIT	CREDIT	BALANCE		
					DEBIT	CREDIT	
1986 Apr. 30		P8	3041325		3041325		

The Invoice Method. Under the invoice method of accounting for purchases on account, individual posting from the purchases journal is not required. When this plan is followed, it is customary to place a check mark in the Posting Reference column of the purchases journal at the time each invoice is entered.

The Ledger Account Method. If an individual ledger account is kept for each supplier, all transactions representing either increases or decreases in the amount owed to each supplier should be posted individually to the proper account. The posting, usually done with the aid of electronic equipment, will be completed directly from the purchase invoices and other vouchers or documents. As the individual supplier accounts are posted, a check mark ($\sqrt{}$) should be placed in the Posting Reference column of the purchases journal. The ledger account method of accounting for Accounts Payable will be explained in detail in Chapter 8.

A flowchart of the major documents used in the purchases function was presented near the beginning of the chapter. That flowchart can now be updated to include the accounting procedures as follows:

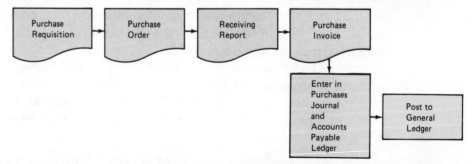

Schedule of Accounts Payable

A list showing the amount due to each supplier as of a specified date is known as a schedule of accounts payable. It is usually advisable to prepare such a schedule at the end of each month. An example for MicroWorld as of March 31, 1986, is provided below. Such a schedule can be prepared easily from the list of supplier accounts in the subsidiary accounts payable ledger or by going through the unpaid invoice file and listing the names of the suppliers and the amount due to each. If the total of the schedule does not agree with the balance of the summary accounts payable account, the error may be in either the subsidiary ledger, the file, or the summary ledger account. The subsidiary ledger could be incorrect because of an error in posting. The file may be incorrect in that one or more paid invoices have not been removed or one or more unpaid ones are missing. Another possibility is that a memorandum of a partial payment was overlooked in preparing the list. The accounts payable account could be incorrect because of an error in posting or because of an error in a journal from which the total purchases were posted. In any event, the postings, journals, and invoices must be examined until the reason for the discrepancy is found so that the necessary correction can be made.

MicroWorld Schedule of Accounts Payable April 30, 1986	
AB Electronics	5349 60
EHM Corp.	2634 80
Microserve, Inc.	3288 00
3D Corp.	997 05
	12269 45

MicroWorld—Schedule of Accounts Payable

Cash Payments Journal

Just as purchase transactions occur frequently in many enterprises, it follows that payment of suppliers' invoices and other obligations of the business will cause cash payment transactions to occur frequently. Such cash transactions may be entered advantageously in a special journal. A journal designed for entering all cash payments (other than petty cash) but only cash payments is called a cash payments journal. The following is a cash payments journal.

CASH PAYMENTS JOURNAL

PAGE 12

DATE	CK. NO.	ACCOUNT DEBITED	POST. REF.	GENERAL DR.	ACCOUNTS PAYABLE DR.	PURCHASES DR.	CASH CR.	
1986 Apr. 2	307	Rent Expense	541	2200 00			2200 00	1
4	308	Telecomp, Inc.	✓		4287 30		4287 30	2
10	309	Compacto Co.	✓		9671 60		9671 60	3
14	310	Advertising Expense	546	2414 90			2414 90	4
22	311	Faye J. Quinn, Drawing	311.1	1500 00			1500 00	5
24	312	EHM Corp.	✓		4184 90		4184 90	6
29	313	Purchases	✓			1141 10	1141 10	7
				6114 90	18143 80	1141 10	25399 80	8
				(✓)	(2/8)	(5/1)	(1/1)	9

Cash Payments Journal

Note that every entry in the cash payments journal includes the following information:

1. Date of the cash payment
2. Number of the check issued
3. Name of the supplier or other account debited
4. Amount of the cash payment, entered in the Cash Cr. column.

The following aspects of cash payment entry procedures should be noted:

1. A payment of an expense—name of expense account is entered in the Account Debited column and the debit amount is entered in the General Dr. column.
2. A cash purchase—"Purchases" is entered in the Account Debited column and the debit amount is entered in the Purchases Dr. column.
3. Payment to a supplier—name of supplier is entered in the Account Debited column and the debit amount is entered in the Accounts Payable Dr. column. If the invoice is past due, "Purchases Discounts Lost/name of supplier" is entered in the Account Debited column and the amount of the discount lost is entered in the General Dr. column, in addition to the debit in the Accounts Payable Dr. column for the net amount of the invoice. The check mark ($\sqrt{}$) entered in the Post Reference column will be discussed in Chapter 8.
4. A cash refund for a sales return or allowance—"Sales Returns and Allowances" is entered in the Account Debited column and the debit amount is entered in the General Dr. column.
5. A payment of a liability—name of the liability account is entered in the Account Debited column and the debit amount is entered in the General Dr. column.
6. Withdrawal by the owner—name of drawing account is entered in the Account Debited column and the debit amount is entered in the General Dr. column.
7. NSF check—"Accounts Receivable/customer's name" is entered in the Account Debited column and the debit amount is entered in the General Dr. column.

Posting From the Cash Payments Journal

Each amount in the General Dr. column of the cash payments journal is posted individually to the ledger account named in the Account Debited column. The notation "CP 12" is entered in the Post. Ref. column of the affected ledger account at the time that the item is posted, and the appropriate account number is entered in the Post. Ref. column of the cash payments journal.

At the end of the month, the four amount columns of the cash payments journal are totaled and the ruling completed as illustrated. The summary posting involves posting the total of the Accounts Payable Dr. column as a debit to Account No. 218, the total of the Purchases Dr. column as a debit to Account No. 511, and the total of the Cash Cr. column as a credit to Account No. 111.

As each total is posted, the notation "CP 12" is entered in the Post. Ref. column of the affected ledger account, and the number of that account is entered in parentheses below the appropriate column total in the cash payments journal. A check mark ($\sqrt{}$) is entered in parentheses below the total of the General Dr. column to indicate that its total is not posted to the ledger.

The summary posting from MicroWorld's cash payments journal to the ledger accounts on April 30 is as follows:

ACCOUNT Accounts Payable   ACCOUNT NO. 218

DATE	ITEM	POST. REF.	DEBIT	CREDIT	BALANCE DEBIT	BALANCE CREDIT
1986 Apr. 30		P8		3041325		3041325
30		CP12	1814380			1226945

ACCOUNT Purchases   ACCOUNT NO. 511

DATE	ITEM	POST. REF.	DEBIT	CREDIT	BALANCE DEBIT	BALANCE CREDIT
1986 Apr. 30		P8	3041325		3041325	
30		CP12	114110		3155435	

ACCOUNT Cash   ACCOUNT NO. 111

DATE	ITEM	POST. REF.	DEBIT	CREDIT	BALANCE DEBIT	BALANCE CREDIT
1986 Apr. 1		$\sqrt{}$			5000000	
30		CP12		2539980	2460020	

Cash Purchases

Cash purchases of merchandise are entered in the cash payments journal by debiting the purchases account (using the "Purchases Dr." column) and by crediting the cash account. Usually cash purchases are not posted to the individual accounts of suppliers. However, if it is desired to post cash purchases to the individual accounts of suppliers, such transactions may be entered both in the purchases journal and in the cash payments journal. In other words, invoices received in connection with cash purchases may be processed in the same manner as invoices for purchases on account. MicroWorld follows the practice of entering cash purchases of merchandise in the cash payments journal and purchases on account in the purchases journal.

COD Purchases

When property is purchased on COD terms, the total amount paid represents the cost of the property. Since payment must be made before possession of the property can be obtained, it is customary to treat such transactions the same as cash purchases. Thus the check issued in payment of a COD purchase is entered in the cash payments journal by debiting the proper account and by crediting the cash account. The proper account to debit depends upon the kind of property purchased. If merchandise is purchased, the purchases account is debited for the cost of the merchandise and the transportation account is debited for the amount of any transportation charges paid. If plant or equipment assets are purchased, the proper asset account is debited for the total cost, including COD fees and transportation charges. If supplies are purchased, the proper supplies account is debited for the total cost of the supplies, including COD fees and transportation charges.

Transportation Charges

Express and freight charges may be prepaid by the shipper or may be paid by the buyer at the time of delivery. Parcel post charges must be prepaid by the shipper. Store-to-door delivery of freight shipments may be made by the transportation companies. However, when freight shipments are not delivered to the buyer's place of business by the transportation company, the buyer either calls for the goods at a nearby freight warehouse or employs a truck to deliver the goods.

Transportation Charges Prepaid. If the transportation charges are prepaid by the shipper, the amount may or may not be added to the invoice, depending upon the terms of the sale. If the shipper has quoted prices FOB destination, it is understood that the prices quoted include transportation charges either to the buyer's place of business or to a nearby freight warehouse and that no additional charge will be made for any transportation charges paid by the shipper.

If the shipper has quoted prices FOB shipping point, it is understood that the prices quoted do not include the transportation charges and that the buyer is expected to pay the transportation costs. If these transportation charges are prepaid by the shipper, the charges will be added to the invoice, and the shipper will be reimbursed by the buyer when the invoice is paid.

Transportation Charges Collect. If prices are quoted FOB shipping point and shipment is made collect, the buyer pays the transportation charges before obtaining possession of the shipment. Such transportation charges represent an addition to the cost of the merchandise or other property purchased. The method of entering the transportation charges in this case is the same as if the charges had been prepaid by the shipper and added to the invoice.

If prices are quoted FOB destination but for some reason shipment is made collect, the buyer pays the transportation charges to obtain possession of the shipment. In such cases the transportation charges paid by the buyer are entered as a debit to the account of the supplier from whom the merchandise or other property was ordered. In other words, the payment of the transportation charges in such case should be treated the same as a partial payment of the amount due the shipper.

Transportation Accounts. As previously explained, transportation charges applicable to merchandise purchased may be entered by debiting the purchases account. However, it is common practice to enter transportation charges on incoming merchandise in a separate account, which may be entitled Freight In or Transportation In. Under these circumstances, a special Freight In or Transportation In column is included in the purchases journal for this purpose, or this type of transaction can be entered in a two-column journal. This account is treated as a subdivision of the purchases account and the balance must be taken into consideration as an addition to purchases in computing the cost of goods sold at the close of each accounting period.

Transportation charges applicable to equipment assets, such as office equipment, store equipment, or delivery equipment, are treated as an addition to the cost of the equipment. It is immaterial whether the freight charges are prepaid by the shipper and added to the invoice or whether shipment is made collect. If the freight is prepaid and added to the invoice, the total cost, including the invoice price and the transportation charges, is entered as a debit to the equipment account in one amount. On the other hand, if shipment is made freight collect, the amount of the invoice and the amount of the freight charges are posted as separate debits to the equipment account.

Parcel Post Insurance. Merchandise or other property mailed parcel post may be insured against loss or damage in transit. Such insurance may be purchased through the U.S. Postal Service, or it may be purchased from private insurance companies. If the cost of insurance is charged to the customer and is added to the invoice, it represents an addition to the cost of the merchandise or other property purchased. Thus, if an invoice is received for merchandise purchased and the merchandise is billed at a total cost of $225 plus postage of $3 and insurance of 90 cents, the total cost of the merchandise is $228.90.

The cost of insurance seldom is entered separately in the accounts of the buyer, but either is charged directly to the purchases account or is included with transportation charges and charged to Freight In.

The purchaser may indicate in placing an order that the merchandise is not to be insured. When this is indicated, the purchaser implies a willingness to assume the risk for any loss or damage sustained to the merchandise in transit. Title to merchandise ordinarily passes to the purchaser when it is placed in the hands of the carrier for delivery.

BUILDING YOUR ACCOUNTING KNOWLEDGE

1. What is the formula for the simple determination of the cost of goods sold?
2. Describe briefly how each of the following accounts is used: (1) Purchases, (2) Purchases Discounts Lost, (3) Purchases Returns and Allowances.
3. Discuss the two major methods of keeping records of the transactions completed with individual suppliers.
4. List four items of information about each purchase normally entered in the purchases journal.
5. List four items of information about each cash payment normally entered in the cash payments journal.
6. List seven kinds of transactions requiring varying entry procedures in the cash payments journal.
7. In what journal does MicroWorld enter cash purchases?
8. Are COD purchases handled the same as cash purchases or the same as purchases on account?
9. If transportation charges are billed collect under normal FOB shipping point terms, what do such charges represent as far as the buyer is concerned?
10. If transportation charges are billed collect under FOB destination terms, how should the buyer treat the payment of these charges?
11. Indicate two alternative means of entering the cost of parcel post insurance.

APPLYING ACCOUNTING CONCEPTS

Exercise 6-4. Determine the cost of goods sold based on the following data taken from the accounts of Arbor Hardware, a small retail business.

Merchandise inventory, beginning of the period $16,000
Purchases during the period 74,000
Purchases discounts lost during the period 2,300
Purchases returns and allowances during the period 4,200
Merchandise inventory, end of the period 17,500

Exercise 6-5. Robert Lee, who operates Lee's Drug Store, completed the following transactions related to purchases of merchandise on account.

Aug. 3 Purchased medicines from MDA Medicines, $245, terms, n/30. Invoice No. 170.

     5 Purchased jewelry from Lynn's Boutique, $75, terms, n/30. Invoice No. 171.

   10 Purchased greeting cards from The Strawberry Patch, $114, terms, n/30. Invoice No. 172.

   16 Purchased film from Jim's Photo Supplies, $57, terms, n/30. Invoice No. 173.

   18 Purchased medicines from Care Medical Supplies, $389, terms, n/30. Invoice No. 174.

(a) Prepare a purchases journal using the same format and account titles as illustrated in the chapter. Enter the purchases in the purchases journal. **(b)** Total and rule the journal.

Exercise 6-6. **(a)** Prepare a cash payments journal using the same format and account titles as illustrated in the chapter. Enter the payments of the transactions from Exercise 6-5 in the cash payments journal. Assume that payments were made 30 days after the date of purchase. Number the checks beginning with 675. **(b)** Enter the following transactions:

Sept. 20 Issued Check No. 680 for $350 to Jahn-Scott Insurance Agency in payment of insurance premium on the drug store.

    25 Issued Check No. 681 for $133 to Parker Brothers for a cash purchase of medicines.

(c) Total and rule the journal.

Report No. 6-2

Complete Report No. 6-2 in the study assignments and submit your working papers to the instructor for approval. Then continue with the textbook discussion in Chapter 7 until Report No. 7-1 is required.

EXPANDING YOUR BUSINESS VOCABULARY

What is the meaning of each of the following items?

Accounts Payable **(p. 187)**
allowance **(p. 181)**
back orders **(p. 172)**
cash discounts **(p. 174)**
cash payments journal **(p. 191)**
COD **(p. 180)**
cost of goods sold **(p. 184)**
credit memorandum **(p. 181)**
debit memorandum **(p. 181)**
drayage bill **(p. 181)**
FOB destination **(p. 195)**
FOB shipping point **(p. 195)**
freight bill **(p. 180)**
gross-price basis **(pp. 174, 186)**
invoice **(p. 171)**
invoice method **(p. 187)**
ledger account method **(p. 187)**
list prices **(p. 172)**
merchandise inventory **(p. 184)**
net-price basis **(p. 175)**

net purchases **(p. 184)**
purchase **(p. 183)**
purchase invoice **(p. 171)**
purchase order **(p. 170)**
purchase requisition **(p. 169)**
purchases allowances **(p. 184)**
purchases discounts **(p. 184)**
purchases journal **(p. 188)**
purchases returns **(p. 184)**
receiving report **(p. 172)**
sales invoice **(p. 171)**
schedule of accounts payable **(p. 191)**
stock in trade **(p. 184)**
subsidiary accounts payable ledger **(p. 188)**
summary posting **(p. 189)**
supplier or vendor **(p. 170)**
trade discounts **(p. 173)**
waybill **(p. 180)**

CHAPTER 7

Accounting for Sales and Collections

CHAPTER OBJECTIVES

Careful study of this chapter should enable you to:

- Describe the various types of sales, including cash sales, sales on account, bank credit card sales, COD sales, sales "on approval," "layaway" sales, installment sales, and consignment sales, and explain the processing of each type of sale.

- Describe retail sales taxes and the related accounting procedure.

- Describe commonly followed practices in processing incoming orders for merchandise, including the use of the following source documents:
  1. Customer purchase order
  2. Sales ticket or invoice
  3. Customer's check
  4. Credit memorandum
- Define the terms sales, sales discounts, sales returns and allowances, net sales, and gross margin (gross profit).

- Describe subsidiary records, specifically:
  1. A file of uncollected charge sale tickets—the "sales ticket" method
  2. A subsidiary accounts receivable ledger—the "ledger account" method
- Explain and use a special journal for sales of merchandise.

- Explain and use a special journal for all cash receipts.

In the calculation of periodic income under the accrual basis, realized revenue of a period is matched with the expenses reasonably assignable to that period. Realized revenue means the receipt of cash or a collectible claim to cash arising from the sale of something of value—usually goods.

The purpose of this chapter is to describe and explain the common accounting practices for handling sales of merchandise and the subsequent collection of remittances for such sales. The setting is the same small retail enterprise introduced in Chapter 6. Commonly used source documents for sales and collections will be discussed and illustrated, and special journals for sales and cash receipts will be introduced and explained.

SOURCE DOCUMENTS AND ASSOCIATED RECORDS FOR SALES AND COLLECTIONS

In order to understand the role of the various source documents and associated records for sales, it is helpful to know the nature of the underlying sales transactions. A variety of types of sales may be identified in the retail business world.

Types of Sales

Eight of these types of sales will be discussed here: (1) cash sales; (2) sales on account; (3) bank credit card sales; (4) COD sales; (5) sales on approval; (6) layaway sales; (7) installment sales; and (8) consignment sales.

(1) Cash Sales. Some businesses sell merchandise for cash only, while others sell merchandise either for cash or on account. A variety of practices are followed in the handling of cash sales. If such transactions are numerous, it is probable that one or more types of electronic cash register will be used. In this instance the original entry of the sales is made in the register. Often, registers have the capability of accumulating more than one total. This means that by using the proper key, each amount that is entered in the register can be classified by type of merchandise, by department, or by salesperson. Where sales tax is involved, the amount of the tax may be separately entered. In accounting terms, a cash sale means that the asset Cash is increased by a debit and the income account Sales and a liability account Sales Tax Payable are credited.

In many retail establishments the procedure in handling cash sales is for the salesclerks to prepare sales tickets in triplicate. (Sales tickets will be discussed and illustrated in a subsequent section.) Sometimes the preparation of the sales tickets involves the use of a cash register that enters the amount of the sale directly on the ticket. Modern electronic cash registers serve as input terminals that are "on line" with computers, that is, in direct communication with the central processor. At the end of each day the cash received is compared with the record that the register provides. The receipts may also be compared with the total of the cash-sales tickets, if the system makes use of the latter. (A daily summary of a cash register tape is illustrated below. The colored numbers in parentheses are keyed to the discussion in this and subsequent paragraphs.)

```
            (1)
      CASH SALES        327.79 +
            (3)
      MCARD/VISA        550.62 +
            (6)
      LAYAWAY            79.50 +
      TOTAL CASH        957.91 ⅹ
            (2)
      CHARGE SALES      543.84 +
            (5)
      APPROVAL          126.58 +
      TOTAL CHARGE      670.42 ⅹ

      TOTAL SALES     1,628.33 Gⅹ
      SALES TAX          81.42 +
                         81.42 ⅹ

      REC'D ON ACCT.    324.51 +
                        324.51 ⅹ

      PAID OUT           76.51 +
                         76.51 ⅹ

      NO SALE             0.00 +
                          0.00 ⅹ


      ⅹ   SUB-TOTAL
      Gⅹ  GRAND TOTAL
```

Cash Register Tape Summary

(2) Sales on Account. Sales on account are often referred to as "charge sales" because the seller exchanges merchandise for the buyer's promise to pay. In accounting terms, this means that the asset Accounts Receivable of the seller is increased by a debit or charge, and the income account Sales is increased by a credit. Selling goods on account is common practice at the retail level of the distribution process. Firms that sell goods on account should investigate the financial reliability of those to whom they sell. A business of some size may have a separate credit department whose major function is to establish credit policies and decide upon requests for credit from persons and firms who wish to buy goods on account. Seasoned judgment is needed to avoid a credit policy that is so stringent that profitable business may be refused, or a credit policy that is so liberal that uncollectible account losses may become excessive.

Generally, no goods are delivered until the salesclerk has been assured that the buyer has established credit—that there is an account for this customer with the company. In the case of many retail businesses, customers with established credit are provided with credit cards or charge plates, which provide evidence that the buyer has an account. These are used in mechanical or electronic devices to print the customer's name and other identification on the sales tickets. In the case of merchants who commonly receive a large portion of their orders by mail or by phone, this confirmation of the buyer's status can be handled as a matter of routine before the goods are delivered.

(3) Bank Credit Card Sales. The use of bank credit cards in connection with retail sales of certain types of goods and services is referred to as bank credit card sales. The two most widely used credit cards of this type in the United States are the VISA card and the MasterCard. Several thousand banks participate in each of these programs. The two systems have much in common.

Participating banks encourage their depositors and other customers to obtain the cards by supplying the necessary information to establish their credit reliability. When this is accomplished, a small plastic card containing the cardholder's name, an identifying number, and an expiration date is issued to the applicant. Both VISA and MasterCard furnish participating businesses with lists of expired or otherwise invalid credit cards at frequent intervals, so that participants can aid the banks in screening out undesirable credit risks.

Merchants and other businesses are invited to participate in the program. If certain conditions are met, the bank will accept for deposit completed copies of the prescribed form of sales invoice (also sometimes called "ticket," or "draft") for goods sold or services rendered to cardholders and evidenced by the invoices bearing the card imprints and the buyers' signatures. The bank, in effect, either "buys" the tickets at a discount (commonly 4%, though it may be more or less depending upon various factors) immediately, or gives the merchant immediate credit for the full amount of the tickets, and, once a month, charges the merchant's account with the total amount of the discount at the agreed rate. The latter practice is more common.

For the merchant, bank credit card sales are nearly the equivalent of cash sales. The service is performed or the goods are sold; and the money is secured. It is then up to the bank to collect from the buyer or bear the loss, if the account proves to be uncollectible.

In most respects, accounting for bank credit card sales is very much the same as accounting for regular cash sales. A regular sales ticket may be prepared as well as the credit card form of invoice. Usually the transactions are accounted for as sales for the full price with the amount of the discount being treated as an expense when the bank makes the monthly charge.

Sales made by certain types of businesses that use other forms of retail credit cards—notably those of petroleum companies, and businesses participating in the "American Express," "Carte Blanche," and

"Diner's Club" programs, are similar in many respects to bank credit card sales.

(4) COD Sales. Collect on Delivery sales (COD sales) are sales of merchandise or other property on COD terms. Under this arrangement, payment must be made at the time the goods are delivered to the buyer by the seller or the agent. The agent usually is an employee of the seller but may also be a messenger, the postal service, an express company, or any common carrier (railroad, truck line, airline, etc.).

In retail merchandising, COD sales tickets are segregated each day and a COD list is prepared for control purposes. The merchandise is then delivered to the customer and the sale price is collected upon delivery. When the money is turned in to the seller, the driver or other agent is given credit for the collection on the COD list and the sale is entered in the same manner as a cash sale. If, for any reason, the customer refuses to accept the merchandise, it is returned to stock and the sale is canceled. Under this plan of handling COD sales, title to the merchandise does not pass to the customer until the goods are delivered and collection has been made; therefore, the merchandise is considered to be part of the inventory of the seller until a remittance is received.

(5) Sales on Approval. Sales that give the customer the right to return the goods within a specified time are called sales on approval. The sale is not complete unless the customer retains the goods. Such sales may be treated as ordinary charge sales, and any returns may be handled as ordinary sales returns. On the other hand, sales on approval may be handled the same as ordinary cash sales. Under this plan a memorandum record of the sale is kept until it is definitely known that the goods will be retained by the customer. The customer must either pay for the goods or return them by a specified date. When a remittance is received, the sale is entered. If the goods are returned, they are put back in stock and the sale is canceled.

(6) Layaway Sales. Sales on approval should not be confused with layaway sales. Layaway sales may be made for cash or on account, but in either case the customer agrees to call later for the goods. Sometimes a deposit is made by the buyer with the understanding that the merchandise will be held until some future date, at which time the buyer either calls for the merchandise or requests that the merchandise be delivered. If instead of calling for the merchandise, the customer requests delivery on a COD basis, a COD slip is made for the proper amount. When the remittance is received, it is entered in the same manner as if the customer had called for the merchandise and paid cash.

Accounting for deposits on layaway sales is not uniform, but the usual method is to enter the deposits in the same manner as cash sales. When this plan is used, a charge sales ticket is prepared for the balance due and is entered by debiting a special accounts receivable control account and crediting the sales account. Individual accounts with layaway customers may be kept in a special subsidiary ledger, sometimes referred to as a layaway ledger.

At the end of the accounting period, the total amount due from customers who made deposits on layaway sales is treated as ordinary accounts receivable. The cost of the merchandise that is being held for future delivery is not included in the inventory because it is considered to be the property of the customer.

(7) Installment Sales. The term installment sales is applied to a variety of arrangements in which the purchaser of goods (and sometimes services) makes a so-called "down payment" and agrees to pay the remainder of the sales price in fractional, periodic amounts over an extended period of time. These arrangements might also be viewed as "installment payments." From the standpoint of the seller, such transactions often are equivalent to cash or bank credit card sales. Frequently, some type of financial institution is a party to the transaction at the outset. The seller gets the money immediately; thus the buyer becomes a borrower who must make payments to a bank or finance company. Interest is always involved. In other cases, the seller does acquire a receivable, but soon "sells" it to a financial institution. Often, the seller must guarantee the collectibility of the receivable. In some cases, the seller "carries the account" and the buyer makes periodic payments directly to the business from whom the goods were purchased. Usually, the payments include an interest component.

If the seller does carry the account, it is desirable to use a special form of subsidiary ledger account that is designed to facilitate entering installment transactions. The subsidiary accounts comprise what is called an "installment ledger" that contains the details of the general ledger account titled Installment Accounts Receivable. At one time, the accounting for installment sales entailed a somewhat complicated procedure that was based on the idea that no gross margin on such sales should be taken into income calculations until the money was received. Each dollar collected, whether from down payment or periodic installments, was considered to be partly a recovery of the cost of what was sold and partly gross margin. If the collection period extended over several years, the recognition of the gross margin on the sale would be spread over those years. This procedure, called the "installment method," is no longer considered to be an acceptable accounting practice except in special and unusual circumstances. Normal practice is to regard installment sales as regular sales on account, that is, all revenue from an installment sale is considered to be realized at the point of sale. For income tax purposes, however, the installment method may be used. Using this method in the calculation of taxable income permits the postponement of payment of taxes until the year that the money is received.

(8) Consignment Sales. An arrangement in which one business, known as the consignor, ships goods to another business, known as the consignee, without any change in the legal ownership of the goods, is called a consignment sale. The consignee acts as an agent for the consignor and attempts to sell the goods, usually at prices specified by the consignor. If the goods are sold, the consignee receives an agreed commission, which is deducted from the proceeds of the sales when remittance of the amount due is made to the consignor. Consigned goods in the hands of the consignee at the end of the accounting period are a part of the consignor's inventory until sold and should be included in that account balance. Sale of such goods is entered by the consignor when they are sold by the consignee.

Sometimes, each party keeps a set of formal memorandum accounts for consignment transactions. In other cases, no formal entries are made until the goods have been sold. Consignment selling is not a widespread practice.

Retail Sales Tax

A tax imposed by many cities and states upon the sale of tangible personal property at retail is known as a retail sales tax. The tax usually is a percentage of the gross sales price or the gross receipts from sales. Retail sales taxes may also include taxes imposed upon persons engaged in furnishing services at retail, in which case the tax is a percentage of the gross receipts for furnishing such services. The rates of the tax vary considerably. In most states the tax is a general sales tax. However, in some states the tax is imposed only on specific items, such as automobiles, cosmetics, radio and television sets, and playing cards, and in other states, food purchased in stores and medicines are exempt from tax.

To avoid fractions of cents and to simplify the determination of the tax, it is customary to use a sales tax table or schedule. For example, where the rate is 5%, the tax may be calculated as shown in the schedule at the top of page 206.

The amount of the tax imposed under the schedule approximates the legal rate. Retail sales tax reports accompanied by remittances for

Amount of Sale	Amount of Tax
1¢ to 10¢	None
11¢ to 29¢	1¢
30¢ to 49¢	2¢
50¢ to 69¢	3¢
70¢ to 89¢	4¢
90¢ to $1.09	5¢

and so on

the amounts due must be filed periodically, either monthly or quarterly, depending upon the law of the state or city in which the business is located.

Customer Purchase Order

The following flowchart shows some of the major documents and procedures commonly used in the sales function of a merchandise business. Each of these documents and procedures is explained in this and the following sections.

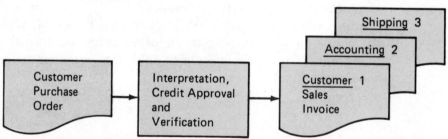

Sales by merchants may be made in response to purchase orders received by mail or telephone. Orders received by mail may be entered on the purchase order form, letterhead, or other stationery of the buyer or on an order blank furnished by the seller. An illustration of a typical purchase order form was shown on page 171. It is probable that upon receiving this order, a rubber stamp impression with spaces to show the date received, credit approval, approval of prices shown, and date of billing was placed on its face. In the process of handling the order, the person or persons involved make appropriate notations. Orders received by telephone are carefully entered on forms provided for that purpose.

Procedure for Handling Incoming Purchase Orders. The procedure in handling purchase orders varies widely with different firms. It is important that there should be a well-organized plan, the purpose of which is to promote efficiency and to maintain an internal check that will tend to prevent mistakes in handling orders. The following five steps constitute the heart of such a plan.

(1) **Interpretation.** Each purchase order received should be interpreted as to (a) identity of the customer and (b) quantity and description of items ordered. Orders may be received from old or new customers. Sometimes it is difficult to identify a new customer, particularly if there had been no previous correspondence or the customer had not been contacted by the seller's representative. In some cases identification of the items ordered is difficult because customers frequently are careless in describing the merchandise wanted. Different items of merchandise may be specified by name or stock number. Care should be used to make sure that the stock number agrees with the description of the item.

(2) **Credit Approval.** All purchase orders received that involve credit in any form should be referred to the store manager or credit department for approval before being billed or shipped. COD orders should also be approved because some customers have a reputation for not accepting COD shipments which are then returned at the seller's expense. Customers who abuse the COD privilege may be required thereafter to send cash with the order, either in full or part payment. Some firms follow a policy of requiring part payment in cash with all orders for merchandise to be shipped COD.

(3) **Verification of Purchase Orders.** The unit prices specified on purchase orders should be verified, the proper extensions should be made, and the total should be entered. Persons performing this function usually use electronic calculating machines.

(4) **Shipping.** In handling each purchase order, it is necessary to determine how shipment will be made and how the transportation charges will be handled. Shipment may be made by parcel post, express, or freight. Parcel post packages may be insured. Express shipments may be made by rail or air. Freight shipments may be made by rail, air, truck, or water.

The transportation charges must be prepaid on shipments made by parcel post. The transportation charges on express and freight shipments may be prepaid by the shipper or may be paid by the customer upon receipt of the shipment. When transportation charges are prepaid by the shipper, they may or may not be added to the invoice, depending upon whether prices have been quoted FOB shipping point or FOB destination.

If shipment is made by freight, it is also necessary to determine the routing of the shipment. The buyer may specify how shipment should be made. When the buyer does not indicate any preference, the shipper must determine whether to make shipment by rail, truck, air, or water, and also frequently must make a choice of transportation companies to be used. Shipment to certain points may be made via a variety of different trucking companies, airlines, or railroads.

A retail merchant like MicroWorld would seldom incur transportation charges in connection with its sales. If any such charges are incurred, they may be charged to an operating expense account entitled Freight Out and entered in the cash payments journal.

(5) Billing. The last step in the handling of an order is billing or preparing the sales ticket or invoice. The sales ticket or invoice usually is prepared on a typewriter, billing machine, or computer-printer. Sales invoices should be numbered consecutively. By using some form of copying equipment, additional copies may be prepared. At least three copies usually are considered necessary. The original should go to the customer as an acknowledgement of the order; a copy should go to accounting personnel for data entry purposes; and a copy should be used as authority for packing and shipping the merchandise.

Additional copies of the sales ticket or invoice may also be used for the following purposes by larger organizations:

1. One copy may go to the salesperson in whose territory the sale is made.
2. One copy may go to a branch office, if the sale is made in a territory served by such an office.
3. One copy may serve as a label to be secured to the carton or package in which shipment is made. Usually this copy is perforated so that only that part containing the name and the address of the customer is used.

Sales Ticket

The source document of a sales transaction is called a sales ticket or sales invoice. Whether merchandise is sold for cash or on account, a sales ticket should be prepared. When the sale is for cash, the ticket may be printed by the cash register at the time that the sale is keyed in. However, some stores prefer to use individually prepared sales tickets whether the sale is for cash or on account. The same flexibility does not prevail in entering charge sales; instead, a sales ticket or charge slip must be prepared for every sale on account. Each salesperson may be provided with a separate pad of sales tickets. Each pad bears a different letter or number that identifies the clerk. The individual sales tickets are also numbered consecutively. This facilitates sorting the tickets by clerks if it is desired to compute the amount of goods sold by each clerk.

The following sales ticket shows the type of information usually obtained.

M MicroWorld   206B

1099 E. Louisiana
Indianapolis, IN 46202-3322

Account No. _____   Sold by _____   Date *4/10/--*

Sold to *James Rovel*

Address *429 S. Holiday Dr.*

City *South Bend* State *IN* Zip *46615-1928*

Send to *same*

Address _____

City _____ State _____ Zip _____

Recd. on Acct. ☐   Charge Sale ☐   Sales Ret./Allow. ☑

QUAN.	ARTICLES	AMOUNT
15	*Double-sided, double*	
	density diskette	63.00
	Tax	3.15
		66.15

James Rovel
CUSTOMER'S SIGNATURE

All claims & returned goods MUST be accompanied by this bill.

Sales Ticket

When merchandise is sold for cash in a state or a city which has a retail sales tax, the transaction results in an increase in the asset cash offset by an increase in sales revenue and an increase in the liability sales tax payable. Such transactions should be entered in a cash receipts journal by debiting Cash for the amount received and by crediting Sales for the sales price of the merchandise, excluding any sales tax, and crediting Sales Tax Payable for the amount of the tax collected. When merchandise is sold on account in such a state or city, the transaction results in an increase in the asset accounts receivable offset by an increase in sales revenue and an increase in the liability sales tax payable. Such transactions should be entered in a sales journal by debiting Accounts Receivable for the total amount charged to the customer and by crediting Sales for the amount of the sale and crediting Sales Tax Payable for the amount of the related tax. Both of the above-mentioned journals are discussed and illustrated later in this chapter.

An alternative procedure that is permissible under some sales tax laws is to credit the total of both the sales and the tax to the sales account in the first place. Periodically—usually at the end of each month—a calculation is made to determine how much of the balance of the sales account is presumed to be tax, and an entry is made to remove this amount from the sales account and transfer it to the sales tax payable account. Suppose, for example, that the tax rate is 5%, and that the sales account includes the tax collected or charged, along with the amount of the sales. In this event, 100/105 of the balance of the account is presumed to be the amount of the sales, and 5/105 of the balance is the amount of the tax. If the sales account had a balance of $10,500, the tax portion would be $500 (5/105 of $10,500). A debit to Sales and a credit to Sales Tax Payable of $500 would remove the tax from the sales account and transfer it to the sales tax payable account.

Discounts. Trade discounts allowed on sales are usually shown as deductions in arriving at the total of the sales ticket or invoice. Such discounts should not be entered in the accounts of the seller, as they represent merely a reduction in the selling price of the merchandise to avoid overly frequent publication of suppliers' catalogs.

Cash discounts offered should be indicated in the terms. Retail merchants seldom allow cash discounts to their customers but their suppliers commonly allow cash discounts to merchants as an inducement for prompt payment of sales invoices. Retail merchants usually make no effort to account for sales discounts separately.

Customer's Check. Assume that MLT Software collects the April 2 invoice of $824.40 on April 14. A copy of the invoice is removed from an "uncollected invoices" file, and a rubber stamp is used to imprint the notation "Received" and the date of collection "4/14/--" on the face of this copy. The check number and amount received are then entered on the proper lines as shown at the top of page 211. Note that the amount received is $807.91, the invoice amount of $824.40 less the 2% cash discount.

The check received from the customer is indorsed for deposit with another rubber stamp, as shown at the bottom of page 211, and deposited in the bank. The copy of the invoice then is placed in a "collected invoices" file in alphabetic order by customer's name.

Credit Memorandum

Merchandise may be returned by the customer for a credit or the customer may ask for an allowance representing a reduction in the price of the merchandise. If credit is given for merchandise returned or

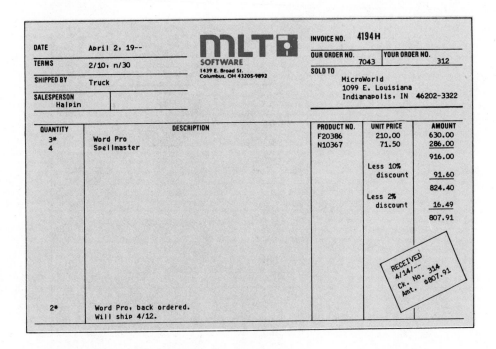

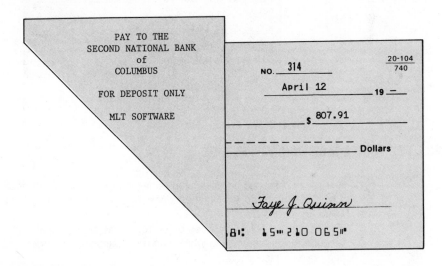

an allowance is made, it is customary to issue a credit memorandum for the amount involved. The following is a filled-in copy of a credit memorandum issued by MicroWorld, authorizing the return of one top-load disk cartridge by Harry Ewing, and granting credit for the price of the top-load disk cartridge and the sales tax.

CREDIT MEMORANDUM   72

H MicroWorld
1099 E. Louisiana
Indianapolis, IN 46202-3322

Date *April 28, 19--*
Name *Harry Ewing*
Address *2730 Bent Brook Dr.*
City *Indianapolis* State *IN* Zip *46250-1998*

Sales Number		OK		
Cash Refund	Mdse. Order	Charge ✓	Gift	Amount *102.90*

QUAN.	ARTICLES	AMOUNT	
1	*Top-load disk cartridge*	98	00
	Tax	4	90
		102	90

One hundred two 90/100 —— DOLLARS
REASON *Not needed*
REC'D. STOCK BY *Laura Murphy*
x *Harry Ewing*
CUSTOMER'S SIGNATURE

Credit Memorandum

BUILDING YOUR ACCOUNTING KNOWLEDGE

1. How is periodic income calculated under the accrual basis of accounting?
2. In what two ways does a bank accept copies of bank credit card sales invoices or tickets for deposit?
3. In what ways do layaway sales differ from sales on approval?
4. Describe the major ways in which financial institutions may get involved in installment sales transactions.
5. Briefly describe the nature of consignment sales.
6. What is the usual basis of measurement for a retail sales tax?
7. What five steps constitute the heart of a plan for proper handling of customer purchase orders?
8. If a sales ticket is prepared in triplicate, what distribution should be made of the copies?
9. What is done with the sales invoice at the time of its collection?
10. Under what circumstances is it customary for a seller of merchandise to issue a credit memorandum?

APPLYING ACCOUNTING CONCEPTS

Exercise 7-1. To simplify the determination of tax, Josie's Party Shoppe uses a sales tax table for calculating the amount of tax to be charged on sales. The rate is 5%. Using the section of a sales tax table presented below, determine the amount of tax that would be added to the price of each item sold and the total to be collected on each individual sale.

Amount of Sale	Amount of Tax
. . .	. . .
$1.10 to 1.29	.06
1.30 to 1.49	.07
1.50 to 1.69	.08
1.70 to 1.89	.09
1.90 to 2.09	.10
2.10 to 2.29	.11
2.30 to 2.49	.12
2.50 to 2.69	.13
2.70 to 2.89	.14
2.90 to 3.09	.15
. . .	. . .

Sale Number	Item	Price	Tax	Total
100	Card	$1.10	$	$
101	Candle	$2.25	$	$
102	Napkins	$2.95	$	$
103	Cup	$1.40	$	$
104	Pen	$1.99	$	$

Exercise 7-2. Morris Office Supply follows the practice of entering sales tax in the sales account. Periodically, the sales tax is determined and forwarded to the state government. The sales account has a balance of $5,465.40. The sales tax rate is 6%.

Determine **(a)** the amount of sales tax that was included in the sales account and **(b)** the price of the merchandise sold.

Exercise 7-3. Barbara McQuaid returned merchandise for a cash refund. The cost of the returned merchandise was $116.47, excluding the sales tax of 5%.

Determine the total amount that should be refunded to McQuaid.

Report No. 7-1

Refer to the study assignments and complete Report No. 7-1. After completing the report, continue with the textbook discussion until the next report is required.

ACCOUNTING PROCEDURES FOR SALES AND COLLECTIONS

In entering transactions concerned with sales of merchandise, it is desirable to keep the following accounts:

1. Sales
2. Sales Tax Payable
3. Sales Returns and Allowances

The following sections include a discussion of each of these accounts, an explanation and illustration of the computation of gross margin, and a discussion of the sales and cash receipts journals.

Sales Account

The sales account is a temporary owner's equity account in which the revenue resulting from sales of merchandise is entered. The account is credited for the selling price of all merchandise sold during the accounting period. If sales are for cash, the credit to Sales is offset by a debit to Cash; if the sales are on account, the debit is made to an asset account, Accounts Receivable.

Sales
Credit
to enter the selling price of merchandise sold.

Sales Tax Payable Account

Where sales tax is imposed on merchandise sold, it is advisable to keep an account for Sales Tax Payable. This is a liability account which is credited for the amount of tax collected or imposed on sales. The account should be debited for the amount of the tax paid to the proper taxing authority or adjustment of tax on merchandise returned by customers. A credit balance in the account at any time indicates the amount of the liability to the tax authority for taxes collected or imposed.

Sales tax accounting may be complicated by such factors as (1) sales returns and allowances and (2) exempt sales. As mentioned above, if the tax is entered at the time the sale is entered, it will be necessary to adjust for the tax when entering sales returns and allowances. If some sales are exempt from the tax, it will be necessary to distinguish

Sales Tax Payable

Debit	Credit
to enter payment of tax to the proper taxing authority or adjustment of tax on merchandise returned by customers.	to enter tax collected or imposed on sales.

between the taxable and the nontaxable sales. A common example of nontaxable sales is sales to out-of-state customers.

Sales Returns and Allowances Account

This account is a temporary owner's equity account in which sales returns and allowances are entered. The account is debited for the selling price (less sales tax) of any merchandise returned by customers or for any allowances made to customers that decrease the selling price of the merchandise sold. The offsetting credit is to Accounts Receivable if the goods are sold on account, or to Cash if a refund was made because the sale was originally for cash. Such allowances may be granted to customers for merchandise delivered in poor condition or for merchandise that does not meet specifications as to quality, weight, size, color, grade, or style.

Sales Returns and Allowances

Debit	
to enter returns and allowances.	

While sales returns and allowances can be debited directly to Sales, it is better to debit Sales Returns and Allowances. The accounts will then show both the amount of gross sales and the amount of returns and allowances. If returns and allowances are large in proportion to gross sales, a weakness in the merchandising operations is indicated; and the trouble should be determined and corrected.

As an example of accounting for sales returns and allowances, consider the credit memorandum illustrated on page 212 for $102.90 which was issued to Harry Ewing for one disk cartridge returned (sales price of merchandise, $98; tax, $4.90). In two-column journal form, the entry is as follows:

Sales Returns and Allowances	98.00	
Sales Tax Payable	4.90	
Accounts Receivable (Harry Ewing)		102.90

If a separate accounts receivable ledger is kept, the amount of $102.90 should also be posted to the credit of the individual account with Harry Ewing in that ledger. This procedure will be discussed further in a subsequent section.

Computation of Gross Margin

An important step in the determination of net income for a merchandising business is the calculation of what is called the gross margin. Gross margin (also known as gross profit) is the difference between net sales and cost of goods sold. Net sales is the total sales (1) less the sales price of any goods returned by customers (sales returns) and (2) less any reduction in price (sales allowances) given to customers. As explained in Chapter 6, cost of goods sold is determined by adding the amount of beginning inventory to the net purchases (purchases less purchases discounts, returns and allowances) and then subtracting the amount of ending inventory. To illustrate the calculation of the gross margin consider the following information:

Sales price of all goods sold and delivered to customers during the current period	$122,000
Sales price of goods returned by customers	8,000
Cost of merchandise (goods) on hand, beginning of period	18,000
Cost of merchandise purchased during the period	96,000
Cost of goods returned to the supplier or allowances made by the supplier (not ordered, damaged or soiled, etc.)	5,000
Cost of merchandise (goods) on hand, end of period	23,000

Based on this information, the gross margin for the period is calculated as follows:

Sales			$122,000
Less sales returns and allowances			8,000
Net sales			$114,000
Cost of goods sold:			
Merchandise inventory, beginning of period		$18,000	
Add purchases............................	$96,000		
Less purchases returns and allowances	5,000		
Net purchases		91,000	
Merchandise available for sale		$109,000	
Less merchandise inventory, end of period		23,000	86,000
Gross margin on sales			$ 28,000

Accounts Receivable

In order that the owner or manager of an enterprise may know the total amount due from charge customers at any time, it is advisable to keep a summary ledger account known as Accounts Receivable. At the beginning of the period, the debit balance of the account represents the total amount due from customers. During the period, the account is debited for the amount of any transactions involving increases and is credited for the amount of any transactions involving decreases in the amounts due from customers. At the end of the period, the debit balance of the account again represents the total amount due from charge customers.

It is also necessary to collect information on the transactions completed with each customer in order that knowledge of the amount due from each customer may be readily available at all times. The following methods of accounting for charge sales are widely used:

The Sales Ticket Method. This method is similar to the invoice method of accounting for purchases, discussed in Chapter 6, page 187. Under this method, it is customary to file the charge sales tickets systematically. All other related source documents representing transactions with customers should be filed with the appropriate sales tickets. Special filing equipment facilitates the use of this method. In some cases, a chronological record of the charge sales tickets is kept as a means of control.

The Ledger Account Method. This method is similar to the ledger account method of accounting for purchases, discussed in Chapter 6, pages 187-188. Under this method it is customary to keep a chronological record of the charge sales tickets. An individual ledger account with each customer is also kept. A separate ledger containing individual accounts with customers arranged in alphabetical order is called a subsidiary accounts receivable ledger. Special electronic equipment may be used in maintaining a permanent file of the charge sales tickets and other documents supporting the accounting records.

Under either of these methods of accounting for transactions with charge customers, it is necessary that a sales ticket or charge slip be prepared for each sale on account. In preparing a charge sales ticket the date, the name and address of the customer, the quantity, a description of the items sold, the unit prices, the total amount of the sale, and the amount of the sales tax should be entered.

Sales Journal

Transactions involving the sale of merchandise on account can be entered in an ordinary two-column journal. However, in merchandising businesses where many sales transactions are made on account, such transactions may be entered advantageously in a special journal. A journal designed for entering only sales on account is called a sales journal. If the business is operated in an area where no sales taxes are imposed, all sales on account can be entered in a sales journal with only one amount column as shown.

	DATE	SALE NO.	TO WHOM SOLD	POST. REF.	AMOUNT	
SALES JOURNAL					PAGE	
1						1
2						2
3						3
4						4
5						5

Sales Journal Without Sales Tax

If the business is operated in an area where sales taxes are imposed, a sales journal with three amount columns, such as the following illustration, is more appropriate. Often, such a journal has both account titles and account numbers in the column headings, or just account numbers as headings. In computer-based accounting systems, account numbers virtually displace account names, except for statement purposes.

	DATE	SALE NO.	TO WHOM SOLD	POST REF.	ACCOUNTS RECEIVABLE DR.	SALES CR.	SALES TAX PAYABLE CR.	
	SALES JOURNAL						PAGE 6	
1	1986 Apr 4	133C	Miguel Lopez	✓	1596 00	1520 00	76 00	1
2	10	134C	Linda Maier	✓	472 50	450 00	22 50	2
3	18	105D	Emily Westcott	✓	1044 75	995 00	49 75	3
4	21	202B	Susan Chen	✓	637 35	607 00	30 35	4
5	24	162A	Amanda Phelps	✓	39 69	37 80	1 89	5
6	28	243C	Helen Armstrong	✓	1333 19	1269 70	63 49	6
7	30	204B	Peter Underwood	✓	302 61	288 20	14 41	7
8					5426 09	5167 70	258 39	8
9					(131)	(411)	(221)	9
10								10
11								11
12								12

Sales Journal With Sales Tax

The transactions entered in the journal were completed by MicroWorld, retail merchant, during the month of April. The store is located in a state that imposes a tax of 5% on the retail sale of all merchandise whether sold for cash or on account.

Note that the following information regarding each charge sales ticket is entered in the sales journal:

1. Date
2. Number of the sales ticket and salesclerk code
3. To whom sold (the customer)
4. Amount charged to customer
5. Amount of sale
6. Amount of sales tax

With this form of sales journal, each transaction can be entered on one horizontal line. The sales ticket should provide all the information needed in entering each charge sale.

If an individual ledger account is not kept with each customer, the charge sales tickets should be filed by customer's name after they have been entered in the sales journal. There are numerous types of devices on the market that are designed to facilitate the filing of charge sales tickets by customer name. Such devices are designed to save time, to promote accuracy, and to provide a safe means of keeping track of the transactions with each charge customer. If an individual ledger account is kept with each customer, the sales tickets normally are used to post the customer accounts. They should then be properly filed.

When a customer makes a partial payment on an account, the amount of the payment should be noted on the most recent charge sales ticket and the new balance should be indicated. Sales tickets paid in full should be receipted and may either be given to the customer or be transferred to another file for future reference. If a customer is given credit for merchandise returned or given an allowance, a notation of the amount of credit should be made on the charge sales ticket to which the credit relates and the new balance indicated on the most recent charge sales ticket. If a credit memorandum is issued to a customer, it should be prepared in duplicate and the copy should be attached to the sales ticket on which the amount is noted.

Posting from the Sales Journal

At the end of the month, the amount columns of the sales journal are footed in small figures. The sum of the totals of the credit columns should be equal to the total of the debit column. The totals are then entered in full-size figures and the ruling completed as illustrated on page 218. The totals should be posted to the general ledger accounts indicated in the column headings. This summary posting should be completed in the following order:

1. Post the total of the Accounts Receivable Dr. column to the debit of Accounts Receivable.
2. Post the total of the Sales Cr. column to the credit of Sales.
3. Post the total of the Sales Tax Payable Cr. column to the credit of Sales Tax Payable.

A proper cross-reference should be provided by entering the page of the sales journal preceded by the initial "S" in the Posting Reference column of the ledger and by entering the account number immediately below the column total of the sales journal. The proper method of completing the summary posting from the MicroWorld sales journal on April 30 is shown in the following accounts affected:

ACCOUNT	Accounts Receivable					ACCOUNT NO.	131	
DATE	ITEM	POST. REF.	DEBIT	CREDIT	BALANCE			
					DEBIT		CREDIT	
1986 Apr 30		S6	5426 09		5426 09			

ACCOUNT	Sales Tax Payable					ACCOUNT NO.	221	
DATE	ITEM	POST. REF.	DEBIT	CREDIT	BALANCE			
					DEBIT		CREDIT	
1986 Apr 30		S6		258 39			258 39	

ACCOUNT	Sales					ACCOUNT NO.	411	
DATE	ITEM	POST. REF.	DEBIT	CREDIT	BALANCE			
					DEBIT		CREDIT	
1986 Apr 30		S6		5167 70			5167 70	

General Ledger Accounts After Posting from Sales Journal

The Sales Ticket Method. Under the sales ticket method of accounting for sales on account, individual posting from the sales journal is not required. When this plan is followed, it is customary to place a check mark in the Posting Reference column of the sales journal at the time of entering each sale.

The Ledger Account Method. If an individual ledger account is kept for each customer, all transactions representing either increases or decreases in the amount due from each customer should be posted individually to the proper account. The posting, usually done with electronic equipment, is completed directly from the charge sales tickets and other documents. As the individual customer accounts are posted, a check mark ($\sqrt{}$) is placed in the Posting Reference column of the sales journal. The ledger account method of accounting for accounts receivable will be explained in detail in Chapter 8.

A flowchart of the major documents and procedures commonly used in the sales function was presented earlier in the chapter. That flowchart can now be updated to include the additional accounting procedures as follows:

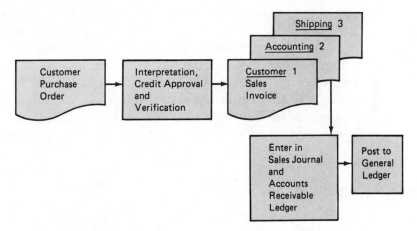

Schedule of Accounts Receivable

A list of customers showing the amount due from each as of a specified date is known as a schedule of accounts receivable. It is usually advisable to prepare such a schedule at the end of each month. An example for MicroWorld as of April 30, 1986, is shown on page 222.

This schedule can be prepared easily from the list of customer accounts in the accounts receivable subsidiary ledger or by going through the sales ticket file and listing the names of the customers and the amount due from each. If the total does not agree with the balance of the summary accounts receivable account, the error may be in the subsidiary ledger, the file, or the ledger account. The subsidiary ledger could be in error because of an error in posting. The file may be

MicroWorld
Schedule of Accounts Receivable
April 30, 1986

Helen Armstrong	400 00
Mona Gibson	474 90
Linda Maier	31 22
Nathaniel Moore	1654 50
Jason Quimby	329 75
Anthony St. James	257 30
Andrea Scott	63 39
	3211 06

MicroWorld—Schedule of Accounts Receivable

incorrect in that either one or more sales tickets on which collection has been made have not been removed or one or more uncollected ones are missing. Another possibility is that a memorandum of a partial collection was overlooked in preparing the list. The accounts receivable account could be incorrect because of an error in posting or because of an error in a journal from which the totals were posted. In any event, the postings, journals, and sales tickets must be reviewed until the reason for the discrepancy is found so that the necessary correction can be made.

Cash Receipts Journal

Just as sales transactions occur frequently in many enterprises, it follows that subsequent collection of customers' accounts, cash and bank credit card sales, and other receipts of the business will cause cash receipt transactions also to occur frequently. Such transactions may be entered advantageously in a special journal. A journal designed for entering all cash receipts is called a **cash receipts journal**. The illustration on page 223 shows a cash receipts journal.

Note that every entry in the cash receipts journal includes the following information:

1. Date of the cash receipt
2. Name of the customer or other account credited
3. Amount of the cash receipt, entered in the Cash Dr. column.

The following aspects of cash receipt entry procedures should be noted:

		CASH RECEIPTS JOURNAL						PAGE 7	
	DATE	ACCOUNT CREDITED	POST. REF.	GENERAL CR.	ACCOUNTS RECEIV. CR.	SALES CR.	SALES TAX PAY. CR.	CASH DR.	
1	1986 April 3	Amanda Phelps	✓		4079			4079	1
2	7	Mona Gibson	✓		12760			12760	2
3	14	Owen Newell	✓		42000			42000	3
4	18	Andrea Scott	✓		31060			31060	4
5	25	Miguel Lopez	✓		131604			131604	5
6	30	Cash & bank cr card sales	✓			261492	130575	274206 7	6
7					221503	261492	130575	296357 0	7
8					(131)	(411)	(221)	(111)	8
9									9

Cash Receipts Journal

1. Cash and bank credit card sales—"Cash and bank credit card sales" is entered in the Account Credited column, the total amount of such sales is entered in the Sales Cr. column, and the total amount of the sales tax is entered in the Sales Tax Payable Cr. column.

2. Collection from customer—name of customer is entered in the Account Credited column and the credit amount is entered in the Accounts Receivable Cr. column. The check mark (√) entered in the Post. Ref. column will be discussed in Chapter 8.

3. Receipt of revenue—name of revenue account is entered in the Account Credited column and the credit amount is entered in the General Cr. column.

Posting from the Cash Receipts Journal

Each amount in the General Cr. column of the cash receipts journal is posted individually to the ledger account named in the Account Credited column. The notation "CR 7" is entered in the Post. Ref. column of the affected ledger account at the time that the item is posted, and the appropriate account number is entered in the Post. Ref. column of the cash receipts journal.

At the end of the month, the five amount columns of the cash receipts journal are totaled and the ruling completed as illustrated. The summary posting involves posting the total of the Accounts Receivable Cr. column as a credit to Account No. 131, the total of the Sales Cr. column as a credit to Account No. 411, the total of the Sales Tax Payable Cr. column as a credit to Account No. 221, and the total of the Cash Dr. column as a debit to Account No. 111.

As each total is posted, the notation "CR 7" is entered in the Post. Ref. column of the affected ledger account, and the number of that account is entered in parentheses below the appropriate column total in the cash receipts journal. A check mark ($\sqrt{}$) is entered in parentheses below the total of the General Cr. column to indicate that its total is not posted to the ledger.

The summary posting from MicroWorld's cash receipts journal to the ledger accounts on April 30 is as follows:

ACCOUNT **Accounts Receivable**   ACCOUNT NO. 131

DATE	ITEM	POST. REF.	DEBIT	CREDIT	BALANCE DEBIT	BALANCE CREDIT
1986 Apr. 30		S6	542609		542609	
30		CR7		221503	321106	

ACCOUNT **Sales Tax Payable**   ACCOUNT NO. 221

DATE	ITEM	POST. REF.	DEBIT	CREDIT	BALANCE DEBIT	BALANCE CREDIT
1986 Apr. 30		S6		25839		25839
30		CR7		130575		156414

ACCOUNT **Sales**   ACCOUNT NO. 411

DATE	ITEM	POST. REF.	DEBIT	CREDIT	BALANCE DEBIT	BALANCE CREDIT
1986 Apr. 30		S6		516770		516770
30		CR7		2611492		3128262

ACCOUNT **Cash**   ACCOUNT NO. 111

DATE	ITEM	POST. REF.	DEBIT	CREDIT	BALANCE DEBIT	BALANCE CREDIT
1986 Apr. 1	Balance	$\sqrt{}$			5000000	
30		CP12		2539980	2460020	
30		CR7	2963570		5423590	

BUILDING YOUR ACCOUNTING KNOWLEDGE

1. Describe how each of the following accounts is used:
   (1) Sales   (2) Sales Tax Payable   (3) Sales Returns and Allowances
2. The gross margin is the difference between what two dollar amounts?

3. Describe the sales ticket method of keeping records of the transactions completed with individual customers.

4. Describe the ledger account method of keeping records of the transactions completed with individual customers.

5. List six items of information about each sale normally entered in the sales journal.

6. In what order should the summary posting from the sales journal to the general ledger be completed?

7. If the schedule of accounts receivable does not agree in total with the balance of the summary accounts receivable account, what major error possibilities exist?

8. List three items of information about each cash receipt normally entered in the cash receipts journal.

9. List three kinds of transactions requiring varying entry procedures in the cash receipts journal.

10. In what journal does MicroWorld enter cash and bank credit card sales.

APPLYING ACCOUNTING CONCEPTS

Exercise 7-4. The following information is from the accounting records of the All Seasons Garden Center.

Sales price of all goods sold and delivered to customers during the current period	$732,000
Sales price of goods returned by customers	48,000
Cost of merchandise (goods) on hand, beginning of the period	108,000
Cost of merchandise purchased during the period	576,000
Cost of goods returned to the supplier or allowances made by the supplier	3,000
Cost of merchandise (goods) on hand, end of current period	138,000

Based on this data, determine the gross margin on sales. Show the calculation using the form illustrated in the chapter.

Exercise 7-5. Janice Drewry Decorations complete the following transactions related to sales of merchandise on account. Sales tax of 5% was included in the amount of each sale.

Mar. 2 Sold wallpaper supplies to Besson Homes, $65.95, terms, n/30. Sale No. 255.

12 Sold paint to Roy Allison, $75, terms, n/30. Sale No. 256.

23 Sold miniblinds to Clydette Collins, $114.83, terms, n/30. Sale No. 257.

24 Sold decorator items to Maureen Caplen, $25.34, terms, n/30. Sale No. 258.

25 Sold paint to Angeline Grasselli, $14.57, terms, n/30. Sale No. 259.

(a) Prepare a sales journal using the same format and account titles as illustrated in the chapter. Enter the above transactions in the sales journal. **(b)** Total and rule the journal.

Exercise 7-6. **(a)** Prepare a cash receipts journal using the same format and account titles as illustrated in the chapter. Enter the receipts from the sales amounts from Exercise 7-5 in the cash receipts journal. Assume that amounts were received 30 days after the date of sale. **(b)** Enter the following transaction:

Apr. 28 Deposited cash and bank credit card sales, $1,532.87 (includes sales tax).

(c) Total and rule the journal.

Report No. 7-2

Refer to the study assignments and complete Report No. 7-2. After completing the report, you may proceed with the textbook discussion in Chapter 8 until the next report is required.

EXPANDING YOUR BUSINESS VOCABULARY

What is the meaning of each of the following terms?

Accounts Receivable **(p. 217)**
bank credit card sales **(p. 202)**
cash receipts journal **(p. 222)**
cash sales **(p. 200)**
COD sales **(p. 203)**
consignee **(p. 205)**
consignment sale **(p. 205)**
consignor **(p. 205)**
cost of goods sold **(p. 216)**
credit cards/charge plates **(p. 201)**
credit memorandum **(p. 211)**
gross margin/gross profit **(p. 216)**
Installment Accounts Receivable **(p. 204)**
installment sales **(p. 204)**

layaway ledger **(p. 204)**
layaway sales **(p. 203)**
net sales **(p. 216)**
realized revenue **(p. 199)**
retail sales tax **(p. 205)**
sales allowances **(p. 216)**
sales journal **(p. 218)**
sales on account **(p. 201)**
sales on approval **(p. 203)**
sales returns **(p. 216)**
sales ticket/sales invoice **(p. 208)**
schedule of accounts receivable **(p. 221)**
subsidiary accounts receivable ledger **(p. 217)**

CHAPTER 8

Accrual Accounting Applied to a Small Retail Business

CHAPTER OBJECTIVES

Careful study of this chapter should enable you to:

- Adapt accrual accounting and the data processing phases of the accounting cycle to a small retail business.

- Explain the application of accounting principles in accounting for:
  1. Uncollectible accounts.
  2. Prepaid expenses.
  3. Depreciation.
- Describe the accounts receivable and accounts payable control accounts in the general ledger, and the three-column account form of their related subsidiary ledgers.

- Explain and prepare a charge customer's statement of account.

A business enterprise that purchases and sells goods on account, maintains a stock of merchandise, and has property, plant or equipment must account for periodic income or loss on the accrual basis. This is necessary to measure the success of the business and to comply with federal and state income tax laws. Several features of accrual accounting were introduced in the preceding chapters. A more detailed consideration of these procedures and the introduction of other major practices that constitute accrual accounting will be presented here and in the two following chapters.

Note that the accrual basis of accounting recognizes revenue in the accounting period in which it is earned, *whether or not* cash has been received, and recognizes expense in the accounting period in which it is incurred, *whether or not* cash has been paid. The cash basis of accounting, on the other hand, recognizes revenue *only* when it is received in cash, and recognizes expense *only* when it is paid in cash.

As an aid in applying the principles and procedures involved in keeping the accounts of a merchandising business on the accrual basis, a system of accounts for the retail computer business called MicroWorld, owned and operated by Faye J. Quinn, will be described. While specific problems may arise in keeping the accounts of a particular enterprise, it should be recognized that most of the principles and procedures discussed and illustrated for MicroWorld are equally applicable to many other types of business.

PRINCIPLES AND PROCEDURES

The discussion will continue to be a blend of accounting principles and practices. It is important to keep in mind that the principles relate to goals and objectives while practices are designed to attain these goals and objectives. Procedures such as double entry and the use of source documents, journals, and ledger accounts are employed to make the processing of accounting data complete, orderly, and as error-free as possible. While most accounting principles are broad enough to allow considerable flexibility, it is in the area of practices that wide latitude is found. Within limits, the records for each business can be styled to meet the particular requirements of the management.

Accrual Accounting

In the opening pages of Chapters 6 and 7, brief mention was made of the accrual basis of accounting which consists of recognizing revenue in the period in which it is earned and recognizing expenses in the period in which they are incurred. The receipt or payment of cash in the same period may or may not be involved. Revenue generally is recognized when services are performed or goods are provided, and is considered to be earned when, in exchange for something of value, money is received or a legal claim to money comes into existence. To a merchant, this normally means the time when the customer buys goods and either pays or agrees to pay for them. In terms of changes in the accounting elements, revenue arises or accrues when an increase in cash or a receivable causes an increase in owner's equity, except in cases where the increase is due to an investment of assets in the business by the owner. In comparable terms, expense accrues or is incurred when either a reduction of an asset (asset outflow) or an increase in a liability causes the owner's equity to be reduced, except in cases where the owner's withdrawal of assets reduces the owner's equity. Expenses should be recognized when goods or services are consumed.

The accrual basis of accounting is widely used by enterprises because it involves the period-by-period matching of revenue with the expenses that caused or aided in producing that revenue. The revenue from sales, for example, must be matched against the cost of the goods sold and the various other expenses that were incurred in earning the revenue. A simple matching of cash received from customers during a period with the cash paid for goods purchased in that period would be almost meaningless in most cases. The collections might relate to sales of a prior period and the payments to purchases of the current period, or vice versa. The expense related to most property, plant or equipment does not arise when such assets are acquired. The expense occurs as these assets' usefulness is gradually exhausted. In computing net income for a specified period, the accrual basis recognizes changes in many types of assets and liabilities—not just changes in the cash account.

In processing business data, accountants must think in terms of time intervals, and must be sure that revenue and expense are accounted for in the proper accounting period. Certain types of revenue and expense do not have to be recognized at the precise moment this revenue or expense arises. For example, the wages of an employee literally accrue minute by minute during each working day but no entry is made of the expense until it is paid at the end of the period. If the employee is not paid by the end of the period, the accountant should enter the payroll expense and the liability that has accrued up to that time. There may be a lag in entering revenue and expense within the accounting period, but steps must be taken at the end of the period to enter all revenue earned and expenses incurred. These steps consist of making what are called end-of-period adjustments in the accounts. It should be mentioned, however, that adjustments normally are not made for trivial amounts. The practice of ignoring matters that are too small to make any significant difference is an application of the practice of materiality. Just how small is "too small" is a question that requires judgment on the part of the accountant. Usually, the judgment is based on the *percentage* which the amount of an item is in relation to the total of similarly classified amounts, rather than on the absolute dollar amount of the item.

Accounting for Uncollectible Accounts Receivable

Businesses that sell goods or services on account realize that from time to time some of the customers do not pay all that they owe. The amounts that cannot be collected from charge customers are called uncollectible accounts expense, bad debts expense or loss from uncollectible accounts. The amount of such expense depends to a large degree upon the credit policy of the business. The seller should seek to avoid the two extremes of either having such a liberal credit policy that uncollectible accounts become excessive or having such a tight credit policy that uncollectible accounts are minimized at the sacrifice of a larger volume of sales and greater net income.

One method of accounting for uncollectible accounts receivable is to recognize the related expense only when a customer's account actually becomes uncollectible, by a debit to Uncollectible Accounts Expense and a credit to Accounts Receivable. A better accounting method is to estimate the amount of uncollectible account losses that will eventually result from the sales of a period and to treat the estimated amount of expected losses as an expense of that same period. This treatment will result in better periodic matching of revenue and expense. In this case, the procedure is to use a contra account entitled Allowance for Doubtful Accounts or Allowance for Bad Debts. The allowance for doubtful accounts is contra to the accounts receivable account, which means its balance will be deducted from the total of the accounts receivable on the balance sheet. Any account having a balance which is intended to be deducted from another related account balance for financial statement purposes is known as a contra account.

Two approaches are commonly used to estimate the allowance for doubtful accounts. With the first approach, at the end of the accounting period, an estimate of uncollectible accounts is made based on a percentage of the sales on account for that period. The adjusting entry is made by debiting Uncollectible Accounts Expense and crediting Allowance for Doubtful Accounts. Any balance already existing in the allowance account is ignored in determining the amount of this entry. To illustrate, assume that in view of past experience it is expected that there will be a loss due to uncollectible accounts of an amount equal to one half of one percent of the sales on account during the year. If the sales on account amounted to $200,000, the estimated uncollectible account losses would be $1,000 ($200,000 × .005), which should be entered as follows:

```
Dec. 31 Uncollectible Accounts Expense ................... 1,000
        Allowance for Doubtful Accounts.................          1,000
        Uncollectible accounts expense provision for the
        year.
```

Accountants who prefer this approach to estimating the allowance argue that it provides a better matching of the uncollectible accounts expense with the related sales revenue.

The second approach to estimating the end-of-period adjustment for uncollectible accounts involves aging the receivables. A detailed analysis is made of the receivables to see what proportions are for recent charges—those that are less than a month old, 30-60 days old, 61-90 days old, etc. Then, guided by past experience, estimates are made of the probable amounts that are likely to be uncollectible for each of the age groups. Generally, the longer a charge has been in the system, the less likely it is that it will ever be collected. The estimates are totaled to determine the appropriate end-of-period (credit) balance in the allowance for doubtful accounts. An adjustment is made to give the allowance account the indicated balance. Note that in contrast to the first approach to estimating the allowance, with this approach any balance already existing in the allowance account should be considered in determining the amount of the entry.

Three possible conditions may be encountered in the allowance for doubtful accounts account:

1. This account may have an existing credit balance.
2. This account may have an existing debit balance.
3. This account may have no balance.

To illustrate Condition (1), assume that after aging the accounts it is estimated that $1,000 will not be collected. Assume also that the allowance account has an existing credit balance of $100. It would appear, in T account form, as follows:

Allowance for Doubtful Accounts

	Bal.	100

The adjusting entry under the aging approach must be for the amount of $900 to bring the allowance account to the desired credit balance. The entry would be as follows:

Dec. 31 Uncollectible Accounts Expense   900
       Allowance for Doubtful Accounts.................   900
       To adjust accounts receivable for uncollectible
       accounts.

After posting the $900 adjusting entry, the two accounts involved will appear, in T account form, as follows:

Uncollectible Accounts Expense	Allowance for Doubtful Accounts
Dec. 31 900	Bal. 100 Dec. 31 900 1,000

To illustrate Condition (2), assume the same $1,000 estimate of uncollectible accounts, but that a $100 debit balance exists in the allowance account as follows:

Allowance for Doubtful Accounts	
Bal. 100	

The adjusting entry must be for the amount of $1,100 to bring the allowance account to the desired credit balance. The entry would be as follows:

```
Dec. 31  Uncollectible Accounts Expense ................... 1,100
             Allowance for Doubtful Accounts. ................         1,100
                 To adjust accounts receivable for uncollectible
                 accounts.
```

After posting the $1,100 adjusting entry, the two accounts involved will appear, in T account form, as follows:

Uncollectible Accounts Expense	Allowance for Doubtful Accounts
Dec. 31 1,100	Bal. 100 | Dec. 31 1,100 1,000

To illustrate Condition (3), assume the same $1,000 estimate of uncollectible accounts, but that *no* balance exists in the allowance account. The adjusting entry would be as follows:

```
Dec. 31  Uncollectible Accounts Expense ................... 1,000
             Allowance for Doubtful Accounts. ................         1,000
                 To adjust accounts receivable for uncollectible
                 accounts.
```

After posting the $1,000 adjusting entry, the two accounts involved will appear in T account form, as follows:

Uncollectible Accounts Expense	Allowance for Doubtful Accounts
Dec. 31 1,000	Dec. 31 1,000

Usually the dollar amount of the estimate of uncollectible accounts arrived at by aging the receivables differs from that arrived at as a percentage of sales on account. However, the amount of the difference is likely to be immaterial. Accountants who prefer the aging approach to estimating the allowance argue that it provides a realistic estimate of the net realizable value (realizable cash value) of the receivables.

Under either approach to estimating the allowance, the amount of the debit balance in the uncollectible accounts expense account is reported in the income statement as an operating expense. The amount of the credit balance in the allowance for doubtful accounts is reported in the balance sheet as a deduction from the receivables, as follows:

```
Accounts receivable..................... $60,000
Less allowance for doubtful accounts ....   1,000 $59,000
```

It should be apparent that the credit part of the adjusting entry cannot be made directly to a specific receivable account because, at the time the entry is made, there is no way of knowing exactly which debtors will not pay. Experience gives virtual assurance that some of the amounts due from customers will be uncollectible but only time will reveal which ones.

When it is determined that a certain account will not be collected, an entry should be made to write off the account and to charge the loss against the allowance. For example, on April 24 of the next year, it is determined that $85 owed by K. W. Chaplin cannot be collected due to either death or bankruptcy. Whatever the circumstance, if it is fairly certain that the amount can never be collected, the following journal entry should be made:

```
Apr. 24  Allowance for Doubtful Accounts...................    85
         Accounts Receivable .............................          85
         To write off account of K. W. Chaplin found to be
         uncollectible.
```

Accounting for Prepaid Expenses

The term prepaid expense is used to describe an item that was purchased and considered to be an asset when acquired, but which will be consumed or used up in the near future and thus become an expense. Supplies of various sorts and prepaid (unexpired) insurance are good examples. At the end of the period, the portions of such assets that have expired or have been consumed must be determined and entries made debiting the proper expense accounts and crediting the proper prepaid expense accounts. For example, a company purchased office supplies for $850 and a three-year fire insurance policy for $390. The entry would appear as follows:

```
Office Supplies............................................   850
Prepaid Insurance.........................................   390
   Cash ...................................................          1,240
      To enter the purchase of office supplies and insurance.
```

If at the end of the accounting period a physical count indicated that there were $150 of office supplies on hand, it can be determined that $700 ($850-$150) of supplies would have been used. The following adjusting entry should be made:

```
Office Supplies Expense ...................................   700
   Office Supplies.........................................          700
      To enter office supplies used.
```

If the insurance policy had been in effect since the beginning of the fiscal year, $130 ($390 ÷ 3 years) of the prepaid insurance would have been consumed during the year. The following adjusting journal entry should be made:

```
Insurance Expense ........................................   130
   Prepaid Insurance.......................................          130
      To enter insurance expired for the year.
```

The chart of accounts for MicroWorld includes two prepaid expense accounts: Supplies, Account No. 151, and Prepaid Insurance, Account No. 155. These accounts are classified as assets in the chart of accounts. The supplies account is debited for the cost of supplies purchased. At the end of the year, the account should be credited for the cost of supplies used during the year with an offsetting debit to Supplies Expense, Account No. 545. The prepaid insurance account is debited for the cost of the insurance purchased during the year. At the end of the year, the account is credited for the portion of the cost that relates to the year then ending with an offsetting debit to Insurance Expense, Account No. 548.

Accounting for Depreciation

Depreciation accounting is the process of allocating the cost of plant and equipment to the periods expected to benefit from the use of these assets. Most of such assets eventually become useless to the business because they either wear out or become inadequate or obsolete. Sometimes all of these causes combine to make the assets valueless except, perhaps, for some small salvage value as scrap or junk.

Generally, in computing depreciation, no consideration is given to what these assets might bring if they were to be sold. Assets of this type are acquired to be used and not to be sold. During their useful lives any current resale value is of no consequence unless the business is about to cease. For a going business, the idea is to allocate the net cost of an asset over the years that it is expected to serve. Net cost means original cost less estimated scrap or salvage value. Usually, there is no way of knowing just how long an asset will serve the business. It is therefore apparent that depreciation expense can be no more than an estimate. However, with past experience as a guide, the estimates can be reasonably reliable.

There are several ways of calculating the periodic depreciation write-off. In the traditional straight-line method, the net cost (original cost less any expected scrap value) of an asset is divided by the number of years that the asset is expected to serve, to arrive at the amount of depreciation expense each year. Because the estimated scrap or salvage value is typically quite small, it is often ignored and the entire original cost of the asset is allocated. Thus, it is common practice to express depreciation as a percentage of the original cost of the asset. For example, in the case of an asset with a 10-year life, 10% of the original cost should be written off each year.

100% ÷ 10 years = 10% per year.

If it has a 20-year life, 5 % should be written off.

100% ÷ 20 years = 5% per year.

In 1954, the Internal Revenue Code was revised to permit taxpayers to use depreciation methods that involve larger depreciation charges in the earlier years of the life of an asset in calculating net income subject to tax. In 1981, the Internal Revenue Code was again revised to permit the use of artificially determined shorter lives for specific classes of assets in calculating taxable income. These methods primarily are useful only in the case of new assets. Except for the first year of asset life under 1981 law, these reducing-charge methods permit larger write-offs in the early years and smaller write-offs in succeeding years. Nevertheless, the straight-line method has been very popular for many years. One of its virtues is simplicity. The straight-line method of accounting for depreciation is used by MicroWorld.

Depreciation expense is handled by an end-of-period adjusting entry that involves debiting one or more depreciation expense accounts and crediting one or more accumulated depreciation accounts. For example, assume that a company purchased a lawn tractor for $3,500 at the beginning of the year, and estimates that it has a useful life of 5 years with no salvage value. The annual depreciation of the lawn tractor under the straight-line method of depreciation would be $700 ($3,500 ÷ 5 years). The entry upon purchase of the equipment would be:

```
Equipment—Tractor.........................................  3,500
   Cash ..................................................          3,500
      To enter purchase of equipment.
```

The adjusting entry for the depreciation at the end of the year would be:

```
Depreciation Expense .......................................   700
   Accumulated Depreciation—Equipment.....................          700
      To enter annual depreciation of equipment.
```

The accumulated depreciation account is a contra account—which means that its balance will be deducted from the related asset that is being depreciated. In theory, there would be no objection to making the credits directly to the asset accounts themselves in the same way that the asset accounts for prepaid expenses are credited to enter their decreases. However, in order that the original cost of the assets will be clearly revealed, portions of the cost written off are credited to the contra accounts. The amounts of the credit balances of the contra accounts are reported in the balance sheet as deductions from the costs of the assets to which they relate.

```
Equipment..............................  $3,500
Less accumulated depreciation ..........     700   $2,800
```

The credit balances in the accumulated depreciation accounts increase year by year. When these amounts are equal to the net cost of the related assets, no more depreciation may be taken.

The similarities and differences between the allowance for doubtful accounts and the accumulated depreciation account should be recognized. Both contra asset accounts are credited by adjusting entries at the end of the period. In both cases, the offsetting debits go to expense accounts. In both cases, the balances in the contra accounts are shown in the balance sheet as subtractions from the amounts of the assets to which they relate. However, Allowance for Doubtful Accounts is decreased or debited whenever an uncollectible account materializes and it is necessary to write off the account. The credit balance of the allowance for doubtful accounts does not continually increase. If it does, this indicates that the estimate of uncollectible account losses has been excessive. In contrast, the credit balances of the accumulated depreciation accounts get larger year by year. The credit balances remain in these accounts for as long as the assets to which they relate are kept in service.

Note also that the purposes of the two contra accounts are not the same. When the balance of the allowance for doubtful accounts is subtracted from the balance of the accounts receivable account, the result is an estimate of how much will be collected from customers—the net realizable value of the receivables. However, when the balance of the accumulated depreciation account is subtracted from the balance of the related asset account, the result is the cost not yet charged to depreciation expense, and will represent the current value of the asset only by sheer coincidence.

Since MicroWorld has only store equipment that is subject to depreciation, there is only one contra account, Accumulated Depreciation—Store Equipment, Account No. 181.1. Depreciation expense is debited to an account so named, Account No. 547.

Accounts with Suppliers and Customers

When the character of the enterprise and the volume of business are such that it is necessary to keep relatively few accounts, it may be satisfactory to keep all of the accounts together in a single general ledger, which may be bound, loose-leaf, a set of cards, or a set of magnetic disks in a computer-based accounting system. As explained in Chapters 6 and 7, records of the amounts due to suppliers for purchases on account and the amounts due from customers for sales on account may be kept without maintaining a separate ledger account for each supplier and for each customer. A file of unpaid suppliers' invoices and another of sales tickets for sales on account may suffice. However, many merchants prefer to keep a separate ledger account for each supplier and for each customer.

Subsidiary Ledgers. When the volume of business and the number of transactions warrant, it may be advisable to subdivide the ledger. In this case, it usually is considered advisable to segregate the accounts with customers and the accounts with suppliers from the other accounts and keep them in separate ledgers called subsidiary ledgers. Separate ledgers containing individual accounts with customers and suppliers are known as accounts receivable subsidiary ledgers and accounts payable subsidiary ledgers, respectively.

Three-Column Account Form. A special account form known as the three-column account form is widely used in keeping the individual accounts with customers and suppliers. While the standard account form shown in the illustration on page 28, or the four-column form illustrated on page 123, may be used, the three-column account form as shown is in frequent use for such accounts. Note that three parallel amount columns are provided for entering debits, credits, and balances. The nature of the account determines whether its normal balance is a debit or a credit. Accounts with customers usually have debit balances; accounts with suppliers usually have credit balances. After each entry, the new balance should be determined and entered in the Balance column.

NAME				ACCOUNT NO.	
ADDRESS					
DATE	ITEM	POST. REF.	DEBIT	CREDIT	BALANCE

Three-Column Account Form

Control Accounts. When subsidiary ledgers are kept for suppliers and for customers, it is customary to keep control accounts for the subsidiary ledgers in the general ledger. Thus, accounts with suppliers are kept in a subsidiary accounts payable ledger, and the control account, Accounts Payable, is kept in the general ledger. Accounts with customers are kept in a subsidiary accounts receivable ledger, and the control account, Accounts Receivable, is kept in the general ledger. The use of control accounts in the general ledger makes it possible to take a trial balance of the general ledger accounts without referring to the subsidiary ledgers.

Accounts Payable Control. A general ledger account, called Accounts Payable—Control, provides a summary of the information entered in the individual accounts with suppliers kept in the subsidiary accounts payable ledger. Transactions affecting suppliers' accounts are posted separately to the individual accounts in the subsidiary ledger. These transactions either are also posted separately, or are summarized periodically and the totals posted, to the control account in the general ledger. As indicated in Chapter 6, the balance of the accounts payable control account may be proved by preparing a schedule of accounts payable.

Accounts with suppliers normally have credit balances. If a supplier's account has a debit balance, the balance may be bracketed or the term "Dr." entered next to the figure in the Balance column. In preparing the schedule of accounts payable, the total of the accounts with debit balances should be deducted from the total of the accounts with credit balances, and the difference should agree with the balance of the accounts payable control account.

Accounts Receivable Control. A general ledger account, called Accounts Receivable—Control, provides a summary of the information entered in the individual accounts with customers kept in the subsidiary accounts receivable ledger. Transactions affecting customers' accounts are posted separately to the individual accounts in the subsidiary ledger. These transactions either are also posted separately, or are summarized periodically and the totals posted, to the control account in the general ledger. As indicated in Chapter 7, the balance of the accounts receivable control account may be proved by preparing a schedule of accounts receivable.

Accounts with customers normally have debit balances. If a customer's account has a credit balance, the balance may be bracketed or the term "Cr." entered next to the figure in the Balance column. In preparing the schedule of accounts receivable, the total of the accounts with credit balances should be deducted from the total of the accounts with debit balances and the difference should agree with the balance of the accounts receivable control account.

Posting to Individual Accounts

It is necessary to post all the amounts that represent increases or decreases to the accounts of each supplier and each customer.

Supplier Accounts. A list of vouchers or other documents that usually represent transactions completed with suppliers is shown below. The usual posting reference is also indicated.

Transaction	Voucher or Document	Posting Reference
Purchase	Purchase invoice No. 1	P1
Return or allowance	Credit memo from supplier No. 1	CM1
Payment on account	Check stub No. 1	Ck1

The purchase invoices and credit memorandums from suppliers are usually numbered consecutively as they are received. These numbers should be not confused with the numbers used by the supplier. The check stub is numbered consecutively to agree with the number of the checks issued. As the direct posting is completed, the proper cross-reference should be made in the Posting Reference column of the account and on the voucher or other document. If a loose-leaf ledger is used and accounts with suppliers are kept in alphabetical order, the posting is indicated by means of a distinctive check mark on the voucher or other document.

Customer Accounts. A list of vouchers or other documents that usually represent transactions completed with customers is shown below. The usual posting reference is also indicated.

Transaction	Voucher or Document	Posting Reference
Sale	Sales ticket No. 1	S1
Return or allowance	Seller's Credit memo No. 1	CM1
Collection on account	Remittance received	CR1

The sales tickets usually are prepared in duplicate or triplicate and are numbered consecutively. Each salesperson may use a different series of numbers. One copy of the sales ticket is retained for accounting use and another copy is given to the customer. Credit memorandums issued to customers in connection with sales returns or allowances usually are prepared in duplicate and are numbered consecutively. One copy of the credit memorandum goes to the customer and the other copy is retained for accounting use. Remittances received from customers may consist of cash or cash items, such as checks, bank drafts, and money orders. When the remittance is in the form of cash, it is customary to issue a receipt. The receipt may be issued in duplicate, in which case the duplicate copy will provide the information needed for the purpose of posting to the customer's account. Sometimes, receipt stubs are used to enter the information for posting purposes. When the remittance is in the form of a check, it is not necessary to issue a receipt as the canceled check will serve as a receipt for the customer.

Posting of a credit to the customer's account may be made directly from the check or from a list of checks received. Sometimes all remittances received daily are listed in such a manner as to provide the information needed for posting purposes. When this plan is followed, accounting need not handle the remittances at all. It is a common practice to use a form of monthly statement of account, the upper portion of which contains the customer's name and address. This portion is detached and returned along with the remittance. The customer notes the amount of the remittance on this slip of paper which then contains all the information needed to post the correct credit to the proper subsidiary ledger account. If the customer does not return the top part of the statement, a receipt or memo is prepared to serve the same purpose. This procedure is especially suitable when it is possible to separate the functions of (1) handling the cash and cash items, and (2) entering the credits to the customers' accounts. As the direct posting is completed, the proper cross-reference should be made in the Posting Reference column of the account and on the voucher or other document. If a loose-leaf ledger is used and accounts with customers are kept in alphabetic order, the posting may be indicated by means of a distinctive check mark or by initialing the voucher or other document.

Accountants generally prefer to post from the basic documents rather than from the books of original entry to the individual accounts with suppliers and customers because such procedure provides better control and promotes accuracy. When a purchase invoice is entered in a purchases journal by one person and is posted directly from the invoice to the proper supplier's account by another person, it is unlikely that both persons will make the same mistake. Even if the posting is done by the person who also handles the purchases journal, there is less likelihood of making a mistake than when the posting is done from the journal entry. If a mistake was made in entering the amount of the invoice in the purchases journal, the same mistake would almost certainly be made in posting from the purchases journal to the supplier's account. The same reasoning may be applied to the entering of sales transactions and all other transactions that affect accounts with suppliers and customers.

Statement of Account

When merchandise is sold on account, it is customary to send a monthly bill to each charge customer. An itemized bill, showing the amount still owed from the previous month and the detailed charges and credits to the customer's account during the current month, is known as a **statement of account**. Usually the statements are mailed as soon as they can be completed following the close of each month or at a time during the month determined by the billing cycle. The use of "billing cycles" is limited, generally, to businesses with hundreds or thousands of customers. In order that statements may be mailed promptly, some firms follow the policy of including transactions completed up to the 25th of the preceding month or five days before the close of the customer's billing cycle. When a remittance is not received from the customer within the usual credit period, a copy of the statement of account may be referred to the credit department for such action as the credit manager may wish to take.

The following is a filled-in copy of a statement of the account of James Rovel for the month ended October 31. It shows (1) the balance at the beginning of the month amounting to $152.75; (2) a charge of $393.75 (for a sale of $375.00 plus tax of $18.75) made on October 22; (3) a credit of $152.75 for cash received on October 28; and (4) the balance at the close of the month amounting to $393.75. Note that the customer is asked to tear off the upper portion of the statement and to return it along with the remittance, after filling in the amount of the remittance.

Statement

M MicroWorld
1099 E. Louisiana
Indianapolis, IN 46202-3322

James Rovel
429 S. Holiday Dr.
South Bend, IN 46615-1928 $ _____
Amount remitted

▲ PLEASE DETACH THIS PORTION AND RETURN WITH YOUR REMITTANCE

DATE	DESCRIPTION	CHARGES	CREDITS	BALANCE
Oct. 1			BALANCE FORWARD	152.75
Oct. 22	Mdse.	393.75		546.50
28	Cash		152.75	393.75

Statement of Account

BUILDING YOUR ACCOUNTING KNOWLEDGE

1. When should revenue be recognized in accrual accounting? in cash accounting?
2. When should expense be recognized in accrual accounting? in cash accounting?
3. Why is it considered better accounting to estimate the amount of uncollectible accounts receivable in advance rather than wait until they become certain?
4. Why is the allowance for doubtful accounts called a contra account?
5. What is the journal procedure when it is determined that a particular customer's account will not be collected?

6. What is meant by the "net cost" of a depreciable asset?
7. Why is the amount of depreciation only an estimate?
8. What are the major differences between the allowance for doubtful accounts and the accumulated depreciation account?

APPLYING ACCOUNTING CONCEPTS

Exercise 8-1. Based on past experience, Marsha's Casual Fashions expects to have a loss due to uncollectible accounts of an amount equal to one half of one percent of the sales on account during the year. Sales on account amounted to $180,000. Give the end-of-period adjusting entry in two-column journal form to enter the estimate for uncollectible account losses.

Exercise 8-2. Color Rite TV Sales and Service estimates the loss for uncollectible accounts using the method based on the aging of accounts receivable. After aging the accounts, it is estimated that $2,500 will not be collected. Give the end-of-period adjusting entry in two-column journal form to enter the estimate for uncollectible account losses assuming the following independent conditions exist prior to the adjustment:

(a) The Allowance for Doubtful Accounts has a credit balance of $200.

(b) The Allowance for Doubtful Accounts has a debit balance of $100.

(c) The Allowance for Doubtful Accounts has no balance.

Exercise 8-3. Great American Suppliers follows the practice of adjusting at the end of the year for an amount estimated to be lost due to uncollectible accounts. On March 17 of the next year, Debbie Buchanan's account in the amount of $345 has been determined to be uncollectible due to bankruptcy. Give the entry in two-column journal form to write off Buchanan's account.

Exercise 8-4. During the year Bandy Air Conditioning and Heating purchased office supplies for $950 and a two-year fire insurance policy for $674. Give the following entries related to these expenditures in two-column journal form:

(a) Entry for the purchase of the office supplies and insurance for cash.

(b) The end-of-period adjusting entry that would be made if there were $380 of office supplies on hand.

(c) The end-of-period adjusting entry that would be made if the insurance policy had been in effect since the beginning of the fiscal year.

Exercise 8-5. On January 5, the beginning of the year, Dial Glass and Mirror purchased a truck on account for $8,700 and estimates that it has a useful life of 4 years with no salvage value.

(a) Give the appropriate entry in two-column journal form upon purchase of the truck.

(b) Assuming that Dial Glass and Mirror uses the straight-line method of depreciation, give the adjusting entry in two-column journal form to enter the depreciation at the end of the year.

**Report
No. 8-1**

Complete Report No. 8-1 in the study assignments and submit your working papers to the instructor for approval. After completing the report, continue with the following textbook discussion until the next report is required.

ILLUSTRATION OF ACCOUNTING PROCEDURE

To apply accrual accounting and the data processing phases of the accounting cycle, the transactions of MicroWorld, a small retail business, will be discussed and illustrated in this chapter and in the next two chapters.

The Chart of Accounts

The importance of classifying accounts was discussed and illustrated in preceding chapters. A chart of accounts is an orderly and systematic list of accounts that identifies each account by means of an assigned number used to assist in locating the account in the ledger. The chart of accounts for the retail business of MicroWorld is shown on page 245. The pattern of numbers or code shown in the illustration is fairly typical of the arrangement used by many businesses.

The chart of accounts usually is arranged in financial statement order—balance sheet accounts followed by income statement accounts. The bold-type headings in the chart of accounts represent major divisions of the financial statements. Interest Expense, Account No. 571, is classified as "Other Expense" instead of being listed under "Operating Expenses" because it represents the expense of obtaining money with which to do business, rather than an expense directly associated with operating the business.

The nature of many of the accounts included in the chart of accounts for MicroWorld should be apparent because they have been described in preceding chapters and their use has been illustrated. In addition, the chart includes certain accounts that are needed in entering several types of transactions and events that were described in the first section of this chapter.

Note that the general ledger illustrated on pages 263-269 does not include account numbers 215, 217, 331, 545, 547, 548, 553, and 554. This is because these accounts are not needed to enter routine transactions. When adjusting entries and closing entries are discussed and illustrated in the following chapters, these accounts will be shown.

MICROWORLD

CHART OF ACCOUNTS

Assets*
Cash
111 Cash
112 Petty Cash Fund

Receivables
131 Accounts Receivable
131.1 Allowance for Doubtful
Accounts

Merchandise Inventory
141 Merchandise Inventory

Supplies and Prepayments
151 Supplies
155 Prepaid Insurance

Property, Plant, and Equipment
181 Store Equipment
181.1 Accumulated Depreciation—
Store Equipment

Liabilities
211 FICA Tax Payable
212 FUTA Tax Payable
213 State Unemployment Tax
Payable
214 Employees Income Tax
Payable
215 Accrued Bank Credit Card
Payable
216 Notes Payable
217 Accrued Interest Payable
218 Accounts Payable
221 Sales Tax Payable

Owner's Equity
311 Faye J. Quinn, Capital
311.1 Faye J. Quinn, Drawing
331 Expense and Revenue
Summary

Revenue
411 Sales
411.1 Sales Returns and Allowances

Cost of Goods Sold
511 Purchases
511.1 Purchases Returns and
Allowances

Operating Expenses
541 Rent Expense
542 Salaries and Commissions
Expense
543 Heating and Lighting Expense
544 Telephone Expense
545 Supplies Expense
546 Advertising Expense
547 Depreciation Expense
548 Insurance Expense
549 Charitable Contributions
Expense
551 Payroll Taxes Expense
552 Bank Credit Card Expense
553 Uncollectible Accounts
Expense
554 Purchases Discounts Lost
562 Miscellaneous Expense

Other Expenses
571 Interest Expense

*Words in bold type represent headings and not account titles.

Books of Account

The books of account used by MicroWorld, owned and operated by Faye J. Quinn, are discussed and illustrated on the following pages. The system includes:

Books of Original Entry	**Books of Final Entry**	**Auxiliary Records**
Purchases journal	General ledger	Petty cash payments
Sales journal	Accounts receivable	record
Cash receipts journal	ledger	Checkbook
Cash payments journal	Accounts payable ledger	Employees' earnings
General journal		records

With the exception of the checkbook and the employees' earnings records, the foregoing books and records are illustrated on pages 259-274 of this chapter.

Purchases Journal. The purchases journal used by MicroWorld is the same as the one illustrated on page 188 and described in detail in Chapter 6. All transactions involving the purchase of merchandise **on account** are entered in this journal. Because the posting of the individual credits to the accounts with suppliers is done directly from the purchase invoices, the only posting required from the purchases journal is the total purchases for each month. This involves a debit to Purchases, Account No. 511, and credit to Accounts Payable, Account No. 218.

Sales Journal. The sales journal used by MicroWorld is the same as the one illustrated on page 218 and described in detail in Chapter 7. All transactions involving the sale of merchandise **on account** are entered in this journal. Because the posting of individual charges to the accounts with customers is done directly from the sales tickets, the only posting required from the sales journal is the total sales for each month. This involves a debit to Accounts Receivable, Account No. 131, and credits to Sales, Account No. 411, and to Sales Tax Payable, Account No. 221.

Cash Receipts Journal. The cash receipts journal used by MicroWorld is the same as the one illustrated on page 223 and described in detail in Chapter 7. All transactions involving the receipt of cash but *only* such transactions are entered in this journal. All amounts entered in the General Cr. column are posted individually as credits to the accounts named in the Account Credited column, and the total is not posted. The totals of the four right-hand amount columns are posted at the end of each month as credits to Accounts Receivable, Account No. 131, Sales, Account No. 411, and Sales Tax Payable, Account No. 221, and as a debit to Cash, Account No. 111.

Cash Payments Journal. The cash payments journal used by MicroWorld is the same as the one illustrated on page 192 and described in detail in Chapter 6. All transactions involving the disbursement of cash but *only* such transactions are entered in this journal. All amounts entered in the General Dr. column are posted individually as debits to the accounts named in the Account Debited column, and the total is not posted. The totals of the three right-hand amount columns are posted at the end of each month as debits to Accounts Payable, Account No. 218, and Purchases, Account No. 511, and as a credit to Cash, Account No. 111.

General Journal. A general journal is used by MicroWorld to enter all transactions that cannot be entered in the special journals. A two-column journal is used for this purpose, and individual amounts are posted separately to the accounts named in the Description column. The totals of this journal are for the purpose of proof only, and are not posted.

General Ledger. A general ledger with the accounts arranged in numerical order is used. A chart of accounts appears on page 245. The four-column account form is used in the general ledger.

Accounts Receivable Ledger. An accounts receivable ledger with the accounts for customers arranged in alphabetic order is used. The three-column account form is used in this ledger. Posting to the individual accounts with customers is done directly from the sales tickets or other documents. As each item is posted, the balance is extended immediately so that reference to the account of any customer at any time will reveal without any delay the amount due. This is important since it is often necessary to determine the status of a particular customer's account before extending additional credit.

Accounts Payable Ledger. An accounts payable ledger with the accounts for suppliers arranged in alphabetic order is used. The three-column account form is used in this ledger also. Posting to the individual accounts with suppliers is done directly from the invoices or other documents. As each item is posted, the balance is extended immediately so that reference to the account of any supplier at any time will reveal the amount owed to that supplier.

Auxiliary Records. As previously stated, certain auxiliary records are used, including a petty cash payments record and a checkbook. The form of petty cash payments record is similar to that illustrated on pages 62 and 63. At the end of each month, when the summary postings from the cash receipts and cash payments journals are completed, the balance of the bank checking account in the ledger should be the same as the balance entered on the check stubs. The earnings records maintained for each of MicroWorld's five employees are similar to the one illustrated on pages 98 and 99.

Accounting Procedure

The books of account containing the transactions completed during the month of December are reproduced on pages 259-276. These books include the purchases journal, the sales journal, the cash receipts journal, the cash payments journal, the general journal, the petty cash payments record, the general ledger, the accounts receivable ledger, and the accounts payable ledger. Before entering the transactions for December, the balance in the petty cash fund was entered in the petty cash payments record. The balance at the beginning of the month of December is shown in each of the accounts in the general, accounts receivable, and accounts payable ledgers. These balances, along with those at the end of the month, are summarized in the trial balance and schedules reproduced on pages 275-276.

Following is a narrative of the transactions completed during December. Transactions that have not been previously introduced are analyzed to show their effect upon the accounts.

MICROWORLD

NARRATIVE OF TRANSACTIONS

Monday, December 1

Issued checks as follows:

No. 257, Burger Realty Co., $2,000, in payment of December rent.
No. 258, The Wichita Express, $287.75, in payment of freight on merchandise purchased.
No. 259, A&J Office Supply Co., $560.25, in payment of invoice of November 2, no discount.

Note that all three checks were entered in the cash payments journal. Check No. 257 was entered by debiting Rent Expense, Account No. 541, and crediting the cash account. Check No. 258 was entered by debiting Purchases, Account No. 511, and by crediting the cash account. Since the freight charge increases the cost of the merchandise, the purchases account was debited. Note that the account titles were entered in the Description column. The account number for Rent Expense was inserted in the Posting Reference column when the individual posting was completed at the end of the week. A check mark was placed in the Posting Reference column for the Purchases entry, because this amount will be posted as a part of the Purchases Dr. column total at the end of the month.

Check No. 259 was entered by debiting Accounts Payable and crediting the cash account, the name of the supplier being written in the Account Debited column. A check mark was placed in the Posting Reference column to indicate that checks issued to suppliers are not posted individually from the cash payments journal. These checks are posted directly to the proper suppliers' accounts in the accounts payable ledger from the information on the check stubs.

Tuesday, December 2

Received the following invoices for merchandise purchased on account:

Diskco, 1700 29th Street, Bakersfield, CA 93301-4747, $1,315, per Invoice No. 94 of November 30. Terms, 2/10 EOM.

Compumate, Inc., 6500 9th Street, New Orleans, LA 70115-1122, $6,494, per Invoice No. 95 of November 30. Terms, 2/10 EOM.

MLT Software, 1439 E. Broad St., Columbus, OH 43205-9892, $1,416, per Invoice No. 96 of November 30. Terms, 2/10-n/30.

Note that after receiving the merchandise and verifying the invoices, transactions were entered net of any discounts in the purchases journal. The account numbers of the suppliers were entered in the From Whom Purchased column. Check marks were placed in the Posting Reference column to indicate that individual posting is not done from the purchases journal. The invoices were then posted directly to the credit of the three suppliers' accounts in the accounts payable ledger, after which the invoices were filed in an unpaid invoice file according to their due dates.

Wednesday, December 3

Received check from James Rovel, $3,891.50.

Note that the credit was immediately posted to the customer's account. The remittance was then entered in the cash receipts journal by debiting the cash account and crediting Accounts Receivable. The name of the customer was entered in the Account Credited column. Since the credit had already been posted to the customer's account, a check mark was placed in the Posting Reference column.

Received a notice from the Third National Bank that $2,156.54 had been deducted from the account of MicroWorld, representing a discount of 4% of the net amount of Visa and MasterCard vouchers that were deposited by MicroWorld relating to such sales (less credits issued to customers for returns) during the preceding month.

Note that this was entered in the cash payments journal as a debit to Bank Credit Card Expense, Account No. 552, and a credit in the Cash Cr. column. (Even though the reduction in the Cash balance was not accomplished by issuing a check, the effect was the same. A subtraction of the amount was made on the next check stub.)

Thursday, December 4

Sold merchandise on account as follows:

No. 71A, James Rovel, 429 S. Holiday Dr., South Bend, IN 46615-1928, $2,995, tax, $149.75.

No. 57B, Helen Armstrong, 1739 Woodsage Trace, Indianapolis, IN 46237-1199, $1,355, tax, $67.75.

No. 35C, Harry Ewing, 2730 Bent Brook Drive, Indianapolis, IN 46250-1998, $980, tax, $49.

Unless otherwise specified, all customer charge accounts are payable by the 10th of the following month. No cash discount is allowed. Note that these transactions were entered in the sales journal. A check mark was placed in the Posting Reference column to indicate that individual posting is not done from the sales journal. The sales tickets were then posted directly to the proper customers' accounts in the accounts receivable ledger, after which each ticket was filed under the name of the customer for future reference. The numbers of the sales tickets indicate that there are four salespersons identified by the letters A, B, C, and D. Each of these persons uses a separate pad of sales tickets numbered consecutively.

Saturday, December 6

Cash (including bank credit card) sales for the week:

Salesperson	Merchandise	Tax	Total
A	$ 3,093.38	$154.67	$ 3,248.05
B	2,651.46	132.57	2,784.03
C	3,977.10	198.86	4,175.96
D	2,651.58	132.58	2,784.16
	$12,373.52	$618.68	$12,992.20

As each cash sale was completed, a sales ticket and a Visa or MasterCard ticket, if necessary, were prepared. The ticket provides the information needed in entering the amount of the sale on the cash register. Each amount was added to the previous total of cash sales made by each salesperson on an electronic accumulator in the register. Usually the total cash sales are entered daily, but to save time and avoid unnecessary duplication of entries, the total cash sales are here entered at the end of each week and on the last day of the month. This transaction was entered in the cash receipts journal by debiting the cash account for $12,992.20 and crediting Sales for $12,373.52 and Sales Tax Payable for $618.68.

End-of-the-Week Work

(1) Proved the footings of the cash receipts journal. (2) Proved the footings of the cash payments journal. (3) Deposited $16,883.70 in the Third National Bank and proved the bank balance, $49,213.44. (4) Posted each entry individually from the General Dr. (Cr.) column of the cash payments journal to the proper general ledger accounts. (5) Proved the footings of the sales journal.

Monday, December 8

Issued checks as follows:

No. 260, AB Electronics, $2,730.78, in payment of invoice of November 29, $2,815.23 less discount of $84.45.

No. 261, Clean Machine Co., $240, in payment of invoice of November 29, no discount.

No. 262, Compacto Co., $6,216.35, in payment of invoice of November 29, $6,343.21 less discount of $126.86.

No. 263, Microserve, Inc., $366.35, in payment of invoice of November 29, $373.83 less discount of $7.48.

No. 264, Pablo Co., $265.60, in payment of invoice of November 29, $271.02, less discount of $5.42.

No. 265, Telecomp, $595.25, in payment of invoice of November 29, $613.66, less discount of $18.41.

Each check was entered in the cash payments journal by crediting the cash account and debiting Accounts Payable for the net amount. The name of the supplier was entered in the Account Debited column and a check mark was placed in the Posting Reference column to indicate that the posting to the individual supplier's account in the accounts payable ledger was not made from this journal. The check stubs provided the information for posting.

Bought services from Clean Machine Co., 5200 N. Keystone Ave., Indianapolis, IN 46220-1986, $250, per Invoice No. 97 of December 5, no discount.

Sold merchandise on account as follows:

No. 59B, Emily Westcott, 1113 Stones Crossing Road, Zionsville, IN 46077-6601, $2,050.40, tax $102.52.

Issued checks as follows:

No. 266, The Indianapolis Times, Inc., $2,682.95, in payment for advertising.

No. 267, State Treasurer, $3,905.36, in payment of sales taxes for November.

Both checks were entered in the cash payments journal by debiting the proper accounts and crediting the cash account. Check No. 266 was charged to Advertising Expense, and Check No. 267 was charged to Sales Tax Payable. The numbers of the checks were entered in the Check No. column and the titles of the accounts to be charged were entered in the Account Debited column.

Tuesday, December 9

Made petty cash payments as follows:

Postage stamps, $20. Petty Cash Voucher No. 83.

Messenger fee, $6. Petty Cash Voucher No. 84.

All payments from the petty cash fund are entered in the petty cash payments record. This record is designed to facilitate the classification of each expenditure. Note that the cost of the postage stamps was entered as a charge to Supplies, Account No. 151, and the messenger fees were charged to Miscellaneous Expense, Account No. 562.

Wednesday, December 10

Issued checks as follows:

No. 268, Diskco, $577.05, in payment of invoice of November 15, $588.83, less discount of $11.78.

No. 269, Compumate, Inc., $6,364.12, in payment of invoice of November 30, $6,494 less discount of $129.88.

No. 270, MLT Software, $1,387.68, in payment of invoice of November 30, $1,416 less discount of $28.32.

A customer who used a MasterCard to purchase a word processor (sales price, $399, sales tax, $19.95) two days before, returned this item because its capacity was too limited. Quinn agreed to take this item back and prepared a MasterCard credit ticket for the full amount, $418.95.

Since the original transaction had been handled as a cash sale, the return was entered in the cash payments journal as a credit of $418.95 in the Cash column with a debit of $399 to Sales Returns and Allowances, Account No. 411.1, and a debit of $19.95 to Sales Tax Payable, Account No. 221. (At the next bank deposit, the amount of the credit ticket will be treated as a deduction from the amount of the tickets being deposited.)

Thursday, December 11

Issued Check No. 271 for $3,327.86 to the Third National Bank, a U.S. depository, in payment of the following taxes:

Employees' income tax withheld during November....		$1,045.90
FICA tax imposed:		
On employees (withheld during November).........	$1,140.98	
On the employer	1,140.98	2,281.96
Total...		$3,327.86

This transaction resulted in a decrease in FICA tax payable and employees income tax payable with a corresponding decrease in the cash account. This was entered in the cash payments journal by debiting FICA Tax Payable for $2,281.96 and Employees Income Tax Payable for $1,045.90 and crediting the cash account for $3,327.86.

Sold merchandise on account as follows:

No. 43D, Michael Taylor, 5850 Wildflower Circle, Bloomington, IN 47401-1230, $1,995, tax, $99.75.

Friday, December 12

Received the following remittances from customers:
Susan Chen, $100, on account.
Mona Gibson, $50, on account.
Jason Quimby, $36.20, in full settlement of account.

Saturday, December 13

Cash and bank credit card sales for the week:

Salesperson	Merchandise	Tax	Total
A	$ 4,021.39	$201.07	$ 4,222.46
B	3,446.90	172.35	3,619.25
C	5,170.23	268.51	5,438.74
D	3,447.05	172.24	3,619.29
	$16,085.57	$814.17	$16,899.74

End-of-the-Week Work

(1) Proved the footings of the cash receipts journal. (2) Proved the footings of the cash payments journal. (3) Deposited $16,666.99 ($17,085.94 − $418.95 credit of December 10) in the Third National Bank and proved the bank balance, $37,221.08. (4) Posted each entry individually from the General Dr. (Cr.) column of the cash payments journal to the proper general ledger accounts. (5) Proved the footings of the petty cash payments record and proved the balance of the petty cash fund, $224. (6) Proved the footings of the sales journal.

Monday, December 15

Issued Check No. 272 payable to Payroll for $2,981.39.

MicroWorld follows the policy of paying employees on the 15th and last day of each month. The following statement was prepared from the payroll register:

Payroll Statement for Period Ended December 15

Total salaries and commissions earned during period ..		$4,001.72
Employees' taxes to be withheld:		
Employees' income tax	$720.30	
FICA tax, 7.5% of $4,001.72........................	300.13	1,020.43
Net amount payable to employees....................		$2,981.29
Employer's payroll taxes:		
FICA tax, 7.5% of $4,001.72.........................		$ 300.13
Unemployment compensation taxes—		
State unemployment tax, 2.7% of $546.30..........		14.75
FUTA tax, 0.8% of $546.30.........................		4.37
Total		$ 319.25

None of the earnings of the five employees has reached the $47,000 point. Accordingly, all of the salaries and commissions earned during the period are subject to the FICA tax. All but one employee (a part-time employee) reached the $7,000 maximum state unemployment and FUTA tax limits in an earlier month. As a result, only $546.30 of salaries and commissions earned during the period is subject to these unemployment taxes.

Two entries were required for the payroll—(1) in the cash payments journal to enter the total earnings of the employees, the amounts withheld for FICA tax and income tax, and the net amount paid; (2) in the general journal to enter the payroll taxes imposed on the employer. The credits in the Cash Payments Journal to FICA Tax Payable, Account No. 211, and Employees' Income Tax Payable, Account No. 214, are entered in the General Dr. (Cr.) column in brackets, to indicate that they are to be posted as *credits* to these two accounts.

Tuesday, December 16

Made the following payments from the petty cash fund: Girl Scouts of America, $20, Petty Cash Voucher No. 85. Faye J. Quinn, $50, for personal use. Petty Cash Voucher No. 86.

Wednesday, December 17

Received the following invoices for merchandise purchased on account:

A&J Office Supply Co., 2805 S. Meridian, Indianapolis, IN 46225-3460, $563.25, per Invoice No. 98 of December 13, Terms, net 30 days.

Compacto Co., 705 Rialto Ave. West, Fresno, CA 93705-7845, $8,880, per Invoice No. 99 of December 15. Terms 2/10, n/40.

EHM Corp., 1728 Camino Real, San Antonio, TX 78238-4420, $4,278, per Invoice No. 100 of December 15. Terms, 3/10, n/30.

Thursday, December 18

Received the following remittances from customers:
Emily Westcott, $129.98, on account.
Stephanie Johnson, $3,800, in full settlement of account.
Peter Underwood, $65.70, in full settlement of account.

Friday, December 19

Sold merchandise on credit as follows:
No. 39C, Jason Quimby, 1327 Vandeman, Indianapolis, IN 46203-5432, $1,120, tax $56.
No. 46D, Miguel Lopez, 5240 Tousley Ct., Indianapolis, IN 46224-5678, $86.40, tax $4.32.

No. 77A, Myron Nash, 581 Acorn Way, Zionsville, IN 46077-2345, $2,995, tax, $149.75.

Saturday, December 20

Cash and bank credit card sales for the week:

Salesperson	Merchandise	Tax	Total
A	$4,176.06	$208.80	$4,384.86
B	3,579.47	178.97	3,758.44
C	5,369.09	268.45	5,637.54
D	3,576.93	178.85	3,755.78
	$16,701.55	$835.07	$17,536.62

End-of-the-Week Work

(1) Proved the footings of the cash receipts journal. (2) Proved the footings of the cash payments journal. (3) Deposited $21,532.30 in the Third National Bank and proved the bank balance, $55,772.09. (4) Posted each entry individually from the General Dr. (Cr.) column of the cash payments journal to the proper general ledger accounts. (5) Proved the footings of the petty cash payments record and proved the balance of the petty cash fund, $154.00. (6) Proved the footings of the sales journal. (7) Proved the footings of the general journal.

Monday, December 22

Received Credit Memorandum No. 91 for $93.25 from A&J Office Supply Co., for merchandise returned; to be applied on Invoice No. 98 received on December 17.

This transaction was entered in the general journal by debiting Accounts Payable and crediting Purchases Returns and Allowances. It was also posted directly to the account of the A&J Office Supply Co. in the accounts payable ledger from the credit memorandum.

Tuesday, December 23

Issued Check No. 273 for $5,500 to Quinn for personal use.
Made petty cash payments as follows:
Advertising, $12.50. Petty Cash Voucher No. 87.
Supplies, $15. Petty Cash Voucher No. 88.
Miscellaneous expense, $4.75. Petty Cash Voucher No. 89.

Wednesday, December 24

Issued Check No. 274 for $28.15 to United Parcel Service in payment of statement for delivery service for month ended December 15.

> Few of the customers of MicroWorld wish to have their purchases delivered. In some special circumstances, one of the employees handles deliveries. In some cases, United Parcel Service is used. Since the monthly amount is small, Miscellaneous Expense is debited when the charge is paid.

Friday, December 26

Issued checks as follows:

No. 275, Compacto Co., $8,702.40, in payment of invoice of December 15, $8,880.00 less discount of $177.60.

No. 276, EHM Corp., $4,149.66, in payment of invoice of December 15, $4,278, less discount of $128.34.

Sold merchandise on credit as follows:

No. 62B, James Rovel, 429 S. Holiday Drive, South Bend, IN 46615-1928, $6,075, tax, $303.75.

No. 49D, Patsy O'Sullivan, 2141 Edgewood Drive, Indianapolis, IN 46219-9876, $6,985, tax, $349.25.

No. 56C, Mona Gibson, 668 Strawbridge, Indianapolis, IN 46237-2876, $3,800, tax, $190.

Saturday, December 27

Received the following remittances from customers:

Myron Nash, $1,500, on account.
Patsy O'Sullivan, $5,000, on account.

Made petty cash payments as follows:

Advertising, $15.50. Petty Cash Voucher No. 90.
Supplies, $20.25. Petty Cash Voucher No. 91.
Miscellaneous expense, $5.85. Petty Cash Voucher No. 92.

Cash and bank credit card sales for the week:

Salesperson	Merchandise	Tax	Total
A	$4,692.98	$234.65	$4,927.63
B	3,650.19	182.51	3,832.70
C	3,128.72	156.44	3,285.16
D	2,861.54	143.08	3,004.62
	$14,333.43	$716.68	$15,050.11

End-of-the-Week Work

(1) Proved the footings of the cash receipts journal. (2) Proved the footings of the cash payments journal. (3) Deposited $21,550.11 in the Third National Bank and proved the bank balance, $58,941.99. (4) Posted each entry individually from the General Dr. (Cr.) column of the cash payments journal to the proper general ledger accounts. (5) Proved the footings of the petty cash payments record and proved the balance of the petty cash fund, $80.15. (6) Proved the footings of the sales journal. (7) Proved the footings of the general journal.

Monday, December 29

Issued Credit Memorandum No. 32 for $315 to Myron Nash for merchandise returned. (Sales price of merchandise, $300, tax, $15. This transaction should be entered in the general journal.)

Issued Check No. 277 for $747.50 to The Indianapolis Times, Inc., in payment of advertising bill.

Received a notice from the Third National Bank that $3,800 had been deducted from the account of MicroWorld, because a check from Stephanie Johnson deposited a few days before had not been paid by Johnson's bank due to insufficient funds. Johnson's check was enclosed with the notice.

> The amount of the check was debited immediately to Johnson's account in the accounts receivable ledger with the notation "NSF" (not sufficient funds). An entry was made in the cash payments journal debiting Accounts Receivable with a credit in the Cash Cr. column. A deduction was made on the following check stub.

Issued checks as follows:

No. 278, The Indiana Bell Telephone Co., $118.40, for telephone service.

No. 279, The Hoosier Gas & Electric Co., $419.28, for gas and electricity.

Tuesday, December 30

Received the following invoices:

Printmaster, 5675 Pulaski Rd., Chicago, IL 60629-6705, $2,270, for merchandise purchased per Invoice No. 101 of December 27. Terms, 4/10, n/30.

AB Electronics, 399 Goodman, Cincinnati, OH 45219-2901, $4,556 per Invoice No. 102 of December 27, Terms 3/10, n/45.

Compacto Co., 705 Rialto Ave. West, Fresno, CA 93705-7845, $2,220 per Invoice No. 103 of December 27. Terms 2/10, n/40.

Compumate, Inc., 6500 9th Street, New Orleans, LA 70115-1122, $4,396 per Invoice No. 104 of December 27. Terms 2/10, EOM.

Microserve, Inc., 691 Drexmore Ave., Charlotte, NC 28209-4678 $222 per Invoice No. 105 of December 27. Terms 2/10, n/30.

3D Corp., 874 Crescent Drive, Flint, MI 48503-7564, $575 purchased per Invoice No. 106 of December 27. Terms 3/10, n/30.

Wednesday, December 31

Cash and bank credit card sales:

Salesperson	Merchandise	Tax	Total
A	$2,346.49	$117.32	$2,463.81
B	1,825.10	91.26	1,916.36
C	1,430.77	71.54	1,502.31
D	1,564.36	78.22	1,642.58
	$7,166.72	$358.34	$7,525.06

Issued Check No. 280 payable to Payroll for $2,951.47.

Payroll Statement for Period Ended December 31

Total salaries and commissions earned during period ..		$3,961.70
Employees' taxes to be withheld:		
Employees' income tax	$713.10	
FICA tax, 7.5% of $3,961.70.........................	297.13	1,010.23
Net amount payable to employees.....................		$2,951.47
Employer's payroll taxes:		
FICA tax, 7.5% of $3,961.70.........................		$ 297.13
Unemployment compensation taxes—		
State unemployment tax, 2.7% of $541.11		14.61
FUTA tax, 0.8% of $541.11.......................		4.33
Total		$ 316.07

Issued Check No. 281 for $169.85 to replenish the petty cash fund.

Statement of Petty Cash Payments for December

Faye J. Quinn, drawing	$50.00
Supplies	55.25
Advertising expense	28.00
Charitable contributions expense	20.00
Miscellaneous expense	16.60
Total payments..	$169.85

Before the foregoing statement was prepared, the totals of the petty cash payments record were entered, along with appropriate single and double rulings. The balance was then entered below the double rulings. The amount received to replenish the fund was added to the balance and the total, $250, was entered in the Description column.

The amount of the check issued was entered in the cash payments journal by debiting the proper accounts and crediting the cash account. It should be remembered that no posting is done from the petty cash payments record; the proper accounts will be charged for the petty cash payments when the posting is completed from the cash payments journal.

ROUTINE END-OF-THE-MONTH WORK

(1) Proved the footings and entered the totals in the cash receipts journal, cash payments journal, sales journal, and the general journal; entered the total in the purchases journal. (2) Deposited $7,525.06 in the Third National Bank and proved the bank balance, $58,260.55. (3) Completed the individual posting from the General Dr. (Cr.) column of the cash payments journal. (4) Completed the summary posting of the columnar totals of the cash receipts journal, cash payments journal, purchases journal, and sales journal to the proper accounts in the general ledger. (5) Entered appropriate rulings in the cash receipts journal, cash payments journal, purchases journal, sales journal, and the general journal. (6) Prepared a trial balance and schedules of accounts receivable and accounts payable.

	PURCHASES JOURNAL			PAGE 22	
DATE	INVOICE NO.	FROM WHOM PURCHASED	POST. REF.	AMOUNT	
19— Dec. 2	94	Diskco -- No. 040	✓	1 288 70	1
2	95	Compumate, Inc. -- No. 032	✓	6 364 12	2
2	96	MLT Software -- No. 132	✓	1 387 68	3
8	97	Clean Machine Co. -- No. 030	✓	250 00	4
17	98	A+J Office Supply Co. -- No. 010	✓	563 25	5
17	99	Compacto Co. -- No. 031	✓	8 702 40	6
17	100	EHM Corp. -- No. 050	✓	4 149 66	7
30	101	Printmaster -- No. 161	✓	2 179 20	8
30	102	AB Electronics -- No. 011	✓	4 419 32	9
30	103	Compacto Co. -- No. 031	✓	2 175 60	10
30	104	Compumate, Inc. -- No. 032	✓	4 308 08	11
30	105	Microserve, Inc. -- No. 130	✓	217 56	12
30	106	3D Corp. -- No. 201	✓	557 75	13
		Purchases Dr. / Accounts Payable Cr.	511/218	36 563 32	14
					15

SALES JOURNAL — PAGE 34

	DATE	SALE NO.	TO WHOM SOLD	POST REF.	ACCOUNTS RECEIVABLE DR.	SALES CR.	SALES TAX PAYABLE CR.
1	Dec. 4	71A	James Rovel -- No. 180	✓	3 144 75	2995 00	149 75
2	4	57B	Helen Armstrong -- No. 010	✓	1 422 75	1355 00	67 75
3	4	35C	Harry Ewing -- No. 050	✓	1 029 00	980 00	49 00
4	8	59B	Emily Westcott -- No. 230	✓	5 596 50 / 2 152 92	5330 00 / 2050 40	266 50 / 102 52
5	11	43D	Michael Taylor -- No. 200	✓	2 094 75	1995 00	99 75
6	19	39C	Jason Quimby -- No. 170	✓	9 844 17 / 1 176 00	9375 40 / 1120 00	468 77 / 56 00
7	19	46D	Miguel Lopez -- No. 120	✓	90 72	86 40	4 32
8	19	77A	Myron Nash -- No. 140	✓	3 144 75	2995 00	149 75
9	26	62B	James Rovel -- No. 180	✓	14 255 64 / 6 378 75	13576 80 / 6075 00	678 84 / 303 75
10	26	49D	Patsy O'Sullivan -- No. 150	✓	7 334 25	6985 00	349 25
11	26	56C	Mona Gibson -- No. 070	✓	3 990 00	3800 00	190 00
12					37 958 64 / 37 958 64	30436 80 / 30436 80	1521 84 / 1521 84
13					(131)	(411)	(221)

MicroWorld—Sales Journal

CASH RECEIPTS JOURNAL — PAGE 42

	DATE	ACCOUNT CREDITED	POST REF.	GENERAL CR.	ACCOUNTS RECEIV. CR.	SALES CR.	SALES TAX PAY. CR.	CASH DR.
1	Dec. 3	James Rovel - No. 180	✓		3891 50			3891 50
2	6	Cash + bank cr. card sales	✓			12373 52	618 68	12992 20
3	12	Susan Chen - No. 030	✓		3891 50 / 100 00	12373 52	618 68	16 883 70 / 100 00
4	12	Mona Gibson - No. 070	✓		50 00			50 00
5	12	Jason Quimby - No. 170	✓		36 20			36 20
6	13	Cash + bank cr. card sales	✓			16085 57	814 17	16899 74
7	18	Emily Westcott - No. 230	✓		4077 70 / 129 98	28459 09	1432 85	33969 64 / 129 98
8	18	Stephanie Johnson - No. 100	✓		3800 00			3800 00
9	18	Peter Underwood - No. 210	✓		65 70			65 70
10	20	Cash + bank cr. card sales	✓			16701 55	835 07	17536 62
11	27	Myron Nash - No. 140	✓		8073 38 / 1500 00	45160 64	2267 92	55501 94 / 1500 00
12	27	Patsy O'Sullivan - No. 150	✓		5000 00			5000 00
13	27	Cash + bank cr. card sales	✓			14333 43	716 68	15050 11
14	31	Cash + bank cr. card sales	✓		14573 38	59497 07 / 7166 72	2987 60 / 358 34	77052 05 / 7525 06
15					14573 38 / 14573 38	66660 79	3342 94	84577 11
16				(✓)	(131)	(411)	(221)	(111)

MicroWorld—Cash Receipts Journal

CASH PAYMENTS JOURNAL   PAGE 48

	DATE	CK. NO.	ACCOUNT DEBITED	POST. REF.	GENERAL DR.	ACCOUNTS PAYABLE DR.	PURCHASES DR.	CASH CR.	
1	Dec 1	257	Rent Expense	541	200000			200000	1
2	1	258	Purchases	✓			28775	28775	2
3	1	259	A+J Office Supply-No.010	✓		56025		56025	3
4	3		Bank Credit Card Expense	552	215654 / 415654	56025	28775	215654 / 500454	4
5	8	260	AB Electronics-No.011	✓		273078		273078	5
6	8	261	Clean Machine Co.-No.030	✓		24000		24000	6
7	8	262	Compacto Co.-No.031	✓		621635		621635	7
8	8	263	Microserve, Inc.-No.130	✓		36635		36635	8
9	8	264	Pablo Co.-No.160	✓		26560		26560	9
10	8	265	Telecomp-No.200	✓		59525		59525	10
11	8	266	Advertising Expense	546	268295			268295	11
12	8	267	Sales Tax Payable	221	390536			390536	12
13	10	268	Diskco-No.040	✓		57705		57705	13
14	10	269	Compumate, Inc.-No.032	✓		636412		636412	14
15	10	270	MLT Software-No.132	✓		138768		138768	15
16	10		Sales Returns and Allow	411.1	39900				16
17			Sales Tax Payable	221	1995			41895	17
18	11	271	FICA Tax Payable	211	228196				18
19			Emp. Inc. Tax Payable	214	104590 / 1449166	1930343	28775	332786 / 3408284	19
20	15	272	Salaries and Comm. Exp	542	400172				20
21			FICA Tax Payable	211	(30013)				21
22			Emp. Inc. Tax Payable	214	(72030) / 1747295	1930343	28775	298129 / 3706413	22
23	23	273	Faye J. Quinn, Drawing	311.1	550000			550000	23
24	24	274	Miscellaneous Expense	562	2815			2815	24
25	26	275	Compacto Co.-No.031	✓		870240		870240	25
26	26	276	EZM Corp.-No.050	✓	2300110	414966 / 3215549	28775	414966 / 5544434	26
27	29	277	Advertising Expense	546	74750			74750	27
28	29		Acc Rec.-Stephanie Johnson	131.1	380000			380000	28
29	29	278	Telephone Expense	544	11840			11840	29
30	29	279	Heating and Lighting Exp	543	41928			41928	30
31	31	280	Salaries and Comm. Exp	542	396170				31
32			FICA Tax Payable	211	(29713)				32
33			Emp. Inc. Tax Payable	214	(71310)			295147	33
34	31	281	Faye J. Quinn, Drawing	311.1	5000				34
35			Supplies	151	5525				35
36			Advertising Expense	546	2800				36
37			Charitable Contr. Exp	549	2000				37
38			Miscellaneous Expense	562	1660			16985	38
39					3120760	3215549	28775	6365084	39
					3120760	3215549	28775	6365084	
40					(✓)	(218)	(511)	(111)	40

MicroWorld—Cash Payments Journal

PAGE *18*   **PETTY CASH PAYMENTS**

	DAY	DESCRIPTION	VOU. NO.	TOTAL AMOUNT	311.1	151
1		AMOUNTS FORWARDED		250.00		
2	9	Postage stamps	83	20 00		20 00
3	9	Messenger fee	84	6 00		
4	16	Girl Scouts of America *224.00*	85	26 00 / 20 00		20 00
5	16	Faye J. Quinn, personal use	86	50 00	50 00	
6	23	Advertising *154.00*	87	96 00 / 12 50	50 00	20 00
7	23	Supplies	88	15 00		15 00
8	23	Miscellaneous expense	89	4 75		
9	27	Advertising	90	15 50		
10	27	Supplies	91	20 25		20 25
11	27	Miscellaneous expense	92	5 85		
12		*80.15*		169 83 / 169 85	50 00 / 50 00	55 25 / 55 25
13	31	Balance		80.15		
14	31	Received in fund		169.85		
15		Total		250.00		
16						

MicroWorld—Petty Cash Payments Record (left page)

     JOURNAL   PAGE *27*

	DATE	DESCRIPTION	POST. REF.	DEBIT	CREDIT	
1	19— Dec 15	Payroll Taxes Expense	551	3 19 25		1
2		FICA Tax Payable	211		3 00 13	2
3		FUTA Tax Payable	212		4 37	3
4		State Unemployment Tax Payable	213		14 75	4
5	22	Accounts Payable—A & J Office Supply	218/1	3 19 25 / 93 25	3 19 25	5
6		Purchases Returns and Allowances	511.1		93 25	6
7	29	Sales Returns and Allowances	411.1	4 12 50 / 3 00 00	4 12 50	7
8		Sales Tax Payable	221	15 00		8
9		Accounts Receivable—Myron Nash	131/1		3 15 00	9
10	31	Payroll Taxes Expense	551	3 16 07		10
11		FICA Tax Payable	211		2 97 13	11
12		FUTA Tax Payable	212		4 33	12
13		State Unemployment Tax Payable	213		14 61	13
14				10 43 57	10 43 57	14

MicroWorld—General Journal

FOR MONTH OF *December* 19--   PAGE *18*

DISTRIBUTION OF DEBITS						ACCOUNT	AMOUNT	
546	549	562						
								1
								2
		600						3
	2000	600						4
								5
	2000	600						6
1250								7
		475						8
1550								9
								10
		585						11
2800	2000	1660						12
2800	2000	1660						13
								14
								15
								16

MicroWorld—Petty Cash Payments Record (right page)

ACCOUNT *Cash*   ACCOUNT NO. *111*

DATE	ITEM	POST. REF.	DEBIT	CREDIT	BALANCE DEBIT	BALANCE CREDIT
19-- Dec 1	Balance	✓			3733428	
31		CR42	8457711		12191139	
31		CP48		6365084	5826055	

ACCOUNT *Petty Cash Fund*   ACCOUNT NO. *112*

DATE	ITEM	POST. REF.	DEBIT	CREDIT	BALANCE DEBIT	BALANCE CREDIT
19-- Dec 1	Balance	✓			25000	

MicroWorld—General Ledger

ACCOUNT Accounts Receivable   **ACCOUNT NO.** 131

DATE	ITEM	POST. REF.	DEBIT	CREDIT	BALANCE DEBIT	BALANCE CREDIT
19-- Dec 1	Balance	✓			1474348	
29		J27		31500	1442848	
29		CP48	380000		1822848	
31		S34	3195864		5018712	
31		CR42		1457338	3561374	

ACCOUNT Allowance for Doubtful Accounts   **ACCOUNT NO.** 131.1

DATE	ITEM	POST. REF.	DEBIT	CREDIT	BALANCE DEBIT	BALANCE CREDIT
19-- Dec 1	Balance	✓				59000

ACCOUNT Merchandise Inventory   **ACCOUNT NO.** 141

DATE	ITEM	POST. REF.	DEBIT	CREDIT	BALANCE DEBIT	BALANCE CREDIT
19-- Dec 1	Balance	✓			9708380	

ACCOUNT Supplies   **ACCOUNT NO.** 151

DATE	ITEM	POST. REF.	DEBIT	CREDIT	BALANCE DEBIT	BALANCE CREDIT
19-- Dec 1	Balance	✓			196555	
31		CP48	5525		202080	

ACCOUNT Prepaid Insurance   **ACCOUNT NO.** 155

DATE	ITEM	POST. REF.	DEBIT	CREDIT	BALANCE DEBIT	BALANCE CREDIT
19-- Dec 1	Balance	✓			306029	

ACCOUNT Store Equipment   **ACCOUNT NO.** 181

DATE	ITEM	POST. REF.	DEBIT	CREDIT	BALANCE DEBIT	BALANCE CREDIT
19-- Dec 1	Balance	✓			2354810	

MicroWorld—General Ledger (continued)

ACCOUNT *Accumulated Depreciation -- Store Equipment* ACCOUNT NO. *181.1*

DATE	ITEM	POST. REF.	DEBIT	CREDIT	BALANCE DEBIT	BALANCE CREDIT
Dec 1	Balance	✓				549364

ACCOUNT *FICA Tax Payable* ACCOUNT NO. *211*

DATE	ITEM	POST. REF.	DEBIT	CREDIT	BALANCE DEBIT	BALANCE CREDIT
Dec 1	Balance	✓				228196
11		CP48	228196		-0-	-0-
15		CP48		30013		30013
15		J27		30013		60026
31		CP48		29713		89739
31		J27		29713		119452

ACCOUNT *FUTA Tax Payable* ACCOUNT NO. *212*

DATE	ITEM	POST. REF.	DEBIT	CREDIT	BALANCE DEBIT	BALANCE CREDIT
Dec 1	Balance	✓				2698
15		J27		437		3135
31		J27		433		3568

ACCOUNT *State Unemployment Tax Payable* ACCOUNT NO. *213*

DATE	ITEM	POST. REF.	DEBIT	CREDIT	BALANCE DEBIT	BALANCE CREDIT
Dec 1	Balance	✓				12350
15		J27		1475		13825
31		J27		1461		15286

ACCOUNT *Employees Income Tax Payable* ACCOUNT NO. *214*

DATE	ITEM	POST. REF.	DEBIT	CREDIT	BALANCE DEBIT	BALANCE CREDIT
Dec 1	Balance	✓				104590
11		CP48	104590		-0-	-0-
15		CP48		72030		72030
31		CP48		71310		143340

MicroWorld—General Ledger (continued)

ACCOUNT Notes Payable   **ACCOUNT NO.** 216

DATE	ITEM	POST. REF.	DEBIT	CREDIT	BALANCE DEBIT	BALANCE CREDIT
19-- Dec 1	Balance	✓				3400000

ACCOUNT Accounts Payable   **ACCOUNT NO.** 218

DATE	ITEM	POST. REF.	DEBIT	CREDIT	BALANCE DEBIT	BALANCE CREDIT
19-- Dec 1	Balance	✓				1155163
22		G27	9325			1145838
31		P22		3656332		4802170
31		CP48	3215549			1586621

ACCOUNT Sales Tax Payable   **ACCOUNT NO.** 221

DATE	ITEM	POST. REF.	DEBIT	CREDIT	BALANCE DEBIT	BALANCE CREDIT
19-- Dec 1	Balance	✓				390536
8		CP48	390536		-0-	-0-
10		CP48	1995		1995	
29		G27	1500		3495	
31		J34		152184		148689
31		CR42		334294		482983

ACCOUNT Faye J. Quinn, Capital   **ACCOUNT NO.** 311

DATE	ITEM	POST. REF.	DEBIT	CREDIT	BALANCE DEBIT	BALANCE CREDIT
19-- Dec 1	Balance	✓				15603053

ACCOUNT Faye J. Quinn, Drawing   **ACCOUNT NO.** 311.1

DATE	ITEM	POST. REF.	DEBIT	CREDIT	BALANCE DEBIT	BALANCE CREDIT
19-- Dec 1	Balance	✓			8250000	
23		CP48	550000		8800000	
31		CP48	5000		8805000	

MicroWorld—General Ledger (continued)

ACCOUNT Sales   ACCOUNT NO. 411

DATE	ITEM	POST. REF.	DEBIT	CREDIT	BALANCE DEBIT	BALANCE CREDIT
19-- Dec. 1	Balance	✓				79364660
31		S34		3043680		82408340
31		CR42		6666079		89074419

ACCOUNT Sales Returns and Allowances   ACCOUNT NO. 411.1

DATE	ITEM	POST. REF.	DEBIT	CREDIT	BALANCE DEBIT	BALANCE CREDIT
19-- Dec. 1	Balance	✓			1270285	
10		CP48	39900		1310185	
29		J27	30000		1340185	

ACCOUNT Purchases   ACCOUNT NO. 511

DATE	ITEM	POST. REF.	DEBIT	CREDIT	BALANCE DEBIT	BALANCE CREDIT
19-- Dec. 1	Balance	✓			56631520	
31		P22	3656332		60287852	
31		CP48	28775		60316627	

ACCOUNT Purchases Returns and Allowances   ACCOUNT NO. 511.1

DATE	ITEM	POST. REF.	DEBIT	CREDIT	BALANCE DEBIT	BALANCE CREDIT
19-- Dec. 1	Balance	✓				846045
22		J27		9325		855370

ACCOUNT Rent Expense   ACCOUNT NO. 541

DATE	ITEM	POST. REF.	DEBIT	CREDIT	BALANCE DEBIT	BALANCE CREDIT
19-- Dec. 1	Balance	✓			2200000	
1		CP48	200000		2400000	

ACCOUNT Salaries and Commissions Expense   ACCOUNT NO. 542

DATE	ITEM	POST. REF.	DEBIT	CREDIT	BALANCE DEBIT	BALANCE CREDIT
19-- Dec. 1	Balance	✓			7968762	
15		CP48	400172		8368934	
31		CP48	396170		8765104	

MicroWorld—General Ledger (continued)

ACCOUNT *Heating and Lighting Expense*   ACCOUNT NO. 543

DATE		ITEM	POST. REF.	DEBIT	CREDIT	BALANCE DEBIT	BALANCE CREDIT
19-- Dec	1	Balance	✓			5096 08	
	29		CP48	419 28		5515 36	

ACCOUNT *Telephone Expense*   ACCOUNT NO. 544

DATE		ITEM	POST. REF.	DEBIT	CREDIT	BALANCE DEBIT	BALANCE CREDIT
19-- Dec	1	Balance	✓			1428 32	
	29		CP48	118 40		1546 72	

ACCOUNT *Advertising Expense*   ACCOUNT NO. 546

DATE		ITEM	POST. REF.	DEBIT	CREDIT	BALANCE DEBIT	BALANCE CREDIT
19-- Dec	1	Balance	✓			35775 24	
	8		CP48	2682 95		38458 19	
	29		CP48	747 50		39205 69	
	31		CP48	28 00		39233 69	

ACCOUNT *Charitable Contributions Expense*   ACCOUNT NO. 549

DATE		ITEM	POST. REF.	DEBIT	CREDIT	BALANCE DEBIT	BALANCE CREDIT
19-- Dec	1	Balance	✓			1250 00	
	31		CP48	20 00		1270 00	

ACCOUNT *Payroll Taxes Expense*   ACCOUNT NO. 551

DATE		ITEM	POST. REF.	DEBIT	CREDIT	BALANCE DEBIT	BALANCE CREDIT
19-- Dec	1	Balance	✓			7443 72	
	15		J27	319 25		7762 97	
	31		J27	316 07		8079 04	

MicroWorld—General Ledger (continued)

ACCOUNT *Bank Credit Card Expense*   ACCOUNT NO. 552

DATE		ITEM	POST. REF.	DEBIT	CREDIT	BALANCE	
						DEBIT	CREDIT
19-- Dec.	1	Balance	✓			2234857	
	3		CP48	215654		2450511	

ACCOUNT *Miscellaneous Expense*   ACCOUNT NO. 562

DATE		ITEM	POST. REF.	DEBIT	CREDIT	BALANCE	
						DEBIT	CREDIT
19-- Dec.	1	Balance	✓			200375	
	24		CP48	2815		203190	
	31		CP48	1660		204850	

ACCOUNT *Interest Expense*   ACCOUNT NO. 571

DATE		ITEM	POST. REF.	DEBIT	CREDIT	BALANCE	
						DEBIT	CREDIT
19-- Dec.	1	Balance	✓			61970	

MicroWorld—General Ledger (concluded)

NAME *Helen Armstrong*   ACCOUNT NO. 010
ADDRESS *1739 Woodsage Trace, Indianapolis,* IN 46237-1199

DATE		ITEM	POST. REF.	DEBIT	CREDIT	BALANCE
19-- Dec.	4		S57B	142275		142275

NAME *Susan Chen*   ACCOUNT NO. 030
ADDRESS 337 *Elm Street, Noblesville,* IN 46060-3377

DATE		ITEM	POST. REF.	DEBIT	CREDIT	BALANCE
19-- Dec.	1	Dr. Balance	✓			15525
	12		CR2		10000	5525

MicroWorld—Accounts Receivable Ledger

NAME *Harry Ewing* ACCOUNT NO. 050
ADDRESS 2730 Bent Brook Dr., Indianapolis, IN 46250-2876

DATE	ITEM	POST. REF.	DEBIT	CREDIT	BALANCE
19-- Dec. 4		S35C	102900		102900

NAME *Mona Gibson* ACCOUNT NO. 070
ADDRESS 668 Strawbridge, Indianapolis, IN 46237-1050

DATE	ITEM	POST. REF.	DEBIT	CREDIT	BALANCE
19-- Dec. 1	Dr. Balance	✓			7950
12		CR3		5000	2950
26		S56C	399000		401950

NAME *Stephanie Johnson* ACCOUNT NO. 100
ADDRESS 6010 South Eaton Ave., Indianapolis, IN 46259-6789

DATE	ITEM	POST. REF.	DEBIT	CREDIT	BALANCE
19-- Dec. 1	Dr. Balance	✓			380000
18		CR6		380000	- 0 -
29	NSF	CP48	380000		380000

NAME *Miguel Lopez* ACCOUNT NO. 120
ADDRESS 5240 Tousley Court, Indianapolis, IN 46224-5678

DATE	ITEM	POST. REF.	DEBIT	CREDIT	BALANCE
19-- Dec. 1	Dr. Balance	✓			302160
19		S46D	9072		311232

NAME *Myron Nash* ACCOUNT NO. 140
ADDRESS 581 Acorn Way, Zionsville, IN 46077-2154

DATE	ITEM	POST. REF.	DEBIT	CREDIT	BALANCE
19-- Dec. 1	Dr. Balance	✓			9800
19		S77Q	314475		324275
27		CR8		150000	174275
29		CM32		31500	142775

MicroWorld—Accounts Receivable Ledger (continued)

NAME *Patsy O'Sullivan*   ACCOUNT NO. *150*
ADDRESS *2141 Edgewood Drive, Indianapolis, IN 46219-9876*

DATE		ITEM	POST. REF.	DEBIT	CREDIT	BALANCE
19-- Dec.	1	Dr. Balance	✓			3465 75
	26		S49D	7334 25		10800 00
	27		CR9		5000 00	5800 00

NAME *Jason Quimby*   ACCOUNT NO. *170*
ADDRESS *1327 Vandeman, Indianapolis, IN 46203-5432*

DATE		ITEM	POST. REF.	DEBIT	CREDIT	BALANCE
19-- Dec.	1	Dr. Balance	✓			36 20
	12		CR4		36 20	- 0 -
	19		S39C	1176 00		1176 00

NAME *James Rovel*   ACCOUNT NO. *180*
ADDRESS *429 South Holiday Dr., South Bend, IN 46615-1928*

DATE		ITEM	POST. REF.	DEBIT	CREDIT	BALANCE
19-- Dec.	1	Dr. Balance	✓			3891 50
	3		CR1		3891 50	- 0 -
	4		S71A	3144 75		3144 75
	26		S62B	6378 75		9523 50

NAME *Michael Taylor*   ACCOUNT NO. *200*
ADDRESS *5850 Wildflower Circle, Bloomington, IN 47401*

DATE		ITEM	POST. REF.	DEBIT	CREDIT	BALANCE
19-- Dec.	11		S43D	2094 75		2094 75

NAME *Peter Underwood*   ACCOUNT NO. *210*
ADDRESS *5260 Eagle Creek Parkway, Indianapolis, IN 46254-8275*

DATE		ITEM	POST. REF.	DEBIT	CREDIT	BALANCE
19-- Dec.	1	Dr. Balance	✓			65 70
	18		CR7		65 70	- 0 -

MicroWorld—Accounts Receivable Ledger (continued)

NAME *Emily Westcott*   ACCOUNT NO. 230
ADDRESS *1113 Stones Crossing Road, Zionsville, IN 46077-6601*

DATE		ITEM	POST. REF.	DEBIT	CREDIT	BALANCE
Dec.	1	Dr. Balance	✓			12998
	8		S59B	215292		228290
	18		CR5		12998	215292

MicroWorld—Accounts Receivable Ledger (concluded)

NAME *A & J Office Supply Co.*   ACCOUNT NO. 010
ADDRESS *2805 South Meridian, Indianapolis, IN 46225-3460*

DATE		ITEM	POST. REF.	DEBIT	CREDIT	BALANCE
Dec.	1	Cr. Balance	✓			56025
	1		Ck259	56025		-0-
	17	12/13-n/30	P98		56325	56325
	22		CM91	9325		47000

NAME *AB Electronics*   ACCOUNT NO. 011
ADDRESS *399 Goodman, Cincinnati, OH 45219-2901*

DATE		ITEM	POST. REF.	DEBIT	CREDIT	BALANCE
Dec.	1	Cr. Balance	✓			273078
	8		Ck260	273078		-0-
	30	12/27-3/10, n/45	P102		441932	441932

NAME *Clean Machine Co.*   ACCOUNT NO. 030
ADDRESS *5200 N. Keystone Ave., Indianapolis, IN 46220-1986*

DATE		ITEM	POST. REF.	DEBIT	CREDIT	BALANCE
Dec.	1	Cr. Balance	✓			24000
	8		Ck261	24000		-0-
	8	12/5-n/30	P97		25000	25000

MicroWorld—Accounts Payable Ledger

NAME *Compacto Co.*   ACCOUNT NO. 031
ADDRESS *705 Rialto Avenue West, Fresno,* CA 93705-7845

DATE		ITEM	POST. REF.	DEBIT	CREDIT	BALANCE
19-- Dec.	1	Cr. Balance	✓			6216 35
	8		Ck 262	6216 35		- 0 -
	17	12/15 - 2/10, n/30	P 99		8702 40	8702 40
	26		Ck 275	8702 40		- 0 -
	30	12/27 - 2/10, n/40	P 103		2175 60	2175 60

NAME *Compumate, Inc.*   ACCOUNT NO. 032
ADDRESS *6500 9th Street, New Orleans,* LA 70115-1122

DATE		ITEM	POST. REF.	DEBIT	CREDIT	BALANCE
19-- Dec.	2	11/30 - 2/10 EOM	P 95		6364 12	6364 12
	10		Ck 269	6364 12		- 0 -
	30	12/27 - 2/10 EOM	P 104		4308 08	4308 08

NAME *Diskco*   ACCOUNT NO. 040
ADDRESS *1700 29th Street, Bakersfield,* CA 93301-4747

DATE		ITEM	POST. REF.	DEBIT	CREDIT	BALANCE
19-- Dec.	1	Cr. Balance	✓			577 05
	2	11/30 - 2/10 EOM	P 94		1288 70	1865 75
	10		Ck 268	577 05		1288 70

NAME *EHM Corp.*   ACCOUNT NO. 050
ADDRESS *1728 Camino Real, San Antonio,* TX 78238-4420

DATE		ITEM	POST. REF.	DEBIT	CREDIT	BALANCE
19-- Dec.	12	12/15 - 3/10, n/30	P 100		4149 66	4149 66
	26		Ck 276	4149 66		- 0 -

NAME *Microserve, Inc.*   ACCOUNT NO. 130
ADDRESS *691 Drexmore Ave., Charlotte,* N.C. 28209-4678

DATE		ITEM	POST. REF.	DEBIT	CREDIT	BALANCE
19-- Dec.	1	Cr. Balance	✓			366 35
	8		Ck 263	366 35		- 0 -
	30	12/27 - 2/10, n/30	P 105		2175 6	2175 6

MicroWorld—Accounts Payable Ledger (continued)

NAME *MLT Software*   **ACCOUNT NO.** *132*
ADDRESS *1439 East Broad St., Columbus, OH 43205-9892*

DATE	ITEM	POST. REF.	DEBIT	CREDIT	BALANCE
19-- Dec. 2	11/30 - 2/10 EOM	P96		138768	138768
10		Ck270	138768		-0-

NAME *Pablo Co.*   **ACCOUNT NO.** *160*
ADDRESS *1894 Winthrop Ave., White Plains, NY 10606-6915*

DATE	ITEM	POST. REF.	DEBIT	CREDIT	BALANCE
19-- Dec. 1	Cr. Balance	✓			26560
8		Ck264	26560		-0-

NAME *Printmaster*   **ACCOUNT NO.** *161*
ADDRESS *5675 Pulaski Rd., Chicago, IL 60629-6705*

DATE	ITEM	POST. REF.	DEBIT	CREDIT	BALANCE
19-- Dec. 30	12/27 - 4/10, n/30	P101		217920	217920

NAME *Telecomp, Inc.*   **ACCOUNT NO.** *200*
ADDRESS *810 Caballero, Simi Valley, CA 93065-2154*

DATE	ITEM	POST. REF.	DEBIT	CREDIT	BALANCE
19-- Dec. 1	Cr. Balance	✓			59525
8		Ck265	59525		-0-

NAME *3D Corp.*   **ACCOUNT NO.** *201*
ADDRESS *874 Crescent Drive, Flint, MI 48503-7564*

DATE	ITEM	POST. REF.	DEBIT	CREDIT	BALANCE
19-- Dec. 30	12/29 - 3/10, n/30	P106		55775	55775

MicroWorld—Accounts Payable Ledger (concluded)

MicroWorld
Schedule of Accounts Receivable

	Nov. 30, 19--	Dec. 31, 19--
Helen Armstrong -- No. 010		142275
Susan Chen -- No. 030	15525	5525
Harry Ewing -- No. 050		102900
Mona Gibson -- No. 070	7950	401950
Stephanie Johnson -- No. 100	380000	380000
Miguel Lopez -- No. 120	302160	311232
Myron Nash -- No. 140	9800	142775
Patsy O'Sullivan -- No. 150	346575	580000
Jason Quimby -- No. 170	3620	117600
James Rovel -- No. 180	389150	952350
Michael Taylor -- No. 200		209475
Peter Underwood -- No. 210	6570	
Emily Westcott -- No. 230	12998	215292
	1474348	3561374

MicroWorld—Schedule of Accounts Receivable

MicroWorld
Schedule of Accounts Payable

	Nov. 30, 19--	Dec. 31, 19--
A & J Office Supply Co. -- No. 010	56025	47000
AB Electronics -- No. 011	273078	441932
Clean Machine Co -- No. 030	24000	25000
Compacto Co. -- No. 031	621635	217560
Compumate, Inc. -- No. 032		430808
Diskco -- No. 040	57705	128870
Microserve, Inc. -- No. 130	36635	21756
Pablo Co. -- No. 160	26560	
Printmaster -- No. 161		217920
Telecomp -- No. 200	59525	
3D Corp. -- No. 201		55775
	1155163	1586621

MicroWorld—Schedule of Accounts Payable

Micro-World
Trial Balance

| | | November 30, 19-- | | December 31, 19-- | |
ACCOUNT	ACCT. No.	DEBIT	CREDIT	DEBIT	CREDIT
1 Cash	111	3733428		5826055	
2 Petty Cash Fund	112	25000		25000	
3 Accounts Receivable	131	1474348		3561374	
4 Allowance for Doubtful Accts	131.1		59000		59000
5 Merchandise Inventory	141	9708380		9708380	
6 Supplies	151	196555		202080	
7 Prepaid Insurance	155	306029		306029	
8 Store Equipment	181	2354810		2354810	
9 Accum. Depr.-Store Equip	181.1		549364		549364
10 FICA Tax Payable	211		228196		119452
11 FUTA Tax Payable	212		2698		3568
12 State Unemployment Tax Pay	213		12350		15286
13 Employees Inc. Tax Payable	214		104590		143340
14 Notes Payable	216		3400000		3400000
15 Accounts Payable	218		1155163		1586621
16 Sales Tax Payable	221		390536		482983
17 Faye J. Quinn, Capital	311		15603053		15603053
18 Faye J. Quinn, Drawing	311.1	8250000		8805000	
19 Sales	411		79364660		89074419
20 Sales Returns and Allowances	411.1	1270285		1340185	
21 Purchases	511	56631520		60316627	
22 Purchases Ret and Allowances	511.1		846045		855370
23 Rent Expense	541	2200000		2400000	
24 Salaries and Commissions Exp	542	7968762		8765104	
25 Heating and Light Expense	543	509608		551536	
26 Telephone Expense	544	142832		154672	
27 Advertising Expense	546	3577524		3923369	
28 Charitable Contributions Exp	549	125000		127000	
29 Payroll Taxes Expense	551	744372		807904	
30 Bank Credit Card Expense	552	2234857		2450511	
31 Miscellaneous Expense	562	200375		204850	
32 Interest Expense	571	61970		61970	
33		101715655	101715655	111892456	111892456

MicroWorld—Trial Balance

BUILDING YOUR ACCOUNTING KNOWLEDGE

1. In MicroWorld's chart of accounts, why is interest expense classified as "Other Expense" instead of being listed as part of "Operating Expenses"?
2. What kinds of transactions are entered in MicroWorld's purchases journal?
3. What kinds of transactions are entered in MicroWorld's sales journal?
4. What kinds of transactions are entered in MicroWorld's cash receipts journal? In MicroWorld's cash payments journal?
5. What kinds of transactions are entered in MicroWorld's general journal?
6. What are the names and account forms of the three ledgers used by MicroWorld?
7. What are the three auxiliary records maintained by MicroWorld?

8. Why are check marks placed in the Posting Reference columns of MicroWorld's purchases and sales journals?

9. Why are check marks placed below the totals of the General Debit and Credit columns of MicroWorld's cash payments and cash receipts journals?

APPLYING ACCOUNTING CONCEPTS

Exercise 8-6. Purple Thumb Nursery uses the following journals: sales, purchases (only for merchandise purchased on account), cash receipts, cash payments, and general. Identify the appropriate journal or journals in which each of the following transactions would be recorded:

(a) Issued check in payment of invoice for merchandise purchased on account.

(b) Recorded cash sales for the week.

(c) Sold merchandise on account.

(d) Received check from a customer for merchandise sold on account.

(e) Received an invoice for merchandise purchased on account.

(f) Received a notice from the bank for an amount deducted from the company's bank account for Bank Credit Card Expense related to Visa and MasterCard sales.

(g) Replenished the petty cash fund.

(h) A customer returned an item that had been purchased the prior day using a MasterCard. A MasterCard credit ticket was prepared for the full amount.

(i) Issued check payable to Payroll for weekly payroll and entered liability for payroll taxes.

(j) Received credit memorandum for merchandise returned that was purchased on account by the company earlier in the month.

Exercise 8-7. Give the appropriate entries in two-column journal form for the weekly payroll and for the employer's liability associated with the payroll.

The payroll statement for the period ended November 15 is as follows:

Total salaries and commissions			$4,275.00
Employees' taxes withheld:			
Employees' income tax		$875.00	
FICA tax, 7.5% of $4,275		320.63	1,195.63
Net amount payable to employees			$3,079.37
Employer's payroll taxes:			
FICA tax, 7.5% of $4,275			$ 320.63
Unemployment compensation taxes:			
State unemployment tax, 2.7% of $765	$ 20.66		
FUTA tax, 0.8% of $765	6.12		26.78
Total.....................................			$ 347.41

Exercise 8-8. The Statement of Petty Cash Payments for Judi's Cupboard indicates the following expenditures have been made during the month of March:

J. E. Ellis, drawing................... $200
Supplies   25
Advertising expense   8
Charitable contributions expense   50
Miscellaneous expense   7
    Total payments................... $290

Give the entry in two-column journal form for the check to replenish the petty cash fund at the end of the month.

Report No. 8-2

Complete Report No. 8-2 in the study assignments and submit your working papers to the instructor for approval. After completing this report, continue with the textbook discussion in Chapter 9 until the next report is required.

EXPANDING YOUR BUSINESS VOCABULARY

What is the meaning of each of the following terms?

Accounts Payable—Control **(p. 238)**

Accounts Receivable—Control **(p. 239)**

accrual basis of accounting **(p. 227)**

bad debts expense **(p. 230)**

cash basis of accounting **(p. 228)**

chart of accounts **(p. 244)**

contra account **(p. 230)**

control accounts **(p. 238)**

depreciation accounting **(p. 234)**

end-of-period adjustments **(p. 229)**

general journal **(p. 247)**

loss from uncollectible accounts **(p. 230)**

materiality **(p. 229)**

net cost **(p. 235)**

prepaid expense **(p. 233)**

reducing-charge methods **(p. 235)**

statement of account **(p. 241)**

straight-line method **(p. 235)**

subsidiary ledgers **(p. 237)**

three-column account form **(p. 238)**

uncollectible accounts expense **(p. 230)**

CHAPTER 9

The Periodic Summary

CHAPTER OBJECTIVES

Careful study of this chapter should enable you to:

- Prepare a ten-column end-of-year work sheet for a retail business, including the following adjustments:
  1. The two adjustments needed to combine the beginning and ending merchandise inventory components of cost of goods sold.
  2. The adjustment needed to recognize accrued interest payable.
  3. The adjustment needed to recognize accrued bank credit card payable.
  4. The two adjustments needed to recognize the cost of supplies and insurance premiums applicable to the year just ended.
  5. The two adjustments needed to recognize the amount of uncollectible accounts expense expected to result from the past year's charge sales and the amount of depreciation of property, plant, and equipment during the past year.
- Prepare the financial statements of a retail merchandising business.
- Analyze financial statements using some basic techniques.
- Describe the business owner's, as distinguished from the business', responsibility for income and self-employment taxes.

One of the major reasons for having an accounting system is to accumulate information that will make it possible to prepare periodic summaries for (1) the revenue and expenses of the business during a specified period and (2) the assets, liabilities, and owner's equity of the business at a specified date. A trial balance of the general ledger accounts provides most of the information that is required for these summaries (the income statement and the balance sheet). However, the trial balance does not supply the data in a form that is easily interpreted, nor does it reflect changes in the accounting elements that

have not been represented by ordinary business transactions. Therefore, at the end of a fiscal period, it is necessary (1) to determine the
kinds and amounts of changes that the accounts do not reflect and
adjust the accounts accordingly and (2) to recast the information into
the form of an income statement and a balance sheet. These two steps
are often referred to as the periodic summary.

END-OF-PERIOD WORK SHEET

It has already been explained in Chapter 5 that an end-of-period
work sheet is a device that assists the accountant in three ways. It
facilitates (1) the preparation of the financial statements, (2) the making of needed adjustments in the accounts, and (3) the closing of the
temporary owner's equity accounts. In most cases, management is
interested in reviewing the income statement and the balance sheet as
soon as possible after the period has ended.

Work sheets are not financial statements; they are devices used to
assist the accountant in performing certain tasks. Ordinarily, it is only
the accountant who uses a work sheet. For this reason, a work sheet is
usually prepared in pencil or with the aid of a microcomputer.

A Work Sheet For A Retail Store

While an end-of-period work sheet can be in any one of several
forms, a common and widely used arrangement involves ten amount
columns consisting of five pairs. The first pair of amount columns is
for the trial balance. The data to be entered consist of the name,
number, and debit or credit balance of each account. Debit balances
should be entered in the left-hand column and credit balances in the
right-hand column. The second pair of amount columns is used to
enter end-of-period adjustments. The third pair of amount columns is
used to show the account balances as adjusted. This pair of amount
columns is headed "Adjusted Trial Balance" because its purpose is to
show that the debit and credit account balances as adjusted are equal
in amount. The fourth pair of columns is for the adjusted balances of
the expense and revenue accounts and is headed "Income Statement"
since the amounts shown will be reported in that statement. The fifth
and last pair is headed "Balance Sheet" and shows the adjusted
account balances that will be reported in that statement. A ten-column end-of-year work sheet for MicroWorld is illustrated on page 282.

To illustrate the preparation and use of the end-of-period work
sheet, the example of the accounts of MicroWorld will be continued.

The journals and ledgers for this business for the month of December were reproduced in the preceding chapter. In this chapter, the income statement for the year and the balance sheet at the end of the year are reproduced, and the use of a work sheet as a device for summarizing the data to be presented in those statements will be demonstrated.

The Work Sheet for MicroWorld

Following is a description and discussion of the steps taken in the preparation of the work sheet on page 282. Each step should be studied carefully with frequent reference to the work sheet.

Trial Balance Columns. The trial balance of the general ledger accounts as of December 31 is entered in the first pair of amount columns. This trial balance is the same as the one shown on page 276 except that all of the account titles shown in the chart of accounts on page 245 are included in the work sheet list even though some of the accounts have no balances at this point.

The Trial Balance Debit and Credit columns are then totaled. The totals should be equal. If not, the discrepancy must be found and corrected before the preparation of the work sheet can proceed.

Adjustments Columns. The second pair of amount columns on the work sheet is used to make entries that reflect the changes that occurred during the year in some of the accounting elements. In this case, adjustments are needed: (a) and (b) to remove the amount of the beginning-of-year merchandise inventory and to enter the amount of the end-of-year inventory; (c) to enter the amount of interest expense incurred but not paid; (d) to enter the amount of bank credit card expense for December that will not be deducted from the bank account until early in the following month; (e) and (f) to enter the portions of supplies used and prepaid insurance expired during the year; (g) to enter the estimated amount of expected uncollectible accounts expense; and (h) to enter the estimated depreciation expense for the year.

Eight complete entries are made in the Adjustments columns to reflect these changes. When an account is debited or credited, the amount is entered on the same horizontal line as the name of the account and in the appropriate Adjustments Debit or Credit column. Each adjusting entry made on the work sheet is identified by a small letter in parentheses to facilitate cross-reference. Following is an explanation of each entry:

Microworld
Work Sheet
For the Year Ended December 31, 19--

#	Account Title	Acct. No.	TB Debit	TB Credit	Adj. Debit	Adj. Credit	ATB Debit	ATB Credit	IS Debit	IS Credit	BS Debit	BS Credit
1	Cash	111	5826055				5826055				5826055	
2	Petty Cash Fund	112	25000				25000				25000	
3	Accounts Receivable	131	3561374				3561374				3561374	
4	Allow. for Doubtful Accounts	131.1		59000		(b) 301263		360263				360263
5	Merchandise Inventory	141	9708380		(a) 10269520	(a) 9708380	10269520				10269520	
6	Supplies	151	202080			(a) 122080	80000				80000	
7	Prepaid Insurance	155	306029			(f) 153015	153014				153014	
8	Store Equipment	181	2354810				2354810				2354810	
9	Accum. Depr. Store Equip.	181.1		549364		(d) 235481		784845				784845
10	FICA Tax Payable	211		119452				119452				119452
11	FUTA Tax Payable	212		3568				3568				3568
12	State Unempl. Tax Payable	213		15286				15286				15286
13	Employees Inc. Tax Payable	214		143340				143340				143340
14	Accrued Bank C. Card Payable	215				(e) 9299		9299				9299
15	Notes Payable	216		3400000				3400000				3400000
16	Accrued Interest Payable	217				(c) 28333		28333				28333
17	Accounts Payable	218		1586621				1586621				1586621
18	Sales Tax Payable	221		482983				482983				482983
19	Faye J. Quirke, Capital	311		15603053				15603053				15603053
20	Faye J. Quirke, Drawing	311.1	8805000				8805000				8805000	
21	Expense + Revenue Summary	331			(a) 9708380	(a) 10269520	9708380	10269520	9708380	10269520		
22	Sales	411		8907449				8907449		8907449		
23	Sales Returns and Allow.	411.1	1340185				1340185		1340185			
24	Purchases	511	60316627				60316627		60316627			
25	Purchase Returns and Allow.	511.1		855370				855370		855370		
26	Rent Expense	541	2400000				2400000		2400000			
27	Salaries and Comm. Expense	542	8765104				8765104		8765104			
28	Heating and Lighting Expense	543	551536				551536		551536			
29	Telephone Expense	544	154672				154672		154672			
30	Supplies Expense	545			(a) 122080		122080		122080			
31	Advertising Expense	546	3923369				3923369		3923369			
32	Depreciation Expense	547			(d) 235481		235481		235481			
33	Insurance Expense	548			(f) 153015		153015		153015			
34	Charitable Contr. Expense	549	127000				127000		127000			
35	Payroll Taxes Expense	551	807904				807904		807904			
36	Bank Credit Card Expense	552	2450511		(e) 9299		2459810		2459810			
37	Uncollectible Accounts Expense	553			(b) 301263		301263		301263			
38	Miscellaneous Expense	562	204850				204850		204850			
39	Interest Expense	571	61970		(c) 28333		90303		90303			
			111892456	111892456	20827371	20827371	122736352	122736352	91661579	100199309	31074773	22537043
40	Net Income								8537730			8537730
									100199309	100199309	31074773	31074773

MicroWorld—Ten-Column Work Sheet

Entry (a)

Expense and Revenue Summary 97,083.80
Merchandise Inventory 97,083.80

This entry is the first of two entries that adjust for the cost of goods sold. In order to remove the amount of the beginning merchandise inventory from the asset account and at the same time include it in the determination of net income for the current year, Expense and Revenue Summary, Account No. 331, is debited and Merchandise Inventory, Account No. 141, is credited for $97,083.80. This amount had been in the merchandise inventory account as a debit since the accounts were adjusted as of December 31, a year ago. The amount of the beginning merchandise inventory is debited to Expense and Revenue Summary because it is, in effect, a part of the cost of goods sold.

Entry (b)

Merchandise Inventory 102,695.20
Expense and Revenue Summary 102,695.20

The second entry of this two-step procedure that adjusts for the cost of goods sold enters the calculated cost of the merchandise on hand December 31—often referred to as the year-end inventory. The calculation was based on a physical count of the merchandise in stock at the close of the year. The cost of the merchandise in stock at year end is entered by debiting Merchandise Inventory, Account No. 141, and crediting Expense and Revenue Summary, Account No. 331, for $102,695.20. The amount of ending inventory is credited to Expense and Revenue Summary because this amount is, in effect, a deduction in the calculation of the cost of goods sold, as follows:

Merchandise inventory, January 1		$ 97,083.80
Purchases	$603,166.27	
Less purchases returns and allowances	8,553.70	
Net purchases		594,612.57
Merchandise available for sale		$691,696.37
Less merchandise inventory, December 31		102,695.20
Cost of goods sold		$589,001.17

Ending inventory is the portion of the merchandise available for sale, defined as beginning inventory plus net purchases, that is still on hand at year end.

Entry (c)

Interest Expense 283.33
Accrued Interest Payable 283.33

This accrual adjustment enters the accrued interest expense that was incurred but not paid by debiting Interest Expense, Account No. 571, and by crediting Accrued Interest Payable, Account No. 217, for $283.33. The $34,000 note payable in the December 31 trial balance represents a 10%, 6-month note dated December 1. Interest on this note at the rate of 10% per year for 30 days (December 1 to December 31) is $283.33.

Entry (d)

Bank Credit Card Expense	92.99	
Accrued Bank Credit Card Payable		92.99

This adjustment enters the expense of the deduction that will be made by the bank during January for Visa and MasterCard vouchers deposited during December. These amounted to $2,324.76. The bank will deduct 4% of this amount, or $92.99 ($2,324.76 × .04), from the checking account. Since this $92.99 is really an expense for the year just ended, the adjustment is needed to include the expense in the calculation of net income for the past year. The adjustment is recorded by a debit to Bank Credit Card Expense, Account No. 552, and a credit to Accrued Bank Credit Card Payable, Account No. 215.

Entry (e)

Supplies Expense	1,220.80	
Supplies		1,220.80

This adjustment enters the calculated cost of the supplies used during the year by debiting Supplies Expense, Account No. 545, and crediting Supplies, Account No. 151, for $1,220.80. This amount was determined as follows: The December 31 trial balance shows that Supplies has a debit balance of $2,020.80, which is the cost of supplies on hand at the start of the year, plus the cost of supplies purchased during the year. A physical count made of the supplies on December 31 determined the cost of the supplies on hand to be $800. Thus, the cost of the supplies used during the year amounted to $1,220.80 ($2,020.80 − $800.00).

Entry (f)

Insurance Expense	1,530.15	
Prepaid Insurance		1,530.15

This adjustment enters the insurance expense for the year by debiting Insurance Expense, Account No. 548, and crediting Prepaid Insurance, Account No. 155, for $1,530.15. The December 31 trial balance shows that Prepaid Insurance has a debit balance of $3,060.29. This amount is the cost of a 2-year policy dated January 2 of the year under consideration. By December 31, one year had elapsed; therefore one half of the premium paid had become an expense.

Entry (g)

```
Uncollectible Accounts Expense ......................    3,012.63
    Allowance for Doubtful Accounts ...................               3,012.63
```

This adjustment enters the estimated uncollectible accounts expense for the year by debiting Uncollectible Accounts Expense, Account No. 553, and crediting Allowance for Doubtful Accounts, Account No. 131.1 for $3,012.63. Guided by past experience, MicroWorld estimated that uncollectible account losses will be approximately one percent of the total sales on account for the year. Investigation of the records revealed that such sales amounted to $301,262.73. One percent of this amount is $3,012.63.

Entry (h)

```
Depreciation Expense ...............................    2,354.81
    Accumulated Depreciation—Store Equipment .........               2,354.81
```

This adjustment enters the depreciation expense for the year by debiting Depreciation Expense, Account No. 547, and crediting Accumulated Depreciation—Store Equipment, Account No. 181.1 for $654.11. The December trial balance shows that Store Equipment has a debit balance of $23,548.10. This balance represents the cost of various items of property that have been owned the entire year. This equipment is being depreciated at the rate of 10% a year, or $2,354.81 ($23,548.10 × .10).

After making the required entries in the Adjustments columns of the work sheet, the columns are totaled to prove the equality of the debit and credit entries.

Adjusted Trial Balance Columns. The third pair of amount columns of the work sheet is for the adjusted trial balance, which is a trial balance after the adjustments have been applied. To determine the balance of each account after making the required adjustments, it is necessary to take into consideration the amounts entered in the first two pairs of amount columns (Trial Balance and Adjustments columns).

When an account balance is not affected by entries in the Adjustments columns, the amount in the Trial Balance columns is extended directly to the Adjusted Trial Balance columns. When an account balance is affected by an entry in the Adjustments columns, the balance to be entered in the Adjusted Trial Balance columns is increased or decreased by the amount of the adjusting entry. For example, Accumulated Depreciation—Store Equipment is listed in the Trial Balance Credit column as $5,493.64. Since there is an entry of $2,354.81 in the Adjustments Credit column, the amount extended to the Adjusted Trial Balance Credit column is $7,848.45 ($5,493.64 + $2,354.81). Prepaid Insurance is listed in the Trial Balance Debit column as $3,060.29. Since there is an entry of $1,530.15 in the Adjustments Credit column, the amount extended to the Adjusted Trial Balance Credit column is $1,530.14 ($3,060.29 − $1,530.15).

There is one exception to the procedure just described. It relates to the debit and the credit in the Adjustments columns for Expense and Revenue Summary, Account No. 331. While $5,611.40 is the excess of the $102,695.20 credit (the amount of the end-of-year merchandise inventory) over the $97,083.80 debit (the amount of the beginning-of-year merchandise inventory) and this excess amount can be extended to the Adjusted Trial Balance Credit column, it is better to extend both the debit and credit amounts into the Adjusted Trial Balance columns. The reason is that both amounts are used in the preparation of the cost of goods sold section on the income statement and, therefore, both amounts should appear in the Income Statement columns.

The Adjusted Trial Balance columns are then totaled to prove the equality of the debits and the credits.

Income Statement Columns. The fourth pair of columns of the work sheet shows the amounts that will be reported in the income statement. The manner of extending both the debit and credit amounts on the line for Expense and Revenue Summary was described previously. The amounts for sales and purchases returns and allowances are extended to the Income Statement Credit column. The amounts for sales returns and allowances, purchases, and all expenses are extended to the Income Statement Debit column.

The Income Statement columns are then totaled. The difference between the totals of these columns is the net income or net loss during the accounting period. If the total of the credits exceeds the total of the debits, the difference represents the increase in owner's equity due to net income; if the total of the debits exceeds the total of the credits, the difference represents the decrease in owner's equity due to net loss.

The Income Statement columns of MicroWorld's work sheet on page 282 show that the total of the credits amounts to $1,001,993.09

and the total of the debits amounts to $916,615.79. The difference, $85,377.30, is the net income for the year.

Balance Sheet Columns. The fifth pair of columns of the work sheet shows the amounts that will be reported in the balance sheet. The amounts for assets are extended to the Balance Sheet Debit column. The amounts for liabilities and owner's equity are extended to the Balance Sheet Credit column.

The Balance Sheet columns are then totaled. The difference between the totals of these columns also is the amount of net income or net loss for the accounting period. If the total of the debits exceeds the total of the credits, the difference represents net income; if the total of the credits exceeds the total of the debits, the difference represents net loss. This difference should be the same as the difference between the totals of the Income Statement columns.

The Balance Sheet columns of the work sheet of MicroWorld show that the total of the debits amounts to $310,747.73 and the total of the credits amounts to $225,370.43. The difference of $85,377.30 represents the amount of net income for the year.

Completing the Work Sheet. The difference ($85,377.30) between the totals of the Income Statement columns and the totals of the Balance Sheet columns is entered on the next horizontal line below the totals. Since the difference represents net income, it is entered in the Income Statement Debit and in the Balance Sheet Credit columns. If a net loss resulted, the amount would be so designated and entered in the Income Statement Credit and in the Balance Sheet Debit columns. After the net income (or net loss) has been entered, double rulings are placed immediately below the totals.

Proving the Work Sheet. The work sheet provides proof of the arithmetical accuracy of the data that it summarizes. The totals of the Trial Balance columns, the Adjustments Columns, and the Adjusted Trial Balance columns must be equal. The amount of the difference between the totals of the Income Statement columns must be exactly the same amount as the difference between the totals of the Balance Sheet columns.

The reason why the same amount will balance both the Income Statement columns and the Balance Sheet columns is provided by an understanding of (1) the real nature of net income (or net loss) and (2) the basic difference between the income statement accounts and the balance sheet accounts. The reality of net income is that the assets have increased, or that the liabilities have decreased, or that some combination of both events has taken place during a period of time. Most of these changes are entered day after day in the asset and liability accounts in order that they may be kept up to date. However, the effect of the changes on the owner's equity element is not entered in the permanent owner's equity account. Instead, the changes are entered in the temporary owner's equity accounts—the revenue and expense accounts.

At the end of the period after the asset and liability accounts have been adjusted, each of these accounts reflects all of the changes of the period. In contrast, all of the changes in owner's equity for the period are reflected in the revenue and expense accounts and in the drawing account.

As applied to the work sheet, this means that the Balance Sheet column totals are out of balance by the amount of the change in owner's equity due to net income or net loss for the period involved. In other words, the asset and liability accounts reflect the net income of the period, but the owner's capital account at this point does not. It is only after the temporary accounts are closed at the end of the period and the amount of the net income for the period has been transferred to the owner's capital account that this account reflects the net income of the period.

The owner's capital account lacks two things to bring its balance up to date: (1) the decrease due to any withdrawals during the period, which is reflected in the debit balance of the drawing account and (2) the increase due to any net income (or the decrease due to any net loss) for the period. On the work sheet, the debit balance of the drawing account is extended to the Balance Sheet Debit column. Thus, all that is needed to cause the Balance Sheet columns to be equal is the amount of the net income (or loss) for the year—the same amount that is the difference between the totals of the Income Statement columns.

BUILDING YOUR ACCOUNTING KNOWLEDGE

1. In what three ways does an end-of-period work sheet assist the accountant?
2. Explain the purpose of each of the eight adjustments on the MicroWorld work sheet.
3. Why are both the debit and credit amounts in the Adjustments columns on the Expense and Revenue Summary line of the work sheet extended to the Adjusted Trial Balance columns?
4. What two amounts from the Income Statement Debit column are added and what amount from the Income Statement Credit column is then subtracted to determine the amount of merchandise available for sale?
5. What amount from the Income Statement Credit column is subtracted from the merchandise available for sale to calculate the cost of goods sold?
6. What does the difference between the totals of the Income Statement columns represent? What does the difference between the Balance Sheet column totals represent?

7. What two things does the owner's capital account lack to bring its balance up to date?

APPLYING ACCOUNTING CONCEPTS

Exercise 9-1. Provide the adjusting entries in two-column journal form that are needed for the following situations. The end of the accounting period is December 31, 19--.

1. The supplies account has a balance of $750. An inventory of the supplies on hand indicates that $215 is available at the end of the year.
2. Interest is owed on a $2,500, 13%, 60-day note payable. The note is dated December 15 of the current year.
3. Visa and MasterCard vouchers in the amount of $7,528 were deposited on December 29. The vouchers are subject to a bank credit card expense of 4%.
4. The prepaid insurance account has a balance of $646. This represents the premium for a two-year fire policy. The policy was effective as of September 1 of the current year.
5. The office equipment is depreciated at the rate of 10%. The balance in the office equipment account is $8,635.
6. Sales on account for the year totaled $96,820. Based on past experience, losses for uncollectible accounts are estimated to be three-fourths of 1% of sales on account.

Exercise 9-2. Identify the financial statement (or statements) on which each of the following accounts would be shown. Assume that each account has a normal balance. Copy the account numbers and on the same line write an "I" if the account goes on the income statement and a "B" if the account goes on the balance sheet. Indicate next to the financial statement designation a DR or a CR to show the normal balance of the account.

1. Accounts Payable
2. Accounts Receivable
3. Accumulated Depreciation—Store Equipment
4. Accrued Bank Credit Card Payable
5. Accrued Interest Payable
6. Allowance for Doubtful Accounts
7. Advertising Expense
8. Bank Credit Card Expense
9. Cash
10. B. J. Evans, Capital
11. Depreciation Expense
12. B. J. Evans, Drawing
13. Employees Income Tax Payable
14. Expense and Revenue Summary
15. FICA Tax Payable
16. FUTA Tax Payable
17. Insurance Expense
18. Merchandise Inventory (beginning of the period)
19. Merchandise Inventory (end of the period)
20. Payroll Taxes Payable
21. Petty Cash Fund
22. Prepaid Insurance
23. Purchases
24. Purchases Returns and Allowances
25. Revenue from Fees
26. Sales
27. Sales Returns and Allowances
28. Sales Tax Payable
29. Store Equipment
30. Uncollectible Accounts Expense

**Report
No. 9-1**

Complete Report 9-1 in the study assignments and submit your working papers to the instructor for approval. After completing the report, continue with the following textbook discussion until the next report is required.

THE FINANCIAL STATEMENTS

The financial statements of a small retail business usually include (1) an income statement and (2) a balance sheet. In addition, a third statement, called the "Statement of Changes in Financial Position," is normally prepared by larger enterprises. The purpose of an income statement is to summarize the results of operations during an accounting period. The income statement provides information as to the sources of revenue, types of expenses, and the amount of the net income or the net loss for the period. The purpose of a balance sheet is to provide information as to the status of a business at a specified date. The balance sheet shows the kinds and amounts of assets and liabilities and the owner's equity in the business at a specified point in time—usually at the close of business on the last date of the accounting period.

The Income Statement

A formal statement of the results of the operation of a business during an accounting period is called an income statement. Other titles commonly used for this statement include statement of earnings, operating statement, profit and loss statement, and income and expense statement. The purpose of the statement is to show the types and amounts of revenue and expenses that the business had during the accounting period involved, and the resulting net income or net loss for this period.

Importance of the Income Statement. The income statement is generally considered to be the most important financial statement of a business. A business normally cannot survive for very long unless it makes a profit. The income statement is essentially a "report card" of the enterprise. The statement provides a basis for judging the overall effectiveness of the management. Decisions as to whether to continue a business, to expand it, or to contract it are often based upon the results as reported in the income statement. Actual and potential creditors are interested in income statements because one of the best reasons for extending credit or for making a loan is that the business is profitable.

Various government agencies are interested in income statements of businesses for a variety of reasons. Regulatory bodies are concerned with the earnings of the enterprises they regulate, such as airlines, banks, insurance companies, public utilities and railroads, because a part of the regulation usually relates to the prices, rates, or fares that may be charged. If the enterprise is either exceptionally profitable or unprofitable, some change in the allowed prices or rates may be needed. Income tax authorities—federal, state, and local—have an interest in business income statements. Net income determination for tax purposes differs somewhat from the calculation of net income for financial reporting purposes, but for a variety of reasons, the tax authorities are interested in both sets of calculations.

Form of the Income Statement. It is essential that the income statement be properly headed. The name of the business (or of the individual if it is a professional practice or is named for the owner) should be shown first. The name of the statement is then shown followed by the period of time that the statement covers, for example, "For the Year Ended December 31, 1986."

The body of the income statement depends, in part, upon the type of business. Two types of income statement forms are commonly used—the single step and the multiple step. The single-step form of income statement lists all revenue items and their total first, followed by all expense items and their total, to produce a difference which is either net income or net loss.

The multiple-step form of income statement is commonly used for merchandising businesses. The term "multiple-step" is applied because the final net income is calculated on a step-by-step basis. The amount of gross sales is shown first with sales returns and allowances deducted, resulting in a difference called net sales. (Many published income statements begin with the amount of net sales.) Cost of goods sold is next subtracted to arrive at gross margin (sometimes called gross profit). The portion of the statement down to this point is sometimes called the "trading section." Operating expenses are listed next, and the total of their amounts is subtracted from the gross margin to arrive at the amount of operating income. Finally, the amounts of any other revenue are added and any other expenses are subtracted to arrive at the final amount of net income (or net loss). Interest expense is classified as "other expense" because it is an expense of financing the business, rather than an expense of operating the business.

The spread sheet analysis, formatting, and word processing capabilities of microcomputers make it easy to prepare the original statements as computer print-outs which can be photocopied. The photocopies can then be presented to the owners of a business and to potential creditors or other interested parties. The multiple-step income statement for MicroWorld for the year ended December 31, 19--, is shown on the next page. The information needed in preparing the statement was obtained from the work sheet shown on page 282. Note that the operating expenses are arranged in descending size order (except for Miscellaneous Expense), which is a fairly common approach.

The Balance Sheet

A formal statement of the assets, liabilities, and owner's equity of a business at a specified date is known as a balance sheet. The title of the statement had its origin in the equality of the elements, that is, the sum of the assets equals the sum of the liabilities and owner's equity. Sometimes, the balance sheet is called a statement of financial position, a statement of condition, or a statement of assets and liabilities. Many accountants now believe that the title statement of financial position is more descriptive of what is shown on the balance sheet. Various other titles are used occasionally.

Importance of the Balance Sheet. The balance sheet of a business is of considerable interest to various parties for several reasons. The owner or owners of a business are interested in the kinds and amounts of assets and liabilities and the amount of the owner's equity or capital element.

Creditors of the business are interested in the financial position of the enterprise, particularly as it pertains to the claims they have and the prospects for prompt payment. Potential creditors are concerned about the financial position of the business. Their decision as to whether to extend credit or to make loans to the business may depend, in large part, upon the condition of the enterprise as revealed by a balance sheet.

Persons considering buying an ownership interest in a business are greatly interested in the character and amount of the assets and liabilities, in addition to the future earnings possibilities of the business.

Finally, various regulatory bodies are interested in the financial position of the businesses that are under their jurisdiction.

Form of the Balance Sheet. It is essential that the balance sheet be properly headed. The name of the business (or the name of the individual if it is a professional practice or is named for the owner), should be shown first. This is followed by the name of the statement—usually just "Balance Sheet," and then the date—month, day, and year. It

MicroWorld
Income Statement
For the Year Ended December 31, 19--

Operating revenue:
Sales			$890,744.19
Less sales returns and allowances			13,401.85
Net sales			$877,342.34

Cost of goods sold:
Merchandise inventory, January 1		$ 97,083.80	
Purchases	$603,166.27		
Less purchases returns and allowances	8,553.70		
Net purchases		594,612.57	
Merchandise available for sale		$691,696.37	
Less merchandise inventory, December 31 ..		102,695.20	
Cost of goods sold			589,001.17
Gross margin on sales......................			$288,341.17

Operating expenses:
Salaries and commissions expense		$ 87,651.04	
Advertising expense		39,233.69	
Bank credit card expense..................		24,598.10	
Rent expense		24,000.00	
Payroll taxes expense		8,079.04	
Heating and lighting expense		5,515.36	
Uncollectible accounts expense		3,012.63	
Depreciation expense......................		2,354.81	
Telephone expense........................		1,546.72	
Insurance expense		1,530.15	
Charitable contributions expense		1,270.00	
Supplies expense		1,220.80	
Miscellaneous expense		2,048.50	
Total operating expenses			202,060.84
Operating income			$ 86,280.33

Other expenses:
Interest expense			903.03
Net income .....'..........................			$ 85,377.30

MicroWorld—Income Statement

must be remembered that a balance sheet relates to a particular moment of time.

Traditionally, balance sheets have been presented either in account form or in report form. Each of these forms was discussed briefly in Chapter 5. In the account form, the assets are listed on the left side of the page or on the left of two facing pages, and the liabilities and owner's equity are listed on the right. This form is similar to the debit-side and credit-side arrangement of the standard ledger account. The balance sheet of MicroWorld as of December 31, 19--, in account form is reproduced on pages 296 and 297. The data for the preparation of the statement were taken from the work sheet.

When the report form of the balance sheet is followed, the assets, liabilities, and owner's equity elements are exhibited in that order on the page. The balance sheet of Vance Zarmer, Computer Consultant, was shown in report form on page 142. This arrangement is generally preferable if the statement is to be printed out on regular letter-size paper ($8\frac{1}{2}''$ × $11''$).

Classification of Data in the Balance Sheet. The purpose of the balance sheet and of all other financial statements and reports is to convey as much information as possible. This aim is furthered by the classification of the data being reported. As applied to the balance sheet, it has become almost universal practice to classify both assets and liabilities into those that are considered current and those that are considered noncurrent or long-term.

Current Assets. Current assets include cash and all other assets that may be reasonably expected to be converted to cash or sold or consumed within one year or the normal operating cycle of the business, whichever is longer. In a merchandising business, the current assets usually include cash, receivables (such as accounts receivable), merchandise inventory, and temporary investments. Prepaid expenses, such as unused supplies and unexpired insurance, are also generally treated as current assets. This is not because these items will be realized in cash, but because they will probably be consumed in a relatively short time.

The asset cash may be represented by one or more accounts, such as bank checking accounts, bank savings accounts, or a petty cash fund. The MicroWorld balance sheet on pages 296-297 shows that cash is listed at $58,510.55, which is made up of two items as shown in the work sheet on page 282: the balance in the checking account at the Third National Bank, $58,260.55, and the amount of the petty cash fund, $250.

Temporary investments are those assets that have been acquired with money that would otherwise have been temporarily idle and unproductive. Such investments usually take the form of corporate stocks, bonds, notes, or any of several types of government bonds, notes, or bills. Quite often, the policy is to invest in securities that can be liquidated in a short time with little chance of loss. The account entitled Marketable Securities is frequently used to describe temporary investments.

Assets of the same type may be owned by a business for many years. Under such circumstances, they would be classified as long-term investments and included in a separate asset classification entitled Investments. The intention of the business indicates whether the investments are to be classified as temporary and included in the current assets as marketable securities or considered as long-term investments and included in a separate asset classification entitled Investments. Presently, MicroWorld has no investments, but Quinn might be well advised to invest a portion of the relatively large cash balance in high-yield short-term securities.

Property, Plant, and Equipment. Assets that are used in the operation of a business, such as land, buildings, office equipment, store equipment, and delivery equipment are called property, plant, and equipment. Of these assets, only land is permanent; however, all of these assets have a useful life that is comparatively long.

The balance sheet of MicroWorld shows that store equipment is the only such asset. The amount of the accumulated depreciation is shown as a deduction from the cost of the equipment. The difference represents the undepreciated cost of the equipment which is the amount that will be written off as depreciation expense in future periods.

Current Liabilities. Current liabilities include those obligations that will be due within one year or the normal operating cycle of the business, whichever is longer, and paid with monies provided by the current assets. As of December 31, the current liabilities of MicroWorld consist of FICA tax payable, FUTA tax payable, state unemployment tax payable, employees income tax payable, accrued bank credit card payable, notes payable, accrued interest payable, accounts payable, and sales tax payable.

Long-Term Liabilities. Long-term liabilities include those obligations that will extend beyond one year or one normal operating cycle, whichever is longer. The most common long-term liability is a mortgage payable.

Mortgage Payable is an account that is used to reflect a debt or an obligation that is secured by a mortgage on certain property. A mortgage is a written agreement specifying that if the borrower does not repay a debt, the lender has the right to take over the property to satisfy the debt. When the debt is paid, the mortgage becomes void. A mortgage payable is similar to an account payable or a note payable except that the creditor holds the mortgage as security for the payment of the debt. Usually, debts secured by mortgages run for a longer

Micro
Balance
December

Assets

Current assets:

Cash		$ 58,510.55
Accounts receivable	$35,613.74	
Less allowance for doubtful accounts	3,602.63	32,011.11
Merchandise inventory......................................		102,695.20
Supplies		800.00
Prepaid insurance		1,530.14
Total current assets		$195,547.00

Property, plant, and equipment:

Store equipment	$23,548.10	
Less accumulated depreciation	7,848.45	
Total property, plant, and equipment		15,699.65

Total assets..		$211,246.65

MicroWorld—Balance Sheet (left side)

period of time than ordinary notes payable or accounts payable. A mortgage payable is classified as a long-term liability if the maturity date extends beyond one year or the normal operating cycle of the business, whichever is longer. MicroWorld has no long-term liabilities.

Owner's Equity. Accounts relating to the owner's equity element may be either permanent or temporary. The permanent owner's equity accounts which are used to accumulate the results of the operations of a particular enterprise are determined by the type of organization, that is, whether the enterprise is organized as a sole proprietorship, as a partnership, or as a corporation.

In a sole proprietorship, one or more accounts representing the owner's interest or equity in the assets may be kept. The chart of accounts on page 245 shows that the following accounts are classified as owner's equity accounts for Faye J. Quinn:

> Faye J. Quinn, Capital—Account No. 311
> Faye J. Quinn, Drawing—Account No. 311.1
> Expense and Revenue Summary—Account No. 331

World
Sheet
31, 19--

Liabilities

Current liabilities:
FICA tax payable	$ 1,194.52	
FUTA tax payable	35.68	
State unemployment tax payable	152.86	
Employees income tax payable	1,433.40	
Accrued bank credit card payable	92.99	
Notes payable	34,000.00	
Accrued interest payable	283.33	
Accounts payable	15,866.21	
Sales tax payable	4,829.83	
Total current liabilities		$ 57,888.82

Owner's Equity

Faye J. Quinn, capital:
Capital, January 1		$156,030.53
Net income	$85,377.30	
Withdrawals	88,050.00	(2,672.70)
Capital, December 31		153,357.83
Total liabilities and owner's equity		$211,246.65

MicroWorld—Balance Sheet (right side)

Account No. 311 reflects the amount of Quinn's equity. It may be increased by additional investments and net income for the accounting period of the enterprise; it may be decreased by withdrawals and by sustaining a net loss for the accounting period. Except for additional investments, there will be no change in the balance of this account during the accounting period, in which case the balance represents the owner's investment in the business as of the beginning of the accounting period and until such time as the books are closed at the end of the accounting period.

Account No. 311.1 is Quinn's drawing account. This account is charged for any withdrawals of cash or other property for personal use. It is a temporary account in which the owner's personal drawings during the accounting period are entered. Ordinarily such drawings are made in anticipation of earnings rather than as withdrawals of capital. The balance of the account, as shown by the trial balance at the close of an accounting period, represents the total amount of the owner's drawings during the period.

The work sheet shown on page 282 reveals that the balance of Quinn's drawing account is listed in the Balance Sheet Debit column. This is because there is no provision on a work sheet for making deductions from owner's equity except by listing them in the Debit column. Since the balance of the owner's capital account is listed in the Balance Sheet Credit column, the listing of the balance of the owner's drawing account in the Debit column is equivalent to deducting the amount from the balance of the owner's capital account.

Account No. 331 is used only at the close of the accounting period to adjust the merchandise inventory account and summarize the temporary owner's equity accounts. Sometimes this account is referred to as a clearing account. No entries appear in this account before the books are adjusted and closed at the end of the accounting period.

The owner's equity section of the balance sheet of MicroWorld is arranged to show the major changes that took place during the year in the owner's equity element of the business. Quinn's interest in the business amounted to $156,030.53 at the beginning of the period. The interest increased $85,377.30 as the result of profitable operations and decreased $88,050.00 as the result of withdrawals during the year. Thus, the owner's equity element of the business on December 31 amounted to $153,357.83 ($156,030.53 + $85,377.30 − $88,050.00).

Analysis of Financial Statements

There are various procedures employed to assist in the interpretation of income statements.

Income Statement Analysis. Income statements may be presented for two or more periods of comparable length in comparative form. The figures for the two periods are shown in adjacent columns and a third column shows the amount of increase or decrease in each element. This will call attention to changes of major significance.

Another analytical device is to express all or at least the major items on the statement as a percent of net sales and then to compare these percentages for two or more periods. The income statement of MicroWorld on page 293 is used to illustrate this approach. If the net sales of $877,342.34 for the year just ended are treated as 100%, the cost of goods sold, which amounted to $589,001.17, is equal to 67.13% ($589,001.17 ÷ $877,342.34) of net sales; the gross margin, which amounted to $288,341.17, is equal to 32.87% ($288,341.17 ÷ $877,342.34) of net sales; operating expenses, which amounted to $202,060.84, are equal to 23.03% ($202,060.84 ÷ $877,342.34) of net sales; operating income (gross margin less operating expenses), which amounted to $86,280.33, is equal to 9.84% ($86,280.33 ÷ $877,342.34) of net sales; interest expense, which amounted to $903.03, is equal to .10% ($903.03 ÷ $877,342.34) of net sales; and net income, which amounted to $85,377.30, is equal to 9.74% ($85,377.30 ÷ $877,342.34) of net sales.

Net sales	$877,342.34	100.00%
Less cost of goods sold	589,001.17	67.13
Gross margin on sales	$288,341.17	32.87
Operating expenses	202,060.84	23.03
Operating income	$ 86,280.33	9.84
Interest expense	903.03	.10
Net income	$ 85,377.30	9.74%

A comparison of these percentages with the same data (if available) for one or more prior years would reveal trends that would be of interest, and perhaps of real concern, to the management of the business. Also, a comparison of these percentages with benchmark data for retail computer businesses of about the same size with respect to assets and net sales would be useful. Such data are available from the U.S. Department of Commerce.

Balance Sheet Analysis. The information provided by a balance sheet can be analyzed in several ways to assist in judging the financial position and soundness of the business. A few of the major analytical procedures will be briefly considered.

A balance sheet as of one date may be compared with a balance sheet as of another date to determine the amount of the increase or the decrease in any of the accounts or groups of accounts. Sometimes, balance sheets as of two or more dates are prepared in comparative form by listing the amounts as of different dates in parallel columns. Thus, if balance sheets as of the close of two consecutive calendar years are compared, it is possible to determine the amount of the increase or the decrease during the intervening period in any of the accounts or groups of accounts involved. If the comparison reveals an increase in accounts receivable, it may indicate either a business expansion or that collections were not as favorable as they were during the preceding period. If the comparison reveals an increase in accounts payable, it may indicate either business expansion or an inability to pay current bills because of insufficient cash. If the comparison reveals an increase in the current assets without a corresponding increase in the current liabilities, it may indicate an improved financial position or status.

Too much emphasis should not be placed upon an increase or decrease in cash. Some individuals are inclined to judge the results of operations largely by the cash balance. This practice may be misleading. The net results of operations can be properly determined only by the comparison of all assets and liabilities.

The ability of a business to meet its current obligations may be determined largely by an analysis of its current assets and current liabilities. In a merchandising enterprise in which the capital invested is a material revenue-producing factor, the current ratio, which is the ratio of the current assets to the current liabilities, may be important.

$$\text{Current ratio} = \frac{\text{Current assets}}{\text{Current liabilities}}$$

The balance sheet shown on pages 296 and 297 reveals that the total current assets amount to $195,547.00 and the total current liabilities amount to $57,888.82, a ratio of 3.38 to 1 ($195,547.00 ÷ $57,888.82). This ratio is sufficiently high to indicate a very favorable financial position. The rough "rule of thumb" traditionally has been that a current ratio should be about 2 to 1, but many businesses operate successfully on a minimum current ratio of 1.5 to 1.

Banks often consider the ratio of current assets to current liabilities when considering the advisability of making a loan. It is not expected that the property, plant and equipment assets will be sold to realize sufficient funds with which to pay a short-term loan. If the balance sheet seems to indicate that a sufficient amount of cash will not be realized from the collection of accounts receivable or from the sales of service or merchandise to repay a loan at maturity, the bank may consider the loan inadvisable.

Other measures sometimes used in analyzing a firm's ability to meet its current obligations are the quick ratio and the amount of working capital. Quick assets include cash and all other current assets that are readily realizable in cash, such as accounts receivable, and temporary investments in the form of marketable securities and short-term certificates of deposit. The ratio of quick assets to current liabilities is called the quick ratio.

$$\text{Quick ratio} = \frac{\text{Quick assets}}{\text{Current liabilities}}$$

The balance sheet shown on pages 296 and 297 reveals total quick assets of $90,521.66 and a quick ratio of 1.56 to 1 ($90,521.66 ÷ $57,888.02). This means that quick assets are more than adequate to meet current obligations. Again, the rough "rule of thumb" traditionally has been that a quick ratio should be about 1 to 1, but many businesses operate successfully on a minimum quick ratio of 0.6 to 1.

The excess of the amount of current assets over the amount of current liabilities is called working capital or net current assets.

Working capital = Current assets — Current liabilities

Working capital is an indicator of the funds available with which to carry on current business operations. MicroWorld's working capital at year-end amounts to $137,658.18 ($195,547.00 — $57,888.82), which is nearly 90% ($137,658.18 ÷ $153,357.83) of owner's equity.

It is difficult to estimate what the proper current ratio, quick ratio, or amount of working capital should be, because of the variations in enterprises and industries. A 2 to 1 ratio of current assets to current liabilities, while more than sufficient in some enterprises, may be inadequate in others. In the milk distribution business, for example, a 1 to 1 ratio of current assets to current liabilities is considered satisfactory. The reasons are that very little capital is tied up in inventory, the amount of accounts receivable is comparatively small, and the terms on which the milk is purchased from farmers are such that settlements are slow and comparatively large amounts are due to farmers at all times. Another reason is that a large amount of capital is invested in property, plant and equipment, such as equipment for treating the milk and delivering it to customers.

Interstatement Analysis. A comparison of the relationships between certain amounts in the income statement and certain amounts in the balance sheet may be informative. A good example of this type is the ratio of net income to owner's equity in the business, which is known as return on owner's equity or return on investment (ROI).

$$\text{Return on owner's equity (ROI)} = \frac{\text{Net income}}{\text{Owner's equity}}$$

The owner's equity of MicroWorld was $156,030.53 on January 1. The net income for the year of $85,377.30 is 55% ($85,377.30 ÷ $156,030.53) of the owner's equity. A comparison of this ratio with the return on owner's equity in prior years should be of interest to the owner. It may also be of interest to compare the return on owner's equity of MicroWorld with the same ratio for other stores of comparable nature and size. It is important to note, however, that the net income of MicroWorld was computed without regard to any salary or other compensation for the services of Quinn. In comparing the results of operations of MicroWorld with those of other retail computer businesses, some appropriate adjustment of the salary and other compensation data might be needed in order to impute the value of Quinn's services and make the comparison valid.

Another ratio involving both balance sheet and income statement accounts is the rate of inventory turnover for each accounting period— the number of times the merchandise available for sale is turned during the accounting period. The rate of inventory turnover is determined by the following:

$$\frac{\text{Cost of goods sold for the period}}{\text{Average inventory}}$$

If inventory is taken only at the end of each accounting period, the average inventory for the period may be calculated by adding the beginning and ending inventories and dividing their sum by two. The turnover of MicroWorld for the year ended December 31, is computed as follows:

Beginning inventory	$ 97,083.80
Ending inventory	102,695.20
Cost of goods sold for the period	589,001.17

$$\text{Average inventory} = \frac{\text{Beginning inventory (\$97,083.80} + \text{Ending inventory (\$102,695.20)}}{2}$$

$$= \$99,889.50$$

$$\text{Rate of turnover} = \frac{\text{Cost of goods sold for the period (\$589,001.17)}}{\text{Average inventory (\$99,889.50)}} = 5.9$$

This calculation indicates that, on the average, the merchandise turns over almost once every 2 months. A careful analysis of the theory involved in computing the rate of inventory turnover will indicate that the greater the rate of turnover, the smaller the margin need be on each dollar of sales to produce a satisfactory total dollar amount of gross margin. This is because the increase in numbers of units sold offsets the smaller amount of gross margin earned per unit.

Income and Self-Employment Taxes

The discussion of accounting for the revenue and expenses of a business enterprise has included frequent references to income tax considerations. It is important to note that an unincorporated business owned by one person is not taxed. The owner—not the business—is subject to income taxes. Business revenue and business expenses must be reported on the owner's personal tax return regardless of the amount of money or other property that was withdrawn from the business during the year. As mentioned in Chapter 1, in the case of a sole proprietorship, there is no legal distinction between the business and its owner.

To bring a large class of self-employed individuals into the federal social security program, the law requires all self-employed persons (except those specifically exempted) to pay a self-employment tax. The rate of tax is about 2.5% more than the prevailing FICA rate, but the base of the self-employment income tax is the same as the base for the FICA tax. If it is assumed that the combined FICA tax rate is 7.5%, the self-employment income tax rate would be about 10% on the assumed base of $47,000. Self-employment income means the net income of a trade or business conducted by an individual or a partner's distributive share of the net income of a partnership whether or not any cash is distributed. Earnings of less than $400 from self-employment are ignored. The actual rate and base of the tax may be changed by Act of Congress at any time.

A taxable year for the purpose of the tax on self-employment income is the same as the taxpayer's taxable year for federal income tax purposes. The self-employment tax is reported along with the regular federal income tax. For calendar-year taxpayers, the tax return and full or final payment are due on April 15 following the close of the year. Like the personal income tax, the self-employment tax is treated as a personal expense of the owner, and thus its cost would not appear on the financial statements of the business. If the taxes are paid with business funds, the amount should be charged to the owner's drawing account and will thus appear on the balance sheet opposite the "Less withdrawals" caption.

BUILDING YOUR ACCOUNTING KNOWLEDGE

1. Explain why the income statement is essentially a "report card" of the enterprise.
2. Describe the nature of the two forms of income statement.
3. How did the title "balance sheet" originate? What title do many accountants now believe to be more descriptive?
4. What is the major difference between the two forms of balance sheet?
5. What determines the permanent owner's equity accounts used to accumulate the results of operations of a particular enterprise?
6. What are the two major analytical devices used to assist in the interpretation of income statements?
7. Explain why it is difficult to say what is a proper ratio of current assets to current liabilities.
8. Describe the use of the return on owner's equity (ROI) ratio; the use of rate of inventory turnover.
9. How should the amount of the self-employment tax be accounted for if the tax is paid with business funds?

APPLYING ACCOUNTING CONCEPTS

Exercise 9-3. The adjusted trial balance for Buttons & Bows Fabrics is shown below:

Buttons & Bows Fabrics
Adjusted Trial Balance
For the Year Ended December 31, 19--

	Debit	Credit
Cash	5,507	
Accounts Receivable	12,310	
Allowance for Doubtful Accounts		369
Merchandise Inventory	43,790	
Supplies	1,285	
Prepaid Insurance	984	
Office Equipment	8,750	
Accumulated Depreciation—Office Equipment		3,500
Accrued Bank Credit Card Payable		64
Notes Payable		4,625
Accrued Interest Payable		75
B. L. Merle, Capital		55,232
B. L. Merle, Drawing	7,200	
Expense and Revenue Summary	51,876	43,790
Sales		154,737
Sales Returns and Allowances	3,715	
Purchases	96,238	
Purchases Returns and Allowances		5,412
Salaries and Commissions Expense	30,750	
Depreciation Expense	1,750	
Insurance Expense	328	
Bank Credit Card Expense	2,189	
Uncollectible Accounts Expense	345	
Interest Expense	637	
Miscellaneous Expense	150	
Totals	267,804	267,804

Prepare **(a)** a multiple-step income statement and **(b)** a classified balance sheet in report form.

Exercise 9-4. The following amounts were taken from the income statement for Edgewood Frame Gallery for the month ended November 30, 19--:

Net sales	$293,073
Cost of goods sold	203,640
Operating expenses	36,763
Other expenses	490

Using net sales as the base, calculate the percent of net sales for each of the following items: **(a)** Net sales; **(b)** Cost of goods sold; **(c)** Gross margin on sales; **(d)** Operating expenses; **(e)** Operating income; **(f)** Other expenses; **(g)** Net income.

Exercise 9-5.   The following are amounts that were summarized from the April 30, 19--, balance sheet for Mead Office Products:

Cash	$ 8,506
Accounts receivable (net amount)	3,413
Merchandise inventory, April 1	14,077
Merchandise inventory, April 30	14,292
Total current assets	26,549
Total assets	28,821
Total current liabilities	9,078
L. R. Mead, capital, April 1	19,130
Net income	12,380
L. R. Mead, drawing	11,767
Cost of goods sold for April	85,405

Determine the following ratios that might be significant in evaluating the status of Mead Office Products. **(a)** Current ratio; **(b)** Quick ratio; **(c)** Working capital; **(d)** Return on owner's equity; **(e)** Rate of inventory turnover.

Exercise 9-6.   Cindi Rozell owns Cindi's Inside Story, an unincorporated interior decorating consulting agency. Rozell is self-employed. Her company had a net income of $63,975 for the current fiscal year.

Assume that self-employment income tax rate is 10% and the base on which the tax is assessed is $47,000. Determine the amount of self-employment tax owed by Rozell.

Report No. 9-2

> *Complete Report No. 9-2 in the study assignments and submit your working papers to the instructor for approval. After completing the report, you may continue with the textbook discussion in Chapter 10 until the next report is required.*

EXPANDING YOUR BUSINESS VOCABULARY

What is the meaning of each of the following terms?

account form **(p. 293)**

adjusted trial balance **(p. 285)**

balance sheet **(p. 292)**

clearing account **(p. 298)**

current assets **(p. 294)**

current liabilities **(p. 295)**

current ratio **(p. 300)**

gross margin/gross profit **(p. 291)**

income statement **(p. 290)**

income and expense statement **(p. 290)**

inventory turnover **(p. 302)**

long-term liabilities **(p. 295)**

Marketable Securities **(p. 294)**

merchandise available for sale **(p. 283)**

mortgage **(p. 295)**

Mortgage Payable **(p. 295)**

multiple-step form **(p. 291)**

net current assets **(p. 301)**

net sales **(p. 291)**

operating income **(p. 291)**

operating statement **(p. 290)**

periodic summary (p. 280)

profit and loss statement (p. 290)

property, plant, and equipment (p. 295)

quick assets (p. 300)

quick ratio (p. 300)

report form (p. 294)

return on investment (ROI) (p. 301)

return on owner's equity (p. 301)

self-employment income (p. 303)

single-step form (p. 291)

statement of assets and liabilities (p. 292)

statement of condition (p. 292)

statement of earnings (p. 290)

statement of financial position (p. 292)

temporary investments (p. 294)

undepreciated cost (p. 295)

work sheet (p. 280)

working capital (p. 301)

CHAPTER 10

Adjusting and Closing Accounts at End of Accounting Period

CHAPTER OBJECTIVES

Careful study of this chapter should enable you to:

- Explain and perform the steps in the accounting cycle that are needed to:
  1. Journalize and post adjusting entries and update the ledger account balances.
  2. Journalize and post closing entries and update the ledger account balances.
  3. Take a post-closing trial balance.
  4. Journalize and post reversing entries.

As explained in the preceding chapter, the adjustment of certain accounts at the end of the accounting period is required because changes that have occurred during the period are not reflected in the accounts. Since the purpose of the temporary owner's equity accounts is to assemble information relating to a specified period of time, the balances of these accounts must be closed out at the end of the period to prepare the accounts for the following period.

The purpose of this chapter is to acquaint you with those end-of-period activities in the accounting cycle that deal with adjusting entries, closing entries, the post-closing trial balance and reversing entries. The adjusting and closing entries are the clean-up activities that prepare the ledger for the new accounting period and transfer the results of current operations from the revenue and expense and drawing accounts to the permanent owner's equity account. The post-closing trial balance serves as an end-of-period accuracy check, and the reversing entries simplify the proper separation of revenues and expenses between successive accounting periods.

ADJUSTING ENTRIES

Entries required at the end of an accounting period to bring certain account balances up to date are known as adjusting entries. In preparing the work sheet for MicroWorld (reproduced on page 282), adjustments were made to accomplish the following purposes:

1. To transfer the amount of the merchandise inventory at the beginning of the accounting period to the expense and revenue summary account.
2. To enter the calculated cost of the merchandise inventory at the end of the accounting period.
3. To enter the amount of interest accrued on notes payable.
4. To enter the amount of accrued bank credit card payable.
5. To enter the cost of supplies used during the year.
6. To enter the amount of insurance premium expired during the year.
7. To enter the amount of uncollectible accounts estimated to result from the sales on account made during the year.
8. To enter the estimated amount of depreciation of property, plant and equipment (store equipment) for the year.

The effect of these adjustments was reflected in the financial statements reproduced on pages 293 and 296-297. To bring the ledger into agreement with the financial statements, the adjustments should be entered in the proper accounts. It is customary, therefore, at the end of each accounting period to journalize the adjustments and post them to the proper accounts.

Journalizing the Adjusting Entries

Adjusting entries are made in a general journal. The following is a portion of a general journal showing the adjusting entries of MicroWorld. Since the heading "Adjusting Entries" explains the nature of the entries, a separate explanation of each adjusting entry is unnecessary. The information needed in journalizing the adjustments was obtained from the Adjustments columns of the work sheet reproduced on page 282. The account numbers were not entered in the Posting Reference column at the time of journalizing but were entered when the posting was completed.

	DATE		DESCRIPTION	POST. REF.	DEBIT	CREDIT	
	19--		JOURNAL — PAGE 28				
1	Dec	31	Adjusting Entries				1
2			Expense and Revenue Summary	331	9708380		2
3			Merchandise Inventory	141		9708380	3
4			Merchandise Inventory	141	10269520		4
5			Expense and Revenue Summary	331		10269520	5
6			Interest Expense	571	28333		6
7			Accrued Interest Payable	217		28333	7
8			Bank Credit Card Expense	552	9299		8
9			Accrued Bank Credit Card Payable	215		9299	9
10			Supplies Expense	545	122080		10
11			Supplies	151		122080	11
12			Insurance Expense	548	153015		12
13			Prepaid Insurance	155		153015	13
14			Uncollectible Accounts Expense	553	301263		14
15			Allowance for Doubtful Accounts	131.1		301263	15
16			Depreciation Expense	547	235481		16
17			Accumulated Depr - Store Equip.	181.1	20827371	235481	17
						20827371	17
18							18
19							19
20							20

MicroWorld—Adjusting Entries

Posting the Adjusting Entries

The adjusting entries are posted individually to the proper ledger accounts. The accounts of MicroWorld that were affected by the adjusting entries are reproduced on pages 310-312. The entries in the accounts for December transactions that were posted prior to the adjusting entries are the same as in the accounts reproduced on pages 263-269. The number of the general journal page on which the adjusting entries are to be found was entered in the Posting Reference column of the general ledger accounts, and the account numbers were entered in the Posting Reference column of the general journal as the posting was completed. This provided a cross-reference in both books.

ACCOUNT *Allowance for Doubtful Accounts*   ACCOUNT NO. 131.1

DATE		ITEM	POST. REF.	DEBIT	CREDIT	BALANCE DEBIT	BALANCE CREDIT
19-- Dec.	1	Balance	✓				59000
	31		J28		301263		360263

ACCOUNT *Merchandise Inventory*   ACCOUNT NO. 141

DATE		ITEM	POST. REF.	DEBIT	CREDIT	BALANCE DEBIT	BALANCE CREDIT
19-- Dec.	1	Balance	✓			9708380	
	31		J28		9708380		
	31		J28	10269520		10269520	

ACCOUNT *Supplies*   ACCOUNT NO. 151

DATE		ITEM	POST. REF.	DEBIT	CREDIT	BALANCE DEBIT	BALANCE CREDIT
19-- Dec.	1	Balance	✓			196555	
	31		CP48	5525		202080	
	31		J28		122080	80000	

ACCOUNT *Prepaid Insurance*   ACCOUNT NO. 155

DATE		ITEM	POST. REF.	DEBIT	CREDIT	BALANCE DEBIT	BALANCE CREDIT
19-- Dec.	1	Balance	✓			306029	
	31		J28		153015	153014	

ACCOUNT *Accumulated Depreciation—Store Equipment*   ACCOUNT NO. 181.1

DATE		ITEM	POST. REF.	DEBIT	CREDIT	BALANCE DEBIT	BALANCE CREDIT
19-- Dec.	1	Balance	✓				549364
	31		J28		235481		784845

ACCOUNT *Accrued Bank Credit Card Payable*   ACCOUNT NO. 215

DATE		ITEM	POST. REF.	DEBIT	CREDIT	BALANCE DEBIT	BALANCE CREDIT
19-- Dec.	31		J28		9299		9299

MicroWorld—General Ledger Accounts After Posting Adjusting Entries

ACCOUNT *Accrued Interest Payable*					ACCOUNT NO. *217*	
DATE	ITEM	POST. REF.	DEBIT	CREDIT	BALANCE DEBIT	CREDIT
19-- Dec. 31		J28		28333		28333

ACCOUNT *Expense and Revenue Summary*					ACCOUNT NO. *331*	
DATE	ITEM	POST. REF.	DEBIT	CREDIT	BALANCE DEBIT	CREDIT
19-- Dec. 31		J28	9708380			
31		J28		10269520		

ACCOUNT *Supplies Expense*					ACCOUNT NO. *545*	
DATE	ITEM	POST. REF.	DEBIT	CREDIT	BALANCE DEBIT	CREDIT
19-- Dec. 31		J28	122080		122080	

ACCOUNT *Depreciation Expense*					ACCOUNT NO. *547*	
DATE	ITEM	POST. REF.	DEBIT	CREDIT	BALANCE DEBIT	CREDIT
19-- Dec. 31		J28	235481		235481	

ACCOUNT *Insurance Expense*					ACCOUNT NO. *548*	
DATE	ITEM	POST. REF.	DEBIT	CREDIT	BALANCE DEBIT	CREDIT
19-- Dec. 31		J28	153015		153015	

ACCOUNT *Bank Credit Card Expense*					ACCOUNT NO. *552*	
DATE	ITEM	POST. REF.	DEBIT	CREDIT	BALANCE DEBIT	CREDIT
19-- Dec. 1	Balance	✓			2234857	
3		CP48	215654		2450511	
31		J28	9299		2459810	

MicroWorld—General Ledger Accounts After Posting Adjusting Entries
(continued)

ACCOUNT *Uncollectible Accounts Expense*					ACCOUNT NO. 553	
DATE	ITEM	POST. REF.	DEBIT	CREDIT	BALANCE	
					DEBIT	CREDIT
19-- Dec. 31		J28	301263		301263	

ACCOUNT *Interest Expense*					ACCOUNT NO. 571	
DATE	ITEM	POST. REF.	DEBIT	CREDIT	BALANCE	
					DEBIT	CREDIT
19-- Dec. 1	Balance	✓			61970	
31		J28	28333		90303	

MicroWorld—General Ledger Accounts After Posting Adjusting Entries (concluded)

BUILDING YOUR ACCOUNTING KNOWLEDGE

1. Give a brief explanation of the purpose of each of the eight end-of-period adjusting entries made by MicroWorld.
2. In what type of journal are adjusting entries made?
3. Where is the information obtained that is needed in journalizing the adjustments?
4. When is the account number of each adjusted ledger account entered in the Posting Reference column of the general journal?
5. In the posting process, how is a cross-reference provided both to the general journal and to the general ledger?

APPLYING ACCOUNTING CONCEPTS

Exercise 10-1. Creative Frame and Gallery is in the process of preparing end-of-the-period financial statements. The accountant for the company has summarized the following data related to entries that need to be made in order to bring the accounts up to date prior to preparing the statements.

Merchandise inventory, January 1	$77,667
Merchandise inventory, December 31	82,156
Insurance premiums expired.............................	1,224
Supplies used	976
Interest accrued on notes payable	226
Accrued bank credit card payable	74
Estimated uncollectible accounts (based on sales on account)	2,410
Depreciation on store equipment	1,886

Give the eight adjusting entries in two-column journal form to bring the accounts up to date.

Exercise 10-2.   A partial work sheet for Crown Office Supplies appears below:

Crown Office Supplies
Work Sheet
For the Year Ended December 31, 19--

Account	Trial Balance Debit	Trial Balance Credit	Adjusted Trial Balance Debit	Adjusted Trial Balance Credit
Cash	29,131		29,131	
Accounts Receivable	17,802		17,802	
Allowance for Doubtful Accounts		293		1,799
Merchandise Inventory	48,544		51,347	
Supplies...........................	1,019		409	
Prepaid Insurance	1,536		771	
Store Equipment	11,771		11,771	
Accumulated Depreciation—Store Equipment.......................		2,745		3,922
Accrued Bank Credit Card Payable ..				46
Notes Payable		1,700		1,700
Accrued Interest Payable				141
R. C. Crown, Capital		17,854		17,854
R. C. Crown, Drawing	44,025		44,025	
Expense and Revenue Summary			48,544	51,347
Sales..............................		445,378		445,378
Purchases 301,583			301,583	
Supplies Expense			610	
Depreciation Expense			1,177	
Insurance Expense..................			765	
Bank Credit Card Expense	12,250		12,296	
Uncollectible Accounts Expense			1,506	
Interest Expense	309		450	
Totals 467,970		467,970	522,187	522,187

Analyze the trial balance and the adjusted trial balance to enter the eight end-of-period adjustments that were made. Proceed as follows: **(a)** Determine the change in each balance (increase, decrease, or no change). **(b)** Determine if the change is a debit or credit. **(c)** Locate the related debit and credit. For example, insurance expense and prepaid insurance would be related accounts. **(d)** Enter in two-column journal form the eight entries that were made to adjust the trial balance totals to obtain the amounts shown in the adjusted trial balance.

Report No. 10-1

Complete Report No. 10-1 in the study assignments and submit your working papers to the instructor for approval. Continue with the following textbook discussion until Report No. 10-2 is required.

CLOSING PROCEDURE

After the adjusting entries have been posted, all of the temporary owner's equity accounts should be closed. This means that the accountant must close out (1) the balance of each account that enters into the calculation of the net income (or net loss) for the accounting period and (2) the balance of the owner's drawing account. The purpose of the closing procedure is to transfer the balances of the temporary owner's equity accounts to the permanent owner's equity account, and entries made to accomplish this are known as closing entries. This is accomplished by means of the same four procedures that were described in Chapter 5. Specifically, each revenue and expense account is (1) debited or (2) credited with an offsetting credit or debit to the permanent owner's equity account, or to a summarizing account called Expense and Revenue Summary (sometimes called Income Summary, Profit and Loss Summary, or just Profit and Loss). The resulting balance of the expense and revenue summary account, which is the net income or net loss for the period, is then (3) transferred to the permanent owner's equity account.

The final step in the closing procedure is to (4) transfer the balance of the owner's drawing account to the permanent owner's equity account. After the temporary owner's equity and drawing accounts are transferred to the permanent owner's equity account, only the asset accounts, the liability accounts, and the permanent owner's equity account will have balances. The sum of the balances of the asset accounts (less balances of any contra accounts) will be equal to the sum of the balances of the liability accounts plus the balance of the permanent owner's equity account. The accounts will agree exactly with what is shown in the balance sheet as of the close of the period. The balance sheet of MicroWorld as of December 31, reproduced on pages 296 and 297, shows that the assets, liabilities, and owner's equity as of December 31 may be expressed in equation form as follows:

ASSETS	=	LIABILITIES	+	OWNER'S EQUITY
$211,246.65		$57,888.82		$153,357.83

The flowchart at the top of page 315 illustrates the closing process and the accounts involved.

Journalizing the Closing Entries

Closing entries, like adjusting entries, are entered in a general journal. A portion of a general journal showing the closing entries for

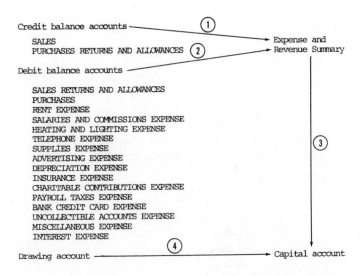

Credit balance accounts ①

    SALES   → Expense and
    PURCHASES RETURNS AND ALLOWANCES ②   → Revenue Summary

Debit balance accounts

    SALES RETURNS AND ALLOWANCES
    PURCHASES
    RENT EXPENSE
    SALARIES AND COMMISSIONS EXPENSE
    HEATING AND LIGHTING EXPENSE
    TELEPHONE EXPENSE
    SUPPLIES EXPENSE
    ADVERTISING EXPENSE   ③
    DEPRECIATION EXPENSE
    INSURANCE EXPENSE
    CHARITABLE CONTRIBUTIONS EXPENSE
    PAYROLL TAXES EXPENSE
    BANK CREDIT CARD EXPENSE
    UNCOLLECTIBLE ACCOUNTS EXPENSE
    MISCELLANEOUS EXPENSE
    INTEREST EXPENSE   ④

Drawing account ─────────────────────────→ Capital account

MicroWorld is shown on page 316. Since the heading "Closing Entries" explains the nature of the entries, a separate explanation of each closing entry is not necessary. The information required in preparing the closing entries was obtained from the Income Statement columns of the work sheet illustrated on page 282.

The first closing entry was made to close the sales and purchases returns and allowances accounts. Since these accounts have credit balances, each account must be debited for the amount of its balance in order to close it. The debits to these two accounts are offset by a credit of $899,297.89 to Expense and Revenue Summary.

The second closing entry was made to close the sales returns and allowances, purchases, and all of the expense accounts. Since these accounts have debit balances, each account must be credited for the amount of its balance in order to close it. The credits to these accounts are offset by a debit of $819,531.99 to Expense and Revenue Summary.

The posting of the first two adjusting entries and the first two closing entries causes the expense and revenue summary account to have a credit balance of $85,377.30, which is the net income for the year. At this point, the account has served its purpose and must be closed. The third closing entry accomplishes this by debiting the expense and revenue summary account and crediting Faye J. Quinn, Capital, for $85,377.30. The fourth closing entry was made to close the Faye J. Quinn, Drawing account. Since this account has a debit balance, a

	DATE	DESCRIPTION	POST. REF.	DEBIT	CREDIT	
1	19-- Dec. 31	Closing Entries				1
2		Sales	411	89074419		2
3		Purchases Returns and Allowances	511.1	855370		3
4		Expense and Revenue Summary	331		89929789	4
5		Expense and Revenue Summary	331	81953199		5
6		Sales Returns and Allowances	411.1		1340185	6
7		Purchases	511		60316627	7
8		Rent Expense	541		2400000	8
9		Salaries and Commissions Expense	542		8765104	9
10		Heating and Lighting Expense	543		551536	10
11		Telephone Expense	544		154672	11
12		Supplies Expense	545		122080	12
13		Advertising Expense	546		3923369	13
14		Depreciation Expense	547		235481	14
15		Insurance Expense	548		153015	15
16		Charitable Contributions Expense	549		127000	16
17		Payroll Taxes Expense	551		807904	17
18		Bank Credit Card Expense	552		2459810	18
19		Uncollectible Accounts Expense	553		301263	19
20		Miscellaneous Expense	562		204850	20
21		Interest Expense	571		90303	21
22		Expense and Revenue Summary	331	8537730		22
23		Faye J. Quinn, Capital	311		8537730	23
24		Faye J. Quinn, Capital	311	8805000		24
25		Faye J. Quinn, Drawing	311.1		8805000	25
26				18922578	18922578	26
27						27

MicroWorld—Closing Entries

credit is required to close it. The offsetting entry is a debit of $88,050.00 to Faye J. Quinn, Capital.

The account numbers shown in the Posting Reference column were not entered at the time of journalizing the closing entries. They were entered as the posting was completed. Quinn's capital account, updated at year-end, is as shown:

MicroWorld—Owner's Capital Account at Year-End

Posting the Closing Entries

Closing entries are posted in the usual manner and proper cross-references are provided by using the Posting Reference columns of the general journal and the ledger accounts. After all the closing entries are posted, the accounts affected appear as shown below and on pages 318-321. Note that as each account was closed, the "no balance" symbol "—0—" was placed in each column.

Observe that the first two adjusting entries described and illustrated on pages 308-309 serve to adjust the merchandise inventory account by removing the amount of the beginning inventory and by entering the amount of the ending inventory. These two entries also facilitate the closing process in that they cause the two amounts that go into the calculation of net income or net loss to be entered in the Expense and Revenue Summary. Once the expense and revenue summary account has been closed to the owner's equity account, the income and expense accounts are ready to perform their function in the following period.

MicroWorld—General Ledger Accounts After Posting Closing Entries

ACCOUNT *Expense and Revenue Summary*   ACCOUNT NO. 331

DATE	ITEM	POST. REF.	DEBIT	CREDIT	BALANCE DEBIT	BALANCE CREDIT
19-- Dec 31		J28	9708380			
31		J28		10269520		
31		J29		89929789		
31		J29	81953199			
31		J29	8537730		- 0 -	- 0 -

ACCOUNT *Sales*   ACCOUNT NO. 411

DATE	ITEM	POST. REF.	DEBIT	CREDIT	BALANCE DEBIT	BALANCE CREDIT
19-- Dec 1	Balance	✓				79364660
31		S34		3043680		82408340
31		CR42		6666079		89074419
31		J29	89074419		- 0 -	- 0 -

ACCOUNT *Sales Returns and Allowances*   ACCOUNT NO. 411.1

DATE	ITEM	POST. REF.	DEBIT	CREDIT	BALANCE DEBIT	BALANCE CREDIT
19-- Dec 1	Balance	✓			1270285	
10		CR48	39900		1310185	
29		J27	30000		1340185	
31		J29		1340185	- 0 -	- 0 -

ACCOUNT *Purchases*   ACCOUNT NO. 511

DATE	ITEM	POST. REF.	DEBIT	CREDIT	BALANCE DEBIT	BALANCE CREDIT
19-- Dec 1	Balance	✓			56631520	
31		P22	3656332		60287852	
31		CR48	28775		60316627	
31		J29		60316627	- 0 -	- 0 -

ACCOUNT *Purchases Returns and Allowances*   ACCOUNT NO. 511.1

DATE	ITEM	POST. REF.	DEBIT	CREDIT	BALANCE DEBIT	BALANCE CREDIT
19-- Dec 1	Balance	✓				846045
22		J27		9325		855370
31		J29	855370		- 0 -	- 0 -

MicroWorld—General Ledger Accounts After Posting Closing Entries (continued)

ACCOUNT *Rent Expense*   **ACCOUNT NO.** 541

DATE		ITEM	POST. REF.	DEBIT	CREDIT	BALANCE DEBIT	BALANCE CREDIT
19-- Dec	1	Balance	✓			2200000	
	1		CP48	200000		2400000	
	31		J29		2400000	-0-	-0-

ACCOUNT *Salaries and Commissions Expense*   **ACCOUNT NO.** 542

DATE		ITEM	POST. REF.	DEBIT	CREDIT	BALANCE DEBIT	BALANCE CREDIT
19-- Dec	1	Balance	✓			7968762	
	15		CP48	400172		8368934	
	31		CP48	396170		8765104	
	31		J29		8765104	-0-	-0-

ACCOUNT *Heating and Lighting Expense*   **ACCOUNT NO.** 543

DATE		ITEM	POST. REF.	DEBIT	CREDIT	BALANCE DEBIT	BALANCE CREDIT
19-- Dec	1	Balance	✓			509608	
	29		CP48	41928		551536	
	31		J29		551536	-0-	-0-

ACCOUNT *Telephone Expense*   **ACCOUNT NO.** 544

DATE		ITEM	POST. REF.	DEBIT	CREDIT	BALANCE DEBIT	BALANCE CREDIT
19-- Dec	1	Balance	✓			142832	
	29		CP48	11840		154672	
	31		J29		154672	-0-	-0-

ACCOUNT *Supplies Expense*   **ACCOUNT NO.** 545

DATE		ITEM	POST. REF.	DEBIT	CREDIT	BALANCE DEBIT	BALANCE CREDIT
19-- Dec	31		J28	122080		122080	
	31		J29		122080	-0-	-0-

MicroWorld—General Ledger Accounts After Posting Closing Entries (continued)

ACCOUNT _Advertising Expense_   ACCOUNT NO. 546

DATE	ITEM	POST. REF.	DEBIT	CREDIT	BALANCE DEBIT	BALANCE CREDIT
19-- Dec 1	Balance	✓			3577524	
8		CP48	268295		3845819	
29		CP48	74750		3920569	
31		CP48	2800		3923369	
31		J29		3923369	-0-	-0-

ACCOUNT _Depreciation Expense_   ACCOUNT NO. 547

DATE	ITEM	POST. REF.	DEBIT	CREDIT	BALANCE DEBIT	BALANCE CREDIT
19-- Dec 31		J28	235481		235481	
31		J29		235481	-0-	-0-

ACCOUNT _Insurance Expense_   ACCOUNT NO. 548

DATE	ITEM	POST. REF.	DEBIT	CREDIT	BALANCE DEBIT	BALANCE CREDIT
19-- Dec 31		J28	153015		153015	
31		J29		153015	-0-	-0-

ACCOUNT _Charitable Contributions Expense_   ACCOUNT NO. 549

DATE	ITEM	POST. REF.	DEBIT	CREDIT	BALANCE DEBIT	BALANCE CREDIT
19-- Dec 1	Balance	✓			125000	
31		CP48	2000		127000	
31		J29		127000	-0-	-0-

ACCOUNT _Payroll Taxes Expense_   ACCOUNT NO. 551

DATE	ITEM	POST. REF.	DEBIT	CREDIT	BALANCE DEBIT	BALANCE CREDIT
19-- Dec 1	Balance	✓			744372	
15		J27	31925		776297	
31		J27	31607		807904	
31		J29		807904	-0-	-0-

MicroWorld—General Ledger Accounts After Posting Closing Entries (continued)

ACCOUNT *Bank Credit Card Expense*   ACCOUNT NO. 552

DATE		ITEM	POST. REF.	DEBIT	CREDIT	BALANCE DEBIT	BALANCE CREDIT
19-- Dec	1	Balance	✓			2234857	
	3		CP48	215654		2450511	
	31		J28	9299		2459810	
	31		J29		2459810	-0-	-0-

ACCOUNT *Uncollectible Accounts Expense*   ACCOUNT NO. 553

DATE		ITEM	POST. REF.	DEBIT	CREDIT	BALANCE DEBIT	BALANCE CREDIT
19-- Dec	31		J28	301263		301263	
	31		J29		301263	-0-	-0-

ACCOUNT *Miscellaneous Expense*   ACCOUNT NO. 562

DATE		ITEM	POST. REF.	DEBIT	CREDIT	BALANCE DEBIT	BALANCE CREDIT
19-- Dec	1	Balance	✓			200375	
	24		CP48	2815		203190	
	31		CP48	1660		204850	
	31		J29		204850	-0-	-0-

ACCOUNT *Interest Expense*   ACCOUNT NO. 571

DATE		ITEM	POST. REF.	DEBIT	CREDIT	BALANCE DEBIT	BALANCE CREDIT
19-- Dec	1	Balance	✓			61970	
	31		J28	28333		90303	
	31		J29		90303	-0-	-0-

MicroWorld—General Ledger Accounts After Posting Closing Entries
(concluded)

Post-Closing Trial Balance

A trial balance of the general ledger accounts taken after the temporary owner's equity accounts have been closed is usually referred to as a post-closing trial balance. The purpose of the post-closing trial balance is to prove that the general ledger is in balance at the beginning of a new accounting period before any transactions for the new accounting period are entered.

The post-closing trial balance contains the same accounts and amounts that appear in the Balance Sheet columns of the work sheet, except that (1) the owner's drawing account is omitted because it has been closed, and (2) the owner's capital account has been adjusted for the amount of the net income (or net loss) and the amount of drawings.

A post-closing trial balance of the general ledger of MicroWorld is shown on page 323. The post-closing trial balance may be dated either as of the close of the old accounting period or as of the beginning of the new accounting period. In this illustration, the trial balance is dated December 31, 19--, the end of the period.

Completing the Accounting Cycle

In Chapter 5, page 151, the nine steps involved in handling the effect of all transactions and events completed during an accounting period, beginning with entries in the books of original entry and ending with the post-closing trial balance, were referred to collectively as the accounting cycle. A tenth step—journalizing and posting reversing entries—needs to be added if the accrual basis of accounting is being used.

Reversing Entries for Accrual Adjustments. The purposes of reversing entries are (1) to make possible the entering of the transactions of the succeeding accounting period in a routine manner, (2) to assure that the proper amount of revenue is credited in the period in which it is earned, and (3) to assure that the proper amount of expense is charged to the period in which it is incurred. A convenient rule for determining whether a reversing entry is needed is as follows: If reversing entries are used, any adjusting entry that creates a balance sheet account at the end of the preceding accounting period should be reversed at the beginning of the new accounting period.

A case in point is interest expense. Assume that interest of $350 had accrued on a $3,500 loan in the year 1986. To adjust for the interest expense for 1986, Interest Expense must be debited and Accrued Interest Payable must be credited, as follows:

MicroWorld
Post-Closing Trial Balance
December 31, 19--

Account	Acct No.	Dr. Balance	Cr. Balance
Cash	111	5826055	
Petty Cash Fund	112	25000	
Accounts Receivable	131	3561374	
Allowance for Doubtful Accounts	131.1		360263
Merchandise Inventory	141	10269520	
Supplies	151	80000	
Prepaid Insurance	155	153014	
Store Equipment	181	2354810	
Accumulated Depreciation—Store Equipment	181.1		784845
FICA Tax Payable	211		119452
FUTA Tax Payable	212		3568
State Unemployment Tax Payable	213		15286
Employees Income Tax Payable	214		143340
Accrued Bank Credit Card Payable	215		9299
Notes Payable	216		3400000
Accrued Interest Payable	217		28333
Accounts Payable	218		1586621
Sales Tax Payable	221		482983
Faye J. Quinn, Capital	311		15335783
		22269773	22269773

MicroWorld—Post-Closing Trial Balance

Interest Expense	350	
Accrued Interest Payable		350

To simplify the entry for the payment of the note and interest in 1987, the adjusting entry for 1986 needs to be reversed at the beginning of the 1987 accounting period by debiting Accrued Interest Payable and crediting Interest Expense, as follows:

Accrued Interest Payable	350	
Interest Expense		350

In this manner, when a check for $4,025 is written in 1987, in payment of the note and interest that has accrued in prior and present periods, a simple entry can be made by debiting Notes Payable and Interest Expense and crediting Cash, as shown:

Notes Payable	3,500	
Interest Expense	525	
Cash		4,025

As a result of this entry and the reversing entry made at the beginning of the period, the interest expense account will have a balance of $175, as shown below. This $175 is the correct amount of interest expense on this loan to be charged to 1987.

Interest Expense

Interest paid	525	Accrued from prior accounting period (reversing entry)	350
Bal. 175			

Note that if the 1986 adjusting entry had not been reversed, it would be necessary to debit the accrued interest payable account for $350 as well as debit the interest expense account for the $175 interest accrued in 1987 at the time the note was paid.

Journalizing the Reversing Entries. Reversing entries, like adjusting and closing entries, are made in a general journal. A portion of a general journal showing the reversing entries of MicroWorld is reproduced at the top of page 325. Usually the reversing entries are made immediately after closing the books at the end of an accounting period. However, the entries should be dated as of the first day of the succeeding accounting period. Thus, the reversing entries for MicroWorld are dated January 1. Since the heading "Reversing Entries" explains the nature of the entries, a separate explanation of each reversing entry is unnecessary. Each of the reversing entries shown is discussed in the following section.

Posting the Reversing Entries. Reversing entries are posted in the usual manner and proper cross-references are provided by using the Posting Reference columns of the general journal and the ledger accounts. After the reversing entries have been posted, the accounts affected appear as shown at the bottom of page 325 and on page 327.

	DATE	DESCRIPTION	POST. REF.	DEBIT	CREDIT	
		JOURNAL			PAGE 30	
1	19-- Jan. 1	Reversing Entries				1
2		Accrued Interest Payable	217	28333		2
3		Interest Expense	571		28333	3
4		Accrued Bank Credit Card Payable	215	9299		4
5		Bank Credit Card Expense	552		9299	5
6				37632	37632	6

MicroWorld—Reversing Entries

Accrued Interest Payable. The adjusting entry on December 31 for MicroWorld reproduced below shows that Interest Expense, Account No. 571, was debited and Accrued Interest Payable, Account No. 217, was credited for $283.33 to enter the interest accrued on a 6-month, 10% interest-bearing note for $34,000 issued on December 1. To reverse the adjusting entry it is necessary to debit Accrued Interest Payable, Account No. 217, and to credit Interest Expense, Account No. 571, for $283.33. The accounts affected by the entry are as follows:

ACCOUNT Accrued Interest Payable   ACCOUNT NO. 217

DATE	ITEM	POST. REF.	DEBIT	CREDIT	BALANCE DEBIT	BALANCE CREDIT
19-- Dec. 31		J28		28333		28333
Jan. 1		J30	28333		-0-	-0-

ACCOUNT Interest Expense   ACCOUNT NO. 571

DATE	ITEM	POST. REF.	DEBIT	CREDIT	BALANCE DEBIT	BALANCE CREDIT
19-- Dec. 1	Balance	✓			61970	
31		J28	28333		90303	
31		J29		90303	-0-	-0-
19-- Jan. 1		J30		28333		28333

MicroWorld—Accrued Interest Payable and Interest Expense After Posting of Reversing Entry

Note that after posting the reversing entry, the account Accrued Interest Payable has a zero balance and the account Interest Expense has a credit balance of $283.33. If the note for $34,000 plus interest is paid on June 1, the payment will amount to $35,700 ($34,000, principal of note, plus $1,700, interest at 10% for 6 months). The payment is entered by a debit to Notes Payable, Account No. 216, for $34,000 and Interest Expense, Account No. 571, for $1,700 and a credit to Cash, Account No. 111, for $35,700. After posting this entry, the interest expense account will have a debit balance of $1,416.67 ($1,700 minus $283.33). This balance of $1,416.67 represents the amount of interest expense incurred in the year in which the note matures. If the adjusting entry were not reversed, an analysis would have to be made before entering the payment on June 1 to determine the amount of interest expense incurred in the preceding year and the amount of interest expense incurred in the current year. It would be necessary to debit Accrued Interest Payable for $283.33 and Interest Expense for $1,416.67 so that each year might be charged with the correct interest expense. If the adjustment is reversed, however, this analysis becomes unnecessary.

The reversal procedure is particularly useful if the year-end adjustment for interest expense, incurred but not paid, relates to interest accrued on several interest-bearing obligations. When the adjustment is reversed, all future payments of interest can be debited to the interest expense account without any concern as to when the expense for each amount paid was incurred. The portion of any payments that is an expense of the new period will automatically emerge as the balance of the interest expense account.

Accrued Bank Credit Card Payable. The adjusting entry for MicroWorld shows that Bank Credit Card Expense, Account No. 552, was debited and Accrued Bank Credit Card Payable, Account No. 215, was credited for $92.99 to enter the expense for December which the bank will not deduct from MicroWorld's checking account until early in January. The reversing entry is a debit to the accrual account, Accrued Bank Credit Card Payable (No. 215), and a credit to the expense account, Bank Credit Card Expense (No. 552), for $92.99. The result of the reversing entry is to remove the credit balance in the liability account and give the expense account a credit balance of $92.99. The accounts after the reversing entry has been posted are shown on page 327.

The entry for the bank's deduction of this expense is a debit to Bank Credit Card Expense and a credit to the cash account. If this entry is made in early January for the calculated amount, $92.99, the

ACCOUNT *Accrued Bank Credit Card Payable*					ACCOUNT NO. 215	
DATE	ITEM	POST. REF.	DEBIT	CREDIT	BALANCE DEBIT	CREDIT
19-- Dec. 31		J28		9299		9299
Jan. 1		J30	9299		-0-	-0-

ACCOUNT *Bank Credit Card Expense*					ACCOUNT NO. 552	
DATE	ITEM	POST. REF.	DEBIT	CREDIT	BALANCE DEBIT	CREDIT
19-- Dec. 1		✓			2234857	
3		CP48	215654		2450511	
31		J28	9299		2459810	
31		J29		2459810	-0-	-0-
19-- Jan. 1		J30		9299		9299

**MicroWorld—Accrued Bank Credit Card Payable and Bank Credit Card Expense
After Posting of Reversing Entry**

expense account will be in balance, which reflects the fact that this amount is an expense of the year just ended, not of the new year. If the reversing entry had not been made, the accountant would have had to remember that the January debit had to be different from the other eleven months. This is not a serious problem, but whenever possible it is better not to disturb the regular routine of entering transactions. Reversing entries for accrued expense and revenue help to accomplish this objective.

BUILDING YOUR ACCOUNTING KNOWLEDGE

1. Where is the information obtained that is needed in journalizing the closing entries?
2. Explain the function of each of the four closing entries made by MicroWorld.
3. What is the purpose of a post-closing trial balance?
4. In what two ways does the information in the post-closing trial balance differ from the information in the Balance Sheet columns of the work sheet?
5. What is the tenth and last step in the accounting cycle?
6. What is the purpose of reversing entries for accruals?
7. What is the customary date for reversing entries?

APPLYING ACCOUNTING CONCEPTS

Exercise 10-3. Refer to the Adjusted Trial Balance of Crown Office Supplies in Exercise 10-2. **(a)** Draw T accounts for Expense and Revenue Summary and for R. C. Crown, Capital. Post the beginning and ending inventory amounts to Expense and Revenue Summary and the beginning balance to the capital account. **(b)** Prepare in two-column journal form the closing entries that would be made. **(c)** As you journalize, post all closing entries that affect the expense and revenue summary and capital accounts.

Exercise 10-4. Refer to Exercises 10-2 and 10-3. Prepare a Post-Closing Trial Balance as of December 31 for Crown Office Supplies.

Exercise 10-5. Refer to Exercise 10-2. Enter in two-column journal form the reversing entries that Crown Office Supplies would make as of January 1 of the next year so that the transactions involving the adjusting entries for accruals might be entered in a routine manner.

Report No. 10-2

Complete Report No. 10-2 in the study assignments and submit your working papers to the instructor for approval. You will then be given instructions as to the work to be done next.

EXPANDING YOUR BUSINESS VOCABULARY

What is the meaning of each of the following terms?

accounting cycle **(p. 322)**
adjusting entries **(p. 308)**
closing entries **(p. 314)**
Expense and Revenue Summary **(p. 314)**
Income Summary **(p. 314)**

post-closing trial balance **(p. 322)**
Profit and Loss or Profit and Loss Summary **(p. 314)**
reversing entries **(p. 322)**

CHAPTER 6–10

Supplementary Practical Accounting Problems

PROBLEM 6-A Purchases Journal or Two-Column Journal; Individual and Summary Posting to General Ledger

Jack Schipp operates an office furniture and supply store. The books of original entry consist of four different journals including a two-column journal and a purchases journal. Schipp uses the invoice method of accounting for purchases on account. The first page of the two-column journal is Page 6. The first page of the purchases journal is Page 9. The gross-price basis is used in entering purchases in the purchases journal. The selected general ledger accounts and their balances as of April 1 are as follows:

	Account	Balance, April 1
218	Accounts Payable	$ 6,946.30
511	Purchases	22,097.26
511.1	Purchases Returns and Allowances	664.38
521	Freight In	443.49

The following transactions related to purchases occurred during the month of April:

April 2 Received Invoice No. 193 dated March 31 from McNeil's for desks purchased, $1,658.78. Desks were shipped FOB shipping point; terms 2/10, net/30.

5 Received freight bill from Keepon Trucking Co., $57.95 for delivery charges on the desks purchased from McNeil's.

6 Received Invoice No. 194 dated April 5 from Duper's Supply Co. for memo books purchased, $267.71; terms, 10 days.

April   9   Received Invoice No. 195 dated April 7 from Southlake Office Supply Co. for ledger outfits purchased, $247; terms, 10 days.

12   Received Invoice No. 196 dated April 9 from Clayton Chair, Inc., for chairs purchased, $939.48; terms, 2/10, net /30. Chairs were shipped FOB destination so freight charges of $84.30 were not included in the invoice.

14   Received Invoice No. 197 dated April 13 from Strock's Furniture for tables purchased, $435.13; terms, 45 days.

15   Received Invoice No. 198 dated April 14 from Greise Co. for chairs purchased, $316; terms, 30 days.

19   Received a credit memorandum from Clayton Chair, Inc., for one chair returned, $156.58, because it had the wrong fabric.

21   Received Invoice No. 199 dated April 20 from Sander's for desk sets, $477.90; terms, 10 days.

23   Received a credit memorandum from Strock's Furniture Co. for $42, an allowance for damage during shipment of tables purchased on Invoice No. 197.

27   Received Invoice No. 200 dated April 26 from McNeil's for filing cabinets purchased, $240. Cabinets were shipped FOB shipping point and a separate freight bill for $33.60 was received with the invoice. Terms, 2/10, net/30. (Two entries are required.)

28   Received Invoice No. 201 dated April 27 from Greenwood's Furniture Co. for desks purchased, $1,100; terms, 60 days.

30   Received Invoice No. 202 dated April 28 from IBM Corp. for typewriters purchased, $2,375.50; terms 2/10, net/30.

Required: (1) Enter each transaction in a purchases journal, using a sheet of paper ruled like that shown in the illustration on page 188, or in a two-column journal, using a sheet of paper ruled like that shown in the illustration on page 262. (2) Foot and rule the purchases journal. (3) Open accounts for the four accounts indicated with the related balances, using the four-column ledger form. Complete the summary posting of the purchases journal and the individual posting of the two-column journal for April.

PROBLEM 6-B   (See Problem 6-A.)

Assume that Schipp uses the net-price basis in entering purchases in the purchases journal.

Required: Perform steps (1) - (3) as described in Problem 6-A.

PROBLEM 6-C Cash Payments Journal; Summary Posting to General Ledger

Janice Ventura operates a novelty store under the name of The Dungeon. The books of original entry include a cash payments journal, which will be used for this problem. All merchandise purchases on account were entered in the purchases journal on a gross-price basis.

For the cash payments journal, use a sheet of paper ruled like that shown on page 192. Assume that the first page of the cash payments journal for March is Page 3. The following accounts are used:

		Balance, March 1, 19--
111	Cash	$10,888.28 (Dr.)
218	Accounts Payable	8,642.79 (Cr.)
511	Purchases	15,375.88 (Dr.)
511.2	Purchases Discounts	327.40 (Cr.)

The following transactions relating to cash payments occurred during the month of March:

Mar. 1 Issued Check No. 488 for $380 in payment of rent (Rent Expense) for March.

4 Issued Check No. 489 to Wacko Wacko Supply Co. in payment on account, $750 less 5% discount.

7 Issued Check No. 490 to Crazy George's in payment on account, $340 less 1% discount.

7 Issued Check No. 491 for $35 to Ace Janitorial Service for services rendered (Janitorial Expense).

9 Issued Check No. 492 to United Supply Co. in payment for cash purchase, $365.

16 Issued Check No. 493 to Potatohead, Inc., in payment on account, $845 less 3% discount.

17 Issued Check No. 494 for $38.69 to Northwest Utilities for the monthly electric bill (Utilities Expense).

22 Issued Check No. 495 to Connie's Costume House in payment for cash purchase, $288.

26 Issued Check No. 496 to United Supply Co. in payment for cash purchase, $540.

28 Issued Check No. 497 to Wimple's in payment on account, $605 less 2% discount.

Required: (1) Enter each transaction in the cash payments journal. (2) Foot and rule the cash payments journal. (3) Open accounts for the four accounts indicated with the related balances, using the four-column ledger form. Complete the summary posting of the cash payments journal for March, and update the account balances.

PROBLEM 6-D   (See Problem 6-C.)

Assume that all of Ventura's merchandise purchases on account were entered in the purchases journal on a net-price basis. In addition, also assume that the following accounts are used:

		Balance, March 1, 19--
111	Cash	$10,888.28 (Dr.)
218	Accounts Payable	8,499.07 (Cr.)
511	Purchases	15,048.48 (Dr.)

Required: Perform steps (1) - (3) as described in Problem 6-C. For the cash payments journal, use a sheet of paper ruled like that shown on page 192.

PROBLEM 7-A   Sales Journal; Two-Column Journal; Individual and Summary Posting to General Ledger

J. W. Namath operates a sporting goods store under the name of The Super Store. This problem involves the use of the sales journal and two-column journal only.

For the sales journal, use a sheet of paper ruled like that shown on page 218. For the two-column journal, use a sheet of paper like that shown in the illustration on page 262. Assume that the first page of each journal in September is Page 9. The following accounts are used:

111	Cash		311	J. W. Namath, Capital
131	Accounts Receivable		411	Sales
221	Sales Tax Payable		411.1	Sales Returns and Allowances

The following selected transactions were completed during the month of September:

Sept.   1   Invested $30,000 in the business.

        2   Sold merchandise on account to R. S. Boyle, $55, tax, $2.20. Sale No. 104.

        5   Sold merchandise on account to J. A. Lee, $108.50, tax, $4.34. Sale No. 105.

Sept. 6 R. S. Boyle returned goods for credit. Sales price, $13, tax, $0.52.

9 Sold merchandise on account to D. R. Tenoose, $204.33, tax, $8.17. Sale No. 106.

14 Sold merchandise on account to K. C. Tekulve, $210, tax, $8.40. Sale No. 107.

19 D. R. Tenoose returned some merchandise for credit. Sale price, $48, tax, $1.92.

26 Sold merchandise on account to S. J. Stringer, $39.95, tax, $1.60. Sale No. 108.

28 Sold merchandise on account to B. J. McGraph, $68.05, tax, $2.72. Sale No. 109.

30 Sold merchandise on account to P. A. Birac, $187, tax, $7.48. Sale No. 110.

Required: (1) Enter each transaction in the proper journal. (2) Enter the totals and rule the sales journal and the two-column journal. (3) Open the necessary accounts using the four-column form of ledger paper. Post the sales journal and two-column journal entries for September.

PROBLEM 7-B Cash Receipts Journal; Summary Posting to General Ledger

Bill Doranski operates an antique shop called Bill's Antiques. The books of original entry include a cash receipts journal, which will be used for this problem.

For the cash receipts journal, use a sheet of paper ruled like that shown on page 223. Assume that the first page of the cash receipts journal for November is Page 11. The following accounts are used:

		Balance, Nov. 1, 19--
111	Cash	$ 12,647.39 (Dr.)
131	Accounts Receivable	37,608.12 (Dr.)
221	Sales Tax Payable	842.12 (Cr.)
411	Sales	151,096.97 (Cr.)

The following selected transactions were completed during the month of November.

Nov. 1 Received $750 from B. Griggs on account.

2 Received $205 from S. Kelley on account.

5 Cash and bank credit card sales for the week, $3,995.70, tax, $199.79.

Nov.   9   Received $350 from B. Burpee on account.

12   Cash and bank credit card sales for the week, $2,435.22, tax, $121.76.

18   Received $1,200 from B. Lillis on account.

19   Cash and bank credit card sales for the week, $4,115.08, tax, $205.75.

22   Received $100 from K. Judge on account.

26   Received $700 from J. Butcher on account.

26   Cash and bank credit card sales for the week, $1,977.47, tax, $98.87.

29   Received $335 from L. Popescu on account.

Required: (1) Enter each transaction in the cash receipts journal. (2) Enter the totals and rule the journal. (3) Open the four accounts indicated above with the related balances. Post the cash receipts journal entries for November.

PROBLEM 9-A   Adjustments in Work Sheet

Bill Biambee is in the business of retail heating and cooling. Merchandise is sold for cash and on account. On the next page is a reproduction of the Trial Balance columns of the work sheet for the year ended December 31. The following adjustments are to be made before the close of the accounting period:

a. Merchandise inventory, end of year, $29,843.16.
b. Accruals:
   Interest accrued on notes payable, $57.16.
   Accrued bank credit card payable, $213.21.
c. Prepaid expenses:
   Prepaid insurance unexpired, $720.
   Supplies on hand, $135.66.
d. Depreciation:
   Store equipment, 10% a year, $1,080.
e. Uncollectible accounts expense:
   Increase allowance for doubtful accounts $169 to provide for estimated loss.

Required: Prepare a ten-column work sheet making the necessary entries in the Adjustments columns.

Note: Problems 9-B and 10-A are also based on Biambee's work sheet. If these problems are to be solved, the work sheet prepared in Problem 9-A should be retained for reference until after they are solved, when the solutions of all three problems may be submitted to the instructor.

PROBLEM 9-B   Financial Statements

Refer to the work sheet for Bill Biambee (based on Problem 9-A) and from it prepare the following financial statements:

1. An income statement for the year ended December 31.
2. A balance sheet in account form as of December 31.

BILL BIAMBEE
Work Sheet
For The Year Ended December 31, 19--

Account	Acct. No.	TRIAL BALANCE	
		Debit	Credit
Cash	111	11,513.28	
Petty Cash Fund	112	200.00	
Accounts Receivable	131	15,418.27	
Allowance for Doubtful Accounts	131.1		214.50
Merchandise Inventory	141	22,934.80	
Supplies	151	412.15	
Prepaid Insurance	155	1,116.20	
Store Equipment	181	10,800.00	
Accumulated Depr.—Store Equipment	181.1		1,080.00
FICA Tax Payable	211		751.00
FUTA Tax Payable	212		125.16
State Unemployment Tax Payable	213		173.25
Employees Income Tax Payable	214		842.72
Accrued Bank Credit Card Payable	215		
Notes Payable	216		6,000.00
Accrued Interest Payable	217		
Accounts Payable	218		13,927.50
Sales Tax Payable	221		1,214.80
Bill Biambee, Capital	311		58,194.92
Bill Biambee, Drawing	311.1	15,600.00	
Expense and Revenue Summary	331		
Sales	411		112,413.82
Sales Returns and Allowances	411.1	411.22	
Purchases	511	79,297.08	
Purchases Returns and Allowances	511.1		406.18
Rent Expense	541	6,600.00	
Salaries Expense	542	24,998.00	
Supplies Expense	545		
Advertising Expense	546	850.00	
Depreciation Expense	547		
Insurance Expense	548		
Charitable Contributions Expense	549	510.00	
Payroll Taxes Expense	551	1,815.60	
Bank Credit Card Expense	552	2,563.47	
Uncollectible Accounts Expense	553		
Miscellaneous Expense	562	231.18	
Interest Expense	571	72.60	
		195,343.85	195,343.85

PROBLEM 10-A   Adjusting, Closing, and Reversing Entries

Refer to the work sheet for Bill Biambee (based on Problem 9-A) and prepare the general journal entries required: **(1)** To adjust the general ledger accounts so that they will be in agreement with the financial statements; **(2)** To close the temporary owner's equity accounts on December 31; and **(3)** To reverse the accrual adjustments as of January 1.

PROBLEM 10-B   Complete Accounting Cycle

Molly Goodshoes, as a sole owner, operates a merchandising business known as Molly's Boutique. The business keeps a purchases journal, a sales journal, a cash receipts journal, a cash payments journal, a general journal, and a general ledger. While a petty cash fund is maintained, no payments are made from the fund in December.

Number the pages of the journals as follows:

Purchases Journal, Page 34
Sales Journal, Page 46
Cash Receipts Journal, Page 42
Cash Payments Journal, Page 37
General Journal, Pages 49-51

The four-column form of ledger account is used. Individual accounts with customers and suppliers are not kept in ledger form; however, the purchase invoices and sales tickets are filed in such a manner that the amounts owed to suppliers and the amounts due from customers can be determined at any time.

At the end of the eleventh month of this year, the trial balance appeared as shown on page 339. The following transactions occurred during the month of December:

Narrative of Transactions for December

Dec. 1 (Tuesday) Purchased merchandise from Marsh Co., $3,365. Invoice No. 61, dated November 30. Terms, 30 days.

2 Paid the December rent, $1,235. Check No. 124.

2 Paid the telephone bill, $104.65. Check No. 125.

3 Paid Wellesly Co. $4,637.22 in full settlement of December 1 balance. Check No. 126.

Dec. 5 Sold merchandise on account to Tom Dorsett, $216.30, tax, $8.65. Sale No. 121.

5 Purchased merchandise from Malice, Inc., $2,410. Invoice No. 62, dated December 5. Terms, 30 days.

7 Received $675 from Alex Trevino in full settlement of his account.

8 Paid Marsh Co. $3,365.00 in settlement of their invoice of November 30. Check No. 127.

8 Received $362.15 from Jenny Sullivan in full settlement of her account.

9 Sold merchandise on account to Mary McCord, $82.95, tax, $3.32. Sale No. 122.

9 Received a notice from F & M Bank that $509.07 had been deducted from the account of Molly's Boutique, representing a discount of 4% on the amount net of returns of Visa and MasterCard vouchers that had been deposited during November.

10 Purchased merchandise from the Zeimba Mfg. Co., $916. Invoice No. 63 dated December 9. Terms, 30 days.

11 Sold merchandise on account to Karen Maxwell, $36, tax, $1.44. Sale No. 123.

12 Issued Check No. 128 to F & M Bank, a U. S. depository, in payment of the following taxes:

a. Employees' income tax withheld during
   November.. $509.70
b. FICA tax:
   On employees (withheld during November) $197.20
   On employer 197.20   394.40
        Total $904.10

14 Sold merchandise on account to Lisa McCarty, $211.05, tax $8.44. Sale No. 124.

15 Issued Check No. 129 payable to State Treasurer for $1,281.04 for November sales tax.

17 Molly Goodshoes withdrew $1,500 for personal use. Check No. 130.

19 Gave Karen Maxwell credit for $12.48 because a part of the merchandise sold to her on the 11th was returned. (Sales price, $12, tax $.48.)

19 Sold merchandise on account to Bill Thayer, $385.08, tax, $15.40. Sale No. 125.

21 Purchased merchandise from Toni Thomas, Inc., $2,487.23. Invoice No. 64, dated December 20. Terms, 30 days.

Dec. 22 Received $24.96 from Karen Maxwell for balance of Sale No. 123.

23 Paid bill for advertising, $375. Check No. 131.

24 Sold merchandise on account to Will Estes, $304.50, tax, $12.18. Sale No. 126.

26 Purchased merchandise from Marsh Co. $1,648.31. Invoice No. 65, dated December 23. Terms, 30 days.

26 Received a check for $125 from Tom Dorsett to apply on account.

26 Sold merchandise to Karen Maxwell, $194.75, tax, $7.79. Sale No. 127.

26 Sent the Zeimba Mfg. Co. a check for $458 to apply on account. Check No. 132.

28 Sold merchandise on account to Anthony Gentile, $655.95, tax, $26.24. Sale No. 128.

28 Purchased store equipment from Mutz & Co., $1,260. Terms, 60 days.

29 Received $86.27 from Mary McCord in payment of Sale No. 122.

29 Received credit from Marsh Co. for $88.40 because a part of the merchandise purchased on the 26th was returned by agreement.

29 Sold merchandise on account to Mary McCord, $408.22, tax, $16.33. Sale No. 129.

31 Cash and bank credit card sales for month, $31,755.42, tax, $1,270.22.

31 Issued Check No. 133 payable to Payroll for $4,231.57.

PAYROLL STATEMENT FOR MONTH ENDED DECEMBER 31

Total salaries and commissions earned during period		$5,368.08
Employees' taxes to be withheld:		
a. Employees' income tax	$733.90	
b. FICA tax, 7.5%	402.61	1,136.51
Net amount payable to employees..............		$4,231.57
Employer's payroll taxes:		
a. FICA tax, 7.5%		$402.61
b. Unemployment compensation taxes:		
State, 2.7%	$144.94	
Federal, 0.8%	42.94	187.88
Total		$590.49

(In addition to entering the amounts withheld from employees' wages for FICA and income tax purposes, the payroll taxes imposed on the employer should also be entered.)

MOLLY'S BOUTIQUE
Trial Balance
November 30, 19--

ACCOUNT	ACCT. NO.	TRIAL BALANCE DEBIT	TRIAL BALANCE CREDIT
Cash	111	26,328.42	
Petty Cash Fund	112	200.00	
Accounts Receivable	131	43,864.15	
Allowance for Doubtful Accounts	131.1		830.08
Merchandise Inventory	141	104,600.00	
Supplies	151	360.00	
Prepaid Insurance	155	2,946.75	
Store Equipment	181	8,074.50	
Accumulated Depr.—Store Equipment	181.1		1,614.90
FICA Tax Payable	211		394.40
FUTA Tax Payable	212		112.35
State Unemployment Tax Payable	213		151.99
Employees Income Tax Payable	214		509.70
Accrued Bank Credit Card Payable	215		
Notes Payable	216		4,800.00
Accrued Interest Payable	217		
Accounts Payable	218		21,084.50
Sales Tax Payable	221		1,281.04
Molly Goodshoes, Capital	311		153,488.24
Molly Goodshoes, Drawing	311.1	20,625.00	
Expense and Revenue Summary	331		
Sales	411		331,690.70
Sales Returns and Allowances	411.1	509.15	
Purchases	511	228,091.00	
Purchases Returns and Allowances	511.1		643.90
Rent Expense	541	13,585.00	
Salaries and Commissions Expense	542	51,365.67	
Supplies Expense	545		
Advertising Expense	546	7,428.50	
Depreciation Expense	547		
Insurance Expense	548		
Payroll Taxes Expense	551	3,724.36	
Bank Credit Card Expense	552	3,648.54	
Uncollectible Accounts Expense	553		
Miscellaneous Expense	562	1,084.51	
Interest Expense	571	166.25	
		516,601.80	516,601.80

The following adjustments are to be made before the close of business for the year ended December 31:

a. Merchandise inventory, end of year, $99,400.
b. Accruals:
   Interest accrued on notes payable, $50.
   Accrued bank credit card payable, $385.77.

    c.   Prepaid expenses:
        Prepaid insurance unexpired, $840.
        Supplies on hand, $105.
    d.   Depreciation:
        Store equipment, 10% a year, $807.45.
    e.   Uncollectible accounts expense:
        Increase allowance for doubtful accounts $267.22 to provide for
        estimated loss.

Required: (1) Journalize the December transactions. (2) Open the necessary ledger accounts and enter the December 1 balances, using the November 30 trial balance as the source of the needed information. Complete the individual and summary posting from the books of original entry. (3) Take a trial balance of the general ledger accounts. (4) Prepare a ten-column work sheet making the required adjustments. (5) Prepare an income statement for the year ending December 31 and a balance sheet in report form as of December 31. (6) Enter the adjusting entries in the general journal and post. (7) Enter the closing entries in the general journal and post. (8) Place "no balance" symbols in the accounts that are in balance after the adjusting and closing entries have been posted. (9) Take a post-closing trial balance. (10) Enter the necessary reversing entries as of January 1 in the general journal and post. Place "no balance" symbols in the accounts that are in balance after the reversing entries have been posted.

CHAPTER 11

Accounting for Notes and Interest

CHAPTER OBJECTIVES

Careful study of this chapter should enable you to:

- Describe and explain the nature and use of promissory notes and compute any related interest on such notes.

- Describe and process transactions that involve notes receivable and to prepare a notes receivable register.

- Describe and process transactions that involve notes payable and to prepare a notes payable register.

- Explain and process end-of-period adjustments for:

  1. Interest earned but not yet collected, and
  2. Interest incurred but not yet paid.

- Describe and illustrate the various types of indorsement on notes.

A major characteristic of modern business is the extensive use of credit. Each day hundreds of millions of transactions involve the sale of goods or services in return for promises to pay at a later date. Sales of this type are said to be "on credit" or "on account," and are often described as charge sales. As mentioned in Chapter 7, to facilitate such transactions, the use of credit cards has become commonplace. When opening a credit card account, a form or document is signed that obligates the customer to pay for all purchases within a specific number of days after a bill for the purchases is received from the business. When making a purchase, the buyer then merely signs a sales slip or sales ticket that acknowledges the receipt of the merchandise or service.

This chapter deals with credit transactions that are both less common and more formal than such "open account" or credit card sales transactions. Specifically, the use of and accounting for promissory notes are explained.

The Promissory Note

A promise to repay a borrowed sum of money nearly always takes the form of a promissory note (usually just called a note). The extension of credit for periods of more than 60 days, or for large amounts of money, may result in the use of notes. Such notes have certain legal characteristics that cause them to be negotiable commercial paper. In order to be considered negotiable commercial paper, a promissory note must:

1. Be in writing and signed by the person or persons agreeing to make payment;
2. Be an unconditional promise to pay a certain amount of money;
3. Be payable either on demand or at a definite future time;
4. Be payable to the order of a specified person or firm, or to the bearer.

The following is a promissory note which has all the characteristics of a negotiable commercial paper. William Alverson is known as the maker of the note because he promises to pay a certain amount of money ($1,542.50) at a definite future time (90 days after June 9). Susan Lavin is called the payee of the note because she is the one who is to receive the specified amount of money. Notice that to William Alverson it is a note payable while to Susan Lavin it is a note receivable.

Notes may be interest-bearing or non-interest-bearing. The note illustrated is interest-bearing, with interest at 9% per year. Sometimes no rate of interest is specified on the note; however, the transaction will result in some interest. For example, a borrower might give a $1,000 non-interest-bearing note, payable in 60 days to a bank in return for a loan of $985. The $15 difference between the amount received ($985) and the amount that must be repaid ($1,000) when the note matures (is due) will truly become interest expense at maturity. Interest accrues gradually as time passes. Accounting for this type of transaction is explained on page 352.

Promissory Note

Calculating Interest

In calculating interest on notes, it is necessary to take the following factors into consideration:

1. The principal of the note.
2. The rate of interest.
3. The period of time involved.

The principal of the note is the face amount of the note that the maker promises to pay at maturity separate from any specified interest. The principal is the base on which the interest is calculated.

The rate of interest usually is expressed in the form of a percentage, such as 8% or 10%. Ordinarily the rate is an annual percentage rate, but in some cases the rate is quoted on a monthly basis, such as 1 1/2% a month. A rate of 1 1/2% a month is equivalent to a rate of 18% a year payable monthly (1 1/2% × 12 = 18%). When a note is interest-bearing but the rate is not specified on the face of the note, it is subject to the legal rate, which varies under the laws of the different states.

The time of the note consists of the days or months from the date of issue of a note to the date of its maturity (or the interest payment date if it comes earlier). When the time is specified in months, the interest is calculated on the basis of months rather than days. For example, if a note is payable 3 months from date, the interest should be calculated on the basis of 3 months or 1/4 of a year (3 mos. ÷ 12 mos. = 1/4 yr.). However, when the time of a note is specified in days or when the due date is specified in a note, the interest should be computed using the exact number of days that will elapse from the date of the note to the date of its maturity. For example, if a $1,000, 9% note is dated March 1, and the due date is specified as June 1, the time should be computed as shown:

Days in March	31
Deduct date of note, March 1	1
Days remaining in March	30
Add: Days in April	30
Days in May	31
Note matures on June	1
Total time in days	92

Notice that in this computation the date of maturity was counted but the date of the note was not counted. If the note had specified "3 months after date" instead of June 1, the interest should be computed on the basis of 90 days instead of 92 days since a month, when specified as such, is assumed to have 30 days.

In computing interest, it is customary to consider 360 days as a year. Most banks and business firms follow this practice, though some banks and government agencies use 365 days as the base in computing daily interest. In any case, the formula for computing interest is:

$$I = PRT, \text{ where:}$$
$$I = \text{amount of interest}$$
$$P = \text{amount of principal}$$
$$R = \text{rate of interest}$$
$$T = \text{time (usually a fraction}$$
$$\text{of a 360-day year)}$$

Thus, for the $1,000, 9% note described above, interest on the due date would be $23 ($1,000 × 9% × 92/360). The gradual accumulation of interest on the note to a maturity value of $1,023 is shown by the following time line:

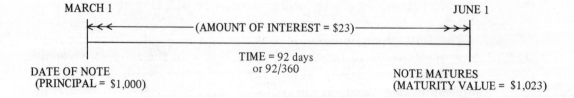

MARCH 1   JUNE 1

(AMOUNT OF INTEREST = $23)

TIME = 92 days
or 92/360

DATE OF NOTE   NOTE MATURES
(PRINCIPAL = $1,000)   (MATURITY VALUE = $1,023)

In the case of long-term notes, the interest may be payable periodically, such as semiannually or annually.

The 30-Day, 12% Method. There are short cuts that may be used in computing interest on the basis of a 360-day year. The interest on any amount for 30 days at 12% can be determined simply by moving the decimal point in the amount two places to the left. The reason for this is that 30 days is 1/12 of a year, and interest on any amount at 12% for 1/12 of a year is the same as the interest at 1% for a full year. Thus, the interest on $650 for 30 days at 12% is $6.50.

The 30-day, 12% method may be used to advantage in many cases even though the actual time may be other than 30 days and the actual rate other than 12%. The following examples will serve to illustrate this fact.

Factors

1. Principal of note, $3,000
2. Time, 30 days
3. Rate of interest, 8%

Calculation

Interest at 12% for 30 days = $30
Interest at 8% = 8/12 × $30 = $20

Factors

1. Principal of note, $4,000
2. Time, 90 days
3. Rate of interest, 10%

Calculation

Interest at 12% for 30 days = $40
Interest at 12% for 90 days = $120
Interest at 10% = 10/12 × $120 = $100

Sometimes it is helpful to determine the interest for 3 days at 12% and then use the result as the basis for calculating the actual interest. Since the interest on any sum for 3 days at 12% may be determined simply by moving the decimal point three places to the left, the interest on $1,000 at 12% for 3 days is $1. If the actual time is 24 days instead of 3 days, the interest will be eight times $1 or $8. This method differs from the 30-day, 12% method only in that 3 days and 12% are used in the basic computation instead of 30 days and 12%.

Published tables are available for reference in determining the amount of interest on stated sums at different rates for any length of time. These tables are widely used by financial institutions and by other business firms.

Accounting for Notes Receivable Transactions

Businesses other than lending institutions such as commercial banks and savings and loan associations generally encounter four types of transactions involving notes receivable:

1. Note received from customer to obtain an extension of time for payment of an obligation.
2. Note collected at maturity.
3. Note renewed at maturity.
4. Note dishonored.

Note Received from Customer to Obtain an Extension of Time for Payment. To obtain an extension of time for the payment of an account, a customer may issue a note for all or part of the amount due. A merchant may be willing to accept the note because it is a written acknowledgment of the debt and undoubtedly will bear interest.

Assume that Chris McLean owes the Lehman Hardware Co. $862.31 on open account. The account is past due and Lehman insists upon a settlement. McLean offers to give a 60-day, 9% note dated May 12, and Lehman accepts McLean's offer. The note is entered in the books of the Lehman Hardware Co. in two-column journal form as follows:

```
May 12  Notes Receivable ...............................   862.31
            Accounts Receivable ..........................              862.31
            Received a note from Chris McLean.
```

If instead of giving a note for the full amount, McLean gives a check for $62.31 and a note for the $800 balance, the transaction would be entered in Lehman's books in two-column journal form as follows:

```
May 12  Cash .............................................    62.31
        Notes Receivable ...............................   800.00
            Accounts Receivable ..........................              862.31
            Received check and note from Chris McLean.
```

The foregoing entry can be entered in a combination journal, cash receipts journal, or any other appropriate book of original entry. This observation applies to all illustrations of entries involving the receipt of cash.

Note Collected at Maturity. When a note receivable matures, it may be collected by the holder or it may be left at a bank for collection. If the maker of the note resides in another locality, the note may be forwarded to a bank in that locality for collection. Usually the maker is notified a few days before the maturity of a note so that the maker may be reminded of the due date, the amount that must be paid, and where the amount is to be paid. When the bank makes the collection, it notifies the holder, on a form similar to the following credit advice, that the net amount has been credited to the holder's account.

ADVICE OF CREDIT   **CENTERRE BANK**
                                                               Bonne Terre, Missouri

TO _____ Lehman Hardware Co. _____

         Account No. 315 30959   July 11   19 86

                WE CREDIT YOUR ACCOUNT AS FOLLOWS:

Chris McLean's note $862.31

Interest for 60 days at 9%   12.93

                                           $875.24

Less collection charge   10.00 $ 865.24

OFFSETTING DR.   APPROVED R. Shaw

Credit Advice

To illustrate the necessary accounting procedure, assume that Lehman left McLean's 60-day, 9% note for $862.31 at Centerre Bank for collection, and on July 11 received notice that the note had been collected including the accrued interest of $12.93. The bank fee for collecting the note amounted to $10.

The transaction is entered in Lehman's books as follows:

July 11 Cash	865.24	
Collection Expense.............................	10.00	
Notes Receivable		862.31
Interest Revenue..............................		12.93
Received credit for the proceeds of Chris McLean's note collected by the bank.		

Note Renewed at Maturity. If the maker of a note is unable to pay the amount due at maturity, it may be possible to renew all or part of the note. If, instead of paying the note for $862.31 at maturity, McLean is allowed to pay only the interest, $12.93, and give another note for 60 days at the same rate of interest, the transaction is entered in the books of the Lehman Hardware Co. in two-column journal form as follows:

```
July 11  Cash .............................................   12.93
         Notes Receivable (new note) ..................... 862.31
         Notes Receivable (old note) ....................          862.31
         Interest Revenue................................          12.93
             Received a new note for $862.31 from Chris Mc-
             Lean in renewal of his note due today and
             $12.93 in cash for the interest on the old note.
```

Note Dishonored. If the maker of a note refuses or is unable to pay or renew it at maturity, the note is said to be dishonored. It thereby loses the quality of negotiability which means that it loses its legal status as a note receivable. Usually the amount is transferred from the notes receivable account to the accounts receivable account pending final disposition of the obligation involved. For example, if Lehman is unable to collect the interest-bearing note for $862.31 received 60 days before from McLean, the following two-column journal entry is made in the books of the Lehman Hardware Co.:

```
July 11  Accounts Receivable ........................... 875.24
         Notes Receivable .............................          862.31
         Interest Revenue.............................          12.93
             Chris McLean's note dishonored.
```

If the claim against McLean should turn out to be completely worthless, the $875.24 will be removed from the accounts receivable account and recognized as an uncollectible account expense. The manner of accounting for this type of transaction was discussed in Chapter 8.

Notes Receivable Register

When many notes are received in the usual course of business, it may be advisable to keep an auxiliary record. An auxiliary record of notes receivable that provides more detailed information than a ledger account is usually known as a notes receivable register. One form of a notes receivable register is reproduced at the top of pages 350 and 351. The notes shown in the illustration were those received by the V. J. Nooney Co. during the period indicated by the record. The information contained in the register is obtained directly from the notes received. The notes are numbered consecutively as they are entered in the register. (This number should not be confused with the maker's number in the lower left-hand corner of the note, as shown in the illustration on page 343.) The due date of each note is determined and entered in the proper When Due column. The interest to maturity is calculated and entered in the Interest Amount column. When a remittance or a new note is received in settlement of a note, the date is entered in the Date Paid column.

Notes Receivable Account

The information contained in the notes receivable account should agree with that entered in the notes receivable register. The following account contains a record of the notes that were entered in the notes receivable register of the V. J. Nooney Co. Notice that each note is

DATE		ITEM	POST. REF.	DEBIT	CREDIT	BALANCE DEBIT	BALANCE CREDIT
ACCOUNT Notes Receivable						ACCOUNT NO. 121	
1986 Apr.	4	No. 1	CR3	4 6 8 12		4 6 8 12	
	21	No. 2	CR3	6 0 0 00		1 0 6 8 12	
May	2	No. 3	CR4	7 5 7 20		1 8 2 5 32	
	19	No. 4	CR4	8 2 0 00		2 6 4 5 32	
June	1	No. 3	CR5		7 5 7 20	1 8 8 8 12	
	3	No. 1	CR5		4 6 8 12	1 4 2 0 00	
	20	No. 2	CR5		6 0 0 00	8 2 0 00	
	20	No. 5	CR5	5 0 0 00		1 3 2 0 00	

identified by the number assigned to the note. If the notes are not numbered, each note should be identified by writing the name of the maker in the Item column of the account.

Proving The Notes Receivable Account

Periodically (usually at the end of each month) the notes receivable account is proved by comparing the balance of the account with the total of the notes owned as shown by the notes receivable register. Note that the following schedule of notes owned on June 30 has the same total as the balance in the notes receivable account illustration.

Schedule of Notes Owned

No. 4	$ 820
No. 5	500
	$1,320

DATE RECEIVED		No.	BY WHOM PAYABLE	WHERE PAYABLE		DATE MADE		
				BANK OR FIRM	ADDRESS	MO.	DAY	YEAR
1986 Apr.	4	1	L.A. Peters	First State Bank	Eureka	Apr.	4	'86
	21	2	J.M. Slawski	Commerce Bank	University City	Apr.	21	'86
May	2	3	S.M. Alpart	Farmers' Bank	Kirksville	May	2	'86
	19	4	L.L. Sheinbein	Central Trust	Jefferson City	May	19	'86
June	20	5	J.M. Slawski	Commerce Bank	University City	June	20	'86

PAGE 2 — NOTES RECEIVABLE REGISTER

Notes Receivable Register (Left Page)

Accrued Interest Receivable

While interest on a note literally accrues day by day, it is impractical to keep a daily record of such accruals. If the life of a note receivable is within the accounting period, no entry is made for the interest until the amount is received.

If, however, the business owns some interest-bearing notes receivable at the end of the accounting period, neither the net income for the period nor the assets at the end of the period will be correctly stated unless the interest accrued on notes receivable is taken into consideration. The amount of the accrued interest may be computed by reference to the notes themselves or to the data provided by a notes receivable register. The accounts are then adjusted by debiting Accrued Interest Receivable and by crediting Interest Revenue for the amount of interest that has accrued to the end of the period. Assume that at the end of a fiscal year ending June 30, a business owns four interest-bearing notes as shown in the following schedule:

Schedule of Accrued Interest on Notes Receivable

Principal	Date of Issue	Rate of Interest	Days From Issue Date to June 30	Accrued Interest June 30
$800.00	April 15	9%	76	$15.20
500.00	May 5	10%	56	7.78
545.80	May 29	9%	32	4.37
700.00	June 12	9%	18	3.15
Total accrued interest on notes receivable				$30.50

When the amount involved is so small, some accountants would ignore it on the ground of immateriality, but technical accuracy requires the following two-column journal entry as of June 30:

	WHEN DUE					AMOUNT			INTEREST			DISCOUNTED		DATE PAID		REMARKS
TIME	J	J	J	A	D				RATE	AMT.		BANK	DATE			

NOTES RECEIVABLE REGISTER   PAGE 2

TIME	WHEN DUE					AMOUNT				INTEREST RATE	INTEREST AMT.		DISCOUNTED BANK	DISCOUNTED DATE	DATE PAID		REMARKS
60 da.	3					4	6	8	12	8%	6	24			June	3	
60 da.	20					6	0	0	00	9%	9	00			June	20	Renewal for $500
30 da.	1					7	5	7	20	9%	5	68			June	1	Sent for coll. 5/30
90 da.			17			8	2	0	00	9%	18	45					
60 da.			19			5	0	0	00	9%	7	50					Renewal of Note No. 2

Notes Receivable Register (Right Page)

June 30 Accrued Interest Receivable....................... 30.50
            Interest Revenue 30.50
            Interest accrued on notes receivable as of June
            30.

In preparing the financial statements at the end of the year, the balance of the interest revenue account (which will include the $30.50 earned but not yet received) will be reported in the income statement, while the balance of the account, Accrued Interest Receivable, will be reported in the balance sheet as a current asset.

Accounting for Notes Payable Transactions

There are generally four types of transactions involving notes payable:

1. Note issued to a supplier to obtain an extension of time for payment of an obligation.
2. Note issued as security for cash loan.
3. Note paid at maturity.
4. Note renewed at maturity.

Note Issued to a Supplier to Obtain an Extension of Time for Payment. When a firm wishes to obtain an extension of time for the payment of an account, a note for all or part of the amount due may be acceptable to the supplier. Assume that Lehman Hardware Co. owes Wigington & Co. $654.70. By agreement, on June 11 Lehman issues to Wigington a check on the Centerre Bank for $54.70 and a 90-day, 10% interest-bearing note for $600. This transaction is entered in the

books of the Lehman Hardware Co. in two-column journal form as
follows:

June 11 Accounts Payable 654.70
              Cash 54.70
              Notes Payable 600.00
              Issued check for $54.70 and note for $600 to
              Wigington & Co.

Note Issued as Security for Cash Loan. Many firms experience brief
periods during the year in which receipts from customers are not adequate to finance their operations. During such periods, business firms
commonly borrow money from banks on short-term notes to help
finance their business operations. Assume that on June 16, Lehman
borrows $6,000 from the Centerre Bank on a 60-day, 10 1/2% interest-
bearing note. The transaction is entered in two-column journal form as
follows:

June 16 Cash 6,000
              Notes Payable................................   6,000
              Borrowed $6,000 at the bank on a 60-day,
              10 1/2% note.

Commercial banks often deduct interest in advance, and this procedure is known as *discounting.* For example, instead of the transaction
previously described, suppose that Lehman borrowed on a $6,000, 60-
day, non-interest-bearing note which the bank discounted at 10 1/2%.
The bank would calculate the implied interest on the note to maturity, known as *bank discount,* and deduct this amount from the $6,000
face of the note. This transaction may be illustrated in time-line form
as follows:

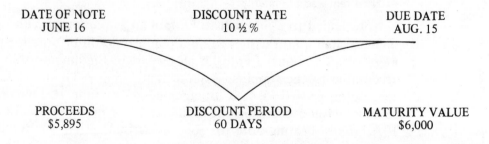

DATE OF NOTE	DISCOUNT RATE	DUE DATE
JUNE 16	10 ½ %	AUG. 15

PROCEEDS	DISCOUNT PERIOD	MATURITY VALUE
$5,895	60 DAYS	$6,000

The formulas for determining how much cash the Lehman Hardware Co. would receive on June 16 are as follows:

1. **Face   + Interest =** <u>**Maturity Value**</u>
   $6,000 +   0   = $6,000

2. **Maturity Value × Discount Rate × Discount Period =** <u>**Discount Amount**</u>
   $6,000   ×   10 1/2%   ×   60/360   = $105

3. **Maturity Value − Discount Amount =** <u>**Proceeds**</u>
   $6,000   − $105   = $5,895

Thus, Lehman Hardware Co. would receive only $5,895 proceeds ($6,000 − $105), and the transaction would be entered as follows:

June 16 Cash	5,895	
Discount on Notes Payable	105	
Notes Payable....................................		6,000
Discounted at 10 1/2%, a $6,000, 60-day, non-interest-bearing note.		

The $105 debit to the discount on notes payable account represents an offset to the $6,000 note payable. Lehman's liability at this time is only $5,895, which is the net amount or proceeds received from the bank. Discount on Notes Payable is a contra-liability account. The $105 discount becomes interest expense gradually each day. It is recognized in full when the note matures on August 15, and the $6,000 principal amount of the note is repaid. Accordingly, Lehman Hardware Co. will enter the payment of the note at maturity in two-column journal form as follows:

Aug. 15 Notes Payable	6,000	
Interest Expense...................................	105	
Cash...		6,000
Discount on Notes Payable.......................		105
Paid 60-day, non-interest-bearing note due today, and recognized interest expense at 10 1/2%.		

Note that, even though the stated rate of interest was 10 1/2% in both cases, the money received was less in amount and therefore more expensive in the second case. In the first case, $6,000 was obtained for 60 days at a cost of $105—exactly 10 1/2% ($105 ÷ $6,000 = 1.75% for 60 days; 10.5% for 360 days). In the second case, $105 was paid for the use of \$5,895 for 60 days—a rate of nearly 10.7%, which is known as the effective rate of interest (\$105 ÷ \$5,895 = 1.781% for 60 days; 10.687% for 360 days). (While notes receivable may also be discounted, small businesses deal with notes payable transactions much more frequently than with notes receivable transactions.)

Note Paid at Maturity. A note made payable to a bank for a loan commonly is paid at that bank upon maturity. When notes made payable to other payees mature, payment may be made directly to the holder or to a bank where the note was left for collection. The maker knows who the payee is but may not know who the holder is at maturity because the payee may have transferred the note to another party. When a note is left with a bank for collection, it is customary for the bank to mail the maker a notice of maturity. For example, assume that Wigington & Co. forwards the 90-day, 10% note for \$600 received from Lehman on June 11 to the Centerre Bank for collection. The bank would notify Lehman before the maturity date by sending a notice similar to the following illustration:

CENTERRE BANK

Bonne Terre, Missouri

Your note described below will be due

MAKER-COSIGNER-COLLATERAL	NUMBER	DATE DUE	PRINCIPAL	INTEREST	TOTAL
A. M. Lehman Lehman Hardware Co.	19360	9/9/86	\$600.00	\$15.00	\$615.00

ENDORSER

TO

A. M. Lehman
Lehman Hardware Co.
Box 362
Bonne Terre, MO 63628-5544

Note: Please bring this notice with you.   PAYABLE AT   Centerre Bank

Notice of Maturity of Note

Upon receiving this notice, Lehman issues a check to the bank for \$615 in payment of the note and interest. The transaction is entered in the books of the Lehman Hardware Co. in two-column journal form as follows:

```
Sept. 9  Notes Payable .......................................  600
         Interest Expense ......................................   15
            Cash ...............................................        615
               Paid note issued June 11 to Wigington & Co., plus in-
               terest.
```

Note Renewed at Maturity. If the maker is unable to pay a note in full at maturity, it may be possible to renew all or a part of the note. For example, on September 9, Lehman might pay the $15 interest and $100 on the principal of the note ($600, issued to Wigington & Co. on June 11), and give a new 60-day, 10% note for $500. This transaction should be entered in two-column journal form as follows:

```
Sept. 9  Notes Payable (old note) .............................  600
         Interest Expense ......................................   15
            Cash ...............................................        115
            Notes Payable (new note) ...........................        500
               Issued a check for $115 and a note for $500 to Wig-
               ington & Co. in settlement of a note for $600 plus in-
               terest.
```

Notes Payable Register

When many notes are issued in the usual course of business, it may be advisable to keep an auxiliary record. An auxiliary record of notes payable that provides more detailed information than a ledger account is usually known as a notes payable register. One form of such a register is reproduced on pages 356 and 357. The notes shown in the illustration were those issued by the V. J. Nooney Co. during the period indicated by the record.

The information contained in the register may be obtained directly from the note before it is mailed or given to the payee, or from a note stub. Blank notes are usually made up in pads with stubs attached on which spaces are provided for entering such essential information as amount, payee, where payable, date, time, rate of interest, and number. The due date of each note is determined and entered in the proper When Due column of the register. The interest at maturity is also calculated and entered in the Interest Amount column. When a note is paid, the date is entered in the Date Paid column.

PAGE 1

NOTES PAYABLE REGISTER

| DATE ISSUED | No. | TO WHOM PAYABLE | WHERE PAYABLE | | DATE MADE | | |
			BANK OR FIRM	ADDRESS	MO.	DAY	YEAR
1986 Apr. 14	1	J.L. Knoop	First State Bank	Eureka	Apr.	14	'86
May 13	2	Commerce Bank	Commerce Bank	Univ. City	May	13	'86
June 2	3	Bloodgood Brothers	Commerce Bank	Univ. City	June	2	'86

Notes Payable Register (Left Page)

Notes Payable Account

The information contained in the notes payable account should agree with that entered in the notes payable register. The following account contains a record of the notes that were entered in the notes payable register of the V. J. Nooney Co.

| ACCOUNT Notes Payable | | | | | | ACCOUNT NO. 216 | | |
| DATE | ITEM | POST. REF. | DEBIT | CREDIT | BALANCE | | |
					DEBIT	CREDIT	
1986 Apr. 14	No. 1	CP3		2 1 4 9 61		2 1 4 9 61	
May 13	No. 2	CP4		8 0 0 0 00		10 1 4 9 61	
June 2	No. 3	CP5		1 3 5 7 35		11 5 0 6 96	
13	No. 1	CP5	2 1 4 9 61			9 3 5 7 35	

Proving the Notes Payable Account

Periodically (usually at the end of each month), the notes payable account is proved by comparing the balance of the account with the total notes outstanding as shown by the notes payable register. Note that the following schedule of the notes outstanding on June 30 has the same total as the balance in the notes payable account illustration.

																	INTEREST				
	WHEN DUE														AMOUNT	RATE	AMOUNT	DATE PAID	REMARKS			
TIME	J	F	M	A	M	J	J	A	S	O	N	D										
60 da.						13									2149 61	9%	32 24	June 13	Settlement of Feb. 14 inv.			
90 da.							11								8000 00	10%	200 00					
30 da.					2										1357 35	11%	12 44		Settlement of Apr. 2 inv.			

NOTES PAYABLE REGISTER   **PAGE 1**

Notes Payable Register (Right Page)

Schedule of Notes Outstanding

No. 2 .... $8,000.00
No. 3 .... 1,357.35
                                        $9,357.35

Accrued Interest Payable

Neither the expenses for a period nor the liabilities at the end of the period will be correctly stated unless the interest accrued on notes payable is taken into consideration. The mechanics of calculating the amount of interest accrued on notes payable are the same as in the case of notes receivable. If a notes payable register is kept, it should provide the information needed in computing the amount of interest accrued on notes payable. If the total amount of such accrued interest was calculated to be $269.12, and the fiscal period ended June 30, the proper adjusting entry may be made as follows:

June 30 Interest Expense	269.12	
Accrued Interest Payable		269.12
Interest accrued on notes payable as of June 30.		

In preparing the financial statements at the end of the year, the balance of the interest expense account, which will include the $269.12 incurred but not yet paid, will be reported in the income statement, while the balance of the account, Accrued Interest Payable, will be reported in the balance sheet as a current liability.

Indorsement of Notes

A promissory note is usually made payable to a specified person or firm, though some notes are made payable to "Bearer." If the note is payable to the order of a specified party, that party must indorse the note to transfer the promise to pay to another party. To indorse means to sign one's name as payee on the back of a note.

The two major types of indorsements are (1) the blank indorsement and (2) the special indorsement. The indorsement is called a blank indorsement when only the payee's name is signed on the left end of the back of the note. The indorsement is called a special indorsement if the words "Pay to the order of" followed by the name of a specified party and the payee's signature appear on the back of the note. The legal effect of both types of indorsement is much the same. However, a blank indorsement makes a note payable to the bearer, while a special indorsement identifies the party to whose order payment is made.

Under certain circumstances, the maker of a note may arrange for an additional party to join in the promise to pay, either as a cosigner or as an indorser of the note. A cosigner signs below the maker's signature on the face of the note. If the other party makes a blank indorsement on the back of the note, it is called an accommodation indorsement. In either event, the payee of the note has an additional person responsible for payment, which is intended to add security to the note.

If a partial payment is made on a note, it is common practice to record the date of the payment and the amount paid on the back of the note, which is called indorsing the payment.

Shown on page 359 is a reproduction of the promissory note originally made payable to the order of Susan Lavin. (See illustration of note on page 343.) The maker of the note, William Alverson, had Darlene Gubuan become an accommodation indorser. Later, the payee, Lavin, transferred the note to T. L. Fischer by a special indorsement. On July 9, $500 was paid on the note.

BUILDING YOUR ACCOUNTING KNOWLEDGE

1. What form does a promise to repay a borrowed sum of money nearly always take?

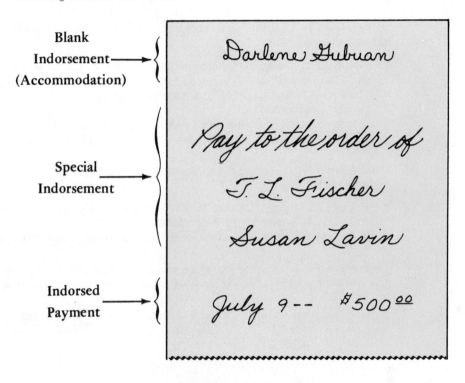

Indorsements on Note

2. What are the four characteristics that a promissory note must evidence in order to be considered negotiable commercial paper?
3. What three factors must be taken into consideration in calculating interest on notes?
4. In computing the exact number of days of interest on a note, what date is counted? What date is not counted?
5. What number of days is considered as a year by most banks and business firms in computing interest?
6. What generally are the four types of transactions involving notes receivable and how do they differ from one another?
7. What generally are the four types of transactions involving notes payable and how do they differ from one another?
8. How are accrued interest receivable and accrued interest payable reported on the balance sheet?

APPLYING ACCOUNTING CONCEPTS

(Use a 360-day year in all of these exercises.)

Exercise 11-1. Compute the amount of interest on each of the following notes.

1. $1,000, 60 days, 11%.
2. $800, 90 days, 13%.
3. $1,200, 120 days, 10%.

Exercise 11-2. Prepare the appropriate two-column journal entry for each of the following transactions.

1. Received a 90-day, 10% note for $912 from a customer in payment of an account receivable.
2. Received $73 and a 60-day, 11% note for $700 from a customer in payment of an account receivable.
3. Received notice from the bank that the note in transaction number (2) was collected at maturity. The bank fee for collecting the note was $11.

Exercise 11-3. Prepare the appropriate two-column journal entry for each of the following transactions.

1. Received a 60-day, 11% note for $875, plus interest of $21.88, in settlement of a 90-day, 10% note for $875 due today.
2. A 60-day, 12% note receivable for $1,200 due today was dishonored.

Exercise 11-4. Assume that at the end of the fiscal year ending July 31, a business owns three interest-bearing notes as shown in the following schedule.

Principal	Date of Issue	Rate of Interest
$1,000.00	May 15	12%
1,200.00	May 30	11%
900.00	June 25	12%

Prepare the adjusting entry at July 31 to recognize the accrued interest receivable on these notes.

Exercise 11-5. Prepare the appropriate two-column journal entry for each of the following transactions.

1. Issued a check for $29.25 and a 60-day, 12% note for $400 to a supplier in payment of an account.
2. Paid the $400 note in transaction number (1) at maturity.

Exercise 11-6. Prepare the appropriate two-column journal entry for each of the following transactions.

1. Borrowed $8,000 from the bank on a 90-day, 13% note.
2. Borrowed money from the bank on a $4,000, 90-day, non-interest-bearing note which the bank discounted at 12%. (You must compute the proceeds of this note.)
3. Issued a check for $260 and a note for $8,000 at 13.5% in settlement of the note in transaction number (1).
4. Paid the $4,000 non-interest-bearing note in transaction number (2) at maturity.

Exercise 11-7. Assume that the total amount of accrued interest on notes payable at the fiscal year end is $81.65. Prepare the adjusting entry at the fiscal year end to recognize the accrued interest payable on these notes payable.

Report No. 11-1

Complete Report No. 11-1 in the study assignments and submit your working papers to the instructor for approval. Then proceed with the textbook discussion in Chapter 12 until Report No. 12-1 is required.

EXPANDING YOUR BUSINESS VOCABULARY

What is the meaning of each of the following terms?

accommodation indorsement **(p. 358)**

bank discount **(p. 352)**

blank indorsement **(p. 358)**

contra-liability **(p. 353)**

cosigner **(p. 358)**

credit advice **(p. 347)**

discount amount **(p. 353)**

discounting **(p. 352)**

dishonored **(p. 348)**

effective rate **(p. 354)**

indorse **(p. 358)**

indorsing the payment **(p. 358)**

maker of the note **(p. 342)**

maturity value **(p. 353)**

negotiable commercial paper **(p. 342)**

notes payable register **(p. 355)**

notes receivable register **(p. 348)**

notice of maturity **(p. 354)**

payee of the note **(p. 342)**

principal of the note **(p. 343)**

proceeds **(p. 353)**

promissory note **(p. 342)**

rate of interest **(p. 343)**

special indorsement **(p. 358)**

time of the note **(p. 343)**

CHAPTER 12

Accounting for Inventory and Prepaid Expenses

CHAPTER OBJECTIVES

Careful study of this chapter should enable you to:

- Describe and contrast the two principal systems of accounting for inventory—the periodic system and the perpetual system.

- Explain the procedures involved in determining the end-of-period physical quantity of goods on hand, and to prepare an inventory sheet.

- Explain and contrast the specific identification, fifo, weighted average, and lifo methods of cost assignment to inventory; and to use the lower of cost or market rule in connection with the specific identification, fifo, and weighted average methods.

- Explain the gross margin and simplified retail methods of estimating the amount to be assigned to the end-of-period inventory.

- Explain and contrast the asset method and the expense method of accounting for supplies and prepayments.

Merchandise inventory and prepaid expenses have an important characteristic in common: both represent costs incurred in one accounting period that are expected in part to benefit the following period. Because the benefit is expected to be realized within a relatively short time, these assets are considered to be current rather than long-term. In most cases, the dollar amount of merchandise inventory is much larger than that for prepaid expenses. For this reason, accounting for merchandise inventory poses a much greater problem and receives much more attention.

MERCHANDISE INVENTORY

One of the major reasons for processing accounting information is to determine the net income (or net loss) of a business on a periodic basis. If the business purchases and sells merchandise, it is essential that the cost of all merchandise available for sale during the accounting period (goods on hand at the start of the period plus net purchases) be apportioned in a reasonable manner between the expense called cost of goods sold (merchandise inventory expense) and the asset commonly called merchandise inventory. The routine involved in accounting for merchandise, using accounts for purchases, purchases returns and allowances, purchases discount, and merchandise inventory, has been discussed and illustrated in preceding chapters. The problem of determining the quantity of goods on hand at the end of the period and of assigning cost to these goods remains to be considered.

Types of Inventory Systems

There are two principal systems of accounting for inventory — (1) the periodic system and (2) the perpetual system. In the periodic system, the merchandise inventory account balance is merely a record of the most recent physical inventory count, usually made only once a year when the stock is low or business is slow. As discussed in Chapter 6, the purchases account is debited with the cost of all goods bought at their respective invoice prices. As discussed in Chapter 7, the sales account is credited with the respective selling prices of all goods sold. The cost of goods sold is not determined until the end of the accounting period, at which time the following formula is applied:

Beginning Inventory (last year's physical count)	+	Net Purchases (account balance at end of this year)	−	Ending Inventory (this year's physical count)	=	Cost of Goods Sold (for entire period)

Purchases returns and allowances and purchases discounts are subtracted from the purchases account to arrive at net purchases.

In the perpetual system, the merchandise inventory account is an active account. It is debited with the cost of all goods bought at their respective invoice prices, and credited with the assumed cost of all goods sold, as well as the cost of any inventory returns, allowances, or discounts. Thus, the balance of the account represents the cost of goods on hand at all times. No purchases or contra purchases accounts are kept. A cost of goods sold account is kept, and when goods are sold, it is debited for the same amount that Merchandise Inventory is credited. At the same time, Accounts Receivable (or Cash) is debited and Sales is credited for the selling prices of all goods sold. Thus, *two* entries are required for each sale as follows:

```
1. Accounts Receivable (or Cash) ........................... xxxx
     Sales.................................................         xxxx
2. Cost of Goods Sold........................................ xxxx
     Merchandise Inventory .....................................     xxxx
```

Taking a Physical Inventory

Under the periodic inventory system, businesses do not maintain a record that shows the quantity and the cost of the merchandise on hand. Lacking such a record, the first step in attempting to apportion merchandise costs between sold and unsold goods consists of counting or measuring the goods that are on hand at the end of the period. This process is called taking a physical inventory.

Taking a physical inventory of a stock of merchandise can be a sizable task. Frequently, it is done after regular business hours. Some firms cease operations for a few days to take inventory. The ideal time to count the goods is when the quantity on hand is at its lowest level. If a fiscal year is selected so as to start and end at the time that the stock of goods is normally at its lowest level, it is known as a natural business year. Such a year is used by many businesses for accounting purposes.

It is desirable for all goods on hand to be inventoried in as short a time as possible. Extra help may be employed in order to take the inventory. Even if this is done, however, the taking of an inventory may require several days. If regular business is carried on during this time, special records must be kept of additions to and subtractions from the stock during the inventory-taking period. In this way, the quantities of goods that are on hand at the end of the last day of the fiscal period can be determined.

Various procedures are followed in taking an inventory so as to be sure that no items are missed, and that no items are included more than once. Frequently, persons taking inventory work in pairs; one counts the items and calls out the information to the other who records it. Usually this information is entered on a special form. This form, known as an inventory sheet, is arranged with columns to show the description of each type of item, the quantity on hand, the cost per unit, and the extension — the amount that results from multiplying the quantity by the unit cost. (The cost per unit usually is determined and the extensions completed after the count is finished.) Inventory sheets commonly provide spaces for (1) the date of the inventory count, (2) the location of the items listed, and (3) the names or initials of the persons who did the calling, recorded the quantities, entered the unit costs, made the extensions, and verified the information. The following is a reproduction of part of an inventory sheet of a furniture store. Two extension columns are provided so that subtotals may be separated from extensions.

INVENTORY Aug. 31   19 86   Page 1

Sheet No. 1   Costed by V.E.R.

Called by W.L.M.   Department A   Extended by V.E.R.

Entered by K.N.   Location Storeroom   Examined by C.J.C.

Description	Quantity	Unit	Unit Cost	Extensions	
Table lamp	20	ea.	52.80	1,056.00	
Wall rack	18	ea.	9.70	174.60	
Bookcase	7	ea.	88.10	616.70	
End table	13	ea.	33.20	431.60	
Desk	6	ea.	108.30	649.80	
Total					4,465.10

Inventory Sheet

In taking a physical inventory, it is very important to be sure that only the goods that are the property of the firm are included. The two main problems in determining the items to be included in physical inventory are (1) goods acquired and later sold on consignment and (2) goods in transit. The important thing to remember about goods on consignment is that they remain the property of the shipper (consignor) and should not be included in the inventory of the company holding the goods (consignee). Thus, if a company has acquired goods on consignment, they should not be included in that company's inventory. If a company has shipped goods on consignment for later sale, they should be included in that company's inventory.

In determining whether goods in transit at year end should be included in inventory, it is necessary to know the FOB terms. If goods are shipped FOB shipping point, the goods are the property of the buying company as soon as they are shipped. If goods are shipped FOB destination, the goods are the property of the selling company until they are received by the buying company.

Assigning Cost to the Inventory

After the quantities of goods owned have been determined at the end of the accounting period, the next step is to decide how much cost should be assigned to each unit. This might seem to be an easy, though perhaps a time-consuming job. If all purchases of the same article were made at the same price per unit, the unit cost times the number of units in the inventory would give the total cost to be assigned to those units. Frequently, however, identical articles are purchased at different times at different costs per unit. The question then arises as to which unit costs should be assigned to the goods in the inventory. If it is possible to separately identify and price items on hand when they are sold, this approach to cost assignment is preferred, and is known as specific identification costing. Often there is no way of knowing exactly which price was paid for the specific goods that are on hand. If so, one of three other methods of cost apportionment normally is adopted. These methods are (1) first-in, first-out costing, (2) weighted average costing, and (3) last-in, first-out costing.

Specific Identification Costing. A method of assigning merchandise cost which requires that each item that is sold and each item remaining in inventory be separately identified with respect to its purchase cost is called the specific identification method. This method is practical only for businesses in which sales volume is relatively low, inventory unit value is relatively high, and items can be distinguished easily from each other. Otherwise, record keeping becomes expensive and time consuming, if not impractical.

To illustrate how this method works, assume the following data for a particular item of merchandise:

	Units	Unit Price	Total Cost
On hand at start of period..................	400	$5.15	$ 2,060
Purchased during period:			
1st purchase	300	5.35	1,605
2nd purchase............................	700	5.75	4,025
3rd purchase	600	5.95	3,570
Number of units available for sale	2,000		$11,260
On hand at end of period	500		
Number of units sold during period	1,500		

Of the 1,500 units sold during the period, it is known for certain that 300 were from the beginning inventory, 200 were from the first purchase, 500 were from the second purchase, and 500 were from the last purchase. The cost of goods sold and the value of inventory at the end of the period are determined as follows:

	Cost of Goods Sold	Value of Ending Inventory
Beginning inventory	300 units @ $5.15 = $1,545	100 units @ $5.15 = $ 515
From 1st purchase	200 units @ 5.35 = 1,070	100 units @ 5.35 = 535
From 2nd purchase	500 units @ 5.75 = 2,875	200 units @ 5.75 = 1,150
From 3rd purchase........	500 units @ 5.95 = 2,975	100 units @ 5.95 = 595
Total	1,500 units $8,465	500 units $2,795

First-In, First-Out Costing. Another widely used method of allocating merchandise cost is called the first-in, first-out or fifo method. This costing method assumes that the first goods bought were the first goods sold and that, therefore, the latest goods bought remain in inventory. Applying this method to the data given at the top of the page, the cost of goods sold and the value of inventory at the end of the period are determined as follows:

	Cost of Goods Sold	Value of Ending Inventory
Beginning inventory	400 units @ $5.15 = $2,060	-0-
From 1st purchase	300 units @ 5.35 = 1,605	-0-
From 2nd purchase	700 units @ 5.75 = 4,025	-0-
From 3rd purchase........	100 units @ 5.95 = 595	500 units @ $5.95 = $2,975
Total	1,500 units $8,285	500 units $2,975

Note that the 500 items on hand at the end of the period are considered to be those most recently purchased. The term "fifo" relates to the goods *sold* during the accounting period and *not* to the goods in inventory at the end of the period.

First in, first out costing is widely used because of two features: (1) Whenever the flow of merchandise can be controlled, the business will see to it that the older goods are moved out first. Thus fifo costing is often in harmony with the actual physical movement of the goods. (2) Fifo costing assigns the most recent purchase costs to the ending inventory shown in the balance sheet. This satisfies those accountants who contend that inventory should be shown on the balance sheet at the most current cost possible.

Another reason for the continuing widespread use of fifo costing is that firms have used this method for a long time. Accountants are reluctant to change a long-followed method of accounting when such a change would affect the comparability of their income calculations over a period of years. Consistency based on comparability is important in accounting.

Weighted Average Costing. Another method of allocating merchandise cost is called the weighted average cost method, also known as the average cost method. This costing method is based on the average cost of identical units.

Using the data shown on page 367, the average cost of identical units is determined by dividing the total cost of units available for sale ($11,260) by the total number of units available for sale (2,000).

$$\frac{\$11,260 \text{ (cost of units available for sale)}}{2,000 \text{ (units available for sale)}} = \begin{array}{c} \$5.63 \text{ weighted average} \\ \text{cost per unit} \end{array}$$

The cost of goods sold and the value of the end-of-period inventory are calculated as follows:

Cost of goods sold	1,500 units @ $5.63	=	$ 8,445
Value of ending inventory	500 units @ 5.63	=	2,815
Total	2,000 units		$11,260

There is a logical appeal to the use of the weighted average basis to allocate cost between goods sold and goods on hand. In this example, one fourth (500) of the total units available (2,000) were unsold. The average cost basis assigns one fourth ($2,815) of the total cost ($11,260) to these goods.

Last-In, First-Out Costing. A fourth method of allocating merchandise cost is called the last-in, first-out or lifo method. It assumes that all of the sales in the period were made from the most recently purchased goods and that, therefore, the earliest goods bought remain in inventory. Applying this method to the data given on page 367, the cost of goods sold and the value of inventory at the end of the period are determined as follows:

	Cost of Goods Sold			Value of Ending Inventory		
Beginning inventory		-0-		400 units @ $5.15 =	$2,060	
From 1st purchase	200 units @ $5.35 =	$1,070		100 units @ 5.35 =	535	
From 2d purchase	700 units @ 5.75 =	4,025		-0-		
From 3d purchase	600 units @ 5.95 =	3,570		-0-		
Total	1,500 units	$8,665		500 units	$2,595	

Note that the 500 units on hand at the end of the period are considered to be the 400 units that were on hand at the start of the period plus 100 of the units from the first purchase. The term "lifo" relates to the goods *sold* during the accounting period and *not* to the goods in inventory at the end of the period.

Sometimes the lifo method has been justified on the grounds that the physical movement of goods in some businesses is actually last-in, first-out. This is rarely the case, but the method has become popular for other reasons. One persuasive argument for the use of the lifo method is that it matches the most current cost of items purchased against the current sales revenue. In many cases in which the lifo method is used, the calculated amount for inventory that has been sold, called cost of goods sold, is really the cost to replace the goods sold. When this amount is subtracted from sales revenue, the resulting gross margin figure is neither inflated nor deflated by gain or loss due merely to price changes. In the opinion of many accountants, this is proper and desirable.

Probably, the major reason for the growing popularity of the lifo method is the fact that when prices are rising, net income calculated by using the lifo method is smaller than the amount determined from using either the fifo or the weighted average method. As a result, the related income tax is smaller. The reverse would be true if prices were falling, but periods of falling prices have been few and brief in the past two centuries.

The lifo method is used by firms in many industries. In fact, procedures have been developed to apply the lifo principle to situations in which the goods sold are not literally replaced. High-fashion merchandise is an example. Suitable adjustments are made to state costs on a lifo basis.

Opponents of the lifo method contend that its use causes old, out-of-date inventory costs to be shown in the balance sheet. The theoretical and practical merits of fifo and lifo are the subject of much professional debate.

Physical Flows and Cost Flows. It is important to recognize that of the four inventory costing methods described, only the specific identification costing method will necessarily reflect cost flows that match physical flows of goods. Each of the other three methods—fifo, weighted average, and lifo—is based on assumed cost flows which are not required to reflect the actual physical movement of goods within the company. Any one of the three assumed cost flow methods may be used under any set of physical flow conditions.

Comparison of Methods. To compare the results obtained by the use of the four cost assignment methods discussed, assume that the 1,500 units were sold for $12,000. The following tabulation contrasts the cost assigned to the ending inventory and cost of goods sold, and the resultant gross margin under each of the four methods. It must be remembered, however, that the example relates to a period in which costs and prices were rising.

	Specific Identification	Fifo	Weighted Average	Lifo
Sales	$12,000	$12,000	$12,000	$12,000
Cost of goods sold:				
Beginning inventory	$ 2,060	$ 2,060	$ 2,060	$ 2,060
Purchases	9,200	9,200	9,200	9,200
Merchandise available for sale ...	$11,260	$11,260	$11,260	$11,260
Less ending inventory	2,795	2,975	2,815	2,595
Cost of goods sold..............	$ 8,465	$ 8,285	$ 8,445	$ 8,665
Gross margin	$ 3,535	$ 3,715	$ 3,555	$ 3,335

Note that in all cases, the total cost of merchandise available for sale ($11,260) is the same. It is the apportionment between goods sold and goods on hand at the end of the period that differs. For example, under fifo costing, $8,285 is apportioned to cost of goods sold and $2,975 to ending inventory. Under conditions of rising prices, the gross margin is lowest if lifo is used because the most recent, and therefore the highest purchase costs are matched against sales revenue. Under conditions of falling prices, the gross margin would be lowest if fifo were used because the earliest and therefore the highest purchase costs would be matched against sales revenue.

It is common practice to describe the methods that have been discussed as methods of inventory valuation. It should be apparent, however, that this process also values the cost of goods sold. The term "valuation" is somewhat misleading, since what is involved is really cost apportionment.

Lower of Cost or Market Method of Inventory Valuation

It is a well-established tradition in accounting that unrealized gains should not be recognized except in very unusual cases. If the value of an asset increases while it is being held, no formal entry of the gain is made on the books because it has not been actually realized. On the other hand, if the value or usefulness of an asset declines while it is being held, it is generally considered proper to recognize and enter the loss, even though it has not yet been realized. This is in keeping with the convention of conservatism, which states that gains should not be anticipated, but that all potential losses should be recognized.

The assignment of the lower of cost or market to the items that comprise the inventory of merchandise at the end of an accounting period is an important application of the convention of conservatism. Cost in this usage means the amount calculated using either the specific identification, fifo, or weighted average method. In determining the cost to be assigned to goods in an inventory, it is proper to assign to the goods on hand a fair share of any transportation costs that were incurred when the goods were purchased. In other words, cost means cost at the buyer's place of business, not cost at the supplier's shipping point. In some cases, transportation charges are an important part of the total cost of merchandise acquired. In addition, costs should be reduced by the amount of any purchases returns, allowances, or discounts taken.

Market in this usage means the cost to replace. It is the prevailing price in the market in which goods are purchased—not the prevailing price in the market in which they are normally sold—that is involved. An improved statement of the practice is the lower of cost or cost to replace. Accountants have assigned upper and lower limits to the market value that may be used in particular cases. The meaning and calculation of these limits is a topic for a more advanced course. Suffice it to say that market may neither exceed the calculated upper limit nor be less than the calculated lower limit.

To illustrate the application of the lower of cost or market rule, assume the following end-of-period data with respect to an inventory consisting of three items:

Item	Recorded Purchase Cost	End-of-Period Market Value	Lower of Cost or Market
1	$ 8,000	$ 7,000	$ 7,000
2	9,000	10,000	9,000
3	7,000	6,500	6,500
	$24,000	$23,500	$22,500

The illustration demonstrates two possible ways of making the lower of cost or market calculation. First, the lower of cost or market rule can be applied to the total inventory. In the foregoing illustration, this would involve comparing the $24,000 total cost with the $23,500 total market value. Under the second approach, the rule is applied to each item in inventory. In the foregoing illustration, this would involve comparing $24,000 total cost with $22,500 lower of cost or market value determined by comparing cost with market for each item. The approach chosen should be applied consistently between periods. The difference between the cost and market value is considered a loss due to holding inventory and typically is included in cost of goods sold on the income statement.

The Gross Margin Method of Inventory Estimation

Taking a physical inventory often is such a sizable task that it is attempted only once a year. If interim income statements and balance sheets are to be prepared, the portions of the cost of goods available for sale during the interim period to be allocated to goods sold during the period and to goods on hand at the end of the period must be estimated. One way of doing this is to apply the gross margin method, in which the amount of sales during the period is reduced by the normal percentage of gross margin (gross profit) to determine the estimated cost of goods sold. Deducting this amount from the total cost of goods available for sale gives the estimated amount of the ending inventory.

To illustrate, assume the following data with respect to a particular firm, which must be available if the method is to be usable:

1. Net sales, first month $110,000
2. Normal gross margin as a percentage of sales 40%
3. Inventory, start of period .... $ 80,000
4. Net purchases, first month 70,000

The estimated cost of goods sold during the month and the estimated merchandise inventory at the end of the month would be determined as shown at the top of page 373.

This computation is applicable only if the normal gross margin on sales has prevailed during the immediate past period and is expected to prevail during the following periods when the goods in the inventory will be sold. This type of calculation also can be used to evaluate the reasonableness of the amount of an inventory that was computed on the basis of a physical count. Any sizable difference in the two

1. Estimated cost of goods sold:
   Net sales.. $110,000
   Normal gross margin ($110,000 × 40%) 44,000
   Estimated cost of goods sold................................ $ 66,000
2. Cost of goods available for sale:
   Inventory, start of period .... $ 80,000
   Net purchases, first month 70,000
   Cost of goods available for sale $150,000
3. Estimated inventory at end of month:
   Cost of goods available for sale $150,000
   Less estimated cost of goods sold........................... 66,000
   Estimated end-of-month inventory .... $ 84,000

calculations might indicate a possible mistake in the count, in costing the items, or a marked change in the realized rate of gross margin. The gross margin procedure also can be used to estimate the cost of an inventory that may have been destroyed by fire or other casualty. Such a calculation might be useful in negotiating an insurance settlement.

The Retail Method of Inventory Estimation

Many retail merchants use a variation of the gross margin method to calculate cost of goods sold and ending inventory for interim-statement purposes. The procedure employed, called the retail method of inventory, requires keeping records of the selling prices of all goods purchased. This information, together with the record of the cost of goods purchased, makes it possible to compute the ratio between cost and retail prices. When the amount of retail sales is subtracted from the retail value of all goods available for sale, the result is the estimated retail value of the ending inventory. Multiplying this amount by the ratio of cost to selling price gives the estimated cost of the ending inventory.

Following is an example of the calculation of the estimated cost of an inventory of merchandise by the retail method:

	Cost	Retail
Inventory, start of period	$ 60,000	$ 85,000
Net purchases during period	126,000	163,000
Merchandise available for sale..........................	$186,000	$248,000
Less sales for period.....................................		180,000
Inventory, end of period, at retail		$ 68,000
Ratio of cost to retail prices of merchandise available for sale ($186,000 ÷ $248,000)		75%
Estimated inventory, end of period, at cost (75% of $68,000)	$ 51,000	

The foregoing example was simplified by assuming that there were no changes in the prices at which the goods were marked to sell. In practice, such changes as additional markups, markup cancellations, and markdowns are commonplace and the calculation must take such adjustments into consideration.

In addition to using the retail method in estimating the cost of inventory for interim-statement purposes, the cost-retail ratio that is developed can be used to convert the amount of a physical inventory which originally has been priced at retail to its approximate cost.

Perpetual Inventory Records

Firms that deal in certain types of merchandise sometimes find it feasible to keep up-to-date records continuously of the quantities and costs of goods on hand, known as perpetual inventory records. The general ledger account for Merchandise Inventory under such a system is somewhat like the account for Cash; a chronological record of each addition (purchase) and subtraction (sale) is maintained. The balance of the account at any time shows the cost of goods that should be on hand.

When perpetual inventory records are kept, the merchandise inventory account in the general ledger is usually a control account. A subsidiary ledger with an account for each type of goods is maintained. These accounts are often in the form of cards or computer disks which are formatted to handle additions, subtractions, and the balance after each change. Goods sold can be assigned cost on either a specific identification, fifo, weighted average, or lifo basis.

Assume that 1,000 units of NELZA were acquired by a firm on August 12 for a total of $2,000, and that the entire quantity was sold on September 9 for $2,750. The necessary entries under a perpetual inventory system would appear in two-column journal form as follows:

1. At time of purchase:

Aug. 12 Merchandise Inventory	2,000	
Accounts Payable or Cash........................		2,000
Bought 1,000 units of NELZA @ $2.		

2. At time of sale:

Sept. 9	Accounts Receivable or Cash...................... 2,750	
	Sales...	2,750
	Sold 1,000 units of NELZA @ $2.75.	
9	Cost of Goods Sold.............................. 2,000	
	Merchandise Inventory	2,000
	Cost of 1,000 units of NELZA sold today.	

Perpetual inventories do not eliminate the need for taking periodic physical inventories. The records must be examined from time to time to discover and correct any errors. However, it is not always necessary to count everything at the same time. The stock can be counted and the records verified by groups of items, by departments, or by sections as time permits, so long as the inventory is completely verified within a single accounting period.

A business that sells a wide selection of comparatively low-cost goods (such as a limited-price variety store) may not find it practical to keep a perpetual inventory. In contrast, a business that sells a relatively few high-cost items (an automobile dealer, for example) can maintain such a record without incurring excessive processing cost. The increasing use of the microcomputer and "point-of-sale" recording probably will cause more of the former types of businesses to switch from periodic to perpetual inventories.

Many types of businesses often keep supplementary or auxiliary records of inventory items in terms of quantities only, called stock records. Stock records serve as a guide in purchasing operations, may help to reveal any shortages, and may provide information as to the goods on hand as a basis for assigning merchandise cost for interim-statement purposes.

BUILDING YOUR ACCOUNTING KNOWLEDGE

1. What are the fundamental differences between the periodic system of accounting for inventory and the perpetual system of accounting for inventory?

2. What is the first step in attempting to apportion merchandise costs between sold and unsold goods?

3. If it is assumed that the first units purchased were the first ones sold, what is assumed about the source of the units left at the end of the accounting period?

4. What two factors are taken into account by the weighted average costing method of merchandise cost allocation?

5. If it is assumed that all sales in the accounting period were of the goods most recently purchased, what is assumed about the source of the units left at the end of the accounting period?

6. When "lower of cost or market" is assigned to the items that comprise the ending merchandise inventory, what does "cost" mean? What does "market" mean?

7. For what two major purposes is the gross margin method of inventory estimation utilized?

8. For what two major purposes is the retail method of inventory estimation utilized?

APPLYING ACCOUNTING CONCEPTS

Exercise 12-1. Assume the following data for a single item of merchandise sold by Posh Company.

	Units	Unit Price	Total Cost
On hand at start of period	500	$4.00	$2,000
Purchased during the period:			
1st purchase	400	$4.10	1,640
2nd purchase	700	$4.20	2,940
Number of units available for sale	1,600		$6,580
On hand at end of period	600		
Number of units sold during period	1,000		

Compute the cost of goods sold and ending inventory for Posh Company under each of the following methods.

1. Specific identification. (Of the 1,000 units sold, 400 were from the beginning inventory, 300 were from the first purchase, and 300 were from the last purchase.)
2. First-in, first-out.
3. Weighted average.
4. Last-in, first-out.

Exercise 12-2. Assume that Shore Company has three items of inventory with costs and market values at year end as follows.

Item	Cost	Market value
1	$ 6,000	$ 5,000
2	$ 9,000	$10,000
3	$12,000	$11,000

Compute the amount of Shore's inventory at year end using (1) the lower of cost or market rule applied to the total inventory, and (2) the lower of cost or market rule applied to each item in the inventory.

Exercise 12-3. Assume the following data for Gromar Company.

Net sales, January $120,000
Normal gross margin as a percentage of sales 30%
Inventory, January 1 .... $ 90,000
Net purchases, January .... $ 80,000

Use the gross margin method to estimate the cost of goods sold for January and the inventory at January 31.

Exercise 12-4. Assume the following data for Remet Company.

	Cost	Retail
Inventory, April 1	$ 50,000	$ 70,000
Net purchases, April	104,000	150,000
Merchandise available for sale	$154,000	$220,000
Less sales, April		170,000
Inventory, April 30, at retail............................		$ 50,000

Use the retail method to estimate the inventory at April 30.

Exercise 12-5. On August 15, Perle Company sold inventory with a cost of $700 for $1,050 cash. Prepare the necessary entries for this sale under a perpetual inventory system.

Report No. 12-1

Complete Report No. 12-1 in the study assignments and submit your working papers to the instructor for approval. Then continue with the following textbook discussion until Report No. 12-2 is required.

PREPAID EXPENSES

Office supplies, store supplies, advertising supplies, and other purchased supplies may not be wholly consumed in the period in which they are acquired. The premiums on insurance policies covering merchandise, equipment, and buildings are often prepaid, but the terms of the policies may extend beyond the current accounting period. Rent and interest may be paid in advance, but the expenses may not be wholly incurred in the same accounting period. The cost of unused supplies on hand at the close of the accounting period and the portion of prepayments such as insurance, rent and interest that will benefit future periods are known as prepaid expenses. Prepaid expenses should be treated as current assets because the benefits will be realized within a comparatively short time.

When accounts are kept on the accrual basis, it is necessary to adjust certain of them at the close of each accounting period for the following:

1. Supplies or services purchased during the period that were entered as **assets** at time of purchase and a portion of which was consumed or used during the period.
2. Supplies or services purchased during the period that were entered as **expenses** at time of purchase and a portion of which was not consumed or used during the period.

Asset Method of Accounting for Prepaid Expenses

Supplies and services that may not be wholly consumed in the period in which they are purchased may be entered as assets at the time of purchase. Under the asset method of accounting, it is necessary to adjust the accounts at the end of each accounting period in order that the used portions may be recorded as expenses. A delay in the recognition of an expense already paid (or of revenue already received) is known as a deferral. On the other hand, as mentioned previously, recognition of an expense that is owed at the end of an accounting period but has not yet been paid (or revenue that is earned but has not yet been received) is known as an accrual.

Supplies. Supplies such as office supplies, store supplies, advertising supplies, fuel, and postage, which may not be wholly consumed in the accounting period in which they are acquired, are usually entered as assets at the time of purchase. Office supplies include letterheads, envelopes, pencils, adding machine and computer tape, notebooks, computer diskettes, typewriter ribbons, and other miscellaneous supplies that are normally consumed in the operation of an office. Transactions arising from the purchase of supplies on account are entered in a multi-column purchases journal with one debit column for entering merchandise purchases and a second debit column for entering purchases of supplies. When supplies are purchased for cash, the transactions are entered in the cash payments journal. In either case, the purchases are posted to the office supplies account in the general ledger.

At the end of each accounting period, an inventory of the office supplies on hand is taken, and an adjusting entry is made for the amount of the office supplies consumed during the period. For example, if at the end of the accounting period, the office supplies account shows a debit balance of $984.26 and a physical inventory count reveals that the cost of supplies on hand amounts to $540, it is assumed that the supplies expense during the period is $444.26 ($984.26 – $540). The adjusting entry is as follows:

Office Supplies Expense	444.26	
Office Supplies		444.26
Office supplies consumed during period.		

After this entry is posted, the office supplies account will have a debit balance of $540, which is reported in the balance sheet as a current asset. The office supplies expense account will have a debit balance of $444.26, which is reported in the income statement as an operating expense. To illustrate, using T accounts:

Office Supplies		Office Supplies Expense	
984.26	444.26	444.26	
Bal. 540.00			

Store supplies include wrapping paper, twine, cellophane tape, corrugated board, paper bags, containers, cleaning supplies, and other miscellaneous supplies that are normally consumed in the operation of a store. Advertising supplies include catalogs, circulars, price lists, order blanks, and other miscellaneous supplies that are normally consumed in an advertising program. Transactions arising from the purchase of such supplies should be entered in the same manner as transactions arising from the purchase of office supplies. The end-of-period adjusting process and resulting treatment of asset and expense elements on the financial statements are similar.

Postage. The cost of postage purchased is usually treated as a current asset and entered by debiting Postage and by crediting the cash account. Some of the postage may be used on packages, and some on ordinary mail. If postage used on packages is billed to the customer, the entry for the sale will include a credit to the postage account. Usually no entry is made when postage is used on ordinary mail each day, but periodically the postage on hand is counted (or valued, if a postage meter is used). The difference between the amount of the unused postage on hand and the debit balance of the postage account represents the amount of postage used and not billed to customers. This requires an adjusting entry to the postage account.

If the account for postage is debited (1) for the amount of postage on hand at the beginning of the month, $76, and (2) for the amount of postage purchased during the month, $261.80, and is credited (3) for the amount of postage used on packages during the month, $95, the account will have a debit balance of $242.80 at the end of the month. If at that time, the actual amount of postage on hand is found to be $62.40, the difference of $180.40 represents the amount of postage that appears to have been used and not billed to customers during the month. The following adjusting entry will be made:

Postage Expense... 180.40
   Postage 180.40
     Amount of postage used on ordinary mail.

After this is posted, the postage account will have a debit balance of $62.40, which is reported in the balance sheet as a current asset. The postage expense account will have a debit balance of $180.40, which is reported as an operating expense in the income statement. To illustrate, using T accounts:

Postage		Postage Expense	
76.00	95.00	180.40	
261.80	180.40		
Bal. 62.40			

A business may meet its postage requirements by (1) buying postage stamps, (2) making a deposit under the postal permit system for a certain amount of postage, or (3) using a postage meter. In the third case, a certain amount of postage is paid for, and the meter is set so that the postage may be used as needed. Regardless of how postage is purchased, the accounting procedure can be the same. The prepaid postage is charged to the postage account and the amount of stamps used or postage consumed is charged to the proper expense account.

Insurance. A variety of risks are assumed in the operation of a business. Property such as buildings, furniture, machinery, supplies, and merchandise inventory may be damaged or destroyed by fire, water, earthquake, windstorm, or other natural disaster. Many types of property, especially money, may be stolen by burglars and sometimes by employees. State laws impose liability on the part of an employer to employees for injury or death arising out of the employees' work. The hazards connected with the ownership and operation of motor vehicles are well known. Accidents to persons unconnected with the business but occurring on business premises pose the threat of lawsuits and possibly large settlements. Loss of income as a result of the interruption of business operations because of a fire or a flood is a possibility.

It is possible to obtain insurance against these types of losses and certain others not mentioned. A separate insurance policy relating to each type of risk can be obtained, but in recent years, the practice of obtaining one policy covering most or all of the risks has become commonplace. Such contracts are described as "package," "blanket," or "multi-peril" policies. In total, the cost of such types of insurance is lower than a collection of policies for separate individual risks.

A contract under which an insurance company (the insurer) agrees to protect the business (the insured) from loss is known as an insurance policy. The amount that the insured is required to pay for insurance protection is known as the premium. The premium is usually stated as a specified rate per $1,000 of insurance for one or more years. Rates for workers' compensation insurance and automobile insurance are subject to change each year even though the coverage is part of a policy that includes other matters. The rate for the other features may be for a 3-year period. The premium for a 3-year coverage is usually less than 3 times the 1-year rate, which is a type of quantity discount. Since insurance is usually purchased for a period of one or more years and the premium is paid in advance by the insured, the amount paid is usually charged to a prepaid insurance account. This account is classified as a current asset.

Expired Insurance. The prepaid insurance account gradually decreases in value as the life of the insurance policy grows shorter. It is customary to enter at the close of each accounting period the total amount of prepayment that expired during the period just ended. The expired amount is entered as an expense. If the management of the business does not see a need for any breakdown of the insurance expense, an end-of-year adjusting entry such as the following would suffice:

Insurance Expense   xxx
    Prepaid Insurance   xxx
        Insurance expired during the year.

The amount in the foregoing entry may be determined by referring to the policy (or policies) and calculating the portion of the premium that relates to the year just ended. The amount of the premium for each major type of coverage is shown on the face of the policy. If more detail about the insurance expense is wanted, it would be possible to analyze the total and to classify it into, perhaps, delivery equipment insurance expense, fire insurance expense (with subclassifications relating to building, to furniture and fixtures, and to merchandise), workers' compensation insurance expense, and public liability insurance expense. Separate accounts can be established to provide as much detail as needed.

If a business has several insurance policies, it may be useful to maintain an auxiliary record known as an Insurance Policy Register. This record provides spaces to show the date and number of each policy, name of the insurer, type and amount of coverage, total term, expiration date, total premium, and columns to show the premium applicable to each month. Usually, a separate page is used for each year.

Canceled Insurance. The insurance company or the insured may cancel an insurance policy at any time before the expiration of the policy. If a policy is canceled, the insured is entitled to receive a refund of that part of the premium applicable to the unexpired period. The amount of the refund will depend upon whether the policy is canceled by direct action of the insurance company or at the request of the insured. When the policy is canceled directly by the insurance company, the premium for the expired period is computed on a pro rata basis. When the policy is canceled at the request of the insured, the premium for the expired period is usually computed on a short-term rate basis, which means that the insurance company's refund to the insured is less than the amount of the unexpired premium. The amount refunded is entered by debiting the cash account and by crediting the prepaid insurance account. The remaining unexpired premium, if any, is then debited to Insurance Expense and credited to Prepaid Insurance.

Prepaid Rent. When business property is rented for more than one accounting period on the basis of a lease agreement, and the lease payment is made in advance, it is usual to regard the amount of the lease payment as prepaid rent. Prepaid rent is classified as a current asset.

At the end of the accounting period, the amount of rent expense relating to the period just ended should be determined, and an adjusting entry made to transfer that portion of the lease payment from the prepaid rent account to the rent expense account. For example, assume that on July 1, an office building was leased by the business for a 3-year period, and a lease payment of $36,000 was made in advance. The entry for the lease payment is as follows:

```
July 1 Prepaid Rent..................................... 36,000
        Cash ..........................................          36,000
              Three-year lease of office building.
```

On December 31, it was determined that one-sixth of the lease had expired; therefore, the following adjusting entry was made:

```
Dec. 31 Rent Expense...................................  6,000
         Prepaid Rent ...................................          6,000
              Prepaid rent transferred to rent expense.
```

After the foregoing entry is posted, the prepaid rent account will have a debit balance of $30,000, which represents 2 1/2 years that the lease will remain active. The $30,000 of prepaid rent is reported in the balance sheet as a current asset. The $6,000 debit balance of the rent expense account is reported in the income statement under the heading of "Operating expenses" (and the subheading of "Administrative expenses" if operating expenses are subclassified).

One advantage of using the asset method of accounting for prepaid expenses is that the adjusting entries required at the end of the period are of the write-off type. Such adjustments do not need to be reversed at the start of the new period.

Expense Method of Accounting for Prepaid Expenses

Supplies and services that may not be wholly consumed in the period in which they are purchased may be entered as expenses at the time of purchase. Under the expense method of accounting, it is necessary to adjust the accounts at the end of each accounting period in order that the unused portions may be entered as assets. For example, if office supplies purchased during an accounting period are charged to the office supplies expense account, it will be necessary to adjust the account at the end of the period for the cost of the supplies on hand. To illustrate, assume that Office Supplies Expense had been charged for a total of $425 during the period and an inventory taken at the end of the period shows that supplies on hand amount to $150. The following adjusting entry is made:

Office Supplies	150	
Office Supplies Expense		150
Office supplies on hand.		

After this entry is posted, the office supplies expense account will have a debit balance of $275, which is reported in the income statement as an operating expense. The office supplies account will have a debit balance of $150, which is reported in the balance sheet as a current asset. To illustrate, using T accounts:

Office Supplies		Office Supplies Expense	
150		425	150
	Bal. 275		

When the expense method of accounting is followed, the adjustments made at the end of the period are called deferral adjustments, because they defer expenses to the next period. Adjustments of this type should be reversed at the start of the new period. In the foregoing example relating to office supplies, the reversing entry would be:

Office Supplies Expense	150	
Office Supplies		150

The effect of the adjusting, closing, and reversing procedure is (1) to remove the unused or unexpired amount from an expense account at the end of the period, (2) to transfer the remaining amount to the expense and revenue summary account, and (3) at the start of the new period, to transfer back to the expense account the amount of expense that previously had been deferred.

The asset and expense methods of accounting for prepaid expenses give the same final result. In the asset method, an amount that will eventually become the expense of current and future periods is first put into an asset account, and at the end of each period, a proper portion is transferred to an expense account. In the expense method, the original amount is first put into an expense account. At the end of each accounting period, the portion that will be an expense of future periods is moved into an asset account and subsequently brought back into the related expense account by a reversing entry at the start of the new period.

BUILDING YOUR ACCOUNTING KNOWLEDGE

1. What are the two methods of entering the amounts of supplies or services purchased when accounts are kept on the accrual basis?
2. How is the value of office supplies, store supplies, advertising supplies, or postage on hand at the end of the accounting period determined?
3. Under what heading should supplies or postage on hand be reported in the balance sheet?
4. Under what heading should supplies or postage expense be reported in the income statement?
5. Why has the practice of obtaining a single "multi-peril" insurance policy become commonplace in recent years?
6. Under what heading should prepaid insurance be reported in the balance sheet? Prepaid rent?
7. What type of end-of-period adjusting entries are required when the asset method of accounting for prepaid expenses is used? Do such adjustments need to be reversed?
8. What type of end-of-period adjusting entries are required when the expense method of accounting for prepaid expenses is used? Do such adjustments need to be reversed?

APPLYING ACCOUNTING CONCEPTS

Exercise 12-6. Use the asset method to account for the following prepaid expenses of Prep Company, which just started in business.

1. Office supplies were purchased for $850 cash.
2. Rent was paid in advance for a two-year period, $20,000.

At the end of the accounting period, prepare adjusting entries for the following:

3. Office supplies on hand, $160.
4. Six months rent has expired.

Exercise 12-7. Assume the same events as in Exercise 12-6. Use the expense method to account for the four events of Prep Company.

Report No. 12-2

Complete Report No. 12-2 in the study assignments and submit your working papers to the instructor for approval. Then continue with the textbook discussion in Chapter 13 until Report No. 13-1 is required.

EXPANDING YOUR BUSINESS VOCABULARY

What is the meaning of each of the following terms?

accrual **(p. 378)**   asset method **(p. 378)** average cost **(p. 368)**

convention of conservatism **(p. 371)**

consignee **(p. 366)**

consignment **(p. 366)**

consignor **(p. 366)**

cost **(p. 371)**

cost apportionment **(p. 370)**

deferral **(p. 382)**

deferral adjustments **(p. 384)**

expense method **(p. 383)**

first-in, first-out (fifo) **(p. 367)**

gross margin method **(p. 372)**

insurance policy **(p. 381)**

in transit **(p. 366)**

inventory sheet **(p. 365)**

last-in, first-out (lifo) **(p. 368)**

lower of cost or cost to replace **(p. 371)**

lower of cost or market **(p. 371)**

market **(p. 371)**

natural business year **(p. 364)**

periodic system **(p. 363)**

perpetual inventory records **(p. 374)**

perpetual system **(p. 363)**

premium **(p. 381)**

prepaid expenses **(p. 378)**

retail method **(p. 373)**

short-term rate basis **(p. 382)**

specific identification **(p. 366)**

stock records **(p. 375)**

taking a physical inventory **(p. 364)**

weighted average cost **(p. 368)**

CHAPTER 13

Accounting for Property, Plant, and Equipment

CHAPTER OBJECTIVES

Careful study of this chapter should enable you to:

- Determine the cost of property, plant, and equipment.

- Explain the nature and purpose of depreciation, the different acceptable depreciation methods and their possible effects on net income.

- Account for the acquisition, disposition, and depreciation of property, plant, and equipment.

- Prepare a property, plant, and equipment record.

- Describe the reporting of depreciation in financial statements.

- Explain the nature of wasting assets and the two different methods of accounting for their depletion.

Many types of business assets, acquired with the expectation that they will remain in service for a number of accounting periods, are called property, plant, and equipment or long-term assets. The descriptions fixed assets and capital assets also are used sometimes. Such assets can be classified in various ways. From a legal standpoint, all property is either real property or personal property. Real property (realty or real estate) includes land and anything attached to the land. In nearly all cases, any real property owned by a business is considered to be a long-term asset. Real estate acquired as a short-term investment is an exception. Personal property includes everything else that can be owned other than real property. Many kinds of personal property also are classified as property, plant, and equipment. Furniture, equipment, motor vehicles, machinery, patents, and copyrights are common examples of personal property that is owned and used by a business for a number of accounting periods.

Another way of classifying long-term assets is on the basis of tangibility. All real property is tangible (has physical substance). The same is true of such personal property as furniture, equipment, and machinery. Major examples of intangible (no physical substance) assets are patents, copyrights, leases, franchises, trademarks, and goodwill. These are considered long-term assets because they are expected to bring future economic benefit for more than one year and, except for goodwill, have a legal status that allows them to be classified as property. The subject of goodwill will be considered in Chapter 16.

Sometimes businesses own interests in other incorporated businesses in the form of capital stock, bonds, or long-term notes. Government bonds or notes are also commonly owned. If these investments are temporary in nature, they are considered marketable securities and should be classified as current assets. If these assets are expected to be owned for a long time, they are considered long-term investments and should be shown in the balance sheet under the heading Investments

For accounting purposes, a common classification of property, plant, and equipment is on the basis of how the original cost of the property is handled in the process of determining net income. The cost of land used only as a site for a store, a factory, a warehouse, or a parking lot is normally left undisturbed in the accounts as long as the land is owned. Because land does not lose its capability to serve these purposes, it does not depreciate. Tangible assets such as buildings, furniture, and equipment are usually called depreciable assets, because they wear out or are used up as time passes. In determining net income, a portion of the cost of such assets is charged off as depreciation expense. In a similar fashion, the cost of such intangible properties as patents, copyrights, and leaseholds is gradually charged off as expense to the periods benefited by the assets. As applied to intangible assets, however, the periodic write-off is termed amortization in contrast to depreciation of certain tangible assets. Actually, the meaning of the word amortization is broad enough to include depreciation, but customarily the write-off of the cost of most tangible long-term assets is called depreciation, while the write-off of the cost of intangible long-term assets is called amortization.

Certain long-term assets whose physical substance is consumed in the operation of a business are called wasting assets Common examples include mines, stands of timber, and oil and gas wells. The cost of such property is allocated to the periods in which its removal or exhaustion occurs. This periodic write-off is called depletion.

For the sake of brevity, land, buildings, and various types of equipment will often be referred to in the following sections simply as long-term assets. It should be understood that these assets are all in the tangible category.

LAND, BUILDINGS, AND EQUIPMENT

In accounting for tangible long-term assets, two major issues need to be addressed: (1) what elements should be included in the cost of a particular asset or group of assets and (2) how the cost should be allocated or apportioned to those future accounting periods that will benefit from the use of such an asset or group of assets.

Cost of Long-Term Assets

Long-term assets may be purchased for cash or on account. The amount at which long-term assets should be entered initially is the total of all outlays needed to put them in use. This total may include the purchase price, transportation charges, installation costs, and any other costs that are incurred up to the point of placing the asset in service. In some cases, interest may be included in the cost. For example, if money is borrowed for the purpose of constructing a building or other facility, it is considered sound accounting to add the interest incurred during the period of construction to the cost of such building or facility. It is important that the total cost of a depreciable asset be properly accounted for, because this cost becomes the basis for the periodic depreciation write-off.

Transactions involving the purchase of property, plant, and equipment may be entered initially in the appropriate book by debiting the proper asset account and by crediting the cash account for the amount paid, or by crediting the proper liability account, such as Accounts Payable, Notes Payable, or Mortgage Payable, for the obligation incurred.

Additions or improvements represent an increase in the value of long-term assets and should be entered by debiting the proper asset account and by crediting the cash account or the proper liability account. For example, if an addition to a building is constructed, the total cost incurred should be debited to the building account. In the same manner, the cost of improvements, such as the installation of partitions, shelving, hardwood or tile floors, sprinkler systems, air conditioning systems, or any other improvements that increase the usefulness of the property, should be entered by debiting the building or building improvement account. The costs of landscaping grounds surrounding an office or factory building represent improvements in the land which enhance its value. Assessments for street improvements, sidewalks, sewers, flood prevention, or parks also represent improvements in, or enhancement of the value of the land. Such costs and assessments should be entered by debiting the land account.

Depreciation of Long-Term Assets

The central task in attempting to determine net income or loss on a periodic basis is to allocate revenue to the period in which it is earned and to assign expenses to the periods that are benefited from the outlays. Long-term assets frequently last for many years and, accordingly, benefit a number of periods. The process of determining and entering the depreciation of most long-term assets is carried on in an effort to assign their cost to the periods that they benefit or serve.

It should be emphasized that depreciation is a process of cost allocation, not a process of valuation. Many factors cause the values of long-term assets to change over time, and the assignment of long-term costs to future accounting periods is very unlikely to produce net amounts in the asset accounts that represent current values. These net amounts (cost less accumulated depreciation) are merely the portions of the original costs which have not yet been allocated to expense.

Causes of Depreciation. Most long-term assets lose their usefulness over time. The allocation of the cost or other recorded value of a long-term asset over those future periods expected to benefit from its use is called depreciation. There are two major types of depreciation: (1) physical and (2) functional.

Physical depreciation refers to the loss of usefulness because of deterioration from age and from wear. It is generally continuous, though not necessarily uniform from period to period. Assets exposed to the elements may wear out at a fairly regular rate. Assets not exposed to the elements may slowly deteriorate whether in use or not, but the speed at which they deteriorate often is related to the extent to which they are used.

Functional depreciation refers to the loss of usefulness because of inadequacy or obsolescence. The growth of a business may result in some of its long-term assets becoming inadequate. The assets remain capable of doing the job for which they were acquired, but the job has become too big for them. Assets may become obsolete because of a change in the demand for products or services, or because of the development of new methods, equipment, or processes which either reduce costs, or increase quality, or both.

Calculating the Amount of Depreciation for a Period. The net cost of an asset should be apportioned over the periods the asset is expected to serve. Net cost means original cost less scrap or salvage value. Scrap or salvage value is quite difficult to predict in most cases. Unless such value is expected to be a significant fraction of original cost, it usually is ignored (considered to be zero). Scrap or salvage value normally is a significant amount in the case of automobiles and trucks. Although the estimation of salvage value can be difficult, the major challenge in depreciation accounting is to attempt to foretell either how many periods the assets will serve or how many units of service the asset will provide. If it were possible to know that a machine could operate a total of 100,000 hours, it would be easy to decide that 5% of its net cost should be charged to the first year if during that year the machine operated 5,000 hours. Likewise, a certain knowledge that an asset would last 10 years and equally serve each of those years would solve the problem of how to apportion its cost. Unfortunately, there is no way of knowing exactly how long an asset will last or exactly what its output will be. All that can be done is to make estimates based upon past experience. In attempting to make such estimates, the accountant may be assisted by information relating to assets previously owned by the business or be guided by the experience of others. Statistics supplied by trade associations and government agencies (such as the Internal Revenue Service) may help. Opinions of engineers or appraisal companies may be sought. Past experience with respect to physical depreciation may be a very good guide for the future. Past events, however, are not much help in attempting to predict depreciation caused by inadequacy or obsolescence. Uncertainty surrounds all depreciation calculations.

Methods of Calculating Depreciation. There are several different ways of calculating the amount of depreciation each period. The most commonly used methods are the following:

1. Straight-line method.
2. Declining-balance method.
3. Sum-of-the-years-digits method.
4. Units-of-output method.
5. ACRS depreciation.

Depreciation may be taken into consideration in calculating income subject to federal and state income taxes. A business is not required to calculate depreciation in the same way for both income tax and business accounting purposes. However, because depreciation is only an estimate, many firms adopt depreciation practices for business accounting purposes that are also acceptable for income tax determination purposes. This does not impose severe limitations, since the tax laws generally allow any method that is reasonable and consistently followed, although the first three methods named above are specifically mentioned in the law for depreciable long-term assets acquired prior to 1981.

Straight-Line Method. The depreciation method in which the net cost of an asset is apportioned equally over its estimated useful life in terms of months or years is called the straight-line method. For example, assume that a new asset with a cost of $1,000, an expected life of 4 years, and a $100 estimated salvage value at the end of its useful life, is to be depreciated on a straight-line basis. The amount of depreciation each year would be $225, computed as follows:

$$\frac{\$1,000 \text{ (cost)} - \$100 \text{ (salvage value)}}{4 \text{ years}} = \$225 \text{ annual depreciation}$$

The annual rate of depreciation would be 25% (100% ÷ 4 years).

A month is usually the shortest period that is considered in depreciation accounting. An asset purchased on or before the fifteenth of the month is considered to have been owned for the full month. An asset purchased after the fifteenth of the month is considered to have been acquired the first of the next month.

The difference between the cost of an asset and the total amount charged off as depreciation as of a certain date is its undepreciated cost (sometimes called book value). In the foregoing illustration, the undepreciated cost of the asset after the first year, assuming it was in use for 12 months, would be $775 [$1,000 (cost) − $225 (depreciation)]. When the straight-line method is used, the undepreciated cost of the asset decreases uniformly period by period. As shown on the following graph, the undepreciated cost over a number of periods is a downward-sloping, but perfectly straight line. That is how the method got its name.

The straight-line method's outstanding advantage is its simplicity. Since depreciation is based upon estimates, many business people and accountants believe that the use of more complicated procedures is not warranted. The calculation of depreciation on a straight-line basis

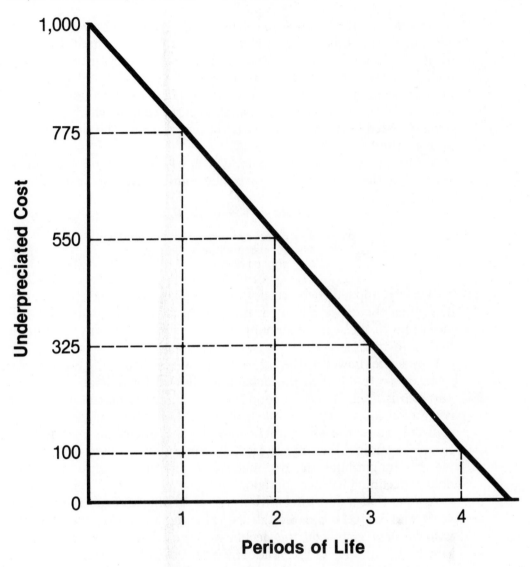

is still a widely followed practice when other methods offer no particular advantage.

Declining-Balance Method. Many long-term assets require repairs and replacement of parts to keep them in service. Such expenses usually increase as the assets grow older. Some accountants believe that depreciation expense should be higher in early years to offset the higher repair and maintenance expenses of the later years. Another reason advanced in support of an accelerated depreciation method is the contention that assets contribute proportionately more to the business during the years that the assets are comparatively new. For these reasons, it may be desirable to calculate depreciation in a way that will give larger write-offs in the early years of the life of the unit. One way to accomplish this result is to apply a fixed or uniform rate to the undepreciated cost of the property each year. The depreciation method using a fixed or uniform rate applied to the undepreciated cost, resulting in successively smaller depreciation charges as the undepreciated cost diminishes year by year is called the declining-balance method.

A formula to calculate a rate which will leave a predetermined amount at the end of a predetermined number of years is as follows:

$$\text{Rate} = 1 - n\sqrt[n]{s \div c}$$

Where n = number of years of estimated life
s = estimated salvage value
c = original cost

This rate is applied each year to the undepreciated cost of the asset to determine the depreciation for the year. Any rate less than 100% will never reduce the original amount to zero, so that some salvage value is built into this method.

In practice, however, the rate used is rarely calculated by a formula. Instead, a rate equal to the maximum allowed for federal income tax purposes is used. If certain conditions are met, the maximum allowed is either twice the straight-line rate, 1-1/2 times the straight-line rate, or 1-1/4 times the straight-line rate. In the discussion that follows, twice the straight-line rate is used. Because a rate is used that is double the straight-line rate, this method is sometimes referred to as the double-declining-balance method.

Assume that a new asset with a cost of $1,000, an expected life of 4 years, and a $100 estimated salvage value at the end of its useful life, is to be depreciated on the declining-balance basis. The depreciation rate to be applied to the undepreciated cost of the asset each year would be 50%, computed as follows:

Straight-line rate = 25% (100% ÷ 4 years)
Declining-balance rate = 50% (2 × 25%)

The undepreciated cost at the end of each year would be as shown at the top of page 395.

As shown on the following graph, the undepreciated cost declines rapidly in the early years and more slowly in the later years of an asset's life.

Note that although salvage value is not considered directly in the determination of the depreciation amount, the asset should not be

Year	Undepreciated Cost Beginning of Year	Rate	Annual Depreciation	Accumulated Depreciation End of Year	Undepreciated Cost End of Year
1	$1,000.00	50%	$500.00	$500.00	$500.00
2	500.00	50	250.00	750.00	250.00
3	250.00	50	125.00	875.00	125.00
4	125.00	50	25.00	900.00	100.00

depreciated below its estimated salvage value. Thus, as shown in the illustration and graph, the amount of depreciation actually recorded in the final year (Year 4) is limited to $25 ($125 − $100).

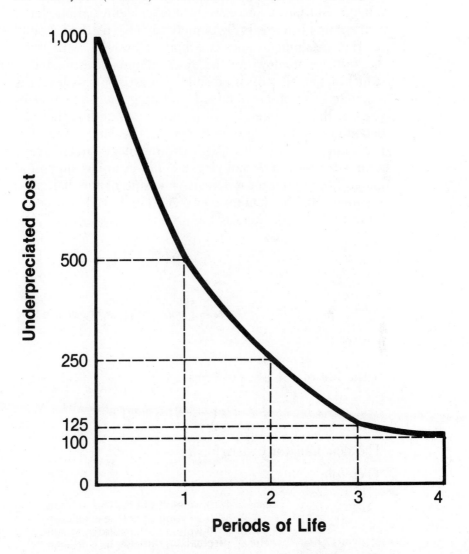

If the business qualifies for the use of declining-balance depreciation for income tax purposes, the declining-balance rate can be abandoned at any time, and the undepreciated cost at that date, less any estimated salvage value, can be written off in equal installments over the estimated remaining life. For example, in the foregoing illustration, suppose that at the end of the second year when the asset had an undepreciated cost of $250, it appeared likely that the salvage value would be zero. Accordingly, $125 ($250 ÷ 2) depreciation could be taken for each of the two remaining years.

Sum-of-the-Years-Digits Method. The depreciation method using a steadily decreasing rate applied to net cost (original cost less salvage value), resulting in successively smaller depreciation charges is known as the sum-of-the-years-digits method. This method is similar in effect to the declining-balance method. However, with the years-digits method, a write-down to the exact amount of estimated salvage value (which might be zero) is possible. The write-off each year is based on a schedule of fractions obtained by listing the digits that represent the years of the estimated life of the asset and adding these digits to get a denominator for all of the fractions. The largest year-digit is used as the numerator for the first year, the next largest year-digit as the numerator for the second year, etc. For example, suppose that the estimated life of an asset is 4 years. The sum of the digits (4 + 3 + 2 + 1) equals 10 (the denominator). A formula can also be used to determine the denominator, as follows:

$$S = N\left(\frac{N + 1}{2}\right)$$

S = sum of the digits
N = number of years of estimated life

If the life of the asset is 4 years:

$$S = 4\left(\frac{4 + 1}{2}\right) = 4(2\frac{1}{2}) = 10$$

The denominator equals 10.

Therefore:

Year 1: 4/10 write-off of cost less salvage
2: 3/10 write-off of cost less salvage
3: 2/10 write-off of cost less salvage
4: 1/10 write-off of cost less salvage

As applied to an asset costing $1,000, with an estimated salvage value of $100, the results would be as follows:

Year	Net Cost	Rate	Annual Depreciation	Accumulated Depreciation End of Year	Undepreciated Cost End of Year
1	$900	4/10	$360	$360	$640
2	900	3/10	270	630	370
3	900	2/10	180	810	190
4	900	1/10	90	900	100

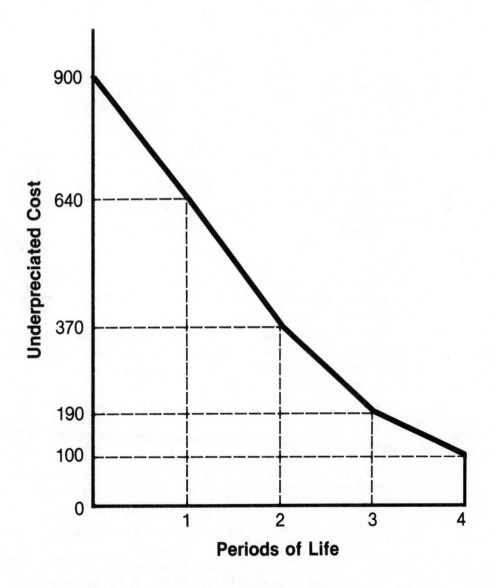

If an asset is acquired during an accounting period, a slight modification of the sum-of-the-years-digits method becomes necessary. Assume that the $1,000 asset described earlier was acquired on April 1 of Year 1. The application of the method would require modification as follows:

Year	Net Cost	Rate	Depreciation	Accumulated Depreciation End of Year	Undepreciated Cost End of Year
1	$900	4/10	$270.00 (3/4 yr.)	$270.00	$730.00
2	900	4/10	90.00 (1/4 yr.)	562.50	437.50
2	900	3/10	202.50 (3/4 yr.)		
3	900	3/10	67.50 (1/4 yr.)	765.00	235.00
3	900	2/10	135.00 (3/4 yr.)		
4	900	2/10	45.00 (1/4 yr.)	877.50	122.50
4	900	1/10	67.50 (3/4 yr.)		
5	900	1/10	22.50 (1/4 yr.)	900.00	100.00

Note that the final result is the same as in the previous example. The differences are in the amounts of accumulated depreciation at year-end (less in years 1 through 4) and in the amounts of undepreciated cost at year-end (more in years 1 through 4).

Units-of-Output Method. The depreciation method that estimates the number of units of service or output that can be secured from an asset and allocates the net cost of the asset to the periods it serves on the basis of the use or output during each period is called the units-of-output or units-of-production method. This measure of service does not exist for many assets.

The units-of-output method may be used for certain types of machinery, equipment, and vehicles. For example, assume that a company finds from experience that it can obtain 70,000 miles of service from certain types of trucks before they become so worn out that the need for extensive repairs and replacements makes it advisable for the company to dispose of them. The company purchases a new truck of this type at a cost (apart from tires, which are separately depreciated) of $10,000. The company expects that the truck can be traded in for $3,000 after 70,000 miles of service. The estimated net cost to be charged to operations during the life of the truck, the depreciation per mile, and the first-year depreciation are therefore:

Net cost = $10,000 cost − $3,000 salvage = $7,000

$$\text{Depreciation per mile} = \frac{\$7,000 \text{ net cost}}{70,000 \text{ total miles}} = 10 \text{ cents}$$

First year depreciation = 28,000 miles @ 10 cents = $2,800.

Accelerated Cost Recovery System (ACRS) Depreciation. The Economic Recovery Tax Act of 1981 introduced ACRS (accelerated cost recovery system) depreciation. This method permits extremely rapid depreciation of long-term business assets for income tax purposes. A business can decrease its income tax expense by claiming large depreciation expense deductions in the early years of a long-term asset's life.

ACRS increases the rate of asset cost write-off by:

1. Designating four "recovery" periods of artificial length over which the costs of long-term assets can be written off. Most business property can be placed into one of three ACRS classifications—3-year, 5-year, and 18-year. These periods are noticeably shorter than the designated assets' useful lives:
   (a) Automobiles, light trucks, and special tools—3-year write off.
   (b) Heavy trucks, machinery, and equipment—5-year write-off.
   (c) Buildings and land improvements—18-year write-off if purchased after March 15, 1984.
2. Using a modified declining-balance depreciation rate, as the following table indicates:

ACRS Depreciation Rates

Year	3-Year Property	5-Year Property	18-Year Property
1	25	15	10
2	38	22	9
3	37	21	8
4		21	7
5		21	6
6			6
7			5
8			5
9			5
10			5
11			5
12			5
13			4
14			4
15			4
16			4
17			4
18			4
	100	100	100

For example, assume that a light delivery truck costing $15,000 is acquired. Even though its estimated useful life is four years, this truck qualifies as three-year ACRS property. The following schedule shows the calculation of the depreciation expense deduction for federal income tax purposes for each of the three years.

Delivery Truck Depreciation
Deduction Schedule
(ACRS for Income Tax)

Year	Calculation	Expense Deduction	Accumulated Depreciation	Undepreciated Cost
1	($15,000 × 25%)	$3,750	$ 3,750	$11,250
2	(15,000 × 38%)	5,700	9,450	5,550
3	(15,000 × 37%)	5,550	15,000	-0-

Observe that the undepreciated cost is zero at the end of Year 3. ACRS ignores salvage value. Another feature of the ACRS method is that for 3- and 5-year property there is no concern for fractional periods. Regardless of the time of year that an asset in these classes is acquired, depreciation is taken for a full year. Fractional periods are considered for 18-year property.

Comparison of Methods

The results of the different depreciation methods are experienced in two ways: (1) through the pattern of depreciation charges and the resultant periodic undepreciated cost amount on the balance sheet, and (2) through the periodic determination of net income on the income statement.

Depreciation Pattern and Undepreciated Costs. The following tabulation contrasts the results of using straight-line, declining-balance, and sum-of-the-years digits depreciation methods for an asset costing $1,000, with a 10 year estimated life and an estimated salvage value of $100:

Year	Straight-Line Method Depreciation Charge	Straight-Line Method Undepreciated Cost End of Year	Declining-Balance Method Depreciation Charge	Declining-Balance Method Undepreciated Cost End of Year	Sum-of-the Years-Digits Method Depreciation Charge	Sum-of-the Years-Digits Method Undepreciated Cost End of Year
1	$90.00	$910.00	$200.00	$800.00	$163.64	$836.36
2	90.00	820.00	160.00	640.00	147.27	689.09
3	90.00	730.00	128.00	512.00	130.91	558.18
4	90.00	640.00	102.40	409.60	114.55	443.63
5	90.00	550.00	81.92	327.68	98.18	345.45
6	90.00	460.00	65.54	262.14	81.82	263.63
7	90.00	370.00	52.43	209.71	65.45	198.18
8	90.00	280.00	41.94	167.77	49.09	149.09
9	90.00	190.00	33.55	134.22	32.73	116.36
10	90.00	100.00	26.84	107.38	16.36	100.00

Under the straight-line method, the annual depreciation charge was determined by dividing the net cost of $900 ($1,000 cost − $100 salvage value) by 10 years.

Under the declining-balance method, salvage value was ignored since it is a built-in factor, and twice the straight-line rate was applied to the undepreciated cost at the start of each year. With a 10-year life, the straight-line rate is 10%, so twice this is 20%. The undepreciated cost at the end of 10 years ($107.38) is very close to the estimated salvage value of $100. If this were not the case, the declining-balance procedure could have been dropped at some point and in the years remaining, equal charges could have been made to write off all but the estimated salvage value.

Under the sum-of-the-years digits method, salvage value was taken into consideration. The sum of the digits, 1 through 10, is $55 \left[10\left(\dfrac{10 + 1}{2}\right) \right]$. Therefore, the charge was 10/55 of the net cost in the first year, 9/55 in the second year, and so on.

Effect on Net Income Calculation. Over a number of years, the total of the amounts of the calculated annual net income will be about the same regardless of the method of depreciation used. For any one year, however, the method of depreciation used may make a significant difference in the amount of the calculated net income. For example, assume that a business acquired a number of new depreciable assets at a cost of $60,000, with an estimated life of 10 years and an estimated scrap value of $6,000. For the first year of operation, revenue was $150,000 and all costs and expenses except depreciation amounted to $120,000. Following is a comparison of three very condensed income statements of the new business showing the net income for the first year after applying the three depreciation methods:

	Straight-Line Depreciation Method Used		Declining-Balance Depreciation Method Used		Sum-of-the-Years-Digits Depreciation Method Used	
Revenue		$150,000		$150,000		$150,000
Costs and expenses other than depreciation	$120,000		$120,000		$120,000	
Depreciation	5,400	125,400	12,000	132,000	9,818	129,818
Net income		$ 24,600		$ 18,000		$ 20,182

To verify the depreciation calculation, refer to Year 1 of the example on page 400 and multiply by 60, since that example was based on a

$1,000 asset, and this illustration assumes that the depreciable assets cost $60,000.

Note that the calculated amount of net income in the first case is over one third greater than the amount in the second case. In contrast, the effect on net income will reverse itself in later years. During those years the reported net income will be larger for the accelerated methods than for the straight-line method. Clearly significant differences in net income may result from the choice of depreciation methods.

In the preceding chapter, the effects of the choice of inventory method on net income were noted. It is apparent that periodic business income calculation is not an exact science, but rather an art involving careful judgment based on an understanding of acceptable alternatives and the consequences of their use.

BUILDING YOUR ACCOUNTING KNOWLEDGE

1. Describe five different ways of classifying long-term assets.
2. What may be included in the total amount at which a long-term asset is entered initially?
3. How should additions or improvements representing an increase in the value of long-term assets be entered?
4. How should the cost of such activities as landscaping grounds be entered?
5. What are the two major causes of depreciation?
6. What is meant by the "net cost" of a long-term asset?
7. What are the five most commonly used methods of calculating depreciation, and how do they differ in their application?
8. Why cannot the units-of-output method of depreciation be applied to all depreciable long-term assets?
9. What are the three types of business assets and respective recovery periods in ACRS depreciation?

APPLYING ACCOUNTING CONCEPTS

Exercise 13-1.   A light truck is purchased on January 1 at a cost of $10,500. It is expected to serve for 5 years and to have a trade-in value of $1,500. Calculate the depreciation expense for the first and third years of use of the truck using the

1. Straight-line method.
2. Declining-balance method.
3. Sum-of-the-years-digits method.

Exercise 13-2.   The truck purchased in Exercise 13-1 is expected to be used for 90,000 miles over its 5-year life. Calculate the depreciation expense for the first and third years of use if the truck is driven 25,000 miles in year 1 and 15,000 miles in year 3.

Exercise 13-3.   The truck purchased in Exercise 13-1 is classified as 3-year property according to ACRS depreciation. Using the ACRS depreciation rates provided in the chapter, calculate the depreciation expense for tax purposes in the first and third years of use of the truck.

Report No. 13-1

Complete Report No. 13-1 in the study assignments and submit your working papers to the instructor for approval. Then continue with the textbook discussion until Report No. 13-2 is required.

ACCOUNTING PROCEDURE

The number of accounts for tangible long-term assets that will be kept in the general ledger will depend upon the number of depreciable assets, the type of information required by the management, and in the case of all but land, the sort of depreciation procedure that is to be followed. Land is not subject to depreciation in business accounting. If there are very few long-term assets, a separate account for each one with a related depreciation account can be kept in the general ledger. In such a case, the periodic depreciation for each asset should be calculated and entered separately.

Entering Depreciation

Depreciation usually is entered at the end of the period, along with other necessary adjusting entries. One or more depreciation expense accounts may be debited, and one or more accumulated depreciation accounts may be credited. The number of each of these accounts depends upon the degree of detail that is desired in the general ledger accounts and for the periodic statements. Often there is one depreciation expense account for each major type of asset, such as Depreciation Expense — Buildings, Depreciation Expense — Furniture and Fixtures, and Depreciation Expense — Delivery Equipment. A business that classifies expenses on a departmental basis may use a large number of depreciation expense accounts.

In the normal course of events, the only entries in the accumulated depreciation accounts are those made at the end of each period to enter the depreciation for the period then ended. When some disposition is made of a depreciable asset (such as its sale, exchange, retirement, or destruction by fire), depreciation should be entered for the interval between the date of the last regular adjustment of the accounts and the date of the disposition of the asset. Usually, the depreciation is calculated to the nearest full month.

To illustrate the depreciation accounting process, assume that a delivery truck was acquired on January 6, 1986 with a cost of $10,000, an estimated useful life of 4 years, and an estimated salvage value of $4,000. The annual depreciation using the straight-line method would be calculated as follows:

$$\frac{\$10,000 \text{ cost} - \$4,000 \text{ salvage}}{4 \text{ year life}} = \$1,500 \text{ annual depreciation}$$

The entry for the annual depreciation on the truck as of December 31, 1986 would appear in two-column form as follows:

```
Depreciation Expense—Delivery Truck ...................... 1,500
    Accumulated Depreciation—Delivery Truck ................         1,500
    Annual depreciation on truck.
```

The foregoing entry would be repeated each succeeding December 31 until the delivery truck was either fully depreciated or disposed of.

Assume that the truck was sold on May 1, 1989. The entry for the depreciation through the date of the sale of the asset would be as follows:

Depreciation Expense—Delivery Truck	500	
Accumulated Depreciation—Delivery Truck		500
Depreciation on truck for 1/3 year.		

Disposition of Long-Term Assets

A long-term asset may be disposed of in any one of the following ways:

1. It may be discarded or retired.
2. It may be sold.
3. It may be exchanged or traded in for property of like kind or for other property.

Discarding or Retiring Long-Term Assets. A long-term asset may be discarded or retired whether or not it has been fully depreciated. If it has been fully depreciated, no gain or loss will be realized. If it has not been fully depreciated, the undepreciated cost of the discarded asset will represent a loss. Such a loss may be the result of underestimating the depreciation of the asset for the period of time that it has been in use, or it may be the result of obsolescence. Often, it is better to scrap an obsolete machine and buy a new one even though a loss is realized on the old machine.

To illustrate, on July 15, postal scales that had no exchange or sale value were discarded. The property, plant, and equipment record indicated that the scales originally had cost $150 and that depreciation totaling $120 had been entered as a credit to the accumulated depreciation—store equipment account. This event involved a loss of $30 ($150 − $120) that was the undepreciated cost of the discarded asset. The transaction was entered as indicated by the following two-column journal entry:

Loss on Discarded Store Equipment	30	
Accumulated Depreciation—Store Equipment	120	
Store Equipment		150
Discarded postal scales.		

When this entry is posted, the debit of $120 to the accumulated depreciation account and the credit of $150 to the store equipment account will remove the amounts relating to the postal scales from the balances of these accounts. The debit of $30 to Loss on Discarded Store Equipment represents the realized loss that will be reflected on the income statement.

When a long-term asset is discarded after it has been fully depreciated, even though no gain or loss results from the transaction, the amounts relating to the discarded asset should be eliminated from the account balances by debiting the accumulated depreciation account and by crediting the asset account with the amount of the original cost of the asset.

Selling Long-Term Assets. If a long-term asset is sold, it is necessary to know its undepreciated cost before the proper amount of any gain or loss resulting from the transaction can be determined. The undepreciated cost of an asset is the difference between its cost and the total amount of accumulated depreciation entered to the date of sale. When a long-term asset is sold at its undepreciated cost, no gain or loss results from the transaction; when it is sold for more than its undepreciated cost, the difference represents a gain; when it is sold for less than its undepreciated cost, the difference represents a loss.

Assume that an electronic calculator costs $350, has no estimated salvage value, and depreciates at the rate of 10% a year. The annual depreciation is entered in two-column journal form as follows:

Depreciation Expense—Office Equipment	35	
Accumulated Depreciation—Office Equipment		35

$$\frac{\$350 \text{ cost} - 0 \text{ salvage}}{10\text{-year life}} = \$35 \text{ annual depreciation}$$

At the end of the 3 years, the undepreciated cost of the calculator will be $245, the difference between the cost price ($350) and the accumulated depreciation ($105).

$350 cost − ($35 annual depreciation × 3) = $350 − $105 = $245.

If the calculator was sold at the end of 3 years for $275 cash, the transaction should be entered in two-column journal form as follows:

Cash	275	
Accumulated Depreciation—Office Equipment	105	
Office Equipment..		350
Gain on Sale of Office Equipment		30
Sold calculator.		

When this entry is posted, the debit of $105 to the accumulated depreciation account will offset the amounts entered previously as credits to the accumulated depreciation account over a period of 3 years. The amount credited to Office Equipment will offset the purchase price of $350 previously entered as a debit to Office Equipment. These entries have the effect of completely eliminating the amounts relating to the old calculator from the office equipment and accumulated depreciation accounts. The gain of $30 ($275 sales price − $245 undepreciated cost) realized from the sale of the calculator is reported as a Gain on Sale of Office Equipment. This gain should be listed under the heading of "Other revenue" in the income statement.

If the calculator was sold at the end of 3 years for $225 instead of $275, there would be a loss of $20 ($245 undepreciated cost − $225 sales price), instead of a gain of $30. The transaction should be entered in two-column journal form as follows:

Cash	225	
Accumulated Depreciation—Office Equipment	105	
Loss on Sale of Office Equipment	20	
Office Equipment		350
Sold calculator.		

When this entry is posted, the debit of $105 to the accumulated depreciation account and the credit of $350 to the office equipment account will eliminate the amounts relating to the old calculator from these accounts. The loss resulting from the sale of the old calculator for $20 less than its undepreciated cost will be reported as a Loss on Sale of Office Equipment. This loss should be listed under the heading of "Other expense" in the income statement.

Exchange or Trade-In of Long-Term Assets. A long-term asset may be exchanged or traded in for other property. Accepted financial accounting treatment, in most cases, is based on the fair market values of the asset exchanged. **Fair market value** is a value that is agreed upon in a current sales transaction by a willing buyer and a willing seller. On the other hand, tax regulations often allow the asset acquired to be assigned a cost equal to the undepreciated cost of the asset given up.

If one asset is traded in on the purchase of another, a trade-in allowance frequently is granted which may be equal to, greater than, or less than the undepreciated cost of the asset traded in. Trade-in allowances frequently do not reflect fair market values, so that any gain or loss calculated based on a trade-in allowance may not be an accurate measurement of the situation.

In financial accounting, long-term assets are classified into two categories for purposes of exchange or trade-in: similar (the tax laws refer to these as "of like kind") and dissimilar (the tax laws refer to these as "not of like kind"). In accounting for exchanges of similar assets, financial accounting recognizes all losses but no gains. For tax purposes, neither gains nor losses are recognized on such exchanges. In contrast, in accounting for exchanges of dissimilar assets, both financial accounting and the tax laws recognize gains and losses on the exchanges.

To illustrate the exchange or trade in of similar assets ("like kind"), assume that a delivery truck that cost $6,500 and has been owned for 3 years is traded in for another delivery truck which is to be used for a similar purpose. Depreciation in the amount of $1,800 has been taken each year—a total of $5,400. Thus, the undepreciated cost of the truck is $1,100 ($6,500 − $5,400). If the trade-in value of the old truck is $1,500 and the new truck has a fair market value of $8,000, $6,500 would be paid in cash ($8,000 − $1,500). This $6,500 balance paid to the supplier on the long-term asset trade-in is known as boot. The transaction should be entered in two-column journal form as follows:

Delivery Equipment (new truck) 7,600		
Accumulated Depreciation—Delivery Equipment 5,400		
Delivery Equipment (old truck)	6,500	
Cash	6,500	
Purchased a new truck.		

The new truck's cost ($7,600) is the sum of the undepreciated cost of the old truck ($1,100) and the boot paid ($6,500). This cost becomes the basis for future depreciation charges. Note that this journal entry does not recognize the $400 gain, which is the difference between the undepreciated cost of $1,100 and the trade-in value of the old truck of $1,500. When this entry is posted, the cost of the old truck will be eliminated from the delivery equipment account and that account will be charged with the cost of the new truck. The accumulated depreciation on the old truck will also be eliminated from the accumulated depreciation account, and no gain will be recognized in recording the transaction. This method of accounting also conforms to the tax laws.

If the fair market value of the new truck had been only $7,500, and the trade in value of the old truck only $1,000, boot of $6,500 would still be paid. Proper financial accounting would require the following two-column journal entry:

```
Delivery Equipment (new truck) .............................. 7,500
Accumulated Depreciation—Delivery Equipment ............. 5,400
Loss on Exchange of Delivery Equipment....................  100
    Delivery Equipment (old truck) ...........................         6,500
    Cash .................................................................         6,500
        Purchased a new truck.
```

Note that in this situation the new truck is entered at its fair market value and that a $100 loss (the excess of the undepreciated cost over the trade-in allowance) on the exchange is charged to a special loss account. This method of accounting does not conform to the tax laws, because losses for tax purposes (like gains for tax purposes) are not recognized in connection with a "like kind" exchange. The proper entry for tax purposes would be the same as the entry previously illustrated on page 408 where a gain on the exchange was involved but not entered.

To illustrate the trade-in of dissimilar assets (not of like kind), assume that a typewriter that cost $300 and has been owned for 2 years is traded in for a new cash register. Depreciation in the amount of $60 has been taken each year for a total of $120. Thus the undepreciated cost of the typewriter is $180 ($300 − $120). The new cash register has a fair market value of $625. A trade-in allowance of $200 is granted, and the balance, $425, is paid in cash as boot. Since this transaction involves an exchange of dissimilar assets, any gain or loss should be recognized. Because $200 was allowed for an asset that had an undepreciated cost of $180 ($300 cost of asset − $120 accumulated depreciation), the transaction involved a gain of $20. The transaction should be entered in two-column journal form as follows:

```
Office Equipment........................................................ 625
Accumulated Depreciation—Office Equipment ................ 120
    Office Equipment.......................................................         300
    Cash .......................................................................         425
    Gain on Exchange of Office Equipment......................          20
        Purchased a new cash register.
```

When this entry is posted, the debit of $120 to the accumulated depreciation account will offset the amounts entered previously as credits to that account over a period of 2 years. The amount credited to Office Equipment will offset the purchase price of the typewriter previously entered as a debit to that account. These entries have the effect of completely eliminating the amounts relating to the old typewriter from the office equipment account and the accumulated depreciation account. The gain realized on the old typewriter is reported as a Gain on Exchange of Office Equipment. Had the trade-in allowance been less than the undepreciated cost of the typewriter, the difference would have represented a loss to be reported as a Loss on Exchange of Office Equipment.

The following chart summarizes the financial accounting and income tax accounting rules for recognition of gain or loss in "like kind" and "not of like kind" exchanges of long-term assets.

Asset

	Like Kind		Unlike Kind	
	Recognition of			
	Gain	Loss	Gain	Loss
Financial Accounting	No	Yes	Yes	Yes
Tax Accounting	No	No	Yes	Yes

Property, Plant, and Equipment Records

If the business has a large number of depreciable long-term assets, it is likely that a summary general ledger account will be kept for each major class of assets, such as one account for buildings, one for machinery and equipment, one for office furniture and equipment, and one for delivery trucks. Each of these summary accounts will have a related accumulated depreciation account. It is highly desirable that such summary accounts be supported by some sort of supplementary or subsidiary records. If depreciation is calculated on a unit basis (meaning a separate calculation and record of depreciation for each unit), it is common practice to maintain a subsidiary record of each unit. Such records commonly take the form of cards or computer disks. Space is provided on each card or disk record to show the details about the asset, including the cost of the unit (which supports the debit in the general ledger asset account), and the amount of depreciation taken each period (which supports the credits in the general ledger accumulated depreciation account). Space is also provided to enter the disposition of the asset. The following is a typical property, plant, and equipment record. Note that salvage value was considered in arriving at the amount of annual depreciation, $150 [($900 original cost − $150 estimated salvage value) ÷ 5 years]. Also note that the 20% rate

PROPERTY, PLANT, AND EQUIPMENT RECORD

Description   Typewriter   Account   Office Equipment

Age when acquired   New   Estimated salvage value $150

Estimated life   5 years   Rate of annual depreciation based on cost
                                                      less salvage value   20%

COST				DEPRECIATION RECORD			
Date Purchased		Description	Amount	Year	Rate	Amount	Total To Date
1984 Jan.	9	IBM Selectric II typewriter,	900 00	19 84	20%	150 00	150 00
		Serial No. 8403637		19 85	20%	150 00	300 00
		Fletcher Typewriter Company, City		19 86	20%	75 00	375 00
		Less estimated salvage value	150 00	19			
		Net cost	750 00	19			
				19			
				19			
				19			
				19			

SOLD, EXCHANGED, OR DISCARDED						19		
Date	Explanation	Amount Realized	More than / Less than	✓Undepr. Cost	Accum. Depr.	19		
1986 July	1	Sold	550 00		25 00	375 00	19	
							19	
							19	

Property, Plant, and Equipment Record

(100% ÷ 5 years) is applied to the original cost of $900, less the $150 estimated salvage value.

Following is a narrative of the transactions that were entered on the record:

January 9, 1984. Purchased IBM Selectric II typewriter, No. 8403637, from the Fletcher Typewriter Company, City, for $900.

December 31, 1984. Depreciation of typewriter at annual rate of $150 [($900 cost − $150 salvage value) × .20].

December 31, 1985. Depreciation of typewriter at annual rate of $150.

July 1, 1986. Depreciation of typewriter for one-half year, $75. Sold typewriter for $550 cash.

Note that before the sale of the typewriter on July 1, 1986, was entered, depreciation for the half year, amounting to $75, was entered on the card or disk record. The sale was also entered on the record, after which the record was transferred from a file of assets owned to a file of assets sold, exchanged, or discarded. (In a computer-based accounting system, the record would be transferred electronically from an "active asset" disk to an "inactive asset" disk.) Such an asset record, when properly kept, will provide all the information needed in claiming the proper amount of depreciation on each long-term asset as a deduction from gross income in the annual income tax returns.

Fully Depreciated Long-Term Assets

A long-term asset is said to be fully depreciated when the accumulated depreciation is equal to the cost of the asset. When an asset is fully depreciated, no further depreciation should be entered. Since the rate of depreciation is based on its estimated useful life, an asset may still be used after it is fully depreciated. In this case, the cost of the asset and an equal amount of accumulated depreciation are usually retained in the accounts. When a fully depreciated asset is scrapped, the cost of the asset and the total amount of depreciation should be removed from the accounts. Such an adjustment involves a debit to the proper accumulated depreciation account and a credit to the proper long-term asset account for the cost of the asset.

In some states a taxable value is placed on a fully depreciated long-term asset if the asset is in continued use. Under such circumstances, the taxable value of the fully depreciated asset should be stated in the property, plant, and equipment record as a guide in preparing the property tax schedule. The taxable values of fully depreciated long-term assets and the undepreciated costs of other long-term assets should be listed so that the total taxable value of the long-term assets may be determined.

Depreciation in the Financial Statements

Most accountants and business people consider depreciation to be an operating expense and so classify it in the income statement. There may be as much subclassification as the management desires. Depreciation of delivery equipment, for example, may be classed as a selling expense, while depreciation of office furniture and equipment may be classed as an office or general administrative expense.

In view of the close relationship between long-term asset accounts and their accumulated depreciation accounts, the accepted practice in the preparation of balance sheets is to show the amount of the accumulated depreciation as a deduction from the cost of the asset. The difference, representing undepreciated cost, is extended to be included in the asset total.

Accumulated depreciation accounts, like allowances for doubtful accounts, are sometimes called asset valuation accounts. An accumulated depreciation account, however, only values the asset in a very limited and remote sense. The difference between the cost of the asset and the balance of the accumulated depreciation account is not expected to have any relation to the market value of the asset. Such assets are not intended for sale. What they might bring, if sold, is usually of small consequence. The difference between the gross amount of the long-term assets and the related accumulated depreciation accounts simply represents costs not yet charged to operations. Some companies so describe this difference in their balance sheets.

Wasting Assets

A wasting asset is any real property which is acquired for the purpose of removing or extracting the valuable natural resource on or in the property. Stands of timber, mines, oil wells, gas wells, or land acquired in the belief that the property contains minerals, oil, or gas that can be extracted, are examples of wasting assets because, in most cases, it is expected that the valuable product eventually will be removed or exhausted so as to leave the property relatively valueless. In the case of many types of mines and wells, only the valuable materials below the surface are owned. The land, as such, may not be owned by the mining, oil, or gas company.

Depletion. The consumption or exhaustion of wasting assets is called depletion. Apart from income tax considerations, the accounting problem is to apportion the cost of such assets to the periods in which they are consumed. The procedure called cost depletion is very similar to that involved in computing depreciation on a units-of-output basis. The cost of the property is reduced by estimated salvage or residual value, if any, and the difference is divided by the estimated number of units that the property contains. The result is the depletion expense per unit. This amount times the number of units removed and sold during the period will give the depletion expense for the period.

To illustrate the computation of and proper accounting for depletion, consider the following example. A coal mine is acquired at a cost of $1,000,000. No salvage value is expected. The estimated number of units available for production is 1,000,000 tons. During the current year, 180,000 tons of coal are mined and sold. The computation of the amount of depletion expense is as follows:

$1,000,000 ÷ 1,000,000 tons = $1 per ton
180,000 tons × $1 per ton = $180,000 depletion expense

The depletion is entered in two-column journal form as follows:

Depletion Expense 180,000
   Accumulated Depletion—Coal Mine....................   180,000
     Depletion based on 180,000 tons of coal @ $1 a ton.

The difference between the cost of the mine and the amount of the accumulated depletion is the undepleted cost of the property:

Cost of coal mine $1,000,000
Less accumulated depletion   180,000
Undepleted cost of mine.............. $ 820,000

It is customary to show the accumulated depletion as a deduction from the property account in the balance sheet in order to indicate the undepleted cost of the property. Depletion Expense is a temporary account that is closed into Expense and Revenue Summary at the end of the accounting period. It should be reported as an operating expense in the income statement. It is an expense that may be deducted in calculating taxable income.

From time to time the estimate of the quantity of the resource that remains in the property has to be changed. The usual practice is to make a new calculation of the depletion per unit, starting with the most recently determined undepleted cost of the property and dividing that amount (less estimated salvage value, if any) by the number of units extracted during the current year plus the current estimate of the number of units remaining. For example, the mine mentioned in the previous illustration had an undepleted cost of $820,000 at the start of the second year. Assume that during that year, 275,000 tons were extracted, and at the end of the year the engineers estimate that 925,000 tons remain. The calculation of the revised depletion expense per unit and depletion expense for the second year would be as follows:

$$\frac{\$820{,}000}{275{,}000 \text{ tons } + 925{,}000 \text{ tons}} = 68.33\text{¢ per ton}$$

275,000 tons × 68.33¢ = $187,907.50 depletion expense

Depletion Expense for Federal Income Tax Purposes. Special rules govern the amount of the deduction for depletion expense that can be taken for federal income tax purposes. The taxpayer may compute the amount in the cost depletion manner explained in the preceding paragraphs. However, certain taxpayers who own and operate oil and gas wells (basically where the resource is regulated or sold under a fixed contract) and certain types of mines may use percentage depletion. Under this method, depletion is equal to certain specified percentages (which vary from 5% to 22%) of the amount of the sales of the period subject to stated maximum and minimum limits. The dollar amount deductible is limited to 50% of the taxable income exclusive of any depletion deduction.

BUILDING YOUR ACCOUNTING KNOWLEDGE

1. For what time interval should depreciation be entered when a depreciable asset is disposed of?
2. What are the three major ways in which a long-term asset may be disposed of?
3. From what two major causes may a loss result when a long-term asset is discarded or retired? Will a gain or loss result if a discarded or retired asset has been fully depreciated?
4. When a long-term asset is sold, what must be known about the asset in order to determine the proper amount of gain or loss on the sale?
5. Describe the major differences between accounting for a "similar" (or "like kind") exchange of long-term assets, and accounting for a "dissimilar" (or "not of like kind") exchange. Indicate the ways in which financial accounting and income tax procedures differ in dealing with long-term asset exchanges.
6. What details about a particular long-term asset are provided by a property, plant, and equipment record?
7. What does the difference between the gross amount of long-term assets and the related accumulated depreciation accounts represent to accountants?
8. What depreciation method is very similar to cost depletion? How does percentage depletion differ from cost depletion?

APPLYING ACCOUNTING CONCEPTS

Exercise 13-4. Shelving units which had cost $2,800 and had accumulated depreciation of $2,580 were discarded. Prepare the journal entry for this transaction.

Exercise 13-5. A delivery truck which had cost $11,000 and had accumulated depreciation of $8,900 was sold for $2,800.

(a) Prepare the journal entry for this transaction. **(b)** Assuming that the truck was sold for $1,900, prepare the journal entry for this transaction.

Exercise 13-6. A drill press which had cost $20,000 and had accumulated depreciation of $11,400 was traded in for a new drill press with a fair market value of $23,000. The old drill press and $13,000 in cash were given for the new drill press.

(a) Prepare the journal entry for this transaction. **(b)** Assuming that the old drill press and $15,000 in cash were given for the new drill press, prepare the journal entry for this transaction.

Exercise 13-7. Office partitions which had cost $2,400 and had accumulated depreciation of $1,900 were traded in on new typewriters with a fair market value of $2,100. The partitions and $1,150 were given for the typewriters. Prepare the journal entry for this transaction.

Exercise 13-8. A gravel pit was acquired at a cost of $900,000. It is estimated that the pit will produce 600,000 cubic yards of gravel. During Year 1, 180,000 cubic yards of gravel were mined and sold.

(a) The proper depletion expense for Year 1 is _____.

(b) During Year 2, 200,000 cubic yards of gravel were mined and sold. At the end of the year, it is estimated that 300,000 cubic yards of gravel remain to be mined. The proper depletion expense for Year 2 is _____.

Report No. 13-2

Complete Report No. 13-2 in the study assignments and submit your working papers for approval. Then continue with the textbook discussion in Chapter 14 until Report No. 14-1 is required.

EXPANDING YOUR BUSINESS VOCABULARY

What is the meaning of each of the following terms?

ACRS depreciation **(p. 399)**   book value **(p. 392)**
amortization **(p. 388)**   boot **(p. 408)**

capital assets **(p. 387)**

cost allocation **(p. 390)**

cost depletion **(p. 413)**

declining-balance method
   (p. 394)

depletion **(pp. 388, 413)**

depreciable assets **(p. 388)**

depreciation **(pp. 388, 390,
   399)**

fair market value **(p. 407)**

fixed assets **(p. 387)**

functional depreciation **(p. 390)**

intangible **(p. 388)**

Investments **(p. 388)**

long-term assets **(p. 387)**

marketable securities **(p. 388)**

net cost **(p. 391)**

percentage depletion **(p. 415)**

personal property **(p. 387)**

physical depreciation **(p. 390)**

property, plant, and equipment
   assets **(p. 387)**

real property **(p. 387)**

straight-line method **(p. 392)**

sum-of-the-years-digits method
   (p. 396)

tangible **(p. 388)**

trade-in allowance **(p. 407)**

undepreciated cost **(p. 392)**

unit basis **(p. 410)**

units-of-output (production)
   method **(p. 398)**

wasting assets **(pp. 388, 413)**

CHAPTER 14

Internal Accounting Control

CHAPTER OBJECTIVES

Careful study of this chapter should enable you to:

- Define internal accounting control and to explain its importance in operating a business.

- Identify the basic elements of good internal accounting control.

- Explain the application of internal accounting control concepts in the two major operating cycles of every business: **(1)** the expenditure cycle and **(2)** the revenue cycle.

There are enormous variations in size, type of operation, and product lines of companies. Each of these factors affects the type of control system appropriate for a particular company. For example, a very small business often uses only a limited number of formal control procedures and has little segregation of duties because there are few people to perform the duties in the first place. The key internal control element in this situation is the owner-manager who personally supervises the activities of the business. On the other hand, as the size and nature of a business become larger and more complex, it becomes impossible for the owner to maintain such close contact with all the activities of the business. Consequently, the owner must rely more on a formal internal accounting control system to ensure that the activities of the business are being conducted properly and errors or fraud are prevented or promptly detected. It is important to recognize that it is impossible to define the "correct" system of internal accounting control for all businesses.

In this chapter, certain basic internal accounting control concepts are explained and many aspects of the application of these concepts are illustrated. Some of the internal accounting controls, such as the use of prenumbered documents, are relevant for virtually every business. Other controls, such as an ideal segregation of duties, are not feasible for very small firms. Clearly, the exact system of internal accounting control for a given firm should be developed based on that firm's needs and business environment.

INTERNAL ACCOUNTING CONTROL CONCEPTS

In order to appreciate why many documents, records and procedures exist and are used in particular ways in accounting, an understanding of the concept of internal accounting control and the key elements of internal accounting control is needed.

Meaning and Importance of Internal Control

An internal accounting control system is defined as all the procedures, documents, and records used by a business to protect its assets and to ensure that the activities of the business are properly performed and documented. The system should provide assurance that (1) all transactions are properly authorized and accounted for, (2) access to assets is permitted only to authorized parties for authorized purposes, and (3) records of assets are verified periodically by examining the related physical properties.

Internal accounting control is essential to the functioning of a business. There is hardly an aspect of a business that is not affected by it. For example, the system must ensure that purchases are made only of goods to be used in the business and that bills are paid only for goods and services actually purchased and received by the business. Similarly, when shipments are made to customers, the system must ensure that the customers are billed and the related amounts collected. Then, the system must ensure that cash receipts from sales are received and entered by the business and not kept by an employee. In addition, management decisions often are based on accounting information; the control system must ensure that this information is accurate and up to date.

Internal accounting control systems can take many different forms in different businesses; they can be quite simple or very complex. Regardless of their form, however, internal accounting controls are critical to the efficient functioning of a business.

Key Elements of Internal Control

Before looking at specific applications of internal accounting control in individual areas of a business, it will help to examine the basic elements or principles underlying the entire concept. Four key elements of internal accounting control can be identified:

1. Segregation of duties.
2. Authorization procedures and related responsibilities.
3. Accounting procedures.
4. Independent checks on performance.

Segregation of Duties. Segregation of duties involves assigning duties in such a way that (1) different employees are responsible for different parts of a transaction, and (2) employees who maintain accounting records do not have custody of the firm's assets. Appropriate segregation of duties helps to detect errors promptly and reduces the possibility of employee fraud. For example, assume that one employee is responsible for ordering goods, a second employee for receiving goods, a third employee for paying for goods based on proper evidence of purchase, and a fourth employee for accounting for the purchase of and payment for the goods. Such a segregation of duties provides a built-in check of one employee on another in that the amounts ordered, received, paid for, and entered in the accounting records must agree; otherwise some error has occurred. Similarly, no one of these four employees can obtain goods for personal use or make improper payments for goods without being caught.

The duties of accounting and asset custody should be segregated in order to prevent employees from stealing business assets and concealing their theft by modifying the accounting records. For example, assume that one employee is responsible for receiving customer remittances on account, and a second employee is responsible for entering sales and customer remittances in the accounting records. This segregation of duties prevents the first employee from keeping the customers' remittances because the customer would complain if billed by the second employee for amounts that already had been remitted. Similarly, the second employee has no incentive to make improper entries in the accounting records because of lack of access to cash receipts.

Authorization Procedures and Related Responsibility. Sound authorization procedures involve assigning responsibilities so that only properly authorized activities take place in the business and the persons responsible for such activities and the related assets are identified at every step in the process. Basically, this element of internal accounting control should ensure that transactions do not occur without sufficient authorization. For some transactions this authorization can be general.

For example, a sales clerk in a department store has general authorization to make sales of particular goods using a particular cash register and perhaps keying in a specific clerk number. For other transactions, the authorization is likely to be specific. For example, major production equipment of a business normally is bought or sold only if specific written authorization is obtained from management at a relatively high level. Whether the authorization is general or specific, the control concept remains the same; someone should be responsible for every activity in which a business engages. Unless someone has authorized and assumed responsibility for an action, that action should not be taken by the business. Correspondingly, after some activity has occurred, it should be possible to determine who authorized it and therefore is held responsible.

Accounting Procedures. Proper accounting procedures include use of accounting records and documents in such a way that whenever business activities occur, the accounting system reacts. A major dimension of this internal accounting control element is the use of prenumbered documents that must be generated promptly when an activity occurs and then subsequently accounted for. Subsequent accounting for prenumbered documents can be simplified by entering the data and filing the documents in numerical order. This element of internal accounting control helps ensure that all valid activities of the business are included in the records and that only valid activities are included. For example, assume that prenumbered sales receipts are used, that one copy of the receipt is issued to a customer whenever a sale occurs and the other copy is retained in the firm's files. In this situation, if the numerical sequence of receipts is complete and there are no duplicate receipts entered, it is reasonable to assume that all sales transactions are accounted for and only valid sales transactions are entered.

Independent Checks on Performance. This last key element of internal accounting control includes the various methods used by a business to ensure that management's accounting rules and regulations are being followed. Perhaps the most easily recognized type of independent check on performance is that provided by the internal audit department of a business. The internal audit department has broad responsibility to see that the internal accounting control system is effective. This includes responsibilities for determining (1) that the system is properly designed and (2) that there is compliance with the segregation of duties, with authorization, and with accounting procedures dictated by the system. The first responsibility is fulfilled primarily by making sure that the system is characterized by the key elements of internal control that are described in this section. The second responsibility is fulfilled by testing and analyzing the business activities that occur during the year. For example, the numerical sequence of sales invoices or checks can be accounted for by maintaining numerical order. The sum of the balances in the accounts receivable ledger can be verified by comparing it with the general ledger accounts receivable balance. A bank reconciliation can be prepared. Canceled checks can be traced to appropriate supporting documents.

In addition to the specific performance checks provided by the internal audit department, a system of independent checks is built into many phases of the business. For example, if the accounts receivable records, sales journal, and general ledger are maintained by three different people in the accounting department, each of these employees provides an automatic independent check on a part of the work of the other two employees. If any one of these employees does not perform the prescribed procedures correctly, the accounting records will not agree. Another type of independent check built into the system literally involves some duplication of work. This happens whenever an employee is responsible for verifying the work of a fellow employee, such as when the price, quantity, and total dollar amount of a sales invoice must be verified by a second employee before it is mailed to a customer. Many of these built-in checks can exist throughout a company's accounting system and can help provide assurance that various procedures are being properly performed.

BUILDING YOUR ACCOUNTING KNOWLEDGE

1. Why is it impossible to define the "correct" system of internal accounting control for all businesses?
2. What assurance should be provided by an internal accounting control system?
3. How would appropriate segregation of duties prevent an employee responsible for receiving customer remittances on account from keeping the customers' remittances?
4. How do sound authorization procedures contribute to internal accounting control?
5. Why should documents be prenumbered and subsequently accounted for?
6. What are the responsibilities of an internal audit department?

APPLYING ACCOUNTING CONCEPTS

Exercise 14-1. Selected acquisition and payment transactions of Fraum Co. for the first month of operations are as follows:

1. Purchased equipment on account from Supay Co., $1,297.
2. Purchased merchandise for cash, $803.
3. Purchased merchandise on account from Selby Co., $915.
4. Paid $700 on account to Supay Co.
5. Purchased merchandise on account from Vency Co., $548.
6. Paid $600 on account to Selby Co.

(a) Prepare appropriate two-column journal entries for the above transactions. (b) Post appropriate entries to the accounts payable subsidiary ledger and to the accounts payable account. (Use T account forms.) (c) Prove the balance of the accounts payable account by preparing a schedule of accounts payable.

Exercise 14-2. Selected sales and collection transactions of Busher Co. for the first month of operations are as follows:

1. Sold merchandise on account to P. Cusae, $419.
2. Sold merchandise for cash, $610.
3. Sold merchandise on account to R. Clibee, $264.
4. Collected $300 on account from P. Cusae.
5. Sold merchandise on account to N. Percy, $317.
6. Collected $150 on account from R. Clibee.   •

(a) Prepare appropriate two-column journal entries for the above transactions. (b) Post appropriate entries to the accounts receivable subsidiary ledger and to the accounts receivable account. (Use T account forms.) (c) Prove the balance of the accounts receivable account by preparing a schedule of accounts receivable.

**Report
No. 14-1**

Complete Report No. 14-1 in the study assignments and submit your working papers to the instructor for approval. Then continue with the textbook discussion until Report No. 14-2 is required.

APPLICATION IN THE EXPENDITURE CYCLE

The expenditure cycle includes all of the functions involved in acquiring and receiving goods from suppliers and in making payments for the goods purchased. Diagramming and briefly explaining the expenditure cycle will assist in understanding internal accounting control in the expenditure cycle. A flowchart of the basic elements of the expenditure cycle appears on the following page. Many variations of the expenditure cycle are possible for different businesses. For example, in a small business, all the purchasing and payment activities might be performed by a single owner/manager. Purchases might be

FLOWCHART OF EXPENDITURE CYCLE

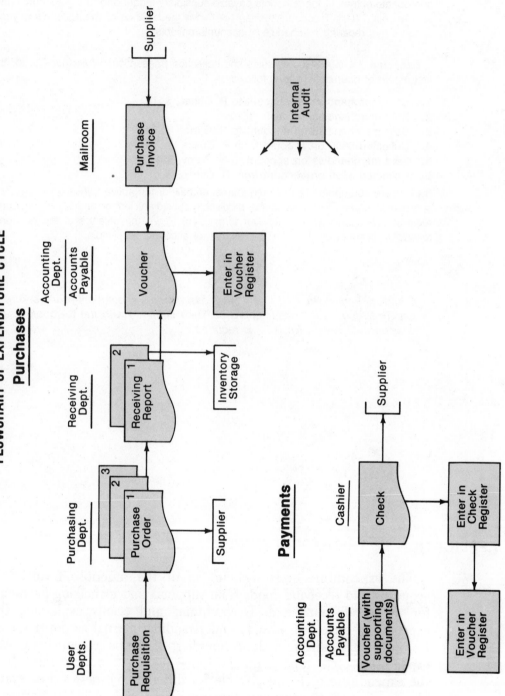

made directly from sales representatives who visit the store, perhaps with the goods ready for delivery. At the other extreme, in very large firms two or three different levels of authorization might be required in order to make expenditures above a specified dollar amount. The flowchart presented here assumes a medium-sized business that purchases tangible products.

The Purchases portion of the flowchart shows that any department or person in the firm wanting to purchase goods must prepare an authorized purchase requisition and forward it to the purchasing department. The purchasing department examines the purchase requisition and prepares a purchase order and sends it to the appropriate supplier. When the goods arrive from the supplier, a receiving report is prepared in the receiving department. This receiving report and a copy of the purchase order are sent to the accounting department where eventually they are matched with the purchase invoice received from the supplier. The purchase order, receiving report, and purchase invoice provide the basis for preparing a voucher, which is a document used to authorize payments for goods and services. The voucher is entered in the voucher register, an accounting record similar to a purchases journal.

The Payments portion of the flowchart indicates that the voucher and supporting documents are used by the cashier as a basis for preparing a check that is sent to the supplier in settlement for the goods received. The cashier also enters in the check register the date, amount, and payee of the check. The voucher and supporting documents are then returned to the accounts payable section where they are used to enter in the voucher register the fact that the voucher has been paid.

The Internal Audit Department has responsibility to oversee and monitor the entire system of internal accounting control shown in the flowchart. Its functions might include seeing that purchases are made only on the basis of authorized purchase orders or that all payments are properly entered.

Internal accounting control over the expenditure cycle will now be discussed in some detail. The partial records of Spinner & Thomas, a partnership engaged in the bakery business, are illustrated. The organization of this discussion follows the outline suggested by the expenditure flowchart.

Acquisition of Goods

A firm must have an internal accounting control system that ensures that it purchases only those goods and services that are necessary for the efficient and effective operation of the business. Documents and procedures that are relevant for controlling the purchasing process are illustrated and explained in the following sections.

Purchase Requisition. The purchase requisition is a document requesting that the purchasing department order specific goods. The following is a purchase requisition used by Spinner & Thomas. Purchase requisitions should be prenumbered and subsequently accounted for by number. This is to ensure that all requisitions are properly handled by the purchasing department and that the individual responsible for requesting that any merchandise be purchased can be subsequently identified if necessary.

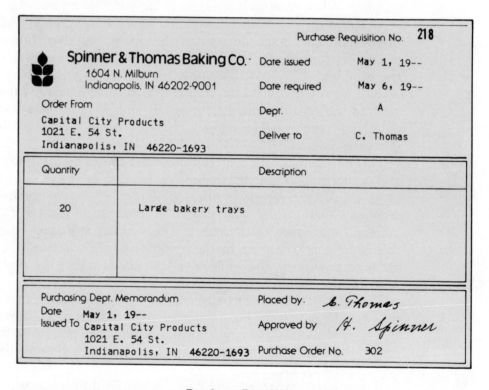

Purchase Requisition

The purchase requisition itself does not authorize a purchase. The requisition must first be approved. For a minor purchase, the approval might come from a department supervisor, whereas a major purchase should be approved at a higher level of management. When approved, the purchase requisition authorizes the purchasing department to generate a purchase order.

Purchase Order. The purchase order is an explicit request by the firm to buy goods from a supplier. The following purchase order prepared by Spinner & Thomas was based on the purchase requisition illustrated on page 426. Purchase orders should be prenumbered and subsequently accounted for by number, in order to ensure either that all of the goods on an order are received or that the order is canceled, and that only goods that have been ordered are received and paid for subsequently. The number of copies of the purchase order that are prepared depends on the particular accounting information system. There are likely to be at least three copies. One copy is sent to the

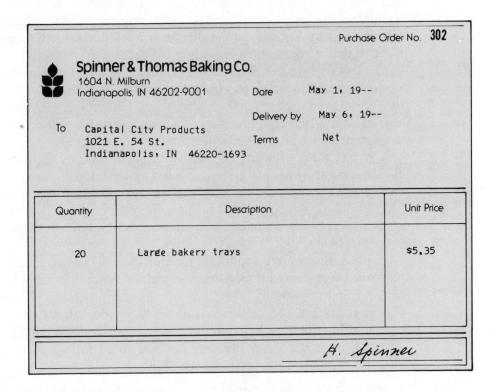

Purchase Order No. **302**

Spinner & Thomas Baking Co.
1604 N. Milburn
Indianapolis, IN 46202-9001

Date   May 1, 19--

Delivery by   May 6, 19--

To   Capital City Products
      1021 E. 54 St.   Terms   Net
      Indianapolis, IN 46220-1693

Quantity	Description	Unit Price
20	Large bakery trays	$5.35

H. Spinner

Purchase Order

supplier, a second copy goes to the accounting department, and the third copy is retained by the purchasing department for its files. A fourth copy could be sent to the individual who requisitioned the goods, and a fifth copy could be sent to the receiving department for use as a receiving report.

Receiving Report. Whether or not a copy of the purchase order is used for this purpose, a document called a receiving report should be prepared promptly by the receiving department for all goods received by the firm. Receiving reports should be prenumbered and subsequently accounted for by number to ensure that all goods received are properly entered. There are normally two copies of the receiving report. One copy is sent to the accounting department, and the other remains with the goods for forwarding to the inventory storage area.

PAYMENT FOR GOODS USING THE VOUCHER SYSTEM

Much of the material covered thus far in this chapter was addressed previously in other sections of the text. For example, basic features of accounting for purchases and payments were explained in Chapter 6, and accounting for sales and collections was addressed in Chapter 7. For this reason, data entry procedures in these areas generally have not been explained and illustrated in detail in this chapter. However, the accounting system used to *control* payments for items purchased by the business warrants further attention. Therefore, the data entry aspects of internal accounting control over payments will be explained in greater detail in this section.

A system for controlling expenditures that is used by many businesses is known as a voucher system. Such a system is very useful for controlling cash payments, because written authorization is required for each payment. A voucher system usually involves the use of vouchers, a voucher register, a vouchers payable account in the general ledger, voucher checks, and a check register. There are several alternative accounting procedures applicable to the voucher system. For instance, ordinary checks may be used and entered in a simple cashbook or in a cash payments journal. Like most accounting processes, the voucher system is flexible and readily adaptable to various situations.

The use of the voucher system of accounting is not advisable under all conditions, but it usually may be used to advantage when one or more of the following circumstances exist:

1. When the volume of transactions is large enough to require a system of control over expenditures.
2. When the nature of the business is such that it is desirable to enter invoices at the time that they are received rather than when payment is made.
3. When it is the custom of the firm to pay all invoices in full at maturity instead of making partial or installment payments.

There are generally five key documents in a voucher system: a purchase order, a receiving report, a purchase invoice, a voucher, and a check. Purchase orders and receiving reports were described previously. The purchase invoice and voucher will now be explained.

Purchase Invoice. A purchase invoice is the supplier's bill for goods, materials, or other assets purchased or for services rendered. The following is a purchase invoice received by Spinner & Thomas for the purchase of bakery trays from Capital City Products. When the purchase invoice is received by the accounts (or vouchers) payable sec-

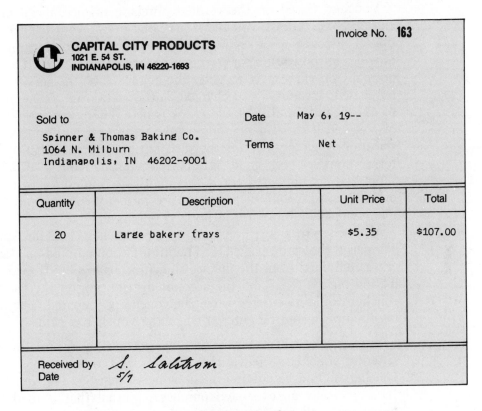

Purchase Invoice

tion of the accounting department, it should be compared with the purchase order and receiving report on file in that department to determine that the invoice is for the quantity ordered and received and for the proper price. In addition, mathematical accuracy of the invoice should be verified and the account to be charged for the purchase should be determined.

An alternative approach to purchase invoice verification used by some firms is to have the different employees responsible for ordering and receiving goods participate in the verification process. The receiving clerk would verify receipt of the assets purchased and the purchasing agent would verify the quantities, prices, and terms of the order. The accounting department would then verify the mathematical accuracy of the invoice and determine the account distribution.

Voucher. Based on the verified purchase invoice, receiving report, and purchase order, a voucher is prepared by the vouchers payable section. The voucher is a key internal accounting control document which provides authorization for payment for goods or services. The voucher normally provides space to enter the invoice date, the goods or services purchased, accounts to be charged, authorization for payment, date of payment, and number of the check issued. There is no standard form of voucher; it varies depending on the nature of the business, the classification of accounts, and the distribution desired. Regardless of its form, however, for good internal accounting control the voucher should be prenumbered and subsequently accounted for by number in order to ensure that all payments are properly entered and that payments are made only for authorized purchases.

A voucher that was prepared by the voucher clerk for Spinner & Thomas is shown on page 431. The information entered on this voucher was obtained from the invoice shown on page 429. All of the information on the front and the account distribution on the back of this voucher would be entered when the voucher is prepared. The payment information would be entered when the voucher is paid.

Entering Vouchers. There are two accounting records involved in entering vouchers: the voucher register and the general ledger. All vouchers should be entered in the voucher register. The voucher register is basically an expanded purchases journal that is used to enter purchases of all types of assets and services. The voucher register represents the first point at which purchases activities are reflected in the accounting records. In addition, each entry in the voucher register is a key step leading to the payment of a specific amount. This makes the voucher register particularly important from a control standpoint. To the extent feasible, vouchers should be entered in the voucher register in numerical order to facilitate accounting for the numerical sequence of the vouchers.

The columnar headings of a voucher register depend upon the nature of the business and the desired classification of purchases and expenses. One form of voucher register is shown on page 432. That illustration shows that Voucher No. 164, which is reproduced on page 431, was entered by debiting Store Equipment, Account No. 181, and by crediting Vouchers Payable, Account No. 218, for $107.

Spinner & Thomas Baking Co.

1604 N. Milburn
Indianapolis, IN 46202-9001

VOUCHER No. 164

Date Issued ___ May 7 ___ 19 _ _ Terms _Net_ Due ___ May 7 ___ 19 _ _

To _Capital City Products_

Address ___ 1021 E. 54 St., Indianapolis, IN 46220-1693 ___

Invoice Date	Description	Amount
May 6	20 Large bakery trays	$107 00

Authorized by	Prepared by
H. Spinner	S. Salstrom
	Voucher Clerk

Voucher *(front)*

DISTRIBUTION

Purchases		Operating Expenses		Sundry Accounts	
Dept. A	Dept. B	Acct. No.	Amount	Acct. No.	Amount
				181	107 00

PAYMENT

Date of Payment ___ May 7 ___ 19 _ _ Check No. ___ 519 ___ Amount $ _107.00_

CERTIFICATION

This voucher has been audited carefully and is correct in every respect.

J. Davis

Accountant

Voucher *(back)*

VOUCHER REGISTER FOR MONTH OF May 19 --   PAGE 13

PURCHASES DR. DEPT. A	DEPT. B	OPERATING EXPENSES DR. ACCT. NO.	AMOUNT	√	SUNDRY ACCOUNTS DR. ACCT. NO.	AMOUNT	√	DAY	VOU. NO.	TO WHOM ISSUED	SUNDRY ACCOUNTS CR. ACCT. NO.	AMOUNT	√	VOUCHERS PAYABLE CR.	DATE	CK. NO.
										AMOUNTS FORWARDED						
		5443	1 500 00					1	158	Estate Leasing Co.				2 500 00	5/1	511
		5406	1 000 00													
2 928 00	1 291 00							5	159	Flowers Baking Co.				4 219 00	5/7	514
1 206 00	2 647 00							5	160	Helleman Baking Co.				3 853 00	5/7	515
2 033 00	2 034 00							5	161	International Bakers				4 067 00	5/7	516
4 114 00								5	162	Omar Bakeries				4 114 00	5/7	517
1 460 00	2 764 00							5	163	Tri-Baking Co.				4 224 00	5/7	518
					181	107 00		7	164	Capital City Products				107 00	5/7	519
		5433	186 00					8	165	Indianapolis Star				186 00	5/8	522
		5431	899 00					16	166	Payroll	211	268 00		5 016 00	5/16	520
		5432	994 00								214	576 00				
		5401	1 567 00													
		5402	1 200 00													
		5434	1 200 00													
52 940 00	39 143 00		14 824 00			4 917 00						1 728 00		110 096 00		
52 940 00	39 143 00		14 824 00			4 917 00						1 728 00		110 096 00		
(511)	(521)		(541)			(√)						(√)		(218)		

Spinner & Thomas Voucher Register—(Partial)

Following is a description of the vouchers that have been entered in the voucher register:

May 1 No. 158, Estate Leasing Co.; store and office rent, Account No. 5443, $1,500, and Account No. 5406, $1,000.

5 No. 159, Flowers Baking Co.; merchandise, Account No. 511, $2,928, and Account No. 521, $1,291.

5 No. 160, Heileman Baking Co.; merchandise, Account No. 511, $1,206, and Account No. 521, $2,647.

5 No. 161, International Bakers; merchandise, Account No. 511, $2,033, and Account No. 521, $2,034.

5 No. 162, Omar Bakeries; merchandise, Account No. 511, $4,144.

5 No. 163, Tri-Baking Co.; merchandise, Account No. 511, $1,460, and Account No. 521, $2,764.

7 No. 164, Capital City Products; bakery trays, Account No. 181, $107.

8 No. 165, Indianapolis Star; advertising, Account No. 5433, $186.

16 No. 166, Payroll, May 1-16, $5,016. Distribution: Store Clerks Wage Expense, Account No. 5431, $899; Truck Drivers Wage Expense, Account No. 5432, $994; Office Salaries Expense, Account No. 5401, $1,567; Harlan Spinner, Salary Expense, Account No. 5402, $1,200; Carol Thomas, Salary Expense, Account No. 5434, $1,200. Taxes withheld: FICA Tax Payable, Account No. 211, $268; Employees Income Tax Payable, Account No. 214, $576.

Voucher No. 166 was based on a report of the payroll clerk. The amount payable is the net amount of the payroll after deducting the taxes withheld. The total wages and salaries earned during the pay period ended May 16 amounted to $5,860 represented by:

Store clerks wage expense	$ 899.00
Truck drivers wage expense	994.00
Office salaries expense	1,567.00
Harlan Spinner, salary expense	1,200.00
Carol Thomas, salary expense	1,200.00
Total	$5,860.00

Note that five lines were required to enter this transaction in the voucher register. This was because of the five entries in the Operating Expenses Dr. column.

To prove the voucher register, it is only necessary to determine that the sum of the debit footings is equal to the sum of the credit footings. The footings should be proved before the totals are forwarded and before the summary posting is completed.

Both individual posting and summary posting from the voucher register to the general ledger are required. In addition, individual posting from the voucher register to the operating expense ledger is required. (Use of the operating expense ledger is explained in Chapter 17.) The individual posting involves posting each item entered in the Sundry Accounts Dr. and Cr. Amount columns to the proper account in the general ledger, and posting each item in the Operating Expense Dr. Amount column to the proper account in the operating expense subsidiary ledger. As each item is posted, a check mark should be placed beside it in the check ($\sqrt{}$) column of the voucher register. The page number of the voucher register should also be entered in the Posting Reference column of the ledger account to which the amount is posted.

The summary posting of the voucher register required each month involves the following procedures:

1. The total of the column headed Purchases—Dept. A should be posted as a debit to the purchases—Dept. A account in the general ledger.
2. The total of the column headed Purchases—Dept. B should be posted as a debit to the purchases—Dept. B account in the general ledger.
3. The total of the column headed Operating Expenses Dr. should be posted as a debit to the operating expenses account in the general ledger, which is the control account for the operating expenses subsidiary ledger.
4. The total of the column headed Vouchers Payable Cr. should be posted as a credit to the vouchers payable account in the general ledger.

As the total of each column is posted from the voucher register, the account number should be entered in parentheses immediately below the total. The page number of the voucher register should also be entered in the Posting Reference column of the ledger account to which it is posted. Check marks in parentheses should be entered below the totals of the Sundry Accounts Dr. and Cr. amount columns in the voucher register to indicate that these totals should not be posted.

Paying Vouchers. After the vouchers are entered in the voucher register, they may be filed according to due date or alphabetically by supplier name in an unpaid vouchers file. Regardless of the way in which the vouchers are filed, they should be paid according to the terms stated in the invoice. Delay in payment may result in discounts being lost or in the loss of credit standing.

When they become due, the vouchers and supporting documents should be presented to the cashier or other proper disbursing officer for payment. The disbursing officer should review each voucher and supporting documents for propriety of the expenditure, prepare and sign the check, and mail it directly to the supplier. In no case should a check be written without a supporting voucher and documentation. Ordinary checks may be used. In some cases, however, a voucher check is used, which is a check with space for entering data from the invoice or other sources of information concerning the voucher to which the check relates. In the following illustration, a voucher check issued to Capital City Products in payment of its invoice of May 6 is reproduced. The statement attached to it provides space for details of the invoice, including its date, number, description, amount, deductions, if any, and net amount. The information given on the statement attached to the check is for identification purposes and serves as a remittance advice to the payee of the check. Whether an ordinary check or a voucher check is used, the checks should be prenumbered and subsequently accounted for by number to ensure that no unauthorized payments occur.

No. 519		**Spinner & Thomas Baking Co.** 1604 N. Milburn Indianapolis, IN 46202-9001					3-4 740
Date __May 7, 19--__		May 7 _____ 19 _ _					No. 519
To __Capital City__		Pay to the order of __Capital City Products__				$ 107.00	
Products		One hundred seven 00/100 -					Dollars
Voucher No. 164		*FEDERAL NATIONAL BANK*			*Harlan Spinner*		
Amount of Voucher __$107.00__		*Indianapolis, Indiana* ⑈074000009⑈ 92 641 8 ⑆					Treasurer
		Detach this statement before depositing check.					
Discount _____		Date __May 7, 19--__					
Amount of Check __$107.00__		Attached voucher check is full settlement of the following:					

Invoice		Description	Invoice Amount	Deductions		Net Amount
Date	Number			For	Amount	
May 6	163	20 Large bakery trays	107 00			107 00

Voucher Check

After the voucher has been paid, the disbursing officer should cancel the voucher and supporting documents to indicate payment. This ensures that a voucher will not be processed again to generate a duplicate payment. The canceled voucher and supporting documents are then returned to the vouchers payable section for filing either numerically or alphabetically in a paid vouchers file. In either case, the numerical sequence should be strictly controlled for possible missing or duplicate vouchers.

Entering Checks. Three accounting records are affected by the check entering process: the check register, voucher register, and general ledger. All checks issued in payment of vouchers may be entered in a check register. A check register is an accounting record of all checks written by a firm. When the charges pertaining to each voucher have been entered in the voucher register, it is not necessary to make provision for distribution of charges in the check register. It is not unusual, however, to find that columns are provided in the check register to enter deductions that may be made at the time of payment, such as purchases discounts. The form of check register shown below does not have such a column. After checks are entered in the check register, an entry should also be made in the Disposition columns of the voucher register to show that the voucher has been paid, as illustrated in the disposition columns of the voucher register on page 432. This entry, which would be made by the vouchers payable clerk based on a canceled voucher, serves the same purpose as a debit entry in a supplier's ledger account.

CHECK REGISTER FOR MONTH OF *May*   19 --   PAGE *13*

| VOUCHERS PAYABLE DR. | | DAY | DRAWN TO THE ORDER OF | CASH CR. | | |
NO.	AMOUNT			CHK. NO.	AMOUNT	
1			**AMOUNTS FORWARDED**			1
158	2 5 0 0 00	1	Estate Leasing Co.	511	2 5 0 0 00	2
149	2 6 0 00	2	Walnut Paper	512	2 6 0 00	3
154	7 4 00	5	Stansifer's Garage	513	7 4 00	4
159	4 2 1 9 00	7	Flowers Baking Co.	514	4 2 1 9 00	5
						20
	99 1 8 6 00				99 1 8 6 00	21
	99 1 8 6 00				99 1 8 6 00	
	(2 1 8)				(1 1 1)	22

Spinner & Thomas' Check Register (*Partial*)

Following is a description of the checks that have been entered in the check register reproduced on page 436.

May 1 No. 511, Estate Leasing Co., $2,500, in payment of Voucher No. 158.

   2 No. 512, Walnut Paper, $260, in payment of Voucher No. 149.

   5 No. 513, Stansifer's Garage, $74, in payment of Voucher No. 154.

   7 No. 514, Flowers Baking Co., $4,219, in payment of Voucher No. 159.

To prove the check register, it is only necessary to determine that the footing of the Cash Cr. column is equal to the footing of the Vouchers Payable Dr. column. The footings should be proved before the totals are forwarded and before the summary posting is completed.

No individual posting from the check register is required. It is only necessary to complete the summary posting at the end of each month.

The summary posting procedure is as follows:

1. The total of the column headed Vouchers Payable Dr. should be posted as a debit to the vouchers payable account in the general ledger.

2. The total of the column headed Cash Cr. Amount should be posted as a credit to the cash account in the general ledger.

As the total of each column is posted from the check register, the account number in parentheses should be entered immediately below the total. The page number of the check register should also be entered in the Posting Reference column of the ledger account to which the amount is posted.

Proving Vouchers Payable. When the voucher system is used, it is possible to dispense with a subsidiary accounts payable ledger. The file of unpaid vouchers serves as the detail to support the balance of the vouchers payable account after all posting has been completed. The voucher register itself partially performs this function. Every blank in the Disposition columns of the register shows that the indicated voucher is unpaid. The unpaid vouchers file can be consulted if more detail about any item is needed.

When a trial balance is prepared at the end of a period, the balance of the vouchers payable account should be verified by preparing a list of the vouchers contained in the unpaid vouchers file. The total amount of this list should be equal to the balance of the account.

If a subsidiary accounts payable ledger is not maintained and if unpaid vouchers are filed according to due date, there is no way of quickly finding out how much is owed to a particular supplier. This may not be considered important. Businesspeople using the voucher system tend to think in terms of unpaid invoices rather than being primarily concerned with the total amount owed to each of their suppliers. However, if the latter information is needed, copies of the vouchers may be filed according to the names of the suppliers. In addition, a subsidiary accounts payable ledger may be maintained if one is desired.

Purchases Returns and Allowances. When a voucher system of accounting is used, purchases returns and allowances must be entered in such a way that the accounts currently reflect such transactions, that the voucher register shows the proper amounts payable, and that the amount of the affected unpaid voucher is reduced. A commonly used procedure involves three steps:

1. A notation of the return or allowance is made on the affected voucher and the credit memo is attached to it.
2. A notation of the reduction is made in the voucher register beside the amount of the affected voucher.
3. The transaction is formally entered in the general journal.

A return or allowance relating to a merchandise purchase would require a debit to Vouchers Payable and a credit to Purchases Returns and Allowances. If the return or allowance is related to a purchase of a long-term asset or to some expense, the credit in the entry would be to the asset or expense account.

Partial Payments. When a business using the voucher system makes partial payments on invoices, special handling is required. If it is known at the outset that an invoice will be paid in installments, a separate voucher for each installment should be prepared in the first place. If it is decided to make a partial payment on an invoice already vouchered and entered, the original voucher should be canceled and two or more new ones issued. The total amount of the new vouchers should be equal to that of the old voucher. The vouchers would be entered in the voucher register by a debit to Vouchers Payable in the Sundry Accounts—Dr. column for the amount of the old voucher, and by a credit to Vouchers Payable in the Vouchers Payable Cr. column for the amounts of the new vouchers. A note should be entered in the Disposition columns of the voucher register indicating that the old voucher has been canceled and showing the numbers of the new vouchers issued. Payments of the vouchers should then be entered in the usual manner.

BUILDING YOUR ACCOUNTING KNOWLEDGE

1. What functions are included in the expenditure cycle?

2. Purchase orders are typically prepared in multiple-copy form. What is done with the different copies of the purchase order?

3. Why is a voucher system very useful for controlling cash payments?

4. Under what circumstances is there usually an advantage in using a voucher system?

5. What two accounting records are involved in entering vouchers?

6. What are the appropriate procedures for paying vouchers?

7. Why should the disbursing officer cancel a voucher and supporting documents to indicate payment after the voucher is paid?

8. When a voucher system is used, how is the vouchers payable account balance verified at the end of a period?

APPLYING ACCOUNTING CONCEPTS

Exercise 14-3. The following transactions occurred during the first month of operations of Lewell Co.

Sept.   2 Received an invoice for $800 from Klew Realty Co. for rent. (Rent Expense, Account No. 5443.)

5 Received an invoice for $1,520.85 from Cray Supply House for merchandise.

10 Received an invoice for $910.90 from Reese Equipment Co. for office furniture. (Office Equipment, Account No. 191.)

16 Received a bill for $110.07 for telephone service and installation from Inlet Telephone Co. (Telephone Expense, Account No. 5409.)

19 Received an invoice for $87.50 from the Daily Herald for advertising. (Advertising Expense, Account No. 5433.)

26 Received an invoice for $1,110.55 from Lema Co. for merchandise.

Enter the foregoing transactions in a voucher register similar to the one on page 432.

Exercise 14-4. The following payments were made during the first month of operations of Lewell Co. (See Exercise 14-3.)

Sept.   3 Issued Check No. 1 in payment of invoice from Klew Realty Co.

16 Issued Check No. 2 in payment of invoice from Cray Supply House.

17 Issued Check No. 3 in payment of invoice from Reese Equipment Co.

26 Issued Check No. 4 in payment of invoice from the Daily Herald.

Enter the foregoing transactions in a check register similar to the one on page 436.

Exercise 14-5. See Exercises 14-3 and 14-4.

(a) Foot the Vouchers Payable column in the voucher register and in the check register. Open a T-account for vouchers payable and post the footings to it. **(b)** Prove the balance of the vouchers payable account by preparing a schedule of unpaid vouchers from the voucher register.

Report No. 14-2

Complete Report No. 14-2 in the study assignments and submit your working papers to the instructor for approval. Then continue with the textbook discussion until Report No. 14-3 is required.

APPLICATION IN THE REVENUE CYCLE

The revenue cycle includes all the functions involved in receiving customer orders, providing goods and services, billing customers, and collecting payments—either on account or for cash sales. Diagramming and briefly explaining the revenue cycle will assist in understanding internal accounting control in the revenue cycle. A flowchart of the basic elements of the revenue cycle appears on the following page. Many variations of the revenue cycle are possible for different businesses. The flowchart shown here assumes a medium-sized business that deals in a tangible product.

The Credit Sales portion of the flowchart shows that a customer who purchases merchandise on account usually sends a purchase order to a particular business. In response to this order, a sales order would be generated by the business. This sales order is the basis for preparing a shipping order which causes goods to be shipped to the customer. One copy of the shipping order is sent to the customer with the goods and a second copy is sent to the Billing section so that a bill, the sales invoice, will be sent to the customer. A second copy of the sales invoice is sent to the General Accounting and Accounts Receivable sections for entry in the accounting system.

The Collections and Cash Sales portion of the flowchart depicts the processing of both collections on account and collections from cash sales. Collections on account are generally received by mail from customers. Normally included with the check is a remittance advice, which is a document indicating the purpose of the payment, that is, the bill that is being paid. Remittance advices are sent to the General Accounting and Accounts Receivable sections for entering in the accounting records and the checks are sent to the cashier, who prepares a deposit slip and sends it with the checks to the bank. The bank returns a validated deposit slip to the Accounting Department.

FLOWCHART OF REVENUE CYCLE

Credit Sales

Collections and Cash Sales

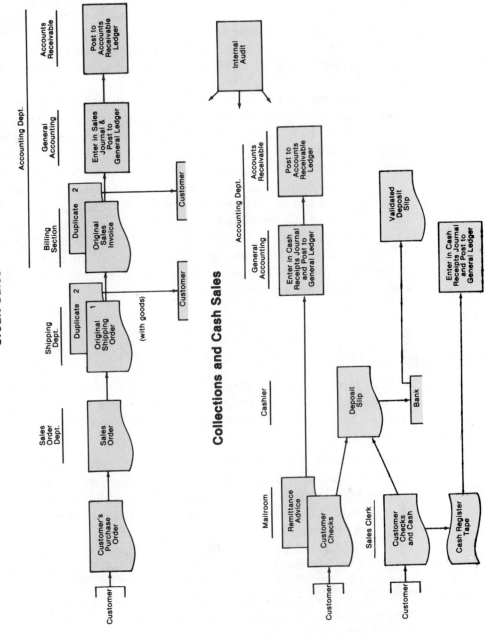

Sales clerks normally use cash registers to handle cash sales. Customer remittances of cash or checks are forwarded to the cashier, who prepares a deposit slip and sends the deposit to the bank. The cash register tape is sent to the Accounting Department for entering. A validated deposit slip is returned to the Accounting Department by the bank.

The Internal Audit Department has responsibility to oversee or monitor the entire system of internal accounting control depicted in the flowchart. Its functions might include making sure that goods are shipped only on the basis of authorized shipping orders or that all collections on account are properly entered in the accounting records.

Internal accounting control over the revenue cycle will now be discussed in some detail. The partial records illustrated are those of Spinner & Thomas. The merchandise accounts are kept on a departmental basis—Dept. A handles pastries and cakes, Dept. B handles bread and rolls. Since internal accounting controls relevant for cash sales differ significantly from those relevant for credit sales, cash sales and credit sales are discussed separately here.

Cash Sales

Most businesses make at least a portion of their sales for cash rather than on account. Regardless of the percentage of sales made for cash, certain basic internal accounting control procedures should be employed.

Cash Register Tapes and Sales Tickets. Receipts from cash sales are generally controlled by the use of a cash register that generates a cash register tape in duplicate; one copy for the customer and one copy to be retained for the firm's records. At the end of each day, the cash and any checks received from customers are sent to the cashier for preparation of the bank deposit, and the cash register tapes are either picked up by or sent to the accounting department for entry in the accounting records.

An alternative system for handling cash sales that is used by many businesses is the preparation of a separate sales ticket for each transaction. A salesclerk prepares a sales ticket in duplicate for each sale, and these tickets and the related cash receipts are then handled in a manner similar to that used for cash register tapes and related cash receipts. The only additional control necessary when sales tickets are used is that the tickets should be prenumbered and subsequently accounted for by number.

Deposit Slip. The cashier prepares a deposit slip in duplicate for the cash and checks received from the salesclerks and sends both copies with the deposit to the bank. The validated deposit slip should be returned by the bank to the firm's accounting department.

Accounting Procedures for Cash Sales. The first accounting record affected by cash sales is the cash receipts journal. The cash register tapes, the sales tickets, or a listing of the tickets are the basis for the entries in the cash receipts journal. Examples of entries of cash sales can be seen in the portion of the cash receipts journal of Spinner & Thomas illustrated on page 452.

The second accounting record affected by cash sales is the general ledger. At the end of each month, a summary posting is made from the cash receipts journal to the general ledger cash and sales accounts for the appropriate amounts.

When each validated deposit slip is returned by the bank to the firm's accounting department, the amount deposited is compared with the amount entered in the cash receipts journal based on the cash register tapes or sales tickets. This procedure ensures that all cash sales collected by the salesclerks and forwarded to the cashier were in fact properly deposited.

This system appears to control adequately what happens to cash once a proper cash register or sales ticket record is made of each cash sale. A question might be raised, however, as to the control that exists over the salesclerks to see that a valid cash register entry or sales ticket is prepared in the first place. The answer essentially is the customer. Any customer purchasing merchandise expects to receive some kind of receipt for the amount remitted. In order to provide such a receipt, the salesclerk must generate either a cash register entry or a sales ticket. It would still be possible for the salesclerk to alter a sales ticket subsequently, but if these documents are reviewed by the accounting department or internal audit staff, frequent alterations in sales tickets would be questioned.

Credit Sales

Internal accounting control procedures for credit sales typically are more complicated than those for cash sales. By their nature, credit sales involve more documents, more people, and more accounting records.

Customer Purchase Order. The customer's purchase order initiates a sales transaction. Since the customer intends to purchase goods from another business, clearly one firm's purchase is another firm's sale. Customer orders can be received either by mail or by telephone. If an order is received by telephone, the customer order document usually is generated internally by the seller. Based on the customer order, a sales order is prepared.

Sales Order. The sales order is a document prepared by the sales order department which authorizes sales of merchandise to a customer. It would be possible to use the customer order as a sales order, but control and handling efficiency are improved if a separate sales order is generated. The following is a sales order prepared by Spinner & Thomas Baking Co. for a sale to Heritage House. Sales orders should be prenumbered and subsequently all numbers should be accounted for. If any numbers are missing, this would suggest that some orders have been lost and not properly processed. Sales orders are often prepared in duplicate so that the sales order department can retain one copy for its files. Many companies also have a separate credit department. If a credit department exists, the sales order is sent to the credit department to obtain approval of a sale to any charge customer. Note the credit approval that appears on the Spinner & Thomas sales order. After credit is approved, the sales order is sent to the shipping department.

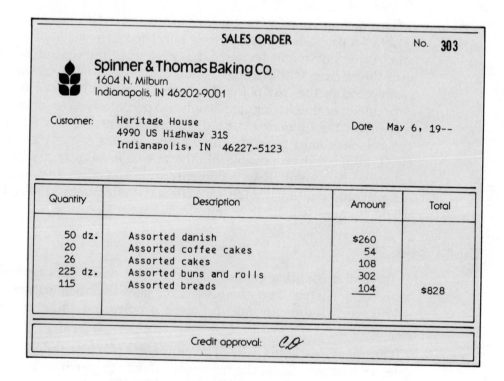

Sales Order

Shipping Order. The shipping order is the document that provides authorization to ship merchandise. It is an important control document in a firm's information system. An example of a shipping order for a shipment from Spinner & Thomas to Heritage House is shown below. This shipping order was prepared based on the preceding sales order. Shipping orders should be prenumbered and subsequently accounted for by number in order to ensure that all shipments are properly entered and that all goods shipped are billed to the purchasers. One copy of the shipping order is sent to the customer with the goods and the other copy is sent to the billing section so that a sales invoice can be prepared.

SHIPPING ORDER   No. **295**

Spinner & Thomas Baking Co.
1604 N. Milburn
Indianapolis, IN 46202-9001

Customer:

   Heritage House
   4990 US Highway 31S
   Indianapolis, IN 46227-5123

Date   May 6, 19--
Shipping instructions   Our truck
To be delivered   May 7, 19--

Quantity	Description	Amount	Total
50 dz.	Assorted danish	$260	
20	Assorted coffee cakes	54	
26	Assorted cakes	108	
225 dz.	Assorted buns and rolls	302	
115	Assorted breads	104	$828

Shipping Order

Sales Invoice. A multiple-copy sales invoice, which is the company's bill to the customer, is prepared in the billing section of the accounting department as soon as the copy of the shipping order has been received, indicating that the goods have been shipped. The following is a copy of a summary sales invoice that was generated based on the shipping order reproduced above. In Spinner & Thomas' system, this invoice showing sales summarized in terms of pastries and breads is supported by a detailed sales invoice (not shown) listing items

| SUMMARY SALES INVOICE | | No. 291 |

Spinner & Thomas Baking Co.
1604 N. Milburn
Indianapolis, IN 46202-9001

Customer: Date   May 7, 19--
  Heritage House
  4990 US Highway 31S
  Indianapolis, IN 46227-5123

Description	Amount	Total
Pastries Breads	$422 406	$828

Summary Sales Invoice

purchased, unit prices, and extended amounts. This document is extremely important from a control standpoint. In conjunction with the shipping order, the sales invoice provides assurance that all goods shipped are also billed. Sales invoices should be prenumbered and subsequently accounted for by number in order to provide this assurance of proper billing. If any sales invoice number is missing from the sequence, it would suggest that some shipment was not billed or perhaps that the billing was not posted to the accounting records. In addition, each sales invoice should be supported by a shipping order to make certain that sales are entered only for goods actually shipped to customers. One copy of the sales invoice is sent to the customer and a second copy is sent to accounting. Other copies of the sales invoice might also be used in an accounting information system but the two copies described above are the minimum necessary. In many accounting information systems, the sales invoices must be verified as to price, quantity, and extended amounts before they are mailed to customers.

Accounting Procedures for Credit Sales. Accounting procedures for entering sales were explained to a great extent in Chapter 7. That discussion is extended here in order to emphasize the internal accounting control aspects of the data entry process.

The first accounting record affected by sales transactions is a firm's sales journal. The following is a portion of the sales journal for Spinner & Thomas. The individual sales invoices represent the basis for entries in the sales journal. In most accounting information systems, entries to such a journal represent the first point at which sales activities are reflected in the accounting records. Neither the customer order, nor the sales order, nor the shipping order, nor the preparation of the sales invoice directly affects any accounting record. This makes the sales journal particularly important from a control standpoint. Note that the sales invoices are entered in the sales journal not only in chronological order but also in numerical order. This feature of the data entry process makes the sales journal a convenient place to account for the numerical sequence of sales invoices.

SALES JOURNAL FOR MONTH OF May   19 --   PAGE 9

	DEBIT								CREDIT				
	GENERAL LEDGER			ACCOUNTS RECEIVABLE	√	DAY	NAME	SALE NO.	SALES		GENERAL LEDGER		
	ACCT. NO.	AMOUNT	√						DEPT. A	DEPT. B	ACCT. NO.	AMOUNT	√
1				1307 00	√	5	Ayres Department Stores	287	822 00	485 00				1
2				1075 00	√	5	Bakemeier's Bakery	288	672 00	403 00				2
3				798 00	√	5	Methodist Hospital	289	277 00	521 00				3
4				701 00	√	7	Brother Juniper's	290	508 00	193 00				4
5				828 00	√	7	Heritage House	291	422 00	406 00				5
6				645 00	√	7	Houlihan's Place	292	437 00	208 00				6
28				26827 00 / 26827 00					14884 00 / 14884 00	11943 00 / 11943 00				28
29				(131)					(411)	(421)				29

Spinner & Thomas' Sales Journal (Partial)

A second accounting record affected by sales transactions is the accounts receivable ledger. A portion of the accounts receivable ledger for Spinner & Thomas is reproduced on page 448. For good internal accounting control, the individual sales invoices should be the basis for posting to the individual customer accounts in the accounts receivable ledger. Note that the individual postings for sales invoices Nos. 287, 288, and 289 appear in these customer accounts, just as they appeared in the preceding sales journal. Posting to the individual customer accounts from the sales invoices rather than from the sales journal provides an independent check on the posting process. If the postings of

NAME Ayres Department Stores   **TERMS** Net

ADDRESS 1 W. Washington St., Indianapolis, IN 46204-5174

DATE		ITEM	POST. REF.	DEBIT	CREDIT	BALANCE
19-- May	1	Balance	√			9 76 00
	5		S287	1 3 0 7 00		2 2 8 3 00

NAME Bakemeier's Bakery   **TERMS** Net

ADDRESS 2039 N. Capitol Ave., Indianapolis, IN 46202-4240

DATE		ITEM	POST. REF.	DEBIT	CREDIT	BALANCE
19-- May	1	Balance	√			4 91 00
	5		S288	1 0 75 00		1 5 6 6 00

NAME Methodist Hospital   **TERMS** Net

ADDRESS 1604 N. Capitol Ave., Indianapolis, IN 46202-5126

DATE		ITEM	POST. REF.	DEBIT	CREDIT	BALANCE
19-- May	1	Balance	√			6 50 00
	5		S289	7 98 00		1 4 4 8 00

Spinner & Thomas' Accounts Receivable Ledger (Partial)

customer accounts were made from the sales journal, any error in posting the sales journal would automatically be carried forward to the accounts receivable ledger. On the other hand, if both the sales journal and the customer accounts are posted from individual sales invoices by different accounting department employees, a posting error by either employee would cause the records to disagree, unless of course, both employees made exactly the same error. The posting error would be discovered at the end of the month because at that time, the individual customer account balances in the accounts receivable ledger would be scheduled, totaled, and compared with the general ledger accounts receivable control, which is posted from the total of the sales journal entries.

The third accounting record affected by sales transactions is the general ledger. As explained in Chapter 7, at the end of the month a summary posting would be made from the sales journal to the appropriate general ledger accounts. The accounts and amounts posted for May are indicated at the bottom of the columns in the sales journal on page 447. The posting that is of particular interest for purposes of the present discussion is the one to accounts receivable for $26,827. The following illustration shows the general ledger accounts receivable control account. After posting from the sales journal, the account has a balance of $33,653. This represents the total balances in all accounts receivable as of the end of May, after posting all charge sales made during May.

ACCOUNT *Accounts Receivable*					ACCOUNT NO. *131*	
DATE	ITEM	POST. REF.	DEBIT	CREDIT	BALANCE DEBIT	BALANCE CREDIT
19-- May 1	Balance	√			6 8 2 6 00	
31		S9	26 8 2 7 00		33 6 5 3 00	

Accounts Receivable Control Account in General Ledger

Remittance Advice and Check. When a customer makes a remittance by mail, it is customary for the customer to include a remittance advice with the check. The remittance advice is a form showing the customer's name and address and the amount of the remittance. A good example of a remittance advice is shown on page 450. For good internal accounting control, the checks and remittance advices should be separated in the mailroom; the checks should be sent to the cashier and the remittance advices to the accounting department. If a customer remittance arrives without a remittance advice, a remittance advice should be prepared in the mailroom for forwarding to the accounting department.

The processing of the checks and remittance advices is designed to ensure that customer remittances on account are properly received, deposited, and entered in the firm's records. If employees in the mailroom attempt to retain any customer remittances for their own use, the fraud will be discovered because mailroom employees do not have access to the accounting records. Consequently, the customer will undoubtedly be billed again for the amount previously remitted but intercepted by the mailroom employees. When the customer complains about the billing, the theft will be discovered. The actions of the cashier who receives the remittances from the mailroom are simi-

Methodist Hospital
1604 N. Capitol Ave.
Indianapolis, IN 46202-4492

Date   May 5, 19--

Enclosed is our payment of the following:

| Invoice | | Description | Amount |
Date	No.		
4/28	279	Assorted pastries, rolls, and breads Deductions Net	$650.00 -0- $650.00

Remittance Advice

larly controlled. The accounting department employees have access to the accounting records and can fraudulently alter them, but these employees have no access to the remittances and therefore, no incentive to modify the accounting records.

Deposit Slip. The cashier prepares a deposit slip in duplicate for the checks and cash received from the mailroom, and sends both copies along with the checks and cash to the bank. The following is a common form of deposit slip. These deposit slips are often prenumbered. The bank validates the deposit slip and returns it to the depositing firm.

DEPOSIT SLIP		3-4 / 740

Spinner & Thomas Baking Co.
1604 N. Milburn
Indianapolis, IN 46202-9001

Currency	2,452	20
Coin	139	80
Checks		
Total from other side		
Total	2,592	00

Date _____ May 2 _____ 19 _ _

**FEDERAL
NATIONAL
BANK**
Indianapolis, Indiana

⑆ 0740000009⑆   92 641 8 ⑉

Deposit Slip

Accounting Procedures for Collections. The first accounting record affected by collections on account is the cash receipts journal, a special journal used to enter all but only cash receipts. The individual remittance advices are the basis for entries in this record. A portion of the cash receipts journal for Spinner & Thomas is shown on page 452.

A second accounting record affected by the collections is the accounts receivable ledger. The receipts are posted to the accounts receivable ledger in chronological order and the source of each receipt is indicated. For good internal accounting control, the individual remittance advices should be used to post to the individual customer accounts in the accounts receivable ledger. The portion of the accounts receivable ledger illustrated on page 448 is reproduced on page 453, with three additional items, the remittances on account by the three customers during May. Note that having different accounting department employees use the remittance advices to post separately to the accounts receivable ledger provides the same type of control over the cash receipts posting process that separate posting to the accounts receivable ledger from the individual sales invoices provided over the sales posting process. If an error was made in posting either to the general ledger or to the accounts receivable ledger, the error would be discovered at the end of the month when the total of the balances

CASH RECEIPTS JOURNAL FOR MONTH OF May 19 --   PAGE 12

| | DEBIT | | | | | | | CREDIT | | | | |
| | GENERAL LEDGER | | | CASH NET AMOUNT | DAY | RECEIVED FROM DESCRIPTION | ACCOUNTS RECEIVABLE | ✓ | CASH SALES | | GENERAL LEDGER | | |
#	ACCT. NO.	AMOUNT	✓						DEPT. A	DEPT. B	ACCT. NO.	AMOUNT	✓
1						AMOUNTS FORWARDED							
2				3368 00	1	Cash Sales			1896 00	1472 00			
3				2592 00	2	Cash Sales			1434 00	1158 00			
4				2941 00	5	Cash Sales			1571 00	1370 00			
5				3260 00	6	Cash Sales			1798 00	1462 00			
6				1232 00	6	Ayres Department Stores	1232 00	✓					
7				977 00	6	Bakemeier's Bakery	977 00	✓					
8				650 00	6	Methodist Hospital	650 00	✓					
27				11072 00 / 11072 00			30500 00 / 30500 00		42451 00 / 42451 00	37186 00 / 37186 00		583 00 / 583 00	
28				(1 1 1)			(1 3 1)		(4 1 1)	(4 2 1)		(✓)	

Spinner & Thomas' Cash Receipts Journal (Partial)

in the accounts receivable ledger is compared with the general ledger accounts receivable control account balance. Even though the individual remittance advices are used to post the subsidiary accounts receivable ledger, the posting reference "CR12" is used to refer to the page of the cash receipts journal on which these collections were entered. This is because no other reference numbers are available for subsequent comparison or verification.

NAME *Ayres Department Stores*   **TERMS** *Net*

ADDRESS *1 W. Washington St., Indianapolis, IN 46204-5174*

DATE		ITEM	POST. REF.	DEBIT	CREDIT	BALANCE
19- May	1	Balance	√			9 7 6 00
	5		S287	1 3 0 7 00		2 2 8 3 00
	6		CR12		1 2 3 2 00	1 0 5 1 00

NAME *Bakemeier's Bakery*   **TERMS** *Net*

ADDRESS *2039 N. Capitol Ave., Indianapolis, IN 46202-4240*

DATE		ITEM	POST. REF.	DEBIT	CREDIT	BALANCE
19- May	1	Balance	√			4 9 1 00
	5		S288	1 0 7 5 00		1 5 6 6 00
	6		CR12		9 7 7 00	5 8 9 00

NAME *Methodist Hospital*   **TERMS** *Net*

ADDRESS *1604 N. Capitol Ave., Indianapolis, IN 46202-5126*

DATE		ITEM	POST. REF.	DEBIT	CREDIT	BALANCE
19- May	1	Balance	√			6 5 0 00
	5		S289	7 9 8 00		1 4 4 8 00
	6		CR12		6 5 0 00	7 9 8 00

Spinner & Thomas' Accounts Receivable Ledger (Partial)

Another accounting record affected by the collections is the general ledger. At the end of each month, a summary posting would be made from the cash receipts journal to the appropriate general ledger accounts. The accounts and amounts posted for May are indicated at the bottom of the columns in the cash receipts journal on page 452. The general ledger accounts receivable control account shown on page 449 is reproduced below, with one additional item, the credit total of $30,500 from the May cash receipts journal. After this posting, the account has a balance of $3,153. This represents the total of the balances in all individual customer accounts receivable as of the end of May, after crediting the customer accounts for all remittances received.

ACCOUNT Accounts Receivable									ACCOUNT NO. 131	
DATE	ITEM	POST. REF.	DEBIT	CREDIT	BALANCE					
					DEBIT		CREDIT			
19– May 1	Balance	√			6 8 2 6 00					
31		S9	26 8 2 7 00		33 6 5 3 00					
31		CR12		30 5 0 0 00	3 1 5 3 00					

Accounts Receivable Control Account in General Ledger

In the previous discussion of deposit slips, it was noted that validated deposit slips are returned by the bank to the firm. Internal control is strengthened if these deposit slips are returned to the accounting department of the firm rather than to the cashier. An accounting department employee should compare the amount shown on the validated deposit slip with the amounts entered in the cash receipts journal as remittances on account. This procedure ensures that customer remittances on account as indicated on the remittance advices and entered in the cash receipts journal were in fact deposited by the cashier.

BUILDING YOUR ACCOUNTING KNOWLEDGE

1. What functions are included in the revenue cycle?
2. What purposes are served by the shipping order?
3. Why should postings to individual customer accounts receivable be made from the sales invoices rather than from the sales journal?
4. Why are checks and remittance advices separated in the mailroom, with the checks being sent to the cashier, and the remittance advices to the accounting department?
5. What control exists over salesclerks to see that a valid cash register entry is made or a sales ticket is prepared when a sale occurs?
6. What three accounting records are affected by collections on account?
7. Why should validated deposit slips be returned by the bank to the accounting department of the firm rather than to the cashier?

APPLYING ACCOUNTING CONCEPTS

Exercise 14-6.   The following sales and collection transactions occurred during the first month of operations of the Robcar Co.

May   4 Made charge sale No. 1 to H. Inger, $310.50.
      6 Made cash sales of $1,412.45.
  11 Made charge sale No. 2 to P. Willems, $283.39.
  12 Made charge sale No. 3 to F. Miller, $402.
  18 Received $200 on account from H. Inger.
  19 Made cash sales of $904.25.
  24 Received $283.39 on account from P. Willems.
  26 Made charge sale No. 4 to L. Fishel, $331.71.
  29 Made charge sale No. 5 to H. Inger, $204.13.

Enter the foregoing transactions in a sales journal similar to the one on page 447 or in a cash receipts journal similar to the one on page 452.

Exercise 14-7.   See Exercise 14-6.

(a) Foot the sales journal and cash receipts journal in Exercise 14-6. **(b)** Post the transactions from Exercise 14-6 to an accounts receivable subsidiary ledger, and the journal totals to an accounts receivable account. (Use T account forms.) **(c)** Prove the accounts receivable balance by preparing a schedule of accounts receivable.

Report No. 14-3

Complete Report No. 14-3 in the study assignments and submit your working papers for approval. Then continue with the textbook discussion in Chapter 15 until Report No. 15-1 is required.

EXPANDING YOUR BUSINESS VOCABULARY

What is the meaning of each of the following terms:

accounting procedures
  (p. 421)
authorization procedures
  (p. 420)
cash receipts journal **(p. 451)**
check register **(pp. 425, 436)**
customer's purchase order
  (p. 443)
independent check **(p. 421)**
internal accounting control system
  (p. 419)
internal audit department **(p. 421)**
purchase invoice **(p. 429)**

purchase order **(p. 427)**
purchase requisition **(p. 426)**
receiving report **(p. 427)**
remittance advice **(p. 449)**
sales invoice **(p. 445)**
sales journal **(p. 447)**
sales order **(p. 444)**
segregation of duties **(p. 420)**
shipping order **(p. 445)**
voucher **(pp. 425, 430)**
voucher check **(p. 435)**
voucher register **(pp. 425, 430)**
voucher system **(p. 428)**

CHAPTER 15

Accounting Concepts and Accepted Practices

CHAPTER OBJECTIVES

Careful study of this chapter should enable you to:

- Describe and explain the basic accounting concepts of:

    1. The Business Entity
    2. The Going Concern
    3. The Monetary Unit
    4. Transaction-Based Records and Historical Cost
    5. Periodicity, Realization, and Matching
    6. The Accrual Basis

- Describe and explain the widely accepted accounting practices of:

    1. Consistency and Comparability
    2. Adequate Disclosure
    3. Objectivity and Verifiability
    4. Materiality and Practicality
    5. Conservatism
    6. Legality

The framework that underlies modern business accounting is a blend of various assumptions, conventions, requirements, practical compromises, and constraints. Because these factors are so interrelated, it is not possible to list them in an unquestioned order of importance. The student should remember this in the discussion that follows. In the organization of this chapter, the various matters are grouped according to (1) those that can be regarded as concepts and (2) those that may be classed as accepted practices. However, it will soon become apparent that there is some overlap between the categories.

BASIC CONCEPTS IN FINANCIAL ACCOUNTING

The basic concepts in financial accounting include: (1) the business entity, (2) the going concern, (3) the monetary unit, (4) transaction-based records and the related concept of historical cost, (5) periodicity and the related concepts of realization and matching, and (6) the accrual basis.

The Business Entity

As applied to business accounting, the entity concept means that the business to which the records (or financial statements) relate is treated as a separately identifiable economic unit. This economic unit can be defined in various ways without regard to legal considerations of who actually owns the property and who is liable for the debts. In connection with the discussions and illustrations of the accounts of a single-owner business (a sole proprietorship), it was stressed that while the owner might possess various properties, only the property used in the business was taken into account. Likewise, the record of liabilities excluded any of the proprietor's debts of a nonbusiness or personal nature. Consequently, there was no accounting for any type of revenue and expense not connected with business operations. Of course, a business could be considered to include other, perhaps wholly unrelated, profit-seeking activities if the owner so desires. Or, the accounting entity could consist of the assets used by the business and the liabilities incurred on behalf of the business, even though, legally, the property belonged to the owner who was personally liable for the debts.

In the case of business partnerships, the separate entity is almost a legal reality. Property can be owned by a partnership. However, with limited exceptions, the debts of the firm may become personal liabilities of each of the partners. In the case of business corporations, the business entity is a legal reality, even though corporations are owned by their shareholders or stockholders. Corporations can own property, incur debt, sue, and be sued. The debts of a corporation are debts of the corporate entity, not personal debts of its owners (stockholders). This is one of the reasons for the wide popularity of the corporate form of business organization.

Probably the greatest extension of the entity concept occurs when one corporation owns most or all of another (or perhaps several others). While each corporation is a legal entity and each has a separate set of records, their individual financial statements are combined to present what is known as a consolidated income statement and a consolidated balance sheet. From the viewpoint of the stockholders of the parent corporation (the corporation that controls the other corporations in the consolidated group), there is, in effect, just one entity.

The Going-Concern

A well-established tradition in business accounting is that in the absence of strong reason to believe otherwise, a business should be assumed to have a continuing, indefinite life. This is called the going-concern concept, or concept of continuity. Several arguments are offered in support of this concept. Corporations can have virtually perpetual existence. In the other two forms of business organizations, proprietors and partners will die, but the businesses involved can be continued by others—perhaps by those who inherit the business, by remaining partners, or by those to whom the business may be sold. It is argued that, in most cases, the owners and managers of a business intend and hope that the business will continue indefinitely. They usually make decisions with a view to maintaining the existence of the business, often in the hope of expanding it.

The reality of the economic world does not give full support to the going-concern concept. Business failures are commonplace. The mortality rate among new businesses is especially high. However, the alternative to assuming that a business will continue indefinitely would be to make an estimate of its probable life. What is a reasonable estimate? Two years? Five years? Ten years? Whatever the estimated life, it would mean that the acquisition of a depreciable asset with a potential useful life greater than the expected life of the business might seem inadvisable. Whenever long-term assets were acquired, the nature of depreciation calculations could be affected. The estimated life of the business rather than the estimated useful life of the asset might become the controlling element. In addition, the longer a business were to survive, the greater would be the chance for its continued existence; thus some depreciation rates might have to be revised and rerevised. Since this alternative to a continuity concept is so unattractive (perhaps unworkable), the going-concern concept seems the more sensible alternative.

The Monetary Unit

The monetary unit concept means that business transactions are measured in terms of money and the purchasing power of money is assumed to be stable. The monetary unit used by American accountants (United States and Canada) to measure financial transactions is the dollar. In Great Britain, the unit is the pound, and in West Germany, the unit is the mark. Whatever form of monetary unit is used, it is not as reliable a measuring unit as is a physical measure, such as the meter or kilogram, because the value of money fluctuates. This can cause the monetary unit to have different values at different points in time.

For several decades, the question of whether changes in the value of the dollar should be recognized in the accounting process has been discussed and debated. It is well known that the purchasing power of the dollar is constantly changing—nearly always declining. The impact of this on the financial statements is greatest in the case of long-term assets. Quite apart from the question of whether the amounts reported on a balance sheet should approximate current market values of the assets as opposed to historical cost, is the problem that the amounts shown as the costs of long-term assets may be a mixture of some dollars spent perhaps 25 years ago, some 20 years ago, some 10 years ago, and some more recently. Almost certainly, the value of the dollar was not the same at those different times. The amount charged to depreciation expense would be, in consequence, a mixture of different-valued dollars. To a lesser extent, all this may apply to shorter-term assets whose costs become expenses within a shorter period of time; for example, inventories. Another point is that the dollars of revenue for a single period generally represent similar purchasing power, while the dollars of expense deducted may be a diverse mixture.

Awareness of the limitations of the monetary unit as a measuring device is not lacking. Accounting reports necessarily are limited in scope by the use of the monetary measure. Such matters as competitive advantage or disadvantage, employee attitudes, management talents, and working conditions often cannot be stated adequately in dollar terms. Accountants simply feel that the interpretation of the effects of any changes in the value of money should be made by the users of the accounting reports rather than by the accountants.

The effects of the instability of the dollar on accounting reports may be illustrated as follows. Assume that a business bought equipment for $50,000 ten years ago and it now costs $100,000 to replace the equipment because inflation has cut the value of the dollar in half during the ten-year period. If the old equipment is fully depreciated and the net income of the business over the ten-year period was equal to $50,000, this implies that the cost of the old equipment has been recovered and the firm has had a profit of $50,000. However, the firm has not really had a profit at all, because it will require both the recovered cost of the old equipment ($50,000) and the $50,000 of reported net income to purchase the new equipment for $100,000. Thus, the reported net income might be viewed as a mirage.

The monetary unit concept continues to be accepted, because money is still a common ingredient of all business transactions and does provide a practical measurement unit capable of lending objectivity and uniformity to financial data. Nevertheless, there is a growing interest in reporting accounting information either adjusted for general price level changes or in terms of replacement costs.

Transaction-Based Records and Historical Cost

Fundamental to business accounting is the idea that there is nothing to account for until a transaction occurs. Closely allied to this notion is the requirement that the amount to be entered when the transaction involves the acquisition of an asset is the acquisition cost, or historical cost, of that asset. The historical cost concept holds that, generally, no adjustment will be made to this amount in later periods, except to allocate the original cost of the asset to periodic expense as the asset is consumed.

Accountants do not deny that changes in the values of assets occur over time. Rather, accountants generally insist on objective, verifiable evidence before they are willing to enter information in the accounts. (Objective, verifiable evidence is discussed in a later section of this chapter.) Differences between the historical cost of a business's assets and the various market values of those assets that may exist at some later date may be difficult to measure and may never materialize. Consequently, accountants are reluctant to enter such value changes in the accounts. In contrast, when a transaction occurs, the objective, verifiable evidence that the accountant seeks becomes available. Add to this the application of the realization concept discussed in the next section and the case for transaction-based historical cost accounting gains strength.

Periodicity, Realization, and Matching

Central to business accounting is the concept that income determination may be made on a periodic basis, known as the periodicity concept. This means that income should always be determined annually, and in addition, sometimes for shorter periods, such as quarterly or monthly. Any period shorter than a year is described as an interim period. The requirement that income be determined on a periodic basis causes most of the problems associated with income measurement.

In order to determine income on a periodic basis, the accountant must decide when to recognize revenue and expenses. Revenue is recognized in accordance with the realization concept. Revenue generally is considered to be realized when there is a receipt of cash or a claim to cash in exchange for goods or services. For example, a car is taken to a service station for a tankful of gasoline (goods) and a car wash (services). The dealer may either receive cash or allow the use of a credit card (a claim to cash) in settlement. In either event, the dealer is considered to have realized revenue, even though the use of the credit card would create an account receivable on the dealer's books.

Once a decision is made regarding when to recognize revenue (using the realization concept), the expenses must next be recognized in accordance with the matching concept. The matching concept means that expenses incurred to generate particular revenues should be matched with those revenues that they helped to generate. For example, if the dealer in the previous example recorded the sale of gasoline, the cost of the gasoline sold should be matched against the revenue realized from the sale. Uncollectible accounts receivable represent a potential problem if revenue is considered realized when a claim to cash is created. The usual solution is the periodic estimation of uncollectible accounts expense, which then becomes part of the income calculation for the same period in which the receivables were recorded.

It is in attempting to perform the matching process that the periodic-income-determination requirement poses the largest problem. Two outstanding examples of expense-matching problems are: (1) the apportionment of merchandise cost between cost of goods sold and end-of-period inventory, where specific identification of the units sold is not possible, and (2) the allocation of the cost of most long-term assets by means of depreciation, depletion, or amortization. Considerable judgment and estimation are necessary in each of these cases. Nonetheless, the matching of revenues and expenses is a fundamental part of the accrual accounting process.

The Accrual Basis

According to the accrual basis concept, revenue is recognized in the accounting period in which it is earned, and expenses are recognized in the accounting period in which they are incurred, regardless of whether the receipt or disbursement of cash takes place in the same period. Revenue is recognized when money or a legal claim to money is obtained in exchange for something of value. Revenue accrues when an inflow of assets causes an increase in owner's equity other than from an investment of assets in the business by the owner. Expense accrues when an asset outflow or an additional liability causes owner's equity to decrease other than from a withdrawal of assets by the owner or owners.

The accrual basis of accounting involves the periodic matching of revenue with the expenses related to its realization. Revenue from sales must be matched with the cost of goods sold and the various other expenses incidental to conducting a business. The simple matching of cash receipts for a particular period with the cash paid for goods or services acquired in that period is meaningless for the most part. Collections may relate to sales of the current period and payments may relate to purchases during a previous period or vice versa. The expenses related to most long-term assets occur as the property loses its usefulness. The accrual basis recognizes changes in a variety of assets and liabilities in determining periodic net income—not just cash changes.

It is the combined effect of the realization and matching concepts coupled with the accrual basis concept, that provides some assurance that income is accurately measured and reported each period.

BUILDING YOUR ACCOUNTING KNOWLEDGE

1. Does the business entity concept identify only the legal property and legal debts of the business enterprise or may it be broader than this? Discuss.
2. What attribute of corporations supports the going-concern concept? What experiences of proprietors and partners support it?
3. Since the realities of the economic world do not fully support the going-concern concept, how is it justified by accountants? Discuss.
4. How do accountants justify the use of the monetary unit as a measuring device?
5. How is the historical cost concept related to transaction-based records?
6. How do the realization and matching concepts relate to the periodicity concept? Give two examples of this relationship.
7. When is revenue considered to be earned on the accrual basis? When is expense considered to be incurred on this basis?
8. What problems are created by a simple matching of cash received from customers during an accounting period with the cash paid for goods or services purchased in that same period?

APPLYING ACCOUNTING CONCEPTS

Exercise 15-1. J. Seary, who owns and operates J. S. Lock Service, engaged in the following transactions during the past month.

1. Received $85 for repairing lock on customer safe.
2. Paid $62 shop electric bill.
3. Paid $37 dental bill for daughter.
4. Received $140 for installing new bolt locks on customer doors.
5. Received $67 from sale of son's bicycle.
6. Paid $70 for cleaning service at shop.

Prepare two-column journal entries for each of the above transactions that should be considered part of J.S. Lock Service operations.

Exercise 15-2. K. Pearson purchased new office equipment for $3,000. The equipment is expected to last 10 years and have no salvage value. Pearson plans to sell the business in which the equipment is used in three years.

Compute the appropriate depreciation expense for the equipment for the first year of use, using the straight-line method.

Exercise 15-3. Prepare appropriate two-column journal entries for each of the following events and transactions that should be reflected in the accounting records.

1. Purchased manufacturing equipment for $3,400 on account.
2. Purchased merchandise for $1,550 cash.
3. Determined that the equipment in transaction (1) could now be purchased for $2,900.
4. Determined that the merchandise in transaction (2) could now be sold for $1,875.
5. Sold the merchandise in transaction (2) for $1,840 cash.

Exercise 15-4. U. Trust, who runs a car lot, engaged in the following transactions:

1. Acquired a used Mustang at auction for $3,100.
2. Acquired a used Omega at auction for $3,750.
3. Sold the Mustang for $4,050.
4. Acquired a used Dodge at auction for $2,940.
5. Sold the Omega for $4,800.
6. Paid lot rental and utilities of $360.

(a) Compute the amount of gross margin on the sale of the Mustang. **(b)** Compute the amount of the gross margin on the sale of the Omega. **(c)** Compute the net income from operating the lot during this time period.

**Report
No. 15-1**

Complete Report No. 15-1 in the study assignments and submit your working papers to the instructor for approval. Then continue with the textbook discussion until Report No. 15-2 is required.

ACCEPTED ACCOUNTING PRACTICES

In an attempt to serve the interests of various groups of people concerned with business affairs as reported in periodic financial statements, several practices have become widely accepted in the accounting profession. Some of these practices have grown out of the concepts that have been discussed. Others are intended to help make accounting reports easier to understand. Many involve a compromise between partially-conflicting objectives. Six of the most important of these practices are discussed in the paragraphs that follow.

Consistency and Comparability

It has already been noted that the problems posed by the periodicity and matching concepts (which are fundamental to business accounting) preclude the attainment of absolute accuracy in the calculation of periodic income. Nevertheless, the users of financial statements invariably want to make comparisons between current and past results. This combination of circumstances makes it necessary to have a degree of consistency (e.g., the use of the same inventory or depreciation method from period to period) in accounting methods which makes comparability (the ability to identify similarities and differences in performance) between periods possible. One example of this need is found in the choice of an accounting method for merchandise inventory. Regardless of whether fifo or lifo is considered best, it is not difficult to imagine the possible consequence of switching from one to the other each year. This switching might make any comparison of the results of operations for several years almost meaningless. Frequent changes of the depreciation method could produce a similar undesirable result. Stated loosely, the rule is: "If you cannot be completely certain of your choice of method, at least use it consistently."

The consistency practice must not be carried to such an extreme that it is taken to mean that a method of accounting once adopted must never be changed. Changing circumstances may require a change in accounting method, but it is not expected that numerous and substantial changes will be needed each year. When important changes are made, it is essential that the financial statements clearly indicate (by footnote or otherwise) the changes made and the reasons therefor. Sometimes data are included in the explanation to show what the result might have been if the change had not been made. The act of providing an explanation of what was done, and why, is an example of compliance with the practice of adequate disclosure.

Adequate Disclosure

For at least the following three reasons, the practice of adequate disclosure must be followed in the preparation of accounting reports:

1. Financial statement users want to know which of the various generally accepted accounting principles and practices have been used.
2. There is a danger that significant facts about what has taken place during the period under review will somehow get "buried" among all the other information that the report contains or else remain undisclosed.
3. There has been an increasing demand from users of financial reports for more information about the business.

To meet the adequate disclosure requirement, a number of procedures have evolved. The use of explanatory notes, either in the body of financial statements or as footnotes, has become widespread. (Mention was made in the previous section of the importance of disclosing any important changes in the use of an accounting method.) What is termed the "all inclusive" type of income statement has become widely used. Such a statement not only shows the composition of the income (loss) from regular operations for the period, but, in addition, any unusual gains or losses that have occurred.

The annual reports of large corporations often include an assortment of tables and graphs intended to emphasize significant trends in their corporate business affairs. Often statistical data of a nonfinancial nature are included, such as the number of employees or the number of units produced. Annual reports of this type always include a message from the company president or board chairperson that draws attention to important things that happened during the year, including any major changes in management personnel and a general forecast for the year or years ahead.

In the interest of adequate disclosure, multiproduct-line companies are now required to provide information about major segments or product lines of the business by both the Securities and Exchange Commission and the Federal Trade Commission. It has also been proposed that annual reports should include a financial budget (forecast) so that interested parties can have an idea of "what's coming." Professional ethics rules prohibit auditors from vouching for the achievability of forecast data, although there is no rule against vouching for the basic assumptions and calculations involved. However, a published forecast might reveal information useful to competitors, and since the reported plans may not work out, many business managers and accountants fear that such a procedure might do more harm than good. Just how far adequate disclosure should go is an unsettled issue. Nevertheless, the inclusion of forecast data in published annual reports is increasing.

Objectivity and Verifiability

Data that are entered in the accounting records and later reported in the financial statements of a business generally should be supported by source documents or other records that are both objective and verifiable forms of evidence that certain transactions occurred. This is the practice of objectivity and verifiability. Sales tickets, purchase invoices, and employee paychecks are examples of source documents that provide objective evidential matter. When evidence is not completely objective, as in the case of doubtful accounts receivable or long-term asset depreciation, the most objective evidence available should be used. Records of past experience in collecting accounts receivable are an example of objective evidence for entering doubtful accounts expense.

The notion of objectivity is that such source documents or records of past experience provide unbiased, factual evidence of real transactions and events that have occurred. The notion of verifiability is that any two accountants looking independently at the same evidence probably would make the related entry in the same way.

Materiality and Practicality

In the field of law, there is a maxim of *de minimis non curat lex,* which means that the law is not concerned with trifles. The same can be said of accounting. In accounting, what is called the practice of materiality and practicality means that the concepts of accrual accounting need not be followed in the case of amounts that are too small to make any real difference. For example, even though a waste basket that cost $5 may be expected to be useful for many years, it is not necessary to account for it as an asset to be depreciated. Simply treat the expenditure as, perhaps, miscellaneous expense. It is an almost universal practice for each business to establish some "cut-off point" that the accountant should follow in entering such expenditures. In the case of a small business, the point might be $25 or $50; larger businesses may have a higher limit. Consistency of treatment is, of course, necessary.

In the handling of certain year-end adjustments, the amount involved may dictate whether an adjustment should be made. For example, it may be unnecessary to bother with accrued interest payable or receivable in the amount of $2.65 or to enter the fact that $15 of the supplies expense account balance (amounting to more than $400) actually relates to supplies that are still on hand.

Probably the most important application of the practice of materiality is in connection with the financial statements. Adequate disclosure does not require that a petty cash fund of $100 be shown by itself rather than being lumped together with cash in bank, or that the detail be shown for prepaid expenses whose total is equal to one percent of total assets. In fact, the interests of adequate disclosure are best served by preparing financial statements and schedules that are not so filled with detail that the significant matters may be obscured.

Another widespread practice that is followed in the interest of eliminating the immaterial aspects of financial statements is to eliminate cents; instead, each amount is rounded to the nearest dollar. In fact, the financial statements of very large companies frequently show amounts rounded to the nearest $1,000.

Conservatism

The customs, concepts, and conventions of modern business accounting involve a tendency (some say a bias) toward conservatism. Generally, this means that when two or more acceptable ways of allocating the cost of an asset between benefiting periods can be used, the one that causes reported assets and periodic income to be smaller usually is chosen. The widely-used "cost or market, whichever is lower" method for assigning a value to the end-of-period merchandise inventory will cause both the inventory and the income for the period just ended to be smaller than otherwise. As applied to depreciation, if equally good reasons exist to use either a ten-year or a twelve-year estimated life for a depreciable asset, most accountants would use the shorter life. For the years the asset is used, both the income of each of the periods and the undepreciated cost of the asset at the end of each period will be smaller than if the longer life were used. When the question arises whether to charge the total cost of an item to expense immediately or to treat it as an asset to be amortized, the "expense-it-now" option usually is followed.

Probably the most all-encompassing example of the practice of conservatism stems from the historical-cost and realization concepts, which do not permit "writing up" assets even if they are thought at a later date to be worth more than the accounts show. Some accountants contend that refusing to show current or present values for all assets causes many balance sheets to be almost worthless. However, if such write-ups were to become accepted practice, either accountants would have to be trained as appraisers or appraisers would have to be employed. It is questionable whether the values thus determined would qualify as objective, verifiable evidence. Historical costs, generally, do meet this test. Further, either the amount of the write-up would have to be considered as revenue even though there were no inflows of cash or receivables (or other assets), or provision would have to be made in the accounts for unrealized revenue. In the opinion of many accountants and business executives, so-called unrealized revenue is not revenue at all.

The conservatism practice is thought to have become deeply imbedded in accounting for two major reasons: (1) If unquestioned absolute accuracy in accounting is not possible, there is probably less danger of damaging the interests of existing and prospective owners and creditors by following conservative practices. (2) Conservative accounting practices lead to lower reported income for tax purposes and therefore lower taxes. Income tax laws do not require that most items be handled in the same way for tax purposes as they are in the accounts, but businesses typically find it easier to account for their activities in the same way for financial reporting purposes as for tax purposes. Further, a tax approach is easier to defend if it corresponds to what is done in the accounts.

Legality

Accounting records and reports must conform with certain legal requirements, such as tax regulations, contract provisions, and state incorporation laws, that relate to specific business transactions. This is the practice of legality. For example, it is illegal to evade taxes or reduce the required tax payments by ignoring or flaunting the law. It is also illegal to fail or refuse to enter payroll tax deductions when keeping employee payroll records. The structure of the equity section of a corporation balance sheet often is affected by the laws of the state in which the firm is incorporated. In addition, the ability of a corporation to pay dividends can be determined by state incorporation laws. The accounting system must be maintained in such a way that compliance with applicable laws can be determined.

BUILDING YOUR ACCOUNTING KNOWLEDGE

1. Why are consistency and comparability closely associated in business accounting?
2. If an important change in accounting method takes place, how should it be indicated to users of financial statements?
3. Give three reasons for observing the practice of adequate disclosure.

4. What attributes make source documents both objective and verifiable?
5. Explain why materiality is closely associated with practicality.
6. What is the relationship between materiality and adequate disclosure?
7. Give three examples of the application of the practice of conservatism.
8. Give two examples of legal requirements to which accounting records and reports must conform.

APPLYING ACCOUNTING CONCEPTS

Exercise 15-5. Massage Co. is considering making three accounting changes in the current year.

1. From FIFO to LIFO inventory. FIFO inventory cost is $7,000, whereas LIFO inventory cost would be $5,200.
2. From straight-line to declining-balance depreciation. Straight-line depreciation is $6,600, whereas declining-balance depreciation would be $8,900.
3. From amortizing goodwill over 12 years to amortizing it over 5 years. Goodwill amortization on a 12-year basis is $2,000, whereas on a 5-year basis it would be $4,800.

If Massage Co's net income for the year is $12,300 based on FIFO inventory, straight-line depreciation, and 12-year goodwill amortization, compute the net income if all three accounting changes are made.

Exercise 15-6. Matty Co. reported net income of $38,000 for the current year. In reviewing Matty's records, you discover the following items for which no adjustments were made at the end of the period.

1. Supplies of $27 were on hand.
2. Interest revenue of $5 had accrued for four days on a note receivable.
3. Delivery charges of $13 on packages received in the current period were not entered until paid in the following period.
4. Petty cash expenditures of $7 were not entered because reimbursement of petty cash was not made at the end of the period.
5. Interest expense of $10 had accrued for six days on a note payable.

(a) Compute the net income of Matty Co. for the year if adjustment were made for these items. **(b)** What accounting practice would support Matty's not making these adjustments?

**Report
No. 15-2**

Complete Report No. 15-2 in the study assignments and submit your working papers for approval. Then continue with the textbook discussion in Chapter 16 until Report No. 16-1 is required.

EXPANDING YOUR BUSINESS VOCABULARY

What is the meaning of each of the following terms?

accrual basis concept **(p. 461)**

adequate disclosure **(p. 464)**

concept of continuity **(p. 458)**

conservatism **(p. 467)**

consistency and comparability
  (p. 464)

consolidated balance sheet
  (p. 458)

consolidated income statement
  (p. 458)

entity concept **(p. 457)**

going-concern concept **(p. 458)**

historical cost concept **(p. 460)**

interim period **(p. 461)**

legality **(p. 468)**

matching concept **(p. 461)**

materiality and practicality
  (p. 466)

monetary unit concept **(p. 459)**

objectivity **(p. 466)**

periodicity concept **(p. 460)**

realization concept **(p. 461)**

unrealized revenue **(p. 468)**

verifiability **(p. 466)**

CHAPTERS 11-15

Supplementary Practical Accounting Problems

PROBLEM 11-A Notes receivable register

Ann Allen is a dealer in paintings and framing materials. In accounting for notes received from customers in return for extensions of time in paying their obligations, Allen uses a notes receivable register similar to the one reproduced on pages 350 and 351. Following is a narrative of transactions involving notes received from customers during the current year.

Mar. 6 Received from Frank Soambee a 60-day, 12% note (No. 1) for $850 dated March 5, and payable at First National Bank, Willow Brook.

Apr. 27 Received from John Henry a 90-day, 10% note (No. 2) for $900 dated April 26, and payable at Second National Bank, Mayfield.

May 4 Received a check for $867.00 in payment for Frank Soambee's note due today plus interest.

20 Received from Knapp Logger a 60-day, 13% note (No. 3) for $1,200 dated May 19, and payable at Northern Trust Company, Park Ridge.

July 18 Received a check for $1,226.00 in payment for Knapp Logger's note due today plus interest.

25 Received a check for $922.50 in payment for John Henry's note due today plus interest.

Sept. 8 Received from Earl Fishhead a 90-day, 11% note (No. 4) for $800 dated September 7, and payable at Monroe State Bank, Monroe.

Dec. 6 Received a check from Monroe State Bank for $812.00 in payment of the note due yesterday plus interest less a $10 collection charge.

Required: (1) Prepare entries in two-column journal form for the transactions. Foot the amount columns as a means of proof. (2) Make the required entries in a notes receivable register similar to the one reproduced on pages 350 and 351, to provide a detailed auxiliary record of the notes received by Allen.

PROBLEM 11-B   Notes payable

Denton Fenders operates a department store. Sometimes, Fenders finds it necessary to issue notes to suppliers to obtain extensions of time for payment of accounts. Unless otherwise stated, all notes are made payable to the Brown County Bank, Newburg. Following is a narrative of transactions involving notes issued by Fenders during the current year:

Feb.   3   Borrowed $1,500 from the bank on a 90-day, 11% note (No. 1).

Mar. 10   Issued a 60-day, 9% note (No. 2) for $660 to Budd & Decker Co.

Apr. 15   Issued a 60-day, 13% note (No. 3) for $1,000 to R. U. Irish & Co.

May   4   Issued a check for $1,541.25 to the bank in payment of note due today plus interest.

       9   Gave Budd & Decker Co. a check for $9.90 in payment of the interest due today and a new note (No. 4), for $660, due in 60 days, with interest at 9%, in settlement of the note due today.

June 14   Issued a check for $1,021.67 to R.U. Irish & Co. in payment of note due today plus interest.

July   1   Borrowed $5,000 from the bank on a 90-day, 13% note (No. 5).

       8   Issued a check for $669.90 to Budd & Decker Co. in payment of note due today plus interest.

Sept. 29   Gave Brown County Bank a check for $162.50 in payment of the interest due today and a new note (No.6) for $5,000.00, due in 60 days with interest at 13%, in settlement of the note due today.

Nov. 28   Issued a check for $5,108.33 to the bank in payment of note due today plus interest.

Required: (1) Prepare entries in two-column journal form for the transactions. Foot the amount columns as a means of proof. (2) Make the required entries in a notes payable register similar to the one reproduced on pages 356 and 357, to provide a detailed auxiliary record of the notes issued.

PROBLEM 12-A Application of fifo, weighted average, and lifo methods

The Earthbound Company is in the wholesale hardware business. Stock record cards are kept of all merchandise handled. The data with respect to Article X were assembled from the stock record cards and appeared as follows.

On hand at beginning of period............ 760 units
First purchase during period.............. 850 units @ $42
Second purchase during period........... 800 units @ $50
Last purchase during period.............. 900 units @ $48
In stock at end of period .... 750 units

Earthbound Company had sales of $173,000 during the period.

Assume that the units in stock at the beginning of the period were assigned a cost of $41 each under the fifo method, $39 each under the weighted average method, and $37 each under the lifo method.

Required: Compute ending inventory, cost of goods sold, and gross margin under (1) the fifo method, (2) the weighted average method, and (3) the lifo method of cost assignment. (Carry the weighted average unit cost to four decimal places.)

PROBLEM 12-B Application of the lower of cost or market rule

Stanfield Distributors has four items in its ending inventory: Products W, X, Y, and Z. The quantities, costs, and market values of these items are given below:

Product	Quantity	Cost	Market
W	311	$12	$13
X	429	15	13
Y	223	18	19
Z	489	17	16

Assume that Stanfield uses the fifo lower of cost or market method of cost assignment.

Required: Calculate the dollar amount of ending inventory by applying the lower of cost or market rule to: (1) the total inventory, and (2) each item in the inventory.

PROBLEM 12-C   Postage account

Watkins & Sinclair is a mail-order house. Metered postage is used on parcel post packages. Deposits are made for postage under the postal permit system. Postage stamps are purchased for other purposes. All prepaid postage is charged to Postage, Account No. 154, and periodically the postage used is charged to the following expense accounts:

> 557   Freight Out (Parcel Post)
> 558   Advertising Postage Expense
> 559   General Postage Expense

During the month of June, the postage used on parcel post packages amounted to $1,039, and on advertising matter, $516. On June 30, the unused stamps on hand amounted to $116, and the unused metered postage amounted to $437.

Required: (1) Open the necessary accounts and enter the debit balance of the postage account before adjustment, $2,432. (2) Make the required adjusting entry in general journal form for all postage expense for the month. (3) Post the entry to the appropriate accounts.

PROBLEM 13-A   Depreciation of long-term assets; trade in

On February 1, 19A Simonis & Kosiba, a partnership, began the wholesale distribution of heating equipment. In accounting for their long-term assets, the following accounts are used:

> 171   Office Equipment
> 171.1   Accumulated Depreciation—Office Equipment
> 181   Store Equipment
> 181.1   Accumulated Depreciation—Store Equipment
> 183   Delivery Equipment
> 183.1   Accumulated Depreciation—Delivery Equipment
> 218   Accounts Payable
> 547   Depreciation Expense—Office Equipment
> 554   Depreciation Expense—Store Equipment
> 555   Depreciation Expense—Delivery Equipment

The following is a narrative of transactions involving the purchase of long-term assets during the year ended December 31, 19A:

Feb. 12   Invoice No. 218—Purchased cabinet file for office use on account from The Ironcase Co., $490; estimated useful life, 10 years; estimated trade-in value at end of 10 years, $70.

Mar. 7   Invoice No. 232—Purchased a small truck for delivery purposes on account from Mercurial Motors, Inc., $7,200; estimated useful life, 4 years; estimated trade-in value at end of 4 years, $900.

Apr. 18   Invoice No. 239—Purchased an office table on account from The City Furniture Co., $360; estimated useful life, 20 years; no salvage value.

July 2   Invoice No. 274—Purchased showcases on account from Campbell Co., $600; estimated useful life, 15 years; no salvage value.

Aug. 28   Invoice No. 291—Purchased used double-pedestal desk for use in storeroom on account from Harper Store Equipment Co., $280; estimated useful life, 20 years; no salvage value.

Sept. 9   Invoice No. 312—Purchased used Magic-write typewriter, No. 5837852-11 on account from Magic Corporation, $375; estimated useful life, 5 years; estimated trade-in value at end of 5 years, $75.

On February 7, 19C, after entering twenty-three months' depreciation, the delivery truck purchased on March 7, 19A, was traded in for a new truck with a market value of $7,900, and $4,000 in cash also was paid.

Required: (1) Enter the foregoing transactions in proper two-column journal form. (2) Foot the amount columns. (3) Determine the annual rate of depreciation (straight-line method) applicable to the net cost of each of the long-term assets purchased, compute the amount of depreciation accumulated during the current year ended December 31, 19A, and prepare an entry in two-column journal form for the depreciation. Depreciation is taken for a full month on assets purchased by the 15th of a month. (4) Prepare a two-column journal entry for the transaction on February 7, 19C. Recognize the gain or loss, if appropriate, for financial accounting purposes.

PROBLEM 13-B   Wasting asset—depletion and sale

Graves Enterprises, Inc., owns a gravel pit that was purchased a few years before for $150,000. Depletion has been calculated on the basis of 20 cents for every cubic yard of gravel excavated. At the beginning of the current year, the balance of the accumulated depletion account was $9,350. During the first four months of this year, 19A, 60,000 cubic yards of gravel were excavated, and on May 2, 19A the pit was sold for $140,000 cash.

Required: Prepare entries in general journal form, for (1) the depletion accumulated for the first four months of the year, and (2) the sale of the gravel pit, recognizing any gain or loss on the sale.

PROBLEM 14-A Voucher register; check register; schedule of unpaid vouchers

Voltaic Electronics, a business just organized, uses a voucher register and a check register similar to those shown on pages 432 and 436.

Vouchers were entered using the gross-price basis. Checks were issued in payment of any invoices subject to discount on the day preceding the last day of the discount period.

The narrative of transactions of the month is as follows:

Oct. 3 Issued Voucher No. 1 for $200 to establish a petty cash fund and cashed Check No. 1 for that amount. (Petty Cash Fund, Account No. 112.)

3 Received an invoice for $695 from the Multnomah Real Estate Co. for rent. Issued Check No. 2 in payment of the invoice. (Rent Expense, Account No. 5443.)

4 Received an invoice for $2,193.75 from the Earblast Radio-Stereo Manufacturers, Inc., for merchandise. Date of invoice, September 29; terms, 1/10, n/30.

5 Received an invoice for $479 from Sturdee Equipment Co. for an office desk purchased. Date of invoice, October 3; terms, net 30 days. (Office Equipment, Account No. 191.)

6 Received a bill for telephone service from the Monopoly Telephone Co. and issued Check No. 3 for $27.80 in payment. (General Office Expense, Account No. 5418.)

Oct. 7 Received a bill for office supplies from Paper Chase Co. and issued Check No. 4 for $73.50 in payment. (Office Supplies, Account No. 152.)

8 Received an invoice for $894.50 from the Trendy Corporation for a shipment of merchandise. Date of invoice, October 6; terms, 2/15, n/60.

12 Received an invoice for $543.50 from the Radunn Advertising Agency for advertising service. Issued Check No. 6 in payment. (Advertising Expense, Account No. 5433.)

13 Received an invoice for $92.50 from the AllLand Insurance Co. for insurance. Issued Check No. 7 in payment. (Prepaid Insurance, Account No.155.)

14 Received an invoice for $2,197.25 from the Dundee Manufacturing Co. for a shipment of radio parts. Date of invoice, October 11; terms, 1/10, n/30.

15 Issued Payroll Voucher No. 11 covering wages earned for the half month as follows:

> Warehouse salaries,$1,350.00
> Delivery salaries, $170.00
> Office salaries, $1,100.00
> Sales salaries, $1,010.00
>
> Taxes withheld:
>   FICA tax, $243.00
>   Employees' income tax, $768.50

Issued Check No. 8 in payment of Payroll Voucher No. 11. The following accounts will be affected in entering the payroll:

> 111   Cash
> 211   FICA Tax Payable
> 214   Employees' Income Tax Payable
> 218   Vouchers Payable
> 5401 Office Salaries Expense
> 5431 Sales Salaries Expense
> 5432 Delivery Salaries Expense
> 5439 Warehouse Salaries Expense

17 Issued a voucher for $100 to be used in purchasing stamps for the office. Cashed Check No. 9 for this amount and obtained the stamps. (Charge to Office Supplies, Account No.152.)

19 Received from the Last National Bank a notice of the maturity of a $1,500 non-interest-bearing note dated

September 30 due them. Issued Check No. 10 for that amount. (Notes Payable, Account No. 216.)

Oct. 20 Received an invoice from Toolers for $81.19, the cost of repairs on warehouse machinery. Issued Check No. 11 in payment. (Repairs, Account No. 5442.)

21 Received an invoice for $1,540.30 from Ultimate Radio & TV for a shipment of merchandise. Date of invoice, October 20; terms, 1/10, n/30.

24 Received an invoice for $219.00 for warehouse supplies purchased from the Central Container Co.; terms, on account. (Warehouse Supplies, Account No. 153.)

26 Received an invoice from Nuland Lifts for $10,279, the cost of a lift truck for use in the warehouse. Terms, net 30 days. (Warehouse Equipment, Account No. 182.)

28 Received an invoice for $1,160.00 from the Private Electric Co. for a shipment of merchandise. Date of invoice, October 27; terms, 2/10, n/30.

31 Issued Payroll Voucher No. 19 covering wages earned for the half month as follows:

> Warehouse Salaries, $1,300.00
> Delivery Salaries, $170.00
> Office Salaries, $1,050.00
> Sales Salaries, $1,070.00
>
> Taxes withheld:
> FICA Tax, $240.53
> Employees' Income Tax, $770.15

Issued Check No. 15 in payment of Payroll Voucher No. 19.

Required: (1) Enter the foregoing transactions in the voucher register and check register. (2) Foot and prove the footings of both the voucher register and the check register. (3) Open an account for vouchers payable and post to it the footings of the Vouchers Payable columns in the voucher register and the check register. Use a T form of account. (4) Prove the balance of the vouchers payable account by preparing a schedule of the unpaid vouchers from the voucher register.

PROBLEM 14-B Cash sales and sales on account

Linda Fergy is the owner of a radio, television, and stereo equipment store. Following is a list of the general ledger accounts that are affected by this problem with the September 1 balances indicated:

111   Cash, $2,937.80
131   Accounts Receivable, $4,194.67
411   Sales, $30,657.18

As of September 1, the accounts receivable had debit balances as follows:

Hank Thun, 1512 Blackburn St., Wheaton; $583.22
Allen Gist, 1586 Briarcliffe Blvd., Lombard; $1,093.44
Ursula Flitner, 122 Main St., Wheaton; $1,215.67
Tim Gulstrom, 655 Roosevelt Rd., Glen Ellyn; $659.18
Pat Guhin, 542 Kenilworth, Batavia; $643.16

The narrative of September sales and collections transactions is as follows:

Sept. 1 (Wednesday) Charge sale No. 362, Tim Gulstrom, $408.
       3 Cash sales of $512.
       4 Collected $1,215.67 on account from Ursula Flitner.
       6 Charge sale No. 363, Hank Thun, $167.
       8 Collected $659.18 on account from Tim Gulstrom.
      10 Charge sale No. 364, Allen Gist, $830.
      11 Cash sales of $434.
      14 Cash sales of $618.
      16 Collected $583.22 on account from Hank Thun.
      18 Charge sale No. 365, Pat Guhin, $188.
      20 Collected $1,093.44 on account from Allen Gist.
      22 Cash sales of $294.
      24 Charge sale No. 366, Ursula Flitner, $167.
      25 Cash sales of $609.
      27 Collected $643.16 on account from Pat Guhin.
      29 Charge sale No. 367, Tim Gulstrom, $544.

Required: (1) Open the necessary general ledger accounts and enter the September 1 balances, using four-column ledger paper. (2) Open the accounts receivable ledger and enter the September 1 balances, using three-column ledger paper. (3) Enter the charge sales for September and post directly to the proper customers' accounts, using a sales journal similar to the one reproduced on page 447. (4) Enter the cash sales and collections on account for September and post the collections directly to the proper customers' accounts, using a cash receipts journal similar to the one reproduced on page 452. (5) Foot, prove the footings, enter the totals, and rule the sales journal and the cash receipts journal. Complete the summary posting and update the account balances. (6) Prove the balance of the accounts receivable account by preparing a schedule of the accounts receivable as of September 30.

PROBLEM 15-A   The business entity

Ward's Bakery, owned and operated by Lew D. Ward, is in the process of separating the assets and liabilities of the business enterprise from Ward's personal assets and liabilities as of December 31, 19--. Ward has solicited your help.

The list of assets, liabilities, income, and withdrawals is given below:

Cash in bank (Lyon National Bank) for business affairs	$13,950
Cash in bank (Washington Bank) for personal affairs	26,870
Accounts receivable owed to Ward's Bakery	18,470
Allowance for doubtful accounts on Ward's Bakery accounts receivable	795
Merchandise inventory of Ward's Bakery	68,440
Prepaid insurance:	
Lew D. Ward	400
Ward's Bakery	350
Supplies:	
Ward's Bakery	90
Lew D. Ward	115
Store equipment	9,900
Accumulated depreciation on store equipment	4,400
Delivery truck used by the business	9,500
Accumulated depreciation on delivery truck	3,500
Automobile for personal use	8,200
Store building owned as a personal asset (net)	12,600
Real estate investment owned by Ward	7,400
Notes payable to outsiders by Ward	2,000
Notes payable to outsiders by Ward's Bakery	4,000
Accrued interest payable on notes:	
Ward's Bakery	50
Lew D. Ward	40
Accounts payable to outsiders by:	
Lew D. Ward	3,000
Ward's Bakery	10,115
Sales tax owed by bakery	1,865
Taxes payable withheld—Ward's Bakery	880
Notes receivable owed to Ward	3,000
Mortgage due on Ward's home	28,800
Net income of Ward's Bakery for 19--	29,900
Lew D. Ward's withdrawals for 19--	21,000

Required: From the above list (1) separate those items that clearly relate to Ward's Bakery, and prepare a balance sheet as of December 31, 19--, in report form. (2) The separation of business assets and liabilities from personal assets and liabilities is an adaptation of what accounting concept?

## CHAPTER 16

Accounting for Owner's Equity

CHAPTER OBJECTIVES

Careful study of this chapter should enable you to:

- Explain the characteristics, advantages, and disadvantages of the single proprietorship form of business operation, and to account for proprietary transactions.

- Explain the nature of a business partnership and its advantages and disadvantages.

- Explain the manner in which a partnership is formed, and to recognize a partnership agreement.

- Explain and prepare the accounting entries needed for:

    1. The formation of a partnership.
    2. The admission of a new partner, including the possible accounting for goodwill.
    3. The compensation of partners.
    4. The allocation of partnership profits and losses.
    5. The dissolution of a partnership.

- Prepare the owners' equity section of a partnership balance sheet.

- Explain the nature of business corporations and the accounting for corporate owners' (stockholders') equity, including:

    1. The advantages and major disadvantage of a private business corporation.
    2. The manner in which a corporation is organized.
    3. The nature of the ownership interest in a corporation and the nature of its operation.
    4. The preparation of the accounting entries peculiar to a business corporation.
    5. The preparation of the entries required for the incorporation of a single proprietorship and of a partnership.
    6. The preparation of the owners' equity section of a corporation balance sheet.

The accounting equation—ASSETS = LIABILITIES + OWN-ER'S EQUITY—reflects the fact that both outsiders and insiders have interests in the assets of a business. The claims of the outsiders are known as the liabilities of the business, while the interests of the insiders are known as the owners' or stockholders' equity in the assets of the business. Proper accounting for owners' equity in three types of business organizations will be discussed in this chapter: (1) the single proprietorship, (2) the partnership, and (3) the corporation. Whether an enterprise is operated by an individual as a single proprietorship, by two or more individuals as a partnership, or by stockholders through directors and officers as a corporation has little or no bearing on proper accounting procedure for entering routine transactions. However, there are significant differences in the owners' equity structures of these three types of businesses, and therefore differences in the accounting for and reporting of owners' or stockholders' equity transactions.

THE SINGLE PROPRIETORSHIP

A business that is owned and operated by one person is known as a single proprietorship. When there is only one owner, the amount of the owner's interest in the business is called owner's equity. Sometimes the designations net worth or capital are used.

In small merchandising enterprises and in personal service enterprises the single proprietorship form of organization predominates. The professions of medicine and dentistry, for example, are composed largely of individuals who are engaged in practice as sole owners. One reason for the popularity of the single proprietorship form of operation is that it is easily organized and does not involve formal legal agreement with others as to ownership or conduct. Anyone may engage in a lawful enterprise merely by complying with state and local laws.

Organization of a Single Proprietorship

When operating an enterprise as a sole owner, an individual decides the amount and the nature of the property that will be invested in the business. The original investment may consist of cash only, or of cash and any other property, such as merchandise, office equipment, store equipment, or delivery equipment. The property invested usually is segregated and accounted for separately from other property that may be owned by the proprietor, in accordance with the business entity concept. An individual may engage in more than one enterprise and may operate each enterprise separately as a single proprietorship. In such cases, it may be desirable to keep separate records of the activities of each enterprise.

In comparison with other forms of business organization, the single proprietorship offers certain advantages, such as:

1. Simplicity of organization.
2. Freedom of initiative and industry.
3. Minimizing of government reporting requirements.
4. Strengthening of incentive to individual effort.

The single proprietorship form of organization has some disadvantages, of which the following are the most significant:

1. The amount of available capital may be limited.
2. The amount of available credit may be restricted.
3. The proprietor has sole responsibility for all debts incurred.
4. The proprietor is legally obligated to assume all debts of the business as personal debts.

Accounting Procedure

The accounting procedure for handling the transactions uniquely related to a single proprietorship can be classified into six topics as follows:

1. Owner's equity accounts.
2. Opening entries.
3. Current period proprietary transactions.
4. Closing revenue, expense, and summary accounts.
5. Closing the owner's drawing account.
6. Owner's equity section of a single proprietorship balance sheet.

Owner's Equity Accounts. There are two types of owner's equity accounts: (1) permanent and (2) temporary.

In a single proprietorship, the owner's capital account is the only permanent owner's equity account. The account is usually given the name of the owner of the enterprise followed by "Capital" or "Proprietor."

The temporary owner's equity accounts are those in which increases and decreases in owner's equity arising from the transactions completed during an accounting period are entered, such as the owner's drawing or personal account and all of the revenue and expense accounts. At the end of each year, it is customary to close the temporary revenue and expense accounts by transferring their balances to one or more summary accounts. These summary accounts are then closed to the permanent owner's equity account. The owner's drawing account is also closed to the permanent owner's equity account.

Opening Entries. An individual may invest cash and other property in a single proprietorship enterprise. If the investment consists solely of cash, the opening entry will involve a debit to Cash and a credit to the owner's capital account for the amount invested.

If cash and other property, such as office equipment or store equipment are invested, the opening entry will involve a debit to Cash for the amount of the cash invested, debits to appropriate equipment accounts for the amounts of the other property invested, and a credit to the owner's capital account for the total amount of the investment.

If, at the time of organizing an enterprise, there are any liabilities applicable to the property invested, such as accounts payable, notes payable, or mortgages payable, the amounts of the liabilities should be credited to appropriate liability accounts and the owner's capital account should be credited only for the excess of the amount of the assets invested over the total amount of the liabilities.

For example, assume that Mary Roback starts a merchandising business by investing cash, $8,000, office equipment, $2,000, and store equipment, $1,500. Roback owes $600 on the office equipment. The opening entry in general journal form for the investment is:

Cash	8,000	
Office Equipment	2,000	
Store Equipment	1,500	
Accounts Payable		600
Mary Roback, Capital		10,900
Investment in business.		

Some small business enterprises start and operate with very few records. No journals or ledgers are used. Cash receipts and payments are kept on check stubs. The amounts of accounts receivable and payable can be found only by consulting files of uncollected charge-sales slips and unpaid bills. At the end of a period, various calculations relating to inventory, doubtful accounts, expired insurance, depreciation, and accruals are made in informal fashion and the several bits of information are pieced together to prepare an income statement and a balance sheet. These statements are often incorrect. Conditions and facts may have been overlooked. Business papers may have been lost. The absence of double-entry records means that one method of verifying the mathematical accuracy of the assembled figures is not available.

While such informal accounting practices may barely suffice when the enterprise is small and transactions are few, the time will come when a formal accounting information system is needed. To start such a system, it is necessary to prepare a balance sheet from the information at hand and to use this as a basis for an opening journal entry for the assets, liabilities, and owner's equity of the enterprise.

For example, assume that H. A. Erk has been operating a business without any formal, double-entry accounting records. After several months, Erk decides that proper records are necessary. With the help of an accountant, the following balance sheet for the business is constructed. The information supplied by the balance sheet is used in preparing the general journal entry shown at the top of page 486.

H. A. ERK
Balance Sheet
December 31, 1986

Assets			Liabilities		
Cash		$ 4,550			
Accounts receivable	$ 7,200		Notes payable..........	$ 4,000	
Less allowance for			Accounts payable	5,800	
doubtful accounts	800	6,400	Total liabilities		$ 9,800
Merchandise inventory..		17,340			
Store equipment	$10,000		**Owner's Equity**		
Less accumulated			H.A. Erk, capital.......		27,490
depreciation	1,000	9,000	Total liabilities and		
Total assets...........		$37,290	owner's equity		$37,290

Jan. 2	Cash	4,550	
	Accounts Receivable	7,200	
	Merchandise Inventory	17,340	
	Store Equipment	10,000	
	Notes Payable		4,000
	Accounts Payable		5,800
	Allowance for Doubtful Accounts		800
	Accumulated Depreciation—Store Equipment		1,000
	H.A. Erk, Capital		27,490

After the necessary accounts in the general ledger have been opened, the debits and the credits of the opening journal entry are posted in the usual manner. Each asset account is debited and each liability account, the allowance for doubtful accounts, and accumulated depreciation are credited for the respective amounts shown in the balance sheet. Erk's capital account is credited for the equity in the business. In opening the accounts receivable ledger, the balances of the accounts with customers are entered directly from a schedule of accounts receivable. In opening the accounts payable ledger, the balances of the accounts with suppliers are entered directly from a schedule of accounts payable.

Current Period Proprietary Transactions. Certain types of transactions may be referred to as proprietary transactions because they affect either the owner's drawing account or the capital account. The following are typical proprietary transactions:

1. Periodic withdrawals of cash for personal use of owner.
2. Payment of owner's personal or family bills with business cash.
3. Withdrawal of cash or other assets by the owner intended as a partial liquidation of the business.
4. Investment of cash or other assets by owner intended as a permanent increase in assets and owner's equity.

Cash withdrawn periodically by the owner for personal use is charged to the owner's drawing or personal account on the assumption that such amounts represent withdrawals in anticipation of income. These withdrawals are sometimes regarded as salary or compensation for personal services rendered; however, they actually represent decreases in the owner's equity in the business and cannot be treated as operating expenses of the enterprise.

The payment of personal or family bills with business funds should be entered as a withdrawal of cash by the owner. It is quite common for a sole owner of a business or professional enterprise to pay all personal, family or household bills by issuing checks against the same bank account that is used for business expenditures of the enterprise. However, care should be used in entering all checks issued. Those representing personal or family expenditures should be charged to the owner's drawing or personal account. Those representing business expenditures should be charged to the proper expense, asset, or liability accounts.

An owner may, at any time, permanently withdraw a portion of the cash or other assets invested in the business, or make additional investments in the business in the form of cash or other property. Withdrawals are considered to be decreases in the permanent invested capital and should be charged to the capital account. Additional investments are considered to be increases in capital and should be credited to the capital account.

Closing Revenue, Expense, and Summary Accounts. At the end of each year, it is customary to close the temporary owner's equity accounts. As the temporary accounts are closed, their balances usually are transferred to an account entitled Expense and Revenue Summary.

In a merchandising enterprise, however, there also may be a summary account called Cost of Goods Sold. In the closing process, the cost of goods sold account is debited for (1) the amount of the merchandise inventory at the beginning of the year, and (2) the amount of the purchases for the year; it is credited for (1) the amount of purchases returns and allowances for the year, and (2) the amount of the merchandise inventory at the end of the year. After transferring these amounts, the balance of the account represents the cost of goods sold during the year, and it is in turn transferred to Expense and Revenue Summary. Note that this is a more indirect closing procedure than the approach using only the Expense and Revenue Summary that was discussed in Chapter 10.

The difference between the amount of debits and the amount of credits to the Expense and Revenue Summary represents the amount of the net income or the net loss for the year. If the summary account has a credit balance, it represents net income; if the account has a debit balance, it represents net loss. The balance of the expense and revenue summary account at the end of the accounting period is then transferred to the owner's capital account by means of a journal entry. If the expense and revenue summary account has a credit balance, the journal entry will involve a debit to Expense and Revenue Summary and a credit to the owner's capital account for the amount of the net income. If the summary account has a debit balance, the journal entry will involve a debit to the owner's capital account and a credit to Expense and Revenue Summary for the amount of the net loss.

Closing the Owner's Drawing Account. The owner's drawing account usually is closed at the end of each year by transferring its balance directly to the owner's capital account. The drawing account usually has a debit balance, and it may be closed by means of a journal entry debiting the owner's capital account and crediting the drawing account for the amount of its balance.

After transferring the balances of the expense and revenue summary account and the owner's drawing account to the owner's capital account, the balance of the owner's capital account represents the owner's equity in the enterprise at the end of the year.

Owner's Equity Section of a Single Proprietorship Balance Sheet. The method of exhibiting the owner's equity of a single proprietorship in the balance sheet is shown on pages 11, 142, and 296. There may be some variation in the account titles used by different enterprises. However, the final results should be the same since the balance sheet is an exhibit of the accounting elements: (1) the assets, (2) the liabilities, and (3) the owner's equity. The owner's equity section of the balance sheet should be arranged to show the owner's equity in the business at the beginning of the accounting period, the net increase or the net decrease in the equity during the period, and the amount of equity at the end of the period.

BUILDING YOUR ACCOUNTING KNOWLEDGE

1. Identify four advantages of a single proprietorship in comparison with other forms of business organization.
2. Identify four disadvantages of a single proprietorship form of business organization.
3. What are the two types of owner's equity accounts? Give examples of each in a single proprietorship.

4. When a set of formal, double-entry accounting records is started by a single proprietor for the first time, what is the source of information for preparing the opening entry?

5. How should the payment of personal or family bills using business funds be entered by the single proprietorship?

6. Describe the use of a summary cost of goods sold account in the closing process of a merchandising type of enterprise.

7. How is the owner's drawing account usually closed at the end of each year?

8. How should the owner's equity section of a single proprietorship balance sheet be arranged?

APPLYING ACCOUNTING CONCEPTS

Exercise 16-1. Sherbette Drewry started her merchandising business on November 1 by investing cash, $9,500, office equipment, $6,000, and store furniture and fixtures, $4,500. Drewry owes $2,500 on the store furniture and fixtures.

Give the general journal entry for opening the business.

Exercise 16-2. Bob Petersen has been operating a small retail business without maintaining any formal, double-entry accounting records. On April 30 he decided that proper records are necessary and, with the help of his accountant, constructed a current balance sheet that consists of the following accounts:

Cash	$ 5,650
Accounts receivable	8,300
Allowance for doubtful accounts	1,900
Merchandise inventory	18,440
Store equipment	21,000
Accumulated depreciation on store equipment.................	12,000
Notes payable	5,100
Accounts payable	6,900
Bob Petersen, capital...............	27,490

Using this information from the balance sheet, prepare in general journal form the opening entry for Petersen's business.

**Report
No. 16-1**

Complete Report No. 16-1 in the study assignments and submit your working papers to the instructor for approval. Then continue with the following textbook discussion until Report No. 16-2 is required.

THE PARTNERSHIP

When two or more individuals engage in an enterprise as co-owners, the organization is known as a partnership. This form of organization is common to practically all types of enterprises. However, it is more popular among personal service enterprises than among merchandise enterprises. For example, the partnership form of organization is quite common in the legal and public accounting professions.

Organization of a Partnership

The Uniform Partnership Act states that "a partnership is an association of two or more persons who carry on, as co-owners, a business for profit." The partners may, by agreement, unite their capital, labor, skill, or experience in the conduct of a business for their mutual benefit. While under certain circumstances a partnership may be formed by means of an oral or implied agreement, it is desirable that a partnership agreement be evidenced by a written contract. A written agreement containing the various provisions under which a partnership is to operate is known as a partnership agreement. There is no standard form of partnership agreement, but there are certain provisions that are essential, such as:

1. Date of agreement.
2. Names of the partners.
3. Kind of business to be conducted.
4. Length of time the partnership is to run.
5. Name and location of the business.
6. Investment of each partner.
7. Basis on which profits or losses are to be shared by the partners.
8. Limitation of partners' rights and activities.
9. Salary allowances to partners.
10. Division of assets upon dissolution of the partnership.
11. Signatures of the partners.

The conventional form of partnership agreement is reproduced on the following page.

In comparison with the single proprietorship form of organization, the partnership form offers certain advantages, such as the following:

PARTNERSHIP AGREEMENT

THIS CONTRACT, made and entered into on the first day of July 1, 19--, by and between Harlan Spinner of Indianapolis, Indiana, and Carol Thomas of the same city and state.

WITNESSETH: That the said parties have this day formed a partnership for the purpose of engaging in and conducting a wholesale and retail business in the city of Indianapolis under the following stipulations which are a part of this contract:

FIRST: The said partnership is to continue for a term of twenty-five years from July 1, 19--.

SECOND: The business is to be conducted under the firm name of Spinner & Thomas, at 1604 N. Milburn, Indianapolis, Indiana.

THIRD: The investments are as follows: Harlan Spinner, cash, $35,000; Carol Thomas, cash, $20,000. These invested assets are partnership property.

FOURTH: Each partner is to devote his/her entire time and attention to the business and to engage in no other business enterprise without the written consent of the other partner.

FIFTH: During the operation of this partnership, neither partner is to become surety or bonding agent for anyone without the written consent of the other partner.

SIXTH: Each partner is to receive a salary of $28,800 a year, payable $1,200 in cash on the fifteenth day and last business day of each month. At the end of each annual fiscal period, the net income or the net loss shown by the income statement, after the salaries of the two partners have been allowed, is to be shared as follows: Harlan Spinner, 60 percent; Carol Thomas, 40 percent.

SEVENTH: Neither partner is to withdraw assets in excess of his/her salary, any part of the assets invested, or assets in anticipation of net income to be earned, without the written consent of the other partner.

EIGHTH: In the case of the death or the legal disability of either partner, the other partner is to continue the operations of the business until the close of the annual fiscal period on the following June 30. At that time the continuing partner is to be given an option to buy the interest of the deceased or incapacitated partner at not more than 10 percent above the value of the deceased or incapacitated partner's proprietary interest as shown by the balance of his/her capital account after the books are closed on June 30. It is agreed that this purchase price is to be paid one half in cash and the balance in four equal installments payable quarterly.

NINTH: At the conclusion of this contract, unless it is mutually agreed to continue the operation of the business under a new contract, the assets of the partnership, after the liabilities are paid, are to be divided in proportion to the net credit of each partner's capital account on that date.

IN WITNESS WHEREOF, the parties aforesaid have hereunto set their hands and affixed their seals on the day and year above written.

Harlan Spinner (Seal)

Carol Thomas (Seal)

Partnership Agreement

1. The ability and the experience of the partners are combined in one enterprise.
2. More capital may be raised because the resources of the partners are combined.
3. Credit may be improved because each general partner is personally liable for partnership debts.

There are some disadvantages that are peculiar to the partnership form of organization, such as the following:

1. Each partner is individually liable for all of the debts of the partnership. The liability of each partner is not limited to a pro rata share of the partnership debts. Each partner is personally liable for all of the debts of the business to the same extent as if the business were a sole proprietorship. Under the laws of some states, certain partners may limit their liability. At least one partner, however, must be a general partner who is responsible for all of the debts of the partnership.
2. The interest of a partner in the partnership cannot be transferred without the consent of the other partners.
3. Termination of the partnership agreement, bankruptcy of the firm, or death of one of the partners dissolves the partnership.

Accounting Procedure

In accounting for the operations of a partnership, it is necessary to keep a separate capital account for each partner. It is also customary to keep a separate drawing or personal account for each partner. While no new principles are involved in keeping these accounts, care should be used in preparing the opening entry and in entering any transactions thereafter that affect the respective interests of the partners.

Opening Entries Partners may invest cash and other property in the partnership. Certain liabilities may be assumed by the partnership, such as accounts payable, notes payable, and mortgages payable. In opening the books for a partnership, it is customary to prepare a separate journal entry for the investment of each partner. The proper asset accounts should be debited for the amounts invested, the proper liability accounts should be credited for the amounts of obligations assumed, and each partner's capital account should be credited for the residual equity in the assets. The opening entries for Spinner & Thomas based on the partnership agreement reproduced on page 491 may be made in general journal form, as follows:

Cash 35,000
  Harlan Spinner, Capital   35,000
    H. Spinner invested $35,000 in cash.

Cash 20,000
  Carol Thomas, Capital   20,000
    C. Thomas invested $20,000 in cash.

If, instead of investing $35,000 in cash, Spinner invested office equipment valued at $4,000 on which is owed $1,050, delivery equipment valued at $4,600 on which is owed $950 represented by a note, and $28,400 in cash, the proper opening entry in general journal form for the investment should be as follows:

Cash 28,400
Office Equipment 4,000
Delivery Equipment 4,600
  Vouchers Payable   1,050
  Note Payable   950
  Harlan Spinner, Capital   35,000
    H. Spinner's investment in partnership.

Two or more individuals who have been engaged in business as sole owners may form a partnership for the purpose of combining their businesses. Their respective balance sheets may be the basis for the opening entries for the investments of such partners. For example, assume that on April 1, S. H. Schoen and L. A. Starks form a partnership under the firm name of Schoen & Starks to continue the conduct of the businesses which they have been operating as sole owners. The balance sheets reproduced on page 494 are made a part of the partnership agreement. They agree to invest their assets and also that the partnership shall assume the liabilities shown in their respective balance sheets. Each partner is to receive credit for the equity in the assets invested, and the profits and losses are to be shared on a 50-50 basis. In case of dissolution, the assets are to be distributed between the partners in the ratio of their capital interests at the time of dissolution.

S. H. SCHOEN
Balance Sheet
March 31, 1986

Assets			Liabilities		
Cash		$ 3,172	Notes payable.	$ 1,800	
Accounts receivable	$ 2,762		Accounts payable	5,041	
Less allowance for			Total liabilities		$ 6,841
doubtful accounts	215	2,547			
Merchandise inventory. .		12,287			
Store equipment	$ 1,920		**Owner's Equity**		
Less accumulated					
depreciation	500	1,420	S. H. Schoen, capital . . .		12,585
Total assets.		$19,426	Total liabilities and		
			owner's equity		$19,426

L. A. STARKS
Balance Sheet
March 31, 1986

Assets			Liabilities		
Cash		$ 1,772	Notes payable.	$ 3,000	
Accounts receivable	$ 2,640		Accounts payable	6,619	
Less allowance for			Total liabilities		$ 9,619
doubtful accounts	360	2,280			
Merchandise inventory. .		14,846			
Supplies		143			
Office equipment	$ 2,160		**Owner's Equity**		
Less accumulated					
depreciation	550	1,610	L.A. Starks, capital		12,832
Store equipment	$ 2,400				
Less accumulated					
depreciation	600	1,800	Total liabilities and		
Total assets.		$22,451	owner's equity		$22,451

When two single proprietors decide to combine their businesses, generally accepted accounting principles usually require that non-cash assets (primarily inventories and long-term assets) be taken over at their fair market values as of the date of formation of the partnership. Since it probably cannot be determined as of March 31, 1986, which of the accounts receivable may later prove to be uncollectible in whole or in part, the amount of each accounts receivable balance cannot be adjusted for the currently accumulated allowance for doubtful accounts. It is, therefore, usual practice to enter the full amount of the accounts receivable as a debit and the amount of the allowance for doubtful accounts as a credit in placing each partner's investment in the books of the partnership. In this way, the accounts receivable are entered at their approximate fair market value. Subsequent end-of-period adjustments of the allowance for doubtful accounts on the books of the partnership will reflect future collection experience with respect to the combined accounts receivable of Schoen & Starks. Any accounts receivable on either set of books considered to be uncollectible as of March 31, 1986, should be written off by a debit to the Allowance for Doubtful Accounts and a credit to Accounts Receivable. None was so considered in this case.

Because both Schoen & Starks had been using the fifo method of inventory costing, the values shown for merchandise inventories on their respective balance sheets are mutually acceptable as approximations of fair market value as of March 31, 1986. This is because under the fifo method, the most recently purchased inventory is considered to be still on hand. If Schoen or Starks had been using some other inventory costing method, the merchandise inventory amounts might require restatement to reflect the appropriate fair market value, with effects on the partner's capital accounts similar to those for long-term assets discussed below.

It is determined that the fair market value of Schoen's store equipment as of March 31, 1986, is $1,800, so this amount should be entered on the books of the new partnership, rather than the undepreciated cost of $1,420 ($1,920 − $500) shown on Schoen's balance sheet as of that date. In like manner, it is determined that the fair market values of Starks' office equipment and store equipment as of March 31, 1986, are $1,925 and $2,100 respectively, so these amounts should be entered on the books of the new partnership, rather than the respective undepreciated costs of $1,610 ($2,160 − $550) and $1,800 ($2,400 − $600) shown on Starks' balance sheet as of that date. The differences between the fair market values and the undepreciated costs of the long-term assets contributed by each partner are reflected in the respective credits to the partners' capital accounts of $12,965 and $13,447 shown in the opening entries at the top of the following page.

For tax purposes, S. H. Schoen must use the undepreciated cost of $1,420 to value the store equipment investment, and L. A. Starks must use the undepreciated costs of $1,610 and $1,800 to value the office equipment and store equipment respectively. Their net capital investments for tax purposes would thus be $12,585 and $12,832 respectively, which are the amounts shown as owner's equity on their March 31, 1986, balance sheets.

April 1	Cash	3,172	
	Accounts Receivable	2,762	
	Merchandise Inventory	12,287	
	Store Equipment	1,800	
	Notes Payable		1,800
	Accounts Payable		5,041
	Allowance for Doubtful Accounts		215
	S. H. Schoen, Capital		12,965*
	S. H. Schoen's investment in partnership.		

*S. H. Schoen, Capital (before partnership)		$12,585
Add: Fair market value of store equipment	$1,800	
Undepreciated cost	1,420	380
		$12,965

April 1	Cash	1,772	
	Accounts Receivable	2,640	
	Merchandise Inventory	14,846	
	Supplies	143	
	Office Equipment	1,925	
	Store Equipment	2,100	
	Notes Payable		3,000
	Accounts Payable		6,619
	Allowance for Doubtful Accounts		360
	L. A. Starks, Capital		13,447*
	L. A. Starks' investment in partnership.		

*L. A. Starks, Capital (before partnership)			$12,832
Add: Fair market value of office equipment	$1,925		
Undepreciated cost	1,610	$315	
Fair market value of store equipment	$2,100		
Undepreciated cost	1,800	300	615
			$13,447

Observe that the ratio of the partners' investments in the partnership ($12,965 to $13,447) is not exactly the same as their profit-and-loss sharing ratio (50% each). The basis on which profits and losses are to be shared is a matter of agreement between the partners, and not necessarily the same as their investment ratio. There are factors other than the assets invested that may enter into a profit-and-loss sharing agreement. For example, one partner may contribute most of the assets but render no services, while the other partner may contribute less in assets but devote full time to the activities of the partnership.

Admitting a New Partner. A new partner may be admitted to a partnership by agreement among the existing partners. The admission of a new partner calls for the dissolution of the old partnership and the creation of a new partnership. A new partnership agreement that includes all of the necessary provisions should be prepared. For example, assume that Schoen and Starks admit G. E. Monahan as a new partner as of July 1, and agree to share profits and losses on the basis of their capital interests. If Monahan's investment consisted of cash only, the proper entry to admit Monahan to the partnership would involve a debit to the cash account and a credit to Monahan's capital account for the amount invested. If Monahan has been operating a business as a sole owner and the business is taken over by the partnership, Monahan's balance sheet reproduced below will serve as a basis for preparing the opening entry. Assume that, as of July 1, Monahan

G. E. MONAHAN
Balance Sheet
June 30, 1986

Assets			Liabilities		
Cash		$ 2,992	Notes payable.......... $ 4,524		
Accounts receivable .... $ 7,145			Accounts payable 3,775		
Less allowance for			Total liabilities		$ 8,299
doubtful accounts	539	6,606			
Merchandise inventory..		13,645			
			Owner's Equity		
			G.E. Monahan, capital ..		14,944
			Total liabilities and		
Total assets............		$23,243	owner's equity		$23,243

was admitted to the partnership. The assets listed in the balance sheet are taken over, the liabilities are assumed, and Monahan is given credit for the equity in the assets of the business.

The proper entry in general journal form to admit Monahan as a partner is as follows:

July 1	Cash	2,992	
	Accounts Receivable	7,145	
	Merchandise Inventory	13,645	
	Notes Payable		4,524
	Accounts Payable		3,775
	Allowance for Doubtful Accounts		539
	G.E. Monahan, Capital		14,944
	G.E. Monahan admitted to partnership.		

Because Monahan has no knowledge of any uncollectible accounts receivable as of June 30, 1986, and has been using the fifo method of inventory costing, no fair market value adjustments of the noncash asset account balances were made for purposes of this entry.

Goodwill. Some business organizations earn profits that are very large in relation to the stated amounts of the assets. The unique earning power of a business, which may be due to exceptional management, good location, or other factors, is called goodwill. Since goodwill is difficult to measure and may not prove to be permanent, accountants do not permit its formal recognition as an asset unless it has been purchased.

For example, assume that Schoen & Starks purchased the business of G. E. Monahan for $20,000 cash, acquiring all of the business assets except cash and assuming the business liabilities. If the book values of Monahan's net accounts receivable and merchandise inventory were considered to be reasonable approximations of their fair market values ($6,606 + $13,645 = $20,251), and Monahan's total liabilities of $8,299 were assumed, Schoen & Starks paid $20,000 for assets with net values of $11,952 ($20,251 − $8,299). The $8,048 difference between the $20,000 paid and the $11,952 of specific assets acquired may be considered to be the price paid for the goodwill of Monahan's business. The transaction may be entered as follows:

July 1	Accounts Receivable	7,145	
	Merchandise Inventory	13,645	
	Goodwill	8,048	
	Notes Payable		4,524
	Accounts Payable		3,775
	Allowance for Doubtful Accounts		539
	Cash		20,000
	Purchased G.E. Monahan's business.		

It is also permissible to recognize goodwill if a new partner is taken into a firm and is allowed a capital interest in excess of the net assets that were invested. For example, suppose that instead of purchasing Monahan's business, Schoen and Starks had agreed to give Monahan a capital interest of $22,992 in exchange for Monahan's business assets and liabilities (including the business cash). Also assume that, as in the previous case, the book values of Monahan's noncash assets were considered to be reasonable approximations of their fair market values. Monahan's investment may be entered as follows:

July 1	Cash	2,992	
	Accounts Receivable	7,145	
	Merchandise Inventory	13,645	
	Goodwill	8,048	
	Notes Payable		4,524
	Accounts Payable		3,775
	Allowance for Doubtful Accounts		539
	G.E. Monahan, Capital		22,992
	G.E. Monahan admitted to partnership.		

Goodwill is considered to be an intangible long-term asset. It is usually reported in the balance sheet as the last item in the asset section. Under present accounting rules, it may be amortized over a future period not to exceed 40 years.

Compensation of Partners. The compensation of partners (other than their share of profits) may be in the nature of salaries, royalties, commissions, bonuses, or other compensation. The amount of each partner's compensation and the method of accounting for it should be stated in the partnership agreement. For example, the partnership agreement between Spinner & Thomas shown on page 491 states that each partner is to receive a salary of $2,400 a month. When all partners receive the same salaries and when profits and losses are shared equally, it is immaterial whether the salaries are treated as an expense of the partnership or as withdrawals of anticipated profits. Under the federal income tax law, salaries or other compensation paid to partners for services rendered may not be claimed as a deduction from gross income in the income tax information return of the partnership unless such salaries are guaranteed. In such event, the amounts may be treated as deductions. (The partners, of course, must report compensation income in their individual returns.) However, apart from income tax considerations, the partnership agreement may provide that partners' salaries are to be treated as operating expenses in computing the net income or the net loss to be shared by the partners.

If partners' salaries are treated as operating expenses, it is usually advisable to keep a separate salary account for each partner. For example, the salaries specified in the partnership agreement between Harlan Spinner and Carol Thomas are to be treated as operating expenses. If the salaries are paid regularly, such as monthly or semi-monthly, it will be necessary only to debit each partner's salary account and to credit the cash account. Instead of paying partners' salaries regularly in cash, they may be credited to the partners' drawing accounts. The partners may then draw against such salaries at will. Under this plan, the proper entry for each partner's salary on each payday is to debit the salary account and to credit the drawing account for the proper amount. If partners' salaries are not treated as an expense of the partnership, it is not necessary to keep a salary account for each partner. Thus, amounts withdrawn by the partners as compensation for services may simply be charged to their respective drawing accounts.

Allocation of Partnership Profits and Losses. The partnership agreement should specify the basis on which profits and losses are to be shared by the partners. In the absence of any agreement between the partners, profits and losses must be shared equally regardless of the ratio of the partners' investments. If the partnership agreement specifies how profits are to be shared but does not specify how losses are to be shared, the losses must be shared on the same basis as that indicated for the profits.

After closing the temporary accounts into Expense and Revenue Summary at the end of the accounting period, the balance of the summary account represents either net income or net loss. If the account has a credit balance, it represents net income; if the account has a debit balance, it represents net loss.

The balance of the expense and revenue summary account should be allocated in accordance with the partnership agreement. If the account has a credit balance, the entry to close the account requires a debit to Expense and Revenue Summary and credits to the partners' drawing or capital accounts for the proper share of the net income in each case. Because the partners may formally or informally agree that they will not withdraw any of their permanent investments without mutual consent, it may be preferable to credit their drawing accounts with their respective shares of net income. Any credit balances in partners' drawing or personal accounts can then be reduced by withdrawals without restriction.

Dissolution of a Partnership. Dissolution of a partnership may be brought about through bankruptcy or the death of one of the partners. No partner can retire from the partnership without the consent of the remaining partners. To do so would constitute a violation of the partnership agreement and would make the retiring partner liable to the remaining partners for any loss resulting from the retirement.

By agreement, a partner may retire and be permitted to withdraw assets equal to, less than, or greater than the amount of the retiring partner's interest in the partnership. The book value of a partner's interest is shown by the credit balance of the partner's capital account after all profits or losses have been allocated in accordance with the agreement and the books are closed. If upon retirement cash or other assets equal to the credit balance of the retiring partner's capital account are withdrawn, the transaction will have no effect upon the capital of the remaining partners.

Suppose, for example, that sometime after G. E. Monahan had been taken into the partnership of Schoen & Starks, Monahan expressed a desire to retire and the partners agreed to the withdrawal of cash equal to the amount of Monahan's equity in the assets of the partnership. After closing the temporary owner's equity accounts into Expense and Revenue Summary, and after allocating the net income and closing the partners' drawing accounts, assume that the partners' capital accounts had credit balances as follows:

S. H. Schoen $11,000
L. A. Starks.................... 14,000
G. E. Monahan 19,000

This indicates that the book value of Monahan's interest in the partnership amounts to $19,000. If this amount is withdrawn in cash, the entry in general journal form for the transaction on the books of the partnership is as follows:

G. E. Monahan, Capital.................................. 19,000
   Cash 19,000
     G. E. Monahan retired, withdrawing $19,000 in equity settlement.

While the transaction involves a decrease in cash with a corresponding decrease in the total capital of the partnership, it does not affect the equity of the remaining partners. Schoen still has an equity of $11,000 and Starks an equity of $14,000 in the partnership assets.

If a retiring partner agrees to withdraw less than the book value of the interest, the effect of the transaction will increase the capital accounts of the remaining partners. To enter such a transaction it is necessary to debit the retiring partner's account for the amount of its credit balance, to credit the assets withdrawn, and to credit the difference to the capital accounts of the remaining partners. Thus, if Monahan agreed to withdraw only $15,000 in settlement of the interest, the transaction should be entered in the books of the partership as follows:

G. E. Monahan, Capital	19,000	
Cash		15,000
S. H. Schoen, Capital		1,760
L. A. Starks, Capital		2,240
G. E. Monahan retired, withdrawing $15,000 in equity settlement.		

The difference between Monahan's equity in the assets of the partnership and the amount of cash withdrawn is $4,000 ($19,000 − $15,000). This difference is divided between the remaining partners on the basis stipulated in the partnership agreement; i.e., the ratio of their capital interests after allocating net income and closing their drawing accounts. On this basis, Schoen is credited for 11/25 [$11,000 ÷ ($11,000 + $14,000)] of $4,000, or $1,760, while Starks is credited for 14/25 [$14,000 ÷ ($11,000 + $14,000)] of $4,000, or $2,240.

If a partner is permitted to withdraw more than the book value of the interest, the effect of the transaction will decrease the capital accounts of the remaining partners. Thus, if Schoen and Starks agreed to the withdrawal of $25,000 in settlement of Monahan's interest, the transaction should be entered in the books of the partnership as follows:

G.E. Monahan, Capital	19,000	
S.H. Schoen, Capital	2,640	
L.A. Starks, Capital	3,360	
Cash		25,000
G.E. Monahan retired, withdrawing $25,000 in equity settlement.		

The excess of the amount of cash withdrawn over Monahan's equity in the partnership ($6,000) is divided between the remaining partners on the basis stipulated in the partnership agreement. Thus, Schoen is debited for 11/25 of $6,000 or $2,640, while Starks is debited for 14/25 of $6,000 or $3,360.

When a partner retires from the business, the partner's interest may be purchased by one or more of the remaining partners or by an outside party. If the retiring partner's interest is sold to one of the remaining partners, the retiring partner's equity is merely transferred to the other partner. Thus, if instead of withdrawing cash in settlement of the equity in the partnership, Monahan's equity is sold to Schoen, the entry for the transaction on the books of the partnership is as follows:

G.E. Monahan, Capital....................................	19,000	
S.H. Schoen, Capital		19,000
S.H. Schoen purchased G.E. Monahan's interest in the partnership.		

The amount paid to Monahan by Schoen is a personal transaction not entered on the books of the partnership. Any gain or loss resulting from the transaction is a personal gain or loss of the withdrawing partner and not of the firm. Thus, whatever amount is involved, the credit in Monahan's account is to be transferred to Schoen's account.

Owners' Equity Section of a Partnership Balance Sheet. The method of showing the equity of the partners in the balance sheet of a partnership is similar to that of a single proprietorship, except that the equity of each partner should be shown separately. An illustration of the owners' equity section of a balance sheet for the partnership of Schoen and Starks is shown below, assuming the following:

Net income for the year	$25,000
Profit and loss ratio	50-50
Withdrawals during the year:	
Schoen.............................	$5,000
Starks	6,000

Owners' Equity

S.H. Schoen:			
Capital, April 1, 1986...............................		$12,965	
Net income (50% of $25,000)......................	$12,500		
Less withdrawals	5,000	7,500	
Capital, March 31, 1987			$20,465
L.A. Starks			
Capital, April 1, 1986...............................		$13,447	
Net income (50% of $25,000)......................	$12,500		
Less withdrawals	6,000	6,500	
Capital, March 31, 1987			19,947
Total owners' equity			$40,412

BUILDING YOUR ACCOUNTING KNOWLEDGE

1. Identify eleven essential provisions of a partnership agreement.
2. Identify three advantages of a partnership in comparison with a single proprietorship.
3. Identify three disadvantages of a partnership form of business organization.
4. When two single proprietors decide to combine their businesses, at what values do generally accepted accounting principles usually require that noncash assets be taken over by the partnership?
5. When a new partner who has been the sole owner of a business is admitted to a partnership by having the partnership take over the old business, what usually serves as the basis for preparing the opening entry?
6. Why do accountants not permit the formal recognition of goodwill as an asset unless it has been purchased? Over what maximum future period may goodwill be amortized?
7. In the absence of any agreement between the partners, how must profits and losses be shared? If the partnership agreement specifies how profits are to be shared, in the absence of any agreement between the partners as to how losses are to be shared, what must be true with respect to losses?
8. Identify two ways in which a partnership may be dissolved without the consent of the remaining partners. What form of partnership dissolution requires the consent of the remaining partners?

APPLYING ACCOUNTING CONCEPTS

Exercise 16-3. J.R. Scronce and S.L. Machol agreed on September 1 to go into business as partners. According to the agreement, Scronce is to contribute $45,000 in cash. Machol is to contribute office equipment valued at $3,000 on which $1,000 is owed, delivery equipment valued at $3,500 on which $850 is owed in the form of a note, and enough cash to make his capital investment equal to that of Scronce.

Provide the opening entry in general journal form for the investment.

Exercise 16-4. Designer Carpets, owned by Larry Smythe, and Rudy's Carpets, owned by Rudy Reaves, have decided to combine their business on January 1.

Designer Carpets has the following assets and liabilities:

Cash	$ 25,145
Accounts receivable	32,000
Allowance for doubtful accounts	1,600
Store equipment	27,000
Accumulated depreciation on store equipment	9,000
Merchandise inventory	115,000
Notes payable	65,000
Accounts payable	38,000

Rudy's Carpets has the following assets and liabilities:

Cash...	$ 36,362
Accounts receivable	25,500
Allowance for doubtful accounts...................	1,300
Merchandise inventory	69,000
Office equipment	33,000
Accumulated depreciation on office equipment	11,000
Notes payable	30,000
Accounts payable.................................	57,500

Smythe and Reaves agree that since both have been using the fifo method of valuing the inventory, these amounts are stated at fair market value. The fair market value of the store equipment is $16,000 and the fair market value of the office equipment is $20,000.

Prepare the opening entries in general journal form to enter the investments of Smythe and Reaves.

Exercise 16-5. Smythe and Reaves decided to admit Ralph Anderson, the sole owner of another carpet store, as a new partner on January 1. Anderson's business has the following assets and liabilities:

Cash...	$ 30,993
Accounts receivable	18,200
Allowance for doubtful accounts...................	1,600
Merchandise inventory	85,600
Notes payable	30,000
Accounts payable.................................	10,100

Anderson has no knowledge of any uncollectible accounts receivable as of January 1 and has been using the fifo method of inventory costing, so that no fair market value adjustments of the noncash asset account balances are necessary.

Give the entry in general journal form to admit Ralph Anderson as a partner.

Exercise 16-6. Refer to Exercise 5. Assume that Smythe and Reaves purchased the Anderson business for $77,100 cash, acquiring all of the noncash business assets and assuming the business liabilities. Determine the price paid for the goodwill of Anderson's business and give the entry in general journal form to enter the transaction in the accounting records of the Smythe and Reaves partnership.

Exercise 16-7. Refer to Exercise 16-4. Assume the following end-of-the-year information related to the Smythe and Reaves partnership. Net income for the year was $88,000; Smythe received 60% of the profits and Reaves received 40%; Smythe withdrew $16,000 during the year and Reaves withdrew $12,000.

Prepare the owners' equity section of the balance sheet for the partnership as of December 31, 19--.

**Report
No. 16-2**

Complete Report No. 16-2 in the study assignments and submit your working papers to the instructor for approval. Then continue with the textbook discussion until Report No. 16-3 is required.

THE CORPORATION

A private corporation is an artificial person created by law for a specific purpose. A corporation differs from a single proprietorship or a partnership with respect to organization, ownership, and distribution of net income or net loss.

In comparison with a partnership, the corporate form of organization has several advantages. The most important of these are:

1. Except in very unusual cases, the owners (stockholders) have no personal liability for the debts of the corporation.
2. The shares of ownership are easily transferred from one person to another.
3. The corporation has a perpetual life that is independent of the lives of its owners.
4. More capital may be raised because the resources of numerous stockholders are combined.

A major disadvantage of the corporate form of organization is that the net income of a corporation is taxed and any cash dividends resulting from that income are also taxable to the stockholders, resulting in so-called double taxation.

Organization of a Corporation

In order to incorporate an enterprise, a charter must be obtained from the state in which the corporation is to be formed. The persons who file articles of incorporation are known as the incorporators. Such persons must be competent to contract, some or all of them must be citizens of the state in which the articles are to be filed, and usually each incorporator is required to be a subscriber for one or more shares of the capital stock. All of the incorporators must sign the articles of incorporation.

The procedure in incorporating an enterprise must conform to the laws of the state in which it is desired to incorporate. The laws of the different states vary considerably in their provisions relating to the organization of corporations. Persons desiring to incorporate a business should acquaint themselves with the laws of the particular state in which they wish to incorporate, as it will be necessary to comply with the laws of that state.

Ownership of a Corporation. The owners' equity in a corporation is called capital stock. To make it possible to have many owners—often with different ownership interests—the capital stock is divided into

units called shares. The persons forming a corporation (the incorporators) and those who wish to become owners subscribe for shares. Each
subscriber agrees to buy a certain number of shares for a certain
amount per share. Typically, payment is made in cash, although assets
other than cash are used sometimes. All parties owning shares of stock
in a corporation are known as stockholders (sometimes called
shareholders).

Capital Stock. The charter obtained by a business corporation specifies the amount of capital stock that it is authorized to issue. Capital
stock may or may not have par value. Par value is a technical legal
matter. In general, par value represents the smallest amount that the
corporation can accept in exchange for a share of stock at the time it is
originally issued without the buyer of the stock incurring some liability
to the corporation. In many states, par-value stock cannot be sold originally by the corporation for less than par value, but can be sold either
above or below par value after the original sale. In most states, it is
possible for corporations to issue stock that has no par value.

If the corporation issues only one type of capital stock, it is called
common stock. The stockholders own the corporation "in common."
Among other things, the stockholders have the right to vote for directors and upon certain other matters, and the right to share in dividends. Dividends are distributions to stockholders resulting either
from profitable operations or from the fact that the corporation is
being dissolved. In all cases, these rights are in direct proportion to the
number of shares of stock owned.

Some corporations have more than one class or type of stock. The
classes differ with respect to the rights which go with the ownership of
the stock. In addition to common stock, a corporation may have one
or more types of preferred stock, which may entitle the owner to
receive a limited share of the earnings before the common stockholders receive any dividends or may involve a prior claim upon assets in
the event that the corporation is dissolved. Sometimes preferred stock
has a preference as to both dividends and assets. Frequently, preferred
stockholders do not have voting rights.

Transactions and Accounts Unique to a Corporation

The day-to-day operating transactions of a corporation are similar to
those of a single proprietorship or of a partnership of a like nature.
Certain transactions involving the owners' equity of a business are
unique if the enterprise is incorporated. Examples of such transactions
include:

1. Capital stock subscriptions.
2. Amounts received to apply on capital stock subscriptions.
3. Issuance of capital stock to subscribers.
4. Transfer of capital stock from one stockholder to another stockholder.
5. Declaration and payment of dividends.

In order to account for these types of transactions, certain accounts are required by a corporation. The following is a list of the major accounts and related classifications that are unique to the corporate form of organization:

Account	Classification
Capital Stock	Owners' equity
Subscriptions Receivable	Asset
Capital Stock Subscribed	Owners' equity
Retained Earnings (sometimes called Earnings Retained in the Business)	Owners' equity
Dividends Payable	Liability

Accounting Procedure

In accounting for the operations of a corporation, two major stockholders' equity or owners' equity accounts are kept—Capital Stock and Retained Earnings. In addition, an asset account—Subscriptions Receivable—and an owners' equity account—Capital Stock Subscribed—are kept to enter unpaid subscriptions to capital stock. A liability account—Dividends Payable—is kept to enter the corporation's liability for any dividends declared but not yet paid. The use of these accounts will be discussed fully in the remainder of this chapter.

Owners' Equity Accounts. One of the features of accounting for corporate owners' equity is the distinction that is maintained in the records between owners' equity that results from investments by stockholders—referred to as paid-in capital; and owners' equity that results from profitable operations—referred to as retained earnings. In the case of certain types of corporate transactions, this distinction as to the source of the owners' equity is not evident, but in most cases the difference is reflected in the accounts. For example, when the corporation exchanges its stock for cash or other property equal in amount to the par value of the shares issued, the transaction is entered by debiting the proper asset account and by crediting Capital Stock. If there is more than one type of capital stock, there should be an account for each type.

Starting a Business Corporation. A business corporation may be started in a variety of ways. A corporation may sell its stock directly to new stockholders for cash or may obtain subscriptions to its stock. A subscription is an agreement to buy a certain number of shares at an agreed price and to pay for them at or within a specified time, either in full at one time or in installments over a period of time. For example, assume that a subscription is received for 1000 shares at a price of $10 each (assumed to be the par value of each share in this case). The transaction is entered by debiting Subscriptions Receivable and by crediting Capital Stock Subscribed for $10,000. Collections on the subscription are debited to Cash (or whatever is accepted in lieu of cash) and credited to Subscriptions Receivable. When the subscription is paid in full, the stock is issued and an entry is made debiting Capital Stock Subscribed and crediting Capital Stock for $10,000. As long as the subscriptions receivable account has a balance representing an amount that is expected to be collected, the account is treated as an asset and is shown on the balance sheet. Capital Stock Subscribed is a stockholders' equity account, the balance of which indicates the amount that eventually will be added to Capital Stock.

Following is a narrative of selected corporate common stock transactions with illustrative general journal entries:

(1) The Hilgert Company, Inc., was incorporated with an authorized issue of 10,000 shares of common stock, par value $10 per share. (This would be indicated by the following memorandum in the Description column of the general journal: "Aug. 1. The Hilgert Company, Inc., is authorized to issue 10,000 shares of common stock, par value of $10 per share.") At the time of incorporation, subscriptions had been received as follows:

R. L. Hilgert	5000 shares
Sue Cohen	2500 shares
Sharon Tucker	2500 shares

The stock was subscribed for at par value and one half of the subscription price was paid in cash, the balance to be paid on demand.

To enter this transaction completely, it is necessary (a) to enter the stock subscriptions received, and (b) to enter the cash received to apply on the subscription price. These entries may be made in general journal form as follows:

(a)

Subscriptions Receivable..............................	100,000	
Capital Stock Subscribed...........................		100,000

Received subscriptions to capital stock at par, as follows:

    R.L. Hilgert, 5000 shares
    Sue Cohen, 2500 shares
    Sharon Tucker, 2500 shares

(b)

Cash..	50,000	
Subscriptions Receivable...........................		50,000

Received cash on account for subscriptions to capital stock, as follows:

    R.L. Hilgert, $25,000
    Sue Cohen, $12,500
    Sharon Tucker, $12,500

(2) Received cash from subscribers to capital stock in settlement of balances due, as follows:

R.L. Hilgert...........................	$25,000
Sue Cohen	12,500
Sharon Tucker	12,500

This transaction involves an increase in the asset Cash and a decrease in the asset Subscriptions Receivable. The transaction may be entered in general journal form, as follows:

Cash...	50,000	
Subscriptions Receivable...........................		50,000

Received cash in settlement of the balance due from subscribers to capital stock, as follows:

    R.L. Hilgert, $25,000
    Sue Cohen, $12,500
    Sharon Tucker, $12,500

(3) Issued certificates of stock to the following subscribers who had remitted their subscriptions in full:

R.L. Hilgert.........................	5000 shares
Sue Cohen	2500 shares
Sharon Tucker	2500 shares

Usually, certificates of stock are not issued until subscriptions are remitted in full. In this case, the subscribers remitted their subscriptions in full and the stock certificates are issued. The transactions are entered in general journal form, as follows:

Capital Stock Subscribed	100,000	
Capital Stock[1]		100,000
Capital stock issued to subscribers as follows:		
R.L. Hilgert, 5000 shares		
Sue Cohen, 2500 shares		
Sharon Tucker, 2500 shares		

After posting the above entry, the capital stock account will have a credit balance of $100,000, which is the par value of the capital stock outstanding.

(4) R. L. Hilgert's stock certificate for 5000 shares was returned and Hilgert requested that 2000 shares be transferred to G. B. Waymire. A new certificate for 3000 shares is to be issued to Hilgert.

This transaction indicates that out of 5000 shares owned by Hilgert, 2000 shares were sold to Waymire. Transferring capital stock from one stockholder to another involves the cancellation of the old certificate and the issuance of new certificates for the proper numbers of shares. In this case, it is necessary to cancel the original certificate for 5000 shares issued to Hilgert and to issue two new certificates, one to Waymire for 2000 shares and the other to Hilgert for 3000 shares. This transaction has no effect upon the assets, liabilities, or capital of the corporation. It is merely a transfer of stock between stockholders and the only entry required is a transfer entry in the capital stock records kept by the corporation.

Corporation Profits, Losses, and Dividends. At the end of each accounting period, the balance of the expense and revenue summary account is transferred to the retained earnings account. If a corporation is operated at a loss, the amount of the net loss which is transferred from the expense and revenue summary account to the retained earnings account might result in the retained earnings account having a debit balance. This balance is termed a deficit and will appear as a deduction in the stockholders' equity section of the corporation's balance sheet.

A decision on the part of the directors of a corporation to pay a dividend is commonly referred to as a declaration of dividends. The directors usually specify that the dividends shall be paid to the stockholders of record as of a certain date, which means that only stock-

[1]When both common stock and preferred stock are authorized in the charter of a corporation, separate accounts should be kept for each class of stock. A memorandum entry of the number of shares authorized should be entered in the item column of each capital stock account.

holders whose stock is entered in their names on that date are entitled to receive dividends. Any stockholder who acquires stock after that date is not entitled to share in the dividend previously declared.

Dividends may be paid immediately upon being declared or at some later date. Large corporations usually do not pay dividends until some time after the date of declaration. When dividends are declared and such dividends are payable in cash at a later date, the dividends declared represent a liability of the corporation. It is customary to enter the declaration by debiting Retained Earnings and by crediting Dividends Payable.

To illustrate, assume that the board of directors at its annual meeting held on July 15 voted to pay a cash dividend of 90¢ per share to be paid on Aug. 1 to stockholders of record July 15. As of the date of declaration, there are 10,000 shares issued and outstanding. The transaction may be entered in general journal form, as follows:

```
July 15   Retained Earnings..............................   9,000
            Dividends Payable...........................          9,000
            Dividend declared by board of directors.
```

The dividends payable account will have a credit balance until all dividends declared are paid in full. When dividends are paid immediately upon being declared, there is no need for setting up a dividends payable account.

To enter the payment of the dividend declared in the foregoing transaction, it is necessary to debit Dividends Payable and to credit the cash account, as follows:

```
Aug. 1    Dividends Payable..............................   9,000
            Cash .........................................          9,000
            Paid dividend declared July 15.
```

This transaction has the effect of decreasing the liability, Dividends Payable, by $9,000 with a similar decrease in the asset Cash. After the transaction is posted, the dividends payable account will have no balance.

Incorporating a Single Proprietorship. The legal steps involved in incorporating a single proprietorship are the same as in organizing a new corporation. Usually, the sole proprietor becomes the principal stockholder in the corporation and transfers the assets of the proprietorship business to the corporation in exchange for capital stock. The business liabilities may also be assumed by the corporation. The same books of account may be continued or an entirely new set of books may be installed.

Assume that The Binder Company, Inc., was organized to take over the business formerly conducted by J. J. Binder as sole owner. Binder subscribes for 5000 shares of the capital stock of The Binder Company, Inc., at $10 per share and transfers the equity in the proprietorship (on a fair market value basis, as usually required by generally accepted accounting principles) to apply on the subscription. Just before the transfer at the end of the year, the balance sheet of the business appeared as reproduced below.

J. J. BINDER
Balance Sheet
December 31, 1986

Assets			Liabilities		
Cash		$ 7,400	Notes payable..........	$ 1,800	
Accounts receivable	$ 5,930		Accounts payable	4,990	
Less allowance for			Total liabilities		$ 6,790
doubtful accounts	620	5,310			
Merchandise inventory..		12,410			
Office equipment	$ 2,400				
Less accumulated					
depreciation	600	1,800			
Store equipment	$ 1,900				
Less accumulated			**Owner's Equity**		
depreciation	500	1,400	J.J. Binder, capital		23,730
Delivery equipment	$ 4,600				
Less accumulated					
depreciation	2,400	2,200	Total liabilities and		
Total assets...........		$30,520	owner's equity		$30,520

Binder's net accounts receivable are believed to be collectible and the merchandise inventory is costed on a fifo basis. However, the fair market values of the long-term assets as of December 31, 1986, are considered to be: office equipment, $2,100; store equipment, $1,700; and delivery equipment, $2,400. A comparison of these values with the undepreciated cost amounts shown in the balance sheet reveals that the fair market values are larger by a total of $800 ($6,200 fair market value − $5,400 undepreciated costs). Thus, Binder's equity in the business is considered to be $24,530, or $800 more than the amount of $23,730 that is shown on the balance sheet dated December 31, 1986.

The following entry is made on Binder's books to recognize the fair market values of the long-term assets:

```
Office Equipment ......................................      300
Store Equipment .......................................      300
Delivery Equipment ....................................      200
    J.J. Binder, Capital...................................              800
    Adjustment of long-term assets to fair market values.
```

If Binder intends to continue to use the same set of books with only those modifications needed because of the change to the corporate form of enterprise, the entries for the subscription and its partial payment by the transfer of the business assets and liabilities to the corporation should be as follows:

```
Subscriptions Receivable ..............................    50,000
    Capital Stock Subscribed ...........................             50,000
    J.J. Binder subscribed for 5000 shares of stock at par.


J.J. Binder, Capital...................................    24,530
    Subscriptions Receivable ...........................             24,530
    Assets and liabilities of J.J. Binder transferred to cor-
    poration at fair market value.
```

After the foregoing entries are posted, Binder's capital account will have no balance. The corporate accounts listed below will take the place of Binder's capital account in the general ledger:

Capital Stock   Capital Stock Subscribed
Subscriptions Receivable

As in the case of the Schoen & Starks partnership, for tax purposes, Binder must use the undepreciated costs of the three long-term assets as shown by the December 31, 1986, balance sheet on page 513, and the net capital investment for tax purposes would be considered to be $23,730, as shown also by the balance sheet.

If, instead of using the same books of account that were used by Binder, a new set of books is installed by the corporation, a general journal entry should be made for the transfer of the accounts of the single proprietorship to the corporation. Since the long-term assets are being taken over at their fair market values, they should be entered on the books of the corporation at these values, which represent the costs of the assets to the corporation. The accounts of Binder are then transferred to The Binder Company, Inc., by means of a general journal entry on the books of the corporation, as follows:

Cash	7,400	
Accounts Receivable	5,930	
Merchandise Inventory	12,410	
Office Equipment	2,100	
Store Equipment	1,700	
Delivery Equipment	2,400	
Notes Payable		1,800
Accounts Payable		4,990
Allowance for Doubtful Accounts		620
Subscriptions Receivable		24,530
Assets and liabilities of J.J. Binder transferred to corporation at fair market value.		

Assuming that the balance due on the subscription was paid, a stock certificate for 5000 shares is issued to Binder and the transactions are entered on the books of the corporation, as follows:

Cash	25,470*	
Subscriptions Receivable		25,470
Cash received from J.J. Binder in settlement of balance due on subscription to capital stock.		

*$50,000 Subscriptions Receivable Dr.
less $24,530 Subscriptions Receivable Cr.

Capital Stock Subscribed	50,000	
Capital Stock		50,000
Issued 5000 shares of capital stock to J.J. Binder.		

Incorporating a Partnership. When a partnership is incorporated, the partners may become stockholders of the corporation. The same books of account may be continued or a new set of books may be installed by the corporation. Assume that The Madeo Company, Inc., is organized with an authorized capital of $200,000 to take over the business formerly conducted by Madeo & Madeo, a partnership. The partners subscribe for capital stock of the corporation, as follows:

Larry Madeo, 6000 shares @ $10....... $60,000
Silvia Madeo, 4000 shares @ $10....... $40,000

Madeo & Madeo, as individuals, are to receive credit toward their subscription for their respective equities in the assets of the partnership.

The subscriptions to the capital stock should be entered as indicated in the following general journal entry:

Subscriptions Receivable.............................	100,000	
Capital Stock Subscribed		100,000
Received subscriptions to capital stock as follows:		
Larry Madeo, 6000 shares		
Silvia Madeo, 4000 shares		

The following balance sheet for the partnership was prepared just prior to the time of incorporating the business on April 1, 1986. It has already been adjusted to recognize the fair market values of the inventory and long-term assets as of that date, and the Madeos had no

---

MADEO & MADEO
Balance Sheet
March 31, 1986

Assets			Liabilities		
Cash		$17,000	Notes payable.........	$ 6,000	
Notes receivable	$ 2,000		Accounts payable	9,720	
Accounts receivable	9,900		Total liabilities		$15,720
	$11,900				
Less allowance for					
doubtful accounts	800	11,100			
Merchandise inventory..		25,500			
Office equipment	$ 4,000				
Less accumulated			**Owners' Equity**		
depreciation	1,200	2,800	Larry Madeo, capital....	$25,368	
Delivery equipment	$ 3,200		Silvia Madeo, capital ...	16,912	
Less accumulated			Total owners' equity ..		42,280
depreciation	1,600	1,600	Total liabilities and		
Total assets...........		$58,000	owners' equity		$58,000

knowledge of any specific uncollectible accounts receivable at the date of incorporation.

If the books of the partnership are to be continued in use by the corporation, the transfer of the partners' equities to the corporation may be made by means of the following general journal entry:

Larry Madeo, Capital	25,368	
Silvia Madeo, Capital	16,912	
Subscriptions Receivable		42,280
Assets and liabilities of Madeo & Madeo transferred to corporation at fair market value.		

After this entry is posted, the partners' accounts will have no balances.

As in the previous cases, for tax purposes, Madeo & Madeo must use the undepreciated costs of their long-term assets and the book value of their inventory as of March 31, 1986, prior to any fair market value adjustments, and value their net capital investments accordingly.

If instead of using the same books of account that were used by Madeo & Madeo, a new set of books is installed by the corporation, a general journal entry on the books of the corporation is required to transfer the accounts of the partnership to the corporation. This journal entry is:

Cash	17,000	
Notes Receivable	2,000	
Accounts Receivable	9,900	
Merchandise Inventory	25,500	
Office Equipment	2,800	
Delivery Equipment	1,600	
Notes Payable		6,000
Accounts Payable		9,720
Allowance for Doubtful Accounts		800
Subscriptions Receivable		42,280
Assets and liabilities of Madeo & Madeo transferred to corporation at fair market value.		

Assuming that Madeo & Madeo paid the balance due on their subscriptions and that stock certificates were issued to them, the transactions should be entered on the books of the corporation, as follows:

```
Cash...............................................  57,720
    Subscriptions Receivable...........................          57,720
    Received cash from subscribers as follows:
        Larry Madeo, $34,632
        Silvia Madeo, $23,088


Capital Stock Subscribed..............................  100,000
    Capital Stock .......................................         100,000
    Issued capital stock to subscribers.
```

Owners' Equity Section of a Corporation Balance Sheet. The difference between the amounts of the assets and of the liabilities of a corporation is called either "Capital" or "Stockholders' Equity" and is so described in the balance sheet of the corporation. Generally, the amount resulting from the issuance of capital stock and the amount resulting from undistributed earnings are shown. At the end of the first year of operations, the owners' equity section of the balance sheet of The Madeo Company, Inc., appeared as follows:

Stockholders' Equity

Capital stock (20,000 shares authorized;	
10,000 shares issued and outstanding)	$100,000
Retained earnings.......................	32,000
Total stockholders' equity	$132,000

Because of differences in capital structure, there may be considerable variation in the capital sections of balance sheets prepared for different corporations. If more than one kind of capital stock is issued, each kind should be listed separately. There may be retained earnings (accumulated income) or a deficit (accumulated losses) at the end of the year. A deficit should be shown as a deduction from the amount resulting from the issuance of the capital stock in arriving at the total stockholders' equity of a corporation.

BUILDING YOUR ACCOUNTING KNOWLEDGE

1. Identify four advantages of the corporate form of business organization in contrast to a partnership. Identify a major disadvantage of the corporate form.
2. What qualifications are necessary to be one of the incorporators of a corporation?
3. What are the usual rights of common stockholders?

4. Identify the five major accounts unique to the corporate form of business organization and give their balance sheet classifications.
5. Describe the accounting effect and the necessary entry or entries for the transfer of shares from one corporate stockholder to another.
6. When do dividends become a liability of the corporation?
7. When an existing single proprietorship or partnership is incorporated, at what values do generally accepted accounting principles usually require that noncash assets be taken over by the corporation?
8. Identify the two major divisions of the stockholders' equity section of a corporate balance sheet.

APPLYING ACCOUNTING CONCEPTS

Exercise 16-8. Space Center Industries was incorporated on April 1, 19--, with an authorized issue of 10,000 shares of common stock, par value of $10 per share. At the time of incorporation, subscriptions had been received from Amelia Eckart for 5,000 shares and from Tina Wyckott for 2,500 shares. The stock was subscribed for at par value, and one half of the subscription price was paid in cash with the balance to be paid on the first day of the following month.

In general journal form, enter the following transactions: **(a)** memorandum entry to be made on April 1; **(b)** stock subscriptions received; **(c)** cash received to apply on the subscription price; **(d)** receipt of final cash payment on the stock subscriptions; and **(e)** issue of the capital stock.

Exercise 16-9. The board of directors of Space Center Industries, Inc., at its annual meeting held on June 15, voted to pay a cash dividend of $3 per share on July 15 to stockholders of record on June 30. As of the date of declaration, there were 7,500 shares issued and outstanding.

Enter the following transaction in general journal form: **(a)** declaration of the dividend, and **(b)** payment of the dividend.

Exercise 16-10. Sunshine Health Foods, owned by Josefa Remalius, has been operating as a sole proprietorship. On December 31, Remalius decided to incorporate and subscribed for 1,000 shares of the capital stock of Sunshine Health Foods, Inc., at $100 par value per share and transferred the equity in the proprietorship (on a fair market value basis) to apply on the subscription.

Prior to the incorporation at the end of the year, the balance sheet of the proprietorship showed the following assets and liabilities:

Cash...	$ 8,500
Accounts receivable	6,059
Allowance for doubtful accounts..................	950
Merchandise inventory	33,040
Office equipment	3,600
Accumulated depreciation on office equipment	900
Delivery equipment	5,700
Accumulated depreciation on delivery equipment ...	2,000
Notes payable	2,900
Accounts payable................................	5,690
Josefa Remalius, capital	44,459

The net accounts receivable are believed to be collectible and the merchandise inventory is costed on a fifo basis. The fair market value of the office equipment is $2,500 and the fair market value of the delivery equipment is $4,200.

(a) Assuming that Remalius intends to continue with the same set of books with only those modifications needed to change to the corporate form of organization, give the entries in general journal form to enter the following transactions:

1. Adjustment of long-term assets to fair market value.
2. Subscription for the 1,000 shares of stock at par value.
3. Transfer of assets and liabilities to the corporation at fair market value.

(b) Assuming that Remalius intends to open a new set of books for the corporation, give the general journal entry for the transfer of the accounts of the single proprietorship to the corporation.

**Report
No. 16-3**

Complete Report No. 16-3 in the study assignments and submit your working papers to the instructor for approval. Then continue with the textbook discussion in Chapter 17 until Report No. 17-1 is required.

EXPANDING YOUR BUSINESS VOCABULARY

What is the meaning of each of the following terms?

capital (p. 482)

capital stock (p. 506)

common stock (p. 507)

corporation (p. 506)

declaration of dividends (p. 511)

deficit (p. 511)

dividends (p. 507)

double taxation (p. 506)

goodwill (p. 498)

incorporators (p. 506)

net worth (p. 482)

owner's equity (p. 482)

paid-in capital (p. 508)

par value (p. 507)

partnership (p. 490)

partnership agreement (p. 490)

preferred stock (p. 507)

retained earnings (p. 508)

shares (p. 507)

single proprietorship (p. 482)

stockholders (or shareholders)
   (p. 507)

stockholders' equity (p. 518)

stockholders of record (p. 512)

subscription (p. 509)

CHAPTER 17

Accrual Accounting Applied to a Medium-Scale Wholesale-Retail Business

---

CHAPTER OBJECTIVES

Careful study of this chapter should enable you to:

- Describe how accrual accounting is applied to a medium-size wholesale-retail business with two departments operated as a partnership.

- Explain for such a business the information processing phases of the accounting cycle (source documents, books of original entry, ledgers, and auxiliary records).

- Prepare the following new books of original entry:

  1. Departmental sales journal
  2. Departmental cash receipts journal
  3. General journal with special columns

- Describe the accounting for temporary investments, using the account for government notes as an example.

- Describe the use of departmental cost of goods sold accounts.

- Prepare a subsidiary operating expense ledger with its own chart of accounts.

In the wholesale portion of a wholesale-retail merchandising enterprise, the merchandise handled is usually purchased directly from manufacturers, importers, or producers. The merchandise is sold to retailers and distributors, who in turn sell to consumers at retail prices. The wholesaler usually buys in sizable quantities and has storage facilities that make it possible to carry a large stock of merchandise. Goods may be purchased for cash or on account and, likewise, the goods may be sold for cash or on account. A large percentage of the wholesale business involves the use of credit. The retail portion of such a business is handled in a manner similar to that explained and illustrated in Chapters 8, 9, and 10.

This chapter introduces departmental accounting and applies it to a partnership operated both as a wholesaler and as a retailer. It also illustrates the use of a departmental sales journal, a departmental cash receipts journal, and a general journal with special columns. The voucher register and check register introduced in Chapter 14 are also utilized here. Temporary investment accounts and departmental cost of goods sold accounts are introduced. Finally, a subsidiary operating expense ledger with a separate chart of accounts is utilized for the first time.

Factors Affecting Accounting Records Used

The books of account and the auxiliary records of a wholesale-retail business will vary depending upon a number of factors, such as the following:

1. Type of business organization.
2. Volume of business.
3. Office equipment used.
4. Information desired by the management and others concerned with the operation of the business.

Type of Business Organization. A wholesale-retail merchandising enterprise may be conducted as a single proprietorship, a partnership, or a corporation. The type of organization will affect the accounts that are kept. In a single proprietorship, it may be necessary to keep two accounts for the proprietor—one for capital and the other for personal transactions. In a partnership, it is necessary to keep separate accounts for each partner. In the case of a corporation, it is necessary to keep separate accounts for capital stock, retained earnings, and dividends payable.

Volume of Business. The volume of business is an important factor in determining the types of records and the number of accounts to be maintained. Obviously, the records and the accounts of a firm with annual sales of a million dollars or more will differ considerably from one with annual sales of only $50,000 a year. In a business with numerous departments, management may demand more financial statistical information and have a greater need for adequate control.

When manual methods are used, there is a fairly direct relationship between the size of a business and the number of persons engaged in keeping its records. When several persons are required, the work must be divided in some logical fashion. This means that a separate record or book of original entry will be kept for each major type of business transaction. For example, one journal may be provided to enter purchases, another to enter sales, another to enter cash receipts, another to enter checks written, and a general journal to enter transactions that cannot be entered in the special journals. The books of final entry (the ledgers) also will be subdivided. It is likely that there will be one or more subsidiary ledgers to enter the details about some of the elements that are shown in summary in some of the general ledger accounts. For example, one subsidiary ledger may be for individual customers' accounts (accounts receivable) and another may be for individual operating expense accounts. (A subsidiary ledger for individual accounts payable would not be used if a voucher system is maintained.) Each employee engaged in an accounting activity may specialize in keeping one of these records.

A functional division of the accounting activity may have many advantages. Some of the more important ones are that the functional division:

1. Becomes an integral part of the internal control system, as discussed in Chapter 14.
2. Makes possible a more equitable distribution of the work load among several employees.
3. Provides for a more detailed classification of transactions in the books of original entry.
4. Makes possible periodic summary posting to the general ledger.

Office Equipment. The accounting system is certain to be affected by the use of various types of office equipment. In recent years there has been a great expansion in the use of computer-based accounting systems. In the modern office of a big business enterprise, a large share of the data entry work is done with the aid of electronic data processing equipment. Many companies utilize personal computers and other associated equipment.

Regardless of the extent to which equipment is used in performing the accounting function, the fundamental principles involved in keeping the accounts continue to apply. A knowledge of accounting theory and practice on the part of those employed in accounting positions is just as essential as if no machines were used.

Information Desired. The accounting information system must be designed to provide the desired information for management and others concerned with the operation of a business. Management would like to know where the business stands financially from time to time, as well as the results of operations for given periods of time. Accounting may be required to supply such information of a statistical nature as well as the usual accounting reports. For example, the accounts must be kept so as to provide all the information needed for the various tax reports required by the federal, state, and local governments. In recent years there has been a tremendous increase in the number of tax reports and in the amount of tax information that must be furnished. Many large firms have found it necessary to organize a tax accounting department separate from the general accounting department.

Accounting Procedure

Harlan Spinner and Carol Thomas are partners who conduct a wholesale-retail bakery business. Pastries and cakes are handled in Department A, breads and rolls in Department B. Such merchandise is purchased on account from various bakery suppliers. The bakery products are sold primarily for cash to retail customers. A small number of sales on account also are made to restaurants and wholesale customers. In the following sections, the books of account and accounting procedures for Spinner & Thomas are explained and illustrated.

Books of Account

The records maintained by Spinner & Thomas consist of the following:

1. Books of original entry
   (a) Voucher register
   (b) Sales journal
   (c) Cash receipts journal
   (d) Check register
   (e) General journal
2. Books of final entry
   (a) General ledger
   (b) Subsidiary ledgers:
         Accounts receivable ledger
         Operating expense ledger
3. Auxiliary records
   (a) Petty cash payments record
   (b) Long-term asset record

Voucher Register. A comparison of the format of Spinner & Thomas' voucher register shown on pages 542-543 with that of the voucher register reproduced on page 432 reveals that they are identical. This form of voucher register was described in detail in Chapter 14.

Sales Journal. Spinner & Thomas keeps a multi-column sales journal as illustrated on page 544. Since there is no sales tax on food sales in the state in which Spinner & Thomas operates, no sales tax collections are necessary. Note that General Ledger Debit amount, Credit amount, and Account No. columns are provided. In addition, a special debit amount column is provided for Accounts Receivable, and special credit columns are provided for (1) Sales, Department A, and (2) Sales, Department B. A Sale No. column is provided to tie in the entry for each sale with the related source document.

Proving the Sales Journal. The sales journal may be footed and the footings proved daily or periodically by comparing the sum of the debit footings with the sum of the credit footings. When a page is filled and the amount columns footed, the footings should be proved, and the totals carried forward to the top of the next page. It is customary to start a month at the top of a new page.

Posting from the Sales Journal. Completing the posting from the sales journal involves both individual and summary posting. Individual posting is required from the General Ledger Debit and Credit columns, and may be required from the Accounts Receivable Debit column in some accounting information systems. In Spinner & Thomas' system, however, individual posting to the accounts receivable ledger is done directly from the sales invoices. This posting usually is done daily. As each item is posted, a check mark is entered in the Check (√) column following the General Ledger Debit, Accounts Receivable Debit, or General Ledger Credit Amount column of the sales journal.

The summary posting usually is completed at the end of each month and involves the following procedure (Account Nos. relate to the chart of accounts shown on page 530).

1. The total of the column headed Accounts Receivable should be posted as a debit to Accounts Receivable, Account No. 131, in the general ledger.

2. The total of the column headed Sales, Dept. A, should be posted as a credit to Sales—Department A, Account No. 411, in the general ledger.

3. The total of the column headed Sales, Dept. B, should be posted as a credit to Sales—Department B, Account No. 421, in the general ledger.

As the total of each column is posted, the account number should be written in parentheses immediately below the total in the sales journal. The final step in both individual and summary posting to the general ledger is to enter the initials "SJ" and the page number of the sales journal in the Posting Reference column of the proper general ledger account to the left of the amount posted. The final step in individual posting to the accounts receivable ledger is to enter the letter "S" and the sale number in the Posting Reference column of the proper customer's account to the left of the amount posted. A check mark should be placed in parentheses below the totals of the General Ledger Debit and Credit columns to indicate that these totals are not posted.

Cash Receipts Journal. Spinner & Thomas keeps a multi-column cash receipts journal. In the cash receipts journal reproduced on page 545, General Ledger Debit amount, Credit amount, and Account No. columns are provided. In addition, a special debit amount column is provided for Cash. All cash and cash items are entered by debiting the cash account immediately. This practice usually is followed when a business deposits all its cash receipts in a bank on the day they are received and makes all its payments (other than petty cash) by check. On the credit side, special amount columns are provided for Accounts Receivable, Cash Sales—Department A, and Cash Sales—Department B.

Proving the Cash Receipts Journal. The cash receipts journal may be footed and the footings proved daily or periodically by comparing the sum of the debit footings with the sum of the credit footings.

When a page is filled, the amount columns should be footed, the footings proved, and the totals carried forward to the top of the next page. It is customary to start a month at the top of a new page.

Posting from the Cash Receipts Journal. Completing the posting from the cash receipts journal involves both individual posting and summary posting. Individual posting is required from the General Ledger Debit and Credit columns. Individual posting to the accounts receivable ledger is done directly from the remittance advices. This posting usually is done daily. As each item is posted, a check mark is entered in the Check (√) column following the General Ledger Debit, Accounts Receivable Credit, or General Ledger Credit Amount column of the cash receipts journal.

The summary posting usually is completed at the end of each month and involves the following procedure:

1. The total of the column headed Cash should be posted as a debit to Cash, Account No. 111, in the general ledger.
2. The total of the column headed Accounts Receivable should be posted as a credit to Accounts Receivable, Account No. 131, in the general ledger.
3. The total of the column headed Cash Sales, Dept. A, should be posted as a credit to Sales—Department A, Account No. 411, in the general ledger.
4. The total of the column headed Cash Sales, Dept. B, should be posted as a credit to Sales—Department B, Account No. 421, in the general ledger.

As the total of each column is posted, the account number should be written in parentheses immediately below the total in the cash receipts journal. The final step in both individual and summary posting to the general ledger is to enter the initials "CRJ" and the page number of the cash receipts journal in the Posting Reference column of the proper general ledger account to the left of the amount posted. The final step in individual posting to the accounts receivable ledger is to enter the letter "C" (for collection) in the Posting Reference column of the proper customer's account to the left of the amount posted. A check mark should be placed in parentheses below the totals of the General Ledger Debit and Credit columns to indicate that these totals are not posted.

Check Register. A comparison of the format of Spinner & Thomas's check register reproduced on page 546 with that of the check register reproduced on page 436 will reveal that the formats are identical. This form of check register was described in detail in Chapter 14.

General Journal. The general journal is used for entering all transactions that cannot be entered in the special journals. Spinner &

Thomas uses a general journal (reproduced on page 547) with three amount columns—Detail, Debit, and Credit—as well as an Account No. column. The Detail column is used to enter debits to specific operating expense ledger accounts to support each of the debits to the control account, Operating Expenses, Account No. 541 in the general ledger. Adjusting, closing, and reversing entries also are entered in the general journal.

Proving the General Journal. The general journal may be footed and the footings proved daily or periodically by comparing the Debit footing with the Credit footing. When a page is filled, the three amount columns should be footed, the Debit and Credit footings proved, and the totals carried forward to the top of the next page. It is customary to start a month at the top of a new page.

Posting from the General Journal. Completing the posting from the general journal involves only individual posting from the Detail, Debit and Credit columns. This posting usually is done daily. Since the account numbers normally are entered in the Acct. No. column when the entries are made, posting is indicated by entering a check mark in the Check ($\sqrt{}$) column following each of the amount columns as each item is posted. The initials "GJ" and the page number of the general journal then should be entered in the Posting Reference column of the proper general ledger (or operating expense ledger) account to the left of the amount posted.

Although no summary posting is required, a check mark should be placed in parentheses below the Detail, Debit, and Credit column totals at the end of each month to indicate that these totals are not posted. Check marks should also be placed in parentheses below the proving totals of the adjusting and closing entries in the general journal after each of these sets of entries has been posted.

General Ledger. Spinner & Thomas uses a general ledger with four-column ledger account format. The accounts are arranged in this ledger in numerical order according to the chart of accounts reproduced on page 530. Note that the chart includes some accounts not used in previous presentations. A brief discussion of these new accounts follows.

Government Notes, Account No. 121. This account is used to enter the cost of United States government notes owned by Spinner & Thomas. From time to time, the partners find that the firm's bank balance is larger than necessary. To supplement earnings from regular operations, the excess cash is temporarily invested in certain types of government notes which earn a relatively high rate of return. The

SPINNER & THOMAS

CHART OF GENERAL LEDGER ACCOUNTS

Current Assets*

Cash
111 Cash
112 Petty Cash Fund

Temporary Investments
121 Government Notes

Receivables
122 Accrued Interest Receivable
131 Accounts Receivable
    131.1 Allowance for Doubtful
    Accounts

Inventories
141 Merchandise Inventory—
Department A
142 Merchandise Inventory—
Department B

Supplies and Prepayments
151 Store Supplies
152 Office Supplies
155 Prepaid Insurance

Long-Term Assets
181 Store Equipment
    181.1 Accumulated
    Depreciation—Store
    Equipment
185 Delivery Equipment
    185.1 Accumulated
    Depreciation—Delivery
    Equipment
191 Office Equipment
    191.1 Accumulated
    Depreciation—Office
    Equipment

Current Liabilities
211 FICA Tax Payable
212 FUTA Tax Payable
213 State Unemployment Tax
Payable
214 Employees Income Tax
Payable
216 Notes Payable
217 Accrued Interest Payable
218 Vouchers Payable

Owners' Equity
311 Harlan Spinner, Capital
    311.1 Harlan Spinner, Drawing
321 Carol Thomas, Capital
    321.1 Carol Thomas, Drawing
331 Expense and Revenue
Summary

Revenue from Sales
411 Sales—Department A
    411.1 Sales Returns and
    Allowances—Department
    A
421 Sales—Department B
    421.1 Sales Returns and
    Allowances—Department
    B

Other Revenue
431 Interest Earned

Cost of Goods Sold
511 Purchases—Department A
    511.1 Purchases Returns and
    Allowances—Department
    A
521 Purchases—Department B
    521.1 Purchases Returns and
    Allowances—Department
    B
531 Cost of Goods Sold—
Department A
532 Cost of Goods Sold—
Department B

Operating Expenses
541 Operating Expenses

Other Expenses
571 Interest Expense

*Words in bold type represent headings and not account titles.

notes can be sold or redeemed with little risk of loss. Because there is
no intention to hold the notes for a long period of time, they are
regarded as temporary investments and classified as a current asset of
the firm. In the end-of-period adjustment process, any interest accrued
on the notes is entered as a debit to Accrued Interest Receivable,
Account No. 122 and a credit to Interest Earned, Account No. 431.

**Cost of Goods Sold—Department A and Cost of Goods Sold—
Department B, Account Nos. 531 and 532.** These two accounts are
similar to Expense and Revenue Summary in that they are used only
at the end of the accounting period in the closing process. Each of
these accounts is used to summarize the elements that enter into the
calculation of the cost of goods sold by each department. The debit
balances of the merchandise inventory account (representing the
beginning inventory) and the purchases account, together with the
credit balance of the purchases returns and allowances account, are
closed to the cost of goods sold account. When the amount of the
ending inventory is entered by a debit to the merchandise inventory
account, the cost of goods sold account is credited. The balance of this
account then represents the cost of goods sold for the indicated
department. These balances then are closed to the expense and revenue summary account.

Accounts Receivable Ledger. Spinner & Thomas uses an accounts
receivable ledger with balance-column account format. The accounts
are arranged in this ledger in alphabetical order. A control account,
Accounts Receivable (Account No. 131), is kept in the general ledger.
At the end of each month, it is customary to prepare a schedule of the
accounts receivable, the total of which should be the same as the balance of the accounts receivable control account.

Posting to the customers' accounts in the accounts receivable ledger
may be done either from the books of original entry or directly from
the documents that represent the transactions. The accountant for
Spinner & Thomas follows the latter practice, using copies of sales
invoices, remittance advices, and credit memorandums. A check mark
is placed in the Check ($\sqrt{}$) column next to the Accounts Receivable
amount column either in the sales journal or cash receipts journal, or
next to the credit column in the general journal, each time an entry is
made. This reminds the accountant that posting is done directly from
source documents.

Operating Expense Ledger. Spinner & Thomas uses an operating
expense ledger with balance-column account format. The accounts are
arranged in numerical order. A chart of the accounts for Spinner &

Thomas appears below. A control account, Operating Expenses (Account No. 541), is kept in the general ledger. At the end of each month, it is customary to prepare a schedule of the operating expenses, the totals of which should be the same as the balance of the operating expenses control account.

SPINNER & THOMAS

CHART OF OPERATING EXPENSE LEDGER ACCOUNTS

Administrative Expenses

5401 Office Salaries Expense
5402 Harlan Spinner, Salary Expense
5403 Office Supplies Expense
5404 Depreciation of Office Equipment
5405 Office Equipment Insurance Expense
5406 Office Rent Expense
5407 Payroll Taxes Expense
5408 Heat, Light, and Water Expense
5409 Telephone Expense
5416 Postage Expense
5417 Uncollectible Accounts Expense
5422 Miscellaneous General Expense

Selling Expenses

5431 Store Clerks Salary Expense
5432 Truck Drivers Wage Expense
5433 Advertising Expense
5434 Carol Thomas, Salary Expense
5435 Depreciation of Delivery Equipment
5436 Delivery Equipment Insurance Expense
5437 Depreciation of Store Equipment
5438 Store Equipment Insurance Expense
5441 Truck Gas and Oil Expense
5442 Truck Repairs & Maintenance Expense
5443 Store Rent
5444 Store Supplies Expense
5452 Miscellaneous Selling Expense

All posting to the operating expense accounts is done from the books of original entry. As each item is posted, the initials and the page of the journal from which it is posted are entered in the Posting Reference column of the account.

As each entry involving an operating expense account is made in either the voucher register or general journal, the appropriate subsidiary ledger account number is written in the Acct. No. column to the left of the proper amount column. Then, when each of these amounts is posted to the operating expense ledger, a check mark is placed in the Check ($\sqrt{}$) column just to the right of the proper amount column.

Auxiliary Records. Spinner & Thomas keeps certain auxiliary records such as a petty cash payments record, a long-term asset record, voucher check stubs, and vouchers.

The format of the petty cash payments record is similar to that of the petty cash payments record illustrated on pages 262 and 263 of Chapter 8. The format of the long-term asset record is similar to the format of the long-term asset record illustrated on page 411 of Chapter 13. The voucher check and voucher formats were illustrated on pages 435 and 431 of Chapter 14. To conserve space, Spinner & Thomas' auxiliary records are not illustrated in this chapter.

Accounting Procedure Illustrated

The accounts of Spinner & Thomas are kept on the basis of a fiscal year ending June 30. The books of original entry (voucher register, sales journal, cash receipts journal, check register, and general journal) are shown on pages 542-543, 544, 545, 546, and 547. The general ledger and subsidiary ledgers are not reproduced in this illustration. Following is a narrative of the June transactions that are shown entered in the illustrations.

SPINNER & THOMAS

Narrative of Transactions

Monday, June 2

Issued Voucher No. 196 to Estate Leasing Co., Indianapolis, for $2,500, of which $1,500 represents store rent expense and $1,000 represents office rent expense.

Since the type of voucher used by Spinner & Thomas was illustrated in Chapter 14, it will not be illustrated in this chapter. Instead, sufficient detail will be given to explain each entry in the voucher register illustrated on pages 542-543. The voucher register illustration also begins with three unpaid vouchers from the previous month, May.

Issued Check No. 601 in payment of Voucher No. 171, and Check No. 602 in payment of Voucher No. 196.

The voucher register illustration on page 542 shows the payees and amounts of these two checks. Note that, in addition to the check register entries, the date and number of each check are written in the Disposition columns of the voucher register.

Cash sales for the day were $1,882 for Dept. A and $1,718 for Dept. B.

Cash sales are entered in the cash receipts journal illustrated on page 545. Note that the cash sales of Dept. A bakery goods are carefully separated from the cash sales of Dept. B bakery goods.

Tuesday, June 3

Received checks from customers on account as follows:
Brother Juniper's, $808, for merchandise sold on May 29.
Houlihan's Place, $514, for merchandise sold on May 29.
The Tin Star, $782, for merchandise sold on May 29.

Checks sent in by customers are accompanied by remittance advices, which are used to enter the transactions in the cash receipts journal illustrated on page 545 and to post to the individual customer accounts receivable ledger (not shown).

Cash sales for the day were $1,782 for Dept. A and $1,675 for Dept. B.

Wednesday, June 4

Issued Checks Nos. 603 and 604 in payment of Vouchers Nos. 194 and 195.

Issued Voucher No. 197 to Walnut Paper, Indianapolis, for store paper supplies, $201. (Charged to Account No. 151.)

Made charge sales as follows:

Bakemeier's Bakery, Indianapolis, pastries, $734; breads, $269; Sale No. 297.

Heritage House, Indianapolis, pastries, $392; breads, $354; Sale No. 298.

Sam's Deli, Indianapolis, pastries, $234; breads, $504; Sale No. 299.

Entries in the sales journal and postings to individual customer accounts receivable (not shown) are made from copies of the sales invoices. The sales journal is illustrated on page 544. Note that pastries are Dept. A sales and breads are Dept. B sales. All sales are numbered consecutively.

Cash sales for the day were $1,681 for Dept. A and $1,524 for Dept. B.

Thursday, June 5

Issued Voucher No. 198 to Indiana Bell, Indianapolis, for June telephone service, $101.

Received checks from customers on account as follows:

Ayres Department Stores, $1,180, for merchandise sold to them on May 31.

Bakemeier's Bakery, $983, for merchandise sold to them on May 31.

Methodist Hospital, $605, for merchandise sold to them on May 31.

Cash sales for the day were $1,808 for Dept. A and $1,402 for Dept. B.

Friday, June 6

Issued vouchers as follows:

Voucher No. 199 to Flowers Baking Co., Indianapolis, $4,566; pastries, $2,960; breads, $1,606.

Voucher No. 200 to International Bakers, Anderson, $4,373; pastries, $2,136; breads, $2,237.

Voucher No. 201 to Omar Bakeries, Indianapolis, pastries, $4,460.

Invoices for the previous week's purchases are received from suppliers on Friday and on the last day of the month for any other purchases through that date.

Made charge sales as follows:

Ayres Department Stores, Indianapolis, pastries, $767; breads, $421; Sale No. 300.

Brother Juniper's, Indianapolis, pastries, $450; breads, $152; Sale No. 301.

Houlihan's Place, Indianapolis, pastries, $332; breads, $148; Sale No. 302.

Cash sales for the day were $1,582 for Dept. A and $1,336 for Dept. B.

Saturday, June 7

Cash sales for the day were $1,566 for Dept. A and $1,361 for Dept. B.

End-of-the-Week Work

(1) Footed the amount columns in the books of original entry, entered the footings in small figures immediately below the line on which the last entry appeared, and proved the footings. (2) Proved the cash balance in the following manner:

Cash balance, June 1	$26,122*
Add receipts June 1-7 per cash receipts journal	24,189
Total	$50,311
Subtract checks issued June 1-7 per check register	12,186
Cash balance, June 7	$38,125

*From General Ledger Account No. 111 not shown in this illustration.

(3) Completed the individual posting from the books of original entry to the general ledger and operating expenses ledger accounts. (Accounts receivable ledger accounts were posted directly from the sales invoices and remittance advices.)

Monday, June 9

Issued Credit Memorandum No. 7 to Brother Juniper's, $7, as an allowance for having delivered the wrong pastry order.

The pastry had been billed as a part of Sale No. 301. The allowance transaction was entered in the general journal illustrated on page 547, after which the credit memorandum was posted immediately as a credit to the account of Brother Juniper's in the accounts receivable ledger. ("CM" stands for credit memorandum in the journal entry explanation.)

Cash sales for the day were $1,715 for Dept. A and $1,433 for Dept. B.

Tuesday, June 10

Received checks from customers on account as follows:
Bakemeier's Bakery, $1,003, for merchandise sold on June 4.
Heritage House, $746, for merchandise sold on June 4.
Sam's Deli, $738, for merchandise sold on June 4.
Cash sales for the day were $1,777 for Dept. A and $1,484 for Dept. B.

Wednesday, June 11

Issued Checks Nos. 605, 606, 607, and 608 in payment of Vouchers Nos. 197, 199, 200, and 201.
Made charge sales as follows:
Bakemeier's Bakery, Indianapolis, pastries, $631; breads, $308; Sale No. 303.

Methodist Hospital, Indianapolis, pastries, $236; breads, $506; Sale No. 304.

The Tin Star, Indianapolis, pastries, $312; breads, $215; Sale No. 305.

Cash sales for the day were $1,738 for Dept. A and $1,446 for Dept. B.

Thursday, June 12

Issued Voucher No. 202 to Indianapolis Power & Light, Indianapolis, for May electricity bill, $239.

Received checks from customers on account as follows:

Ayres Department Store, $1,188, for merchandise sold on June 6.

Brother Juniper's, $595, for merchandise sold on June 6, less the $7 allowance for having delivered the wrong pastry order.

Houlihan's Place, $480, for merchandise sold on June 6.

Cash sales for the day were $1,812 for Dept. A and $1,532 for Dept. B.

Friday, June 13

Issued Vouchers as follows:

Voucher No. 203 to Heileman Baking Co., Fort Wayne, $3,860; pastries, $1,256; breads, $2,604.

Voucher No. 204 to Omar Bakeries, Indianapolis, pastries, $4,410.

Voucher No. 205 to Tri-Baking Co., Indianapolis, $4,236; pastries, $1,459; breads, $2,777.

Made charge sales as follows:

Ayres Department Stores, Indianapolis, pastries, $763; breads, $482; Sale No. 306.

Brother Juniper's, Indianapolis, pastries, $436; breads, $145; Sale No. 307.

Houlihan's Place, Indianapolis, pastries, $342; breads, $227; Sale No. 308.

Cash sales for the day were $1,524 for Dept. A and $1,201 for Dept. B.

Saturday, June 14

Issued Voucher No. 206 to Indianapolis Water Co., Indianapolis, for May water bill, $172.

Cash sales for the day were $1,423 for Dept. A and $1,120 for Dept. B.

End-of-the-Week Work

(1) Footed the amount columns in the books of original entry, entered the footings in small figures immediately below the line on which the last entry appeared, and proved the footings. (2) Proved the cash balance in the following manner.

Cash balance, June 1	$26,122
Add receipts, June 1-14 per cash receipts journal	47,144
Total	$73,266
Subtract checks issued June 1-14 per check register	25,786
Cash balance, June 14	$47,480

(3) Completed the individual posting from the books of original entry to the general ledger and operating expenses ledger accounts.

Monday, June 16

Issued Voucher No. 207 to the Federal National Bank for the payment of the following taxes:

Employees' income tax (withheld during May)................		$1,120
FICA tax imposed —		
on employees (withheld during May).................	$569	
on the employer....................................	569	1,138
Total		$2,258

Issued Voucher No. 208 to Payroll for the semimonthly wages, $5,452.

Spinner & Thomas follows the policy of paying employees on the 15th (or the next business day) and the last day of each month. The business is subject to the taxes imposed under the Federal Insurance Contributions Act (for old-age benefits and hospital insurance), and the Federal Unemployment Tax Act (for unemployment insurance purposes), and is required to make contributions to the state unemployment compensation fund. The company is also required to withhold a percentage of employees' wages both for FICA and for income tax purposes. In addition to the wages paid to employees, the Spinner & Thomas partnership agreement provides that each partner is to receive a salary of $2,400 a month, payable semimonthly. The salaries of the partners constitute an operating expense of the business and do not represent "wages" as defined in the social security and income tax laws; hence, their salaries are not subject to the FICA tax imposed upon employers and employees. Neither are such salaries subject to withholding for employee's income tax.

Each payday the accountant is supplied with a report prepared by the payroll clerk showing the total amount of wages and salaries earned during the pay period, the amount of payroll deductions, and the net amount of cash needed for payroll purposes. The report for June 16 appears on page 539.

PAYROLL STATEMENT
Period Beginning June 1 and Ending June 16

Classification	Total Earnings	DEDUCTIONS		Net Amount Payable
		FICA Tax	Employee's Income Tax	
Store Clerks Wages	1,000.00	75.00	119.80	805.20
Truck Drivers Wages	1,104.00	82.80	154.50	866.70
Office Salaries	1,736.00	130.20	225.70	1,380.10
Partners' salaries:				
H. Spinner	1,200.00	None	None	1,200.00
C. Thomas	1,200.00	None	None	1,200.00
	6,240.00	288.00	500.00	5,452.00

Employer's payroll taxes:
(a) FICA tax, 7.5% of $3,840.00 .... $288.00
(b) Unemployment compensation taxes—
State unemployment compensation tax,
5.4% of $1,200 .... $64.80
FUTA tax, 0.8% of $1,200 .... 9.60   74.40
Total $362.40

A check made payable to Payroll is issued for the net amount payable. This check is then cashed at the Federal National Bank to obtain currency in the denominations necessary to pay each employee. The accountant is instructed to deposit Spinner's and Thomas' salaries in their individual bank accounts and to furnish them with copies of the deposit tickets.

The payroll voucher was entered in the voucher register by debiting the proper salary accounts for the earnings, by crediting the proper liability accounts for the taxes withheld, and by crediting the vouchers payable account for the amount of the check to be subsequently issued. The payroll taxes imposed on the employer were entered in the general journal by debiting Operating Expenses in the Debit column, by debiting Payroll Taxes Expense in the Detail column, and by crediting the proper liability accounts for the taxes imposed.

Issued Checks Nos. 609 and 610 in payment of Vouchers Nos. 207 and 208.

Spinner reported that interest coupons amounting to $600 from government notes were deposited in the Federal National Bank. This transaction was entered in the cash receipts journal.

Cash sales for the day were $1,726 for Dept. A and $1,476 for Dept. B.

The white space appearing at this point in the illustrated records indicates omission of the transactions completed on the days between June 16 and 30.

Monday, June 30

Issued vouchers as follows:

Voucher No. 219 to Flowers Baking Co., Indianapolis, $4,044; pastries, $1,211; breads, $2,833.

Voucher No. 220 to Omar Bakeries, Indianapolis, pastries, $2,500.

Voucher No. 221 to U.S. Post Office for postage, $59.

Voucher No. 222 to Petty Cash to replenish the petty cash fund. The following report was submitted by the clerk responsible for the fund.

Statement of Petty Cash Payments for June

Acct. No.	Description	Amount
5409	Telephone Expense	$ 3.00
5422	Miscellaneous General Expense	79.00
5433	Advertising Expense	13.00
5441	Truck Gas & Oil Expense	12.00
5452	Miscellaneous Selling Expense	30.00
	Total Disbursements	$137.00

Issued Voucher No. 223 to Payroll for the semimonthly wages, $5,503, in accordance with the payroll statement for the period June 16-30, shown on page 541.

Issued Checks Nos. 638, 639, and 640 in payment of Vouchers Nos. 221, 222, 223.

Received checks from customers on account as follows:

Heritage House, $829, for merchandise sold on June 25.

The Tin Star, $714, for merchandise sold on June 25.

Cash sales for the day were $1,850 for Dept. A and $1,615 for Dept. B.

End-of-the-Month Work

(1) Footed the amount columns, proved the footings, entered the totals, and ruled each of the books of original entry. (2) Proved the cash balance in the following manner:

Cash balance, June 1	$ 26,122
Total receipts for June per cash receipts journal	103,790
Total	$129,912
Less total checks issued during June per check register	95,477
Cash balance, June 30	$ 34,435

PAYROLL STATEMENT Period Beginning June 16 and Ending June 30				
Classification	Total Earnings	DEDUCTIONS		Net Amount Payable
		FICA Tax	Employee's Income Tax	
Store Clerks Wages	1,023.00	76.78	122.40	823.82
Truck Drivers Wages	1,126.00	84.45	157.00	884.55
Office Salaries	1,757.00	131.77	230.60	1,394.63
Partners' Salaries:				
H. Spinner	1,200.00	None	None	1,200.00
C. Thomas	1,200.00	None	None	1,200.00
	6,306.00	293.00	510.00	5,503.00

Employer's payroll taxes:
  (a) FICA tax, 7.5% of $3,906.00 .... $293.00
  (b) Unemployment compensation taxes—
      State unemployment compensation tax,
        5.4% of $1,200 .... $64.80
        FUTA tax, 0.8% of $1,200 .... 9.60   74.40
      Total $367.40

(The accounting procedure used is similar to that shown on pages 538-539 relating to payroll.)

(3) Completed the individual posting from the books of original entry to the general ledger and to the operating expense ledger accounts. (4) Completed the summary posting of the totals of the special columns of each of the books of original entry to the general ledger accounts. (5) Prepared a trial balance and schedules of accounts receivable, vouchers payable, and operating expenses.

Step (5) would be completed as a part of the normal routine at the end of each month. However, since the end of June is also the end of the fiscal year for Spinner & Thomas, the procedure is varied slightly. The preparation of the general ledger trial balance and the schedule of operating expenses is combined with the preparation of the end-of-year work sheets used to assist in producing the income statement for the year and the balance sheet as of June 30. This process is described and illustrated in the following chapter. (The schedule of accounts receivable is shown on page 586.)

VOUCHER REGISTER FOR MONTH OF June   19 --   PAGE 25

Line	PURCHASES DR — DEPT. A	PURCHASES DR — DEPT. B	OPER. EXP. DR — ACCT. NO.	OPER. EXP. DR — AMOUNT	✓	SUNDRY DR — ACCT. NO.	SUNDRY DR — AMOUNT	✓	DAY	VOU. NO.	TO WHOM ISSUED	SUNDRY CR — ACCT. NO.	SUNDRY CR — AMOUNT	✓	VOUCHERS PAYABLE CR	DATE	CK. NO.
1											AMOUNTS FORWARDED						
2									5/27	171	Walnut Paper				282 00	6/2	601
3									5/31	194	Flowers Baking Co.				5 130 00	6/4	603
4									5/31	195	Omar Bakeries				4 274 00	6/4	604
5															9 686 00		
6			5443	1 500 00	✓	151	2 01 00	✓	2	196	Estate Leasing Co.				2 500 00	6/2	602
7			5406	1 000 00	✓												
8									4	197	Walnut Paper				201 00	6/11	605
9			5409	101 00	✓				5	198	Indiana Bell				101 00	6/20	619
10	2 960 00	1 606 00							6	199	Flowers Baking Co.				4 566 00	6/11	606
11	2 136 00	2 237 00							6	200	International Bakers				4 373 00	6/11	607
12	4 460 00								6	201	Omar Bakeries				4 460 00	6/11	608
13	9 556 00	3 843 00	5408	2 601 00 / 239 00			2 01 00		12	202	Indianapolis Power & Light				16 201 00 / 239 00	6/26	627
14	1 256 00	2 604 00							13	203	Heileman Baking Co.				3 860 00	6/17	612
15	4 410 00								13	204	Omar Bakeries				4 410 00	6/17	613
16	1 459 00	2 777 00							13	205	Tri-Baking Co.				4 236 00	6/17	614
17	16 681 00	9 224 00	5408	172 00	✓				14	206	Indianapolis Water Co.				172 00	6/27	631
18				3 012 00		211 / 214	201 00 / 1 138 00 / 1 120 00	✓	16	207	Federal National Bank	211	288 00	✓	29 118 00 / 258 00	6/16	609
19												214	500 00	✓			
20			5431	1 000 00	✓				16	208	Payroll				5 452 00	6/16	610
21			5432	1 104 00	✓												
22			5401	1 736 00	✓												
23			5402	1 200 00	✓												
24			5434	1 200 00	✓												
48	1 211 00	2 833 00							30	219	Flowers Baking Co.				4 044 00		
49	2 500 00								30	220	Omar Bakeries				2 500 00		
50			5416	59 00	✓				30	221	U.S. Post Office				59 00	6/30	638
51	62 720 00 / 62 720 00	41 256 00 / 41 256 00		6 056 00 / 6 056 00			5 444 00 / 5 444 00		30		Carried forward		788 00		1146 88 00		

Voucher Register—Spinner & Thomas

VOUCHER REGISTER FOR MONTH OF June   19 --   PAGE 26

	PURCHASES DR		OPERATING EXPENSES DR			SUNDRY ACCOUNTS DR			DAY	VOU. NO.	TO WHOM ISSUED	SUNDRY ACCOUNTS CR			VOUCHERS PAYABLE CR	DISPOSITION	
	DEPT. A	DEPT. B	ACCT. NO.	AMOUNT	√	ACCT. NO.	AMOUNT	√				ACCT. NO.	AMOUNT	√		DATE	CK. NO.
1	62 720 00	41 256 00		6 056 00			5 444 00	√			AMOUNTS FORWARDED		7 88 00		114 688 00		
2			5409	3 00	√				30	222	Petty Cash				1 37 00	6/30	639
3			5422	79 00	√												
4			5433	13 00	√												
5			5441	12 00	√												
6			5452	30 00	√												
7			5431	10 23	√				30	223	Payroll	211	2 93 00	√	5 503 00	6/30	640
8			5432	11 26	√							214	5 10 00	√			
9			5401	17 57	√												
10			5402	12 00	√												
11			5434	12 00	√								1 5 91 00		120 328 00		
12	62 720 00	41 256 00		12 499 00			5 444 00						1 5 91 00		120 328 00		
13	(5 1 1)	(5 2 1)		(5 4 1)			(√)						(√)		(2 1 8)		

Voucher Register—Spinner & Thomas (concluded)

SALES JOURNAL FOR MONTH OF June 19-- PAGE 27

SALE NO.	DAY	NAME	✓	ACCOUNTS RECEIVABLE (Debit)	SALES DEPT. A (Credit)	SALES DEPT. B (Credit)
297	4	Bakemeier's Bakery	✓	1003 00	734 00	269 00
298	4	Heritage House	✓	746 00	392 00	354 00
299	4	Sam's Deli	✓	738 00	234 00	504 00
300	6	Ayres Department Stores	✓	1188 00	767 00	421 00
301	6	Brother Juniper's	✓	602 00	450 00	152 00
302	6	Houlihan's Place	✓	480 00	332 00	148 00
303	11	Bakemeier's Bakery	✓	939 00	631 00	308 00
304	11	Methodist Hospital	✓	742 00	236 00	506 00
305	11	The Tin Star	✓	527 00	312 00	215 00
306	13	Ayres Department Stores	✓	1245 00	763 00	482 00
307	13	Brother Juniper's	✓	581 00	436 00	145 00
308	13	Houlihan's Place	✓	569 00	342 00	227 00
				9360 00	5629 00	3731 00

	ACCOUNTS RECEIVABLE	SALES DEPT. A	SALES DEPT. B
30	20323 00	11453 00	8870 00
31	20323 00	11453 00	8870 00
32	(131)	(411)	(421)

Sales Journal—Spinner & Thomas

CASH RECEIPTS JOURNAL FOR MONTH OF June 19 —

DEBIT GENERAL LEDGER ACCT. NO.	AMOUNT	√	CASH NET AMOUNT	DAY	RECEIVED FROM—DESCRIPTION	ACCOUNTS RECEIVABLE	√	CREDIT CASH SALES DEPT. A	DEPT. B	GEN. LEDGER ACCT. NO.	AMOUNT	√
			3600 00		AMOUNTS FORWARDED			1882 00	1718 00			
			3457 00	2	Cash sales			1782 00	1675 00			
			808 00	3	Brother Juniper's	808 00	√					
			514 00	3	Houlihan's Place	514 00	√					
			782 00	3	The Tin Star	782 00	√					
			3205 00	3	Cash sales			1681 00	1524 00			
			3210 00	4	Cash sales			1808 00	1402 00			
			1180 00	5	Ayres Department Stores	1180 00	√					
			983 00	5	Bakemeier's Bakery	983 00	√					
			605 00	5	Methodist Hospital	605 00	√					
			2918 00	5	Cash sales			1582 00	1336 00			
			2927 00	6	Cash sales			1566 00	1361 00			
			2418 00	7	Cash sales			1030 00	1388 00			
			3148 00	9	Cash sales			1715 00	1433 00			
			1003 00	10	Bakemeier's Bakery	1003 00	√					
			746 00	10	Heritage House	746 00	√					
			738 00	10	Sam's Deli	738 00	√					
			3261 00	10	Cash sales			1777 00	1484 00			
			3184 00	11	Cash sales			1738 00	1446 00			
			1188 00	12	Ayres Department Stores	1188 00	√					
			595 00	12	Brother Juniper's	595 00	√					
			480 00	12	Houlihan's Place	480 00	√					
			3344 00	12	Cash sales			1812 00	1532 00			
			2725 00	13	Cash sales			1524 00	1201 00			
			2543 00	14	Cash sales			1423 00	1120 00			
			60 00	16	Interest on Gov't Notes					431	60 00	√
			3202 00	16	Cash sales			1726 00	1476 00			
			103790 00			9622 00		20290 00	17232 00		60 00	
			(111)			(131)		(411)	(421)		(√)	

CASH NET AMOUNT	DAY	RECEIVED FROM—DESCRIPTION	ACCOUNTS RECEIVABLE	√	DEPT. A	DEPT. B	AMOUNT
829 00	30	Heritage House	829 00	√			
714 00	30	The Tin Star	714 00	√			
3465 00	30	Cash sales			1850 00	1615 00	
103790 00			18328 00		44875 00	39987 00	60 00
103790 00			18328 00		44875 00	39987 00	60 00
(111)			(131)		(411)	(421)	(√)

Cash Receipts Journal—Spinner & Thomas

CHECK REGISTER FOR MONTH OF June 19 --   PAGE 24

	VOUCHERS PAYABLE DR.				CASH CR.	
	NO.	AMOUNT	DAY	DRAWN TO THE ORDER OF	CHK. NO.	AMOUNT
1				AMOUNTS FORWARDED		
2	171	2 8 2 00	2	Walnut Paper	601	2 8 2 00
3	196	2 5 0 00	2	Estate Leasing Co.	602	2 5 0 00
4	194	5 1 3 00	4	Flowers Baking Co.	603	5 1 3 00
5	195	4 2 7 00	4	Omar Bakeries	604	4 2 7 00
6	197	12 1 8 6 00 / 2 0 1 00	11	Walnut Paper	605	12 1 8 6 00 / 2 0 1 00
7	199	4 5 6 00	11	Flowers Baking Co.	606	4 5 6 00
8	200	4 3 7 00	11	International Bakers	607	4 3 7 00
9	201	4 4 6 00	11	Omar Bakeries	608	4 4 6 00
10	207	25 7 8 6 00 / 2 2 5 8 00	16	Federal National Bank	609	25 7 8 6 00 / 2 2 5 8 00
11	208	5 4 5 2 00	16	Payroll	610	5 4 5 2 00
30	221	5 9 00	30	U.S. Post Office	638	5 9 00
31	222	1 3 7 00	30	Petty Cash	639	1 3 7 00
32	223	5 5 0 3 00	30	Payroll	640	5 5 0 3 00
33		95 4 7 7 00 / 95 4 7 7 00				95 4 7 7 00 / 95 4 7 7 00
34		(2 1 8)				(1 1 1)

Check Register—Spinner & Thomas

GENERAL JOURNAL

PAGE 41

DATE	DESCRIPTION	ACCT. NO.	DETAIL	✓	DEBIT	✓	CREDIT	✓	
19-- June 9	Sales Returns and Allowances—Dept. A	411.1			7 00			✓	1
	Accounts Receivable	131					7 00	✓	2
	Brother Juniper's, CM7								3
16	Operating Expenses	541			3 6 2 40	✓			4
	Payroll Taxes Expense	5407	3 6 2 40	✓					5
	FICA Tax Payable	211					2 8 8 00	✓	6
	FUTA Tax Payable	212					9 60	✓	7
	State Unemployment Tax Payable	213					6 4 80	✓	8
	Payroll taxes—June 16 payroll								9
30	Operating Expenses	541			3 6 7 40	✓			31
	Payroll Taxes Expense	5407	3 6 7 40	✓					32
	FICA Tax Payable	211					2 9 3 00	✓	33
	FUTA Tax Payable	212					9 60	✓	34
	State Unemployment Tax Payable	213					6 4 80	✓	35
	Payroll taxes—June 30 payroll								36
			7 2 9 80 / 7 2 9 80 (✓)		7 5 4 00 / 7 5 4 00 (✓)		7 5 4 00 / 7 5 4 00 (✓)		37

General Journal—Spinner & Thomas

BUILDING YOUR ACCOUNTING KNOWLEDGE

1. What are the differences in the owner's equity accounts that are kept in a single proprietorship, a partnership, and a corporation?
2. Name five separate books of original entry and indicate the type of business transaction normally entered in each.
3. Give four advantages of a functional division of the accounting activity.
4. What kinds of equipment often are used to aid the accounting work in the modern office of a big business enterprise?
5. What special information requirement has led to the organization of specialized accounting departments in large firms?
6. Describe the function of each of the five books of original entry kept by Spinner & Thomas.
7. Describe the function of each of the two subsidiary ledgers kept by Spinner & Thomas.
8. What are the two major auxiliary records that Spinner & Thomas maintain? Name two other auxiliary records that are kept in files by Spinner & Thomas.

APPLYING ACCOUNTING CONCEPTS

Exercise 17-1. Given the following columnar totals from the Voucher Register of Bradshaw's Florist, what should be the total of the vouchers payable column? Identify the total as either a debit or credit balance.

Column	Debit	Credit
Purchases, Department A	$26,270	
Purchases, Department B	14,526	
Operating Expenses	1,656	
Sundry Accounts	4,544	$878
Vouchers Payable	?	?

Exercise 17-2. The following totals were taken from the Sales Journal of Computer Sales and Service. What should be the total of the accounts receivable column? Indicate whether the total is a debit or credit balance.

Column	Debit	Credit
General Ledger	$ 437	$ 250
Accounts Receivable	?	?
Sales, Hardware Department		8,543
Sales, Software Department		7,075

Exercise 17-3. The following are the columnar totals taken from the Cash Receipts Journal of Bay Area Pools. Determine the toal amount of cash sales for Department B. Will the balance be a debit or a credit?

Column	Debit	Credit
General Ledger	$27,123	$ 605
Cash	92,685	
Accounts Receivable		15,763
Cash Sales, Department A		34,015
Cash Sales, Department B	?	?

Exercise 17-4. If the total of the vouchers payable column of the Check Register for Austin's Antiques is $75,974, what should be the total of the Cash column?

Exercise 17-5. Identify the appropriate journal in which the following transactions would be entered:

1. Issued a voucher.
2. Issued a check in payment of a voucher.
3. Entered cash sales for the day.
4. Entered checks received from customers on account.
5. Made a charge sale.
6. Issued a credit memorandum to a customer.
7. Entered the liability for payroll taxes owed.
8. Issued a voucher for payment of payroll taxes.
9. Deposited interest coupons from government notes held by the bank.
10. Issued a voucher to replenish the petty cash fund.
11. Entered expenditures summarized in the Statement of Petty Cash Payments.

Exercise 17-6. In completing the end-of-the-week work on May 13, the following amounts were taken from the accounting records of Victory Home Builders Supply:

Cash balance, May 1	$37,145
Receipts for May 1-13 per cash debit column	
in the cash receipts journal	35,732
Checks issued May 1-13 per cash credit column	
in the check register	23,294

Prove the cash balance as of May 13.

**Report
No. 17-1**

The study assignments contain an analysis test that should be completed at this time. Before beginning work on the test, this chapter should be reviewed thoroughly. The narrative of transactions for June should be compared with the illustrations to see how each transaction is recorded and to note the effect of each transaction on the accounts involved. Special attention should be given to the analysis following certain transactions. Unless the procedure involved in entering the transactions completed by Spinner & Thomas during the month of June is thoroughly understood, you cannot hope to make a satisfactory grade on the test.

EXPANDING YOUR BUSINESS VOCABULARY

What is the meaning of each of the following terms:

cash receipts journal **(p. 527)**   operating expense ledger
Detail column **(p. 529)**   **(p. 531)**
                                          sales journal **(p. 526)**

CHAPTER 18

Accounting Procedure At Year End

CHAPTER OBJECTIVES

Careful study of this chapter should enable you to:

- Prepare a ten-column, end-of-year summary work sheet supplemented by a three-column end-of-year operating expenses work sheet.

- Prepare end-of-year departmental summary accounts for cost of goods sold.

- Prepare adjustments that involve debits to accounts on the operating expenses work sheet (with a summary debit to the general ledger account, Operating Expenses) and credits to various general ledger accounts on the summary work sheet.

- Prepare the adjusting entries and the closing entries in the general journal (using the summary work sheet as a guide) and post to the general ledger end-of-period summary accounts (Expense and Revenue Summary, and the two departmental accounts for cost of goods sold).

- Prepare the post-closing trial balance.

- Prepare any reversing entries required in the general journal as of the first day of the new accounting period.

One of the several reasons for maintaining an accounting information system is to make it possible to prepare periodic financial reports, including an income statement for the fiscal year and a balance sheet as of the close of that year. Long experience has shown that one of the fastest ways to produce these financial statements is (1) to use the information provided by the accounts—as reflected by the year-end trial balance taken after the regular posting has been completed, (2) to determine the needed adjustments, and (3) to bring these amounts together in a manner that facilitates statement preparation. The device most commonly used for these purposes is the work sheet.

This chapter continues the use of the ten-column work sheet in summary form, and also introduces a three-column supplementary work sheet for operating expenses. The use of departmental summary accounts for cost of goods sold as partial substitutes for the expense and revenue summary account is introduced and illustrated. The adjusting and closing process is explained and illustrated for each type of work sheet. Finally, a post-closing trial balance and the one necessary reversing entry are described and illustrated.

SUMMARY AND SUPPLEMENTARY YEAR-END WORK SHEETS

A simple eight-column work sheet for a personal service enterprise was discussed and illustrated in Chapter 5. A ten-column work sheet for a retail merchandising business was introduced in Chapter 9. Following is a discussion and illustration of Spinner & Thomas's ten-column summary work sheet supplemented by a three-column operating expenses work sheet. In the preceding chapter, a partial narrative of transactions for this firm for the month of June, 19-- (the last month of the fiscal year) was given. These transactions were entered in the books of original entry. The books of original entry were reproduced as they would appear after both the individual and the summary posting had been completed. The general ledger accounts and the accounts in each of the two subsidiary ledgers (accounts receivable and operating expenses) were not reproduced. However, it may be assumed that trial balances of these ledgers were taken. The general ledger was found to be in balance and the total of the account balances in each subsidiary ledger was found to agree with the balance of the related control account in the general ledger.

Summary Year-End Work Sheet

The Spinner & Thomas work sheet is shown on pages 554 and 555. It is identical to that used for MicroWorld on page 282. The first step in its preparation was to place the proper heading at the top, to insert the proper heading in the space provided at the top of each of the five pairs of amount columns, and to list the general ledger account titles and numbers in the spaces provided at the left. Note that with one exception the title and number of each general ledger account was listed (refer to the chart of accounts given on page 530 for the complete list) even though some of the accounts had no balances at the time the trial balance was taken. The one exception is Expense and Revenue Summary, Account No. 331. This account is used in the formal process of closing the books but is not needed on the work sheet. Expense and Revenue Summary was included in the MicroWorld work sheet on page 282 because the account was used to adjust the beginning and ending inventories. These inventory adjustments in the Spinner & Thomas work sheet are made using two cost of goods sold accounts that MicroWorld did not maintain. Note also that for Cost of Goods Sold—Department A, Account No. 531, and Cost of Goods Sold—Department B, Account No. 532, two lines were allowed in each case to accommodate the several debits and credits that will be involved. (The purpose of the cost of goods sold account is to provide a means of bringing together all the elements that are involved in calculating the amount of this cost: (1) beginning inventory, (2) purchases, (3) purchases returns and allowances, and (4) ending inventory.) The account balances were entered in the first pair of columns (trial balance) and these columns were totaled to prove their equality.

Adjustment of the Merchandise Accounts. Eight entries (a-h), were made in the adjustments columns of the work sheet to show the calculation of the cost of goods sold for each department and to adjust the merchandise inventory accounts.

Entry (a): The amount of the beginning inventory for Department A, $1,714, was transferred to Cost of Goods Sold— Department A by a debit to that account (No. 531) and by a credit to Merchandise Inventory—Department A, Account No. 141.

Entry (b): The amount of the beginning inventory for Department B, $1,410, was transferred to Cost of Goods Sold— Department B by a debit to that account (No. 532) and by a credit to Merchandise Inventory—Department B, Account No. 142.

SPINNER & THOMAS
Work Sheet
For the Year Ended June 30, 19—

#	ACCOUNT	ACCT. NO.	TRIAL BALANCE DEBIT	TRIAL BALANCE CREDIT	ADJUSTMENTS DEBIT	ADJUSTMENTS CREDIT	ADJ. TRIAL BALANCE DEBIT	ADJ. TRIAL BALANCE CREDIT	INCOME STATEMENT DEBIT	INCOME STATEMENT CREDIT	BALANCE SHEET DEBIT	BALANCE SHEET CREDIT
1	Cash	111	34435.00				34435.00				34435.00	
2	Petty Cash Fund	112	200.00				200.00				200.00	
3	Government Notes	121	10000.00				10000.00				10000.00	
4	Accrued Interest Receivable	122			(i) 50.00		50.00				50.00	
5	Accounts Receivable	131	10978.00				10978.00				10978.00	
6	Allowance for Doubtful Accounts	131.1		60.00		(p) 180.00		240.00				240.00
7	Merchandise Inventory—Dept. A	141	17714.00		(g) 16800.00	(a) 17140.00	16800.00				16800.00	
8	Merchandise Inventory—Dept. B	142	14110.00		(h) 15000.00	(b) 14100.00	15000.00				15000.00	
9	Store Supplies	151	8974.00			(m) 7724.00	1250.00				1250.00	
10	Office Supplies	152	7896.00			(n) 7141.00	755.00				755.00	
11	Prepaid Insurance	155	5532.00			(o) 4650.00	882.00				882.00	
12	Store Equipment	181	19780.00				19780.00				19780.00	
13	Accumulated Depr.—Store Equip.	181.1		1680.00		(j) 1978.00		3658.00				3658.00
14	Delivery Equipment	185	57100.00				57100.00				57100.00	
15	Accumulated Depr.—Del. Equip.	185.1		42800.00		(k) 7138.00		49938.00				49938.00
16	Office Equipment	191	19001.00				19001.00				19001.00	
17	Accumulated Depr.—Off. Equip.	191.1		1415.00		(l) 1848.00		3263.00				3263.00
18	FICA Tax Payable	211		1162.00				1162.00				1162.00
19	FUTA Tax Payable	212		28.00				28.00				28.00
20	State Unemployment Tax Pay.	213		389.00				389.00				389.00
21	Employees Income Tax Pay.	214		1010.00				1010.00				1010.00
22	Notes Payable	216		-0-				-0-				-0-

#	Account	No.	Trial Balance Dr	Trial Balance Cr	Adjustments Dr	Adjustments Cr	Adj. Trial Balance Dr	Adj. Trial Balance Cr	Income Statement Dr	Income Statement Cr	Balance Sheet Dr	Balance Sheet Cr
23	Accrued Interest Payable	217		- 0 -				- 0 -				- 0 -
24	Vouchers Payable	218		34375 00				34375 00				34375 00
25	Harlan Spinner, Capital	311		38731 00				38731 00				38731 00
26	Harlan Spinner, Drawing	311.1	10300 00				10300 00				10300 00	
27	Carol Thomas, Capital	321		16599 00				16599 00				16599 00
28	Carol Thomas, Drawing	321.1	7800 00				7800 00				7800 00	
29	Sales—Dept. A	411		734629 00				734629 00		734629 00		
30	Sales Ret. & Allow.—Dept. A	411.1	376 00				376 00		376 00			
31	Sales—Dept. B	421		620988 00				620988 00		620988 00		
32	Sales Ret. & Allow.—Dept. B	421.1	338 00				338 00		338 00			
33	Purchases—Dept. A	511	628785 00			(c) 628785 00						
34	Purchases Ret. & Allow.—Dept. A	511.1		820 00	(e) 820 00							
35	Purchases—Dept. B	521	461110 00			(d) 461110 00						
36	Purchases Ret. & Allow.—Dept. B	521.1		460 00	(f) 460 00							
37	Cost of Goods Sold—Dept. A	531			(a) 1714 00	(e) 820 00	627999 00		627999 00			
38					(c) 628785 00	(g) 1680 00						
39	Cost of Goods Sold—Dept. B	532			(b) 6410 00	(f) 460 00	465560 00		465560 00			
40					(d) 461110 00	(h) 1500 00						
41	Operating Expenses	541	205712 00		(p) 30659 00		236371 00		236371 00			
42	Interest Earned	431		1295 00		(i) 50 00		1345 00		1345 00		
43	Interest Expense	571	- 0 -				- 0 -		- 0 -			
44			1496441 00	1496441 00	1133188 00	1133188 00	1506355 00	1506355 00	1330644 00	1356962 00	175711 00	149393 00
45	Net Income								26318 00			26318 00
46									1356962 00	1356962 00	175711 00	175711 00

Spinner & Thomas—Ten-Column Work Sheet

Entry (c): The amount of the purchases for the year by Department A, $628,785, was transferred to Cost of Goods Sold—Department A by a debit to that account (No. 531) and by a credit to Purchases—Department A, Account No. 511.

Entry (d): The amount of the purchases for the year by Department B, $466,110, was transferred to Cost of Goods Sold—Department B by a debit to that account (No. 532) and by a credit to Purchases—Department B, Account No. 521.

Entry (e): The amount of the purchases returns and allowances for the year for Department A, $820, was transferred to the proper cost of goods sold account by a debit to Purchases Returns and Allowances—Department A, Account No. 511.1 and by a credit to Cost of Goods Sold—Department A, Account No. 531.

Entry (f): The amount of the purchases returns and allowances for the year for Department B, $460, was transferred to the proper cost of goods sold account by a debit to Purchases Returns and Allowances—Department B, Account No. 521.1, and by a credit to Cost of Goods Sold—Department B, Account No. 532.

Entry (g): The cost assigned to the June 30 merchandise inventory for Department A, $1,680, was debited to that account (No. 141) with an offsetting credit to Cost of Goods Sold—Department A, Account No. 531. Spinner & Thomas uses the periodic method of accounting for inventory. A physical count of the goods on hand at the year's end had been made. Reference to recent purchase invoices provided unit costs for the various items. Each time a physical inventory is taken, the quantities found to be on hand are recorded on detailed physical inventory summary sheets, showing the quantity, unit price, and extension for each pastry and cake item in Department A, and the total extensions.

Entry (h): The cost assigned to the June 30 merchandise inventory of Department B, $1,500, was debited to that account (No. 142) with an offsetting credit to Cost of Goods Sold—Department B, Account No. 532. The procedure followed in determining the inventory cost in Department B was the same as that described above for Department A.

The amount of the cost of goods sold for each department was determined by subtracting the sum of the two credits from the sum of the two debits to each of the cost of goods sold accounts. The amounts, $627,999 for Department A and $465,560 for Department B, were extended to the Adjusted Trial Balance Debit column.

Adjustment of the Interest Accounts. On June 30, Spinner & Thomas owned $10,000 face value, 12% United States government notes. Semiannual interest totaling $600 had been collected on June 16. Since that date, interest for 15 days amounting to $50 had accrued. In order to have the calculation of the net income for the year reflect the correct amount of interest earned, this type of accrual had to be taken into consideration.

Entry (i): The interest receivable on June 30, $50, was entered on the work sheet by debiting Accrued Interest Receivable, Account No. 122, and by crediting Interest Earned, Account No. 431: (Because Spinner & Thomas have no notes payable outstanding on June 30, no adjustment for accrued interest expense or payable is required at this time.)

At this point, work on the summary end-of-year work sheet was suspended temporarily until certain information needed from the supplementary work sheet for operating expenses was determined.

Supplementary Work Sheet for Operating Expenses

To provide the desired information, the income statement that was prepared had to be supplemented by a schedule of operating expenses. The accounting system of Spinner & Thomas includes a subsidiary operating expenses ledger which is controlled by the account Operating Expenses (No. 541) in the general ledger. Many of the operating expense accounts required end-of-year debit adjustments (with, of course, a summary debit to the general ledger control account). These adjustments involved offsetting credits to various general ledger accounts.

SPINNER & THOMAS
Supplementary Operating Expenses Work Sheet
For the Year Ended June 30, 19--

ACCOUNT	ACCT. NO.	TRIAL BALANCE DEBIT	ADJUST-MENTS DEBIT	ADJ. TRIAL BALANCE DEBIT
Office Salaries Expense	5401	4 1 9 2 0 00		4 1 9 2 0 00
Harlan Spinner, Salary Expense	5402	2 8 8 0 0 00		2 8 8 0 0 00
Office Supplies Expense	5403		(n) 7 1 4 1 00	7 1 4 1 00
Depreciation of Office Equip.	5404		(l) 1 8 4 8 00	1 8 4 8 00
Office Equip.—Insurance Exp.	5405		(o) 1 2 0 0 00	1 2 0 0 00
Office Rent Expense	5406	1 2 0 0 0 00		1 2 0 0 0 00
Payroll Taxes Expense	5407	8 7 5 8 00		8 7 5 8 00
Heat, Light & Water Expense	5408	4 5 2 8 00		4 5 2 8 00
Telephone Expense	5409	1 0 2 9 00		1 0 2 9 00
Postage Expense	5416	5 4 9 00		5 4 9 00
Uncollectible Accounts Expense	5417		(p) 1 8 0 00	1 8 0 00
Misc. General Expense	5422	7 5 4 00		7 5 4 00
Store Clerks Wage Expense	5431	2 4 4 1 8 00		2 4 4 1 8 00
Truck Drivers Wage Expense	5432	2 6 3 7 6 00		2 6 3 7 6 00
Advertising Expense	5433	2 5 0 2 00		2 5 0 2 00
Carol Thomas, Salary Expense	5434	2 8 8 0 0 00		2 8 8 0 0 00
Depreciation of Delivery Equip.	5435		(k) 7 1 3 8 00	7 1 3 8 00
Delivery Equip.—Ins. Expense	5436		(o) 2 3 0 0 00	2 3 0 0 00
Depreciation of Store Equip.	5437		(j) 1 9 7 8 00	1 9 7 8 00
Store Equipment Ins. Expense	5438		(o) 1 1 5 0 00	1 1 5 0 00
Truck Gas & Oil Expense	5441	6 2 2 8 00		6 2 2 8 00
Truck Repairs & Maint. Exp.	5442	6 9 6 00		6 9 6 00
Store Rent Expense	5443	1 8 0 0 0 00		1 8 0 0 0 00
Store Supplies Expense	5444		(m) 7 7 2 4 00	7 7 2 4 00
Misc. Selling Expense	5452	3 5 4 00		3 5 4 00
		20 5 7 1 2 00	3 0 6 5 9 00	23 6 3 7 1 00

Spinner & Thomas—Operating Expenses Work Sheet

To assemble all the information needed both for the income statement and for the supporting schedule of operating expenses, and to facilitate the entering of adjustments in the general ledger and subsidiary ledger accounts (which must be done later), a supplementary operating expenses work sheet was used. As will be seen, it is very closely tied in with the summary work sheet. The Spinner & Thomas operating expenses work sheet is reproduced on page 558. Note that it was given an appropriate heading that included the period involved. This work sheet needed only three amount columns: (1) to show the account balances when the trial balance was taken, (2) to provide space for certain adjustments, and (3) to show the adjusted amounts. In every case only debits were involved. The titles and numbers of all the accounts in the subsidiary operating expenses ledger were placed in the columns provided at the left. (Refer to the chart of accounts given on page 530 for the complete list.) Observe that many of the accounts had no balance when the trial balance was taken. The balance of each account was entered in the Trial Balance Debit column. That column was totaled. If the total, $205,712, did not agree with the balance shown on the summary work sheet for Operating Expenses, Account No. 541 (the control account), it would have been necessary to discover and correct the discrepancy before the preparation of either work sheet could proceed.

All the adjustments that follow (for depreciation, supplies used, insurance expired, and the doubtful accounts provision) involved both the summary work sheet and the supplementary work sheet. One or more operating expense accounts were debited on the operating expenses work sheet, and one or more general ledger accounts were credited on the summary work sheet.

Depreciation Expense. In the general ledger of Spinner & Thomas, there are three long-term asset accounts with related accumulated depreciation accounts: Store Equipment, Delivery Equipment, and Office Equipment. In the operating expenses ledger, there are three depreciation expense accounts that correspond to the asset classifications. The firm's policy is that no depreciation is taken on assets owned for less than six months. The schedule on page 560 was prepared to determine the estimated depreciation expense for the year.

Based on the calculations shown on the schedule, the following adjustments were made on the work sheets—the debits on the operating expenses work sheet and the credits on the summary work sheet:

Entry (j): Depreciation of Store Equipment, Account No. 5437, was debited and Accumulated Depreciation—Store Equipment, Account No. 181.1, was credited for $1,978.

Schedule of Depreciation Expense
For the Year Ended June 30, 19--

Asset	Cost	Annual (Straight-Line) Rate of Depreciation	Depreciation For the Year
Store Equipment	$19,780	10%	$1,978
Delivery Equipment	57,100	12½	7,138
Office Equipment	18,480*	10	1,848

*Note that the balance of the office equipment account shown on the work sheet on page 554 is $19,001. That is because the cost of an electronic desk calculator ($521) purchased on June 18 is included. Since this asset has been owned for less than six months, no depreciation is taken on it.

Entry (k): Depreciation of Delivery Equipment, Account No. 5435, was debited and Accumulated Depreciation—Delivery Equipment, Account No. 185.1, was credited for $7,138.

Entry (l): Depreciation of Office Equipment, Account No. 5404, was debited and Accumulated Depreciation—Office Equipment, Account No. 191.1, was credited for $1,848.

Supplies Expense. The general ledger of Spinner & Thomas includes two asset accounts for supplies—Store Supplies and Office Supplies. When purchased, the supplies are entered as assets by debiting the accounts, Store Supplies, Account No. 151, and Office Supplies, Account No. 152. An inventory of unused supplies is taken at the end of the year so that the cost of the supplies used can be calculated and charged to the proper operating expense accounts. The following schedule was prepared to determine the needed adjustments. The amount shown for each type of supplies was determined by a count of

Schedule of Supplies Used
For the Year Ended June 30, 19--

Asset	Account Balance June 30, 19--	Amount on Hand June 30, 19--	Expense For Year
Store Supplies	$8,974	$1,250	$7,724
Office Supplies	7,896	755	7,141

the unopened packages and boxes, which were assigned approximate costs of recent purchases.

Based upon the calculation, the following adjustments were made on the work sheets:

Entry (m): Store Supplies Expense, Account No. 5444, was debited and Store Supplies, Account No. 151, was credited for $7,724.

Entry (n): Office Supplies Expense, Account No. 5403, was debited and Office Supplies, Account No. 152, was credited for $7,141.

Insurance Expense. Prepaid insurance premiums are entered by Spinner & Thomas in the same manner as supplies. At the time of payment of a premium, the amount paid is entered as an asset by debiting Prepaid Insurance, Account No. 155. At the end of the fiscal year, June 30, calculations are made to determine the fraction of the total term of each policy that elapsed during the year. Each amount thus determined is classified according to the type of asset insured and charged to the proper insurance expense account. The operating expenses ledger of Spinner & Thomas includes insurance expense accounts for the insurance on delivery equipment, store equipment, and office equipment.

The following schedule of insurance expense was prepared from a file of information relating to insurance policies.

Schedule of Insurance Expense
For the Year Ended June 30, 19--

Type of Property Insured	Expense for Year
Delivery Equipment	$2,300
Store Equipment	1,150
Office Equipment	1,200
Total	$4,650

Based upon this schedule, the following adjustment was made on the work sheets:

Entry (o): Delivery Equipment Insurance Expense, Account No. 5436, was debited for $2,300; Store Equipment Insurance Expense, Account No. 5438, was debited for $1,150; Office Equipment Insurance Expense, Account No. 5405, was debited for $1,200; and Prepaid Insurance, Account No. 155, was credited for $4,650.

Doubtful Accounts. Spinner & Thomas uses the allowance method of accounting for doubtful accounts. On the basis of "aging" the accounts receivable, it was estimated that $240 of such accounts will not be collected. Since there already is a $60 balance in the allowance for doubtful accounts, $180 more is needed to make the required $240. The following entry was made on the work sheets:

Entry (p): Uncollectible Accounts Expense, Account No. 5417, was debited and Allowance for Doubtful Accounts, Account No. 131.1, was credited for $180.

Completing The Operating Expenses Work Sheet

In order to complete this work sheet, the amount for each operating expense account was extended into the Adjusted Trial Balance column. Note that in every case, the extended amount was either the unadjusted amount or the amount of the adjustment. The Adjustments and Adjusted Trial Balance columns were then totaled. Since only debits were involved in this work sheet, the total of the Adjusted Trial Balance column, $236,371, had to be equal to the sum of the totals of the Trial Balance and Adjustments columns ($205,712 + $30,659). A double rule was placed below the three totals.

Completing The Summary Work Sheet

To complete the adjustments on the summary work sheet, the balance of the control account, Operating Expenses, had to be increased to reflect the total of all of the debits to the operating expenses that had been made on the supplementary work sheet. Accordingly, that total, $30,659, was entered on the line for Operating Expenses, Account No. 541, in the Adjustments Debit column. Note that the debit was identified as "(j-p)," since it was offset by credits to seven general ledger accounts made when adjustments (j) through (p) were entered on the work sheets to adjust the operating expense accounts.

The Adjustments columns were totaled to prove the equality of the debits and credits. The amounts in the Trial Balance columns, adjusted where indicated by amounts in the Adjustments columns, were extended to the Adjusted Trial Balance columns. The latter also were totaled to prove the equality of the debits and credits. Each amount in the Adjusted Trial Balance columns was extended to the proper Income Statement or Balance Sheet column. The last four columns were then totaled.

Note that the Income Statement Credit column exceeded the Debit column by $26,318, and that the Balance Sheet Debit column exceeded the Credit column by the same amount. This means that Spinner & Thomas had a profitable year. "Net Income" was written on the next line at the left, and the amount, $26,318, was placed in the two proper places (Income Statement debit column and Balance Sheet credit column). The Income Statement and Balance Sheet columns were then totaled to prove that each pair was in balance. Double rules were placed below the final totals in all ten columns.

The summary work sheet then can be used to prepare the income statement for the fiscal year (shown on page 579) and the balance sheet as of the last day of that year (shown on page 585). The supplementary work sheet provided the information for the schedule of operating expenses (shown on page 580).

BUILDING YOUR ACCOUNTING KNOWLEDGE

1. What three functions does a work sheet perform in the production of year-end (or other period-end) financial reports?
2. What was the first step in the preparation of the Spinner & Thomas summary work sheet?
3. Why was the Expense and Revenue Summary account omitted from the Spinner & Thomas work sheet when it was included in the MicroWorld work sheet?
4. What is the purpose of each of the cost of goods sold accounts maintained by Spinner & Thomas?
5. How many entries were made in the adjustments columns of the Spinner & Thomas summary work sheet to show the calculation of the cost of goods sold for each department and to adjust the departmental merchandise inventory accounts? Briefly explain the purpose of each of these adjustments.
6. What was the purpose of the only other adjustment made entirely in the summary work sheet?
7. What is the purpose of the supplementary work sheet for operating expenses? How many columns does it have and what is the purpose of each column?
8. How many entries were made both in the adjustments columns of the Spinner & Thomas summary work sheet and in the adjustments column of the supplementary operating expenses work sheet? Briefly explain the purpose of each of these adjustments.

APPLYING ACCOUNTING CONCEPTS

Exercise 18-1. The following amounts were taken from the accounts of Sewell and Cherry, partners of a small retail business. Determine the individual cost of goods sold for Departments A and B for the fiscal year ended June 30, 19--:

Merchandise Inventory, Department A, July 1	$ 1,613
Merchandise Inventory, Department B, July 1	1,309
Merchandise Inventory, Department A, June 30	1,579
Merchandise Inventory, Department B, June 30	1,499
Purchases, Department A	517,675
Purchases, Department B	355,100
Purchases Returns and Allowances, Department A	719
Purchases Returns and Allowances, Department B	359

Exercise 18-2. On June 30, Sewell and Cherry owned United States government notes, face value of $5,000, interest rate 12%. Semiannual interest totaling $300 had been collected on May 15.

Determine the amount of interest earned but not yet received that would be entered as an adjustment on the summary work sheet for the year ended June 30, 19--.

Exercise 18-3. Sewell and Cherry follow the policy of taking depreciation only on assets owned for six months or more. Complete the following schedule to determine the estimated depreciation expense for the year.

Assets	Cost	Annual Rate of Depreciation	Depreciation for the Year
Store Equipment	$14,866	10%	?
Delivery Equipment	34,100*	12 1/2%	?
Office Equipment	12,500	10%	?

*The balance of the delivery equipment account includes $7,800 for a vehicle purchased on September 15.

Exercise 18-4. Sewell and Cherry enter payments for supplies as assets when they are purchased. An inventory of unused supplies is taken at the end of the year so that the cost of the supplies used can be calculated and charged to the proper operating expense accounts.

Complete the following schedule to determine the needed adjustments for the fiscal year ended June 30, 19--.

Asset	Account Balance June 30, 19--	Amount on Hand June 30, 19--	Expense For Year
Store Supplies	$6,748	$750	?
Office Supplies	5,696	255	?

Exercise 18-5. At the time of payment of insurance premiums, Sewell and Cherry enter the amount paid as an asset by debiting Prepaid Insurance. Complete the following schedule to determine the adjustments needed for Insurance Expense for the year ended June 30, 19--.

Type of Property Insured	Account Balance June 30, 19--	Unexpired Insurance Premium	Expense For Year
Delivery Equipment	$1,374	$916	?
Store Equipment	936	468	?
Office Equipment	1,458	972	?

Exercise 18-6. Sewell and Cherry use the allowance method of accounting for doubtful accounts. On the basis of "aging" the accounts receivable, it was estimated that $1,425 of such accounts would not be collected. For each of the following situations, use a T account to show the beginning balance, amount of adjustment, and end-of-the-year balance in the Allowance for Doubtful Accounts.

(a) If the Allowance for Doubtful Accounts already has a credit balance of $75, what is the amount to be entered as an adjustment to Uncollectible Accounts Expense for the current year? **(b)** If the Allowance for Doubtful Accounts has an unadjusted debit balance of $55, what is the amount to be entered as an adjustment to Uncollectible Accounts Expense for the current year?

Report No. 18-1

Complete Report No. 18-1 in the study assignments. Do not submit the report at this time. Since Reports Nos. 18-1 and 18-2 are related, you should retain the working papers until you have completed both reports. Continue with the textbook discussion until Report No. 18-2 is required.

ADJUSTING, CLOSING, AND REVERSING ENTRIES

The most important function of the year-end work sheet is to facilitate the preparation of the income statement and the balance sheet as soon as possible after the end of the accounting period. Having completed the work sheets illustrated and discussed in the preceding pages, the accountant for Spinner & Thomas would next prepare the financial statements. A secondary function of the work sheets is to aid in the process of formally entering adjusting and closing entries in the books. For the purpose of the organization of subject matter in this textbook, adjusting, closing, and reversing entries will be considered next. The financial statements will be illustrated and discussed in Chapter 19.

Journalizing The Adjusting Entries

Adjusting entries as of June 30 were entered in the general journal reproduced on pages 568-569. The form of general journal used by Spinner & Thomas provided a special Detail column for charges to the accounts in the operating expenses subsidiary ledger. Journalizing the adjusting entries involved the use of this column as well as the Debit and Credit columns. Several features of these entries should be noted:

1. The general ledger accounts are debited or credited in the conventional form; each subsidiary ledger account and its detail are also entered. However, the account numbers were entered when the journalizing was done, *not* as a step in the posting.

2. The entries were made in the same order as shown alphabetically (a) through (p), on the work sheets (pages 554-555, and 558). While this order is not essential, the danger of omitting an entry is slightly reduced by using the work sheets as a guide in journalizing the entries.

3. To be sure that the total of the debits equaled the total of the credits, the Debit and Credit columns were footed. The Detail column was footed and found to agree with the total of the Adjustments Debit column on the operating expenses work sheet. Finally, the totals were entered and the usual rulings were supplied.

Posting The Adjusting Entries

As the individual amounts in the Debit and Credit columns were posted to the accounts (indicated by the account numbers), a check mark ($\sqrt{}$) was placed to the right of each amount in the column provided. A check mark also was placed in parentheses below the total of each of these two columns to indicate that the amount was *not* posted to any ledger. In the case of the entries in the Detail column, a check mark was placed to the right of each amount as it was posted. A check mark was also placed in parentheses below the total of that column to indicate that the amount was also *not* posted to any ledger. In both the general ledger and the operating expenses ledger, the page of the general journal (GJ42) was placed in the Posting Reference column as each posting was made.

Journalizing The Closing Entries

The page of the general journal showing the closing entries as of June 30, 19--, is reproduced on page 570. Certain features of these entries should be noted:

1. Each closing entry was made in conventional form—the names of the accounts to be debited or credited were given. The names of the accounts to be credited were slightly indented. As in the case of the adjusting entries, however, the numbers of the accounts were entered at the time of journalizing. The check marks were made later as the posting was completed.

2. The order of the closing entries follows a logical sequence. The revenue accounts are closed first, followed by the expense accounts. The third entry closes the expense and revenue summary account by dividing the income ($26,318) between Spinner & Thomas in a 60-40 ratio as their partnership agreement specifies. The last two closing entries transfer the amount of each partner's withdrawals to the related capital account. The amount columns were footed to prove the equality of the debits and credits.

Note that, while there was a credit of $236,371 to close Operating Expenses, Account No. 541, the individual credits to close the twenty-five accounts in the operating expenses subsidiary ledger were not shown. One reason is that the form of the journal page does not accommodate credits to the operating expenses accounts, because these accounts rarely are credited (except when they are closed). The occasional transaction that requires a credit to an operating expense account can be handled by noting *both* the number of the control account (No. 541) and the number of the subsidiary ledger account in the account number column provided just to the left of the Detail column. The amount of the credit will then be posted as a credit to both accounts.

The operating expense accounts in the subsidiary ledger *must be closed* at the end of the fiscal year. The manner of doing so is illustrated by the reproduction of the account for Advertising Expense, Account No. 5433, shown on page 571. When a general ledger control account is closed, all accounts in a ledger that is subsidiary to that

GENERAL JOURNAL

PAGE 42

	DATE	DESCRIPTION	ACCT. NO.	DETAIL	✓	DEBIT	✓	CREDIT	✓
1	19— June 30	Adjusting Entries							✓
2		Cost of Goods Sold—Dept. A	531			1 7 1 4 00	✓		
3		Merchandise Inventory—Dept. A	141				✓	1 7 1 4 00	✓
4		Cost of Goods Sold—Dept. B	532			1 4 1 0 00	✓		
5		Merchandise Inventory—Dept. B	142				✓	1 4 1 0 00	✓
6		Cost of Goods Sold—Dept. A	531			62 8 7 8 5 00	✓		
7		Purchases—Dept. A	511					62 8 7 8 5 00	✓
8		Cost of Goods Sold—Dept. B	532			46 6 1 1 0 00	✓		
9		Purchases—Dept. B	521					46 6 1 1 0 00	✓
10		Purchases Returns and Allowances—Dept. A	511.1			8 2 0 00	✓		
11		Cost of Goods Sold—Dept. A	531					8 2 0 00	✓
12		Purchases Returns and Allowances—Dept. B	521.1			4 6 0 00	✓		
13		Cost of Goods Sold—Dept. B	532					4 6 0 00	✓
14		Merchandise Inventory—Dept. A	141			1 6 8 0 00	✓		
15		Cost of Goods Sold—Dept. A	531					1 6 8 0 00	✓
16		Merchandise Inventory—Dept. B	142			1 5 0 0 00	✓		
17		Cost of Goods Sold—Dept. B	532					1 5 0 0 00	✓
18		Accrued Interest Receivable	122			5 0 00	✓		
19		Interest Earned	431					5 0 00	✓

Line	Account Title	Acct. No.			
20	Operating Expenses	541	3 0 6 5 9 00 ✓		
21	Office Supplies Expense	5403		7 1 4 1 00 ✓	
22	Office Supplies	152			7 1 4 1 00 ✓
23	Store Supplies Expense	5444		7 7 2 4 00 ✓	
24	Store Supplies	151			7 7 2 4 00 ✓
25	Uncollectible Accounts Expense	5417		1 8 0 0 00 ✓	
26	Allowance for Doubtful Accounts	131.1			1 8 0 0 00 ✓
27	Depreciation of Store Equipment	5437		1 9 7 8 00 ✓	
28	Accumulated Depreciation—Store Equipment	181.1			1 9 7 8 00 ✓
29	Depreciation of Delivery Equipment	5435		7 1 3 8 00 ✓	
30	Accumulated Depreciation—Delivery Equipment	185.1			7 1 3 8 00 ✓
31	Depreciation of Office Equipment	5404		1 8 4 8 00 ✓	
32	Accumulated Depreciation—Office Equipment	191.1			1 8 4 8 00 ✓
33	Delivery Equipment—Insurance Expense	5436		2 3 0 0 00 ✓	
34	Store Equipment—Insurance Expense	5438		1 1 5 0 00 ✓	
35	Office Equipment—Insurance Expense	5405		1 2 0 0 00 ✓	
36	Prepaid Insurance	155			4 6 5 0 00 ✓
37			113 3 1 8 8 00	3 0 6 5 9 00	113 3 1 8 8 00
38			(✓)	(✓)	(✓)
39					

Spinner & Thomas—Adjusting Entries

GENERAL JOURNAL   PAGE 43

DATE	DESCRIPTION	ACCT. NO.	✓	DETAIL	✓	DEBIT	✓	CREDIT	✓	
19— June 30	*Closing Entries*									1
	Sales—Department A	411				73 4 6 2 9 00	✓			2
	Sales—Department B	421				62 0 9 8 8 00	✓			3
	Interest Earned	431				1 3 4 5 00	✓			4
	Expense and Revenue Summary	331						135 6 9 6 2 00	✓	5
	Expense and Revenue Summary	331				133 0 6 4 4 00	✓			6
	Sales Returns and Allowances—Department A	411.1						3 7 6 00	✓	7
	Sales Returns and Allowances—Department B	421.1						3 3 8 00	✓	8
	Cost of Goods Sold—Department A	531						62 7 9 9 9 00	✓	9
	Cost of Goods Sold—Department B	532						46 5 5 6 0 00	✓	10
	Operating Expenses	541						23 6 3 7 1 00	✓	11
	Expense and Revenue Summary	331				2 6 3 1 8 00	✓			12
	Harlan Spinner, Capital	311						1 5 7 9 1 00	✓	13
	Carol Thomas, Capital	321						1 0 5 2 7 00	✓	14
	Harlan Spinner, Capital	311				1 0 3 0 0 00	✓			15
	Harlan Spinner, Drawing	311.1						1 0 3 0 0 00	✓	16
	Carol Thomas, Capital	321				7 8 0 0 00	✓			17
	Carol Thomas, Drawing	321.1						7 8 0 0 00	✓	18
						273 2 0 2 4 00		273 2 0 2 4 00		19
						(✓)		(✓)		20
										21
										22
										23
										24
										25
										26

Spinner & Thomas—Closing Entries

control account also must be closed. The space and time required to list all of the subsidiary ledger accounts, numbers, and balances (twenty-five in the present case) can be saved if all subsidiary ledger expense accounts are closed at the same time that the operating expenses account is closed.

Posting The Closing Entries

The postings were made to the general ledger accounts indicated. A check mark was placed in the column provided in the general journal as each posting was made. The page of the general journal (GJ43) was noted in the Posting Reference column of the account involved. As mentioned in the preceding paragraph, the balance of each account in the subsidiary operating expenses ledger was closed in the manner indicated by the entry on the last line of the illustration of the account for Advertising Expense shown below. (Note that "GJ43" was entered in the Posting Reference column, since that is the page of the general journal on which the closing entry for the operating expenses control account was made.) The other twenty-four operating expense accounts were closed in a similar fashion.

ACCOUNT Advertising Expense						ACCOUNT NO. 5433	
DATE	ITEM	POST. REF.	DEBIT	CREDIT	BALANCE
19– June 1	Dr. Balance	√			2 4 8 9 00
30		VR26	1 3 00		2 5 0 2 00
30		GJ43		2 5 0 2 00	- 0 -

Closed Subsidiary Operating Expense Ledger Account

The expense and revenue summary account and the two cost of goods sold accounts after the adjusting and closing entries had been posted are reproduced on page 572. Note that these accounts are summarizing accounts that are used only at the end of the accounting period. In some accounting systems, cost of goods sold accounts are used throughout the year if such cost is known at the time of sale. This is possible if perpetual inventories are maintained. In the periodic inventory method of Spinner & Thomas, the cost of goods sold accounts are used only at the end of the fiscal year.

ACCOUNT Expense and Revenue Summary						ACCOUNT NO. 331	
DATE	ITEM	POST. REF.	DEBIT	CREDIT	BALANCE DEBIT	BALANCE CREDIT	
19— June 30		GJ43		135696200			
30		GJ43	133064400			2631800	
30	To Close	GJ43	2631800		-0-	-0-	

ACCOUNT Cost of Goods Sold - Department A						ACCOUNT NO. 531	
DATE	ITEM	POST. REF.	DEBIT	CREDIT	BALANCE DEBIT	BALANCE CREDIT	
19— June 30	Beg. Inventory	GJ42	171400				
30	Purchases	GJ42	62878500				
30	Purchases R & A	GJ42		82000			
30	End. Inventory	GJ42		168000	62799900		
30	Exp. & Rev. Summary	GJ43		62799900	-0-	-0-	

ACCOUNT Cost of Goods Sold - Department B						ACCOUNT NO. 532	
DATE	ITEM	POST. REF.	DEBIT	CREDIT	BALANCE DEBIT	BALANCE CREDIT	
19— June 30	Beg. Inventory	GJ42	141000				
30	Purchases	GJ42	46611000				
30	Purchases R & A	GJ42		46000			
30	End. Inventory	GJ42		150000	46556000		
30	Exp. & Rev. Summary	GJ43		46556000	-0-	-0-	

Closed General Ledger Summary Accounts

Post-Closing Trial Balance

After the closing entries were posted, a trial balance of the general ledger accounts that remained open was taken to prove the equality of the debit and credit balances. The post-closing trial balance of the general ledger of Spinner & Thomas is reproduced on page 573.

Account	Acct. No.	Dr. Balance	Cr. Balance
Cash	111	34 4 3 5 00	
Petty Cash Fund	112	2 0 0 00	
Government Notes	121	10 0 0 0 00	
Accrued Interest Receivable	122	5 0 00	
Accounts Receivable	131	10 9 7 8 00	
Allowance for Doubtful Accounts	131.1		2 4 0 00
Merchandise Inventory—Department A	141	1 6 8 0 00	
Merchandise Inventory—Department B	142	1 5 0 0 00	
Store Supplies	151	1 2 5 0 00	
Office Supplies	152	7 5 5 00	
Prepaid Insurance	155	8 8 2 00	
Store Equipment	181	19 7 8 0 00	
Accumulated Depreciation—Store Equip.	181.1		3 6 5 8 00
Delivery Equipment	185	57 1 0 0 00	
Accumulated Depreciation—Delivery Equip.	185.1		49 9 3 8 00
Office Equipment	191	19 0 5 9 00	
Accumulated Depreciation—Office Equip.	191.1		3 2 6 3 00
FICA Tax Payable	211		1 1 6 2 00
FUTA Tax Payable	212		8 6 00
State Unemployment Tax Payable	213		3 8 9 00
Employees Income Tax Payable	214		1 0 1 0 00
Vouchers Payable	218		34 3 7 5 00
Harlan Spinner, Capital	311		44 2 2 2 00
Carol Thomas, Capital	321		19 3 2 6 00
		157 6 6 9 00	157 6 6 9 00

Spinner & Thomas—Post Closing Trial Balance

Some accountants feel that it is necessary to prepare a post-closing trial balance in the form illustrated and file it with various other records. Others think that it is sufficient merely to use an adding machine tape to list and total (1) the amounts of the debit balances and (2) the amounts of the credit balances to be sure that the totals are the same. In the latter case, if the ledger was found not to be in balance, the cause of the discrepancy would have to be located and remedied. Then the tapes would be discarded.

Reversing Entries

One adjusting entry (entry (i)) of the accrual type, Accrued Interest Receivable, was made as of June 30 in the amount of $50. In order that interest collections may be entered in routine fashion in the new period, Spinner & Thomas follows the practice of reversing accrual adjustments. The first entries for the new period are the reversals of the previous accrual adjustments. The reversing entry made on July 1, 19--, is shown below.

	DATE	DESCRIPTION	ACCT. NO.	DETAIL	√	DEBIT	√	CREDIT	√	
21	July 1	Reversing Entry								21
22		Interest Earned	431			50 00	√			22
23		Accrued Interest Receivable	122					50 00	√	23

GENERAL JOURNAL   PAGE 43

Spinner & Thomas—Reversing Entry

BUILDING YOUR ACCOUNTING KNOWLEDGE

1. What is the purpose of the Detail column in Spinner & Thomas' general journal?
2. In what two ways are the accounts identified in entering the adjusting entries in the general journal?
3. Why are the Debit and Credit columns of the general journal footed? Why is the Detail column footed?
4. In what two ways are the accounts identified in entering the closing entries in the general journal?
5. What is the purpose of each of the five closing entries made by Spinner & Thomas?
6. How is the posting of the individual amounts in the adjusting and closing entries indicated in the general journal? In the general and operating expenses ledgers?
7. What is the purpose of the post-closing trial balance? What do some accountants use as a substitute?
8. Why does the accountant for Spinner & Thomas reverse accrual adjustments?

APPLYING ACCOUNTING CONCEPTS

Exercise 18-7. Using a general journal with a special Detail column for charges to the accounts in the operating expenses subsidiary ledger, enter the adjusting entries for the following exercises. Foot and rule the Detail, Debit and Credit columns. (Omit account numbers.)

1. Exercise 18-1.
2. Exercise 18-2.

Exercise 18-8. Enter the adjusting entries for the following exercises in a general journal with a special Detail column for charges to the accounts in the operating expenses subsidiary ledger. Foot and rule the Detail, Debit and Credit columns. (Omit account numbers.)

1. Exercise 18-3.
2. Exercise 18-4.
3. Exercise 18-5.
4. Exercise 18-6 (a).

Exercise 18-9. The following are account balances taken from the accounting records of Sentinel Electronic Equipment.

Sales, Department A	$623,518
Sales, Department B	519,876
Interest Earned	234
Sales Returns and Allowances, Department A	265
Sales Returns and Allowances, Department B	227
Cost of Goods Sold, Department A	516,888
Cost of Goods Sold, Department B	354,450
Operating Expenses	125,260
Charlene Potts, Drawing	10,400
Carol Corley, Drawing	7,900

(a) Using a general journal with a special Detail column for charges to the accounts in the operating expenses subsidiary ledger, enter the necessary closing entries. Divide profits and losses equally. **(b)** Prepare a T account for the expense and revenue summary account. Post the closing entries to this account. **(c)** Foot and rule the columns.

Exercise 18-10. Refer to Exercises 18-7 and 18-8. Prepare in general journal form reversing entries for any accrual type adjustments so that transactions in the new period may be entered in routine fashion.

**Report
No. 18-2**

Complete Report No. 18-2 in the study assignments and submit Reports Nos. 18-1 and 18-2 for approval. Continue with the textbook discussion in Chapter 19 until Report No. 19-1 is required.

EXPANDING YOUR BUSINESS VOCABULARY

What is the meaning of each of the following terms:

adjusting entries **(p. 566)**

closing entries **(p. 567)**

post-closing trial balance
   (p. 572)

reversing entries **(p. 574)**

summary year-end work sheet
   (p. 553)

supplementary work sheet for
   operating expenses **(p. 557))**

CHAPTER 19

The Annual Report

CHAPTER OBJECTIVES

Careful study of this chapter should enable you to:

- Describe and explain the nature of an annual report.

- Prepare a summarized income statement that shows the components and amounts of gross margin on sales by departments and in total, supplemented by schedules of cost of goods sold and of operating expenses.

- Analyze the income statement using percentage analysis, merchandise turnover analysis, and comparative analysis.

- Prepare a balance sheet for a partnership supplemented by a schedule of accounts receivable.

- Analyze the balance sheet using ratio analysis and comparative analysis.

- Perform an analysis of profitability of a business.

- Describe and prepare a statement of changes in financial position (working capital basis), including a supporting schedule of changes in working capital.

The term annual report as applied to a business usually refers to the financial statements and schedules relating to the accounting (fiscal) year of the enterprise. The report generally includes an income statement, a balance sheet, and a statement of changes in financial position. In business corporations with many stockholders (thousands, even hundreds of thousands, in some cases), the annual report may be a thirty- to sixty-page printed publication—sometimes in full color with numerous pictures of the company's products, plants, officers, and various graphs and statistics in addition to the financial statements.

Reports of this type usually include a letter addressed to the stock-holders signed by the president of the corporation or by the chairman of the board of directors and sometimes by both. The letter is printed in the report booklet and is often described as "highlights" of the year. Such annual reports invariably include the opinion (sometimes referred to as the Auditor's Report) of the CPA firm that performed the audit of the company's financial statements.

Annual reports of the elaborate type just mentioned are not used if the business has few owners. In a partnership, it is probable that only the partners and, possibly, one or two of the officials at their bank see the reports. The annual report of Spinner & Thomas consists of the following statements and schedules:

Income Statement for the Year
   Schedule of Cost of Goods Sold
   Schedule of Operating Expenses

Balance Sheet as of June 30
   Schedule of Accounts Receivable

Statement of Changes in Financial Position for the Year (Working Capital Basis)
   Schedule of Changes in Working Capital

THE INCOME STATEMENT

The income statement and schedule of cost of goods sold for the year ended June 30, 19--, for Spinner & Thomas are reproduced on page 579. They were prepared from information provided by the Income Statement columns of the work sheet reproduced on pages 554 and 555. The income statement is arranged to show the sales, cost of goods sold, and the gross margin on sales for each department as well as in total. The schedule of cost of goods sold shows the components that made up the cost of goods sold for each department and the total.

The schedule of operating expenses reproduced on page 580 was prepared from information provided by the operating expenses work sheet shown on page 558. The schedule provides the detail of what makes up the total amount of operating expenses ($236,371) shown on the income statement. If there were only five or ten accounts for operating expenses, it is probable that (1) there would have been no subsidiary ledger for such expenses and (2) the accounts would have been included in the income statement, in which case no schedule would have been needed. There is wide variation in the form and content of financial statements. Some accountants, for example, may present the components of cost of goods sold in the income statement instead of in the "supporting" schedule as illustrated below.

Spinner & Thomas
Income Statement
For the Year Ended June 30, 19--

	Dept. A	Dept. B	Total
Sales	$734,629	$620,988	$1,355,617
Less sales returns and allowances	376	338	714
Net sales	$734,253	$620,650	$1,354,903
Cost of goods sold	627,999	465,560	1,093,559
Gross margin on sales	$106,254	$155,090	$ 261,344
Operating expenses			236,371
Operating income			$ 24,973
Other revenue:			
Interest earned			1,345
Net income			$ 26,318

Spinner & Thomas—Income Statement

Spinner & Thomas
Schedule of Cost of Goods Sold
For the Year Ended June 30, 19--

	Dept. A	Dept. B	Total
Merchandise inventory, July 1, 19--	$ 1,714	$ 1,410	$ 3,124
Purchases	$628,785	$466,110	$1,094,895
Less purchases returns and allowances	820	460	1,280
Net purchases	$627,965	$465,650	$1,093,615
Merchandise available for sale	$629,679	$467,060	$1,096,739
Less merchandise inventory, June 30, 19--	1,680	1,500	3,180
Cost of goods sold	$627,999	$465,560	$1,093,559

Spinner & Thomas—Schedule of Cost of Goods Sold

Spinner & Thomas
Schedule of Operating Expenses
For the Year Ended June 30, 19--

Administrative expenses:

Office salaries expense	$ 41,920
Harlan Spinner, salary expense	28,800
Office supplies expense	7,141
Depreciation of office equipment	1,848
Office equipment insurance expense	1,200
Office rent expense	12,000
Payroll taxes expense	8,758
Heat, light, and water expense	4,528
Telephone expense	1,029
Postage expense	549
Uncollectible accounts expense	180
Miscellaneous general expense	754
Total administrative expenses	$108,707

Selling expenses:

Store clerks wage expense	$ 24,418
Truck drivers wage expense	26,376
Advertising expense	2,502
Carol Thomas, salary expense	28,800
Depreciation of delivery equipment	7,138
Delivery equipment insurance expense	2,300
Depreciation of store equipment	1,978
Store equipment insurance expense	1,150
Truck, gas, and oil expense	6,228
Truck repairs and maintenance expense	696
Store rent expense	18,000
Store supplies expense	7,724
Miscellaneous selling expense	354
Total selling expenses	$127,664
Total operating expenses	$236,371

Spinner & Thomas—Schedule of Operating Expenses

Interpreting The Income Statement

There are numerous ways to analyze an income statement. Three types of analysis will be dealt with in this chapter: (1) percentage analysis, (2) merchandise turnover, and (3) comparative analysis.

Percentage Analysis. In order of importance, the most significant items shown by the annual income statement are the total amounts of (1) net income, (2) sales, (3) cost of goods sold and gross margin (considered together because of the interrelationship), and (4) operating expenses. The dollar amounts of these items take on added meaning if their proportionate relationship to each other is computed and compared. Using Spinner & Thomas's income statement as an example, the customary way of studying these relationships is by percentage analysis, using net sales as the base, 100%.

Net sales	$1,354,903	100.0%
Cost of goods sold	1,093,559	80.7
Gross margin	$ 261,344	19.3%
Operating expenses	236,371	17.5
Operating income	$ 24,973	1.8%
Other revenue	1,345	0.1
Net income	$ 26,318	1.9%

This analysis shows that net income is slightly less than 2% of net sales, with other revenue representing a relatively minor amount. In other words, each dollar of net sales resulted in about two cents of net profit.

Spinner & Thomas may compare these percentages with the same percentages for other similar wholesale/retail bakery businesses, or with their own percentages of operating results for prior years, to determine the relative profitability of their bakery operation.

The same type of analysis can be applied to the data for the net sales, cost of goods sold, and gross margin of each department, as shown below.

	Dept. A		Dept. B	
Net sales	$734,253	100.0%	$620,650	100%
Cost of goods sold	627,999	85.5	465,560	75
Gross margin	$106,254	14.5%	$155,090	25%

Spinner & Thomas might find this analysis useful in the determination of the relative emphasis to place on the output of each department, the possible expansion or contraction of either department, or the need for a review of the pricing policies in either department.

Merchandise Turnover. The data reported in the income statement and in the schedule of cost of goods sold make it possible to compute the merchandise turnover during the year. For the business as a whole, the average inventory was $3,152 ($3,124 beginning inventory plus $3,180 ending inventory, divided by two). Since the total cost of goods sold was $1,093,559, the turnover was almost 347 times ($1,093,559 ÷ $3,152). This means that, on the average, goods remained in stock for about a day, an obviously desirable condition for a bakery. Using the same calculation for each department reveals that the turnover in Department A was 370.1, and in Department B, 320.0. The turnover ratio can help Spinner & Thomas determine whether they are carrying significant amounts of slowmoving bakery products. Based on the departmental turnover ratios, Spinner & Thomas might want to examine in detail the turnover of selected products carried in Department B.

Comparative Analysis. Added meaning is given to the information supplied by an income statement if it is compared with statements for past periods. By using such comparative analysis, answers will be provided to such vital questions as: Are sales growing or shrinking? How much has net income increased or decreased (both absolutely and relatively)? Has the gross margin percentage become larger or smaller? It may be assumed that the first thing each partner did after looking at the income statement for the year just ended was to compare it with the statement for the preceding year—probably for several preceding years. Often, income statements and other financial statements are prepared in comparative form to aid in their interpretation.

BUILDING YOUR ACCOUNTING KNOWLEDGE

1. What three financial statements generally are included in the annual report of a business?
2. Who are likely to be the only users of the annual report of a partnership?
3. What three major items are shown for each department and in total on the Spinner & Thomas income statement?

4. What is the source of the information contained in the schedule of operating expenses?

5. What are the two major categories of expenses shown on the schedule of operating expenses of Spinner & Thomas?

6. What is the customary way of relating cost of goods sold, gross margin, operating expenses, and net income to net sales using percentage analysis? What use is made of such analysis?

7. How is the merchandise turnover for the year computed? What use is made of the turnover ratio?

8. How is the technique of comparative analysis applied to the information supplied by an income statement? What vital questions does comparative analysis help to answer?

APPLYING ACCOUNTING CONCEPTS

Exercise 19-1. The following account balances were taken from the income statement columns of the work sheet of Aztec Sales, a firm owned by Dennis Yee and Alvaro Yepez, partners. Aztec's fiscal year ends on December 31, 19--.

	Dept. A	Dept. B	Total
Sales..................................	$823,518	$519,877	$1,343,395
Sales returns and allowances..........	265	227	492
Merchandise inventory, Jan. 1	1,903	1,309	3,212
Merchandise inventory, Dec. 31	1,579	1,499	3,078
Purchases	517,674	355,009	872,683
Purchases returns and allowances	719	359	1,078
Office salaries expense................			30,800
Office supplies expense			6,030
Uncollectible accounts expense........			179
Miscellaneous general expense			643
Sales salaries expense			1,491
Advertising expense...................			27,700
Depreciation of store equipment			867
Store rent expense....................			12,000
Miscellaneous selling expense			243

Prepare a schedule of cost of goods sold for each department and in total.

Exercise 19-2. Using the appropriate account balances from Exercise 19-1, prepare a schedule of operating expenses in total for Aztec Sales.

Exercise 19-3. Refer to Exercises 19-1 and 19-2 and prepare a summarized income statement. Show the components and amounts of gross margin on sales by department and in total for Aztec Sales.

Exercise 19-4. Refer to Exercise 19-3. Aztec Sales, using net sales as the base, studies the proportionate relationship between net income, sales, cost of goods sold, gross margin, and operating expenses by percentage analysis.

(a) Calculate these percentages in total. Each dollar of net sales resulted in approximately how many cents of net profit? **(b)** Calculate these percentages by department for net sales, cost of goods sold, and gross margin. Which department had a higher cost of goods sold percentage? Which department contributed a greater percentage of gross margin to the total? **(c)** Determine the merchandise turnover. Last year the turnover rate was 300. Is the merchandise selling faster or slower this year?

**Report
No. 19-1**

Complete Report No. 19-1 in the study assignments. Do not submit the report at this time. Since Reports 19-1, 19-2, and 19-3 are related, you should retain the working papers until you have completed all three reports. Continue with the textbook discussion until Report No. 19-2 is required.

THE BALANCE SHEET

The following balance sheet of Spinner & Thomas as of June 30, 19--, is arranged in report form. It was prepared from information pro-

---

SPINNER & THOMAS
Balance Sheet
June 30, 19--

Assets

Current assets:

Cash		$ 34,635	
Government notes		10,000	
Accrued interest receivable		50	
Accounts receivable.....................	$10,978		
Less allowance for doubtful accounts	240	10,738	
Merchandise inventories:			
Department A.........................	$ 1,680		
Department B.........................	1,500	3,180	
Supplies and prepayments...............		2,887	
Total current assets			$ 61,490

Long-term assets:

	Cost	Accum. Depr.	Undepr. Cost	
Store equipment	$19,780	$ 3,658	$ 16,122	
Delivery equipment......................	57,100	49,938	7,162	
Office equipment........................	19,001	3,263	15,738	
Total long-term assets..................	$95,881	$56,859		39,022
Total assets				$100,512

Liabilities

Current liabilities:

Accounts payable	$ 34,375	
Accrued and withheld payroll taxes	2,589	
Total current liabilities..................		$ 36,964

Owners' Equity

	Harlan Spinner	Carol Thomas	
Capital, July 1, 19--	$ 38,731	$ 16,599	
Net income ($26,318, divided 60% — 40%)	15,791	10,527	
Less withdrawals........................	(10,300)	(7,800)	
Capital, June 30, 19--	$ 44,222	$19,326	63,548
Total liabilities and owners' equity			$100,512

Spinner & Thomas—Balance Sheet

vided by the Balance Sheet columns of the work sheet reproduced on pages 554 and 555. Note that the current assets were presented first and arrayed in their probable order of liquidity. Cash was shown first followed by government notes. These notes are regarded as temporary investments since they can be liquidated with relative ease if a shortage of cash should occur. Accrued interest receivable, accounts receivable (less the allowance for doubtful accounts) and merchandise inventories were shown next, and lastly supplies and prepayments. These latter items are included as current assets because their present ownership means that less money will have to be spent for such purposes in the near future. It is not expected that these items will be directly converted into cash. Long-term assets of Spinner & Thomas are the last assets listed. They are shown in columnar form, an approach not previously illustrated, for the purpose of condensing the report.

All of the liabilities of the firm are current liabilities. The owners' equity section is arranged to show the nature and amount of the change in each partner's equity during the year.

The balance sheet is supported by a schedule of accounts receivable as of June 30, 19--. This schedule is just a list of the subsidiary accounts receivable ledger accounts as of the close of the year. It is not an integral part of the balance sheet.

Spinner & Thomas
Schedule of Accounts Receivable
June 30, 19--

Ayres Department Stores	$ 1,915
Bakemeier's Bakery	1,610
Brother Juniper's	1,219
Heritage House	1,278
Houlihan's Place	1,150
Methodist Hospital	1,294
Sam's Deli	1,249
The Tin Star	1,263
	$10,978

Spinner & Thomas—Schedule of Accounts Receivable

Interpreting The Balance Sheet

In interpreting the balance sheet, it is important to remember that the amounts of certain assets as shown on a conventional balance sheet do not necessarily reflect their current values. For example, even though most of Spinner & Thomas's inventory is sold each day, there may be unsalable items in the inventory that remain on hand for another day or more. Also, the undepreciated cost of the long-term assets (the difference between the original cost of these assets and the depreciation so far charged off as expense) does not indicate what these assets would bring if they were to be sold nor does it indicate what it would cost to buy these assets. The difference ($39,022 in total) merely represents the amount, less any expected scrap or salvage value, that is to be charged against future revenues. With these considerations in mind, there are ways to analyze the balance sheet. Two commonly used types of analysis are discussed below: (1) ratio analysis and (2) comparative analysis.

Ratio Analysis. One use of the balance sheet is to aid in judging the liquidity of a business, that is, the ability of the enterprise to meet its current debt obligations. Besides the relative amounts of current assets and current liabilities, the composition of these resources and obligations must also be considered in judging liquidity. Two commonly used measures of liquidity are the current ratio and the quick ratio. The ratio of the current assets ($61,490) to current liabilities ($36,964) of Spinner & Thomas is 1.66 to 1. This is adequate, but of equal or greater significance is the fact that the "quick" assets (cash, temporary investments, and current receivables) total $55,423—1.5 times the current liabilities. This indicates that the firm more than passes the acid test (a ratio of quick assets to total current liabilities of at least 1 to 1).

Comparative Analysis. As in the case of income statements, a comparison of current and past balance sheets may be informative. Comparative balance sheets are often presented in stockholders' reports. In some cases, an analysis that involves expressing one amount as a percent of another may be helpful. In other cases, comparisons of ratios may be more meaningful.

This type of analysis can be illustrated by using the comparative balance sheet summary of Spinner & Thomas on page 596. Note that the current ratio has improved from 1.16 to 1 ($41,750 ÷ $35,885) to 1.66 to 1 ($61,490 ÷ $36,964) from the beginning to the end of the year. In addition, current assets amounted to 61% of total assets at the end of the year, compared with only about 46% at the beginning of the year.

These ratios and percentages indicate that Spinner & Thomas have strengthened their financial control of the business during the year. The percentages also suggest that Spinner & Thomas probably could afford to increase their investment in long-term assets.

Analysis of Profitability

Analysis of profitability involves the use of both income statement and balance sheet data. The amount of annual net income does not mean too much by itself. However, when this amount is contrasted with the volume of sales, the average total amount of the assets, or the average total of the owners' equity element of the business, a better indication of profitability is provided. It was noted on page 581 that Spinner & Thomas had net income equal to almost 2% of net sales. The relationship between Spinner & Thomas' net income and their assets and owners' equity will now be considered.

According to the comparative balance sheet summary on page 596, Spinner & Thomas had average total assets for the fiscal year of $95,863 [($91,215 + $100,512) ÷ 2]. The ratio of net income to average total assets, which is known as return on assets, was therefore 27.5% (net income of $26,318 ÷ average total assets of $95,863).

Spinner & Thomas' average total owners' equity for the fiscal year was $59,439 [($55,330 + $63,548) ÷ 2]. The ratio of net income to average owners' equity, which is known as return on equity, was therefore 44.3% (net income of $26,318 ÷ average owners' equity of $59,439).

Both the return on assets and the return on equity of Spinner & Thomas appear to be very favorable. In judging these relationships, however, it must be remembered that no income tax has been taken into consideration, since partnerships, as such, do not pay income taxes. In their individual income tax returns, Spinner & Thomas must include their shares of the partnership net income along with any "salary" payments or allowances. The amount of any cash or other assets received from the firm is not relevant to the calculation of each partner's taxable income. The amount of income tax that each partner must pay depends upon the total amount of income from various sources, the amount of various deductions and credits that may be taken, and the number of exemptions to which the partner is entitled.

BUILDING YOUR ACCOUNTING KNOWLEDGE

1. In what order are the current assets arrayed on the balance sheet of Spinner & Thomas?
2. Why are supplies and prepayments included among the current assets?
3. What group of assets is listed after the current assets?

4. What is the owner's equity section of the balance sheet arranged to show?
5. Give two examples of balance sheet assets that do not necessarily reflect their current values.
6. What are the current ratio and the quick ratio used to judge or measure?
7. What are the percentage of net income to sales, the return on assets, and the return on owner's equity, used to measure?

APPLYING ACCOUNTING CONCEPTS

Exercise 19-5. The following balances were taken from the balance sheet columns of the end-of-year work sheet of Blue Haven Supplies, a partnership owned by June Betes and Wendy Reed. The fiscal year ends December 31, 19--

Cash	$23,524
Government notes	9,000
Accrued interest receivable	150
Accounts receivable	9,867
Allowance for doubtful accounts	235
Merchandise inventory, Dept. A	1,579
Merchandise inventory, Dept. B	1,499
Supplies and prepayments	1,776
Store equipment	18,670
Accumulated depreciation on store equipment	3,547
Accounts payable	23,264
Accrued and withheld payroll taxes	1,479
June Betes, capital	27,620
Wendy Reed, capital	15,488

Net income for the year was $20,432; profits were split 50-50; and Betes withdrew $14,000 and Reed withdrew $12,000.
Prepare a classified balance sheet in report form for Blue Haven Supplies.

Exercise 19-6.   Refer to Exercise 19-5. Make the following calculations related to the liquidity and profitability of Blue Haven Supplies: **(a)** current ratio, **(b)** quick ratio or acid test, **(c)** percent of current assets to total assets, **(d)** return on assets (total assets were $60,285 at the beginning of the current year), and **(e)** return on equity for each partner and for the partnership.

**Report
No. 19-2**

Complete Report No. 19-2 in the study assignments. Do not submit the report at this time. Since Reports 19-1, 19-2, and 19-3 are related, you should retain the working papers until you have completed all three reports. Continue with the textbook discussion until Report No. 19-3 is required.

THE STATEMENT OF CHANGES IN FINANCIAL POSITION

The annual report of Spinner & Thomas includes a statement of changes in financial position for the year. Since this type of statement has not been discussed or illustrated in earlier chapters, its nature and purpose will be explained before the one for Spinner & Thomas is considered.

Nature and Purpose of the Statement

The managers of a business have the dual objective of generating net income (profitability) and of keeping the enterprise solvent (liquidity). It would seem that success in achievement of the first objective would automatically assure achievement of the second objective. Net income brings in cash—either at once, or as soon as receivables are collected. To assure solvency or liquidity is not that simple, however. The cash inflow resulting from profitable operations may be used to acquire long-term assets, to discharge long-term indebtedness, or it may be withdrawn by the owners. Many profitable and growing businesses suffer from a continual shortage of working capital (current assets minus current liabilities), or may suffer from a chronic *cash* shortage. Sometimes the reverse is the case. There may be little or no net income, and yet by occasional sales of long-term assets, by borrowing on a long-term basis, or by additional investments by the owners, the business maintains ample working capital, or may obtain a supply of ready cash. The increase or decrease in working capital or in cash is the result of the interplay of various management actions and outside influences.

In analyzing the affairs of a business, it is helpful to know the reasons for an increase or a decrease in working capital or in cash during the period under review. To provide this information, a special type of financial statement that explains the change in working capital or in cash has been developed. The preferred title for this financial statement is the statement of changes in financial position. However, it is sometimes called the fund-change statement, the statement of sources and uses of funds, or the statement of changes in working capital.

In ordinary usage, "funds" often is used as a synonym for cash. The term "fund" is used to describe cash or other assets set aside for a specified purpose such as a petty cash fund. In government finance and accounting, a fund is a segregated collection of cash and other assets (and, sometimes, related liabilities) held or used for a certain purpose, such as a highway construction fund. In connection with the Statement of Changes in Financial Position, the word "funds" usually means either working capital or cash. A number of slight variations from these meanings are used in practice, but these are the two basic definitions of "funds." A statement of changes in financial position is a statement explaining the increase or decrease in the working capital or cash of a business during a specified period of time.

At the present time, about an equal number of companies use cash and working capital to express their changes in financial position. Many accountants believe that a statement of sources and uses of cash better explains what is happening to the business. For many purposes, periodic statements of cash receipts and disbursements are needed. But the proper emphasis may be quite different in particular sets of circumstances. To illustrate, consider the following comparative statement of the current assets and current liabilities of a business at the beginning and end of a year:.

	Beginning of Year	End of Year
Current Assets:		
Cash........................	$ 20,000	$100,000
Temporary investments	40,000	10,000
Receivables (net)	80,000	60,000
Inventories and prepayments	60,000	70,000
Total.................................	$200,000	$240,000
Current Liabilities:		
Notes, accounts, and taxes payable	50,000	160,000
Working capital........................	$150,000	$ 80,000

Cash increased 400% but the liquidity position of the company tightened considerably. The current ratio changed from 4 to 1 ($200,000:$50,000) to only 1.5 to 1 ($240,000:$160,000), and the quick (acid-test) ratio from 2.8 to 1 ($140,000:$50,000) to 1.06 to 1 ($170,000:$160,000). In analyzing what has happened in the business, the $70,000 decrease in working capital may prove to be of some future concern despite the increase in cash of $80,000. A statement of changes in financial position based on working capital would shed some light on such a potential problem in this set of circumstances. The working capital approach is explained and illustrated in this chapter. The cash approach will be explained and illustrated in Chapter 28.

Sources of Funds

Funds in the form of working capital may be secured or obtained in four ways:

Investments by Owners. When the owners invest cash or other current assets in the business, working capital is increased.

Profitable Operations. When there has been net income for an accounting period, the increase in cash and receivables due to sales and other revenue must have been more than the total of the decrease in inventory (because of goods sold) and either the decrease in cash or the increase in current payables that took place when expenses were incurred. (The special problem of depreciation and a few other expenses that do not reduce working capital when incurred will be discussed at a later point.)

Long-Term Borrowing. When money is borrowed and the promised date of repayment is two or more years in the future, working capital is increased as a result of a current asset increasing and a long-term liability increasing. (Short-term borrowing does not affect working capital because the increase in cash is exactly offset by the increase in a current liability—usually notes payable.)

Sale of Long-Term Assets. When long-term assets, such as land, buildings, equipment, or trucks are sold, usually either cash or current receivables is increased. In either case, working capital is increased.

Uses of Funds

Funds in the form of working capital may be used or applied in four ways:

Withdrawals by Owners. When the owners of a business take money out either because there has been a profit, or as a withdrawal of their capital investment, working capital is reduced. In corporations, the payment of cash dividends is an example of this type of use of funds.

Unprofitable Operations. When there has been a net loss for an accounting period, either the decrease in cash or the increase in current payables that took place when expenses were incurred plus the decrease in inventory (because of goods sold) must have been more than the increase in cash and receivables due to sales and other revenue.

Repayment of Long-Term Borrowing. When long-term liabilities, such as mortgages payable, are paid, cash and thus working capital are reduced. The discharge of short-term obligations does not affect working capital because the decrease in cash is offset by an equal decrease in a current liability.

Purchase of Long-Term Assets. When a long-term asset (land, building, equipment, etc.) is purchased, usually either cash is reduced or accounts payable is increased. In either case, working capital is diminished.

Direct Financing

There are some changes in financial position in the course of a year that affect only long-term assets and long-term liabilities. For example, buildings or equipment may be acquired in exchange for a mortgage payable over a period of years. In essence, the mortgage payable is a source of funds, and the acquisition of buildings or equipment is a use of funds, but since the source exactly offsets the use, there is no effect on working capital (or cash).

In spite of this, the accounting profession prefers, for purposes of adequate disclosure, that transactions of a direct financing nature (in which the use of funds exactly matches their source) be shown on the statement of changes in financial position. The mortgage payable in the example above may be shown under "Sources" (Long-term Borrowing) and the buildings (or equipment) acquired under "Uses" (Purchase of Long-term Assets).

Simplified Example of Statement of Changes in Financial Position

The statement of changes in financial position is prepared from information supplied by the balance sheets at the beginning and end of the accounting period involved, plus certain other data found in the income statement. To illustrate, the balance sheets of Mach & Mash at the beginning and end of the year 19-- are shown on page 594.

	Beginning of Year	End of Year
Assets:		
Cash	$120,000	$ 160,000
Receivables	360,000	320,000
Inventory	400,000	360,000
Total current assets	$880,000	$ 840,000
Land	80,000	80,000
Building		280,000
Equipment		200,000
	$960,000	$1,400,000
Liabilities and Owners' Equity:		
Notes payable	$ 80,000	$ 120,000
Accounts payable	360,000	240,000
Total current liabilities	$440,000	$ 360,000
Mortgage payable		280,000
Mach, capital	280,000	400,000
Mash, capital	240,000	360,000
	$960,000	$1,400,000

During the year, Mach and Mash each invested an additional $60,000 and each withdrew an additional $20,000. The net income for the year was $160,000.

The amount of working capital at the start of the year was $440,000 ($880,000 − $440,000). At the end of the year, the amount of working capital was $480,000 ($840,000 − $360,000). The change, then, was an increase of $40,000. The objective of the statement of changes in financial position is to explain how this happened.

Comparison of the two balance sheets reveals that the building increased from zero to $280,000 and the equipment increased from zero to $200,000. A building was constructed during the year and completed just before the year ended, directly financed with a $280,000 mortgage. At that time the equipment also was purchased for cash. Acquisition of this asset was a $200,000 use of funds. The owners' equity in the business increased from $520,000 ($280,000 + $240,000) to $760,000 ($400,000 + $360,000). This $240,000 increase in funds came from two sources: (1) the net income for the year, $160,000, and (2) the partners' additional investment of $120,000 in total, less one use: the partners' withdrawals of $40,000 in total. These findings can be classified to produce the statement shown on page 595.

Mach & Mash
Statement of Changes in Financial Position—Working Capital Basis
For the Year Ended December 31, 19--

Sources of funds:			
Net income for the year		$160,000	
Investments by partners:			
Mach	$60,000		
Mash	60,000	120,000	
Issuance of mortgage		280,000	$560,000
Uses of funds:			
Purchase of equipment		$200,000	
Partners' withdrawals:			
Mach	$20,000		
Mash	20,000	40,000	
Construction of building		280,000	520,000
Increase in working capital			$ 40,000

Mach & Mash—Statement of Changes in Financial Position

Assembling the Data for Statement of Changes in Financial Position

There are various techniques for assembling and organizing data to produce a statement of changes in financial position. If the calculations are likely to be complicated, it may be advisable to use a special work sheet, otherwise the use of a work sheet is not warranted. The first step is to summarize, in comparative form, the balance sheets at the beginning and end of the period. Spinner & Thomas used the balance sheet at the close of the preceding year (not reproduced in this textbook) and the balance sheet at the close of the year just ended (reproduced on page 585). The statements were summarized and the changes in each element were noted, as follows:

	Beginning of Year	End of Year	Increase (Decrease)
Cash	$30,602	$ 34,635	$ 4,033
Government notes....................	-0-	10,000	10,000
Receivables (net).....................	5,592	10,788	5,196
Merchandise inventories	3,124	3,180	56
Supplies and prepayments	2,432	2,887	455
Total current assets	$41,750	$ 61,490	$ 19,740
Long-term assets (less accumulated depreciation)......................	49,465	39,022	(10,443)
Total assets.......................	$91,215	$100,512	$ 9,297
Notes and interest payable...........	$ 3,172	-0-	$ (3,172)
Accounts payable	30,263	$ 34,375	4,112
Accrued and withheld payroll taxes....	2,450	2,589	139
Total current liabilities	$35,885	$ 36,964	$ 1,079
Owners' equity......................	55,330	63,548	8,218
Total liabilities and owners' equity ...	$91,215	$100,512	$ 9,297

The foregoing summary shows that working capital increased $18,661 (current assets increased $19,740 while current liabilities increased only $1,079). The purpose of the statement of changes in financial position is to explain this increase. Note that cash only increased $4,033. This was overshadowed by the increase in temporary investments, coupled with the increase in net receivables and the modest increase in the current liabilities. It was mentioned earlier that the change in the amount of cash might not be as significant as the change in working capital, especially when surplus cash is temporarily invested in high-return, relatively liquid securities.

The list of sources and uses of funds was enumerated on pages 592 and 593. The possible sources are: (1) investments by owners, (2) profitable operations, (3) long-term borrowing, and (4) sales of long-term assets. Spinner and Thomas made no investments during the year; there was no long-term borrowing or sale of long-term assets; hence, the only source of funds for the year under review was profitable operations.

The possible uses of funds are: (1) withdrawals by owners, (2) unprofitable operations, (3) repayment of long-term borrowing, and (4) purchase of long-term assets. Items (2) and (3) do not apply since the year had been profitable and there were no long-term debts to repay during the year. Since both partners made withdrawals during the year and a piece of equipment had been purchased, items (1) and (4) are to be considered as uses of funds.

The sources of funds and uses of funds for the Spinner & Thomas business will be explained in the following sections.

Sources of Funds: Operations

The income statement of Spinner & Thomas for the year ended June 30, 19--, revealed a net income of $26,318. This amount represented a source of working capital for the business, which can be explained as follows. There were two types of revenue: sales and interest earned. In both cases, either cash was collected or a current receivable (accounts receivable or accrued interest receivable) was increased, and accordingly, working capital was increased. Almost all expenses that were incurred caused working capital to be reduced. Cost of goods sold reduced the merchandise inventory—an important current asset. Prepaid Insurance, a current asset, was reduced by an amount equal to the cost of the insurance that expired during the period. The allowance for doubtful accounts was, in effect, a reduction of current receivables. Most of the expenses incurred caused either an immediate reduction in cash or an increase in a current payable of some sort. If the current assets are reduced or the current liabilities are increased, working capital is reduced.

The single exception to the above analysis of the effect of expenses upon working capital is depreciation expense. When the depreciation of the three types of long-term assets was entered (refer to adjustments (j), (k), and (l) in the work sheets on pages 554 and 555), the offset to the depreciation expense debit was a credit to the proper accumulated depreciation account. Accumulated depreciation represents the total amount of asset cost charged to operations. An addition to accumulated depreciation is a reduction in the undepreciated cost of the long-term asset—not a reduction in a current asset.

The total amount of Spinner & Thomas' depreciation expense for the year was $10,964 ($1,848 + $1,978 + $7,138). Since this expense did not reduce working capital (as funds are defined here), for purposes of the statement of changes in financial position, the amount of the net income for the year, $26,318, was increased by the amount of the depreciation expense for the year and reported as follows:

Funds provided by current operations:
Net income (per income statement) $26,318
Add expenses not requiring funds:
   Depreciation 10,964
Total funds provided by current operations $37,282

Another method of showing "funds provided by current operations" would be to deduct expenses that reduced working capital from total revenue that increased working capital (sales and interest earned). The difference would be $37,282, the same amount as shown above. Depreciation expense is not mentioned in the statement if this method is used. In the Spinner & Thomas statement, the operating expenses excluding depreciation would total $225,407, and funds provided by current operations would be shown as follows:

Funds provided by current operations:		
Net sales..................................	$1,354,903	
Other revenue.............................	1,345	$1,356,248
Less expenses that reduced working capital:		
Cost of goods sold	$1,093,559	
Operating expense (excluding $10,964 of depreciation expense)	225,407	1,318,966
Funds provided by current operations		$ 37,282

The above method is not as widely used because it is considered desirable to have the statement of changes in financial position start with the amount shown as the net income in the income statement. This treatment serves to tie the financial statements together in a more professional manner.

A great deal of misunderstanding has arisen about depreciation in the statement of changes in financial position. The idea that "depreciation is a source of funds" is entirely incorrect. Depreciation, while difficult to measure on a periodic basis, is a very real expense. It differs from other expenses only in that most expenses reduce working capital, while depreciation expense is a reduction in certain long-term assets. With most other expenses, the payment of cash and recognition of the expense are closely related—money is paid in the same period that the expense is incurred. In a few cases, money was spent in the preceding period, such as payments for inventory and supplies that were not sold or used until the next period; and in some cases, money will not be paid until the next period, such as employer's payroll taxes that relate to one year but are not paid until the next year. Depreciation is considered an expense because cash was paid when the assets that are being depreciated were bought. Depreciation is too often misunderstood because the point in time that the money was spent for the depreciable asset and the point in time when the outlay becomes an expense may be far apart.

Another argument that may be used to show that depreciation is not a source of funds is as follows: Suppose that depreciation expense had been overlooked in calculating the net income for a period. Would the funds provided by current operations be any less? The answer clearly is "no." If Spinner & Thomas had failed to enter the depreciation expense totalling $10,964, the net income for the year would have been incorrectly calculated to be $37,282. In the statement of changes in financial position, that amount would be shown as funds provided by current operations, just as when the net income calculation includes the depreciation expense.

There are some other expenses that have the same characteristics as depreciation. These expenses arise whenever an asset is purchased and gradually written off as an expense over a number of succeeding years. A good example is a patent. Patents have a legal life of 17 years. A company may have purchased a patent soon after it was issued. The management of the acquiring company may not think that the patent will be valuable for 16 to 17 years, but may expect that ownership of the patent will be of benefit, perhaps, for 10 years. Accordingly, one tenth of the cost may be charged to an expense for each of the ten years, which is described as amortizing the cost. The portion written off each year is described as amortization expense. A patent is classified as a long-term asset. As portions of its cost are taken into expense, no decrease in working capital is involved. Accordingly, amortization expense, like depreciation expense, must be "added back" to determine the amount of funds provided by current operations.

Occasions may arise when the net income figure must be further modified to arrive at funds provided by current operations. If, for example, a piece of land that cost $30,000 some years before was sold for $36,000 and the $6,000 gain was reported in the income statement, that amount, $6,000, would have to be excluded from funds provided by current operations. Unless the business was engaged in buying and selling land, such a transaction would not be considered a part of regular operations. The $36,000 received from the sale of the land would be reported separately as a source of funds from the sale of long-term assets in the statement of changes in financial position.

Current operations were the only source of funds for Spinner & Thomas during the year ended June 30, 19--. The two uses of funds during that year will be considered next.

Uses of Funds: Owners' Withdrawals

The owners' equity section of the balance sheet for the year ended June 30, 19--, shown on page 585 indicates that during the year, Spinner withdrew $10,300 and Thomas, $7,800. These amounts are shown in the uses of funds section of the statement of changes in financial position.

Uses of Funds: Purchase of Long-Term Assets

The analysis of the changes in the balance sheets of Spinner & Thomas, shown on page 596, shows a decrease in the total undepreciated cost (cost less accumulated depreciation) of the long-term assets in the amount of $10,443. There was a decrease in the total undepreciated cost amounting to $10,964 caused by depreciation expense for the year. This amount of depreciation, $10,964, was taken into consideration in preparing the income statement. If the decrease in undepreciated cost due to depreciation for the year was $10,964, but the total decrease was only $10,443, there must have been a use of funds in the amount of $521 ($10,964 − $10,443) to purchase some new long-term assets. An examination of the long-term asset accounts revealed that on June 18, an electronic desk calculator was purchased at a cost of $521. Since the bill had been paid, the decrease in cash reduced working capital; hence the purchase of office equipment is a use of funds for the year. This acquisition was so reported in the statement of changes in financial position.

Statement of Changes in Financial Position with Supporting Schedule of Changes in Working Capital

The annual report of Spinner & Thomas includes a statement of changes in financial position with a supporting schedule of changes in working capital. These are reproduced on page 601. The statement of changes in financial position explains the net change in working capital that occurred between the start and the close of the fiscal year. The supporting schedule shows the amounts of the changes in the elements that comprise working capital (current assets and current liabilities). The balance sheets as of the beginning and end of the year provided the data for the schedule. Such a schedule is customarily provided when the working capital approach is used in preparing the statement of changes in financial position. It is important to note that the increase in working capital in the statement itself must agree with the increase in working capital shown in the schedule—$18,661 in this case.

Statements of changes in financial position are not always presented in the form illustrated. One form sometimes used begins with the amount of working capital at the beginning of the period (usually a year). To this are added the sources of funds, appropriately classified. The uses of funds are then shown and their total is subtracted to show the amount of working capital at the end of the period. As was noted earlier, titles other than "statement of changes in financial position" sometimes are used. By whatever name it is called, the inclusion of the statement in the annual report has now become standard practice.

Spinner & Thomas
Statement of Changes in Financial Position
For the Year Ended June 30, 19--

Sources of funds:
  Funds provided by current operations:
    Net income (per income statement) $26,318
    Add expenses not requiring funds:
      Depreciation 10,964
    Total sources of funds $37,282
Uses of funds:
  Partners' withdrawals:
    Harlan Spinner $10,300
    Carol Thomas.. 7,800
  Purchase of office equipment 521
  Total uses of funds... 18,621
Increase in working capital $18,661

Spinner & Thomas—Statement of Changes in Financial Position

Spinner & Thomas
Schedule of Changes in Working Capital
For the Year Ended June 30, 19--

	Beginning of Year	End of Year	Working Capital Increase	Working Capital Decrease
Cash	$30,602	$34,635	$ 4,033	
Government notes....................	-0-	10,000	10,000	
Receivables (net)....................	5,592	10,788	5,196	
Merchandise inventories	3,124	3,180	56	
Supplies and prepayments	2,432	2,887	455	
Notes and interest payable...........	3,172	-0-	3,172	
Accounts payable	30,263	34,375		$ 4,112
Accrued and withheld payroll taxes...	2,450	2,589		139
			$22,912	$ 4,251
Increase in working capital				18,661
			$22,912	$22,912

Spinner & Thomas—Schedule of Changes in Working Capital

BUILDING YOUR ACCOUNTING KNOWLEDGE

1. Why is solvency or liquidity not assured merely because a business is profitable?

2. Give three alternate titles for the statement of changes in financial position.

3. What two meanings does the term "funds" generally have as used in connection with the statement of changes in financial position?

4. What two approaches are used by most companies to express changes in financial position? Which approach is explained and illustrated in this chapter?

5. List four potential sources of funds. List four potential uses of funds.

6. What is the first step in assembling the data for the statement of changes in financial position.

7. What misconception about depreciation in the statement of changes in financial position has arisen? What frequently is the reason for this misunderstanding? Why is the alternative method of showing "funds provided by current operations," discussed on pages 597 and 598, not commonly used in practice?

8. What two types of uses of funds are shown on the Spinner & Thomas statement of changes in financial position?

APPLYING ACCOUNTING CONCEPTS

Exercise 19-7. The summary balance sheets of Kelley and Flanigan's Sporting Goods at the beginning and end of the current year are as follows:

	Beginning of Year	End of Year
Assets:		
Cash	$110,000	$ 130,000
Accounts receivable (net)	340,000	300,000
Merchandise inventory	350,000	380,000
Total current assets	$800,000	$ 810,000
Land	100,000	100,000
Building (book value)		185,000
Equipment (book value)......		145,000
	$900,000	$1,240,000
Liabilities and Owners' Equity:		
Notes payable...............	$ 60,000	$ 110,000
Accounts payable	350,000	210,000
Total current liabilities	$410,000	$ 320,000
Mortgage payable		190,000
Roberta Kelley, capital	260,000	380,000
Cyndy Flanigan, capital	230,000	350,000
	$900,000	$1,240,000

During the year, Kelley and Flanigan each invested an additional $50,000 and each withdrew an additional $15,000. The net income for the year was $170,000. Depreciation on the building was $5,000 and depreciation on the equipment was also $5,000.

(a) Determine the working capital at the beginning and end of the year. **(b)** Determine the change in working capital from the beginning to the end of the year. **(c)** Prepare a statement of changes in financial position using working capital as a basis.

Exercise 19-8. Refer to Exercise 19-7. Prepare a supporting schedule of changes in working capital for Kelley and Flanigan's Sporting Goods.

Report No. 19-3

Complete Report No. 19-3 in the study assignments and submit your working papers for Reports Nos. 19-1, 19-2 and 19-3 for approval. Continue with the textbook discussion in Chapter 20 until Report No. 20-1 is required.

EXPANDING YOUR BUSINESS VOCABULARY

What is the meaning of each of the following terms?

acid test **(p. 587)**
amortization expense **(p. 599)**
annual report **(p. 577)**
Auditor's report **(p. 578)**
comparative analysis **(p. 582)**
direct financing **(p. 593)**
fund **(p. 591)**
fund-change statement **(p. 590)**
highway construction fund **(p. 591)**
liquidity **(p. 587)**
merchandise turnover **(p. 581)**
opinion **(p. 578)**
percentage analysis **(p. 581)**

petty cash fund **(p. 591)**
profitability **(p. 581)**
return on assets **(p. 588)**
return on equity **(p. 588)**
sources of funds **(p. 592)**
statement of changes in financial position **(pp. 590, 591)**
statement of changes in working capital **(p. 590)**
statement of sources and uses of funds **(p. 590)**
undepreciated cost **(p. 587)**
uses of funds **(p. 592)**
working capital **(p. 590)**

CHAPTER 20

Interim Financial Statements

CHAPTER OBJECTIVES

Careful study of this chapter should enable you to:

- Define and describe interim financial statements.

- Explain the reason for preparing interim statements.

- Explain the tentative nature and the limitations of interim financial statements.

- Prepare interim financial statements using the summary-work-sheet technique supplemented by the technique of deriving an interim income statement by the use of successive year-to-date income statements.

- Describe the special problem of accounting for property taxes on an interim basis.

In accounting for business operations, it is general practice to determine income or loss on an annual basis and to prepare balance sheets at annual intervals. While the calendar year is widely used as the fiscal year, many firms adopt the natural business year, which is a year that starts and ends at the time when business activity is at its lowest level. In any case, twelve months is the basic time interval. Interested parties, notably owners and managers, need more frequent reports of the affairs of a business. For this reason, it is common to prepare interim financial statements. Interim means "between." An income statement for a period of time shorter than, and within the limits of, the fiscal year is an interim income statement. A balance sheet as of a date other than the close of the fiscal year is an interim balance sheet.

Interim Statements

Interim statements may be prepared for any segment of a year. However, it is impractical to use a very short period such as a day or a week because of (1) the considerable amount of work involved in producing the statements, and (2) the fact that the shorter the period, the more unreliable the determination of income. Many of the problems of accounting (in contrast to pure data gathering, entering, and storing) arise because numerous items of value are acquired in one period, but are not sold or used entirely within that period. Two important examples are (1) the problem of allocating cost between goods sold (or used) and goods unsold (or unused) at the end of the period, and (2) in the case of most long-term assets, the problem of cost allocation by means of depreciation. The need to allocate inventory costs is a particularly good example of the difficulty of preparing interim statements. At the end of the fiscal year, physical inventories may be taken to determine (or, in some cases, to verify) the quantities of merchandise inventory and various supplies on hand. The procedure is likely to be time consuming and, thus, expensive. It cannot be done at the end of every interim period. Estimates generally have to be used for interim-statement purposes. The shorter the period, the greater the problem.

Because of constraints such as those just mentioned, the month is considered to be the smallest time segment generally feasible for interim-statement purposes. Monthly time segments have the advantage of being universally understood.

Interim statements may be prepared on a quarterly (three months) basis. Quarterly statements tend to be somewhat more reliable than monthly statements. This is because the estimation and allocation methods used for items such as uncollectible accounts, depreciation, and inventories do not have as significant an effect in determining the income for a quarter as they do for a period as short as a month. In addition, quarters are more comparable in length. Quarterly statements in a very condensed form commonly are furnished to the stockholders of large business corporations.

In the majority of cases, interim statements must be regarded as very provisional or tentative in nature. Despite their imperfections, these statements can be useful if they are carefully interpreted.

Using Work Sheets to Produce Interim Financial Statements

It has been demonstrated in previous chapters that the end-of-year work sheet is a useful device to (1) assist in the production of the annual income statement and the year-end balance sheet, and (2) aid in the year-end process of formally adjusting and closing the accounts. The same type of work sheet can materially assist in the production of interim statements. Adjustments are entered on the work sheet, but no formal adjusting or closing of the accounts is done at the end of interim periods.

The use of interim period work sheets is illustrated in this chapter for the preparation of interim financial statements of the Gribbins & Gribbins Wholesale Building Supply Company owned and operated as a partnership by Ronald E. Gribbins and his wife, Martha L. Gribbins. For purposes of this illustration, the business is not departmentalized and the general ledger contains comparatively few accounts. Assume that appropriate books of original entry and auxiliary records are used, and there is no subsidiary operating expenses ledger. The firm uses the calendar year as its fiscal year.

The partners share profits and losses in a 50-50 ratio. The determination of net income takes partners' salaries into account. The accountant for the company prepares monthly income statements and year-to-date income statements, as well as balance sheets, as of the last day of each month. A year-to-date income statement is one that covers a variable time period from the beginning of the fiscal year up to and including the last day of the most current month.

Work Sheet for the First Month of a Fiscal Year

Eight columns of a ten-column work sheet for the first month are reproduced on pages 608 and 609. To conserve space, the Adjusted Trial Balance columns are not shown. For purposes of simplicity, the amounts are rounded to the nearest dollar. The amounts in the Trial Balance columns were taken from the general ledger after the posting for the month of January had been completed. The reasons why some accounts have no balances will become apparent in the discussion that follows.

The following entries were made in the Adjustments amount columns.

Entry (a): The amount of the beginning inventory of merchandise, $3,074,756, was debited to Cost of Goods Sold, Account No. 531, and was credited to Merchandise Inventory, Account No. 141.

Entry (b): The amount of the purchases for the month, $1,882,769, was debited to Cost of Goods Sold, Account No. 531, and was credited to Purchases, Account No. 511.

Entry (c): The amount of the purchases returns and allowances for the month, $23,425, was debited to Purchases Returns and Allowances, Account No. 511.1, and was credited to Cost of Goods Sold, Account No. 531.

Entry (d): The amount of the purchases discount for the month, $40,846, was debited to Purchases Discount, Account No. 511.2, and was credited to Cost of Goods Sold, Account No. 531.

Entry (e): The amount assigned to the merchandise inventory at January 31, $3,066,000, was debited to Merchandise Inventory, Account No. 141, and was credited to Cost of Goods Sold, Account No. 531. The firm uses the perpetual method of inventory accounting and maintains stock records of certain high value items. The stock records indicate the quantities of these items that were presumed to be on hand at January 31. Since very little discrepancy had been found in prior years between these records and the physical counts, the records were considered reliable. Quantities of various low value items were estimated. All quantities were costed by reference to recent purchase invoices.

Entry (f): The interest accrued, $21,875, since January 1, on the $3,000,000 mortgage payable was debited to Interest Expense, Account No. 571, and was credited to Accrued Interest Payable, Account No. 217. Interest at $8\frac{3}{4}\%$ per annum is payable semiannually each January 1 and July 1. Interest for the six months ended last December 31 ($131,250) was paid on January 2 since January 1 was a holiday. The determination of net income or loss for January must take into account the interest that has accrued during the month.

Entry (g): The amount of the insurance expense for January, $5,526,

Account	Acct. No.	TRIAL BALANCE	
		Debit	Credit
Cash	111	81,500	
Accounts Receivable	131	399,232	
Allowance for Doubtful Accounts	131.1		3,992
Merchandise Inventory	141	3,074,756	
Store Supplies	151	16,046	
Prepaid Insurance	155	22,432	
Land	161	1,170,000	
Building	171	4,873,939	
Accumulated Depreciation—Building	171.1		2,452,486
Furniture and Equipment	181	542,131	
Accumulated Depreciation—Furniture and Equipment	181.1		180,558
Delivery Equipment	185	188,173	
Accumulated Depreciation—Delivery Equipment	185.1		92,536
FICA Tax Payable	211		18,932
FUTA Tax Payable	212		790
State Unemployment Tax Payable	213		4,260
Employees Income Tax Payable	214		22,336
Accrued Interest Payable	217		
Accounts Payable	218		469,788
Mortgage Payable	262		3,000,000
Ronald E. Gribbins, Capital	311		2,124,017
Ronald E. Gribbins, Drawing	311.1	11,984	
Martha L. Gribbins, Capital	321		1,749,264
Martha L. Gribbins, Drawing	321.1	9,070	
Sales	411		2,365,812
Sales Returns and Allowances	411.1	23,466	
Sales Discount	411.2	50,462	
Purchases	511	1,882,769	
Purchases Returns and Allowances	511.1		23,425
Purchases Discount	511.2		40,846
Cost of Goods Sold	531		
Partners' Salaries Expense	541	9,600	
Salaries and Commissions Expense	542	157,775	
Utilities Expense	543	4,327	
Telephone Expense	544	1,280	
Supplies Expense	545		
Delivery Expense	546	5,687	
Depreciation Expense	547		
Insurance Expense	548		
Payroll Taxes Expense	551	14,515	
Property Tax Expense	552		
Uncollectible Accounts Expense	553		
Miscellaneous Expense	562	9,898	
Interest Expense	571		
		12,549,042	12,549,042
Accrued Property Tax Payable			
Net Income			

WHOLESALE BUILDING SUPPLY COMPANY
Sheet
January 31, 19--

ADJUSTMENTS Debit	ADJUSTMENTS Credit	INCOME STATEMENT Debit	INCOME STATEMENT Credit	BALANCE SHEET Debit	BALANCE SHEET Credit
				81,500	
				399,232	
	(j) 11,459				15,451
(e) 3,066,000	(a) 3,074,756			3,066,000	
	(h) 4,814			11,232	
	(g) 5,526			16,906	
				1,170,000	
				4,873,939	
	(i) 10,154				2,462,640
				542,131	
	(i) 2,824				183,382
				188,173	
	(i) 3,920				96,456
					18,932
					790
					4,260
					22,336
	(f) 21,875				21,875
					469,788
					3,000,000
					2,124,017
				11,984	1,749,264
				9,070	
			2,365,812		
		23,466			
		50,462			
	(b) 1,882,769				
(c) 23,425					
(d) 40,846					
(a) 3,074,756	(c) 23,425	1,827,254			
(b) 1,882,769	(d) 40,846				
	(e) 3,066,000				
		9,600			
		157,775			
		4,327			
		1,280			
(h) 4,814		4,814			
		5,687			
(i) 16,898		16,898			
(g) 5,526		5,526			
		14,515			
(k) 11,730		11,730			
(j) 11,459		11,459			
		9,898			
(f) 21,875		21,875			
	(k) 11,730				11,730
8,160,098	8,160,098	2,176,566	2,365,812	10,370,167	10,180,921
		189,246			189,246
		2,365,812	2,365,812	10,370,167	10,370,167

Work Sheet for One-Month Period

was debited to Insurance Expense, Account No. 548, and was credited to Prepaid Insurance, Account No. 155. The insurance policy file provides the information needed to calculate the amount.

Entry (h): The estimated cost of store supplies used during the month, $4,814, was debited to Supplies Expense, Account No. 545, and was credited to Store Supplies, Account No. 151. This amount was determined by subtracting the estimated cost of the store supplies on hand, January 31, $11,232, from the balance of the store supplies account, $16,046. Note that the firm uses the asset method of accounting for supplies.

Entry (i): The depreciation for the month, $16,898, was debited to Depreciation Expense, Account No. 547, with credits to Accumulated Depreciation—Building, Account No. 171.1, $10,154, Accumulated Depreciation—Furniture and Equipment, Account No. 181.1, $2,824, and Accumulated Depreciation—Delivery Equipment, Account No. 185.1, $3,920. The firm uses straight line depreciation calculated at the following annual rates; building $2\frac{1}{2}\%$; furniture and equipment, $6\frac{1}{4}\%$ and delivery equipment, 25%. These rates were applied to the cost of the assets as shown in the trial balance, and 1/12 of each resulting amount was taken as the depreciation for January. No long-term assets were purchased during January.

Entry (j): The amount of the adjustment in the doubtful accounts provision for the month, $11,459, was debited to Uncollectible Accounts Expense, Account No. 553, and was credited to Allowance for Doubtful Accounts, Account No. 131.1. Experience has indicated that uncollectible account losses average $\frac{1}{2}$ of 1% of net sales. Net sales for January amounted to $2,291,884 [$2,365,812 (gross sales) − $23,466 (sales returns and allowances) − $50,462 (sales discount)]. One half of 1% of $2,291,884 is $11,459. The January 31 trial balance shows the allowance account to have a credit balance of $3,992, which represents the remainder of an amount determined to be necessary based on a percentage of net sales in one or more previous months. At this time, the $11,459 adjustment for January is added to the balance in the allowance for doubtful accounts of $3,992 to produce a new balance of $15,451. However, this balance will be watched carefully in subsequent months to avoid having it become larger than necessary.

Entry (k): The property tax assignable to January, $11,730, was debited to Property Tax Expense, Account No. 552, and was credited to Accrued Property Tax Payable. Note that the latter title had to be added to the list and that no account number is shown. The reason is that there is no need for such an account in the general ledger. The account is used solely to produce interim financial statements.

Property taxes pose a special accounting problem. Such taxes do not accrue in the conventional sense. Usually the amount of the tax is not known until the tax bill is received several months after the assessment date. The tax may be paid in two installments: one half by a specified day late in the calendar year and the other half by a specified day in the following spring. Property tax expense commonly is accounted for on a cash basis; that is, no record is made until a payment occurs. By the end of the year, the property tax expense account shows the amount of tax actually paid during the year. Gribbins & Gribbins accounts for property taxes in their interim report in the following manner: In the year just ended they paid $67,572 in April, and $70,380 in December. Since another $70,380 must be paid in April of the current year, it seems reasonable to allocate one sixth of the amount to each of the first six months. This is accomplished by a debit to the expense account and a credit to the liability. The purpose of this entry is to give the month of January a reasonable share of the year's property tax expense. Not all accountants treat property tax expense in precisely this manner, but some procedure has to be followed to cause a reasonable amount to be included in the income determination for each interim period.

The work sheet was completed by (1) totaling the Adjustments columns to prove their equality, (2) extending the amounts as adjusted to the proper Income Statement or Balance Sheet columns, (3) footing the last four columns to determine the net income for the month and entering this amount, $189,246, in the Income Statement Debit and the Balance Sheet Credit columns, and (4) entering the totals and making the rulings.

The Interim Statements for January

The income statement for the month of January, 19--, for Gribbins & Gribbins Wholesale Building Supply Company is reproduced on page 612. The balance sheet as of January 31, 19-- is shown on page

613. Note that, in the owners' equity section, the net income for the month is apportioned between the partners in the agreed ratio: 50%-50%.

Gribbins & Gribbins Wholesale Building Supply Company
Income Statement
For the Month of January, 19--

Sales.........		$2,365,812
Less: Returns and allowances		(23,466)
Sales discounts		(50,462)
Net sales.........		$2,291,884
Cost of goods sold:		
Merchandise inventory, January 1........	$3,074,756	
Purchases........	1,882,769	
Less: Returns and allowances	(23,425)	
Purchases discounts	(40,846)	
Cost of merchandise available for sale	$4,893,254	
Less merchandise inventory, January 31	3,066,000	1,827,254
Gross margin on sales		$ 464,630
Operating expenses:		
Partners' salaries expense........	$ 9,600	
Salaries and commissions expense	157,775	
Utilities expense	4,327	
Telephone expense	1,280	
Supplies expense	4,814	
Delivery expense........	5,687	
Depreciation expense	16,898	
Insurance expense.........	5,526	
Payroll taxes expense	14,515	
Property tax expense........	11,730	
Uncollectible accounts expense........	11,459	
Miscellaneous expense........	9,898	
Total operating expenses.........		253,509
Operating income.........		$ 211,121
Interest expense		21,875
Net income.........		$ 189,246

Gribbins & Gribbins Wholesale Building Supply Company—Income Statement

---

The procedure of preparing a work sheet and the interim financial statements is almost identical to the steps that normally are followed at the end of the year. At year-end, however, the work of the accountant will not cease with statement preparation. The adjusting entries

Gribbins & Gribbins Wholesale Building Supply Company
Balance Sheet
January 31, 19--

Assets

Current assets:
Cash		$	81,500
Accounts receivable	$ 399,232		
Less allowance for doubtful accounts	15,451	383,781	
Merchandise inventory		3,066,000	
Store supplies		11,232	
Prepaid insurance		16,906	
Total current assets			$3,559,419

Long-term assets:
Land		$1,170,000	
Building	$4,873,939		
Less accumulated depreciation	2,462,640	2,411,299	
Furniture and equipment	$ 542,131		
Less accumulated depreciation	183,382	358,749	
Delivery equipment	$ 188,173		
Less accumulated depreciation	96,456	91,717	
Total long-term assets			4,031,765
Total assets			$7,591,184

Liabilities

Current liabilities:
FICA tax payable	$	18,932
FUTA tax payable		790
State unemployment tax payable		4,260
Employees income tax payable		22,336
Accrued interest payable		21,875
Accrued property tax payable		11,730
Accounts payable		469,788
Total current liabilities		$ 549,711

Long-term liability:
Mortgage payable	3,000,000
Total liabilities	$3,549,711

Owners' Equity

Ronald E. Gribbins, capital:
Capital, January 1	$2,124,017	
Add net income (50% of $189,246)	94,623	
Less withdrawals	(11,984)	
Capital, January 31		$2,206,656

Martha L. Gribbins, capital:
Capital, January 1	$1,749,264	
Add net income (50% of $189,246)	94,623	
Less withdrawals	(9,070)	
Capital, January 31		1,834,817
Total owners' equity		4,041,473
Total liabilities and owners' equity		$7,591,184

Gribbins & Gribbins Wholesale Building Supply Company—Balance Sheet

have to be journalized and posted, followed by the journalizing and posting of the needed closing entries. It is likely that a post-closing trial balance will have to be taken. In many cases certain reversing entries will have been journalized and posted. At the end of each interim period, however, none of these steps is involved.

Work Sheet for the First Two Months of a Fiscal Year

The work sheet for the first two months is reproduced on pages 616 and 617. The amounts in the Trial Balance columns were the balances of all of the general ledger accounts after the posting for the month of February had been completed. A comparison of the January 31 trial balance on page 608 with the trial balance for February 28 on page 616 reveals that there are no changes in the balances of several accounts. As explained previously, this is because the adjustments made in the work sheet for January were solely to produce interim financial statements for January, and are not made a formal part of the accounting records.

The balance of the merchandise inventory account (No. 141) remains unchanged until the accounts are adjusted at the end of the year. There are no changes in the balances of the land and delivery equipment accounts (Nos. 161 and 185) because no assets of these types were acquired or disposed of during February. None of the accumulated depreciation accounts (Nos. 171.1, 181.1, and 185.1) received any debits, since none of the related assets was retired or sold during February, and the accumulated depreciation accounts will receive no credits until the year-end adjustments are recorded.

Accrued Interest Payable, Account No. 217, has no balance at the end of either month since the accrual is not entered on a monthly basis. There was no transaction during February that affected the balance of Mortgage Payable, Account No. 262. The partners' capital accounts (Nos. 311 and 321) are unchanged, since neither partner made any additional investment in February. The accounts will be unaffected by withdrawals and net income or loss until the annual closing entries are posted at the end of the year. The accounts for Depreciation Expense (No. 547), Insurance Expense (No. 548), Supplies Expense, (No. 545), and Uncollectible Accounts Expense (No. 553), have no balances at the end of either month, since they normally are not debited until the year-end adjustments are made. Property Tax Expense, Account No. 552, and Interest Expense, Account No. 571, have no balances at the end of either month, since no payments of property taxes were made during either month, and the payment of mortgage interest on January 2 discharged the liability entered at the end of the previous year. Cost of Goods Sold, Account No. 531, and Expense and Revenue Summary, Account No. 331 (not shown), have no balances at either date, since these accounts are used solely in the end-of-year process of formally adjusting and closing the accounts.

The entries in the Adjustments columns of the work sheet for the two months ended February 28 involve exactly the same accounts as the entries on the work sheet for the month ended January 31.

Entry (a): Cost of Goods Sold, Account No. 531, was debited and Merchandise Inventory, Account No. 141, was credited for exactly the same amount, $3,074,756, as on the earlier work sheet, since the January 1 inventory was involved in the calculations of cost of goods sold both for January alone and for the two-month period ended February 28.

Entries (b), (c), and (d): The balances of Purchases, Account No. 511, $3,358,352, Purchases Returns and Allowances, Account No. 511.1, $44,507, and Purchases Discount, Account No. 511.2, $77,611, were transferred to Cost of Goods Sold, Account No. 531. In each case, the balance represents the amount for the two months.

Entry (e): Merchandise Inventory, Account No. 141, was debited and Cost of Goods Sold, Account No. 531, was credited for $2,838,000, the estimated amount of the inventory on February 28.

Entry (f): Interest Expense, Account No. 571, was debited and Accrued Interest Payable, Account No. 217, was credited for $43,750, the mortgage interest accrued for the two months.

Entry (g): Insurance Expense, Account No. 548, was debited and Prepaid Insurance, Account No. 155, was credited for $10,965, the

Account	Acct. No.	TRIAL BALANCE	
		Debit	Credit
Cash	111	122,326	
Accounts Receivable	131	488,853	
Allowance for Doubtful Accounts	131.1	7,836	
Merchandise Inventory	141	3,074,756	
Store Supplies	151	19,852	
Prepaid Insurance	155	23,333	
Land	161	1,170,000	
Building	171	4,877,168	
Accumulated Depreciation—Building	171.1		2,452,486
Furniture and Equipment	181	608,670	
Accumulated Depreciation—Furniture and Equipment	181.1		180,558
Delivery Equipment	185	188,173	
Accumulated Depreciation—Delivery Equipment	185.1		92,536
FICA Tax Payable	211		18,175
FUTA Tax Payable	212		1,546
State Unemployment Tax Payable	213		8,350
Employees Income Tax Payable	214		20,458
Accrued Interest Payable	217		
Accounts Payable	218		294,071
Mortgage Payable	262		3,000,000
Ronald E. Gribbins, Capital	311		2,124,017
Ronald E. Gribbins, Drawing	311.1	43,562	
Martha L. Gribbins, Capital	321		1,749,264
Martha L. Gribbins, Drawing	321.1	37,036	
Sales	411		4,494,594
Sales Returns and Allowances	411.1	44,584	
Sales Discount	411.2	95,887	
Purchases	511	3,358,352	
Purchases Returns and Allowances	511.1		44,507
Purchases Discount	511.2		77,611
Cost of Goods Sold	531		
Partners' Salaries Expense	541	19,200	
Salaries and Commissions Expense	542	309,239	
Utilities Expense	543	8,438	
Telephone Expense	544	2,503	
Supplies Expense	545		
Delivery Expense	546	11,144	
Depreciation Expense	547		
Insurance Expense	548		
Payroll Taxes Expense	551	28,450	
Property Tax Expense	552		
Uncollectible Accounts Expense	553		
Miscellaneous Expense	562	18,811	
Interest Expense	571		
		14,558,173	14,558,173
Accrued Property Tax Payable			
Net Income			

BUILDING SUPPLY COMPANY
Sheet
February 28, 19--

ADJUSTMENTS		INCOME STATEMENT		BALANCE SHEET	
Debit	Credit	Debit	Credit	Debit	Credit
				122,326	
				488,853	
	(j) 21,771				13,935
(e) 2,838,000	(a) 3,074,756			2,838,000	
	(h) 9,244			10,608	
	(g) 10,965			12,368	
				1,170,000	
				4,877,168	
	(i) 20,308				2,472,794
				608,670	
	(i) 5,648				186,206
				188,173	
	(i) 7,840				100,376
					18,175
					1,546
					8,350
					20,458
	(f) 43,750				43,750
					294,071
					3,000,000
					2,124,017
				43,562	
					1,749,264
				37,036	
			4,494,594		
		44,584			
		95,887			
	(b) 3,358,352				
(c) 44,507					
(d) 77,611					
(a) 3,074,756	(c) 44,507	3,472,990			
(b) 3,358,352	(d) 77,611				
	(e) 2,838,000				
		19,200			
		309,239			
		8,438			
		2,503			
(h) 9,244		9,244			
		11,144			
(i) 33,796		33,796			
(g) 10,965		10,965			
		28,450			
(k) 23,460		23,460			
(j) 21,771		21,771			
		18,811			
(f) 43,750		43,750			
	(k) 23,460				23,460
9,536,212	9,536,212	4,154,232	4,494,594	10,396,764	10,056,402
		340,362			340,362
		4,494,594	4,494,594	10,396,764	10,396,764

—Work Sheet for Two-Month Period

share of insurance premiums applicable to the two months. (The amount is not exactly twice the amount for January because one policy expired early in February and was renewed at a slightly lower rate.)

Entry (h): Supplies Expense, Account No. 545, was debited and Store Supplies, Account No. 151, was credited for $9,244, which was the calculated cost of supplies used during the two months. This amount was determined by subtracting the estimated cost of supplies on hand February 28, $10,608, from the amount of the balance of the store supplies account on February 28, $19,852.

Entry (i): Depreciation Expense, Account No. 547, was debited for $33,796, and Accumulated Depreciation—Building, Account No. 171.1, was credited for $20,308, Accumulated Depreciation—Furniture and Equipment, Account No. 181.1, was credited for $5,648, and Accumulated Depreciation—Delivery Equipment, Account No. 185.1, was credited for $7,840. In each case, the amount is exactly twice that for January. During February, $66,539 was added to the furniture and equipment account and $3,229 to the building account. Since the partnership does not compute depreciation on assets owned for less than one month, no depreciation was taken on these newly acquired assets.

Entry (j): Uncollectible Accounts Expense, Account No. 553, was debited and Allowance for Doubtful Accounts, Account No. 131.1, was credited for $21,771. This amount was determined by taking ½ of 1% of the net sales for the two months, $4,354,123 ($4,494,594 − $44,584 − $95,887). Since the allowance for doubtful accounts had a debit balance of $7,836, an adjusting entry in the amount of $21,771 produced a credit balance in the allowance for doubtful accounts of $13,935 as of February 28.

Entry (k): Property Tax Expense, Account No. 552, was debited and Accrued Property Tax Payable was credited for $23,460. This amount represents the share of property tax expense for the two months. It is exactly twice the amount of the adjustment for January.

Note that in calculating the amounts of insurance expense, depreciation expense, interest expense and property tax expense, the fact that

January had more days than February was ignored. The month—not the number of days—was the unit of time used.

The work sheet was completed in the usual manner. Net income for the two-month period ended February 28, 19--, in the amount of $340,362 was calculated.

Interim Statements—Successive Periods

The work sheet reproduced on pages 616 and 617 assembled the data needed for an income statement covering the two-month period ended February 28, 19--, and a balance sheet as of the same date. The accountant for the partnership uses the same procedure to develop a succession of year-to-date income statements and month-end balance sheets. Income statements of this type are valuable for comparative purposes. Owners and managers are interested in learning how the progress in the current year compares with that of the preceding years.

In addition to the cumulative, year-to-date-income statement, an interim income statement is needed for each month by itself. Little effort is required to produce such statements using the year-to-date information. The technique is illustrated on page 620. At the left is the income statement of the company for the two-month period ended February 28, 19--. This was prepared from the Income Statement columns of the work sheet reproduced on pages 616 and 617. The income statement for January, 19-- is shown next. This statement is exactly the same as the one shown on page 612 developed from the Income Statement columns of the January work sheet on pages 608 and 609. At the right is the income statement for February, 19--, which was derived by subtracting the amounts in the January statement from those in the January-February statement, with the exception of the February merchandise inventory.

Since the income statements show the calculation of cost of goods sold, the amounts of the beginning and ending merchandise inventories shown in the February statement were not derived by subtraction. The beginning inventory for February, $3,066,000, was the ending inventory for January. The ending inventory for February, $2,838,000, is also the ending inventory for the two-month period.

GRIBBINS & GRIBBINS WHOLESALE BUILDING SUPPLY COMPANY
Income Statements

	For Two Months Ended February 28, 19—		For January, 19—		For February, 19—	
Sales		$4,494,594		$2,365,812		$2,128,782
Less: Returns and allowances		(44,584)		(23,466)		(21,118)
Sales discounts		(95,887)		(50,462)		(45,425)
Net sales		$4,354,123		$2,291,884		$2,062,239
Cost of goods sold:						
Merchandise inventory, beginning of period	$3,074,756		$3,074,756		$3,066,000	
Purchases	3,358,352		1,882,769		1,475,583	
Less: Returns and allowances	(44,507)		(23,425)		(21,082)	
Purchases discounts	(77,611)		(40,846)		(36,765)	
Cost of merchandise available for sale	$6,310,990		$4,893,254		$4,483,736	
Less merchandise inventory, end of period	2,838,000		3,066,000		2,838,000	
		3,472,990		1,827,254		1,645,736
Gross margin on sales		$ 881,133		$ 464,630		$ 416,503
Operating expenses:						
Partners' salaries expense	$ 19,200		$ 9,600		$ 9,600	
Salaries and commissions expense	309,239		157,775		151,464	
Utilities expense	8,438		4,327		4,111	
Telephone expense	2,503		1,280		1,223	
Supplies expense	9,244		4,814		4,430	
Delivery expense	11,144		5,687		5,457	
Depreciation expense	33,796		16,898		16,898	
Insurance expense	10,965		5,526		5,439	
Payroll taxes expense	28,450		14,515		13,935	
Property tax expense	23,460		11,730		11,730	
Uncollectible accounts expense	21,771		11,459		10,312	
Miscellaneous expense	18,811		9,898		8,913	
Total operating expenses		497,021		253,509		243,512
Operating income		$ 384,112		$ 211,121		$ 172,991
Interest expense		43,750		21,875		21,875
Net income		$ 340,362		$ 189,246		$ 151,116

Gribbins & Gribbins Wholesale Building Supply Company—Income Statements

The balance sheet as of February 28, 19--, is reproduced on page 622. This was prepared from the Balance Sheet columns of the work sheet on pages 616 and 617. Note that the owners' equity section shows each partner's equity as of January 1, plus the share of the net income for the two-month period less the withdrawals during the two-month period, to arrive at the amount of each partner's equity on February 28. An alternative would be: Partners' equity on January 31 (as shown in the balance sheet on page 613), plus the share of the February net income less the February withdrawals. The result would have been the same.

It should be evident that a similar procedure would have been employed if quarterly, rather than monthly, interim statements had been prepared.

BUILDING YOUR ACCOUNTING KNOWLEDGE

1. What two circumstances make it impractical to use a very short period for the preparation of interim statements (such as a day or a week)?
2. What advantage do monthly time segments have for interim statement preparation?
3. Why are interim statements which are prepared on a quarterly basis generally more reliable than interim statements prepared on a monthly basis?
4. Why is it unnecessary for an interim-statement work sheet to provide aid in formally adjusting and closing the accounts?
5. Describe how Gribbins & Gribbins determines its ending merchandise inventory for interim statement purposes.
6. Briefly describe the special accounting problem posed by the assessment and collection of property taxes.
7. How did the firm of Gribbins & Gribbins derive the amounts for its February, 19-- income statements?

Gribbins & Gribbins Wholesale Building Supply Company
Balance Sheet
February 28, 19--

Assets

Current assets:

Cash		$ 122,326
Accounts receivable	$ 488,853	
Less allowance for doubtful accounts	13,935	474,918
Merchandise inventory		2,838,000
Store supplies		10,608
Prepaid insurance		12,368
Total current assets			$3,458,220

Long-term assets:

Land		$1,170,000
Building	$ 4,877,168	
Less accumulated depreciation	2,472,794	2,404,374
Furniture and equipment	$ 608,670	
Less accumulated depreciation	186,206	422,464
Delivery equipment	$ 188,173	
Less accumulated depreciation	100,376	87,797
Total long-term assets			4,084,635
Total assets			$7,542,855

Liabilities

Current liabilities:

FICA tax payable	$ 18,175	
FUTA tax payable	1,546	
State unemployment tax payable	8,350	
Employees income tax payable	20,458	
Accrued interest payable	43,750	
Accrued property tax payable	23,460	
Accounts payable	294,071	
Total current liabilities		$ 409,810

Long-term liability:

Mortgage payable		3,000,000
Total liabilities		$3,409,810

Owners' Equity

Ronald E. Gribbins, capital:

Capital, January 1	$2,124,017	
Add net income (50% of $340,362)	170,181	
Less withdrawals	(43,562)	
Capital, February 28		$2,250,636

Martha L. Gribbins, capital:

Capital, January 1	$1,749,264	
Add net income (50% of $340,362)	170,181	
Less withdrawals	(37,036)	
Capital, February 28		1,882,409
Total owners' equity			4,133,045
Total liabilities and owners' equity			$7,542,855

Gribbins & Gribbins Wholesale Building Supply Company—Balance Sheet

APPLYING ACCOUNTING CONCEPTS

Exercise 20-1. The following are the account balances taken from the February 28 trial balance of Tate's Frame and Supplies.

Cash	$17,025
Accounts receivable	16,886
Merchandise inventory	37,456
Prepaid insurance	600
Accounts payable	45,626
A.J. Tate, capital	17,200
A.J. Tate, drawing	9,000
Sales	55,035
Sales returns and allowances	1,500
Purchases	33,520
Purchases returns and allowances	2,100
Utilities expense	2,215
Miscellaneous expense	1,759

(a) Enter the trial balance on a work sheet for the two-month period ended February 28. Include the insurance expense and cost of goods sold accounts. Leave one line blank after cost of goods sold. **(b)** Enter the adjusting entries based on the following: (1) Merchandise inventory, February 28, $35,235, (2) Transfer the Purchases and Purchases returns and allowances to cost of goods sold, (3) Insurance expired, $200. **(c)** Complete the work sheet.

Exercise 20-2. Refer to Exercise 20-1. Prepare a succession of year-to-date income statements: for the two-month period, for January, and for February. Additional amounts related to January are as follows:

Sales	$29,231
Sales returns and allowances	475
Purchases	17,834
Purchases returns and allowances	605
Utilities expense	1,130
Insurance expense	100
Miscellaneous expense	840
Merchandise inventory, January 31	32,026

**Report
No. 20-1**

Complete Report No. 20-1 in the study assignments and submit your working papers to the instructor for approval. The instructor will then give directions as to the work to be done next.

EXPANDING YOUR BUSINESS VOCABULARY

What is the meaning of each of the following terms?

interim balance sheet **(p. 605)**

interim income statement
  (p. 605)

natural business year **(p. 604)**

year-to-date income statement
  (p. 606)

CHAPTERS 16-20

Supplementary Practical Accounting Problems

PROBLEM 16-A Opening entry—Proprietorship

On September 1, Brad Basham organized a photographic equipment and supplies enterprise and opened a new set of books. Following is a list of the assets that were invested in the business.

Cash	$17,235
Office equipment	8,437
Store equipment	4,398
Delivery truck	5,156
Total	$35,226

Basham owed $2,026 on the delivery truck that was purchased on account.

Required: Prepare the opening entry in general journal form.

PROBLEM 16-B Opening entry—proprietorship

Robin Clerman, who has been conducting a wholesale wallpaper and paint enterprise, decides to install a formal set of books as of January 2. The balance sheet prepared as of December 31 is shown below.

Robin Clerman
Balance Sheet
December 31, 19--

Assets			Liabilities		
Cash		$ 4,907	FICA tax payable	$ 213	
Accounts receivable ...	$9,034		Employees income tax		
Less allowance for			payable	247	
doubtful accounts ...	1,127	7,907	Accounts payable	6,011	
Merchandise inventory		17,211	Total liabilities........		$ 6,471
Prepaid insurance		690	**Owner's Equity**		
Store equipment	$8,475		Robin Clerman, capital		25,244
Less accumulated			Total liabilities and		
depreciation	7,475	1,000	owner's equity		$31,715
Total assets		$31,715			

Required: Prepare the opening entry in general journal form.

PROBLEM 16-C Capital account—proprietorship

R. J. Whippet is engaged in the wholesale leather goods business. After closing the revenue and expense accounts for the calendar year ended December 31, the expense and revenue summary account, No. 331, had a credit balance of $36,219. At the same time Whippet's capital account, No. 311, had a credit balance of $80,911, and the drawing account, No. 311.1, had a debit balance of $27,000.

Required: (1) Open Whippet's capital account, drawing account, and expense and revenue summary account, using the four-column account form of ledger paper. Enter the December 31 balances. (2) Assuming that Whippet wishes to have the balances of both the expense and revenue summary and drawing accounts transferred to the capital account, journalize and post the required entries. After posting, account Nos. 331 and 311.1 should show "zero" balances, and account No. 311 should show Whippet's present equity.

PROBLEM 16-D Opening entries—partnership

Bob Russell has been operating a wholesale hardware business as a single proprietor. The balance sheet prepared as of September 30 is shown below.

Bob Russell
Balance Sheet
September 30, 19--

Assets			Liabilities		
Cash		$ 9,270	FICA tax payable	$ 290	
Accounts receivable	$11,490		Employees income		
Less allowance for			tax payable	360	
doubtful accounts	860	10,630	Notes payable	8,000	
Merchandise			Accounts payable	4,320	
inventory		17,560			
Store equipment	$ 8,100		Total liabilities		$12,970
Less accumulated					
depreciation	600	7,500	**Owner's Equity**		
			Bob Russell, capital		31,990
			Total liabilities and		
Total assets		$44,960	owner's equity		$44,960

The fair market value of the equipment on September 30 is $7,900. The book values of the other assets are equal to their approximate fair market values. On October 1 of the current year, Frank Russell is admitted as a partner in the business to be conducted under the firm name of Russell & Russell Hardware. Under the partnership agreement, Frank Russell invests $32,390 in cash. The assets of Bob Russell become the property of the partnership and the liabilities are assumed by the partnership.

Required: Prepare the necessary opening entries in general journal form for the investments of the partners, assuming that a new set of books is installed by the partnership.

PROBLEM 16-E Opening entries—partnership

Barbara Conan and Jane Shanna are competitors in the wholesale drug business. On July 1 of the current year, they form a partnership to be operated under the firm name of Conan & Shanna. Their balance sheets as of June 30 are shown at the top of page 628.

Barbara Conan
Balance Sheet
June 30, 19--

Assets			Liabilities		
Cash		$16,927	FICA tax payable . . . . . $ 682		
Accounts receivable . . $23,460			Employees income		
Less allowance for			tax payable 940		
doubtful accounts . . 1,147		22,313	Notes payable 27,500		
Merchandise inventory		29,436	Accounts payable 15,643		
Delivery equipment . . . $12,468			Total liabilities		$44,765
Less accumulated					
depreciation 3,600		8,868	**Owner's Equity**		
Office equipment $12,387			Barbara Conan,		
Less accumulated			capital		41,966
depreciation 3,200		9,187	Total liabilities and		
Total assets		$86,731	owner's equity		$86,731

Jane Shanna
Balance Sheet
June 30, 19--

Assets			Liabilities		
Cash		$16,437	FICA tax payable . . . . . $ 497		
Accounts receivable . . $24,210			Employees income		
Less allowance for			payable tax 655		
doubtful accounts . . 1,456		22,754	Accounts payable 20,411		
Merchandise			Total liabilities		$21,563
inventory		28,469			
Delivery equipment . . . $11,500					
Less accumulated					
depreciation 2,400		9,100	**Owner's Equity**		
Office equipment $11,667					
Less accumulated			Jane Shanna, capital		65,197
depreciation 1,667		10,000	Total liabilities and		
Total assets		$86,760	owner's equity		$86,760

The partnership agreement provides that the assets are to be taken over at their fair market values and that the liabilities are to be assumed by the partnership. Shanna's balance sheet has already been adjusted to recognize fair market values. The fair market values of Conan's delivery equipment and office equipment are $11,900 and $10,000, respectively. The agreement also provides that to equal Shanna's investment, Conan is to contribute a sufficient amount of additional cash. It is also agreed that the partners will share profits and losses equally.

Required: Prepare the necessary opening entries in general journal form for the investments of the partners, assuming that a new set of books is installed by the partnership.

PROBLEM 16-F Distribution of partner's share

The Natural Upholstering Co., a partnership, is engaged in the wholesale upholstering business. Ownership of the firm is vested in C. Weaver, J. Cutter, W. Evenden and B. Liester. Profits and losses are shared equally.

Cutter died on July 5. In the distribution of the partnership assets, the remaining partners agreed to buy Cutter's widow's interest at 110% of its book value. When the books were closed on July 5, Cutter's capital account had a credit balance of $22,975. On August 15, a partnership check was issued to the widow in final settlement.

Required: Compute the amount to be paid to Cutter's widow under the agreement, and prepare the general journal entry required to enter the check on the books of the partnership.

PROBLEM 16-G Subscriptions Receivable; Capital Stock

On January 2, The Computer Bytes Man Co. was incorporated with an authorized issue of 50,000 shares of common capital stock, par value $20 per share. Subscriptions were received from the following:

J. McCarty	12,000 shares,	$240,000
J. Keller	10,000 shares,	$200,000
D. Hagerup	15,000 shares,	$300,000
E. Korhanen	13,000 shares,	$260,000

On January 6, all subscribers paid the amounts due. The stock certificates were issued on January 10.

Following is a list of the corporate accounts to be kept:

Capital Stock   Capital Stock Subscribed
Subscriptions Receivable

Required: Prepare the general journal entries required for (1) the stock subscriptions received, (2) the cash received to apply on subscriptions, and (3) the capital stock issued.

PROBLEM 16-H   Cash dividend

The following transactions relate to payment of cash dividends by The Gourmet Restaurant Co.:

Mar. 28   The board of directors declared a cash dividend of $6.50 per share, payable May 16, to holders of record April 15. There were 43,980 shares of stock outstanding.

May 16   The company mailed dividend checks amounting to $285,870 to stockholders.

Required: Enter (1) the dividend declaration on March 28 and (2) the dividend payment on May 16, using standard two-column general journal paper.

PROBLEM 16-I   New set of books for a corporation

L. Larson, F. Somes, and L. Bowler are partners under the firm name of Larson, Somes, and Bowler. On January 2, The Emerald City Distributing Co., with an authorized capital of $300,000, consisting of 6,000 shares of common stock, par value $50 per share, was organized to take over the business formerly conducted by the partnership. The following balance sheet of the partnership was prepared at the time of incorporating the business. It has already been adjusted to reflect the fair market values of the inventory and long-term assets as of December 31.

Larson, Somes & Bowler
Balance Sheet
December 31, 19--

Assets			Liabilities		
Cash		$ 27,890	FICA tax payable	$ 980	
Accounts receivable	$46,270		Employees income		
Less allowance for			tax payable	1,215	
doubtful accounts	4,085	42,185	Accounts payable . . .	30,495	
Merchandise			Total liabilities		$ 32,690
inventory		59,843			
Office equipment	$18,435				
Less accumulated			**Owners' Equity**		
depreciation	4,980	13,455	L. Larson, capital . . .	$50,000	
Delivery equipment . .	$21,260		F. Somes, capital . . .	36,000	
Less accumulated			L. Bowler, capital . . .	40,343	126,343
depreciation	5,600	15,660	Total liabilities and		
Total assets		$159,033	owners' equity		$159,033

The partners subscribed for capital stock of the corporation as follows:

L. Larson .... 2,500 shares @ $50, $125,000
F. Somes .... 1,500 shares @ $50, $ 75,000
L. Bowler .... 2,000 shares @ $50, $100,000

The partners, as individuals, received credit toward their subscriptions for their respective equities in the assets of the partnership, and gave their personal checks for the balance of their respective subscriptions. A new set of books is to be installed by the corporation.

Required: Prepare entries in general journal form on the corporation books for the following: (1) the subscriptions to the capital stock of the corporation, (2) the transfer of the assets and liabilities of the partnership to the corporation, (3) the receipt of cash in settlement of the balances due on the respective subscriptions, and (4) the issuance of stock certificates.

PROBLEM 18-A   Summary work sheet; supplementary work sheet

Rose & Thorn are partners in a wholesale mercantile business. Their accounts are kept on a fiscal year basis, with the year ending on May 31. The accounts with customers and operating expenses are kept in subsidiary ledgers with control accounts in the general ledger. Any necessary adjustments in the operating expense accounts are made at the end of each year after a trial balance is taken. Since annual financial statements must be prepared, the accountant prepares a ten-column summary work sheet and a three-column supplementary operating expenses work sheet at the end of each year as a means of compiling and classifying the information needed in financial statement preparation.

The following accounts in the operating expense ledger require adjustment as of May 31:

Office Supplies Expense	5403	
Depreciation of Office Equipment...............	5404	
Postage Expense	5416	$ 926.89
Uncollectible Accounts Expense................	5417	
Depreciation of Delivery Equipment.............	5435	
Insurance Expense	5436	
Depreciation of Store Equipment	5437	
Store Supplies Expense........................	5444	
All Others (to balance)........................		187,371.32
		$188,298.21

The following data provide information needed in adjusting the general ledger accounts and the operating expenses ledger accounts.

Merchandise inventory, May 31	$79,402.65
Insurance expense	1,621.18
Store supplies inventory, May 31	291.40
Postage inventory, May 31	89.95
Depreciation of store equipment	621.16
Depreciation of delivery equipment.....................	2,149.20
Estimated uncollectible accounts expense	396.50
Office supplies inventory, May 31	256.70
Depreciation of office equipment......................	1,256.90
Interest accrued on government notes, May 31	220.00
Interest accrued on notes payable, May 31	364.00

The trial balance of the general ledger taken as of May 31 is shown on page 633. To conserve space, the accounts primarily involved in the adjusting and closing process are given. To make it possible to complete the work sheet, in two cases the balances of several accounts are shown as one amount.

Required: Prepare a ten-column summary work sheet for the year ended May 31, 19--, and a supplementary work sheet for operating expenses. Use as a guide the work sheets reproduced on pages 554-555 and 558. Allow 2 lines for Cost of Goods Sold on the summary work sheet.

Retain the solution to this problem for use in Problems 18-B, 19A, and 19B.

Rose & Thorn
Trial Balance
May 31, 19--

Cash	111	21,497.68	
Government Notes	121	12,000.00	
Accrued Interest Receivable	122		
Accounts Receivable	131	20,163.18	
Allowance for Doubtful Accounts	131.1		563.80
Merchandise Inventory	141	56,062.98	
Store Supplies	151	1,821.30	
Office Supplies	152	1,615.95	
Postage Stamps	153	592.11	
Prepaid Insurance	155	2,857.57	
Long-Term Assets (cost)		26,216.52	
Accumulated Depreciation-Store Equipment	181.1		1,256.36
Accumulated Depreciation-Delivery Equipment	185.1		2,088.37
Accumulated Depreciation-Office Equipment	191.1		1,186.55
Accrued Interest Payable	217		
Other Current Liabilities			16,421.11
W. Rose, Capital	311		82,265.13
W. Rose, Drawing	311.1	17,500.00	
P. Thorn, Capital	321		85,721.61
P. Thorn, Drawing	321.1	18,400.00	
Sales	411		692,117.23
Sales Returns and Allowances	411.1	4,211.18	
Purchases	511	513,674.51	
Purchases Returns and Allowances	511.1		3,961.03
Cost of Goods Sold	531		
Operating Expenses	541	188,298.21	
Interest Earned	431		692.80
Interest Expense	571	1,362.80	
		886,273.99	886,273.99

PROBLEM 18-B Adjusting entries; closing entries; and reversing entries

The work sheets for Rose & Thorn for the year ended May 31, 19--, completed in Problem 18-A, will be used to solve this problem.

Required: (1) Prepare the entries necessary to adjust the general ledger accounts and the operating expense ledger accounts as of May 31, 19--. Use the general journal illustration reproduced on pages 568-569 as a guide. (2) After making the required entries, foot the amount columns of each general journal page to prove the footings. (3) Prepare the entries required to close the following types of accounts in the general ledger: revenue accounts, expense accounts, the expense and revenue summary account, No. 331, and the partners' drawing accounts. Distribute the balance of the expense and revenue summary account equally between the two partners. Use the general journal illustration reproduced on page 570 as a guide. (4) Prepare the necessary entries to reverse the accrual adjustments as of June 1, 19--. Use the general journal illustration reproduced on page 574 as a guide. (5) After making the required entries, foot the amount columns of each general journal page to prove the footings. (6) Assuming that the individual posting to the general ledger accounts and the operating expense ledger accounts has been completed, insert the necessary check marks in the general journal. Enter the totals of the amount columns on each page and rule each page of the general journal. Assuming that the summary posting has been completed, make the necessary notations in the general journal.

PROBLEM 19-A   Income statement; balance sheet

The summary work sheet for Rose & Thorn for the year ended May 31, 19--, completed in Problem 18-A, will be used to solve this problem. Presented below is some detail regarding the summary amounts that were shown on the work sheet:

Long-term assets (cost):	
Store equipment	$ 6,863.52
Delivery equipment	8,432.00
Office equipment	10,921.00
	$26,216.52

Other current liabilities:	
Notes payable	$ 7,000.00
Accounts payable	8,400.10
Accrued and withheld payroll taxes	1,021.01
	$16,421.11

Required: (1) Prepare an income statement for the year ended May 31, 19--. Since the business is not departmentalized, a separate schedule of cost of goods sold is not needed. Use as a guide the statement for MicroWorld illustrated on page 293. However, insufficient data are available either to itemize the operating expenses or to prepare a separate schedule of them. Round all amounts to the nearest dollar. (2) Prepare a balance sheet as of May 31, 19--. Use as a guide the balance sheet illustrated on page 585. While the firm maintains subsidiary ledgers of accounts receivable and accounts payable, trial balances of these are not provided and, thus, the preparation of schedules is not possible. Round all amounts to the nearest dollar.

Retain the solution to this problem for use in Problem 19-B.

PROBLEM 19-B   Statement of changes in financial position; schedule of changes in working capital

Use the work sheets of Rose & Thorn from Problem 18-A or the balance sheet from 19-A. Additional information is given below:

Beginning of Year Balance Sheet Information

Cash...	$ 32,437
Government notes and accrued interest..................	32,072
Accounts receivable (net)	30,209
Merchandise inventory	56,063
Supplies and prepayments	1,180
Total current assets..................................	$151,961
Long-term assets (less accumulated depreciation)	21,685
Total assets	$173,646
Notes and accrued interest payable.....................	$ 2,087
Accounts payable......................................	2,625
Accrued and withheld payroll taxes	947
Total current liabilities	$ 5,659
Owners' equity	167,987
Total liabilities and owners' equity	$173,646

Required: Prepare (1) a statement of changes in financial position for the year ended May 31, 19--, supplemented by (2) a schedule of changes in working capital for that year. Use as a guide the statement and schedule illustrated on page 601.

PROBLEM 20-A   Completing the work sheet

The Heicks are partners in the wholesale grocery business. They share profits and losses in the following ratio: D. Heick, senior partner, 60%; R. Heick, junior partner, 40%. Salaries are included in the profit shares. The calendar year is used as a fiscal year.

The partnership's accountant prepares quarterly and year-to-date income statements, as well as balance sheets, as of the last day of each quarter. The completed trial balance for Heick & Heick for the quarter ended March 31, 19--, is shown on the next page.

Required: (1) Prepare a ten-column work sheet for the quarter ended March 31, 19--. Use as your guide the sample work sheet on pages 608 and 609 except that in the ten-column work sheet, you will have the Adjusted Trial Balance columns. Enter the trial balance in the trial balance columns of the work sheet. From the following data and information, enter the necessary adjustments in the adjustments columns of the ten-column work sheet:

a. Transfer the beginning merchandise inventory to Cost of Goods Sold.
b. Transfer the purchases for the quarter to Cost of Goods Sold.
c. Transfer the purchases returns and allowances for the quarter to Cost of Goods Sold.
d. Amount of ending merchandise inventory, $334,988.
e. Interest accrued on mortgage since January 1, $4,200.
f. Insurance expense for quarter, $564.
g. Store supplies used during quarter, $743.
h. Depreciation of building, $1,050.
Depreciation of furniture and equipment, $318.
i. Estimated uncollectible accounts expense for quarter, $912.
j. Property tax assignable to quarter, $1,350.

(2) Extend the adjusted amounts to the adjusted trial balance columns and foot the columns as a means of proof. (3) Complete the work sheet, determine the amount of net income or net loss, and foot the income statement and balance sheet columns as a means of proof.

The solution to this problem will be needed in solving Problem 20-C.

Heick & Heick
Trial Balance
For the Quarter Ended March 31, 19--

	Acct. No.	Debit	Credit
Cash	111	31,343	
Accounts Receivable	131	44,212	
Allowance for Doubtful Accounts	131.1	224	
Merchandise Inventory	141	381,422	
Store Supplies	151	2,477	
Prepaid Insurance	155	3,866	
Land	161	120,000	
Building	171	390,477	
Accum. Depreciation - Building	171.1		186,659
Furniture and Equipment	181	55,767	
Accum. Depreciation-Furniture & Equip.	181.1		20,913
FICA Tax Payable	211		1,280
FUTA Tax Payable	212		58
State Unemployment Tax Payable	213		380
Employees' Income Tax Payable	214		2,188
Accrued Interest Payable	217		—
Accounts Payable	218		53,897
Mortgage Payable	262		226,000
D. Heick, Capital	311		267,690
D. Heick, Drawing	311.1	3,900	
R. Heick, Capital	321		212,460
R. Heick, Drawing	321.1	3,000	
Sales	411		255,060
Sales Returns and Allowances	411.1	1,815	
Purchases	511	165,290	
Purchases Returns and Allowances	511.1		1,518
Cost of Goods Sold (allow 2 lines)	531		
Partners' Salaries Expense	541	7,500	
Salaries and Commissions Expense	542	14,299	
Utilities Expense	543	416	
Supplies Expense	545	—	
Delivery Expense	546	509	
Depreciation Expense	547	—	
Insurance Expense	548	—	
Payroll Taxes Expense	551	1,040	
Property Tax Expense	552	—	
Uncollectible Accounts Expense	553	—	
Miscellaneous Expense	562	546	
Interest Expense	571	—	
		1,228,103	1,228,103

Accrued Property Tax Payable

PROBLEM 20-B   Completing the work sheet

This is a continuation of Problem 20-A. The completed trial balance for Heick & Heick for the six-month period ended June 30, 19--, is shown on page 639.

Required: (1) Prepare a ten-column work sheet for the six-month period ended June 30, 19--. Use as your guide the sample work sheet on pages 616 and 617, except that in the ten-column work sheet, you will have the Adjusted Trial Balance columns. Enter the trial balance on page 639 in the trial balance columns of the work sheet. From the following data and information, enter the necessary adjustments in the adjustments columns of the ten-column work sheet:

a. Transfer the beginning merchandise inventory to Cost of Goods Sold.
b. Transfer the purchases for the six-month period to Cost of Goods Sold.
c. Transfer the purchases returns and allowances for the six-month period to Cost of Goods Sold.
d. Amount of ending merchandise inventory, $342,695.
e. Interest accrued on mortgage since January 1, $8,400.
f. Insurance expense for six-month period, $1,128.
g. Store supplies used during period, $1,327.
h. Depreciation of building, $2,100.
   Depreciation of furniture and equipment, $636.
i. Estimated uncollectible accounts expense for period, $1,950.
j. Property tax assignable to period, $2,700.

(2) Extend the adjusted amounts to the adjusted trial balance columns and foot the columns as a means of proof. (3) Complete the work sheet, determine the amount of net income or net loss, and foot the income statement and balance sheet columns as a means of proof.

The solution to this problem will be needed in solving Problem 20-C.

Heick & Heick
Trial Balance
For the Six-Month Period Ended June 30, 19--

	Acct. No.	Debit	Credit
Cash	111	26,297	
Accounts Receivable	131	56,243	
Allowance for Doubtful Accounts	131.1	478	
Merchandise Inventory	141	381,422	
Store Supplies	151	3,162	
Prepaid Insurance	155	4,213	
Land	161	120,000	
Building	171	390,477	
Accum. Depreciation-Building	171.1		186,659
Furniture and Equipment	181	55,767	
Accum. Depreciation-Furniture and Equip.	181.1		20,913
FICA Tax Payable	211		1,314
FUTA Tax Payable	212		107
State Unemployment Tax Payable	213		707
Employees' Income Tax Payable	214		2,134
Accrued Interest Payable	217		—
Accounts Payable	218		45,263
Mortgage Payable	262		226,000
D. Heick, Capital	311		267,690
D. Heick, Drawing	311.1	6,000	
R. Heick, Capital	321		212,460
R. Heick, Drawing	321.1	4,700	
Sales	411		505,006
Sales Returns and Allowances	411.1	3,473	
Purchases	511	370,374	
Purchases Returns and Allowances	511.1		3,843
Cost of Goods Sold (allow 2 lines)	531		
Partners' Salaries Expense	541	15,000	
Salaries and Commissions Expense	542	29,236	
Utilities Expense	543	913	
Supplies Expense	545	—	
Delivery Expense	546	931	
Depreciation Expense	547	—	
Insurance Expense	548	—	
Payroll Taxes Expense	551	2,167	
Property Tax Expense	552	—	
Uncollectible Accounts Expense	553	—	
Miscellaneous Expense	562	1,243	
Interest Expense	571	—	
		1,472,096	1,472,096

Accrued Property Tax Payable

PROBLEM 20-C   Interim statements

This is a continuation of Problems 20-A and 20-B. The ten-column work sheets completed in these two previous problems will be used here.

Required: (1) Prepare a year-to-date income statement for the six-month period ended June 30, 19--, an income statement for the quarter ended March 31, 19--, and an income statement for the quarter ended June 30, 19--. Use as your guide the sample comparative income statements on page 620. (2) Prepare a balance sheet in report form as of June 30, 19--, using as your guide the sample balance sheet on page 622.

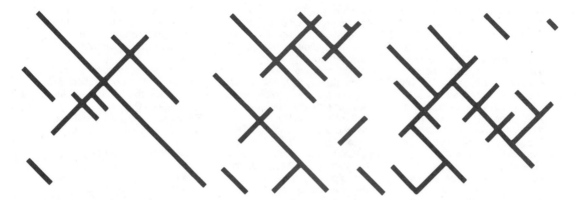

INDEX

-A-

ABA numbers (American Bankers Association), 68
ACRS (accelerated cost recovery system) depreciation, 399
Accepted accounting practices, 464
Accommodation indorsement, 358
Account, 14; books of, 245, 526; capital, 30; cash, 56; checking, 65; clearing, 298; closing owner's drawing, 488; contra, 230; contra-liability, 353; notes payable, 356; notes receivable, 349; payable, 5; purchases discount, 185; purchases discounts lost, 185; purchases returns and allowances, 186; receivable, 4; sales, 214; sales on, 201; sales returns and allowances, 215; sales tax payable, 214; savings, 81; standard form, 14; statement of, 241

Accountant, 4
Account form, 293; of balance sheet, 141; three-column, 238
Accounting, accrual basis, 227; and bookkeeping, 4; business, 3; cash basis, 228; concepts and accepted practices, 456; depreciation, 234; elements, 4; nature of business, 1; payroll, 85; records, 121
Accounting cycle, 151, 322; completing the, 322
Accounting equation, 6; effect of transactions on, 7
Accounting for, a personal service enterprise, 117; cash, 55; depreciation, 234; employee earnings and deductions, 102; employer payroll taxes, 108; inventory and prepaid expenses, 362; notes and interest, 341; notes payable transactions, 351; notes receivable transactions, 345; owner's equity, 481; prepaid expenses, 233, 362,

378, 383; property, plant, and equipment, 387; purchases and payments, 167; sales and collections, 199; uncollectible accounts receivable, 229
Accounting procedures, 26, 248, 421; at year end, 551; collections, 451; credit sales, 446; depreciation, 403; for a corporation, 508; for a partnership, 492; for a single proprietorship, 483; for a whole-sale retail business, 525, 533; for cash sales, 442; purchases and payments, 183; sales and collections, 214
Accounting process, 3
Accounts, adjustment of merchandise, 553; asset, liability, and owner's equity, 16; balancing the closed, 147; chart of, 30, 119, 244; closed general ledger, *illustrated*, 147-149; closing revenue, expense, and summary, 487; contra, 120; control, 238; customer,

240; doubtful, 561; footing, 45; owner's equity, 484, 508; supplier, 239; T, 15; temporary, owner's equity, 20; transportation, 195; updating owner's equity, 150; use of revenue and expense, 20; with suppliers and customers, 237

Accounts payable, 187; control, 238; ledger, 247, *illustrated,* 272-274; schedule of, 191; subsidiary, ledger, 188

Accounts receivable, 217; control, 239; *illustrated,* 449, 454; installment, 204; schedule of, 221

Accounts receivable ledger, 247, 531; *illustrated,* 269-272, 453

Accrual, 378; basis concept, 461; basis of accounting, 227

Accrual accounting, 228; applied to a medium-scale business, 522; applied to a small retail business, 227

Accrual adjustments, reversing entries, 322

Accrued bank credit card payable, 326; and bank credit card expense after posting reversing entry, *illustrated,* 327

Accrued interest payable, 325, 357; and interest expense after posting of reversing entry, *illustrated,* 325

Accrued interest receivable, 350

Acid test, 587

Acquisition of goods, 425

Additional withholding allowances, 90

Adequate disclosure, 465

Adjusted trial balance, 285; columns, 285

Adjusting and closing accounts at end of accounting period, 307

Adjusting entries, 143, 308, 566; *illustrated,* 143, 309; for a personal service enterprise, 143; journalizing, 308, 566; posting, 309, 566

Adjustment of the merchandise accounts, 553

Adjustments, columns, 281; deferral, 384; end-of period, 229

Admitting a new partner, 497

Advice, credit, 347

Allocation, cost, 390; of partnership profits and losses, 500

Allowance, 181; trade-in, 407; special withholding, 90;

withholding, 90

Allowances, purchases, 184

Amortization, 338; expense, 599

Amounts, discount, 353; zero bracket, 90

Analysis, balance sheet, 299; comparative, 582, 587; income statement, 298; interstatement, 301; of financial statements, 298; of profitability, 588; percentage, 581; ratio, 587

Annual report, 577

Application, for Social Security Number (Form SS-5), 89; in the expenditure cycle, 423; in the revenue cycle, 440

Asset, liability, and owner's equity accounts, 16

Asset method of accounting for prepaid expenses, 378

Assets, 4; capital, 387; cost of long-term, 389; current, 141, 294; depreciable, 388; depreciation of long-term, 390; discarding long-term, 405; disposition of long-term, 405; exchange of long-term, 407; fixed, 387; fully depreciated long-term, 412; intangible, 388; long-term, 387; property, plant, and equipment, 387; retiring long-term, 405; return on, 588; sale of long-term, 592; selling long-term, 406; tangible, 388; trade-in of long-term, 407; wasting, 388, 413

Assigning cost to the inventory, 366

Auditing, 2

Auditor's report, 578

Authorization procedures and related responsibility, 420

Automated, systems, 94; teller machines, 72

Auxiliary records, 123, 247, 533

Average cost method, 368

-B-

Back orders, 172

Bad debts expense, 230

Balance, 22, 45; trial, 22

Balance-column account form, 122

Balance sheet, 50, 292, 585; account form, 141, *illustrated,* 52-53, 296-297; analysis, 299; body, 50; classification of data, 294; columns, 287;

consolidated, 458; form of, 292; heading, 50; importance of, 292; interpreting, 586; report form, *illustrated,* 142, 585

Balance sheet owners' equity section of, a corporation, 518; a partnership, 503; a single proprietorship, 488

Balances, credit, 23; debit, 22

Balancing the closed accounts, 147

Bank, 65; credit card sales, 202; discount, 352; keeping a ledger account for each, 80; records kept by a, 75

Banking procedures, 65

Banking transactions, journalizing, 74

Bank statement, 75; reconciliation of, *illustrated,* 78

Basic concepts in financial accounting, 457

Basis, accrual, 461; gross price, 174, 186; net price, 175; short-term rate, 382; unit, 410

Bill, drayage, 181; freight, 180

Billing, 208

Blank indorsement, 66, 358

Book, of original entry, 28; value, 138, 392

Bookkeeper, 4

Bookkeeping, and accounting, 4; double-entry, 13

Books of account, 245, 526

Boot, 408

Borrowing, long-term, 592

Business, enterprises, 118; entity, 4, 457

Business accounting, the nature of, 1, 3

Business organization, type of, 523

Business year, natural, 364, 604

-C-

Calculating, interest, 343; the amount of depreciation for a period, 391

Canceled insurance, 382

Capital, 5, 482; account, 30; assets, 387; paid-in, 508; stock, 506, 507; working, 590

Card, signature, 67

Cash, account, 56; accounting for, 55; discounts, 174; payments, 56, 58; proving, 58; purchases, 194; receipts, 56;

sales, 200; short and over, 58
Cash basis, accounting for a personal, service enterprise, 118; expense, 118; of accounting, 228; revenue, 118
Cash fund, operating a petty, 59
Cash loan, note issued as security, 352
Cash payments journal, 191, 246, *illustrated*, 192, 261; posting from, 193
Cash receipts journal, 222, 246, 451, 527, *illustrated*, 223, 260, 452, 545; posting from, 223, 528; proving, 527
Cash register, 56; tapes, 442
Cash sales, 442; accounting procedures for, 443
Causes of depreciation, 390
Charge, 15; plates, 201
Charges, transportation, 194
Chart of accounts, 30, 119, 244; *illustrated*, 31, 120, 245
Check, 65; book, 72; customer's, 210; indorsing, 66; payroll, 97, *illustrated*, 100; postdated, 71; preparing a, 73; stub, 72; voucher, 435
Checking account, 65; interest-earning, 82; opening a, 67
Check register, 425, 436, 528, *illustrated*, 436, 546
Checks, and stubs, 74; dishonored, 70; electronic processing of, 73; entering, 436, NSF, 70; outstanding, 76
Checkwriter, 73
Classification of data in the balance sheet, 294
Clearing account, 298
Closed general ledger accounts, *illustrated*, 147-149
Closing entries, 144, 314, 566; for a personal service enterprise; journalizing, 314, 567; posting, 571
Closing, owner's drawing account, 488; procedure, 314; revenue, expense and summary accounts, 487
COD, 180; purchases, 180, 194; sales, 203
Collections, accounting procedures, 451
Columns, adjusted trial balance, 285; adjustments, 281; balance sheet, 287; income statement, 286; trial balance, 281
Combination journal, 121, *illustrated*, 122, 128-131
Commercial paper, negotiable, 342

Common stock, 507
Comparability, 464
Comparative analysis, 582, 587
Comparison of, cost assignment methods, 370; depreciation methods, 400
Compensation, of partners, 499; types of, 86
Completing the, accounting cycle, 322; operating expenses work sheet, 562; summary work sheet, 562; work sheet, 287
Compound entry, 64
Computation of gross margin, 216
Concept, accrual basis, 461; entity, 457; going-concern, 458; historical cost, 460; matching, 49, 461; monetary unit, 459; of continuity, 458; periodicity, 460; realization, 461; internal accounting control, 419
Conservatism, 467; convention of, 371
Consignee, 205, 366
Consignment, 366; sales, 205
Consignor, 205, 366
Consistency, 464
Consolidated, balance sheet, 458; income statement, 458
Constructive receipt, 118
Contra accounts, 120, 230
Contra-liability account, 353
Control, accounts, 238; internal, 56, 57; internal accounting, 418
Convention of conservatism, 371
Corporation, 506; accounting procedure, 508; ownership of, 506; organization of, 506; profits, losses, and dividends, 511; starting a business, 509; transactions and accounts unique to, 507
Consigner, 358
Cost, 371; allocation, 390; apportionment, 370; depletion, 413; historical, 460; lower of, 371; net, 235, 391; of goods sold, 184, 216, 531; of long-term assets, 389; to replace, 371; undepreciated, 138, 295, 392, 587
Costing, first-in, first-out, 367; last-in, first-out, 368; specific identification, 366; weighted average, 368
Credit, 15; advice, 75, 347; balances, 23; cards, 201; memorandum, 181, 210, 211

Credit sales, 443; accounting procedures, 446
Credits, and debits, 15
Current assets, 141, 294; net, 301
Current liabilities, 295
Current ratio, 300
Current period proprietary transactions, 486
Customer, accounts, 240; purchase order, 206, 443
Customer's check, 210

-D-

Debit, 15; advice, 70, *illustrated*, 70; balances, 22; memorandum, 181
Declaration of dividends, 511
Declining-balance method, 393, 394
Deductions from total earnings, 88; other deductions, 93
Deferral, 378; adjustments, 384
Deficit, 511
Depletion, 388, 413; cost, 413; expenses for federal income tax purposes, 415; percentage, 415
Deposit, direct, 97; slip, 443, 450; ticket, 67
Deposits, by mail, 69; in transit, 76; making, 67; night, 69
Depreciable assets, 388
Depreciation, 388, 390; accelerated cost recovery system, 399; accounting, 234; accounting procedure, 403; calculating the amount for a period, 391; causes of, 390; entering, 404; expense, 119, 559; functional, 390; in the financial statements, 412; of long-term assets, 390; pattern and undepreciated costs, 400; physical, 390
Depreciation methods, comparison of, 400; of calculating, 391
Determination of total earnings, 87
Direct financing, 593
Discarding long-term assets, 405
Disclosure, adequate, 465
Discount, amount, 353; bank, 352
Discounting, 352
Discounts, 210; cash, 174; purchases, 184; trade, 172, 173

Dishonored, checks, 70; note, 348

Disposition of long-term assets, 405

Dissolution of a partnership, 500

Dividends, 507; declaration of, 511

Double-entry, bookkeeping, 13; framework, 13

Doubtful accounts, 561

Drawee, 66

Drawer, 65

Drayage, bill, 181

-E-

Earnings, determination of total, 87; retained, 508

Earnings record, 93; employee's, 98, illustrated, 98-99

Effect, of transaction on the accounting equation, 7; on net income calculation, 401

Effective rate of interest, 354

Electronic, funds transfer, 82; processing of checks, 73; system, 94

Embezzlement, 56

Employee earnings and deduction, 86; accounting for, 102

Employee's earnings record, 98, illustrated, 98-99

Employees, and independent contractors, 86; FICA tax withheld, 88; income tax payable, 103; income tax withheld, 89

Employer payroll taxes, accounting for, 108; imposed on, 105; journalizing, 109

Employer's, FICA tax, 105; FUTA tax, 106; identification number, 102; quarterly federal tax return and quarterly report form (Form 941), illustrated, 114; state unemployment tax, 106

End-of-period, adjustments, 229; work sheet, 137, 280, illustrated, 137

Entering, checks, 436; depreciation, 404; vouchers, 430

Enterprise, business, 118; manufacturing, 117; mercantile, 117; personal service, 117; professional, 118

Entity, business, 457; concept, 457

Entries, adjusting, 143, 308, 566, illustrated, 143; closing, 144, 314, 567, illustrated, 146; reversing, 566, 574

Entry, compound, 64

Equity, owner's, 5, 30, 296, 482; return on, 588

Exchange of long-term assets, 407

Expenditure cycle, application in, 423; flowchart of, illustrated, 424

Expense, 19; amortization, 599; and revenue, 18; and revenue summary, 314; bad debts, 230; cash basis, 118; depreciation, 119, 559; insurance, 561; payroll, 102; payroll taxes, 108; prepaid, 233, 378; supplies, 560; uncollectible accounts, 230

Expense method of accounting for prepaid expenses, 383

Expired insurance, 381

-F-

Factors affecting accounting records used, 523

Fair market value, 407

Federal tax deposit form, (Form 8109), illustrated, 112

Fee, 86

FICA, and federal income taxes, responsibilities for, 111

FICA tax, employer's, 105; payable, 103, 108; taxes, 88

Filing returns and making payroll tax payments, 111

Financial accounting, basic concepts, 457

Financial data, flow of, illustrated, 48

Financial position, statement of changes in, 591

Financial statements, 10, 48, 141, 290; analysis of, 298; depreciation in, 412; interim, 604

Financing, direct, 593

First-in, first-out (fifo), costing, 367; method 367

Fiscal period, work at close of, 137

Fiscal year, 19

Fixed assets, 387

Flow of financial data, 48

Flowchart, of expenditure cycle, 424; of revenue cycle, 441

FOB, destination, 195; shipping

point, 195

Foot, 45

Footing accounts, 45

Footings proof of, 125

Form, application for social security (Form SS-5), 89; employer's quarterly federal tax return (Form 941), 114; federal tax deposit (Form 8109), 112; multiple-step, 291; of the balance sheet, 292; of the income statement, 291; single-step, 291; wage and tax statement, (Form W-2), 101; withholding allowance certificate (Form W-4), 91

Freight bill, 180

Fully depreciated long-term assets, 412

Functional depreciation, 390

Fund, 591; highway construction, 591; petty cash, 591

Funds, uses of, 592; sources of, 592

Funds transfer, electronic, 82

FUTA tax, 106; employer's, 106; payable, 108

-G-

General journal, 247, 528, illustrated, MicroWorld, 262, Spinner & Thomas, 547; posting from, 529; proving, 529

General ledger, 40, 122, 247, 528, illustrated, MicroWorld, 263-269, Vance Zarmer, 133-136; accounts receivable control account, illustrated, 449, 454

General ledger accounts, after posting adjusting entries, illustrated, 310-312; after posting closing entries, illustrated, 317-321; after posting from sales journal, illustrated, 220

Going-concern concept, 458

Goods, acquisition of, 425

Goodwill, 498

Government notes, 529

Gross, pay, 88; price basis, 174, 186; profit, 216, 291

Gross margin, 216; computation of, 216

Gross margin method, 372; of inventory estimation, 372

-H-

Heading, of a balance sheet, 50; of an income statement, 49
Highway construction fund, 591
Historical cost, 460; concept, 460

-I-

Identification number, 102
Importance of the, balance sheet, 292; income statement, 290
Imprest method, 60
In balance, 23
Income, and expense statement, 290; and self-employment taxes, 302; net, 19; self-employment, 303; summary, 314
Income statement, 10, 48, 290, 578; analysis, 298; body, 49; columns, 286; consolidated, 458; form of, 291; heading, 49; illustrated, 49, 142, 293, 579; importance of 290; interim, 605; interpreting, 580; year-to-date, 606
Income tax payable, employees, 103
Incorporating, a partnership, 515; a single proprietorship, 512
Incorporators, 506
Independent, check on performance, 421; contractor, 86
Indorse, 358
Indorsement, accommodation, 358; blank, 66, 358; of notes, 358, illustrated, 359; restrictive, 66, illustrated, 66; special, 358
Indorsing the, check, 66; payment, 358
Information processor, 4
Input, 12
Installment, accounts receivable, 204; sales, 204
Insurance, 380; canceled, 382; expense, 561; expired, 381; parcel post, 196; policy, 381
In transit, 366
Intangible assets, 388
Interest, calculating, 343; effective rate, 354; rate of, 343
Interest-earning checking accounts, 82
Interest payable, accrued, 357

Interest receivable accrued, 350
Interim, balance sheet, 605; income statement, 605; period, 461
Interim financial statements, 604; using work sheets to produce, 606
Interim statements, 605; first month of fiscal year, illustrated, 612, 613; successive periods, 619, illustrated, 620, 622
Internal, accounting control, 418; accounting control concepts, 419; audit department, 421; control, 56, 57
Internal control, key elements, 420; meaning and importance, 419
Interpreting the, balance sheet, 586; income statement, 580
Interstatement analysis, 301
Inventory, accounting for, 362; assigning cost, 366; merchandise, 184, 363; sheet, 365; taking a physical, 364; turnover, 302
Inventory estimation, gross margin method, 372; retail method, 373
Inventory records, perpetual, 374
Inventory systems, types of, 363
Inventory valuation, lower of cost or market method, 371
Investments, 388; by owners, 592; return on, 301; temporary, 294
Invoice, 171; method, 187, 190; payment of, 178; purchase, 170, 171, 429; sales, 171, 208, 445

-J-

Journal, 27, 28; cash receipts, 223, 246, 451, 527; cash payments, 191, 246; combination, 121, illustrated, 122; general, 247, 528; proving, 36; purchases, 188, 246; sales, 217, 218, 246, 447; two-column, 28, illustrated, 28
Journalizing, 27, 29; adjusting entries, 308, 566; banking transactions, 74; closing entries, 314, 567; employer's payroll taxes, 109; illustrated, 30; payroll transactions, 104; procedure, illustrated, 31-36;

reversing entries, 324; transactions, 27

-K-

Keeping a ledger account for each bank, 80
Key elements of internal control, 420

-L-

Land, buildings, and equipment, 389
Last-in, first-out (lifo), costing, 368; method, 368
Layaway, ledger, 204; sales, 203
Ledger, account method, 187, 190, 217, 221; accounts payable, 247; accounts receivable, 247, 448, 530, illustrated, 453; general, 40, 122, 247, 528; layaway, 204; operating expense, 531; posting to, 39; subsidiary, 237; subsidiary accounts payable, 188; subsidiary accounts receivable, 217
Legality, 468
Liabilities, 5; current, 295; long-term, 141, 295
Liquidity, 587
List prices, 172
Long-term assets, 387, 389; depreciation of, 390; discarding, 405; disposition of, 405; exchange of, 407; fully depreciated, 412; purchase of, 593; sale of, 592; retiring, 405; selling, 406; trade-in, 407
Long-term borrowing, 592; repayment of, 593
Long-term liabilities, 141, 295
Loss, from uncollectible accounts, 230; net, 19
Lower of cost or market, 371; method of inventory valuation, 371

-M-

Machines, automated teller, 72
Maker of the note, 342
Making, deposits, 67; payroll tax payments, filing returns, 111;

withdrawals, 71
Manual system, 93
Manufacturing enterprise, 117
Market, 371
Marketable securities, 294, 388
Matching concept, 49, 461
Materiality, 229, 466
Maturity, note paid, 354; note renewed, 355; value, 353
Meaning and importance of internal control, 419
Mechanical system, 94
Memorandum, credit, 181; debit, 181
Mercantile enterprise, 117
Merchandise, available for sale, 283; inventory, 184, 363; turnover, 581
Merit rating system, 107
Method, asset, 378; average cost, 368; declining-balance, 393, 394; expense, 383; first-in, first-out, 367; gross margin, 372; imprest, 60; invoice, 187, 190; last-in, first-out, 368; ledger account, 187, 190, 217, 221; retail, 373; sales ticket, 217, 220; specific identification, 366; straight-line, 235, 392; sum-of-the-years-digits, 396; thirty-day, 12%, 345; units-of-output, 398; units of production, 398; wage bracket, 91; weighted average cost, 368
Methods, comparison of cost assignment, 370; comparison of depreciation, 400; of calculating depreciation, 391; record-keeping, 93; reducing-charge, 235
MICR numbers, 68
Monetary unit concept, 459
Monthly statement, illustrated, 57
Mortgage, 295; payable, 295
Multiple-step form, 291

-N-

Natural business year, 364, 604
Nature, and purpose of the statement, 590; of business accounting, 1
Negotiable, 66; commercial paper, 342
Net, cost, 235, 391; current assets, 301; income, 19; loss, 19; pay, 88; price basis, 175; sales, 216, 291; worth, 5, 482

Night deposits, 69
Note, collected at maturity, 346; dishonored, 348; issued as security for cash loan, 352; issued to supplier to obtain an extension of time for payment, 351; maker of, 342; notice of maturity, 354; paid at maturity, 354; payee of, 342; principal of, 343; promissory, 342; received from customer to obtain an extension of time for payment, 346; renewed at maturity, 347, 355; time of, 343
Notes, and interest, accounting for, 341; government, 529; indorsement, 358; payable, 5
Notes payable account, 356, illustrated, 356; proving, 356
Notes payable register, 355, illustrated, 356-357
Notes payable transactions, accounting for, 351
Notes receivable account, 349, illustrated, 349; proving, 349
Notes receivable register, 348, illustrated, 350-351
Notes receivable transactions, accounting for, 345
Notice of maturity of note, 354, illustrated, 354
NSF checks, 70

-O-

Objectivity, 466
Opening a checking account, 67
Opening entries, for a partnership 492; for a single proprietorship, 484
Operating, a petty cash fund, 59; expense ledger, 531; income, 291; statement, 10, 290
Operations, profitable, 592; sources of funds, 597; unprofitable, 593
Opinion, 578
Order, customer's purchase, 443; sales, 444; shipping, 445
Organization of, a corporation, 506; a partnership 490; a single proprietorship, 483
Output, 12
Outstanding checks, 76
Overdraft, 70
Owner's capital account at year end, illustrated, 317
Owner's equity, 5, 30, 296, 482; accounting for, 481; return on, 301

Owner's equity accounts, 484, corporation, 508; updating, 105, illustrated, 150
Owner's equity section in, a corporation balance sheet, 518; a partnership balance sheet, 503; a single proprietorship balance sheet, 488
Owners, investment by, 592; withdrawals by 592
Ownership of a corporation, 506

-P-

Paid-in capital, 508
Paid invoice, illustrated, 179
Par value, 507
Parcel post insurance, 196
Partial payments, 438
Partner, admitting a new, 497
Partners, compensation of, 499
Partnership, 490; accounting procedure, 492; agreement, 490, illustrated, 491; incorporating, 515; dissolution of, 500; organization of, 490; profits and losses, allocation of, 500
Passbook, 81
Pay, gross, 88; net, 88
Payable, accounts, 5, 187; accrued bank credit card, 326; accrued interest, 325, 357; employees income tax, 103; FICA tax, 103, 108; FUTA tax, 108; notes, 5; state unemployment tax, 109
Paycheck and deduction stub, illustrated, 100
Payee, 66; of the note, 342
Paying vouchers, 434
Payment, for goods using the voucher system, 428; indorsing, 358; of invoice, 178
Payments, cash, 56, 58; partial, 438
Payroll, accounting, 85; check, 97, illustrated, 100; expense, 102; records, 93; register, 93, illustrated, 96-97; taxes expense, 108; taxes imposed on the employer, 105; transactions, journalizing, 104
Percentage, analysis, 581; depletion, 415
Periodic, summary, 279; system, 363
Periodicity concept, 460
Perpetual, inventory records,

374; system, 363
Personal property, 387
Personal service enterprise, accounting for, 117; adjusting entries for, 143; cash basis accounting for, 118; closing entries for, 144
Petty cash fund, 59, 591
Petty cash payments record, 61, *illustrated,* John E. Berra, 62-63, MicroWorld, 262-263; proving, 63, *illustrated,* 63
Petty cash voucher, 59, *illustrated,* 60
Physical, depreciation, 390; flows and cost flows, 370
Postage, 379
Post-closing trial balance, 322, 572, *illustrated,* 150, 323, 573
Postdated check, 71
Posting, 40; from the cash receipts journal, 223, 528, *illustrated,* 224; from the cash payments journal, 193; from the general journal, 529; from the purchases journal, 189; from the sales journal, 219, 526; summary, 189; the adjusting entries, 309, 566; the closing entries, 571; the reversing entries, 324; to individual accounts, 239; to the ledger, 39, *illustrated,* 41-44
Practicality, 466
Preferred stock, 507
Premium, 381
Prepaid, rent, 382; transportation charges, 194
Prepaid expenses, 233, 378; accounting for, 233, 362; asset method of accounting, 378; expense method of accounting, 383
Preparing, a check, 73; the trial balance, 46
Principal of the note, 343
Principles and procedures, 228
Procedures, accounting, 421; authorization, 420; banking, 65; for handling incoming purchase orders, 206; journalizing, *illustrated,* 31-36
Proceeds, 353
Process, accounting, 3
Processing, 12
Professional enterprises, 118
Profit and loss, 314; statement, 10, 290; summary, 314
Profitable operations, 592
Profitability, 581; analysis of, 588

Promissory note, 342, *illustrated,* 343
Proof of footings, 125
Property, personal, 387; real, 387
Property, plant, and equipment, 141, 295; accounting for, 387; assets, 387; records, 410, *illustrated,* 411
Proprietary transactions, current period, 486
Proprietorship, 5; single, 482
Proved, 125
Proving, cash, 58; the cash receipts journal, 527; the general journal, 529; the journal, 36, *illustrated,* 37-38; the notes payable acccount, 356, the notes receivable account, 349; the petty cash payments record, 63, *illustrated,* 63; the sales journal, 526; the work sheet, 287; vouchers payable, 437
Purchase, 183; of long-term assets, 593
Purchase invoice, 170, 171, 429, *illustrated,* 172, 429; terms, 178; with cash discount, *illustrated,* 176; with series of discounts, *illustrated,* 177; with trade discount, *illustrated,* 173
Purchase order, 170, 427, *illustrated,* 427; billing, 208; credit approval, 207; customer, 206, 443, *illustrated,* 171; interpretation, 207; procedure for handling incoming, 206; shipping, 207; verification of, 207
Purchase requisition, 169, 426, *illustrated,* 169, 426
Purchases, allowances, 184; cash, 194; COD, 180, 194
Purchases discounts, 184; account, 185; lost account, 185
Purchases returns, 184; and allowances account, 186, 438
Purchases and payments, accounting for, 167; accounting procedures, 183
Purchases journal, 188, 246, *illustrated,* 188; posting from, 189

-Q-

Quick assets, 300
Quick ratio, 300

-R-

Rate of interest, 343
Ratio analysis, 587
Realization concept, 461
Realized revenue, 199
Real property, 387
Receipts, cash, 56; constructive, 118
Receivable, account, 4
Receiving report, 172, 427
Reconciliation of bank statement, *illustrated,* 78
Reconciling the bank statement, 76
Record, accounting, 121; earnings, 93; employee's earnings, 98, *illustrated,* 98-99; petty cash payments, 61, *illustrated,* 62-63, 262-263; stockholders of, 511
Record-keeping methods, 93
Records, auxiliary, 123, 533; kept by a bank, 75; payroll, 93; perpetual inventory, 374; property, plant, and equipment, 410; stock, 375; transaction-based, 460
Reducing-charge methods, 235
Register, cash, 56; check, 425, 436, 528; notes payable, 355; notes receivable, 348; payroll, 93, 95, *illustrated,* 96-97; voucher, 425, 430, 526
Remittance advice, 449; *illustrated,* 450; and check, 449
Rent, prepaid, 382
Repayment of long-term borrowing, 593
Report, annual, 577; auditor's, 578
Report form, 294; of balance sheet, 141, *illustrated,* 142, 585
Responsibilities, for FICA and federal income taxes, 111; for state and federal unemployment taxes, 113
Restrictive indorsement, 66, *illustrated,* 66
Retail method, of inventory estimation, 373
Retail sales tax, 205
Retained earnings, 508
Retiring long-term assets, 405
Return on, assets, 588; equity, 588; owner's equity, 301
Returns, purchases, 184; and allowances, 438
Revenue, 18; and expense, 18; cash basis, 118; realized, 199;

unrealized, 468
Revenue cycle, application in,
440; flowchart of, 441
Reversing entries, 566, 574,
illustrated, 325; for accrual
adjustments, 322; journalizing,
324; posting, 324
Rounded amounts in statements
and schedules, 143

-S-

Salary, 86
Sale, merchandise available for,
283; of long-term assets, 592
Sales, account, 214; allowances,
216; bank credit card, 202;
cash, 200, 442; COD, 203;
consignment, 205; credit, 443;
installment, 204; invoice, 208,
445, *illustrated,* 446; layaway,
203; net, 216, 291; on
account, 201; on approval,
203; order, 444, *illustrated,*
444; returns, 216; returns, and
allowances account, 215; tax
payable account, 214; tickets,
442; types of, 200
Sales and collections,
accounting for, 199;
accounting procedures for,
214; source documents and
associated records, 200
Sales journal, 217, 218, 246,
447, 526, *illustrated,* 260, 447,
544; posting from, 219, 526;
proving, 526; with sales tax,
illustrated, 218; without sales
tax, *illustrated,* 218
Sales tax, retail, 205
Sales ticket, 208, *illustrated,* 209;
method, 217, 220
Savings account, 81
Schedule of, accounts payable,
191, 275; accounts receivable,
221, *illustrated,* 222, 275, 586;
changes in working capital,
illustrated, 601; cost of goods
sold, *illustrated,* 579 operating
expenses, *illustrated,* 580
Securities, marketable, 388
Segregation of duties, 420
Self-employment income, 303
Selling long-term assets, 406
Service bureaus, 94
Shareholders, 507
Shares, 507
Shipping, 207; order, 445,
illustrated, 445
Short-term rate basis, 382

Signature card, 67
Single proprietorship, 482;
accounting procedure, 483;
incorporating, 512; opening
entries, 484; organization of,
483
Single-step form, 291
Source document, 27; and
associated records for sales
and collections, 200
Sources of funds, 592;
operations, 597
Special, indorsement, 358;
withholding allowance, 90
Specific identification, costing,
366; method, 366
Starting a business corporation,
509
State, and federal unemployment
taxes, responsibilities for, 113;
and local taxes, 89;
unemploymnet tax, 105;
unemployment tax, employer's,
106; unemployment tax
payable, 109
Statement, bank, 75, *illustrated,*
77; income, 10, 48, 290;
income and expense, 290;
monthly, *illustrated,* 57;
operating, 10, 290; profit and
loss, 10, 290; wage and tax,
101, *illustrated,* 101
Statement of, account, 241,
illustrated, 242; assets and
liabilities, 292; changes in
working capital, 590;
condition, 292; of earnings,
290; financial position, 292;
sources and uses of funds,
590
Statement of changes in
financial position, 590, 591;
assembling the data, 595;
illustrated, 595, 601; simplified
example, 593; with supporting
schedule of changes in
working capital, 600
Statements, and schedules
rounded amounts, 143;
financial, 10, 48, 141, 290;
interim, 605
Stock, capital, 506, 507;
common, 507; in trade, 184;
preferred, 507; records, 375
Stockholders, 507; equity, 518;
of record, 511
Straight-line method, 235, 392,
illustrated, 393
Subscription, 509
Subsidiary ledgers, 237;
accounts payable, 188;
accounts receivable, 217

Summary, expense and revenue,
314; income, 314; posting,
189; profit and loss, 314; year-
end work sheets, 552, 553,
illustrated, 554-555
Sum-of-the-years-digits method,
396, *illustrated,* 397
Supplementary year-end work
sheets, 552, *illustrated,* 558
Supplier, 170; accounts 239
Supplies, 378; expense, 560
System, electronic, 94; internal
accounting control, 419;
manual, 93; mechanical, 94;
merit rating, 107; periodic,
363; perpetual, 363; voucher,
428
Systems, automated, 94; types of
inventory, 363

-T-

T accounts, 15
Taking a physical inventory, 364
Tangible assets, 388
Tapes, cash register, 442
Tax, employer's FICA, 105;
employer's FUTA, 106;
employer's state
unemployment, 106; retail
sales, 205; state
unemployment, 105
Tax withheld, employees'
income, 89; employees' FICA
tax, 88
Taxes, accounting for employer
payroll, 108; FICA, 88; income
and self-employment, 302;
state and local, 89
Temporary, investments, 294;
owner's equity accounts, 20
Terms, purchase invoice, 178
Thirty-day, 12% method, 345
Three-column account form, 238
Ticket, deposit, 67, *illustrated,*
68; sales, 442
Time, of the note, 343; sharing,
95
Total earnings, deductions from,
88
Trade discount, 172, 173
Trade-in, allowance, 407; of
long-term assets, 407
Transaction-based records, 460
Transactions, 7; and accounts
unique to a corporation, 507;
journalizing, 27; journalizing
payroll, 104
Transportation accounts, 195
Transportation charges, 194;

collect, 195; prepaid, 194
Transposition error, 79
Trial balance, 22, 39, 45; adjusted, 295; columns, 281; *illustrated,* 24, 47, 276; post-closing, 322, 573, *illustrated,* 150; preparing, 46
Turnover, merchandise, 581
Two-column journal, 28
Types of, compensation, 86; business organization, 523; inventory systems, 363; sales, 200

-U-

Uncollectible accounts, expense, 230; loss from, 230; receivable, accounting for, 229
Undepreciated cost, 138, 295, 392, 587
Unemployment tax, state, 105
Unit basis, 410
Units, -of-output method, 398; of-production method, 398
Unprofitable operations, 593
Unrealized reveune, 468
Updating owner's equity accounts, 150
Use of revenue and expense accounts, 20
Uses of funds, 592; owners' withdrawals, 599; purchase of long-term assets, 599

Using work sheets to produce interim financial statements, 606

-V-

Value, book, 138, 392; fair market, 407; maturity, 353; par, 507
Vendor, 170
Verifiability, 466
Verification of purchase orders, 207
Volume of business, 524
Voucher, 425, 430; check, 435; petty cash, 59; register, 425, 430, 526
Voucher system, 428; payment for goods, 428
Vouchers, entering, 430; paying, 434
Vouchers payable, proving, 437

-W-

Wage and tax statement, (Form W-2), 101, *illustrated,* 101
Wage-bracket method, 91
Wages, 86
Wasting assets, 388, 413
Waybill, 180
Weighted average, costing, 368
Wholesale-retail business,

accounting procedure, 525, 533
Withdrawals, by owners, 592; making, 71
Withholding allowance, 90; certificate (Form W-4), *illustrated,* 91
Work at close of the fiscal period, 137
Working capital, 301, 590; statement of changes, 590
Work sheet, 280; completing, 287; completing the operating expenses, 562; completing the summary, 562; end-of-period, 137, 280; for a retail store, 280; for the first month of a fiscal year, 606; for the first two months of a fiscal year, 614; proving, 287; summary year-end, 552; supplementary year-end, 552; ten-column, *illustrated,* 282
Write-it-once principle, 94

-Y-

Year-to-date income statements, 606
Year, natural business, 364

-Z-

Zero-bracket amounts, 90